Reading Excellence: Word Attack & Rate Development Strategies

Reading Strategies
~ Applied to ~
Science Passages

Teacher's Guide

Anita L. Archer, Ph.D.
Mary M. Gleason, Ph.D.
Vicky Vachon, Ph.D.

Assisted by
Beth Cooper
Ken Shindledecker
Pat Pielaet
Melody McIntosh

SOPRIS WEST™ EDUCATIONAL SERVICES
A CAMBIUM LEARNING COMPANY

BOSTON, MA • LONGMONT, CO

11 12 13 14 15 TPS 20 19 18 17 16

ISBN 13 Digit: 978-1-59318-285-4
ISBN 10 Digit: 1-59318-285-6
69681/07-16

Illustrations by Kathy Bone

Printed in the United States of America
Published and Distributed by

A Cambium Learning Company

4093 Specialty Place • Longmont, Colorado 80504
(303) 651-2829 • www.sopriswest.com

Cover photograph of Rachel Carson courtesy of Lear Carson Collection,
Connecticut College: Photo by Brooks Studio
Cover photograph of leopard © DigitalVision/PictureQuest
Cover photograph of tornado © Comstock Images
Cover photograph of earth/satellite/sun © Scott Tysick/Masterfile

CONTENTS

ABOUT THE AUTHORS

Anita L. Archer, Ph.D.

Dr. Anita Archer serves as an educational consultant to school districts on effective instruction, classroom management, language arts instruction, and study skills instruction. She has taught elementary and middle school students and is the recipient of eight Outstanding Educator awards. She has been a faculty member at San Diego State University, the University of Oregon, and the University of Washington. Dr. Archer is nationally known for her presentations and publications on instructional procedures and design. She has authored many other curriculum and training materials as well as chapters and books.

Mary M. Gleason, Ph.D.

Dr. Mary Gleason is an educational consultant to school districts on implementation of literacy programs. Previously, Dr. Gleason was Director of Training for the National Institute for Direct Instruction (NIFDI). She began her career by teaching for eight years in general and special education classrooms. For 20 years as a professor at the University of Oregon, she designed and taught more than 40 college courses, including supervision and coaching, instructional design, methods courses for special education and general education, and technology in education courses. She is the author or coauthor of many journal articles, books, and curriculum materials. Her research focuses on academic interventions for students with learning disabilities.

Vicky Vachon, Ph.D.

Dr. Vicky Vachon is an educational consultant to school districts in the United States and Canada. She began her career as a classroom teacher in 1971. In 1983, she completed a master's degree in education at the University of Oregon. Upon returning to Canada, she worked as a teacher for the Toronto Board of Education. She was assigned to a multidisciplinary assessment team at the Child Development Clinic, Hospital for Sick Children, for nine years. In 1995, Dr. Vachon returned to the University of Oregon to complete a doctoral degree in special education. Her doctoral dissertation was about the effects of mastery of multisyllabic word reading component skills and the effects of context on the word and text reading skills of middle school students with reading deficiencies. She is a project director for the National Institute for Direct Instruction, overseeing the usage of language arts and math curricula in several schools.

INTRODUCTION

What is REWARDS Plus*?*

REWARDS Plus is a specialized reading program designed for middle school and high school struggling readers. *REWARDS Plus* expands on the strategies introduced in the original *REWARDS* program. While most students make tremendous gains in decoding long words and in building fluency from participating in the *REWARDS* program, additional practice is often needed to "cement" these skills, to increase transfer to content area reading, and to move secondary students closer to grade level. *REWARDS Plus* has two application books, one that applies the reading strategies to social studies articles and the other with application to science articles. Either or both of these books can be used as a follow-up of the *REWARDS* program, and they can be used in either order. When the term *REWARDS Plus* is used in this *Teacher's Guide*, we will be referring to the application to science book.

Each of the 15 Application Lessons in *REWARDS Plus* requires three to four instructional periods, and each lesson is built around a life science (e.g., viruses, food chains), physical science (e.g., atoms), or earth science (e.g., earthquakes, weather, ecosystems) topic. In addition, articles about two scientists, Antoni van Leeuwenhoek and Rachel Carson, are included. *REWARDS Plus* structures each Application Lesson as follows:

- **Before** reading the passages, students use the *REWARDS* strategies to determine the pronunciation of difficult words. In addition, they are introduced to the meanings of critical vocabulary, and they preview the article.
- **During** passage reading, students are asked questions to build their literal and inferential comprehension, and they complete an Information Web (graphic organizer) that summarizes the critical content.
- **After** passage reading, repeated readings are used to build fluency. Students are also taught a strategy for answering multiple-choice questions, and they complete engaging vocabulary activities to ensure retention of critical vocabulary. Finally, students are taught strategies for writing single-paragraph and multi-paragraph answers.

What are the goals of REWARDS Plus: Reading Strategies Applied to Science Passages*?*

REWARDS Plus is designed to take middle and high school students closer to grade-level expectations. As a result of participation in this program, students will:

- Accurately read more multisyllabic words found in science, social studies, and health textbooks as well as other classroom materials.
- Have extended vocabulary, including technical vocabulary for science and academic vocabulary applicable to many subjects.
- Be able to preview content-area chapters to gain an idea of their content.
- Read content-area passages not only accurately, but fluently.
- Experience increased comprehension as their accuracy and fluency increases.
- Accurately complete challenging multiple-choice items, justifying their answers.
- Write coherent single-paragraph and multi-paragraph answers.
- Have more confidence in their reading and writing abilities.

Which students should participate in REWARDS Plus*?*

REWARDS Plus is designed for struggling readers in middle school and high school (sixth through twelfth grade) who have completed the original *REWARDS* program and would benefit from continued decoding and fluency practice with greater focus on vocabulary, comprehension, and writing.

Where should students be placed in the program?

REWARDS Plus has two possible entry points. Students may enter at the beginning of the Review Lessons or at the beginning of the Application Lessons. If students have recently completed the *REWARDS* program successfully, they should begin *REWARDS Plus* with the Application Lessons. However, if students completed *REWARDS* in the previous year or semester—or if students did not demonstrate mastery of the *REWARDS* decoding strategies—they should begin *REWARDS Plus* by completing the six Review Lessons at the beginning of the program.

In what types of settings has REWARDS Plus *been taught?*

REWARDS Plus has been field-tested in a number of middle and high school settings. It could be used in special reading classes, in remedial or special education settings, or in literacy tutoring programs. *REWARDS Plus* is also appropriate as a part of intensive intervention programs after school, during the summer, or during interim sessions.

What are the components of REWARDS Plus*?*

1. ***Teacher's Guide.*** The *Teacher's Guide* consists of four sections:
   a. **Introduction**
   This section provides information about the *REWARDS Plus* program and how it is implemented. The Introduction should be read carefully before the program is implemented.
   b. **Review Lessons**
   Six Review Lessons are found at the beginning of the program. These lessons should be taught if students completed the *REWARDS* program in the previous year or semester, or did not demonstrate mastery at the end of *REWARDS*. These lessons review the critical preskills needed for the decoding strategies, provide guided and independent practice of the decoding strategies, and provide generalization practice through reading sentences. The sentences in the application to science book are different from those in the application to social studies book.
   c. **Application Lessons**
   Fifteen Application Lessons, each requiring three to four instructional periods, strengthen and expand the skills taught in the original *REWARDS* program.
   d. **Additional Materials**
   In the back of the *Teacher's Guide*, you will find:
   - Blackline masters for Review and Application Lesson overhead transparencies.*
   - Blackline masters for each strategy, plus a Prefixes, Suffixes, and Vowel Combinations Reference Chart, so that students can insert copies of the strategies and the chart into their notebooks (Appendix A).*
   - Blackline masters for the Information Webs (graphic organizers) that will be used in each lesson (Appendix B).*
   - A special activity called Quick Words that provides motivating practice on the vocabulary words that are introduced in each Application Lesson (Appendix C).*
   - A Fluency Graph (Appendix D).*
   - An outline for an optional incentive/grading program that could be used to provide feedback and encouragement (Appendix E).
   - An Activity A word list for the Application Lessons (Appendix F).
2. ***Student Book.*** The *Student Book* contains the stimuli used in the Review and Application Lessons for various teacher-directed and practice activities. Most student materials needed for the program are found in the *Student Book*. In addition, teachers will need to copy the reproducible Information Webs, found in the back of the *Teacher's Guide*, for each student.

What is the content of the REWARDS Plus *Review Lessons?*

The *REWARDS Plus* Review Lessons review the flexible strategies for decoding long words that were introduced in *REWARDS*. These strategies involve peeling off prefixes and suffixes, segmenting the rest of the word into decodable "chunks" using the vowels, saying the word parts, saying the whole word, and making sure the word is a real word.

The ability to decode long words is critical for several reasons. First, word recognition is highly related to comprehension and is one of the greatest challenges facing struggling readers. Poor decoding skills, particularly as applied to long words, account for much of the gap between the reading proficiencies of lower and higher readers. In addition, the number of novel long words that students must read increases significantly in middle and high school textbooks. It is estimated that average students, from fifth grade on, will encounter approximately 10,000 new words in print each year. These longer words are also likely to carry most of the

* A complete set of transparencies may also be purchased separately.

Overt Strategy

1. Circle the prefixes.
2. Circle the suffixes.
3. Underline the vowels.
4. Say the parts of the word.
5. Say the whole word.
6. Make it a real word.

Example:

Covert Strategy

1. Look for prefixes, suffixes, and vowels.
2. Say the parts of the word.
3. Say the whole word.
4. Make it a real word.

meaning in content area textbooks. (A complete review of related research is found in the *REWARDS Teacher's Guide.*)

The steps in the Overt and Covert Strategies presented in *REWARDS* are shown above.

Students receive practice in the necessary preskills for these strategies (e.g., pronunciation of affixes and vowels) and the actual strategies in the six Review Lessons. Each activity found in the Review Lessons is briefly described here and on the following pages.

1. **Vowel Combinations.** Students review the common sounds (major sounds) for high frequency vowel combinations (**ay**, **ai**, **au**, **er**, **ir**, **ur**, **ar**, **a–e**, **o–e**, **i–e**, **e–e**, **u–e**, **oi**, **oy**, **or**, **ee**, **oa**, **ou**) and the major and minor sounds for **ow** (low, down), **oo** (moon, book), and **ea** (meat, thread). After the vowel combinations are presented, they are reviewed in subsequent Review Lessons to ensure accurate and quick recognition. The Vowel Combinations Chart below lists all the vowel combinations that are reviewed and presents a key word to clarify the pronunciation.
2. **Vowel Conversions.** Students are reminded that when they encounter a single vowel letter in a word, they should first try the short sound (referred to as the *sound* of the letter). If the resulting word is not a recognizable word, they should then say the long sound (referred to as the *name* of the letter). In this activity, students practice saying the sound and then the name for the letters **a**, **i**, **o**, **u**, and **e**.
3. **Prefixes and Suffixes.** About 80% of multisyllabic words have one or more affix. Thus, the ability to quickly identify and pronounce prefixes (e.g., **re**, **un**, **dis**) and suffixes (e.g., **tion**, **al**, **able**) facilitates the accurate, fluent decoding of longer words. Prefixes and suffixes have four characteristics: a

Vowel Combinations Chart

(Shown in the order that they are introduced in the Review Lessons. See Appendix A for a vowel combination reference chart grouped by type.)

Vowel Combination	Key Word	Vowel Combination	Key Word
ay	say	**oi**	void
ai	rain	**oy**	boy
au	sauce	**or**	torn
er	her	**ee**	deep
ir	bird	**oa**	foam
ur	turn	**ou**	loud
ar	farm	**ow**	low, down
a–e	make	**oo**	moon, book
o–e	hope	**ea**	meat, thread
i–e	side		
e–e	Pete		
u–e	use		

specific pronunciation, a specific spelling, a specific meaning, and attachment to a root word. Thus, affixes assist us in decoding and spelling the word and, if the root word is known, assist us with word meaning.

However, in many cases the root word is not familiar to us. For example, the root may be an archaic form or has meaning in another language, such as Greek or Latin. In other situations, peeling off the affixes leaves a part that is an unfamiliar root word. In these instances, affixes may be helpful only with decoding and spelling because the affix does not carry a familiar meaning that is easily identifiable. Though these elements may not technically be acting as prefixes and suffixes within a specific word, they are still tremendously useful decoding elements.

In this activity, students review the pronunciation of prefixes and suffixes, practice saying these affixes, and review previously introduced affixes, the goal being accurate and quick pronunciation. The charts on this page and page 5 list affixes that are reviewed and their meanings.

4. **Strategy Instruction.** In this activity, the teacher demonstrates each step in the *REWARDS* Overt Strategy and guides students in applying the strategy steps to decode multisyllabic words.
5. **Strategy Practice.** In each Review Lesson, students practice using the Overt Strategy. Students circle prefixes and suffixes, underline the vowels in the rest of the word, and read the word by parts, thus applying the strategy with less teacher assistance.
6. **Independent Strategy Practice.** In Review Lessons 3-6, students shift to the Covert Strategy. Without circling and underlining, students read the word parts to themselves, then read each word aloud.
7. **Sentence Reading.** Sentence-reading activities are included to promote generalization of the *REWARDS* strategies to daily reading. In this activity, students read sentences laden with multisyllabic words that students had already read.

Prefixes Shown in the Order of Introduction

(Shown in the order that they are introduced in the Review Lessons. See Appendix A for an alphabetized reference chart.)

Prefix	Key Word	Meaning
dis	**discover**	away, apart; negative
mis	**mistaken**	wrong; not
ab	**abdomen**	from; away; off; not
ad	**advertise**	to, toward; against
in	**insert**	in, into; not; really
im	**immediate**	in, into; not
com	**compare**	with; together; really
be	**belong**	really; by; to make
pre	**prevent**	before
de	**depart**	away from; down; negative
re	**return**	again, back; really
pro	**protect**	in favor of; before; forward
con	**continue**	with; together; really
per	**permit**	through; really
un	**uncover**	not; reversal of; remove
a	**above**	in, on, at; not, without
ex	**example**	out, away
en	**entail**	in; within; on

Suffixes Shown in the Order of Introduction

(Shown in the order that they are introduced in the Review Lessons. See Appendix A for an alphabetized reference chart.)

Suffix	Key Word	Meaning
s	birds	more than one, verb marker
ing	running	when you do something; quality, state
ed	landed	in the past; quality
ness	kindness	that which is; state, quality
less	useless	without; not
ic	frantic	like; related to
ate	regulate	to make, act; having the quality of
ish	selfish	like, related to; to make
ist	artist	one who
ism	realism	state, quality; act
est	biggest	the most
ful	careful	full of
or	tailor	one who; that which
er	farmer	more; one who; that which
al	final	related to, like
tion	action	state, quality; act
sion	mission	state, quality; act
ion	million	state, quality; act
tive	attentive	one who; quality of
sive	expensive	one who; quality of
y	industry	having the quality of; in the manner of; small
ly	safely	how something is
ary	military	related to
ity	oddity	quality; state
ant	dormant	one who performs; thing that promotes; being
ent	consistent	one who performs; thing that promotes; being
ment	argument	that which; quality, act
ance	disturbance	action, process; quality or state
ence	essence	action, process; quality or state
ous	nervous	having the quality of
cious	precious	having the quality of
tious	cautious	having the quality of
cial	special	related to; like
tial	partial	related to; like
age	courage	that which; state
ture	picture	state, quality; that which
able	disposable	able to be
ible	reversible	able to be
le	cradle	———

What is the content of REWARDS Plus *Application Lessons?*

1. **Passages.** The science passages were specifically written for *REWARDS Plus* to meet a number of requirements. First, the topics were selected to represent the major areas of science study: life science, physical science, and earth science. Second, the articles needed to be well written, cohesive, interesting, and representative of text commonly found in science materials. Next, the articles needed to require little specialized background knowledge beyond that which could be easily introduced as a part of the lesson. Finally, specifications were followed for long words, readability, and passage length. The passages contain many multisyllabic words and have a readability range from eighth to ninth grade reading level. Because the pronunciations of all the difficult words are pretaught, the students experience a significantly lower readability. The passages vary in length from 643 words to 921 words.
2. **Lesson Activities.** Each of the 15 Application Lessons contains the same activities divided into reading interventions that occur before, during, and after reading of the passage. These research-based interventions are summarized in the chart at the bottom of the page.

BEFORE PASSAGE READING

Before students read the passage, they are taught the pronunciation of the difficult words and their meanings, and they preview the article.

3. **Vocabulary.** To increase students' decoding accuracy, fluency, and comprehension, the most difficult words are taught before the passages are read. Three instructional practices are used: ***tell***, ***strategy***, and ***word families***. First, the teacher ***tells*** students the pronunciation of a set of difficult words that are proper names, irregular words, or words of foreign origin. For the second set of words, students use a *REWARDS* ***strategy*** to determine the pronunciation. For the third set of words, students are presented with groups of related words (***word families***), such as the family **transform**, **transformation**, and **transformer**. Students use the decoding strategies to determine the pronunciation of the words.

   The meaning of each word is also presented along with the pronunciation. A short definition that corresponds to the use of the word in the passage (not necessarily the most common definition) is provided, coupled with the part of speech. Teachers are welcome to provide additional information concerning the definitions including examples, illustrations,

Before Passage Reading Interventions	▪ Introduce the pronunciation of difficult words.
	    ▪ Tell students the pronunciation of irregular words.
	    ▪ Guide students in using their *REWARDS* strategies on regular words.
	▪ Teach the meanings of critical vocabulary.
	▪ Dictate spelling words.
	▪ Preview the passage prior to reading.

During Passage Reading Interventions	▪ Guide students in reading the passage. ▪ Ask students questions to check their understanding and to model active thinking during reading. ▪ While students read the passage, have students complete their Information Webs (graphic organizers).

After Passage Reading Interventions	▪ Engage students in repeated reading activities to increase fluency.
	▪ Guide students in answering multiple-choice questions on the article's content.
	▪ Provide engaging vocabulary practice including activities such as:
	    ▪ Yes/No/Why
	    ▪ Completion Activities
	    ▪ Quick Words
	▪ Guide students in planning, writing, and editing multi-paragraph answers.
	▪ Guide students in writing answers to and discussing "What If?" science questions.

and oral sentences that illustrate the word, depending on the background knowledge of students.

You may wish to select five to ten words from the lists for very explicit instruction. Select words that students might encounter in many of their classes and could incorporate into their written and spoken vocabulary (e.g., from Application Lesson 1—**interactions**, **available**, **requirements,** and **transform**). The following instructional steps would be useful for those words:

Explicit Vocabulary Instruction

Step 1: Introduce the pronunciation of the word and the definition.
Read the word. "obsolete"
Read the definition. "No longer used."

Step 2: Rephrase the definition, asking students to complete a statement.
When something is no longer used, it is ________. "obsolete"

Step 3: Check students' understanding by asking questions.
What causes something to become obsolete?
Are electric can openers obsolete? Why or why not?
Are record players obsolete? Why or why not?
Tell your partner examples of things that are obsolete.

A reproducible vocabulary activity called Quick Words is provided for each lesson (see Appendix C). In this optional activity, students study vocabulary for one minute and then take a one-minute timing in which they record the letter of the vocabulary word that goes with the corresponding definition. This activity is repeated each day that is spent on a lesson so that students can experience progress in their vocabulary knowledge.

4. **Spelling.** Many students who have poor decoding skills also have low spelling knowledge and are intimidated by longer words. In this activity, the teacher dictates a lesson word, and then students say and write the parts of the word. Students then compare their spelling to the correct spelling of the word, cross out any misspellings, and rewrite those words.
5. **Preview of Article.** As we are aware in our own reading, our comprehension is enhanced when we preview the material so that we know what will be covered, how the material is organized, and how our prior knowledge might relate to the article. In this teacher-directed activity, the students and preview the content of the article by examining the title and the headings.

DURING PASSAGE READING

After students have been introduced to the words and have previewed the chapter, they read the related science article in designated sections. The students will first read the section silently. Next, they will read the section orally as an entire group (choral reading), to a partner, or as an individual. Every effort should be made to not embarrass students, since many may have a history of reading difficulties and may be uncomfortable reading in front of the whole group, particularly with no prior practice. After each section, they are asked questions to verify their understanding, to firm up their knowledge, and to model the type of self-questioning that they could utilize. At designated spots in the articles, the students will stop and fill in an Information Web, a graphic organizer that summarizes the information from the article. Later in the lesson, students will use the Information Web to teach the content to their partners and to review the critical information.

AFTER PASSAGE READING

After students have read the passage, they work on building their passage-reading fluency. In addition, they learn comprehension strategies for answering multiple-choice questions, practice their vocabulary terms, and write single-paragraph and multi-paragraph responses to content from the article.

6. **Passage Reading—Fluency.** A number of studies have determined that students' oral reading fluency is correlated with reading comprehension. As students read words more fluently with automaticity, they can turn their attention from decoding to comprehension.

The oral reading rate goals listed below represent the number of words read correctly in one minute at different reading levels (not grade levels).

Oral reading fluency can be increased through repeated readings of passages for which students already have a high level of accuracy. After practicing the passage for the purpose of accuracy, students use a repeated reading procedure to increase their read-

Reading Level	Words Read Correctly in One Minute
Grades 6–8	150–180 words per minute
Grades 9–12	180–200 words per minute

ing fluency. First, students do a "Cold Timing" in which they whisper-read for one minute as the teacher times them. The reading is then practiced one or two more times, having students attempt to beat their Cold Timing. Next, students pair with partners, exchange books, listen to their partners read for one minute, and record their partner's errors and number of correct words read on the "Hot Timing." At the close of this activity, students graph their own number of correctly read words on the Cold Timing and Hot Timing. A Fluency Graph is found on the last page of the *Student Book*. An additional, reproducible copy is found in Appendix D.

7. **Comprehension Questions—Multiple Choice.** On classroom tests as well as on state and district standards tests, students' knowledge is often measured using multiple-choice items. In *REWARDS Plus,* each lesson contains four challenging multiple-choice items including vocabulary, cause/effect, compare/contrast, and main idea items. The distracters include plausible (though incorrect) answers, details drawn from the passage (though irrelevant to the question), and inferences not based on details found in the article.

   Students are taught a strategy for completing these types of items: to read the multiple-choice item, to read all of the choices, to think about why each choice might be correct or incorrect, and finally, to select the best answer. While the strategy is simple, the critical thinking skills necessary to answer challenging multiple-choice items are very demanding and are enhanced through interactive practice. In this exercise, students complete an item and then discuss it with classmates, sharing their answers and rationales.

8. **Vocabulary Activities.** If we would like students to retain the meanings of critical vocabulary, they will need multiple exposures to the word. To be truly effective, the practice activities should (a) require deep processing of the word's meaning, not just mimicking the definition, and (b) when possible, connect the word to the students' prior knowledge. Two research-based practice activities that meet these requirements are used. In the first activity, students answer a question with "yes" or "no" and give a rationale for their answer. The questions are laden with new vocabulary terms, requiring careful comprehension and consideration.

   In the second activity, called a Completion Activity, students are given a word and its definition. They are then presented with a partial sentence (stem) that they must complete using their prior knowledge. Once again, the stem contains the new vocabulary term. These activities are designed to appeal especially to secondary students and to make vocabulary study interesting and engaging.

9. **Expository Writing—Multi-Paragraph Answer.** In each lesson, the students are given a prompt that relates to the article's content and demands a two- or three-paragraph response. Students are taught a six-step writing strategy and how to apply it when responding to the prompt. First, students determine three topics that they will cover in their answer and ***list*** the most important details. Next, they review the list, ***cross out*** any details that don't go with the topic, and ***connect*** details that could combine easily into one sentence. Then, students ***number*** the details in a logical order. Finally, students ***write*** and ***edit*** each of their paragraphs and evaluate them against a rubric. This writing strategy is carefully modeled and practiced with students to ensure coherent, well-written products.

10. **Comprehension—Single-Paragraph Answer.** In science, we constantly speculate—What if this happened? At the end of each lesson, students are given a *What If* question to contemplate, write about, and discuss. When writing their answers, they are taught to use wording from the question in formulating their answer. They are also taught discussion guidelines for the behavior of listeners and speakers.

How are REWARDS Plus *lessons designed in the* Teacher's Guide?

Each lesson contains a set of activities. The activities for the Review Lessons are similar each day, as are the activities for the Application Lessons. For each activity, two "lesson plans" are given. First, there is a general description of the activity. Next, there is a teacher script that includes the wording a teacher could use when teaching the lesson. Please read the lessons prior to instruction, including the activity procedures and the scripts. You may then choose to follow the general procedure or the script, maintaining the essence of the activity in either case.

How can I actively involve my students in the instruction?

Student achievement is highly related to opportunities to respond. When students must constantly say, write, or do things in a lesson, they are much more likely to be attentive and to learn from the resulting practice. The Best Practices for Eliciting Responses Chart below outlines some of the procedures you may wish to use to involve all students in the lessons.

How much time do the lessons take?

The amount of time needed to complete each lesson varies greatly depending on the size of the group, the competency of students, and the pace of the teacher. Generally, each Review Lesson requires one period (45–50 minutes). Because of the extensive vocabulary instruction, fluency building, comprehension items, and writing activities, each Application Lesson requires three to four instructional periods of 45–50 minutes. If

Best Practices for Eliciting Responses Chart

Type of Response	Best Practice
Group Says Answer *(A group response can be used when the wording is short and the same for all students.)*	**If students are looking at the teacher.** **T:** Asks a question. **T:** Raises his/her hands to signal thinking time. **S:** Think of the answer. **T:** Says "Everyone" and lowers hands to signal end of thinking time. **S:** Say the answer. **If students are looking at their work.** **T:** Asks a question or gives a directive. **T:** Gives the students thinking time. **S:** Think of the answer. **T:** Signals audibly (e.g., voice signal, such as "Everyone"). **S:** Respond.
Student Partners Say Answer	**The teacher assigns a response partner to each student and the numbers 1 and 2.** **T:** Asks a question or gives a directive. **T:** Asks Partner 1 to respond. ("Ones, tell your partner . . ."). **S:** Tells the answer to his/her partner. **T:** Monitors the class. **T:** Gives feedback to each group.
Individual Student Says Answer	**T:** Asks a question. **T:** Raises his/her hands to signal thinking time. Gives eye contact to all students to encourage formulation of an answer. **S:** Think of an answer. **T:** Calls on one student. **S:** Gives an answer.
Students Write Answer	**T:** Gives a directive or asks a question. Tells students to put down their pencils and look up when they are done. **S:** Write a response. **T:** Monitors students. **T:** Gives feedback to students.

parts of lessons are not completed during an instructional period, the teacher may wish to review the lesson's content and complete it the next day.

How can I measure my students' progress?

Use the procedures outlined in Appendix G at the back of this *Teacher's Guide*. These procedures include directions for pre/post fluency, writing, and vocabulary measures.

Review Lesson 1

Materials Needed:

- *Student Book:* Review Lesson 1
- Review Overhead Transparency A
- Appendix A Reproducible 1: *REWARDS* Strategies for Reading Long Words
- Appendix A Reproducible 2: Prefixes, Suffixes, and Vowel Combinations Reference Chart
- Paper or cardboard to use when covering the overhead transparency
- Washable overhead transparency pen

Text Treatment Notes:

- Black text signifies teacher script (exact wording to say to students).
- Green text in parentheses signifies directions or prompts for the teacher.
- Green text signifies answers or examples of answers.
- Green graphics treatment signifies reproduction of Overhead information.
- Green text and green graphics treatment do not appear in the *Student Book.*

PREPARATION

- Write the following words on a chalkboard or overhead transparency:

  intentionally
  unconventionality
  inventiveness

- Photocopy and distribute Appendix A Reproducibles 1 and 2 (*REWARDS* Strategies for Reading Long Words and Prefixes, Suffixes, and Vowel Combinations Reference Chart). Have students place the copies in their notebooks or in folders for later reference.

INTRODUCTION

1. In the next few days, we are going to review strategies for reading longer words that you learned in the *REWARDS* program. You will remember how to figure out words such as (point to each word on a chalkboard or the overhead) **intentionally**, **unconventionality**, and **inventiveness**.
2. First, we are going to review the skills you need to read longer words. Then, we will practice reading longer words in sentences and in some of our classroom books.

ACTIVITY A

Vowel Combinations

ACTIVITY PROCEDURE

(See the *Student Book*, page 1.)

In this activity, students review the sound to say when they see a combination of letters. Have students point to the letters in their *Student Books*. Tell students the sound as it is pronounced in the key word. Have students practice saying the sounds.

1. Open your *Student Book* to **Review Lesson 1**, page 1. Find **Activity A**. We are going to review some sounds. You learned all of them in the *REWARDS* program, but you may need a short review.
2. Look at the first line of letter combinations. Point to the letters **a - y**. The sound of these letters is usually /ā/. What sound?_
3. Point to the letters **a - i**. The sound of these letters is usually /ā/. What sound?_
4. Point to the letters **a - u**. The sound of these letters is usually /aw/. What sound?_
5. Look at the second line of letter combinations. Point to the letters **e - r**. The sound of these letters is usually /er/. What sound?_
6. Point to the letters **i - r**. The sound of these letters is usually /er/. What sound?_
7. Point to the letters **u - r**. The sound of these letters is usually /er/. What sound?_
8. Point to the letters **a - r**. The sound of these letters is usually /ar/. What sound?_
9. Go back to the beginning of the first line. Say the sounds again. What sound?_ Next sound?_ Next sound?_
10. (Continue Step 9 until students have reviewed all sounds in the two lines.)

ACTIVITY B
Vowel Conversions

ACTIVITY PROCEDURE

(See the *Student Book*, page 1.)

In this activity, students review how to switch between saying the *sound* and saying the *name* for a particular vowel letter. They review that when they see a vowel letter in a long word, they should first say the sound. If it doesn't make a real word, they will say the name. Have students point to the letter while you tell them the sound, and have them repeat the sound. Then, have students point to the same letter while you tell them the name, and have students repeat the name. Have students practice saying the sound, then the name for each letter.

1. Find **Activity B**. When you are reading words and see these letters, first try the sound. If it doesn't make a real word, then try the name.
2. Point to the first letter. The sound is /ă/. What sound?_ The name is **a**. What name?_
3. Point to the next letter. The sound is /ĭ/. What sound?_ The name is **i**. What name?_
4. Point to the next letter. The sound is /ŏ/. What sound?_ The name is **o**. What name?_
5. First letter again. What sound?_ What name?_
6. Next letter. What sound?_ What name?_
7. Next letter. What sound?_ What name?_

REVIEW LESSON
1

ACTIVITY A *Vowel Combinations*

ay (say)	ai (rain)	au (sauce)	
er (her)	ir (bird)	ur (turn)	ar (farm)

ACTIVITY B *Vowel Conversions*

a   i   o

ACTIVITY C *Prefixes and Suffixes*

discover	dis	advertise	ad
mistaken	mis	insert	in
abdomen	ab	immediate	im

Student Book: Review Lesson 1   1

ACTIVITY C

Prefixes and Suffixes

ACTIVITY PROCEDURE

(See the *Student Book*, page 1.)

In this activity, students review identifying and pronouncing prefixes and suffixes. In this lesson, have students first point to the words, then the circled prefixes, while you pronounce them. Ask students to repeat the words and prefixes after you.

1. Find **Activity C**. Now, we are going to review prefixes. Where do we find prefixes?_
2. Point to the first column. The first word is **discover**. What word?_ Point to the circled prefix. The prefix is /dis/. What prefix?_
3. Point to the next word below. The word is **mistaken**. What word?_ Point to the prefix. The prefix is /mis/. What prefix?_
4. (Repeat with **abdomen** and /ab/.)
5. Point to the third column. The first word is **advertise**. What word?_ The prefix is /ad/. What prefix?_
6. (Repeat with **insert** and /in/ and **immediate** and /im/.)
7. Find the second column. It has prefixes only. Read the prefixes. What prefix?_ Next?_ Next?_
8. Find the last column. What prefix?_ Next?_ Next?_

REVIEW LESSON **1**

ACTIVITY A *Vowel Combinations*

ay (say)	ai (rain)	au (sauce)	
er (her)	ir (bird)	ur (turn)	ar (farm)

ACTIVITY B *Vowel Conversions*

a i o

ACTIVITY C *Prefixes and Suffixes*

discover	dis	advertise	ad
mistaken	mis	insert	in
abdomen	ab	immediate	im

Student Book: Review Lesson 1 1

ACTIVITY D

Strategy Instruction

ACTIVITY PROCEDURE

(See the *Student Book*, page 2.)

In this activity, students practice using all their skills for figuring out longer words. First, use three words to show students how to use the strategy. Then, work with students to apply the strategy to the remaining words. For each word, ask students if the word has prefixes, then circle them. Underline the vowels and have students say the sounds. Finally, have students say the word, first part by part, and then as a whole word.

Use Overhead A: Activity D

1. Turn to page 2. Find **Activity D**.
2. We are going to review the *REWARDS* strategy for figuring out longer words.
3. Look up here. Watch me use the *REWARDS* strategy. (Point to the word **abstract** in Line #1.)
4. First, I circle prefixes. (Circle **ab.** Point to the prefix and ask ...) What prefix?_
5. Next, I underline the vowels in the rest of the word. (Underline **a** in **stract**. Point to the vowel and ask . . .) What sound?_
6. Next, I say the parts in the word. (Loop under each part and say the parts: **ab stract**.)
7. Next, we say the whole word. Remember to make it a real word. What word?_
8. (Repeat Steps 4–7 with **insist** and **impact**.)
9. Let's read some more words.
10. (Point to the word **distraught**.) Does the word have a prefix?_ (If the answer is "yes," circle the prefix and ask . . .) What prefix?_
11. (Underline the vowels in the rest of the word and ask . . .) What sound?_
12. Say the word by parts. (Loop under each part and ask . . .) What part?_ What part?_
13. (Run your finger under the whole word.) What word?_
14. (Repeat Steps 10–13 with **misfit** and **admit**.)

Note: You may wish to provide additional practice by having students read a line to the group or to a partner.

REVIEW LESSON

1

ACTIVITY D *Strategy Instruction*

1.	abstract	insist	impact
2.	distraught	misfit	admit

ACTIVITY E *Strategy Practice*

1.	birthday	misplay	discard
2.	maintain	disband	indistinct
3.	modern	addict	imprint
4.	absurd	insert	railway

ACTIVITY F *Sentence Reading*

1. John wanted to disband his rock group after they played at the birthday party.
2. The author will insist on reading the abstract from his new book.
3. She was very distraught when her mother tried to discard her old clothes.
4. The teacher will maintain that her words were right.
5. They will admit that they left imprints of their hands on the glass.
6. As a misfit, the puppy spent most of its time by itself.
7. Her shouts were so absurd that she was asked to leave.
8. Their modern ways of doing things had a strong impact on the group.
9. He tried his best to help the team, but he would often misplay the baseball.
10. The animal's tracks in the mud were indistinct.

2 *REWARDS Plus: Reading Strategies Applied to Science Passages*

ACTIVITY E

Strategy Practice

ACTIVITY PROCEDURE

(See the *Student Book*, page 2.)

In this activity, students practice using the strategy themselves for figuring out longer words. Have students circle prefixes and underline the vowels. Assist students in checking their work, then reading each word, first part by part, and then as a whole word.

Use Overhead A: Activity E

1. Find **Activity E.**
2. Now, it's your turn. For each word, circle prefixes and underline the vowels in the rest of the word. Be careful. Remember that some words have no prefixes, and some words have one or more prefixes. Look up when you are done._
3. (Show the overhead transparency.) Now, check and fix any mistakes._
4. (When students are done checking, assist students in reading each word on the overhead transparency, beginning with the first word in Line #1.) Look up here._
5. (Loop under each word part in **birth day**.) What part? __ What part?_
6. (Run your finger under the whole word.) What word?_
7. (Repeat Steps 4-6 with all words in Activity E.)

Note: You may wish to provide additional practice by having students read a line to the group or to a partner.

REVIEW LESSON **1**

ACTIVITY D *Strategy Instruction*

1. abstract	insist	impact
2. distraught	misfit	admit

ACTIVITY E *Strategy Practice*

1. birthday	misplay	discard
2. maintain	disband	indistinct
3. modern	addict	imprint
4. absurd	insert	railway

ACTIVITY F *Sentence Reading*

1. John wanted to disband his rock group after they played at the birthday party.
2. The author will insist on reading the abstract from his new book.
3. She was very distraught when her mother tried to discard her old clothes.
4. The teacher will maintain that her words were right.
5. They will admit that they left imprints of their hands on the glass.
6. As a misfit, the puppy spent most of its time by itself.
7. Her shouts were so absurd that she was asked to leave.
8. Their modern ways of doing things had a strong impact on the group.
9. He tried his best to help the team, but he would often misplay the baseball.
10. The animal's tracks in the mud were indistinct.

2 *REWARDS Plus: Reading Strategies Applied to Science Passages*

Sentence Reading

ACTIVITY PROCEDURE

(See the *Student Book,* page 2.)

In this activity, students use the strategy for figuring out longer words in the context of sentences that contain words they have already practiced. Have students read a sentence to themselves. Then, choose from several options of having students read the sentence together, to partners, or individually to the class.

Note: If you are teaching older students for whom "thumbs-up" is inappropriate, have students look at you when they can read the sentence.

1. Find **Sentence #1** in **Activity F.** These sentences include words that we practiced today. Read the first sentence to yourself. When you can read all the words in the sentence, put your thumb up.
2. (When students can read the sentence, use one of the following options:
   a. Ask students to read the sentence together [i.e., choral reading].
   b. Have students read the sentence to their partners. Then, call on one student to read the sentence to the group.
   c. Ask one student to read the sentence to the group.)
3. (Repeat these procedures with the remaining sentences. Be sure that you give ample thinking time for each sentence.)

REVIEW LESSON
1

ACTIVITY D *Strategy Instruction*

1. abstract	insist	impact
2. distraught	misfit	admit

ACTIVITY E *Strategy Practice*

1. birthday	misplay	discard
2. maintain	disband	indistinct
3. modern	addict	imprint
4. absurd	insert	railway

ACTIVITY F *Sentence Reading*

1. John wanted to disband his rock group after they played at the birthday party.
2. The author will insist on reading the abstract from his new book.
3. She was very distraught when her mother tried to discard her old clothes.
4. The teacher will maintain that her words were right.
5. They will admit that they left imprints of their hands on the glass.
6. As a misfit, the puppy spent most of its time by itself.
7. Her shouts were so absurd that she was asked to leave.
8. Their modern ways of doing things had a strong impact on the group.
9. He tried his best to help the team, but he would often misplay the baseball.
10. The animal's tracks in the mud were indistinct.

2 *REWARDS Plus: Reading Strategies Applied to Science Passages*

Review Lesson 2

Materials Needed:

- *Student Book:* Review Lesson 2
- Review Overhead Transparency B
- Paper or cardboard to use when covering the overhead transparency
- Washable overhead transparency pen

Text Treatment Notes:

- Black text signifies teacher script (exact wording to say to students).
- Green text in parentheses signifies directions or prompts for the teacher.
- Green text signifies answers or examples of answers.
- Green graphics treatment signifies reproduction of Overhead information.
- Green text and green graphics treatment do not appear in the *Student Book*.

ACTIVITY A
Vowel Combinations

ACTIVITY PROCEDURE

(See the *Student Book,* page 3.)

In this activity, students review the sounds to say when they see combinations of letters. First, have students point to each combination of letters, and tell students the sound as it is pronounced in the key word. Then, have students practice all the sounds from this and the previous lesson.

1. Open your *Student Book* to **Review Lesson 2**, page 3. Find **Activity A**. We are going to review some sounds. You learned all of them in the *REWARDS* program, but you may need a short review.
2. Look at the line of letter combinations. Point to the letters **a—e**. The sound of these letters is usually /ā/. What sound?_
3. Point to the letters **o—e**. The sound of these letters is usually /ō/. What sound?_
4. Point to the letters **i—e**. The sound of these letters is usually /ī/. What sound?_
5. Point to the letters **e—e**. The sound of these letters is usually /ē/. What sound?_
6. Point to the letters **u—e**. The sound of these letters is usually /ū/. What sound?_
7. Go back to the beginning of the line. Say the sounds again. What sound?_ Next sound?_ Next sound?_ Next sound?_ Next sound?_
8. Point to the letters **e - r** in **Line #1**. What sound?_ Next sound?_ Next sound?_ Next sound?_ Next sound?_
9. (Repeat Step 8 for letters in Lines #2–4.)

REVIEW LESSON **2**

ACTIVITY A *Vowel Combinations*

a—e (make)	o—e (hope)	i—e (side)	e—e (Pete)	u—e (use)

1.	er	ir	au	ai	a—e
2.	ar	u—e	ay	i—e	au
3.	e—e	ir	ai	o—e	u—e
4.	ur	ay	a—e	au	i—e

ACTIVITY B *Vowel Conversions*

a i o u

ACTIVITY C *Prefixes and Suffixes*

compare	com	prevent	pre
belong	be	protect	pro
return	re	depart	de

1.	pro	be	pre	ad	dis	mis
2.	com	in	im	re	ab	de

Student Book: Review Lesson 2 3

ACTIVITY B

Vowel Conversions

ACTIVITY PROCEDURE

(See the *Student Book*, page 3.)

Have students point to the letter while you tell them the sound, and have them repeat the sound. Then, have students point to the same letter while you tell them the name, and have students repeat the name. Have students practice saying the sound, then the name for each letter.

1. Find **Activity B**. When you are reading words and see these letters, first try the sound. If it doesn't make a real word, then try the name.
2. Point to the first letter. The sound is /ă/. What sound?_ The name is **a**. What name?_
3. Point to the next letter. The sound is /ĭ/. What sound?_ The name is **i**. What name?_
4. Point to the next letter. The sound is /ŏ/. What sound?_ The name is **o**. What name?_
5. Point to the next letter. The sound is /ŭ/. What sound?_ The name is **u**. What name?_
6. First letter again. What sound?_ What name?_
7. Next letter. What sound?_ What name?_
8. (Repeat Step 7 for the remaining letters.)

REVIEW LESSON **2**

ACTIVITY A *Vowel Combinations*

a—e (make)	o—e (hope)	i—e (side)	e—e (Pete)	u—e (use)

1.	er	ir	au	ai	a—e
2.	ar	u—e	ay	i—e	au
3.	e—e	ir	ai	o—e	u—e
4.	ur	ay	a—e	au	i—e

ACTIVITY B *Vowel Conversions*

a i o u

ACTIVITY C *Prefixes and Suffixes*

compare	com	prevent	pre
belong	be	protect	pro
return	re	depart	de

1.	pro	be	pre	ad	dis	mis
2.	com	in	im	re	ab	de

Student Book: Review Lesson 2 3

ACTIVITY C

Prefixes and Suffixes

ACTIVITY PROCEDURE

(See the *Student Book*, page 3.)

Tell students the words, then the circled prefixes. Have students repeat the words and prefixes. Then, have students practice saying the new and previously learned prefixes.

1. Find **Activity C**. Now, we are going to review prefixes. Where do we find prefixes?_
2. Point to the first column. The first word is **compare**. What word?_ Point to the circled prefix. The prefix is /com/. What prefix?_
3. Point to the next word below. The word is **belong**. What word?_ Point to the prefix. The prefix is /be/. What prefix?_
4. (Repeat with **return** and /re/.)
5. Point to the third column. The first word is **prevent**. What word?_ The prefix is /pre/. What prefix?_
6. (Repeat with **protect** and /pro/ and **depart** and /de/.)
7. Find the second column. It has prefixes only. Read the prefixes. What prefix?_ Next?_ Next?_
8. Find the last column. What prefix?_ Next?_ Next?_
9. Point to the first prefix in **Line #1**. What prefix?_ Next?_ Next?_ Next?_ Next?_ Next?_
10. (Repeat Step 9 for prefixes in Line #2.)

REVIEW LESSON **2**

ACTIVITY A *Vowel Combinations*

a—e (make)	o—e (hope)	i—e (side)	e—e (Pete)	u—e (use)

1.	er	ir	au	ai	a—e
2.	ar	u—e	ay	i—e	au
3.	e—e	ir	ai	o—e	u—e
4.	ur	ay	a—e	au	i—e

ACTIVITY B *Vowel Conversions*

a i o u

ACTIVITY C *Prefixes and Suffixes*

compare	com	prevent	pre
belong	be	protect	pro
return	re	depart	de

1.	pro	be	pre	ad	dis	mis
2.	com	in	im	re	ab	de

ACTIVITY D

Strategy Instruction

ACTIVITY PROCEDURE

(See the *Student Book*, page 4.)

First, use three words to show students how to use the strategy for figuring out longer words. Then, work with students to apply the strategy to the remaining words. For each word, ask students if the word has prefixes, then circle them. Underline the vowels, and have students say the sounds. Finally, have students say the word, first part by part, and then as a whole word.

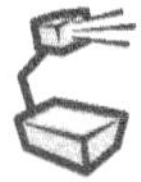
Use Overhead B: Activity D

1. Turn to page 4. Find **Activity D**.
2. We are going to review the *REWARDS* strategy for figuring out longer words.
3. Look up here. Watch me use the strategy. (Point to the word **beside**.)
4. First, I circle prefixes. (Circle **be**. Point to the prefix and ask . . .) What prefix?_
5. Next, I underline the vowels in the rest of the word. (Underline and connect the **i** and **e** in **side**. Point to the vowel and ask . . .) What sound?_
6. Next, I say the parts in the word. (Loop under each part and say the parts: **be side**.)
7. Next, we say the whole word. Remember, it must be a real word. What word?_
8. (Repeat Steps 4–7 with **readjust** and **prepay**.)
9. Let's read some more words.
10. (Point to the word **combine**.) Does the word have a prefix?_ (If the answer is "yes," circle the prefix and ask . . .) What prefix?_
11. (Underline the vowels in the rest of the word and ask . . .) What sound?_
12. Say the word by parts. (Loop under each part and ask . . .) What part?_ What part?_
13. (Run your finger under the whole word.) What word?_
14. (Repeat Steps 10–13 with **provide** and **defraud**.)

Note: You may wish to provide additional practice by having students read a line to the group or to a partner.

REVIEW LESSON
2

ACTIVITY D *Strategy Instruction*

1.	beside	readjust	prepay
2.	combine	provide	defraud

ACTIVITY E *Strategy Practice*

1.	backbone	reprint	costume
2.	mistake	promote	prescribe
3.	obsolete	propose	sunstroke
4.	decode	holiday	subscribe

ACTIVITY F *Sentence Reading*

1. She wanted to subscribe to her favorite magazine.
2. The costume was worn to promote the holiday.
3. Sunstroke can happen if you stay outside in the sun too long.
4. He needed to readjust how he took notes once the splint was put on his arm.
5. It is easy to decode long words such as **provide** and **mistake**.
6. I propose we take a trip on the railway, but we will have to prepay our tickets.
7. When people are brave, they are said to have a lot of backbone.
8. Doctors often prescribe some type of pill when people are not feeling well.
9. The con man tried to defraud the old people of their life savings.
10. The magazine story was obsolete, so we couldn't order a reprint.

4 *REWARDS Plus: Reading Strategies Applied to Science Passages*

ACTIVITY E

Strategy Practice

ACTIVITY PROCEDURE

(See the *Student Book,* page 4.)

Have students circle prefixes and underline the vowels. Assist students in checking their work, then reading each word, first part by part, and then as a whole word.

Use Overhead B: Activity E

1. Find **Activity E**.
2. Now, it's your turn. For each word, circle prefixes and underline the vowels in the rest of the word. Look up when you are done._
3. (Show the overhead transparency.) Now, check and fix any mistakes._
4. (When students are done checking, assist students in reading each word on the overhead transparency, beginning with the first word in Line #1.) Look up here._ (Loop under each word part in **back bone**.) What part?_ What part?_ (Run your finger under the whole word.) What word?_
5. (Repeat Steps 2–4 with all words in Activity E.)

Note: You may wish to provide additional practice by having students read a line to the group or to a partner.

REVIEW LESSON
2

ACTIVITY D *Strategy Instruction*

1. beside	readjust	prepay
2. combine	provide	defraud

ACTIVITY E *Strategy Practice*

1. backbone	reprint	costume
2. mistake	promote	prescribe
3. obsolete	propose	sunstroke
4. decode	holiday	subscribe

ACTIVITY F *Sentence Reading*

1. She wanted to subscribe to her favorite magazine.
2. The costume was worn to promote the holiday.
3. Sunstroke can happen if you stay outside in the sun too long.
4. He needed to readjust how he took notes once the splint was put on his arm.
5. It is easy to decode long words such as **provide** and **mistake**.
6. I propose we take a trip on the railway, but we will have to prepay our tickets.
7. When people are brave, they are said to have a lot of backbone.
8. Doctors often prescribe some type of pill when people are not feeling well.
9. The con man tried to defraud the old people of their life savings.
10. The magazine story was obsolete, so we couldn't order a reprint.

4 *REWARDS Plus: Reading Strategies Applied to Science Passages*

ACTIVITY F

Sentence Reading

ACTIVITY PROCEDURE

(See the *Student Book,* page 4.)

Have students read a sentence to themselves. Then, choose from several options of having students read the sentence together, to partners, or individually to the class.

Note: If you are teaching older students for whom "thumbs-up" is inappropriate, have students look at you when they can read the sentence.

1. Find **Sentence #1** in **Activity F.** These sentences include words that we practiced today. Read the first sentence to yourself. When you can read all the words in the sentence, put your thumb up.
2. (When students can read the sentence, use one of the following options:
   a. Ask students to read the sentence together [i.e., choral reading].
   b. Have students read the sentence to their partners. Then, call on one student to read the sentence to the group.
   c. Ask one student to read the sentence to the group.)
3. (Repeat these procedures with the remaining sentences. Be sure that you give ample thinking time for each sentence.)

REVIEW LESSON
2

ACTIVITY D *Strategy Instruction*

1. beside	readjust	prepay
2. combine	provide	defraud

ACTIVITY E *Strategy Practice*

1. backbone	reprint	costume
2. mistake	promote	prescribe
3. obsolete	propose	sunstroke
4. decode	holiday	subscribe

ACTIVITY F *Sentence Reading*

1. She wanted to subscribe to her favorite magazine.
2. The costume was worn to promote the holiday.
3. Sunstroke can happen if you stay outside in the sun too long.
4. He needed to readjust how he took notes once the splint was put on his arm.
5. It is easy to decode long words such as **provide** and **mistake**.
6. I propose we take a trip on the railway, but we will have to prepay our tickets.
7. When people are brave, they are said to have a lot of backbone.
8. Doctors often prescribe some type of pill when people are not feeling well.
9. The con man tried to defraud the old people of their life savings.
10. The magazine story was obsolete, so we couldn't order a reprint.

4 *REWARDS Plus: Reading Strategies Applied to Science Passages*

Review Lesson 3

Materials Needed:

- *Student Book:* Review Lesson 3
- Review Overhead Transparency C
- Paper or cardboard to use when covering the overhead transparency
- Washable overhead transparency pen

Text Treatment Notes:

- Black text signifies teacher script (exact wording to say to students).
- Green text in parentheses signifies directions or prompts for the teacher.
- Green text signifies answers or examples of answers.
- Green graphics treatment signifies reproduction of Overhead information.
- Green text and green graphics treatment do not appear in the *Student Book*.

ACTIVITY A

Vowel Combinations

ACTIVITY PROCEDURE

(See the *Student Book,* page 5.)

In this activity, students review the sounds to say when they see combinations of letters. First, have students point to each combination of letters, and tell students the sound as it is pronounced in the key word. Then, have students practice all the sounds from this and the previous lessons.

1. Open your *Student Book* to **Review Lesson 3**, page 5. Find **Activity A**. We are going to review some sounds. You learned all of them in the *REWARDS* program, but you may need a short review.
2. Look at the first line of letter combinations. Point to the letters **o - i**. The sound of these letters is usually /oy/. What sound?_
3. Point to the letters **o - y**. The sound of these letters is usually /oy/. What sound?_
4. Point to the letters **o - r**. The sound of these letters is usually /or/. What sound?_
5. Look at the second line of letter combinations. Point to the letters **e - e**. The sound of these letters is usually /ē/. What sound?_
6. Point to the letters **o - a**. The sound of these letters is usually /ō/. What sound?_
7. Point to the letters **o - u**. The sound of these letters is usually /ou/. What sound?_
8. Go back to the beginning of the first line of letter combinations. Say the sounds again. What sound?_ Next sound?_ Next sound?_ Next sound?_ Next sound?_ Next sound?_
9. Point to the letters **e - r** in **Line #1**. What sound?_ Next sound?_ Next sound?_ Next sound?_ Next sound?_
10. (Repeat Step 9 for letters in Lines #2–4.)

REVIEW LESSON **3**

ACTIVITY A *Vowel Combinations*

oi (void)	oy (boy)	or (torn)
ee (deep)	oa (foam)	ou (loud)

1. er	a—e	oi	oy	ee
2. u—e	ou	au	or	oa
3. e—e	ir	ai	i—e	ar
4. o—e	ur	ay	au	ou

ACTIVITY B *Vowel Conversions*

a i o u e

ACTIVITY C *Prefixes and Suffixes*

(con)tinue	con	(a)bove	a
(per)mit	per	(ex)ample	ex
(un)cover	un	(en)tail	en

1. per	con	dis	a	pre	de
2. com	pro	en	ab	im	mis
3. ex	con	un	com	a	pre

Student Book: Review Lesson 3 **5**

ACTIVITY B

Vowel Conversions

ACTIVITY PROCEDURE

(See the *Student Book*, page 5.)

Have students point to the letter while you tell them the sound, and have them repeat the sound. Then, have students point to the same letter while you tell them the name, and have students repeat the name. Have students practice saying the sound and then the name for each letter.

1. Find **Activity B**. When you are reading words and see these letters, what should you try first, the sound or the name?_ If it doesn't make a real word, what should you try?
2. Point to the first letter. The sound is /ă/. What sound?_ The name is **a**. What name?_
3. Point to the next letter. The sound is /ĭ/. What sound?_ The name is **i**. What name?_
4. Point to the next letter. The sound is /ŏ/. What sound?_ The name is **o**. What name?_
5. Point to the next letter. The sound is /ŭ/. What sound?_ The name is **u**. What name?_
6. Point to the next letter. The sound is /ĕ/. What sound?_ The name is **e**. What name?_
7. First letter again. What sound?_ What name?_
8. Next letter. What sound?_ What name?_
9. (Repeat Step 8 for the remaining letters.)

REVIEW LESSON 3

ACTIVITY A *Vowel Combinations*

oi (void)	oy (boy)	or (torn)
ee (deep)	oa (foam)	ou (loud)

1. er	a—e	oi	oy	ee
2. u—e	ou	au	or	oa
3. e—e	ir	ai	i—e	ar
4. o—e	ur	ay	au	ou

ACTIVITY B *Vowel Conversions*

a i o u e

ACTIVITY C *Prefixes and Suffixes*

(con)tinue	con	(a)bove	a
(per)mit	per	(ex)ample	ex
(un)cover	un	(en)tail	en

1. per	con	dis	a	pre	de
2. com	pro	en	ab	im	mis
3. ex	con	un	com	a	pre

Student Book: Review Lesson 3 5

ACTIVITY C

Prefixes and Suffixes

ACTIVITY PROCEDURE

(See the *Student Book*, page 5.)

Tell students the words, then the circled prefixes. Have students repeat the words and prefixes. Then, have students practice saying the new and previously learned prefixes.

1. Find **Activity C**. Now, we are going to review prefixes. Where do we find prefixes?_
2. Point to the first column. The first word is **continue**. What word?_ Point to the circled prefix. The prefix is /con/. What prefix?_
3. Point to the next word below. The word is **permit**. What word?_ Point to the prefix. The prefix is /per/. What prefix?_
4. (Repeat with **uncover** and /un/.)
5. Point to the third column. The first word is **above**. What word?_ The prefix is /ŭ/. What prefix?_
6. (Repeat with **example** and /ex/ and **entail** and /en/.)
7. Find the second column. It has prefixes only. Read the prefixes. What prefix?_ Next?_ Next?_
8. Find the last column. What prefix?_ Next?_ Next?_
9. Point to the first prefix in **Line #1**. What prefix?_ Next?_ Next?_ Next?_ Next?_ Next?_
10. (Repeat Step 9 for prefixes in Lines #2–3.)

REVIEW LESSON 3

ACTIVITY A *Vowel Combinations*

oi (void)	oy (boy)	or (torn)
ee (deep)	oa (foam)	ou (loud)

1.	er	a—e	oi	oy	ee
2.	u—e	ou	au	or	oa
3.	e—e	ir	ai	i—e	ar
4.	o—e	ur	ay	au	ou

ACTIVITY B *Vowel Conversions*

a i o u e

ACTIVITY C *Prefixes and Suffixes*

continue	con	above	a
permit	per	example	ex
uncover	un	entail	en

1.	per	con	dis	a	pre	de
2.	com	pro	en	ab	im	mis
3.	ex	con	un	com	a	pre

Student Book: Review Lesson 3 5

Strategy Practice

ACTIVITY PROCEDURE

(See the *Student Book*, page 6.)

In this activity, have students apply the strategy for figuring out longer words by themselves. Have students circle prefixes and underline the vowels. Have students say the word part by part to themselves and then as a whole word aloud.

Use Overhead C: Activity D

1. Turn to page 6. Find **Activity D**.
2. Circle prefixes and underline the vowels. Look up when you are done._
3. (Show the overhead transparency.) Now, check and fix any mistakes._
4. Go back to the first word._ Sound out the word to yourself. Put your thumb up when you can read the word. Be sure that it is a real word._ What word?_
5. (Continue Step 4 with all words in Activity D.)

Note: You may wish to provide additional practice by having students read a line to the group or to a partner.

REVIEW LESSON
3

ACTIVITY D *Strategy Practice*

1. perturb	uncurl	confess
2. afraid	expert	engrave

ACTIVITY E *Independent Strategy Practice*

1. misinform	disagree	spellbound
2. sweepstake	reproduce	protect
3. turmoil	bemoan	discontent
4. imperfect	boycott	reconstruct

ACTIVITY F *Sentence Reading*

1. Please do not misinform people about the boycott on those items.
2. Don't be afraid to disagree with certain ideas.
3. The man tried to reproduce the painting, but the result was imperfect.
4. He did confess that the turmoil began on the baseball field.
5. I won't bemoan the fact that I did not win the sweepstakes money.
6. It will perturb him to find out that the expert could not protect him.
7. The dancers were so good that they left the people spellbound.
8. Did he engrave the wedding ring for you?
9. They tried to reconstruct the building, but those who paid them were discontent.
10. We always disagree on how much to invest in the stock market.

6 *REWARDS Plus: Reading Strategies Applied to Science Passages*

ACTIVITY E

Independent Strategy Practice

ACTIVITY PROCEDURE

(See the *Student Book,* page 6.)

In this activity, students independently practice using the covert strategy for figuring out longer words. They no longer use overt tasks, such as circling prefixes or underlining vowels. Have students look carefully at each word, locate prefixes and vowels, and figure out the word for themselves. Then, have students say the word aloud.

Use Overhead C: Activity E

Note 1: If students have difficulty decoding a word, demonstrate the strategy on the overhead.

1. Find **Activity E**.
2. Find **Line #1**. Without circling and underlining, look carefully for prefixes. Look for vowels in the rest of the word. If you have difficulty figuring out the word, use your pencil. Put your thumb up when you can say the first word._ (Give ample thinking time.)
3. (When students have decoded the word, ask . . .) What word?_
4. Next word. Put your thumb up when you can say the word._ (Give ample thinking time.) What word?_
5. (Repeat Step 4 for the remaining words in Activity E.)

Note 2: You may wish to provide additional practice by having students read a line to the group or to a partner.

REVIEW LESSON **3**

ACTIVITY D *Strategy Practice*

1.	perturb	uncurl	confess
2.	afraid	expert	engrave

ACTIVITY E *Independent Strategy Practice*

1.	misinform	disagree	spellbound
2.	sweepstake	reproduce	protect
3.	turmoil	bemoan	discontent
4.	imperfect	boycott	reconstruct

ACTIVITY F *Sentence Reading*

1. Please do not misinform people about the boycott on those items.
2. Don't be afraid to disagree with certain ideas.
3. The man tried to reproduce the painting, but the result was imperfect.
4. He did confess that the turmoil began on the baseball field.
5. I won't bemoan the fact that I did not win the sweepstakes money.
6. It will perturb him to find out that the expert could not protect him.
7. The dancers were so good that they left the people spellbound.
8. Did he engrave the wedding ring for you?
9. They tried to reconstruct the building, but those who paid them were discontent.
10. We always disagree on how much to invest in the stock market.

6 *REWARDS Plus: Reading Strategies Applied to Science Passages*

ACTIVITY F

Sentence Reading

ACTIVITY PROCEDURE

(See the *Student Book*, page 6.)

Have students read a sentence to themselves. Then, choose from several options of having students read the sentence together, to partners, or individually to the class.

1. Find **Sentence #1** in **Activity F.** These sentences include words that we practiced today. Read the first sentence to yourself. When you can read all the words in the sentence, put your thumb up.
2. (When students can read the sentence, use one of the following options:
   a. Ask students to read the sentence together [i.e., choral reading].
   b. Have students read the sentence to their partners. Then, call on one student to read the sentence to the group.
   c. Ask one student to read the sentence to the group.)
3. (Repeat these procedures with the remaining sentences. Be sure that you give ample thinking time for each sentence.)

REVIEW LESSON 3

ACTIVITY D *Strategy Practice*

1.	perturb	uncurl	confess
2.	afraid	expert	engrave

ACTIVITY E *Independent Strategy Practice*

1.	misinform	disagree	spellbound
2.	sweepstake	reproduce	protect
3.	turmoil	bemoan	discontent
4.	imperfect	boycott	reconstruct

ACTIVITY F *Sentence Reading*

1. Please do not misinform people about the boycott on those items.
2. Don't be afraid to disagree with certain ideas.
3. The man tried to reproduce the painting, but the result was imperfect.
4. He did confess that the turmoil began on the baseball field.
5. I won't bemoan the fact that I did not win the sweepstakes money.
6. It will perturb him to find out that the expert could not protect him.
7. The dancers were so good that they left the people spellbound.
8. Did he engrave the wedding ring for you?
9. They tried to reconstruct the building, but those who paid them were discontent.
10. We always disagree on how much to invest in the stock market.

6 *REWARDS Plus: Reading Strategies Applied to Science Passages*

Review Lesson 4

Materials Needed:

- *Student Book:* Review Lesson 4
- Review Overhead Transparency D
- Paper or cardboard to use when covering the overhead transparency
- Washable overhead transparency pen

Text Treatment Notes:

- Black text signifies teacher script (exact wording to say to students).
- Green text in parentheses signifies directions or prompts for the teacher.
- Green text signifies answers or examples of answers.
- Green graphics treatment signifies reproduction of Overhead information.
- Green text and green graphics treatment do not appear in the *Student Book*.

ACTIVITY A
Vowel Combinations

ACTIVITY PROCEDURE

(See the *Student Book*, page 7.)

In this activity, students review that sometimes a letter combination has two sounds. They review that when they see this letter combination in a word or word part, they should try the first sound they have learned. If the word doesn't sound right, they should try the second sound they have learned. Have students point to the letter combination. Tell them the sound as it is pronounced in the first key word. Then, tell students what sound to try if the word doesn't sound right. Have students practice what they would say first and what they would say second. Have students practice this sound and sounds from previous lessons. Whenever they come to a boxed letter combination, they should say both sounds.

1. Open your *Student Book* to **Review Lesson 4**, page 7. Find **Activity A**. We are going to review two sounds for these letters. You learned them in the *REWARDS* program, but you may need a short review.
2. Look at the letter combination with word examples. Point to the letters **o - w**. The sound of these letters is usually /ō/, as in **low**. What sound?_ If the word doesn't sound right, try /ou/, as in **down**. What sound?_
3. Let's review. What sound would you try first? /ō/ What would you try next? /ou/

Note: Whenever you come to boxed letters, ask, "What sound would you try first? What sound would you try next?"

4. Point to the letters **o - u** in **Line #1**. What sound?_ Boxed letters. What sound would you try first?_ What sound would you try next?_ Next sound?_
5. (Continue Step 4 for all remaining letters in Lines #1–4.)

REVIEW LESSON 4

ACTIVITY A *Vowel Combinations*

ow
(low) (down)

1.	ou	ow	i—e	oy	ur
2.	oa	a—e	ow	ai	ir
3.	oi	ow	ee	ow	ar
4.	au	or	oy	u—e	ow

ACTIVITY B *Vowel Conversions*

u e i a o

ACTIVITY C *Prefixes and Suffixes*

birds	s	frantic	ic
running	ing	regulate	ate
landed	ed	selfish	ish
		artist	ist
kindness	ness	realism	ism
useless	less	biggest	est
final	al	tailor	or
careful	ful	farmer	er

1.	ab	com	con	dis	pre	re
2.	im	ex	un	per	pro	a
3.	est	ic	ful	or	al	er
4.	ish	ism	less	ate	ness	ist

Student Book: Review Lesson 4 7

ACTIVITY B

Vowel Conversions

ACTIVITY PROCEDURE

(See the *Student Book*, page 7.)

Have students practice saying the sound and then the name for each letter.

1. Find **Activity B**. When you are reading words and see these letters, what should you try first, the sound or the name? If it doesn't make a real word, what should you try?
2. Point to the first letter. What sound? What name?
3. Point to the next letter. What sound? What name?
4. Point to the next letter. What sound? What name?
5. Point to the next letter. What sound? What name?
6. Point to the next letter. What sound? What name?
7. First letter again. What sound? What name?
8. Next letter. What sound? What name?
9. (Repeat Step 8 for the remaining letters.)

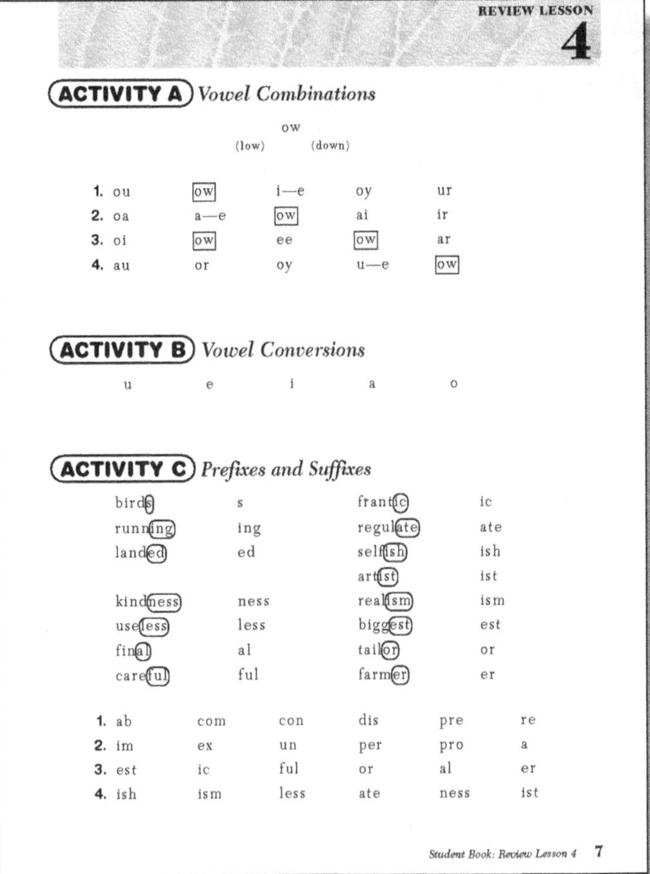

REVIEW LESSON 4

ACTIVITY A *Vowel Combinations*

	ow (low)	ow (down)		
1. ou	ow	i—e	oy	ur
2. oa	a—e	ow	ai	ir
3. oi	ow	ee	ow	ar
4. au	or	oy	u—e	ow

ACTIVITY B *Vowel Conversions*

u e i a o

ACTIVITY C *Prefixes and Suffixes*

birds	s	frantic	ic
running	ing	regulate	ate
landed	ed	selfish	ish
		artist	ist
kindness	ness	realism	ism
useless	less	biggest	est
final	al	tailor	or
careful	ful	farmer	er

1. ab	com	con	dis	pre	re
2. im	ex	un	per	pro	a
3. est	ic	ful	or	al	er
4. ish	ism	less	ate	ness	ist

Student Book: Review Lesson 4 7

ACTIVITY C

Prefixes and Suffixes

ACTIVITY PROCEDURE

(See the *Student Book*, page 7.)

Tell students the words, then the circled suffixes. Have students repeat the words and suffixes. Then, have students practice saying the new and previously learned prefixes and suffixes.

1. Find **Activity C**. Now, we are going to review suffixes. Where do we find suffixes?_
2. Point to the first column. The first word is **birds**. What word?_ Point to the circled suffix. The suffix is /s/. What suffix?_
3. Point to the next word below. The word is **running**. What word?_ Point to the suffix. The suffix is /ing/. What suffix?_
4. (Repeat with **landed** and /ed/, **kindness** and /ness/, **useless** and /less/, **final** and /al/, and **careful** and /ful/.)
5. Point to the third column. The first word is **frantic**. What word?_ The suffix is /ic/. What suffix?_
6. (Repeat with **regulate** and /ate/, **selfish** and /ish/, **artist** and /ist/, **realism** and /ism/, **biggest** and /est/, **tailor** and /or/, and **farmer** and /er/.)
7. Find the second column. It has suffixes only. Read the suffixes. What suffix?_ Next?_ Next?_ Next?_ Next?_ Next?_ Next?_
8. Find the last column. What suffix?_ Next?_ Next?_ Next?_ Next?_ Next?_ Next?_ Next?_
9. Point to the first prefix in **Line #1**. What prefix?_ Next?_ Next?_ Next?_ Next?_ Next?_
10. (Repeat Step 9 for prefixes and suffixes in Lines #2–4.)

REVIEW LESSON 4

ACTIVITY A *Vowel Combinations*

ow (low) (down)

1.	ou	ow	i—e	oy	ur
2.	oa	a—e	ow	ai	ir
3.	oi	ow	ee	ow	ar
4.	au	or	oy	u—e	ow

ACTIVITY B *Vowel Conversions*

u e i a o

ACTIVITY C *Prefixes and Suffixes*

birds	s	frantic	ic
running	ing	regulate	ate
landed	ed	selfish	ish
		artist	ist
kindness	ness	realism	ism
useless	less	biggest	est
final	al	tailor	or
careful	ful	farmer	er

1.	ab	com	con	dis	pre	re
2.	im	ex	un	per	pro	a
3.	est	ic	ful	or	al	er
4.	ish	ism	less	ate	ness	ist

Student Book: Review Lesson 4 7

ACTIVITY D

Strategy Practice

ACTIVITY PROCEDURE

(See the *Student Book*, page 8.)

In this activity, have students apply the strategy for figuring out longer words by themselves. Have students circle prefixes and suffixes and underline the vowels. Have students say the word part by part to themselves and then as a whole word aloud.

Use Overhead D: Activity D

1. Turn to page 8. Find **Activity D**.
2. Circle prefixes and suffixes and underline the vowels. Be careful. Remember that some words have no prefixes or suffixes, and some words have one or more prefixes or suffixes. Look up when you are done.
3. (Show the overhead transparency.) Now, check and fix any mistakes.
4. Go back to the first word. Sound out the word to yourself. Put your thumb up when you can read the word. Be sure that it is a real word. What word?
5. (Continue Step 4 with all words in Activity D.)

Note 1: If students have difficulty finding all the suffixes, remind them to start at the end of the word and work backward.

Note 2: You may wish to provide additional practice by having students read a line to the group or to a partner.

REVIEW LESSON
4

ACTIVITY D *Strategy Practice*

1.	regardless	softness	unfortunate
2.	programmer	slowest	historical
3.	organism	inventor	personal

ACTIVITY E *Independent Strategy Practice*

1.	abnormal	respectful	proposal
2.	exaggerate	exhaust	untruthful
3.	careless	unfaithful	astonish
4.	alarmist	energetic	exclude

ACTIVITY F *Sentence Reading*

1. It is so unfortunate that the programmer quit in the middle of the project.
2. The inventor exaggerated his claims for a modern submarine.
3. Would you be astonished to know that she was excluded from the group?
4. Regardless of how untruthful he was about the money, he is not a careless man.
5. It is not abnormal for many types of organisms to exist in the same area.
6. His proposal was too astonishing to be used, regardless of his background.
7. The historical display exaggerated the inventor's role.
8. She was an alarmist but was not careless with her words or unfaithful to her beliefs.
9. He decided to take the slowest way home for the holidays.
10. She was so energetic that her friends became exhausted whenever they were with her.

8 *REWARDS Plus: Reading Strategies Applied to Science Passages*

ACTIVITY E

Independent Strategy Practice

ACTIVITY PROCEDURE

(See the *Student Book*, page 8.)

In this activity, students independently practice using the covert strategy for figuring out longer words. They no longer use overt tasks, such as circling prefixes and suffixes or underlining vowels. Have students look carefully at each word, locate prefixes, suffixes, and vowels, and figure out the word by themselves. Then, have students say the word aloud.

Use Overhead D: Activity E

Note 1: If students have difficulty decoding a word, demonstrate the strategy on the overhead.

1. Find **Activity E.**
2. Find **Line #1**. Without circling and underlining, look carefully for prefixes and suffixes. Look for vowels in the rest of the word. If you have difficulty figuring out the word, use your pencil. Put your thumb up when you can say the first word._ (Give ample thinking time.)
3. (When students have decoded the word, ask . . .) What word?_
4. Next word. Put your thumb up when you can say the word._ (Give ample thinking time.) What word?_
5. (Repeat Step 4 for the remaining words in Activity E.)

Note 2: You may wish to provide additional practice by having students read a line to the group or to a partner.

REVIEW LESSON

4

ACTIVITY D *Strategy Practice*

1.	regardless	softness	unfortunate
2.	programmer	slowest	historical
3.	organism	inventor	personal

ACTIVITY E *Independent Strategy Practice*

1.	abnormal	respectful	proposal
2.	exaggerate	exhaust	untruthful
3.	careless	unfaithful	astonish
4.	alarmist	energetic	exclude

ACTIVITY F *Sentence Reading*

1. It is so unfortunate that the programmer quit in the middle of the project.
2. The inventor exaggerated his claims for a modern submarine.
3. Would you be astonished to know that she was excluded from the group?
4. Regardless of how untruthful he was about the money, he is not a careless man.
5. It is not abnormal for many types of organisms to exist in the same area.
6. His proposal was too astonishing to be used, regardless of his background.
7. The historical display exaggerated the inventor's role.
8. She was an alarmist but was not careless with her words or unfaithful to her beliefs.
9. He decided to take the slowest way home for the holidays.
10. She was so energetic that her friends became exhausted whenever they were with her.

8 *REWARDS Plus: Reading Strategies Applied to Science Passages*

ACTIVITY F

Sentence Reading

ACTIVITY PROCEDURE

(See the *Student Book*, page 8.)

Have students read a sentence to themselves. Then, choose from several options of having students read the sentence together, to partners, or individually to the class.

1. Find **Sentence #1** in **Activity F.** These sentences include words that we practiced today. Read the first sentence to yourself. When you can read all the words in the sentence, put your thumb up.
2. (When students can read the sentence, use one of the following options:
   a. Ask students to read the sentence together [i.e., choral reading].
   b. Have students read the sentence to their partners. Then, call on one student to read the sentence to the group.
   c. Ask one student to read the sentence to the group.)
3. (Repeat these procedures with the remaining sentences. Be sure that you give ample thinking time for each sentence.)

REVIEW LESSON
4

ACTIVITY D *Strategy Practice*

1.	regardless	softness	unfortunate
2.	programmer	slowest	historical
3.	organism	inventor	personal

ACTIVITY E *Independent Strategy Practice*

1.	abnormal	respectful	proposal
2.	exaggerate	exhaust	untruthful
3.	careless	unfaithful	astonish
4.	alarmist	energetic	exclude

ACTIVITY F *Sentence Reading*

1. It is so unfortunate that the programmer quit in the middle of the project.
2. The inventor exaggerated his claims for a modern submarine.
3. Would you be astonished to know that she was excluded from the group?
4. Regardless of how untruthful he was about the money, he is not a careless man.
5. It is not abnormal for many types of organisms to exist in the same area.
6. His proposal was too astonishing to be used, regardless of his background.
7. The historical display exaggerated the inventor's role.
8. She was an alarmist but was not careless with her words or unfaithful to her beliefs.
9. He decided to take the slowest way home for the holidays.
10. She was so energetic that her friends became exhausted whenever they were with her.

8 *REWARDS Plus: Reading Strategies Applied to Science Passages*

Review Lesson 5

Materials Needed:

- *Student Book:* Review Lesson 5
- Review Overhead Transparency E
- Paper or cardboard to use when covering the overhead transparency
- Washable overhead transparency pen

Text Treatment Notes:

- Black text signifies teacher script (exact wording to say to students).
- Green text in parentheses signifies directions or prompts for the teacher.
- Green text signifies answers or examples of answers.
- Green graphics treatment signifies reproduction of Overhead information.
- Green text and green graphics treatment do not appear in the *Student Book*.

ACTIVITY A

Vowel Combinations

ACTIVITY PROCEDURE

(See the *Student Book*, page 9.)

In this activity, students review the two sounds of another letter combination. Have students point to the letter combination. Tell them the sound as it is pronounced in the first key word. Then, tell students what sound to try if the word doesn't sound right. Have students practice what they would say first and what they would say second. Have students practice this sound and sounds from previous lessons. Remind them to try both sounds when they see boxed letters.

1. Open your *Student Book* to **Review Lesson 5**, page 9. Find **Activity A**. We are going to review two sounds for these letters. You learned them in the *REWARDS* program, but you may need a short review.
2. Look at the letter combination with word examples. Point to the letters **o - o**. The sound of these letters is usually /o͞o/, as in **moon**. What sound?_ If the word doesn't sound right, try /o͝o/, as in **book**. What sound?_
3. Let's review. What sound would you try first? /o͞o/ What would you try next? /o͝o/

Note: Whenever you come to boxed letters, ask, "What sound would you try first? What sound would you try next?"

4. Point to the boxed letters **o - w** in **Line #1**. What sound would you try first?_ What sound would you try next?_ Next sound?_ Next sound?_
5. (Continue Step 4 for all remaining letters in Lines #1–4.)

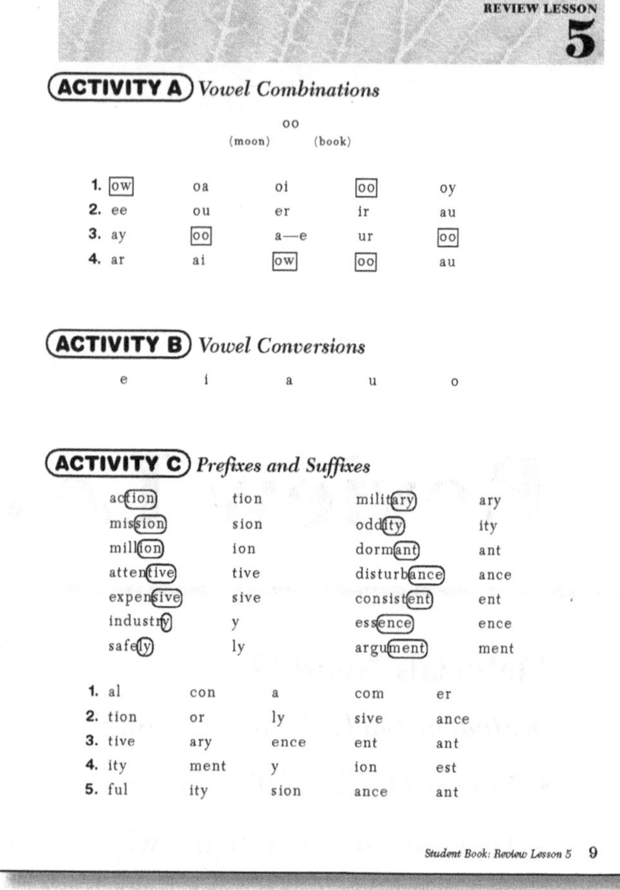

REVIEW LESSON 5

ACTIVITY A *Vowel Combinations*

oo
(moon) (book)

1.	[ow]	oa	oi	[oo]	oy
2.	ee	ou	er	ir	au
3.	ay	[oo]	a—e	ur	[oo]
4.	ar	ai	[ow]	[oo]	au

ACTIVITY B *Vowel Conversions*

e i a u o

ACTIVITY C *Prefixes and Suffixes*

action	tion	military	ary
mission	sion	oddity	ity
million	ion	dormant	ant
attentive	tive	disturbance	ance
expensive	sive	consistent	ent
industry	y	essence	ence
safely	ly	argument	ment

1.	al	con	a	com	er
2.	tion	or	ly	sive	ance
3.	tive	ary	ence	ent	ant
4.	ity	ment	y	ion	est
5.	ful	ity	sion	ance	ant

Student Book: Review Lesson 5 9

ACTIVITY B

Vowel Conversions

ACTIVITY PROCEDURE

(See the *Student Book*, page 9.)

Have students practice saying the sound and then the name for each letter.

1. Find **Activity B**. When you are reading words and see these letters, what should you try first, the sound or the name?_ If it doesn't make a real word, what should you try?_
2. Point to the first letter. What sound?_ What name?_
3. Point to the next letter. What sound?_ What name?_
4. Point to the next letter. What sound?_ What name?_
5. Point to the next letter. What sound?_ What name?_
6. Point to the next letter. What sound?_ What name?_
7. First letter again. What sound?_ What name?_
8. Next letter. What sound?_ What name?_
9. (Repeat Step 8 for the remaining letters.)

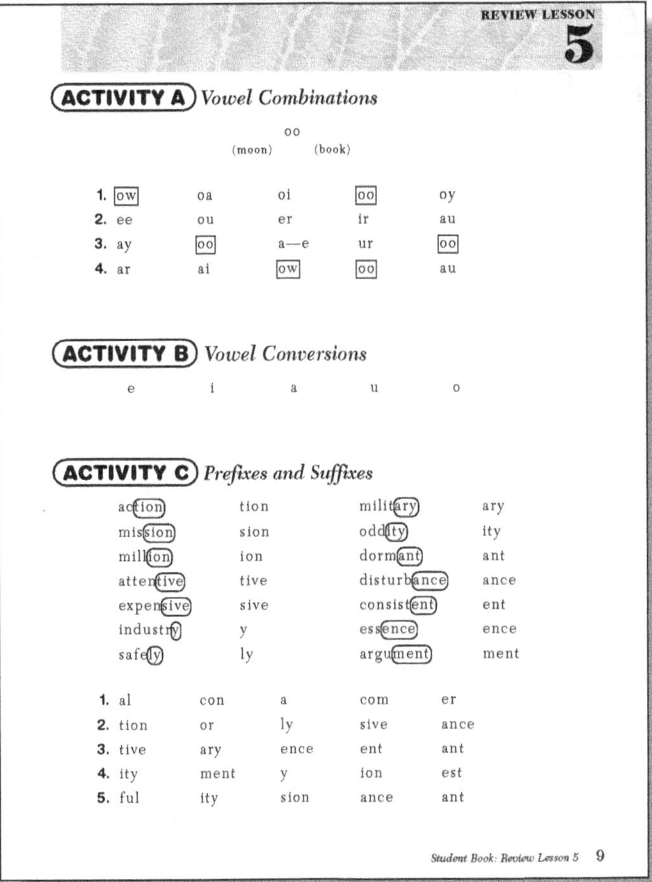

REVIEW LESSON 5

ACTIVITY A *Vowel Combinations*

oo (moon) (book)

1.	ow	oa	oi	oo	oy
2.	ee	ou	er	ir	au
3.	ay	oo	a—e	ur	oo
4.	ar	ai	ow	oo	au

ACTIVITY B *Vowel Conversions*

e i a u o

ACTIVITY C *Prefixes and Suffixes*

action	tion	military	ary
mission	sion	oddity	ity
million	ion	dormant	ant
attentive	tive	disturbance	ance
expensive	sive	consistent	ent
industry	y	essence	ence
safely	ly	argument	ment

1.	al	con	a	com	er
2.	tion	or	ly	sive	ance
3.	tive	ary	ence	ent	ant
4.	ity	ment	y	ion	est
5.	ful	ity	sion	ance	ant

Student Book: Review Lesson 5 9

ACTIVITY C

Prefixes and Suffixes

ACTIVITY PROCEDURE

(See the *Student Book*, page 9.)

Tell students the words, then the circled suffixes. Have students repeat the words and suffixes. Then, have students practice saying the new and previously learned prefixes and suffixes.

1. Find **Activity C**. Now, we are going to review suffixes. Where do we find suffixes?_
2. Point to the first column. The first word is **action**. What word?_ Point to the circled suffix. The suffix is /tion/. What suffix?_
3. Point to the next word below. The word is **mission**. What word?_ Point to the suffix. The suffix is /sion/. What suffix?_
4. (Repeat with **million** and /ion/, **attentive** and /tive/, **expensive** and /sive/, **industry** and /y/, and **safely** and /ly/.)
5. Point to the third column. The first word is **military**. What word?_ The suffix is /ary/. What suffix?_
6. (Repeat with **oddity** and /ity/, **dormant** and /ant/, **disturbance** and /ance/, **consistent** and /ent/, **essence** and /ence/, and **argument** and /ment/.)
7. Find the second column. It has suffixes only. Read the suffixes. What suffix?_ Next?_ Next?_ Next?_ Next?_ Next?_ Next?_
8. Find the last column. What suffix?_ Next?_ Next?_ Next?_ Next?_ Next?_ Next?_
9. Point to **Line #1**. It has a mix of prefixes and suffixes. Point to the first suffix. What suffix?_ Next?_ Next?_ Next?_ Next?_
10. (Repeat Step 9 for suffixes in Lines #2–5).

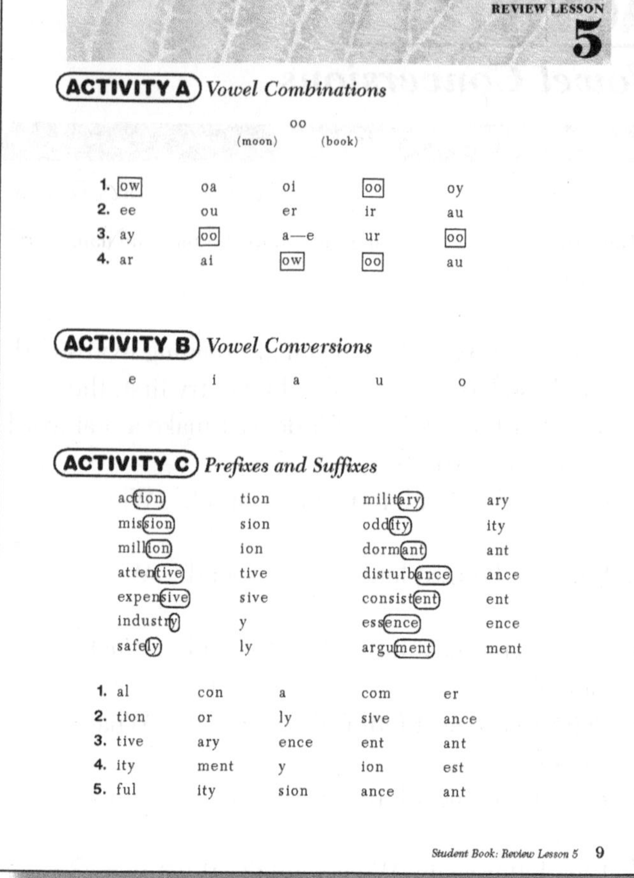

REVIEW LESSON 5

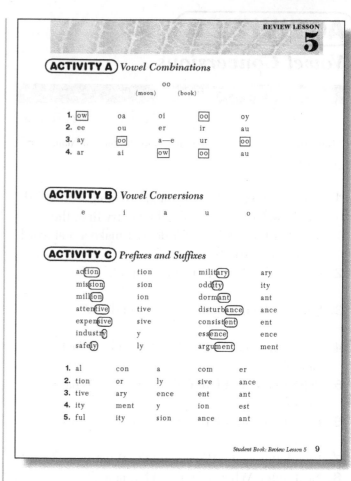

ACTIVITY A *Vowel Combinations*

oo (moon) (book)

1.	ow	oa	oi	oo	oy
2.	ee	ou	er	ir	au
3.	ay	oo	a—e	ur	oo
4.	ar	ai	ow	oo	au

ACTIVITY B *Vowel Conversions*

e i a u o

ACTIVITY C *Prefixes and Suffixes*

action	tion	military	ary
mission	sion	oddity	ity
million	ion	dormant	ant
attentive	tive	disturbance	ance
expensive	sive	consistent	ent
industry	y	essence	ence
safely	ly	argument	ment

1.	al	con	a	com	er
2.	tion	or	ly	sive	ance
3.	tive	ary	ence	ent	ant
4.	ity	ment	y	ion	est
5.	ful	ity	sion	ance	ant

Student Book: Review Lesson 5 9

ACTIVITY D

Strategy Practice

ACTIVITY PROCEDURE

(See the *Student Book,* page 10.)

In this activity, have students apply the strategy for figuring out longer words by themselves. Have students circle prefixes and suffixes and underline the vowels. Have students say the word part by part to themselves and then as a whole word aloud.

Use Overhead E: Activity D

1. Turn to page 10. Find **Activity D.**
2. Circle prefixes and suffixes and underline the vowels. Look up when you are done._
3. (Show the overhead transparency.) Now, check and fix any mistakes._
4. Go back to the first word._ Sound out the word to yourself. Put your thumb up when you can read the word. Be sure that it is a real word._ What word?_
5. (Continue Step 4 with all words in Activity D.)

Note: You may wish to provide additional practice by having students read a line to the group or to a partner.

REVIEW LESSON
5

ACTIVITY D *Strategy Practice*

1.	advertisement	delightful	disinfectant
2.	intentionally	property	expressionless
3.	personality	admittance	incoherence

ACTIVITY E *Independent Strategy Practice*

1.	perfectionist	independently	dictionary
2.	contaminate	precautionary	deductive
3.	inconsistently	excitement	repulsive
4.	opinion	hoodwink	imperfect

ACTIVITY F *Sentence Reading*

1. The members took a precautionary approach when considering her application for admittance to the club.
2. As a perfectionist, she had a strong reaction to the imperfect dictionary.
3. When told that his actions might contaminate the experiment, his face was expressionless.
4. The advertisement for disinfectant was delightful but intentionally inaccurate.
5. He came to his opinion through deductive problem-solving.
6. John came to his own conclusions independently.
7. Unfortunately, the only excitement came at the end of the performance.
8. She did not try to hoodwink him regarding the value of the property.
9. The drawing was imperfect but was not repulsive.
10. The homework assignments were lengthy and were inconsistently completed by most students.

10 *REWARDS Plus: Reading Strategies Applied to Science Passages*

ACTIVITY E

Independent Strategy Practice

ACTIVITY PROCEDURE

(See the *Student Book*, page 10.)

Have students look carefully at each word, locate prefixes, suffixes, and vowels, and figure out the word by themselves. Then, have students say the word aloud.

Use Overhead E: Activity E

Note 1: If students have difficulty decoding a word, demonstrate the strategy on the overhead.

1. Find **Activity E**.
2. Find **Line #1**. Without circling and underlining, look carefully for prefixes and suffixes. Look for vowels in the rest of the word. Put your thumb up when you can say the first word._ (Give ample thinking time.)
3. (When students have decoded the word, ask ...) What word?_
4. Next word. Put your thumb up when you can say the word._ (Give ample thinking time.) What word?_
5. (Repeat Step 4 for the remaining words in Activity E.)

Note 2: You may wish to provide additional practice by having students read a line to the group or to a partner.

REVIEW LESSON
5

ACTIVITY D *Strategy Practice*

1.	advertisement	delightful	disinfectant
2.	intentionally	property	expressionless
3.	personality	admittance	incoherence

ACTIVITY E *Independent Strategy Practice*

1.	perfectionist	independently	dictionary
2.	contaminate	precautionary	deductive
3.	inconsistently	excitement	repulsive
4.	opinion	hoodwink	imperfect

ACTIVITY F *Sentence Reading*

1. The members took a precautionary approach when considering her application for admittance to the club.
2. As a perfectionist, she had a strong reaction to the imperfect dictionary.
3. When told that his actions might contaminate the experiment, his face was expressionless.
4. The advertisement for disinfectant was delightful but intentionally inaccurate.
5. He came to his opinion through deductive problem-solving.
6. John came to his own conclusions independently.
7. Unfortunately, the only excitement came at the end of the performance.
8. She did not try to hoodwink him regarding the value of the property.
9. The drawing was imperfect but was not repulsive.
10. The homework assignments were lengthy and were inconsistently completed by most students.

10 *REWARDS Plus: Reading Strategies Applied to Science Passages*

ACTIVITY F

Sentence Reading

ACTIVITY PROCEDURE

(See the *Student Book*, page 10.)

Have students read a sentence to themselves. Then, choose from several options of having students read the sentence together, to partners, or individually to the class.

1. Find **Sentence #1** in **Activity F.** These sentences include words that we practiced today. Read the first sentence to yourself. When you can read all the words in the sentence, put your thumb up.
2. (When students can read the sentence, use one of the following options:
   a. Ask students to read the sentence together [i.e., choral reading].
   b. Have students read the sentence to their partners. Then, call on one student to read the sentence to the group.
   c. Ask one student to read the sentence to the group.)
3. (Repeat these procedures with the remaining sentences. Be sure that you give ample thinking time for each sentence.)

REVIEW LESSON
5

ACTIVITY D *Strategy Practice*

1.	advertisement	delightful	disinfectant
2.	intentionally	property	expressionless
3.	personality	admittance	incoherence

ACTIVITY E *Independent Strategy Practice*

1.	perfectionist	independently	dictionary
2.	contaminate	precautionary	deductive
3.	inconsistently	excitement	repulsive
4.	opinion	hoodwink	imperfect

ACTIVITY F *Sentence Reading*

1. The members took a precautionary approach when considering her application for admittance to the club.
2. As a perfectionist, she had a strong reaction to the imperfect dictionary.
3. When told that his actions might contaminate the experiment, his face was expressionless.
4. The advertisement for disinfectant was delightful but intentionally inaccurate.
5. He came to his opinion through deductive problem-solving.
6. John came to his own conclusions independently.
7. Unfortunately, the only excitement came at the end of the performance.
8. She did not try to hoodwink him regarding the value of the property.
9. The drawing was imperfect but was not repulsive.
10. The homework assignments were lengthy and were inconsistently completed by most students.

10 *REWARDS Plus: Reading Strategies Applied to Science Passages*

Review Lesson 6

Materials Needed:

- *Student Book:* Review Lesson 6
- Review Overhead Transparency F
- Paper or cardboard to use when covering the overhead transparency
- Washable overhead transparency pen

Text Treatment Notes:

- Black text signifies teacher script (exact wording to say to students).
- Green text in parentheses signifies directions or prompts for the teacher.
- Green text signifies answers or examples of answers.
- Green graphics treatment signifies reproduction of Overhead information.
- Green text and green graphics treatment do not appear in the *Student Book*.

ACTIVITY A

Vowel Combinations

ACTIVITY PROCEDURE

(See the *Student Book*, page 11.)

In this activity, students review the two sounds of another letter combination. Have students point to the letter combination. Tell them the sound as it is pronounced in the first key word. Then, tell students what sound to try if the word doesn't sound right. Have students practice what they would say first and what they would say second. Have students practice this sound and sounds from previous lessons. Remind them to try both sounds when they see boxed letters.

1. Open your *Student Book* to **Review Lesson 6**, page 11. Find **Activity A**. We are going to review two sounds for these letters. You learned them in the *REWARDS* program, but you may need a short review.
2. Look at the letter combination with word examples. Point to the letters **e - a**. The sound of these letters is usually /ē/, as in **meat**. What sound?_ If the word doesn't sound right, try /ĕ/, as in **thread**. What sound?_
3. Let's review. What sound would you try first? /ē/ What would you try next? /ĕ/

Note: Whenever you come to boxed letters, ask, "What sound would you try first? What sound would you try next?"

4. Point to the boxed letters **o - o** in **Line #1**. What sound would you try first?_ What sound would you try next?_ Boxed letters. What sound would you try first?_ What sound would you try next?_
5. (Continue Step 4 for all remaining letters in Lines #1–4.)

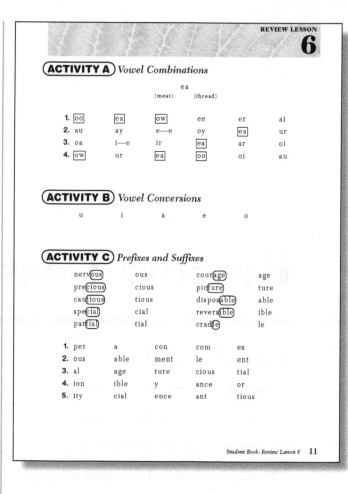

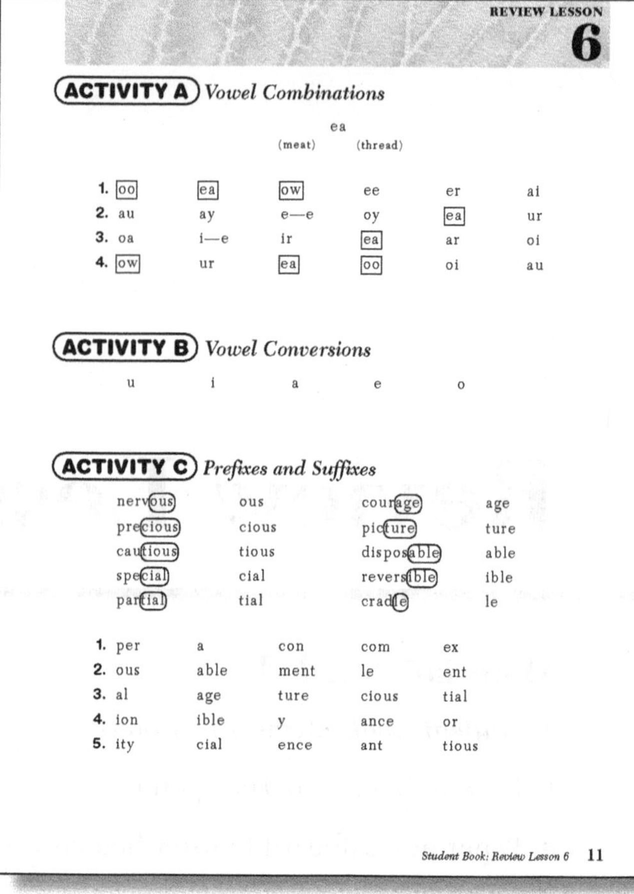

REVIEW LESSON 6

ACTIVITY A *Vowel Combinations*

ea
(meat) (thread)

1.	oo	ea	ow	ee	er	ai
2.	au	ay	e—e	oy	ea	ur
3.	oa	i—e	ir	ea	ar	oi
4.	ow	ur	ea	oo	oi	au

ACTIVITY B *Vowel Conversions*

u i a e o

ACTIVITY C *Prefixes and Suffixes*

nervous	ous	courage	age
precious	cious	picture	ture
cautious	tious	disposable	able
special	cial	reversible	ible
partial	tial	cradle	le

1.	per	a	con	com	ex
2.	ous	able	ment	le	ent
3.	al	age	ture	cious	tial
4.	ion	ible	y	ance	or
5.	ity	cial	ence	ant	tious

Student Book: Review Lesson 6 11

ACTIVITY B

Vowel Conversions

ACTIVITY PROCEDURE

(See the *Student Book,* page 11.)

Have students review saying the sound, then the name for each letter.

1. Find **Activity B**. When you are reading words and see these letters, what should you try first, the sound or the name?_ If it doesn't make a real word, what should you try?_
2. Point to the first letter. What sound?_ What name?_
3. Point to the next letter. What sound?_ What name?_
4. Point to the next letter. What sound?_ What name?_
5. Point to the next letter. What sound?_ What name?_
6. Point to the next letter. What sound?_ What name?_

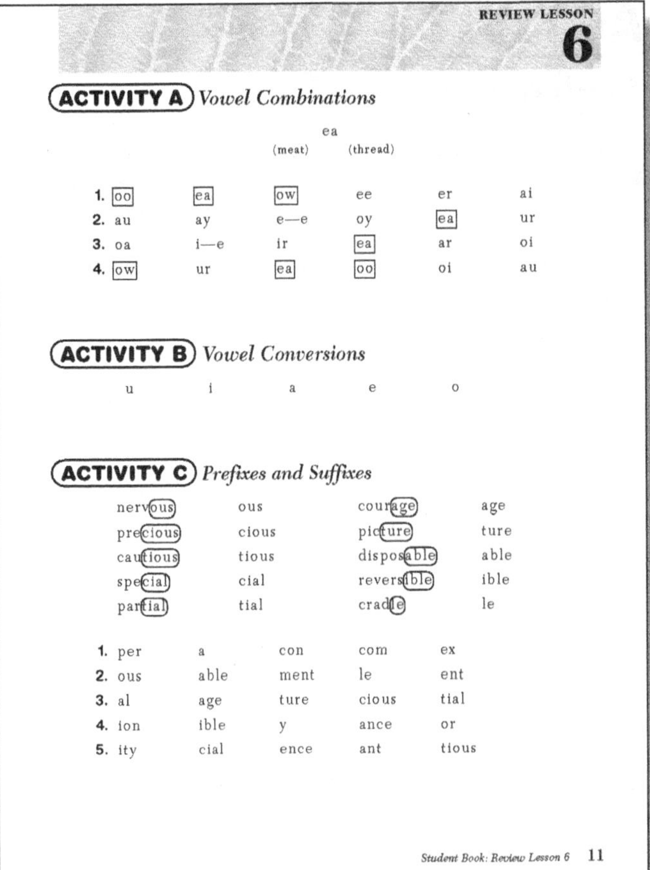
REVIEW LESSON 6

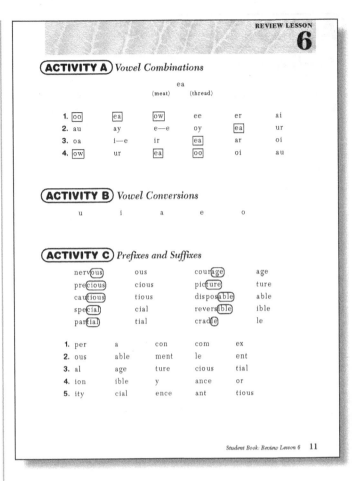

ACTIVITY A *Vowel Combinations*

ea (meat) (thread)

1. oo	ea	ow	ee	er	ai
2. au	ay	e—e	oy	ea	ur
3. oa	i—e	ir	ea	ar	oi
4. ow	ur	ea	oo	oi	au

ACTIVITY B *Vowel Conversions*

u i a e o

ACTIVITY C *Prefixes and Suffixes*

nervous	ous	courage	age
precious	cious	picture	ture
cautious	tious	disposable	able
special	cial	reversible	ible
partial	tial	cradle	le

1. per	a	con	com	ex
2. ous	able	ment	le	ent
3. al	age	ture	cious	tial
4. ion	ible	y	ance	or
5. ity	cial	ence	ant	tious

Student Book: Review Lesson 6 11

ACTIVITY C

Prefixes and Suffixes

ACTIVITY PROCEDURE

(See the *Student Book*, page 11.)

Tell students the words, then the circled suffixes. Have students repeat the words and suffixes. Then, have students practice saying the new and previously learned prefixes and suffixes.

1. Find **Activity C**. Now, we are going to review suffixes.
2. Point to the first column. The first word is **nervous**. What word?_ Point to the circled suffix. The suffix is /ous/. What suffix?_
3. Point to the next word below. The word is **precious**. What word?_ Point to the suffix. The suffix is /cious/. What suffix?_
4. (Repeat with **cautious** and /tious/, **special** and /cial/, and **partial** and /tial/.)
5. Point to the third column of words. The first word is **courage**. What word?_ The suffix is /age/. What suffix?_
6. (Repeat with **picture** and /ture/, **disposable** and /able/, **reversible** and /ible/, and **cradle** and /le/.)
7. Find the second column. It has suffixes only. Read the suffixes. What suffix?_ Next?_ Next?_ Next?_ Next?_
8. Find the last column. What suffix?_ Next?_ Next?_ Next?_ Next?_
9. Point to the first prefix in **Line #1**. What prefix?_ Next?_ Next?_ Next?_ Next?_
10. (Repeat for prefixes and suffixes in Lines #2–5).

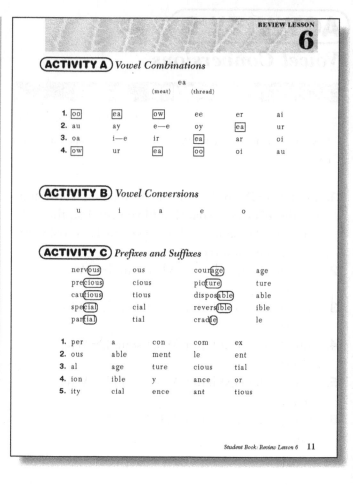

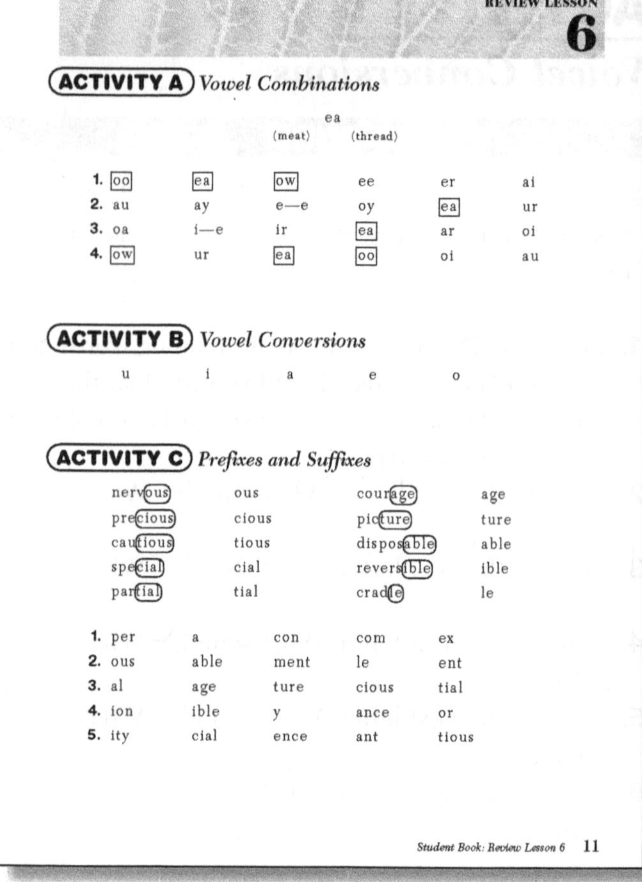

REVIEW LESSON 6

ACTIVITY A *Vowel Combinations*

ea (meat) (thread)

1. oo	ea	ow	ee	er	ai
2. au	ay	e—e	oy	ea	ur
3. oa	i—e	ir	ea	ar	oi
4. ow	ur	ea	oo	oi	au

ACTIVITY B *Vowel Conversions*

u i a e o

ACTIVITY C *Prefixes and Suffixes*

nervous	ous	courage	age
precious	cious	picture	ture
cautious	tious	disposable	able
special	cial	reversible	ible
partial	tial	cradle	le

1. per	a	con	com	ex
2. ous	able	ment	le	ent
3. al	age	ture	cious	tial
4. ion	ible	y	ance	or
5. ity	cial	ence	ant	tious

Student Book: Review Lesson 6 11

ACTIVITY D

Strategy Practice

ACTIVITY PROCEDURE

(See the *Student Book*, page 12.)

Have students circle prefixes and suffixes and underline the vowels. Have students say the word part by part to themselves and then as a whole word aloud.

Use Overhead F: Activity D

1. Turn to page 12. Find **Activity D**.
2. Circle prefixes and suffixes and underline the vowels. Look up when you are done._
3. (Show the overhead transparency.) Now, check and fix any mistakes._
4. Go back to the first word._ Sound out the word to yourself. Put your thumb up when you can read the word. Be sure that it is a real word._ What word?_
5. (Continue Step 4 with all words in Activity D.)

Note: You may wish to provide additional practice by having students read a line to the group or to a partner.

REVIEW LESSON

6

ACTIVITY D *Strategy Practice*

1.	official	substantial	delicious
2.	pretentious	impressionable	incombustible
3.	conjecture	inconspicuous	disadvantage

ACTIVITY E *Independent Strategy Practice*

1.	administrative	performance	threadbare
2.	circumstantial	investigation	professionalism
3.	precipitation	environmentally	communication
4.	unconventional	consolidate	misconception

ACTIVITY F *Sentence Reading*

1. The unprofessional official took a substantial bribe before beginning the investigation.
2. His administrative performance showed tremendous professionalism.
3. Circumstantial evidence was not enough to convict the defendant.
4. Precipitation in the form of sleet leaves motorists at a distinct disadvantage.
5. There was substantial truth in his communication, but it still led to serious misconceptions.
6. If you wish to consolidate services, you will need to ensure environmentally safe conditions for all employees.
7. The unconventional approach to the investigation led to much conjecture.
8. Because she was so impressionable, she was at a disadvantage.
9. Even though her advisor gave good advice, she refused to consolidate her investments.
10. Although his actions were usually pretentious, his presence at the lecture was totally inconspicuous.

12 *REWARDS Plus: Reading Strategies Applied to Science Passages*

ACTIVITY E

Independent Strategy Practice

ACTIVITY PROCEDURE

(See the *Student Book*, page 12.)

Have students look carefully at each word, locate prefixes, suffixes, and vowels, and figure out the word by themselves. Then, have students say the word aloud.

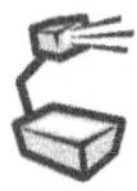

Use Overhead F: Activity E

Note 1: If students have difficulty decoding a word, demonstrate the strategy on the overhead.

1. Find **Activity E**.
2. Find **Line #1**. Put your thumb up when you can say the first word._ (Give ample thinking time.)
3. (When students have decoded the word, ask . . .) What word?_
4. Next word. Put your thumb up when you can say the word._ (Give ample thinking time.) What word?_
5. (Repeat Step 4 for the remaining words in Activity E.)

Note 2: You may wish to provide additional practice by having students read a line to the group or to a partner.

REVIEW LESSON
6

ACTIVITY D *Strategy Practice*

1.	official	substantial	delicious
2.	pretentious	impressionable	incombustible
3.	conjecture	inconspicuous	disadvantage

ACTIVITY E *Independent Strategy Practice*

1.	administrative	performance	threadbare
2.	circumstantial	investigation	professionalism
3.	precipitation	environmentally	communication
4.	unconventional	consolidate	misconception

ACTIVITY F *Sentence Reading*

1. The unprofessional official took a substantial bribe before beginning the investigation.
2. His administrative performance showed tremendous professionalism.
3. Circumstantial evidence was not enough to convict the defendant.
4. Precipitation in the form of sleet leaves motorists at a distinct disadvantage.
5. There was substantial truth in his communication, but it still led to serious misconceptions.
6. If you wish to consolidate services, you will need to ensure environmentally safe conditions for all employees.
7. The unconventional approach to the investigation led to much conjecture.
8. Because she was so impressionable, she was at a disadvantage.
9. Even though her advisor gave good advice, she refused to consolidate her investments.
10. Although his actions were usually pretentious, his presence at the lecture was totally inconspicuous.

12 *REWARDS Plus: Reading Strategies Applied to Science Passages*

ACTIVITY F

Sentence Reading

ACTIVITY PROCEDURE

(See the *Student Book*, page 12.)

Have students read a sentence to themselves. Then, choose from several options of having students read the sentence together, to partners, or individually to the class.

1. Find **Sentence #1** in **Activity F**. These sentences include words that we practiced today as well as words we have not practiced. Read the first sentence to yourself. When you can read all the words in the sentence, put your thumb up.
2. (When students can read the sentence, use one of the following options:
   a. Ask students to read the sentence together [i.e., choral reading].
   b. Have students read the sentence to their partners. Then, call on one student to read the sentence to the group.
   c. Ask one student to read the sentence to the group.)
3. (Repeat these procedures with the remaining sentences. Be sure that you give ample thinking time for each sentence.)

Note: The sentences in this Review Lesson are very similar to the sentences in Lesson 20 of the *REWARDS* program. These sentences contain words that were—and were not—practiced in *REWARDS Plus* Review Lessons. If your students had difficulty with these sentences, you may want to reteach Lessons 13–20 from the original *REWARDS* program before going on to the Application Lessons in *REWARDS Plus*.

REVIEW LESSON
6

ACTIVITY D *Strategy Practice*

1.	official	substantial	delicious
2.	pretentious	impressionable	incombustible
3.	conjecture	inconspicuous	disadvantage

ACTIVITY E *Independent Strategy Practice*

1.	administrative	performance	threadbare
2.	circumstantial	investigation	professionalism
3.	precipitation	environmentally	communication
4.	unconventional	consolidate	misconception

ACTIVITY F *Sentence Reading*

1. The unprofessional official took a substantial bribe before beginning the investigation.
2. His administrative performance showed tremendous professionalism.
3. Circumstantial evidence was not enough to convict the defendant.
4. Precipitation in the form of sleet leaves motorists at a distinct disadvantage.
5. There was substantial truth in his communication, but it still led to serious misconceptions.
6. If you wish to consolidate services, you will need to ensure environmentally safe conditions for all employees.
7. The unconventional approach to the investigation led to much conjecture.
8. Because she was so impressionable, she was at a disadvantage.
9. Even though her advisor gave good advice, she refused to consolidate her investments.
10. Although his actions were usually pretentious, his presence at the lecture was totally inconspicuous.

12 *REWARDS Plus: Reading Strategies Applied to Science Passages*

Application Lesson 1

Materials Needed:

- *Student Book*: Application Lesson 1
- Application Overhead Transparencies 1–4
- Appendix A Reproducible 1: *REWARDS* Strategies for Reading Long Words*
- Appendix A Reproducible 2: Prefixes, Suffixes, and Vowel Combinations Reference Chart*
- Appendix B Reproducible A: Application Lesson 1
- Appendix C Optional Vocabulary Activity: Application Lesson 1
- Paper or cardboard to use when covering the overhead transparency
- Paper or cardboard for each student to use during spelling dictation
- Washable overhead transparency pen

Text Treatment Notes:

- Black text signifies teacher script (exact wording to say to students).
- Green text in parentheses signifies directions or prompts for the teacher.
- Green text signifies answers or examples of answers.
- Green graphics treatment signifies reproduction of Overhead information.
- Green text and green graphics treatment do not appear in the *Student Book*.

* If you did not teach the Review Lessons, copy and distribute Appendix A Reproducibles 1 and 2 to students. Have them place these in a notebook or a folder for future reference.

ACTIVITY A

Vocabulary

ACTIVITY PROCEDURE, List 1

(See the *Student Book*, page 13.)

Tell students each word in the list. Then, have students repeat the word and read the definition aloud. For each definition, provide any additional information that may be necessary. Then, have students practice reading the words themselves.

Note A.1: If you wish to emphasize the part of speech, have students say the part of speech before reading the definition.

Use Overhead 1: Activity A
List 1: Tell

1. (Show the top half of Overhead 1.) Before we read the passage, let's read the difficult words. (Point to **scientists**.) The first word is **scientists**. What word?_ Now, read the definition._
2. (Point to **universe**.) The next word is **universe**. What word?_ Now, read the definition._
3. (Pronounce each word in List 1, and then have students repeat each word and read the definition.)
4. Open your *Student Book* to **Application Lesson 1**, page 13._
5. Find **Activity A**, **List 1**, in your book._ Let's read the words again. First word._ Next word._ (Continue for all words in List 1.)

ACTIVITY PROCEDURE, List 2

(See the *Student Book*, page 13.)

The second list of words can be read using the part-by-part strategy. Have students circle prefixes and suffixes, then underline the vowels. Using the overhead transparency, assist students in checking their work. Next, have students figure out each word to themselves, then say it aloud. Have them read the definition aloud.

Note A.2-1: Provide additional information for any definitions as needed.
Note A.2-2: If you wish to emphasize the part of speech, have students say the part of speech before reading the definition.
Note A.2-3: If you are teaching older students for whom "thumbs-up" is inappropriate, have students look at you when they can read the word.

APPLICATION LESSON **1**

ACTIVITY A *Vocabulary*

List 1: Tell

1. **scientists** *n.* ► (people with expert knowledge of science)
2. **universe** *n.* ► (all things that exist, including our solar system and beyond)
3. **organisms** *n.* ► (all living things, including all plants and animals)
4. **ecosystem** *n.* ► (a living community of organisms and their physical environment)
5. **climate** *n.* ► (the pattern of weather conditions in an area or region)
6. **bacteria** *n.* ► (very tiny single-celled organisms)
7. **fungus** *n.* ► (a plant-like organism without leaves, flowers, or green coloring)
8. **fungi** *n.* ► (more than one fungus; the plural of fungus)
9. **protists** *n.* ► (usually single-celled organisms that have both plant and animal characteristics)

List 2: Strategy Practice

1. **interactions** *n.* ► (actions or influences on each other)
2. **population** *n.* ► (the number of organisms living in an area)
3. **function** *v.* ► (to act or operate normally; to perform)
4. **tropical** *adj.* ► (very humid and hot or having to do with the tropics)
5. **available** *adj.* ► (ready to be used)
6. **requirements** *n.* ► (things that are needed or depended upon)
7. **nutrients** *n.* ► (matter needed by plants and animals so they can live)
8. **predator** *n.* ► (an animal that hunts or kills another for food)
9. **eventually** *adv.* ► (finally)
10. **extinction** *n.* ► (the end of or the dying out of a type of plant or animal)

TALLY ☐ VOCABULARY 5 *Points*

Student Book: Application Lesson 1 13

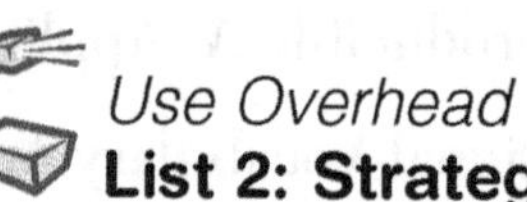

Use Overhead 1: Activity A
List 2: Strategy Practice

1. Find **List 2**. For each word, circle the prefixes and suffixes, and underline the vowels. Look up when you are done._
2. (Show the bottom half of Overhead 1.) Now, check and fix any mistakes._
3. Go back to the first word._ Sound out the word to yourself. Put your thumb up when you can read the word. Be sure that it is a real word._ What word?_ Now, read the definition._
4. (Continue Step 3 with all remaining words in List 2.)

Note A.2-4: You may wish to provide additional practice by having students read words to a partner.

ACTIVITY PROCEDURE, List 1 and 2

(See the *Student Book*, page 13.)

Tell students to look in List 1 or List 2 for a word you are thinking about. Have them circle the number of the word and tell you the word. Explain to students to make a tally mark for each correct word in the Tally box, and then enter the number of tally marks as points in the blank half of the Vocabulary box.

1. For this activity, I will tell you about words I am thinking about. You will have a short time to find those words in either List 1 or List 2, circle the number of that word, and then tell me the word I'm thinking about. Find the Tally box at the bottom of page 13. For every word that you correctly identify, make a tally mark in the Tally box. If you don't identify the correct word, don't do anything.
2. I am thinking of a word. Circle the number of the appropriate word.
   - This animal hunts or kills other animals for food. (Wait.) What word? **predator**
   - When something is ready to be used, that item is this. (Wait.) What word? **available**
   - Weather that is humid and hot is often called this. (Wait.) What word? **tropical**
   - Our influence on others can be a result of these. (Wait.) What word? **interactions**
   - These are very tiny single-celled organisms. (Wait.) What word? **bacteria**
3. Count all the tally marks, and enter that number as points in the blank half of the Vocabulary box.

ACTIVITY PROCEDURE, List 3

(See the *Student Book*, page 14.)

The words in the third list are related. Have students use the *REWARDS* Strategies to figure out the first word in each family. Have them read the definition of the verb and then read the nouns and adjectives that are related to that verb.

Note A.3-1: Provide additional information for any definitions as needed.

Note A.3-2: If you wish to emphasize the part of speech, have students say the part of speech before reading the definition.

Note A.3-3: If you are teaching older students for whom "thumbs-up" is inappropriate, have students look at you when they can read the word.

APPLICATION LESSON
1

List 3: Word Families

	Verb	Noun	Adjective
Family 1	energize (to give energy)	energy energizer	energetic
Family 2	consume (to eat)	consumer consumption	consumable
Family 3	transform (to change)	transformation transformer	
Family 4	capture (to catch or attract)	captive captor	
Family 5	compose (to make or create)	composition composer	composite

ACTIVITY B *Spelling Dictation*

1. energize	4. consume
2. energy	5. consumer
3. energetic	6. consumable

SPELLING 6 Points

14 *REWARDS Plus: Reading Strategies Applied to Science Passages*

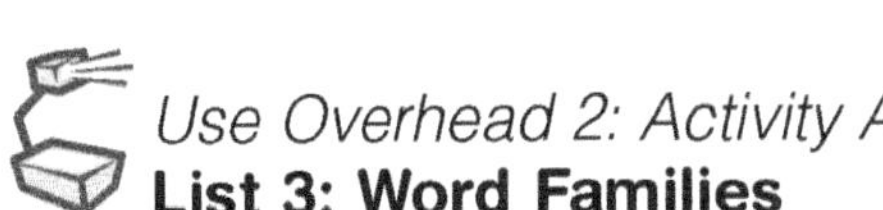

Use Overhead 2: Activity A
List 3: Word Families

1. Turn to page 14._ Find **Family 1** in **List 3**. Figure out the first word. Use your pencil if you wish. Put your thumb up when you know the word._ What word?_ Read the definition of the verb._
2. Look at the nouns in Family 1. Figure out the first word._ What word?_ Next word._ What word?_
3. Look at the adjective in Family 1. Figure out the word._ What word?_
4. (Repeat Steps 1–3 for all word families in List 3.)

Note A.3-4: You may wish to provide additional practice by having students read a word family to the group or to a partner.

Note A.3-5: An additional vocabulary practice activity called Quick Words is provided in Appendix C of this Teacher's Guide. See Appendix C for information about how this optional activity can be used.

ACTIVITY B

Spelling Dictation

ACTIVITY PROCEDURE

(See the *Student Book*, page 14.)

For each word, tell students the word, then have students say the parts of the word to themselves while they write the word. Using the overhead transparency, assist students in checking their spelling and correcting if they misspelled. Then, have students enter the number of correctly spelled words as points in the blank half of the Spelling box.

Note B-1: Distribute a piece of light cardboard to students so they can cover their page during spelling dictation. Students can also use the cardboard as a bookmark to quickly locate pages at the beginning of lessons.

Use Overhead 2: Activity B

1. Find **Activity B.**
2. The first word is **energize**. What word?_ Say the parts in **energize** to yourself as you write the word. (Pause and monitor.)
3. (Show **energize** on the overhead.) Check **energize**. If you misspelled it, cross it out and write it correctly.
4. The second word is **energy**. What word?_ Say the parts in **energy** to yourself as you write the word. (Pause and monitor.)
5. (Show **energy** on the overhead.) Check **energy**. If you misspelled it, cross it out and write it correctly.
6. (Repeat the procedures for the words **energetic**, **consume**, **consumer**, and **consumable**.)
7. Count the number of words you spelled correctly, and record that number as points in the blank half of the Spelling box at the bottom of the page.

APPLICATION LESSON
1

List 3: Word Families

	Verb	Noun	Adjective
Family 1	energize (to give energy)	energy energizer	energetic
Family 2	consume (to eat)	consumer consumption	consumable
Family 3	transform (to change)	transformation transformer	
Family 4	capture (to catch or attract)	captive captor	
Family 5	compose (to make or create)	composition composer	composite

ACTIVITY B *Spelling Dictation*

1. energize	4. consume
2. energy	5. consumer
3. energetic	6. consumable

SPELLING 6 *Points*

14 *REWARDS Plus: Reading Strategies Applied to Science Passages*

ACTIVITY C

Passage Reading and Comprehension

ACTIVITY PROCEDURE

(See the *Student Book*, pages 15–17.)

Have students read the title of the passage and each heading. Ask them to tell their partners two things that the passage will tell about.

Passage Preview

1. Turn to page 15._ Let's preview the passage.
2. Read the title._ What is the whole passage going to tell about?_
3. Now, let's read the headings. Read the first heading._ Read the next heading._ (Continue until students have read all headings.)
4. Turn to your partner. Without looking, tell two things this passage will tell about._

ACTIVITY PROCEDURE

Provide students with an Information Web from Appendix B. Have students read the passage silently to each embedded number, and then reread the same information orally either to a partner, together as a group, or individually. Ask the corresponding comprehension question or questions. Once students finish reading a section labeled A, B, or C, have them fill in the Information Web before going on to the next section.

Note C-1: If students do not finish reading the passage and completing the Information Web during class, have them use their Webs to review the information at the beginning of the next class.

Use Overhead 3: Activity C

Passage Reading

1. (Provide an Information Web for each student.)
2. Turn back to the beginning of the passage. You're going to read the passage and answer questions about what you've read. During passage reading, you are also going to fill in an Information Web to help you remember the important details of the passage. Later, you'll use this Web to review the content of the passage with your partner.

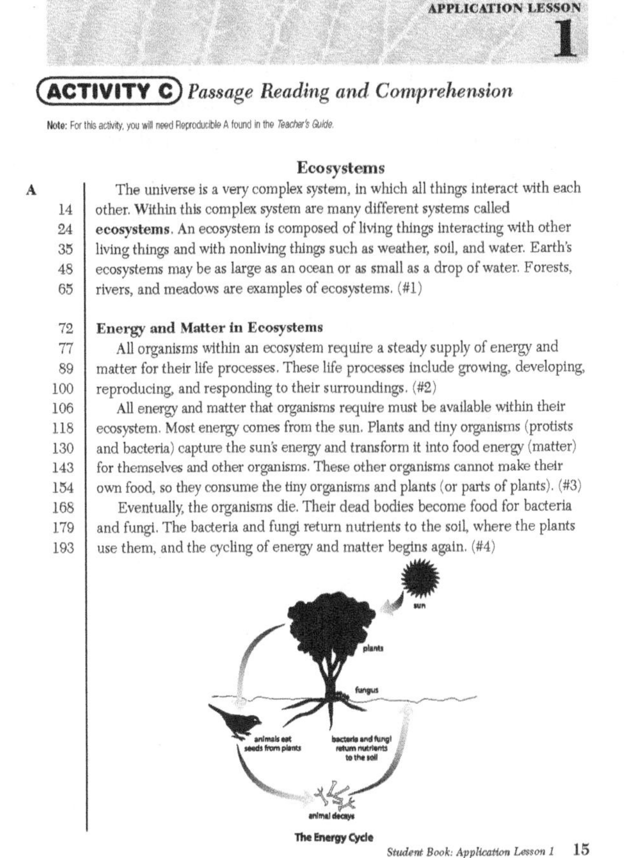

APPLICATION LESSON 1

ACTIVITY C *Passage Reading and Comprehension*

Note: For this activity, you will need Reproducible A found in the *Teacher's Guide*.

Ecosystems

A
The universe is a very complex system, in which all things interact with each
14 other. Within this complex system are many different systems called
24 **ecosystems**. An ecosystem is composed of living things interacting with other
35 living things and with nonliving things such as weather, soil, and water. Earth's
48 ecosystems may be as large as an ocean or as small as a drop of water. Forests,
65 rivers, and meadows are examples of ecosystems. (#1)

72 **Energy and Matter in Ecosystems**
77 All organisms within an ecosystem require a steady supply of energy and
89 matter for their life processes. These life processes include growing, developing,
100 reproducing, and responding to their surroundings. (#2)
106 All energy and matter that organisms require must be available within their
118 ecosystem. Most energy comes from the sun. Plants and tiny organisms (protists
130 and bacteria) capture the sun's energy and transform it into food energy (matter)
143 for themselves and other organisms. These other organisms cannot make their
154 own food, so they consume the tiny organisms and plants (or parts of plants). (#3)
168 Eventually, the organisms die. Their dead bodies become food for bacteria
179 and fungi. The bacteria and fungi return nutrients to the soil, where the plants
193 use them, and the cycling of energy and matter begins again. (#4)

The Energy Cycle

Student Book: Application Lesson 1 15

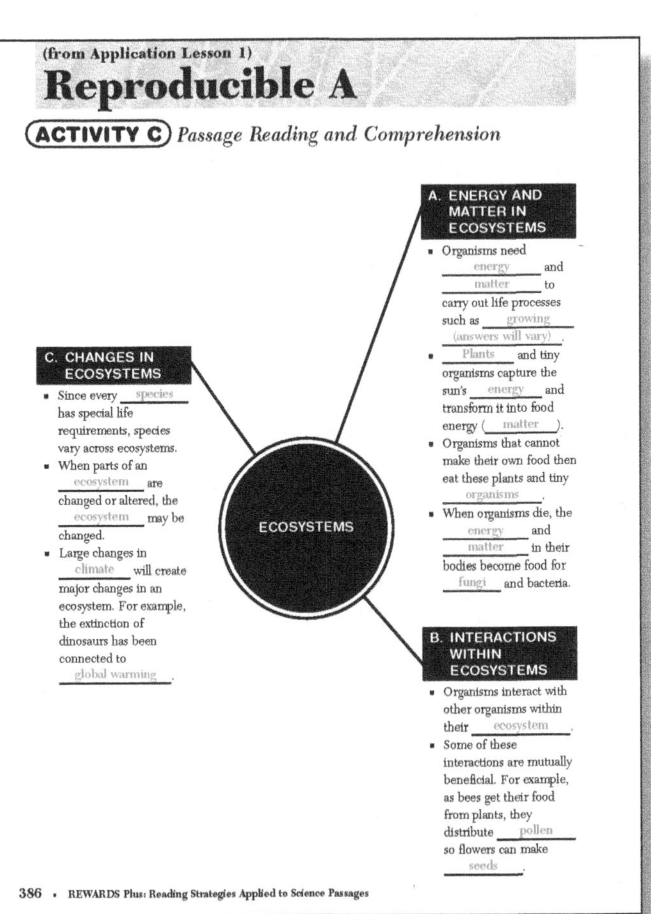

(from Application Lesson 1)

Reproducible A

ACTIVITY C *Passage Reading and Comprehension*

ECOSYSTEMS

A. ENERGY AND MATTER IN ECOSYSTEMS

- Organisms need energy and matter to carry out life processes such as growing (answers will vary).
- Plants and tiny organisms capture the sun's energy and transform it into food energy (matter).
- Organisms that cannot make their own food then eat these plants and tiny organisms.
- When organisms die, the energy and matter in their bodies become food for fungi and bacteria.

B. INTERACTIONS WITHIN ECOSYSTEMS

- Organisms interact with other organisms within their ecosystem.
- Some of these interactions are mutually beneficial. For example, as bees get their food from plants, they distribute pollen so flowers can make seeds.

C. CHANGES IN ECOSYSTEMS

- Since every species has special life requirements, species vary across ecosystems.
- When parts of an ecosystem are changed or altered, the ecosystem may be changed.
- Large changes in climate will create major changes in an ecosystem. For example, the extinction of dinosaurs has been connected to global warming.

386 • REWARDS Plus: Reading Strategies Applied to Science Passages

3. The passage has numbers that appear at the end of one or two paragraphs. Find number 1._ Find number 2._. I will be asking you to read until you reach a number. When you stop, I will ask questions.
4. The passage is also divided into sections A, B, and C. These sections correspond to the Information Web. Find section A in the passage._ Find section B in the passage._ We'll stop at the end of each section and fill in the information on the Web.
5. Turn back to the beginning of the passage once more. Read the title._
6. Find number 1 in the passage._ (Pause). Read down to number 1 silently. Look up when you are done._
7. (Wait for students to complete the reading. Then have students reread the part by having them read orally to a partner, read together orally as a group, or read aloud individually.)
8. (Ask the question or questions associated with each number. Provide feedback to students regarding their answers.)
9. (Repeat steps 6–8 for all paragraphs in Section A.)
10. Now, look at your Information Web. Find the section labeled A._ The information you have just read will help you to fill in this section of the Web.
11. With your partner, fill in the blanks for Section A. You can refer back to the passage for information. Look up when you are done._ (Move around the room and monitor students as they complete the section.)
12. (When the majority of students have finished, show Overhead 3). Look at the overhead and check your work. Fix up or add to any of your answers.
13. Now read down to the next number silently. Look up when you are done._
14. (Repeat steps 7–13 until the students have finished the passage and the Information Web.)
15. Now use your Information Web to retell the important information from the passage to your partner.

APPLICATION LESSON 1

ACTIVITY C *Passage Reading and Comprehension*

Note: For this activity, you will need Reproducible A found in the *Teacher's Guide*.

Ecosystems

A The universe is a very complex system, in which all things interact with each
14 other. Within this complex system are many different systems called
24 **ecosystems**. An ecosystem is composed of living things interacting with other
35 living things and with nonliving things such as weather, soil, and water. Earth's
48 ecosystems may be as large as an ocean or as small as a drop of water. Forests,
65 rivers, and meadows are examples of ecosystems. (#1)

72 **Energy and Matter in Ecosystems**
77 All organisms within an ecosystem require a steady supply of energy and
89 matter for their life processes. These life processes include growing, developing,
100 reproducing, and responding to their surroundings. (#2)
106 All energy and matter that organisms require must be available within their
118 ecosystem. Most energy comes from the sun. Plants and tiny organisms (protists
130 and bacteria) capture the sun's energy and transform it into food energy (matter)
143 for themselves and other organisms. These other organisms cannot make their
154 own food, so they consume the tiny organisms and plants (or parts of plants). (#3)
168 Eventually, the organisms die. Their dead bodies become food for bacteria
179 and fungi. The bacteria and fungi return nutrients to the soil, where the plants
193 use them, and the cycling of energy and matter begins again. (#4)

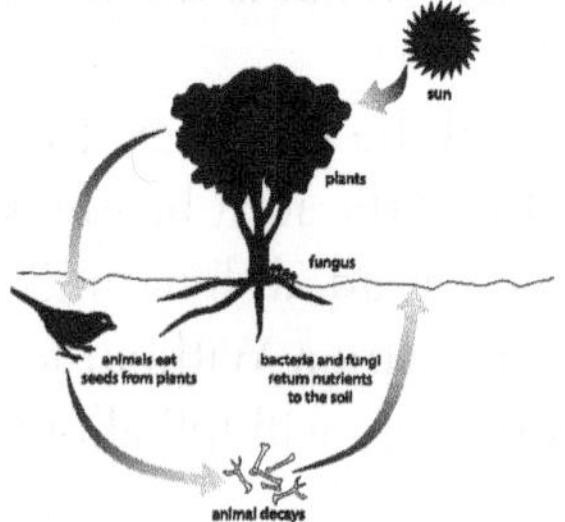

The Energy Cycle

Student Book: Application Lesson 1 15

APPLICATION LESSON 1

B 204 **Interactions Within Ecosystems**
207 Larger organisms not only consume tiny organisms and plants, larger
217 organisms also interact with other organisms within their ecosystem. Sometimes,
227 these interactions are friendly and benefit both organisms. For example, bees
238 benefit when they gather pollen and nectar from flowers. These substances are
250 food for the bees. Flowers benefit because the bees' gathering activities help to
263 move the pollen from one flower to another so the flowers can make seeds. (#5)
277 Another interaction that benefits two organisms is the special relationship
287 that exists when a type of fungus finds a home in and on the roots of trees. This
305 fungus absorbs water and minerals from the surrounding soil and shares these
317 with the tree. The tree uses these raw materials to make a sugary food, which
332 the fungus feeds on. Large forests depend on this special relationship. (#6)

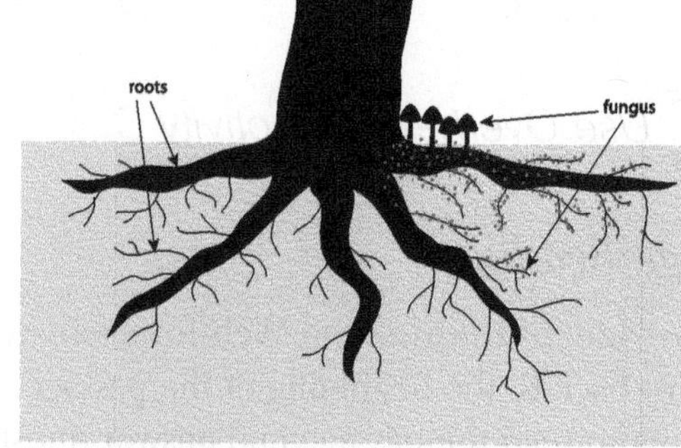

Special Relationship Between Fungus and Tree Roots

343 Other interactions appear not to be so friendly. One example is the predator-
356 prey relationship between the snake and the mouse. It seems as if only the
370 snake benefits from eating the mouse, but actually, the population of mice in the
384 ecosystem is helped. Snakes (the predators) keep the numbers of mice in
396 balance with the supply of mouse food available. (#7)

16 *REWARDS Plus: Reading Strategies Applied to Science Passages*

Comprehension Questions

#1 What things compose or make up an ecosystem?
Living things and nonliving things.

#2 What two things do organisms need to carry out life processes? What are some of the life processes?
Need energy and matter; processes include growing, developing, reproducing, and responding to their surroundings.

#3 Why are plants important within an ecosystem?
Plants (along with protists and bacteria) provide the food energy for all other organisms in an ecosystem.

#4 How can the death of one organism assist other organisms?
Its body becomes food for other organisms, and these organisms return matter to the soil for plants to use.

#5 How does the interaction of bees and flowers benefit both organisms?
Bees get food in the form of pollen and nectar; bees help move pollen from one flower to another so that flowers can make seeds.

#6 How does the interaction of fungi and trees benefit both the fungi and the trees?
The fungi absorb water and minerals from the soil and share these with trees; trees use these materials to make a food that the fungi can eat.

#7 How does the interaction of a snake and a mouse actually benefit both organisms?
Snake eats the mouse for food; there are less mice, thus there is more food available for the mice that are still alive.

#8 Why do the species vary from ecosystem to ecosystem?
Every species has special requirements; every ecosystem has different conditions that support different species.

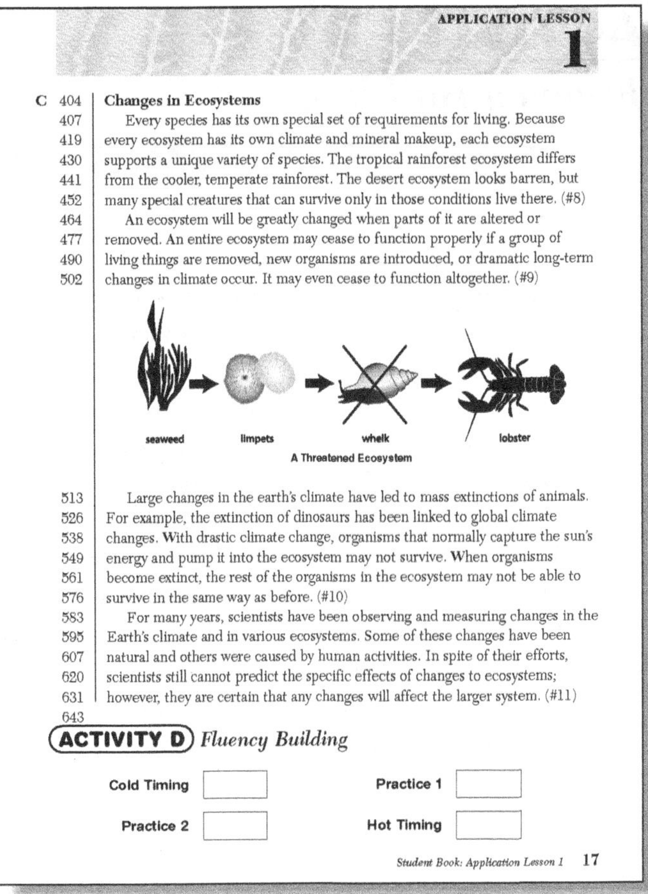

APPLICATION LESSON 1

C 404 **Changes in Ecosystems**
407 Every species has its own special set of requirements for living. Because
419 every ecosystem has its own climate and mineral makeup, each ecosystem
430 supports a unique variety of species. The tropical rainforest ecosystem differs
441 from the cooler, temperate rainforest. The desert ecosystem looks barren, but
452 many special creatures that can survive only in those conditions live there. (#8)
464 An ecosystem will be greatly changed when parts of it are altered or
477 removed. An entire ecosystem may cease to function properly if a group of
490 living things are removed, new organisms are introduced, or dramatic long-term
502 changes in climate occur. It may even cease to function altogether. (#9)

A Threatened Ecosystem

513 Large changes in the earth's climate have led to mass extinctions of animals.
526 For example, the extinction of dinosaurs has been linked to global climate
538 changes. With drastic climate change, organisms that normally capture the sun's
549 energy and pump it into the ecosystem may not survive. When organisms
561 become extinct, the rest of the organisms in the ecosystem may not be able to
576 survive in the same way as before. (#10)
583 For many years, scientists have been observing and measuring changes in the
595 Earth's climate and in various ecosystems. Some of these changes have been
607 natural and others were caused by human activities. In spite of their efforts,
620 scientists still cannot predict the specific effects of changes to ecosystems;
631 however, they are certain that any changes will affect the larger system. (#11)
643

ACTIVITY D *Fluency Building*

Cold Timing		Practice 1	
Practice 2		Hot Timing	

Student Book: Application Lesson 1 17

#9 When a part of the ecosystem is changed or removed, how might it affect the rest of the ecosystem?
Changing a part will change the makeup of the ecosystem; the ecosystem may cease to function altogether.

#10 What is one result of large changes in earth's climate?
Extinction of animals; for example, dinosaurs.

#11 What do scientists know about the effects of changes in an ecosystem?
That changes in one ecosystem can affect the larger system.

ACTIVITY D

Fluency Building

ACTIVITY PROCEDURE

(See the *Student Book*, page 17.)

In this activity, students will be using a repeated reading procedure of the Activity C article to increase their reading fluency. First, have students do a Cold Timing, in which they whisper-read for one minute as you time them. Have them record in their books the number of correct words they read. Then, have students repeat with one or two practice readings to attempt to beat their Cold Timing. Finally, students exchange books in preparation for a Hot Timing. Have students listen to a partner read for one minute, underlining any word errors, and have them determine the number of correct words their partner read. When both students have completed their Hot Timing, they return each other's books and complete their own Fluency Graphs by indicating the number of words they read correctly in the one-minute Cold Timing and the one-minute Hot Timing.

Note D-1: When assigning partners for this activity, have the stronger reader read first. As a result, the other reader will have one additional practice opportunity.

1. Now, it's time for fluency building.
2. Find the beginning of the passage again. (Pause.)
3. Whisper-read. See how many words you can read in one minute. Begin._ (Time students for one minute.) Stop._ Circle the last word that you read._ Count the number of words you read in one minute. (Assist students in determining the number of words by counting from the number at the beginning of the line to the circled word.)_ In your book, find **Cold Timing** in **Activity D** at the bottom of page 17._ Record the number of words you read._
4. Let's practice again. Return to the beginning of the article. Remember to whisper-read. See if you can beat your Cold Timing. Begin._ (Time students for one minute.) Stop._ Put a box around the last word that you read._ Count the number of words you read in one minute._ Find **Practice 1.**_ Record the number of words you read._
5. (Optional) Let's practice one more time before the Hot Timing. Return to the beginning of the article. Remember to whisper-read. See if you can beat your Cold Timing. Begin._ (Time students for one minute.) Stop._ Put a box around the last word that you read._ Count the number of words you read in one minute._ Find **Practice 2.**_ Record the number of words you read._
6. Please exchange books with your partner._ Partner 1, you are going to read first. Partner 2, you are going to listen carefully to your partner as he or she reads. If your partner makes a mistake or leaves out a word, underline that word. Ones, get ready to read quietly to your partner. Begin._ (Time students for one minute.) Stop._ Twos, cross out the last word that your partner read._ Twos, determine the number of words your partner read correctly in one minute._ (Assist students in subtracting the number of mistakes from the number of words read.) Find **Hot Timing.**_ Record the number of words your partner read correctly._
7. Partner 2, you are going to read next. Partner 1, you are going to listen carefully to your partner as he or she reads. If your partner makes a mistake or leaves out a word, underline that word. Twos, get ready to read quietly to your partner. Begin._ (Time students for one minute.) Stop._ Ones, cross out the last word that your partner read._ Ones, determine the number of words your partner read correctly in one minute._ Record the number of words your partner read correctly after **Hot Timing.**_
8. Exchange books._ Turn to the Fluency Graph on the last page of your *Student Book*. First, put a dot and a "C" next to the number that shows how many words you read correctly for your Cold Timing._ Then, put a dot and an "H" next to the number of words you read correctly for your Hot Timing._

seaweed limpets whelk ster

A Threatened Ecosystem

513 Large changes in the earth's climate have led to mass extinctions of animals.
526 For example, the extinction of dinosaurs has been linked to global climate
538 changes. With drastic climate change, organisms that normally capture the sun's
549 energy and pump it into the ecosystem may not survive. When organisms
561 become extinct, the rest of the organisms in the ecosystem may not be able to
576 survive in the same way as before. (#10)
583 For many years, scientists have been observing and measuring changes in the
595 Earth's climate and in various ecosystems. Some of these changes have been
607 natural and others were caused by human activities. In spite of their efforts,
620 scientists still cannot predict the specific effects of changes to ecosystems;
631 however, they are certain that any changes will affect the larger system. (#11)
643

ACTIVITY D *Fluency Building*

Cold Timing		Practice 1	
Practice 2		Hot Timing	

Student Book: Application Lesson 1 17

ACTIVITY E

Comprehension Questions—Multiple Choice

ACTIVITY PROCEDURE

(See the *Student Book*, page 18.)

Have students read each step in the Multiple Choice Strategy. Model item #1 for students. Lead your students through items #2 and #3, proceeding step-by-step. Have students complete the remaining item and provide them with feedback on their answers. Then, have students enter the number of items answered correctly as points in the blank half of the Multiple Choice Comprehension box.

Note E-1: The correct Multiple Choice answers are circled.

1. Turn to page 18. Find **Activity E.** Often in school you take multiple-choice tests. Today, we are going to learn and practice a strategy for doing multiple-choice items.
2. Read **Step 1.** To be sure you understand the item, you may wish to read it more than one time.
3. Read **Step 2.** It is important to **<u>not</u>** make your selection before you have considered all the choices.
4. Read **Step 3.** This is the most critical step in the strategy. For each choice, you must really think about why the choice might be correct or incorrect. It may be necessary to look back in the article.
5. Read **Step 4.** After you have really thought about each choice, you can select the best answer.
6. My turn to do the first item. First, I read the item: **The central vocabulary term in this article is "ecosystem." Which of the following is <u>NOT</u> true of an "ecosystem?"** Now, I have to read each of the choices and think about why the choice might be correct or incorrect.
7. I read choice **a: A forest is an example of an ecosystem**. We know that an ecosystem consists of all living things and their physical surroundings. So a forest is an example of an ecosystem. The question asks which statement is NOT true of an ecosystem so this cannot be the correct choice.
8. I read choice **b: Ecosystems are all very large**. We know that ecosystems vary in size. All ecosystems may not be large. This might be the correct choice.

APPLICATION LESSON
1

ACTIVITY E *Comprehension Questions—Multiple Choice*

Comprehension Strategy—Multiple Choice

Step 1: Read the item.
Step 2: Read all of the choices.
Step 3: Think about why each choice might be correct or incorrect. Check the article as needed.
Step 4: From the possible correct choices, select the best answer.

1. (Vocabulary) **The central vocabulary term in this article is "ecosystem." Which of the following is <u>NOT</u> true of an "ecosystem?"**
   a. A forest is an example of an ecosystem.
   (b.) Ecosystems are all very large.
   c. Organisms in an ecosystem need energy and matter to survive.
   d. A drastic change in climate can threaten the organisms in an ecosystem.
2. (Cause and effect) **If a small organism, such as a crab, does not have a steady supply of energy and matter in its ecosystem, what is most likely to occur?**
   a. The organism would migrate to a new ecosystem.
   b. The organism may need to become a predator in order to have a new food supply.
   (c.) The organism will not survive.
   d. The organism will need to interact with another organism in the ecosystem.
3. (Cause and effect) **Flowers benefit from interacting with bees in an ecosystem because:**
   a. the bees produce honey from the flower's nectar.
   b. the bees move nectar from one flower to another.
   (c.) the bees move pollen from one flower to another.
   d. the flowers use the nectar from other plants to produce seeds.
4. (Main idea) **Which sentence gives the best summary of the article?**
   a. Interactions between organisms in an ecosystem always benefit both organisms.
   b. Ecosystems can be as large as a forest or as small as a drop of water.
   (c.) In an ecosystem, organisms interact with other organisms and must have a supply of energy and matter.
   d. A climate change can lead to extinction of a species.

MULTIPLE CHOICE COMPREHENSION  Points

18 *REWARDS Plus: Reading Strategies Applied to Science Passages*

9. I read choice **c: Organisms in the ecosystem need energy and matter to survive.** All organisms need energy and matter in order to survive and must meet their needs within the ecosystem. This statement is true so it could not be the correct choice.
10. I read choice **d: A drastic change in climate can threaten the organisms in an ecosystem.** Organisms depend on meeting their needs within an ecosystem. Any drastic change could threaten them. This statement is true so it could not be the correct choice.
11. I have thought about all the choices. I ask myself, "Which is the best answer?" I circle choice **b**.
12. Let's do one together. Read item #2.
13. Read choice **a.** Think about why this choice might be correct or incorrect. (Pause. Then, call on individual students.)
14. This is what I was thinking. Organisms need to meet their needs within their ecosystem. A small organism such as a crab would be unable to migrate to a new ecosystem so that is probably not the correct choice.

15. Read choice **b.**_ Think about why this choice might be correct or incorrect. (Pause. Then, call on individual students.)
16. Here's what I think. Organisms that are not already predators, that is, do not hunt and kill other animals for food, could not become predators to get their energy and matter. So, that is probably not the correct choice.
17. Read choice **c.**_ Think about why this choice might be correct or incorrect. (Pause. Then, call on individual students.)
18. This is what I was thinking. If organisms cannot meet their needs for energy and matter within their ecosystems, they may not survive. This could be the correct answer.
19. Read choice **d.**_ Think about why this choice might be correct or incorrect. (Pause. Then, call on individual students.)
20. Here's what I think. Organisms already interact with other organisms within their ecosystems. So interacting with another organism will most likely not help that organism get a steady supply of energy and matter within that ecosystem. This is probably not the correct answer.
21. Which is the best answer?_ Circle it._
22. Let's do the next one together. Read item #3.
23. Read choice **a.**_ Think about why this choice might be correct or incorrect. (Pause. Then, call on individual students.)
24. This is what I was thinking. Bees do produce honey from the nectar in flowers, but this benefits the bees, not the flowers. This is probably not the correct choice.
25. Read choice **b.**_ Think about why this choice might be correct or incorrect. (Pause. Then, call on individual students.)
26. This is what I was thinking. The bees collect nectar from flowers and use it for food for themselves. Again, this would not benefit the flowers so this is probably not the correct choice.
27. Read choice **c.**_ Think about why this choice might be correct or incorrect. (Pause. Then, call on individual students.)
28. This is what I was thinking. Bees moving pollen from one flower to another will benefit the flowers greatly because pollen is used in making new seeds in the process of flowers' reproduction, so this is possibly the best answer.

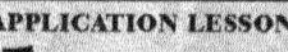
APPLICATION LESSON

1

ACTIVITY E *Comprehension Questions—Multiple Choice*

Comprehension Strategy—Multiple Choice

Step 1: Read the item.
Step 2: Read all of the choices.
Step 3: Think about why each choice might be correct or incorrect. Check the article as needed.
Step 4: From the possible correct choices, select the best answer.

1. (Vocabulary) **The central vocabulary term in this article is "ecosystem." Which of the following is NOT true of an "ecosystem?"**
   - **a.** A forest is an example of an ecosystem.
   - **(b.)** Ecosystems are all very large.
   - **c.** Organisms in an ecosystem need energy and matter to survive.
   - **d.** A drastic change in climate can threaten the organisms in an ecosystem.
2. (Cause and effect) **If a small organism, such as a crab, does not have a steady supply of energy and matter in its ecosystem, what is most likely to occur?**
   - **a.** The organism would migrate to a new ecosystem.
   - **b.** The organism may need to become a predator in order to have a new food supply.
   - **(c.)** The organism will not survive.
   - **d.** The organism will need to interact with another organism in the ecosystem.
3. (Cause and effect) **Flowers benefit from interacting with bees in an ecosystem because:**
   - **a.** the bees produce honey from the flower's nectar.
   - **b.** the bees move nectar from one flower to another.
   - **(c.)** the bees move pollen from one flower to another.
   - **d.** the flowers use the nectar from other plants to produce seeds.
4. (Main idea) **Which sentence gives the best summary of the article?**
   - **a.** Interactions between organisms in an ecosystem always benefit both organisms.
   - **b.** Ecosystems can be as large as a forest or as small as a drop of water.
   - **(c.)** In an ecosystem, organisms interact with other organisms and must have a supply of energy and matter.
   - **d.** A climate change can lead to extinction of a species.

MULTIPLE CHOICE COMPREHENSION

4
Points

18 *REWARDS Plus: Reading Strategies Applied to Science Passages*

29. Read choice **d.**_ Think about why this choice might be correct or incorrect. (Pause. Then, call on individual students.)
30. This is what I was thinking. Flowers do not use nectar from other plants to produce seeds. They use pollen. So this could not be the answer to this question.
31. Which is the best answer?_ Circle it._
32. Use the Multiple Choice Strategy to complete item #4. Be ready to explain why you selected your answer. (Wait while students complete the item. Call on individual students. Ask them why they chose their answer and why they eliminated the other choices. Encourage discussion. Provide students with feedback on their choices, focusing on why or why not those choices might be appropriate.)
33. Count the number of items you got correct, and record that number in the blank half of the Multiple Choice Comprehension box._

ACTIVITY F

Vocabulary Activities

ACTIVITY PROCEDURE

(See the *Student Book*, page 19.)

Model item #1 orally for students, and then have students respond to the question in writing by answering "Yes" or "No" and providing a reason for their answers. Then, model #2 and have students respond in writing. Finally, have students complete the third item orally, provide them with feedback on their answers, and then have students respond in writing.

Yes/No/Why

1. Turn to page 19. Find **Activity F.** Read the first item with me: **Are all organisms predators?** I would answer "No" to this question, and here is my reason. Predators are animals that hunt and kill other animals for food. Many organisms do not get their food by hunting and killing other animals, so I would conclude that all organisms are not predators.
2. Write your answer and your reason for it in the space provided. Look up when you are done.
3. Read item #2 with me: **Do all living things have nutrient requirements?** After thinking about it, I would answer "Yes," because all living things need energy and matter in order to carry out life processes.
4. Write your answer and your reason for it in the space provided. Look up when you are done.
5. Read item #3 with me: **Can ecosystems have tropical climates?** Tell your partner your answer and your reason for it. (Wait. Call on individual students. Provide students with feedback, focusing on the reasons they give for their answers. Encourage discussion.)
6. I would definitely answer "Yes" to this question. Ecosystems exist everywhere on earth and many have tropical climates.
7. Write your answer and your reason for it in the space provided. Look up when you are done.

Note F-1: You may wish to do this as an oral task only rather than an oral and a written task.

APPLICATION LESSON 1

ACTIVITY F *Vocabulary Activities*

Yes/No/Why

1. Are all **organisms predators**?
   Example Answer: No. Predators are animals that hunt and kill other animals for food. Many organisms do not get their food by hunting and killing other animals, so I would conclude that all organisms are not predators.
2. Do all living things have **nutrient requirements**?
   Example Answer: Yes. All living things need energy and matter in order to carry out life processes.
3. Can **ecosystems** have **tropical climates**?
   Example Answer: Yes. Ecosystems exist everywhere on earth and many have tropical climates.

Student Book: Application Lesson 1 19

ACTIVITY PROCEDURE

Model item #1 orally for students, and then have students complete the sentence stem in writing. Have students share answers with partners and with the class. Repeat these steps for the remaining items. Then, have students give themselves points in the blank half of the Vocabulary box.

Completion Activity

1. Turn to page 20. Read the first word and its definition with me: **capture: to catch or attract**.
2. Now, read the sentence stem with me: **You might capture your friends' attention by . . .**
3. When I want to capture my friends' attention, I might signal them, or I might call their names.
4. Think of things you might do to capture your friends' attention and write them. Share your answer with your partner. (Call on a few students to share answers with the class.)
5. Let's do another one. Read the second word and definition with me: **consume: to eat**.
6. Read the sentence stem with me: **When you arrive home from school, you like to consume . . .**
7. I can think of a number of snacks that I'd love to consume after school, including an apple, carrot sticks, and pizza.
8. Think of foods you would like to consume after school and write them. Share your answer with your partner. (Call on a few students to share answers with the class.)
9. (Repeat Steps 5–8 for the rest of the words.)
10. If you participated in answering all seven questions, give yourself seven points in the blank half of the Vocabulary box.

Note F-2: You may wish to do this as an oral task only rather than an oral task and a written task.

APPLICATION LESSON
1

Completion Activity

1. **capture:** to catch or attract
   You might capture your friends' attention by
   Answers will vary.
2. **consume:** to eat
   When you arrive home from school, you like to consume
   Answers will vary.
3. **eventually:** finally
   Homework tasks that you dislike but eventually finish include
   Answers will vary.
4. **extinction:** the end of or the dying out of a type of plant or animal
   Many types of organisms are threatened with extinction as a result of
   Answers will vary.

VOCABULARY 7 Points

20 *REWARDS Plus: Reading Strategies Applied to Science Passages*

ACTIVITY G

Expository Writing—Multi-Paragraph Answer

ACTIVITY PROCEDURE, Plan and Write

(See the *Student Book*, pages 21–23.)

Have students read the prompt and Jacob's three topics. Explain how Jacob made a **LIST** of critical details under each topic. Have students read Jacob's details for topic a. Explain that details that don't go with the topic should be eliminated, and have them **CROSS OUT** the same detail that Jacob crossed out. Next, explain how details can be combined into one sentence, and have students **CONNECT** details as Jacob did in his plan. Have students **NUMBER** their details in the same manner as Jacob. Next, have students read example paragraph a. Guide students in completing the plan for topic b and read example paragraph b. Repeat for topic c. Finally, explain that after they **WRITE**, they should **EDIT** their work, revising for clarity and proofreading for errors in capitalization, punctuation, and spelling.

APPLICATION LESSON **1**

ACTIVITY G *Expository Writing—Multi-Paragraph Answer*

Writing Strategy—Multi-Paragraph Answer

Step 1: LIST (List the details that are important enough to include in your answer.)
Step 2: CROSS OUT (Reread the details. Cross out any that don't go with the topic.)
Step 3: CONNECT (Connect any details that could go into one sentence.)
Step 4: NUMBER (Number the details in a logical order.)
Step 5: WRITE (Write the paragraph.)
Step 6: EDIT (Revise and proofread your answer.)

Prompt: What are three important things about ecosystems?

Plan: Complete the Planning Box with your teacher.

Example Multi-Paragraph Plan

Planning Box
(topic a) *organisms need energy and matter*
① (detail) – *necessary for all life processes*
(detail) – *for growing, developing, reproducing, and responding to environment*
② (detail) – *plants capture energy from sun and make into food for themselves and other organisms*
(detail) – ~~*ecosystems can be very large or very small*~~
(topic b) *organisms interact with other organisms and with nonliving things*
① (detail) – *friendly interactions benefit both organisms*
② (detail) – *some interactions less friendly*
(topic c) *changes in ecosystem can affect how ecosystem functions*
① (detail) – *may not function properly*
(detail) – *may cease to function at all*
② (detail) – *extinction of organisms possible, especially if change in climate*

Student Book: Application Lesson 1 21

Use Overhead 4: Activity G

1. Turn to page 21._ Find **Activity G.**_ Oftentimes, you are asked to write an answer with more than one paragraph. This might be part of an assignment or test. Today, we are going to see how Jacob, another student, applied a strategy to write a multi-paragraph answer. Beginning in the next lesson, you will begin writing similar answers.
2. Find the prompt in the middle of the page._ Read the prompt out loud with me: **What are three important things about ecosystems?** Jacob decided to write a paragraph about each of the three things that were important about ecosystems. Before he wrote his answer, he carefully planned what he wanted to cover. Look at his plan._ First, he wrote a topic for each paragraph. The topic tells what the whole paragraph will tell about. Later, each topic will be incorporated into the first sentence of the paragraph. These sentences are called topic sentences. Read topic a._ Read topic b._ Read topic c._
3. Next, he followed the steps in the Writing Strategy to write his answer. Let's see how he did this. Locate the Writing Strategy at the top of the page._ Read **Step 1** out loud._ Under each topic, Jacob made a **list** of important details. Read topic a._ Now, read the details listed under topic a._ Jacob then listed details for topic b and topic c. Notice that Jacob did not write complete sentences in his plan. He just wrote down short notes that he will later put into sentences.
4. Next, Jacob applied **Steps 2 through 5** to each paragraph.
5. Read **Step 2** out loud._ Before he wrote the first paragraph, Jacob reread his details and **crossed out** any details that did not go with the topic._ (Show Overhead 4.) Look at the overhead._ What detail did he cross out?_ Why do you think this detail was eliminated?_ Cross out the same detail on your paper._
6. Read **Step 3.**_ When you write a paragraph, you want some longer sentences. This can be accomplished by connecting two or three details into one sentence. Look at the overhead._ Jacob **connected** "necessary for all life processes" and "for growing, developing, reproducing, and responding to environment." These details can easily be combined into one sentence. Notice that he did not connect all of the details. He wanted

both short and long sentences. Please draw brackets on your paper to connect the details that Jacob connected._

7. Read **Step 4.**_ Next, Jacob **numbered** the details in the order he wished them to occur in the paragraph. Looking at the overhead, number your details as Jacob did._
8. Read **Step 5.**_ Next, Jacob **wrote** the paragraph. Locate paragraph a on the next page._ (Read paragraph a with your students or to your students.)
9. Jacob then repeated these steps on the remaining two paragraphs. Let's see what he did.
10. Look at the overhead._ First, he looked for details that did not go with the topic. Did he cross out any details?_ Next, he connected details that could go into one sentence. Did he connect any details for this paragraph?_ Next, he numbered the details in a logical order. Number your details as Jacob did._
11. Next, Jacob wrote the paragraph. Locate paragraph b._ (Read paragraph b with your students or to your students.)
12. Jacob then repeated the steps of **cross out, connect,** and **number** with the last topic. Looking at the overhead, make your paper the same as Jacob's for topic c._
13. Finally, he used his plan to write the last paragraph in his answer. Locate paragraph c._ (Read the paragraph with your students or to your students.)
14. Read **Step 6.**_ Jacob **edited** by revising his paragraphs to be sure they were clear and easy to understand and by proofreading them for any errors in capitalization, punctuation, and spelling.

ACTIVITY PROCEDURE, Evaluate

Ask students to read each question in the rubric. Guide them in evaluating the paragraphs using the guidelines. Have students total their points and record them in the blank half of the Writing box.

15. Turn to page 23._ This rubric tells the qualities of good paragraphs. Let's evaluate the paragraphs in Jacob's answer.
16. Read question #1 with me._ Jacob included his topic in the first sentence of each paragraph forming a topic sentence. Circle "Yes" for a, b, and c._

APPLICATION LESSON **1**

ACTIVITY G *Expository Writing—Multi-Paragraph Answer*

Writing Strategy—Multi-Paragraph Answer

Step 1: LIST (List the details that are important enough to include in your answer.)
Step 2: CROSS OUT (Reread the details. Cross out any that don't go with the topic.)
Step 3: CONNECT (Connect any details that could go into one sentence.)
Step 4: NUMBER (Number the details in a logical order.)
Step 5: WRITE (Write the paragraph.)
Step 6: EDIT (Revise and proofread your answer.)

Prompt: What are three important things about ecosystems?

Plan: Complete the Planning Box with your teacher.

Example Multi-Paragraph Plan

Planning Box
(topic a) *organisms need energy and matter*
① { (detail) – *necessary for all life processes*
(detail) – *for growing, developing, reproducing, and responding to environment* }
② (detail) – *plants capture energy from sun and make into food for themselves and other organisms*
(detail) – ~~*ecosystems can be very large or very small*~~
(topic b) *organisms interact with other organisms and with nonliving things*
① (detail) – *friendly interactions benefit both organisms*
② (detail) – *some interactions less friendly*
(topic c) *changes in ecosystem can affect how ecosystem functions*
① { (detail) – *may not function properly*
(detail) – *may cease to function at all* }
② (detail) – *extinction of organisms possible, especially if change in climate*

APPLICATION LESSON **1**

Write: Examine paragraphs a, b, and c with your teacher.

Example Multi-Paragraph Answer

(paragraph a)

One important thing about ecosystems is that all organisms need energy and matter. Energy and matter are necessary for all life processes including growing, developing, reproducing, and responding to the environment. Plants capture energy from the sun and make it into food for themselves and other organisms.

(paragraph b)

In addition, all organisms within an ecosystem interact with other organisms and with nonliving things. In many cases, the interactions between the organisms are friendly and both benefit. For example, both the bee and the flower profit from their interactions. However, some interactions, such as those between prey and predator, are less friendly.

(paragraph c)

Another important idea about ecosystems is that changes in the ecosystem can affect how the ecosystem functions. If a major change occurs, the ecosystem may not function at all or at least not properly. If there is a major change in the climate, this can lead to extinction of organisms within an ecosystem.

17. Read question #2 with me. Jacob only included details that went with each paragraph's topic. Circle "Yes" for a, b, and c.
18. Read question #3 with me. Jacob combined details in his paragraphs so that he would have some short and long sentences. Circle "Yes" for a, b, and c.
19. Read question #4. Raise your hand if you found Jacob's paragraphs easy to understand. Circle "Yes."
20. Read question #5. When Jacob edited his work, he was careful to spell words correctly. In some cases, he looked back in the article to find the spelling of difficult words. Circle "Yes."
21. Read question #6. Jacob capitalized words at the beginning of each sentence. Circle "Yes."
22. Read question #7. Jacob put a period at the end of each sentence. Circle "Yes."
23. Jacob earned a total of 13 points on this activity. Please record 13 in the blank half of the Writing box.
24. Let's review the steps in this strategy. **List, cross out, connect, number, write, edit.** Tell your partner the steps in the strategy.
25. In the next lessons, you will be writing similar paragraphs and eventually longer answers with three paragraphs.

Evaluate: Evaluate the paragraphs using this rubric.

Rubric—Multi-Paragraph Answer	Student or Partner Rating	Teacher Rating
1. Did the author state the topic in the first sentence?	a. (Yes) Fix up b. (Yes) Fix up c. (Yes) Fix up	a. Yes No b. Yes No c. Yes No
2. Did the author include details that go with the topic?	a. (Yes) Fix up b. (Yes) Fix up c. (Yes) Fix up	a. Yes No b. Yes No c. Yes No
3. Did the author combine details in some of the sentences?	a. (Yes) Fix up b. (Yes) Fix up c. (Yes) Fix up	a. Yes No b. Yes No c. Yes No
4. Is the answer easy to understand?	(Yes) Fix up	Yes No
5. Did the author correctly spell words, particularly the words found in the article?	(Yes) Fix up	Yes No
6. Did the author use correct capitalization, capitalizing the first word in the sentence and proper names of people, places, and things?	(Yes) Fix up	Yes No
7. Did the author use correct punctuation, including a period at the end of each sentence?	(Yes) Fix up	Yes No

WRITING 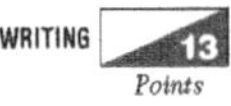

Points

Student Book: Application Lesson 1 23

ACTIVITY H

Comprehension— Single-Paragraph Answer

ACTIVITY PROCEDURE

(See the *Student Book*, pages 24–25.)

Have students read the *What Is* statement and the *What If* question. Explain that in science we often consider or hypothesize about what might happen if circumstances were altered. Tell students that they are first going to write a paragraph in response to the *What If* question and then participate in a discussion. Show them how Jacob took the question and turned it into part of the answer and wrote that down. Then, examine the rest of the paragraph to see how Jacob used evidence from the article and his own experience and knowledge base to respond to the question. Finally, review the discussion behaviors in the "Looks Like/Sounds Like" chart, and have students add their own ideas to Jacob's paragraph. Award points for writing and participating in the discussion.

1. Turn to page 24. Find **Activity H.**
2. At the end of each of our lessons, you are going to contemplate what might happen as a result of an event. You are going to make best guesses or hypotheses about what might happen using information from the article and from your own background knowledge and experience. You will be writing a paragraph that contains your hypotheses and then you will participate in a discussion.
3. When we answer a question in writing, we can use a strategy. Read **Step 1.**
4. Find the *What Is* statement in the middle of the page. Read it out loud with me: **Humans are part of an ecosystem and their activities may change the ecosystem in a number of ways.**
5. Find the *What If* question. Read it with me: **What might happen to the ecosystem if a new, large shopping mall was built on the forested outskirts of a city where there were few houses and roads?**
6. Read **Step 2.** When you answer a question in writing, it is useful to turn the question into part of the answer and to write that down as part of your first sentence in the answer. Look at Jacob's paragraph. Read the first sentence with me: **If a large shopping mall was built on the forested outskirts of a city, a number of things might happen to the ecosystem.**

APPLICATION LESSON

1

ACTIVITY H *Comprehension—Single-Paragraph Answer*

Writing Strategy—Single-Paragraph Answer

Step 1: Read the item.
Step 2: Turn the question into part of the answer and write it down.
Step 3: Think of the answer or locate the answer in the article.
Step 4: Complete your answer.

Prompt:

What Is—Humans are part of an ecosystem and their activities may change the ecosystem in a number of ways.

What If—What might happen to the ecosystem if a new, large shopping mall was built on the forested outskirts of a city where there were few houses and roads?

Write and Discuss: Write a paragraph. Then share your ideas. Use the Discussion Guidelines.

Example Single-Paragraph Answer

If a large shopping mall was built on the forested outskirts of a city, a number of things might happen to the ecosystem. First, because the plants will be destroyed, they will be unable to transform energy from the sun into food needed by other organisms. Therefore, other organisms will not have the energy and matter that they require for life. These organisms will eventually die unless they are able to migrate to surrounding wooded areas. I would not expect a climate change from one mall. However, continued widespread construction might even begin to affect the climate.

24 *REWARDS Plus: Reading Strategies Applied to Science Passages*

7. Why do you think it would be useful to turn the question into part of the answer? (Answers will vary: You would be more likely to focus on the question. Your answer would be more likely to go with the question. You would have a quick way to get going. You would have a longer answer.)
8. Read **Step 3.** After you have created a topic sentence using the wording from the question, you are ready to add ideas. You may think of an answer based on your experience and background knowledge, but you should also include evidence from the article or other materials that you have studied.
9. Let's read the rest of Jacob's answer out loud to see how he used evidence from the article. (Read the remaining sentences with your students.) When you write your own paragraph, you can earn four points: two points for turning the question into part of the answer and two points for using evidence from the article. Award yourself four points for writing now. Write them in the blank half of the Writing box at the bottom of page 25.

10. After you have written a paragraph, we will have a discussion. I can't wait to hear your creative ideas. First, let's review what you already know about discussions. In a discussion, you are both a listener and a speaker.

11. Look at the Discussion Guidelines at the top of page 25. Read to yourself what the speaker should look like and sound like. Circle the speaker behavior that you believe to be most important. (Call on students to share their perspectives.)

12. Look at the Discussion Guidelines again. Read what the listener should look like and sound like. Circle the listener behavior that you believe to be most important. (Call on students to share their perspectives.)

13. Now, read the *What If* question again and think how you might respond. (After giving students time to reread the question, engage them in a discussion.) If you participated in the discussion as a speaker or a good listener, award yourself four points. Write them in the blank half of the Discussion box at the bottom of page 25.

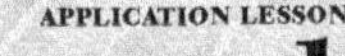

APPLICATION LESSON

1

Discussion Guidelines

Speaker		Listener	
Looks like:	**Sounds like:**	**Looks like:**	**Sounds like:**
• Facing peers • Making eye contact • Participating	• Using pleasant, easy-to-hear voice • Sharing opinions, supporting facts and reasons from the article and from your experience • Staying on the topic	• Facing speaker • Making eye contact • Participating	• Waiting quietly to speak • Giving positive, supportive comments • Disagreeing respectfully

WRITING DISCUSSION

Points *Points*

Student Book: Application Lesson 1 25

Application Lesson 2

Materials Needed:

- *Student Book*: Application Lesson 2
- Application Overhead Transparencies 5–9
- Appendix B Reproducible B: Application Lesson 2
- Appendix C Optional Vocabulary Activity: Application Lesson 2
- Paper or cardboard to use when covering the overhead transparency
- Paper or cardboard for each student to use during spelling dictation
- Washable overhead transparency pen

Text Treatment Notes:

- Black text signifies teacher script (exact wording to say to students).
- Green text in parentheses signifies directions or prompts for the teacher.
- Green text signifies answers or examples of answers.
- Green graphics treatment signifies reproduction of Overhead information.
- Green text and green graphics treatment do not appear in the *Student Book*.

ACTIVITY A

Vocabulary

ACTIVITY PROCEDURE, List 1

(See the *Student Book*, page 27.)

Tell students each word in the list. Then, have students repeat the word and read the definition aloud. For each definition, provide any additional information that may be necessary. Then, have students practice reading the words themselves.

Note A.1: If you wish to emphasize the part of speech, have students say the part of speech before reading the definition.

Use Overhead 5: Activity A
List 1: Tell

1. (Show the top half of Overhead 5.) Before we read the passage, let's read the difficult words. (Point to **photosynthesis**.) The first word is **photosynthesis**. What word?_ Now, read the definition._
2. (Point to **synthesis**.) The next word is **synthesis**. What word?_ Now, read the definition._
3. (Pronounce each word in List 1, and then have students repeat each word and read the definition.)
4. Open your *Student Book* to **Application Lesson 2**, page 27._
5. Find **Activity A**, **List 1**, in your book._ Let's read the words again. First word._ Next word._ (Continue for all words in List 1.)

ACTIVITY PROCEDURE, List 2

(See the *Student Book*, page 27.)

The second list of words can be read using the part-by-part strategy. Have students circle prefixes and suffixes, then underline the vowels. Using the overhead transparency, assist students in checking their work. Next, have students figure out each word to themselves, then say it aloud. Have them read the definition aloud.

Note A.2-1: Provide additional information for any definitions as needed.
Note A.2-2: If you wish to emphasize the part of speech, have students say the part of speech before reading the definition.
Note A.2-3: If you are teaching older students for whom "thumbs-up" is inappropriate, have students look at you when they can read the word.

APPLICATION LESSON **2**

ACTIVITY A *Vocabulary*

List 1: Tell

1. **photosynthesis** *n.* ► (the process by which green plants use the sun's energy to make food)
2. **synthesis** *n.* ► (putting things together)
3. **chlorophyll** *n.* ► (the green substance found in most plants)
4. **chloroplasts** *n.* ► (parts of the leaf in which photosynthesis takes place)
5. **glucose** *n.* ► (a simple sugar)
6. **molecule** *n.* ► (a very small amount, formed by combining atoms)
7. **carbon dioxide** *n.* ► (a colorless, odorless gas occurring naturally)
8. **cellular** *adj.* ► (related to cells)
9. **microbes** *n.* ► (very tiny living organisms)
10. **uniquely** *adv.* ► (unusually)
11. **integral** *adj.* ► (necessary for something to be whole)
12. **resources** *n.* ► (things that are ready to use to meet needs)

List 2: Strategy Practice

1. **respiration** *n.* ► (the action of breathing)
2. **essential** *adj.* ► (absolutely necessary)
3. **chemical** *adj.* ► (related to the properties of substances)
4. **properly** *adv.* ► (correctly)
5. **presence** *n.* ► (the state of being in a place, of being present)
6. **pigment** *n.* ► (a substance that gives color to plant or animal tissues)
7. **release** *v.* ► (to let go)
8. **recombine** *v.* ► (to join together differently)
9. **continuously** *adv.* ► (without end)
10. **existence** *n.* ► (the state of existing or being)

TALLY ____ VOCABULARY 5 Points

Student Book: Application Lesson 2 27

Use Overhead 5: Activity A
List 2: Strategy Practice

1. Find **List 2**. For each word, circle the prefixes and suffixes, and underline the vowels. Look up when you are done._
2. (Show the bottom half of Overhead 5.) Now, check and fix any mistakes._
3. Go back to the first word._ Sound out the word to yourself. Put your thumb up when you can read the word. Be sure that it is a real word._ What word?_ Now, read the definition._
4. (Continue Step 3 with all remaining words in List 2.)

Note A.2-4: You may wish to provide additional practice by having students read words to a partner.

ACTIVITY PROCEDURE, List 1 and 2

(See the *Student Book*, page 27.)

Tell students to look in List 1 or List 2 for a word you are thinking about. Have them circle the number of the word and tell you the word. Explain to students to make a tally mark for each correct word in the Tally box, and then enter the number of tally marks as points in the blank half of the Vocabulary box.

1. For this activity, I will tell you about words I am thinking about. You will have a short time to find those words in either List 1 or List 2, circle the number of that word, and then tell me the word I'm thinking about. Find the Tally box at the bottom of page 27. For every word that you correctly identify, make a tally mark in the Tally box. If you don't identify the correct word, don't do anything.
2. I am thinking of a word. Circle the number of the appropriate word.
   - If you join things together in a different way, you do this to them. (Wait.) What word? **recombine**
   - If something is a necessary part to make a thing whole, it is this to that thing. (Wait.) What word? **integral**
   - When something is absolutely necessary to the success of an action, that thing is this to that action. (Wait.) What word? **essential**
   - An activity that goes on and on without end is said to go on this way. (Wait.) What word? **continuously**
   - When you do something correctly, you are doing it this way. (Wait.) What word? **properly**
3. Count all the tally marks, and enter that number as points in the blank half of the Vocabulary box.

ACTIVITY PROCEDURE, List 3

(See the *Student Book*, page 28.)

The words in the third list are related. Have the students use the *REWARDS* Strategies to figure out the first word in each family. Have them read the definition of the verb and then read the nouns and adjectives that are related to that verb.

Note A.3-1: Provide additional information for any definitions as needed.

Note A.3-2: If you wish to emphasize the part of speech, have students say the part of speech before reading the definition.

Note A.3-3: If you are teaching older students for whom "thumbs-up" is inappropriate, have students look at you when they can read the word.

APPLICATION LESSON **2**

List 3: Word Families

	Verb	Noun	Adjective
Family 1	use (to employ for a purpose)	user usage	usable
Family 2	contain (to hold inside itself)	container	
Family 3	reverse (to change to the opposite)	reversal	reversible
Family 4	combine (to join together)	combination	
Family 5	structure (to arrange or to build)	structure	structural

ACTIVITY B *Spelling Dictation*

1. reverse	4. use
2. reversal	5. user
3. reversible	6. usable

SPELLING 6 *Points*

28 *REWARDS Plus: Reading Strategies Applied to Science Passages*

Use Overhead 6: Activity A
List 3: Word Families

1. Turn to page 28._ Find **Family 1** in **List 3**. Figure out the first word. Use your pencil if you wish. Put your thumb up when you know the word._ What word?_ Read the definition of the verb._
2. Look at the nouns in Family 1. Figure out the first word._ What word?_ Next word._ What word?_
3. Look at the adjective in Family 1. Figure out the word._ What word?_
4. (Repeat Steps 1–3 for all word families in List 3.)

Note A.3-4: You may wish to provide additional practice by having students read a word family to the group or to a partner.

Note A.3-5: An additional vocabulary practice activity called Quick Words is provided in Appendix C of this Teacher's Guide. See Appendix C for information about how this optional activity can be used.

ACTIVITY B

Spelling Dictation

ACTIVITY PROCEDURE

(See the *Student Book*, page 28.)

For each word, tell students the word, then have students say the parts of the word to themselves while they write the word. Using the overhead transparency, assist students in checking their spelling and correcting if they misspelled. Then, have students enter the number of correctly spelled words as points in the blank half of the Spelling box.

Note B-1: Distribute a piece of light cardboard to students so they can cover their page during spelling dictation. Students can also use the cardboard as a bookmark to quickly locate pages at the beginning of lessons.

Use Overhead 6: Activity B

1. Find **Activity B.**
2. The first word is **reverse**. What word?_ Say the parts in **reverse** to yourself as you write the word. (Pause and monitor.)
3. (Show **reverse** on the overhead.) Check **reverse**. If you misspelled it, cross it out and write it correctly.
4. The second word is **reversal**. What word?_ Say the parts in **reversal** to yourself as you write the word. (Pause and monitor.)
5. (Show **reversal** on the overhead.) Check **reversal**. If you misspelled it, cross it out and write it correctly.
6. (Repeat the procedures for the words **reversible**, **use**, **user**, and **usable**.)
7. Count the number of words you spelled correctly, and record that number as points in the blank half of the Spelling box at the bottom of the page.

APPLICATION LESSON
2

List 3: Word Families

	Verb	Noun	Adjective
Family 1	use (to employ for a purpose)	user usage	usable
Family 2	contain (to hold inside itself)	container	
Family 3	reverse (to change to the opposite)	reversal	reversible
Family 4	combine (to join together)	combination	
Family 5	structure (to arrange or to build)	structure	structural

ACTIVITY B *Spelling Dictation*

1. reverse	4. use
2. reversal	5. user
3. reversible	6. usable

SPELLING 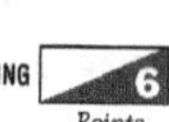 6 Points

28 REWARDS Plus: Reading Strategies Applied to Science Passages

ACTIVITY C

Passage Reading and Comprehension

ACTIVITY PROCEDURE

(See the *Student Book*, pages 29–31.)

Have students read the title of the passage and each heading. Ask them to tell their partners two things that the passage will tell about.

Passage Preview

1. Turn to page 29._ Let's preview the passage.
2. Read the title._ What is the whole passage going to tell about?_
3. Now, let's read the headings. Read the first heading._ Read the next heading._ (Continue until students have read all headings.)
4. Turn to your partner. Without looking, tell two things this passage will tell about._

ACTIVITY PROCEDURE

Provide students with an Information Web from Appendix B. Have students read the passage silently to each embedded number, and then reread the same information orally either to a partner, together as a group, or individually. Ask the corresponding comprehension question or questions. Once students finish reading a section labeled A, B, C, or D, have them fill in the Information Web before going on to the next section.

Note C-1: If students do not finish reading the passage during class, have them use their Information Webs to review the information at the beginning of the next class.

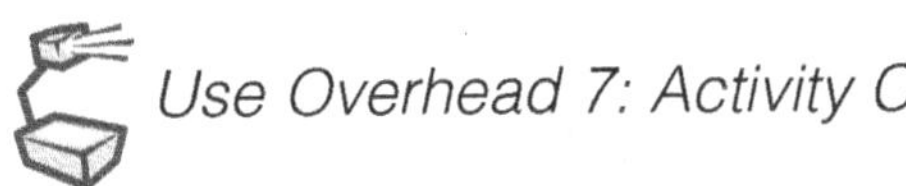

Use Overhead 7: Activity C

Passage Reading

1. (Provide an Information Web for each student.)
2. Turn back to the beginning of the passage. You're going to read the passage and answer questions about what you've read. During passage reading, you are also going to fill in an Information Web to help you remember the important details of the passage. Later, you'll use this Web to review the content of the passage with your partner.
3. Read the title._

APPLICATION LESSON 2

ACTIVITY C *Passage Reading and Comprehension*

Note: For this activity, you will need Reproducible B found in the *Teacher's Guide*.

Plants

A
Many types of plants exist in the world. Plants cover much of the earth's
14 surface. All plants have leaves, but some plants have no flowers, stems, or roots.
28 Nevertheless, plants are essential to the existence of the earth's ecosystems. (#1)
39 Remember that all energy and matter that organisms require must be available
51 within their ecosystem. Just as protists and bacteria do, plants capture the sun's
64 energy and transform it into food energy (matter) for themselves and other
76 organisms. Plants are uniquely structured to make food from the sun's energy and
89 transform the food energy into usable food. In the next section, you will learn how
104 the plant's leaves are integral to the role that a plant plays in its ecosystem. (#2)

B
119 **Photosynthesis in Plants**
122 The job of the plant's leaves is to use light energy from the sun to make food
139 for the plant. This process is called **photosynthesis**. In the word photosynthesis,
151 the "photo" part of the process refers to this light energy being used to split the
167 molecules of water and carbon dioxide. The "synthesis" part refers to putting
179 things together, in this case putting molecules back together to make a sugar
192 called glucose. (#3)

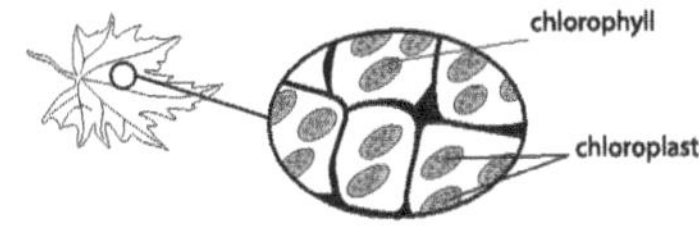
chlorophyll
chloroplasts

194 Photosynthesis occurs only in the presence of chlorophyll. Here's how it
205 works: Leaves contain little packets of green, chlorophyll pigment. These
215 packets, called **chloroplasts**, collect the sun's energy. The leaves then use this
227 light energy from the sun to split water (H_2O) already in the plant into hydrogen
242 and oxygen. The hydrogen stays in the plant, and the oxygen passes out of the
257 leaves and into the air around the plant. Next, the plant recombines the
270 hydrogen molecules (H_2) with carbon dioxide (CO_2) from the air to form a sugar
284 called **glucose** ($C_6H_{12}O_6$), an energy-rich food. The light energy is captured and
297 stored in the chemical bonds of the sugar molecule. In the next section on

Student Book: Application Lesson 2 29

(from Application Lesson 2)

Reproducible B

ACTIVITY C *Passage Reading and Comprehension*

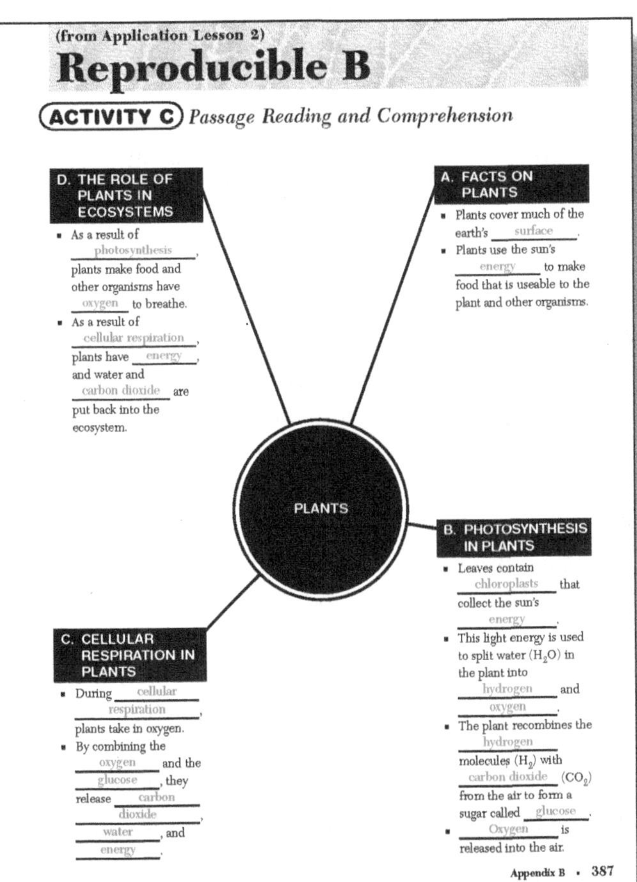
D. THE ROLE OF PLANTS IN ECOSYSTEMS
• As a result of photosynthesis, plants make food and other organisms have oxygen to breathe.
• As a result of cellular respiration, plants have energy, and water and carbon dioxide are put back into the ecosystem.
A. FACTS ON PLANTS
• Plants cover much of the earth's surface.
• Plants use the sun's energy to make food that is useable to the plant and other organisms.
PLANTS
B. PHOTOSYNTHESIS IN PLANTS
• Leaves contain chloroplasts that collect the sun's energy.
• This light energy is used to split water (H_2O) in the plant into hydrogen and oxygen.
• The plant recombines the hydrogen molecules (H_2) with carbon dioxide (CO_2) from the air to form a sugar called glucose.
• Oxygen is released into the air.
C. CELLULAR RESPIRATION IN PLANTS
• During cellular respiration, plants take in oxygen.
• By combining the oxygen and the glucose, they release carbon dioxide, water, and energy.

Appendix B • 387

4. Find number 1 in the passage._ (Pause). Read down to number 1 silently. Look up when you are done._
5. (Wait for students to complete the reading. Then have students reread the part by having them read orally to a partner, read together orally as a group, or read aloud individually.)
6. (Ask the question or questions associated with the number. Provide feedback to students regarding their answers.)
7. (Repeat steps 4–6 for all paragraphs in Section A.)
8. Now, look at your Information Web. Find the section labeled A._ The information you've just read will help you to fill in this section of the Web.
9. With your partner, fill in the blanks for Section A. You can refer back to the passage for information. Look up when you are done._ (Move around the room and monitor students as they complete the section.)
10. (When the majority of students have finished, show Overhead 7). Look at the overhead and check your work. Fix up or add to any of your answers.
11. Now read down to the next number silently. Look up when you are done._
12. (Repeat steps 5–11 until the students have finished the passage and the Information Web.)
13. Now use your Information Web to retell the important information from the passage to your partner.

Comprehension Questions

#1 What parts do all plants have and what parts do some plants not have?

All plants have leaves; some plants have no flowers, stems, or roots.

#2 After a plant captures the sun's energy, what does the plant do with it?

Transforms it into food energy or matter.

#3 What do the parts "photo" and "synthesis" mean in the word "photosynthesis?"

"Photo" refers to the light energy collected from the sun and used to break apart molecules of water and carbon dioxide; "synthesis" means putting things together—in this case putting molecules back together to form glucose.

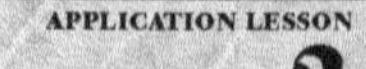

ACTIVITY C *Passage Reading and Comprehension*

Note: For this activity, you will need Reproducible B found in the *Teacher's Guide*.

Plants

A

Many types of plants exist in the world. Plants cover much of the earth's surface. All plants have leaves, but some plants have no flowers, stems, or roots. Nevertheless, plants are essential to the existence of the earth's ecosystems. (#1)

Remember that all energy and matter that organisms require must be available within their ecosystem. Just as protists and bacteria do, plants capture the sun's energy and transform it into food energy (matter) for themselves and other organisms. Plants are uniquely structured to make food from the sun's energy and transform the food energy into usable food. In the next section, you will learn how the plant's leaves are integral to the role that a plant plays in its ecosystem. (#2)

B

Photosynthesis in Plants

The job of the plant's leaves is to use light energy from the sun to make food for the plant. This process is called **photosynthesis**. In the word photosynthesis, the "photo" part of the process refers to this light energy being used to split the molecules of water and carbon dioxide. The "synthesis" part refers to putting things together, in this case putting molecules back together to make a sugar called glucose. (#3)

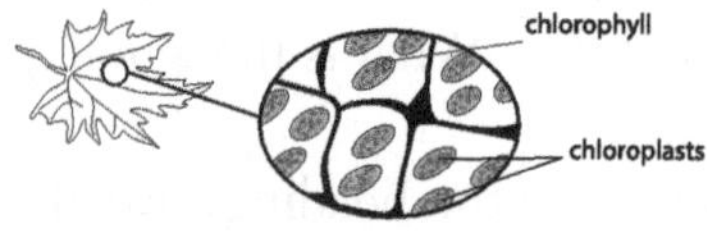

Photosynthesis occurs only in the presence of chlorophyll. Here's how it works: Leaves contain little packets of green, chlorophyll pigment. These packets, called **chloroplasts**, collect the sun's energy. The leaves then use this light energy from the sun to split water (H_2O) already in the plant into hydrogen and oxygen. The hydrogen stays in the plant, and the oxygen passes out of the leaves and into the air around the plant. Next, the plant recombines the hydrogen molecules (H_2) with carbon dioxide (CO_2) from the air to form a sugar called **glucose** ($C_6H_{12}O_6$), an energy-rich food. The light energy is captured and stored in the chemical bonds of the sugar molecule. In the next section on

Student Book: Application Lesson 2 29

(from Application Lesson 2)

Reproducible B

ACTIVITY C *Passage Reading and Comprehension*

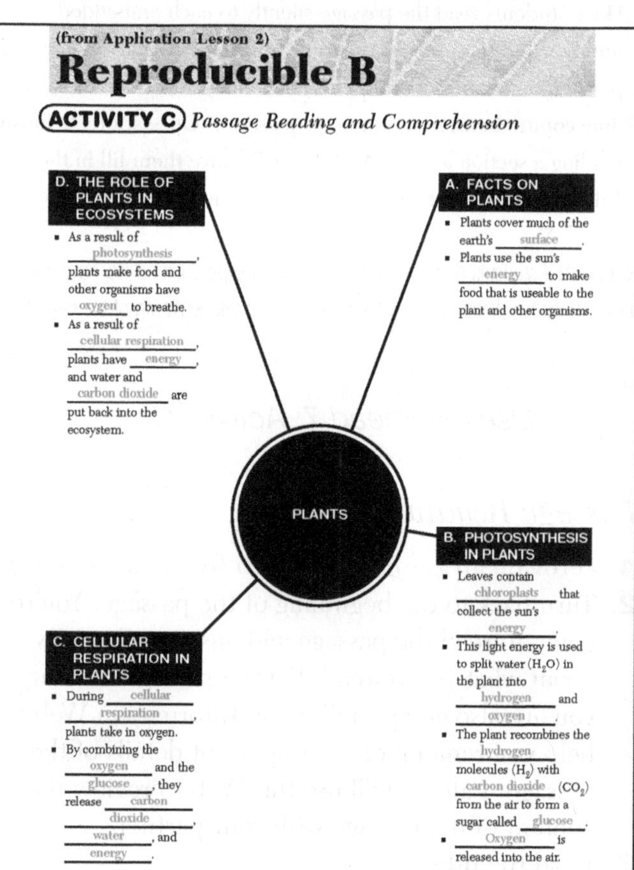
D. THE ROLE OF PLANTS IN ECOSYSTEMS
- As a result of photosynthesis, plants make food and other organisms have oxygen to breathe.
- As a result of cellular respiration, plants have energy, and water and carbon dioxide are put back into the ecosystem.

A. FACTS ON PLANTS
- Plants cover much of the earth's surface.
- Plants use the sun's energy to make food that is useable to the plant and other organisms.

PLANTS

B. PHOTOSYNTHESIS IN PLANTS
- Leaves contain chloroplasts that collect the sun's energy.
- This light energy is used to split water (H_2O) in the plant into hydrogen and oxygen.
- The plant recombines the hydrogen molecules (H_2) with carbon dioxide (CO_2) from the air to form a sugar called glucose.
- Oxygen is released into the air.

C. CELLULAR RESPIRATION IN PLANTS
- During cellular respiration, plants take in oxygen.
- By combining the oxygen and the glucose, they release carbon dioxide, water, and energy.

Appendix B • 387

#4 What is chlorophyll and why is it a necessary component in photosynthesis?

A green pigment found in the leaves; it collects the sun's energy, which is then used to split apart molecules.

#5 Why is it important that plants release oxygen into the air? How much of the earth's oxygen do the plants provide?

Oxygen is the part of the air we breathe; plants provide Earth with half of its oxygen.

#6 During cellular respiration what is taken in? How does that differ from photosynthesis?

During cellular respiration, oxygen is taken in; during photosynthesis, oxygen is released.

#7 What two plant processes are necessary for each ecosystem to function properly?

Photosynthesis and cellular respiration.

cellular respiration, you will learn how the energy is released so that the plant can use it. (#4)

Photosynthesis, or using light energy to transform water and carbon dioxide into glucose sugar, happens every day. As a special waste product, molecules of oxygen (O_2) are released into the air. What a special waste product it is! The oxygen released by plants becomes part of the air we breathe. In fact, plants provide earth with half of its oxygen! Microbes, members of the bacteria and protist kingdoms, also photosynthesize and bring energy into ecosystems. These microbes release the other half of the planet's oxygen. (#5)

C

Cellular Respiration in Plants

Cellular respiration in plants is the energy-releasing process that is the opposite of photosynthesis. During photosynthesis, plants release oxygen. During cellular respiration, they take in oxygen. Even though plants have made energy-rich food (glucose) during photosynthesis, they cannot access the energy in the food unless they also take in oxygen from the air and release the energy. By combining oxygen with the glucose they have made, they release a lot of energy as well as carbon dioxide and water.

When plants combine oxygen from the air with food (glucose), the process of photosynthesis is reversed and the stored energy originally gained from the sun is released to power the plants and help them grow and continue to live. (#6)

D

The Role of Plants in Ecosystems

In order for each ecosystem to function properly, photosynthesis and cellular respiration in plants are both essential. As a result of photosynthesis, plants make their own food, and other organisms have enough oxygen to breathe. As a result of cellular respiration, plants have energy for living and growing, plants provide food for other organisms, and water and carbon dioxide are continuously put back into the ecosystem for plants to use again. If plants had to use up water, carbon dioxide, and oxygen without producing any, the ecosystem would have used up these resources a long time ago. We will learn more about how energy and matter move through ecosystems in the next article. (#7)

ACTIVITY D *Fluency Building*

Cold Timing		Practice 1	
Practice 2		Hot Timing	

Fluency Building

ACTIVITY PROCEDURE

(See the *Student Book*, page 31.)

In this activity, students will be using a repeated reading procedure of the Activity C article to increase their reading fluency. First, have students do a Cold Timing, in which they whisper-read for one minute as you time them. Have them record in their books the number of correct words they read. Then, have students repeat with one or two practice readings to attempt to beat their Cold Timing. Finally, students exchange books in preparation for a Hot Timing. Have students listen to a partner read for one minute, underlining any word errors, and have them determine the number of correct words their partner read. When both students have completed their Hot Timing, they return each other's books and complete their own Fluency Graphs by indicating the number of words they read correctly in the one-minute Cold Timing and the one-minute Hot Timing.

Note D-1: When assigning partners for this activity, have the stronger reader read first. As a result, the other reader will have one additional practice opportunity.

1. Now, it's time for fluency building.
2. Find the beginning of the passage again. (Pause.)
3. Whisper-read. See how many words you can read in one minute. Begin._ (Time students for one minute.) Stop._ Circle the last word that you read._ Count the number of words you read in one minute. (Assist students in determining the number of words by counting from the number at the beginning of the line to the circled word.)_ In your book, find **Cold Timing**. Record the number of words you read._
4. Let's practice again. Return to the beginning of the article. Remember to whisper-read. See if you can beat your Cold Timing. Begin._ (Time students for one minute.) Stop._ Put a box around the last word that you read._ Count the number of words you read in one minute._ Find **Practice 1**._ Record the number of words you read._
5. (Optional) Let's practice one more time before the Hot Timing. Return to the beginning of the article. Remember to whisper-read. See if you can beat your Cold Timing. Begin._ (Time students for one minute.) Stop._ Put a box around the last word that you read._ Count the number of words you read in one minute._ Find **Practice 2**._ Record the number of words you read._
6. Please exchange books with your partner._ Partner 1, you are going to read first. Partner 2, you are going to listen carefully to your partner as he or she reads. If your partner makes a mistake or leaves out a word, underline that word. Ones, get ready to read quietly to your partner. Begin._ (Time students for one minute.) Stop._ Twos, cross out the last word that your partner read._ Twos, determine the number of words your partner read correctly in one minute._ (Assist students in subtracting the number of mistakes from the number of words read.) Find **Hot Timing**._ Record the number of words your partner read correctly._
7. Partner 2, you are going to read next. Partner 1, you are going to listen carefully to your partner as he or she reads. If your partner makes a mistake or leaves out a word, underline that word. Twos, get ready to read quietly to your partner. Begin._ (Time students for one minute.) Stop._ Ones, cross out the last word that your partner read._ Ones, determine the number of words your partner read correctly in one minute._ Record the number of words your partner read correctly after **Hot Timing**._
8. Exchange books._ Turn to the Fluency Graph on the inside back cover. First, put a dot and a "C" next to the number that shows how many words you read correctly for your Cold Timing._ Then, put a dot and an "H" next to the number of words you read correctly for your Hot Timing._

ACTIVITY D *Fluency Building*

Cold Timing		Practice 1	
Practice 2		Hot Timing	

Student Book: Application Lesson 2 31

ACTIVITY E

Comprehension Questions— Multiple Choice

ACTIVITY PROCEDURE

(See the *Student Book,* page 32.)

Review the steps in the Multiple Choice Strategy. Lead students through items #1 and #2, proceeding step-by-step. Have students proceed item by item for the remaining multiple-choice items, reminding them to prepare a rationale for the *best* answer. Have students share their answers and the rationale for their answers. Provide feedback and have students record points for each correct item.

Note E-1: The correct Multiple Choice answers are circled.

APPLICATION LESSON

2

ACTIVITY E *Comprehension Questions—Multiple Choice*

Comprehension Strategy—Multiple Choice

Step 1: Read the item.
Step 2: Read all of the choices.
Step 3: Think about why each choice might be correct or incorrect. Check the article as needed.
Step 4: From the possible correct choices, select the best answer.

1. (Main idea) **If this article needed a new title, which of these would be the best?**
   - **a.** The Parts of Plants
   - **b.** Ecosystems: A Mix of Living and Nonliving Things
   - (**c.**) The Importance of Plants to Ecosystems
   - **d.** The Process of Photosynthesis
2. (Cause and effect) **The leaves are a very important plant structure because:**
   - **a.** they provide shade for other organisms.
   - **b.** they collect fresh water for insects.
   - (**c.**) they use light energy to make food.
   - **d.** they have sugar in them.
3. (Vocabulary) **The word "photosynthesis" contains two meaningful parts. Which best represents the meaning of "photosynthesis?"**
   - **a.** picture + pull apart
   - (**b.**) light + put together
   - **c.** energy + parts
   - **d.** camera + thesis
4. (Cause and effect) **If plants were always covered so sunlight could not reach the leaves, they would not survive because:**
   - **a.** their roots would be unable to get water and minerals.
   - (**b.**) no light energy would be available for the photosynthesis process.
   - **c.** their leaves would wilt.
   - **d.** too much oxygen would be released in the photosynthesis process.

MULTIPLE CHOICE COMPREHENSION 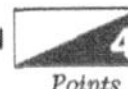

Points

32 *REWARDS Plus: Reading Strategies Applied to Science Passages*

1. Turn to page 32. Find **Activity E.** Let's review the steps in the Multiple Choice Strategy.
2. Read **Step 1.** Remember, to be sure you understand the item, you may wish to read it more than one time.
3. Read **Step 2.** It is important to **<u>not</u>** make your selection before you have considered all the choices.
4. Read **Step 3.** This is the most critical step in the strategy. For each choice, you must really think about why the choice might be correct or incorrect. It may be necessary to look back in the article.
5. Read **Step 4.** After you have really thought about each choice, you can select the best answer.
6. Find question 1. Read it.
7. Read choice **a.** This passage talks about some parts of plants. However parts of plants is not the overall topic of the passage, so this may not be the best answer.
8. Read choice **b.** An ecosystem is a mix of living and nonliving things; however, this passage does not focus on ecosystems. It focuses on a major part of any ecosystem, which is plants. So, this is not the best answer.
9. Read choice **c.** This article <u>is</u> about plants and their importance to ecosystems. This could be the correct choice.
10. Read choice **d.** Photosynthesis was described in this article, but cellular respiration was also described, so this may not be the best choice.
11. Which is the best answer? Circle it.
12. Let's do the next one. Read item #2.
13. Read choice **a.** Think about why this choice might be correct or incorrect. (Pause. Then, call on individual students.)
14. This is what I was thinking. Leaves do provide shade for other organisms, but this is not why these structures are very important to the plant. This is probably not the correct choice.
15. Read choice **b.** Think about why this choice might be correct or incorrect. (Pause. Then, call on individual students.)
16. This is what I was thinking. Leaves do collect fresh water for insects, but, again, this is not why these structures are very important to the plant. This is probably not the correct choice.
17. Read choice **c.** Think about why this choice might be correct or incorrect. (Pause. Then, call on individual students.)
18. This is what I was thinking. Leaves are the structures that capture light energy from the sun to make food for the plant. Plants, like all organisms, need food, thus leaves are very important to plants. This might be the best answer.

19. Read choice **d.**_ Think about why this choice might be correct or incorrect. (Pause. Then, call on individual students.)

20. This is what I was thinking. Sugar is an energy-rich food that plants store, but this is not why leaves are important to plants. So, this is not the correct choice.

21. Which is the best answer?_ Circle it._

22. Use the Multiple Choice Strategy to complete item #3. Be ready to explain why you selected your answer. (Wait while students complete the item. Call on individual students. Ask them why they chose their answer and why they eliminated the other choices. Encourage discussion. Provide students with feedback on their choices, focusing on why or why not those choices might be appropriate.)

23. Use the Multiple Choice Strategy to complete item #4. Be ready to explain why you selected your answer. (Wait while students complete the item. Call on individual students. Ask them why they chose their answer and why they eliminated the other choices. Encourage discussion. Provide students with feedback on their choices, focusing on why or why not those choices might be appropriate.)

24. Count the number of items you got correct, and record that number in the blank half of the Multiple Choice Comprehension box._

APPLICATION LESSON
2

ACTIVITY E *Comprehension Questions—Multiple Choice*

Comprehension Strategy—Multiple Choice

Step 1: Read the item.
Step 2: Read all of the choices.
Step 3: Think about why each choice might be correct or incorrect. Check the article as needed.
Step 4: From the possible correct choices, select the best answer.

1. (Main idea) **If this article needed a new title, which of these would be the best?**
   a. The Parts of Plants
   b. Ecosystems: A Mix of Living and Nonliving Things
   (c.) The Importance of Plants to Ecosystems
   d. The Process of Photosynthesis

2. (Cause and effect) **The leaves are a very important plant structure because:**
   a. they provide shade for other organisms.
   b. they collect fresh water for insects.
   (c.) they use light energy to make food.
   d. they have sugar in them.

3. (Vocabulary) **The word "photosynthesis" contains two meaningful parts. Which best represents the meaning of "photosynthesis?"**
   a. picture + pull apart
   (b.) light + put together
   c. energy + parts
   d. camera + thesis

4. (Cause and effect) **If plants were always covered so sunlight could not reach the leaves, they would not survive because:**
   a. their roots would be unable to get water and minerals.
   (b.) no light energy would be available for the photosynthesis process.
   c. their leaves would wilt.
   d. too much oxygen would be released in the photosynthesis process.

MULTIPLE CHOICE COMPREHENSION 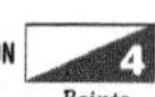 4 Points

32 *REWARDS Plus: Reading Strategies Applied to Science Passages*

ACTIVITY F

Vocabulary Activities

ACTIVITY PROCEDURE

(See the *Student Book*, pages 33–34.)

Model item #1 orally for students, and then have students complete the items. Have students complete the remaining items orally and provide them with feedback on their answers. Have students then respond to each question in writing by answering "yes" or "no" and providing a reason for their answers.

Yes/No/Why

1. Turn to page 33. Find **Activity F.** Read the first item with me: **Is chlorophyll essential**? I would answer "Yes" to this question, and here is my reason. I know that chlorophyll is found in most plants and must be present for photosynthesis to take place. Photosynthesis is a process necessary to convert the sun's energy into food for plants so chlorophyll is essential.
2. Write your answer and your reason for it in the space provided. Look up when you are done.
3. Read item #2. Tell your partner your answer and your reason for it. (Pause. Then call on individual students.)
4. My answer is a definite "No." Carbon dioxide is a gas, and glucose is a sugar, so carbon dioxide could not be a type of glucose.
5. Write your answer and your reason for it in the space provided. Look up when you are done.
6. Read item #3. Tell your partner your answer and your reason for it. (Pause. Then call on individual students.)
7. I would definitely answer "Yes" to this question. Photosynthesis is the process that converts the sun's energy into food for plants, which provide food for most organisms on earth. Without food, we would not live and thus would have no existence.
8. Write your answer and your reason for it in the space provided. Look up when you are done.

Note F-1: You may wish to do this as an oral task only rather than an oral and a written task.

APPLICATION LESSON **2**

ACTIVITY F *Vocabulary Activities*

Yes/No/Why

1. Is **chlorophyll essential**?
Example answer: Yes. Chlorophyll is found in most plants and must be present for photosynthesis to take place. Photosynthesis is a process necessary to convert the sun's energy into food for plants, so chlorophyll is essential.

2. Is **carbon dioxide** a type of **glucose**?
Example answer: No. Carbon dioxide is a gas, and glucose is a sugar, so carbon dioxide could not be a type of glucose.

3. Is our **existence** dependent upon **photosynthesis**?
Example answer. Yes. Photosynthesis is the process that converts the sun's energy into food for plants, which provide food for most organisms on earth. Without food, we would not live and thus would have no existence.

Student Book: Application Lesson 2 33

ACTIVITY PROCEDURE

Have students read the words and definitions and then complete the sentence stems for each vocabulary word. Have them share answers with partners and with the class. Then, have students give themselves points in the blank half of the Vocabulary box.

Completion Activity

1. Turn to page 34._ Read the first word and its definition with me: **combine: to join together**.
2. Now, read the sentence stem with me: **In order to make a great sandwich, you might combine . . .**
3. Think of things that you might combine to make a great sandwich and write them._ Share your answer with your partner._ (Call on a few students to share answers with the class.)
4. Let's do another one. Read the second word and definition with me: **essential: absolutely necessary.**
5. Now, read the sentence stem with me: **In order to drive a car, it is essential that you have . . .**
6. Think of the things that are essential to have in order to drive a car and write them._ Share your answer with your partner._ (Call on a few students to share answers with the class.)
7. (Repeat Steps 4–6 for the rest of the words.)
8. If you participated in answering all seven questions, give yourself seven points in the blank half of the Vocabulary box.

Note F-2: You may wish to do this as an oral task only rather than an oral task and a written task.

APPLICATION LESSON
2

Completion Activity

1. **combine:** to join together
   In order to make a great sandwich, you might combine
   Answers will vary.
2. **essential:** absolutely necessary
   In order to drive a car, it is essential that you have
   Answers will vary.
3. **continuously:** without end
   One example of an activity that goes on continuously is
   Answers will vary.
4. **use:** to employ for a purpose
   Some of the things you use in class include
   Answers will vary.

VOCABULARY 7 Points

ACTIVITY G

Expository Writing—Multi-Paragraph Answer

ACTIVITY PROCEDURE, Plan and Write

(See the *Student Book*, page 35–37.)

Review with students the steps in the Multi-Paragraph Writing Strategy. Have students read the prompt and Veronica's topics. Explain how Veronica made a **LIST** of critical details under each topic. Have students read Veronica's details for topic a and b, then look at topic a again. Explain that details that don't go with a topic should be eliminated, and have them **CROSS OUT** the same detail that Veronica crossed out. Next, explain how details can be combined into one sentence, and have students **CONNECT** details as Veronica did in her plan. Have students **NUMBER** their details in the same manner as Veronica. Next, have students read example paragraph a. Guide students in examining and completing the plan for topic b and writing paragraph b. Finally, explain that after they **WRITE**, they should **EDIT** their work, revising for clarity and proofreading for errors in capitalization, punctuation, and spelling.

Use Overheads 8 and 9: Activity G

1. Turn to page 35._ Find **Activity G.**_ Today we are going to work on writing answers with more than one paragraph. Let's review the strategy for writing a multi-paragraph answer. Read **Step 1** with me: **LIST**. Yes, you will list the important details for each topic. Read **Step 2** with me: **CROSS OUT**. Next, you will cross out any details that don't go with the topic. Read **Step 3**: **CONNECT**. You will connect details that could go into one sentence. Read **Step 4**: **NUMBER**. You will then number the details in a logical order. Read **Step 5**: **WRITE**. Next, you will write the paragraph. After you have used these steps to write each paragraph, you will do **Step 6**. Read **Step 6**: **EDIT**. Finally, you will revise and proofread your paragraph.
2. The steps are **list, cross out, connect, number, write,** and **edit**. Say those steps._ Ones, say the steps to your partner._ Twos, say the steps to your partner._ (Repeat until students can say the steps independently.)
3. Find the prompt in the middle of the page._ Read the prompt out loud with me: **Describe the two processes that plants perform to keep the energy cycle in ecosystems functioning.**

APPLICATION LESSON **2**

ACTIVITY G *Expository Writing—Multi-Paragraph Answer*

Writing Strategy—Multi-Paragraph Answer

Step 1: LIST (List the details that are important enough to include in your answer.)
- **Step 2: CROSS OUT** (Reread the details. Cross out any that don't go with the topic.)
- **Step 3: CONNECT** (Connect any details that could go into one sentence.)
- **Step 4: NUMBER** (Number the details in a logical order.)
- **Step 5: WRITE** (Write the paragraph.)

Step 6: EDIT (Revise and proofread your answer.)

Prompt: Describe the two processes that plants perform to keep the energy cycle in ecosystems functioning.

Plan: Complete the Planning Box with your teacher.

Student Book: Application Lesson 2 35

APPLICATION LESSON **2**

Example Multi-Paragraph Plan

Planning Box
(topic a) *photosynthesis*
(detail) – ~~*much of earth covered with plants*~~
① (detail) – *process for making food*
② (detail) – *leaves contain chloroplasts, which contain chlorophyll*
③ { (detail) – *chloroplasts collect sun's energy*
(detail) – *light energy used to split water into hydrogen & oxygen*
④ { (detail) – *hydrogen stays in plant*
(detail) – *oxygen leaves plant*
⑤ { (detail) – *plant combines hydrogen with carbon dioxide from air to form glucose*
(detail) – *glucose is an energy-rich food*
(topic b) *cellular respiration*
① (detail) – *process of releasing energy*
② { (detail) – *plants take in oxygen from air*
(detail) – *combine oxygen with glucose*
③ (detail) – *release energy & carbon dioxide & water*
④ { (detail) – *stored energy powers the plant*
(detail) – *helps plants live and grow*

Write: Examine paragraph a. Then write paragraph b on a separate piece of paper.

36 *REWARDS Plus: Reading Strategies Applied to Science Passages*

4. Turn to page 36._ First, Veronica recorded the topics for her paragraphs. Read topic a._ Read topic b._ Later, each topic will be incorporated into a topic sentence.
5. Next, she followed the steps in the Writing Strategy to write her answer. What is **Step 1**?_ Read the details **listed** under topic a._ Veronica then listed details for topic b.
6. Next, Veronica applied **Steps 2 through 5** to each paragraph.
7. What is **Step 2**?_ Before she wrote the first paragraph, Veronica reread her details and **crossed out** any details that did not go with the topic._ Look at the overhead._ What detail did she cross out?_ Why do you think this detail was eliminated?_ Cross out the same detail on your paper._
8. What is **Step 3**?_ Look at the overhead._ Veronica **connected** a number of details that can be combined easily into one sentence. Please draw brackets on your paper to connect the details that Veronica connected._
9. What is **Step 4**?_ Next, Veronica **numbered** the details in the order she wished them to occur in the paragraph. Looking at the overhead, number your details as Veronica did._
10. What is **Step 5**?_ Next, Veronica **wrote** the paragraph. Locate paragraph a on the next page._ (Read paragraph a with your students or to your students.)
11. Veronica then repeated these steps on the remaining paragraph. Look at the overhead._ First, she looked for details to **cross out** that did not go with the topic. Did she cross off any details?_ Next, she **connected** details that could go into one sentence. Did she connect any details for this paragraph?_ Next, she **numbered** the details in a logical order. Number your details as Veronica did._
12. Now it's your turn. Take out a blank piece of paper._ Use Veronica's plan and **write** a paragraph describing the process of cellular respiration. If you finish early, please reread and **edit** your paragraph. Don't forget to use the spelling of words in the plan and the article to correct any errors._ (Move around the room and monitor your students as they are writing.)
13. (When the majority of students are done, proceed with the lesson.) What is **Step 6**?_ Veronica edited paragraph a by revising and proofreading for any

---

APPLICATION LESSON **2**

ACTIVITY G *Expository Writing—Multi-Paragraph Answer*

Writing Strategy—Multi-Paragraph Answer

Step 1: LIST (List the details that are important enough to include in your answer.)
Step 2: CROSS OUT (Reread the details. Cross out any that don't go with the topic.)
Step 3: CONNECT (Connect any details that could go into one sentence.)
Step 4: NUMBER (Number the details in a logical order.)
Step 5: WRITE (Write the paragraph.)
Step 6: EDIT (Revise and proofread your answer.)

Prompt: Describe the two processes that plants perform to keep the energy cycle in ecosystems functioning.

Plan: Complete the Planning Box with your teacher.

Student Book: Application Lesson 2 35

APPLICATION LESSON **2**

Example Multi-Paragraph Plan

Planning Box
(topic a) *photosynthesis*
(detail) – ~~*much of earth covered with plants*~~
① (detail) – *process for making food*
② (detail) – *leaves contain chloroplasts, which contain chlorophyll*
③ (detail) – *chloroplasts collect sun's energy*
(detail) – *light energy used to split water into hydrogen & oxygen*
④ (detail) – *hydrogen stays in plant*
(detail) – *oxygen leaves plant*
⑤ (detail) – *plant combines hydrogen with carbon dioxide from air to form glucose*
(detail) – *glucose is an energy-rich food*
(topic b) *cellular respiration*
① (detail) – *process of releasing energy*
② (detail) – *plants take in oxygen from air*
(detail) – *combine oxygen with glucose*
③ (detail) – *release energy & carbon dioxide & water*
④ (detail) – *stored energy powers the plant*
(detail) – *helps plants live and grow*

Write: Examine paragraph a. Then write paragraph b on a separate piece of paper.

36 REWARDS Plus: Reading Strategies Applied to Science Passages

errors in capitalization, punctuation, and spelling. Please carefully read your paragraph. Revise your paragraph so that it is easy to understand and clear. Proofread for any errors in capitalization, punctuation, and spelling. (Give students time to proofread their paragraph.)

ACTIVITY PROCEDURE, Evaluate

Ask students to read each question in the rubric. Guide them in evaluating the paragraphs using the guidelines. Have students total their points and record them in the blank half of the Writing box.

14. Turn to page 37. Veronica has already evaluated paragraph a. Let's evaluate your paragraph.
15. Read question #1 with me. Circle "Yes" for b if your topic sentence includes the topic, cellular respiration.
16. Read question #2 with me. Circle "Yes" for b if all of your details tell about the process of cellular respiration.
17. Read question #3 with me. Circle "Yes" for b if you combined details in a number of sentences.
18. Read question #4. Reread your paragraph. Circle "Yes" if your paragraph is easy to understand.
19. Read question #5. Carefully examine your paragraph. If you think a word is misspelled, underline it and check back in the plan or article and correct the spelling. Circle "Yes" if you believe that you have very few spelling errors.
20. Read question #6. Carefully examine your sentences. Be sure that each sentence begins with a capital. If all sentences begin with a capital, circle "Yes."
21. Read question #7. Examine your sentences. Be sure that each sentence ends with a period. If all sentences end with a period, circle "Yes."
22. This answer only had two paragraphs. As a bonus, circle "Yes" for each c.
23. Count up your points and record them in the blank half of the Writing box.
24. (Show Overhead 9.) Look at the overhead. Let's read Veronica's paragraph. Yours does not have to be the same, but it should be similar. (Read the paragraph to your students or with your students or call on a student to read the example paragraph.)

APPLICATION LESSON **2**

Example Multi-Paragraph Answer

(paragraph a)

The first process that plants perform to keep the energy cycle in ecosystems functioning is photosynthesis. This is the plant's process for making food. The leaves in plants contain chloroplasts, which contain chlorophyll. These chloroplasts collect the sun's energy, which is used to split water into hydrogen and oxygen. The hydrogen stays in the plant while the oxygen leaves the plant. Next, the plant combines the hydrogen with carbon dioxide from the air to form glucose, an energy-rich food for the plant.

Evaluate: Evaluate the paragraphs using this rubric.

Rubric— Multi-Paragraph Answer	Student or Partner Rating	Teacher Rating
1. Did the author state the topic in the first sentence?	a. (Yes) Fix up b. (Yes) Fix up c. (Yes) Fix up	a. Yes No b. Yes No c. Yes No
2. Did the author include details that go with the topic?	a. (Yes) Fix up b. (Yes) Fix up c. (Yes) Fix up	a. Yes No b. Yes No c. Yes No
3. Did the author combine details in some of the sentences?	a. (Yes) Fix up b. (Yes) Fix up c. (Yes) Fix up	a. Yes No b. Yes No c. Yes No
4. Is the answer easy to understand?	(Yes) Fix up	Yes No
5. Did the author correctly spell words, particularly the words found in the article?	(Yes) Fix up	Yes No
6. Did the author use correct capitalization, capitalizing the first word in the sentence and proper names of people, places, and things?	(Yes) Fix up	Yes No
7. Did the author use correct punctuation, including a period at the end of each sentence?	(Yes) Fix up	Yes No

WRITING 13 Points

Student Book: Application Lesson 2 37

25. Let's review the steps in the writing strategy. **List, cross out, connect, number, write, edit.** Tell your partner the steps in the strategy.
26. In the next lesson, you will be writing more paragraphs.

Note G-1: The rubric can be used in a variety of ways. Instead of the students evaluating their own paragraphs, you may wish to have their partners provide feedback. The second column is designed for teacher feedback. If you have a small group, it would be useful to give daily feedback on writing. If the group size is large, you can give feedback to a number of children each day. You may wish to give students bonus points based on your feedback.

ACTIVITY H

Comprehension—Single-Paragraph Answer

ACTIVITY PROCEDURE

(See the *Student Book*, page 38.)

Have students read the *What Is* statement and the *What If* question. Have students turn the question into part of the answer and write down a topic sentence for their answer. Then, have them complete their answer. Encourage them to use evidence from the article and their own experience and background knowledge. Finally, review the discussion behaviors in the "Looks Like/Sounds Like" chart and engage students in a discussion. Award points for writing and participating in the discussion.

Note H-1: To increase the quality of the discussion, the students are asked to think and write about the *What If* before the discussion. However, you may be working with students who have difficulty generating ideas for their paragraph. If that is the case, switch the order of activities: engage the students in a discussion, and then have them write their paragraphs.

1. Turn to page 38._ Find **Activity H.**_
2. Today, you are going to write a paragraph answer to the *What If* question and participate in a discussion. Let's use the strategy to answer the question.
3. Read **Step 1.**_ Find the *What Is* statement in the middle of the page._ Read it out loud with me: **Plants are organisms that transform the sun's energy into energy that is usable by them and other organisms.**
4. Find the *What If* question._ Read it with me: **What would happen if plants couldn't use the sun's light energy to make food?**
5. Read **Step 2.**_ Think how you might turn the question into part of the answer._ Tell me your idea for a topic sentence._ (Example sentence: If plants couldn't use the sun's light energy to make food, a number of things would happen.) Take out a piece of paper and write your topic sentence._ (Move around the room and monitor as students write.)
6. Read **Step 3.**_ After you have created a topic sentence using the wording from the question, you are ready to add ideas. You may think of an answer based on your experience and background knowledge, but you should also include evidence from the article or other materials that you have studied. Take some time to look back in the article and consider how you would respond to this question. Then, add sentences to your paragraph. If you finish early, reread your paragraph and edit it so that it is easy to understand and clear._ (Move around the room and monitor as students write.)
7. Read your paragraph to your partner._
8. You can earn four points for your paragraph: two points for turning the question into part of the answer and two points for using evidence from the article. If you included wording from the question in your answer and added evidence from the article, award yourself four points for writing._ Write them in the blank half of the Writing box.
9. Before we discuss your answers, let's review the discussion guidelines. Look at the Discussion Guidelines at the bottom of the page._ Read to yourself what the speaker should look like and sound like. Circle the speaker behavior that you need to work on._ (Call on students to share their perspectives.)
10. Look at the Discussion Guidelines again._ Read what the listener should look like and sound like.

APPLICATION LESSON **2**

ACTIVITY H *Comprehension—Single-Paragraph Answer*

Writing Strategy—Single-Paragraph Answer

Step 1: Read the item.
Step 2: Turn the question into part of the answer and write it down.
Step 3: Think of the answer or locate the answer in the article.
Step 4: Complete your answer.

Prompt:

What is—Plants are organisms that transform the sun's energy into energy that is usable by them and other organisms.

What if—What would happen if plants couldn't use the sun's light energy to make food?

Write and Discuss: Write a paragraph. Then share your ideas. Use the Discussion Guidelines.

Discussion Guidelines

Speaker		Listener	
Looks like:	**Sounds like:**	**Looks like:**	**Sounds like:**
• Facing peers • Making eye contact • Participating	• Using pleasant, easy-to-hear voice • Sharing opinions, supporting facts and reasons from the article and from your experience • Staying on the topic	• Facing speaker • Making eye contact • Participating	• Waiting quietly to speak • Giving positive, supportive comments • Disagreeing respectfully

WRITING 4 Points | DISCUSSION 4 Points

38 *REWARDS Plus: Reading Strategies Applied to Science Passages*

Circle the listener behavior that you need to work on._ (Call on students to share their perspectives.)

11. (Engage students in a discussion. Award four points to students who are active participants in the discussion, and have them write them in the blank half of the Discussion box.)

Note H-2: If your students are having difficulty writing the *What If* paragraphs, read or show them the following example paragraph:

Example Single-Paragraph Answer

If plants were unable to use the sun's light energy to make food, the effects would be truly devastating. First, plants would be unable to survive if they were unable to produce their necessary food. Second, plants would be unable to provide food to other organisms. Third, these organisms would not only be robbed of necessary food from plants, but they also would not have a ready supply of oxygen that plants would normally release. If plants were unable to produce their own food, life on this planet would cease.

Application Lesson 3

Materials Needed:

- *Student Book*: Application Lesson 3
- Application Overhead Transparencies 10–14
- Appendix A Reproducible 3: Comprehension Strategy—Multiple Choice
- Appendix B Reproducible C: Application Lesson 3
- Appendix C Optional Vocabulary Activity: Application Lesson 3
- Paper or cardboard to use when covering the overhead transparency
- Paper or cardboard for each student to use during spelling dictation
- Washable overhead transparency pen

Text Treatment Notes:

- Black text signifies teacher script (exact wording to say to students).
- Green text in parentheses signifies directions or prompts for the teacher.
- Green text signifies answers or examples of answers.
- Green graphics treatment signifies reproduction of Overhead information.
- Green text and green graphics treatment do not appear in the *Student Book*.

Vocabulary

ACTIVITY PROCEDURE, List 1

(See the *Student Book*, page 39.)

Tell students each word in the list. Then, have students repeat the word and read the definition aloud. For each definition, provide any additional information that may be necessary. Then, have students practice reading the words themselves.

Note A.1: If you wish to emphasize the part of speech, have students say the part of speech before reading the definition.

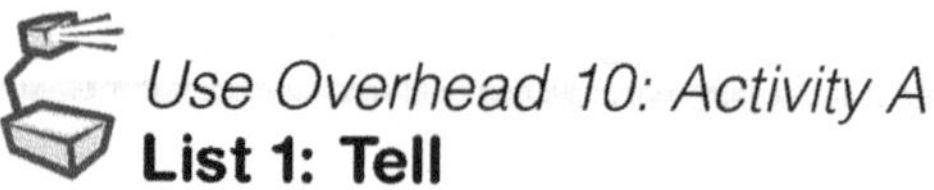

1. (Show the top half of Overhead 10.) Before we read the passage, let's read the difficult words. (Point to **chemosynthesis**.) The first word is **chemosynthesis**. What word?_ Now, read the definition._
2. (Point to **orca**.) The next word is **orca**. What word?_ Now, read the definition._
3. (Pronounce each word in List 1, and then have students repeat each word and read the definition.)
4. Open your *Student Book* to **Application Lesson 3**, page 39._
5. Find **Activity A**, **List 1**, in your book._ Let's read the words again. First word._ Next word._ (Continue for all words in List 1.)

ACTIVITY PROCEDURE, List 2

(See the *Student Book*, page 39.)

The second list of words can be read using the part-by-part strategy. Have students circle prefixes and suffixes, then underline the vowels. Using the overhead transparency, assist students in checking their work. Next, have students figure out each word to themselves, then say it aloud. Have them read the definition aloud.

Note A.2-1: Provide additional information for any definitions as needed.

Note A.2-2: If you wish to emphasize the part of speech, have students say the part of speech before reading the definition.

Note A.2-3: If you are teaching older students for whom "thumbs-up" is inappropriate, have students look at you when they can read the word.

APPLICATION LESSON 3

ACTIVITY A Vocabulary

List 1: Tell

1. **chemosynthesis** *n.* ► (the process by which certain organisms break down energy-rich molecules in order to make their own food)
2. **orca** *n.* ► (a killer whale)
3. **alga** *n.* ► (a simple, nonflowering plant that is usually found in or around water)
4. **algae** *n.* ► (more than one alga; the plural of alga)
5. **lichens** *n.* ► (slow-growing plants composed of algae and fungi)
6. **caribou** *n.* ► (a type of reindeer living in northern Canada and in Alaska)

List 2: Strategy Practice

1. **producers** *n.* ► (organisms that produce their own food)
2. **consumers** *n.* ► (organisms that eat other organisms)
3. **decomposers** *n.* ► (organisms that break down dead organisms)
4. **microscope** *n.* ► (an instrument used to see very small things)
5. **microscopic** *adj.* ► (so small as to be seen only with a microscope)
6. **recycling** *v.* ► (changing waste to reusable items)
7. **arrangement** *n.* ► (the result of being placed, or arranged, in a certain way)
8. **relatively** *adv.* ► (in relation to something else; comparatively)
9. **mutual** *adj.* ► (shared)
10. **parasite** *n.* ► (an organism that lives in or on another organism and receives benefits while harming the other organism)

TALLY ☐ VOCABULARY 5 Points

Student Book: Application Lesson 3 39

Use Overhead 10: Activity A
List 2: Strategy Practice

1. Find **List 2**. For each word, circle the prefixes and suffixes, and underline the vowels. Look up when you are done._
2. (Show the bottom half of Overhead 10.) Before you check your work on List 2, look at item #4. (Point to the second example.) When you completed the *REWARDS* program, you learned to recognize many prefixes and suffixes, but there are many more. (Point to the **micro** that is circled.) From now on, you can also circle **micro**. The prefix is /micro/. Say it._ Look at item #7. (Point to the second example and the **ar** that is circled.) From now on, you can also circle **ar**. The prefix is /ar/. Say it._ Now, go back to item #1. Check and fix any mistakes._
3. Go back to the first word again._ Sound out the word to yourself. Put your thumb up when you can read the word. Be sure that it is a real word._ What word?_ Now, read the definition._
4. (Continue Step 3 with all remaining words in List 2.)

Note A.2-4: You may wish to provide additional practice by having students read words to a partner.

ACTIVITY PROCEDURE, List 1 and 2

(See the *Student Book*, page 39.)

Tell students to look in List 1 or List 2 for a word you are thinking about. Have them circle the number of the word and tell you the word. Explain to students to make a tally mark for each correct word in the Tally box, and then enter the number of tally marks as points in the blank half of the Vocabulary box.

1. Remember, the words I'm thinking about will be in either List 1 or List 2. For every word you correctly identify, circle the number of that word. If the word is correct, make a tally mark in the Tally box. If you don't identify the correct word, don't do anything.
2. I am thinking of a word. Circle the number of the appropriate word.
   - If you share interests with your friends, you are said to have these kinds of interests. (Wait.) What word? **mutual**
   - Something so small that it cannot be seen by your eye is this kind of thing. (Wait.) What word? **microscopic**
   - When people sort their garbage into separate containers so the items can be used again, they are doing this to those items. (Wait.) What word? **recycling**
   - When you place things in a certain way, the result is this. (Wait.) What word? **arrangement**
   - This organism lives in or on other organisms and gains benefits while causing harm to those organisms. (Wait.) What word? **parasite**
3. Count all the tally marks, and enter that number as points in the blank half of the Vocabulary box.

ACTIVITY PROCEDURE, List 3

(See the *Student Book*, page 40.)

The words in the third list are related. Have students use the *REWARDS* Strategies to figure out the first word in each family. Have them read the definition of the verb and then read nouns and adjectives that are related to that verb.

Note A.3-1: Provide additional information for any definitions as needed.

Note A.3-2: If you wish to emphasize the part of speech, have students say the part of speech before reading the definition.

Note A.3-3: If you are teaching older students for whom "thumbs-up" is inappropriate, have students look at you when they can read the word.

APPLICATION LESSON **3**

List 3: Word Families

	Verb	Noun	Adjective
Family 1	cycle (to occur over and over again in a definite order)	cycle	cyclic
Family 2	collect (to put together a group of things)	collection collector	collective
Family 3	reduce (to make smaller in number or size)	reduction reducer	reduced
Family 4	process (to go through a series of actions leading to an end, or to take a course of action)	process processor	
Family 5	require (to have need of)	requirement	

ACTIVITY B *Spelling Dictation*

1. collect	4. reduce
2. collection	5. reduction
3. collective	6. reduced

SPELLING 6 *Points*

40 *REWARDS Plus: Reading Strategies Applied to Science Passages*

Use Overhead 11: Activity A
List 3: Word Families

1. Turn to page 40._ Find **Family 1** in **List 3**. Figure out the first word. Use your pencil if you wish. Put your thumb up when you know the word._ What word?_ Read the definition of the verb._
2. Look at the noun in Family 1. Figure out the word._ What word?_
3. Look at the adjective in Family 1. Figure out the word._ What word?_
4. (Repeat Steps 1–3 for all word families in List 3.)

Note A.3-4: You may wish to provide additional practice by having students read a word family to the group or to a partner.

Note A.3-5: An additional vocabulary practice activity called Quick Words is provided in Appendix C of this Teacher's Guide. See Appendix C for information about how this optional activity can be used.

ACTIVITY B

Spelling Dictation

ACTIVITY PROCEDURE

(See the *Student Book*, page 40.)

For each word, tell students the word, then have students say the parts of the word to themselves while they write the word. Using the overhead transparency, assist students in checking their spelling and correcting if they misspelled. Then, have students enter the number of correctly spelled words as points in the blank half of the Spelling box.

Note B-1: Distribute a piece of light cardboard to students so they can cover their page during spelling dictation. Students can also use the cardboard as a bookmark to quickly locate pages at the beginning of lessons.

Use Overhead 11: Activity B

1. Find **Activity B.**
2. The first word is **collect.** What word?_ Say the parts in **collect** to yourself as you write the word. (Pause and monitor.)
3. (Show **collect** on the overhead.) Check **collect.** If you misspelled it, cross it out and write it correctly.
4. The second word is **collection.** What word?_ Say the parts in **collection** to yourself as you write the word. (Pause and monitor.)
5. (Show **collection** on the overhead.) Check **collection.** If you misspelled it, cross it out and write it correctly.
6. (Repeat the procedures for the words **collective, reduce, reduction,** and **reduced.**)
7. Count the number of words you spelled correctly, and record that number as points in the blank half of the Spelling box at the bottom of the page.

APPLICATION LESSON 3

List 3: Word Families

	Verb	Noun	Adjective
Family 1	cycle (to occur over and over again in a definite order)	cycle	cyclic
Family 2	collect (to put together a group of things)	collection collector	collective
Family 3	reduce (to make smaller in number or size)	reduction reducer	reduced
Family 4	process (to go through a series of actions leading to an end, or to take a course of action)	process processor	
Family 5	require (to have need of)	requirement	

ACTIVITY B *Spelling Dictation*

1. collect	4. reduce
2. collection	5. reduction
3. collective	6. reduced

SPELLING 6 Points

40 *REWARDS Plus: Reading Strategies Applied to Science Passages*

ACTIVITY C

Passage Reading and Comprehension

ACTIVITY PROCEDURE

(See the *Student Book*, pages 41–43.)

Have students read the title of the passage and each heading. Ask them to tell their partners two things that the passage will tell about.

Passage Preview

1. Turn to page 41._ Let's preview the passage.
2. Read the title._ What is the whole passage going to tell about?_
3. Now, let's read the headings. Read the first heading._ Read the next heading._ (Continue until students have read all headings.)
4. Turn to your partner. Without looking, tell two things this passage will tell about._

ACTIVITY PROCEDURE

Provide students with an Information Web from Appendix B. Have students read the passage silently to each embedded number, and then reread the same information orally either to a partner, together as a group, or individually. Ask the corresponding comprehension question or questions. Once students finish reading a section labeled A, B, C, D, E, or F have them fill in the Information Web before going on to the next section.

Note C-1: If students do not finish reading the passage during class, have them use their Information Webs to review the information at the beginning of the next class.

Use Overhead 12: Activity C

Passage Reading

1. (Provide an Information Web for each student.)
2. Turn back to the beginning of the passage. You're going to read the passage and answer questions about what you've read. During passage reading, you are also going to fill in an Information Web to help you remember the important details of the passage. Later, you'll use this Web to review the content of the passage with your partner.
3. Read the title._

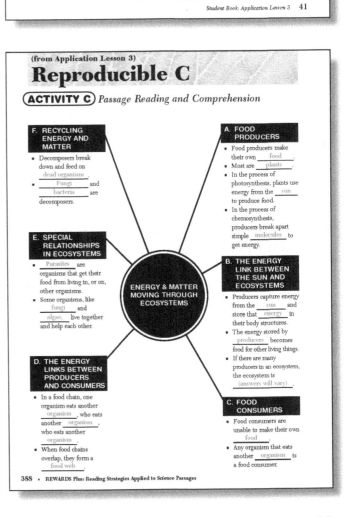

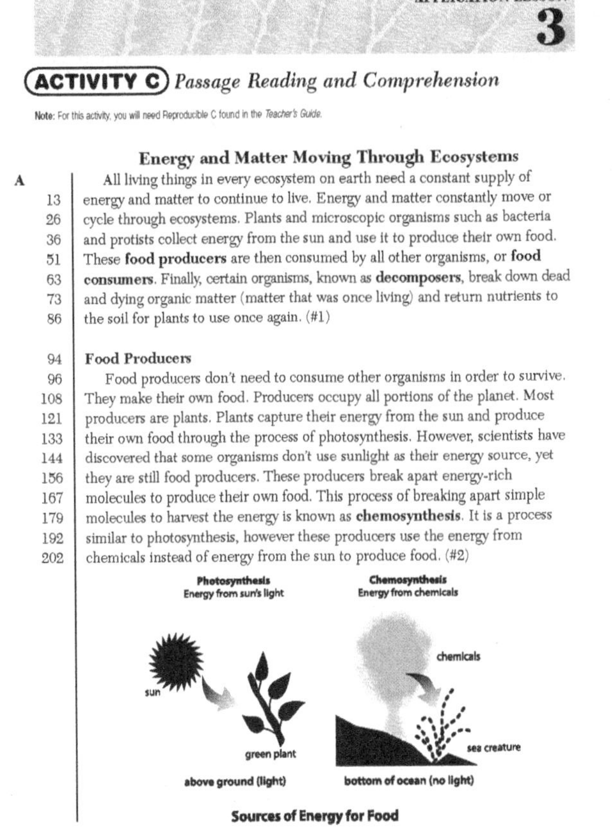

APPLICATION LESSON 3

ACTIVITY C *Passage Reading and Comprehension*

Note: For this activity, you will need Reproducible C found in the *Teacher's Guide*.

Energy and Matter Moving Through Ecosystems

A All living things in every ecosystem on earth need a constant supply of energy and matter to continue to live. Energy and matter constantly move or cycle through ecosystems. Plants and microscopic organisms such as bacteria and protists collect energy from the sun and use it to produce their own food. These **food producers** are then consumed by all other organisms, or **food consumers**. Finally, certain organisms, known as **decomposers**, break down dead and dying organic matter (matter that was once living) and return nutrients to the soil for plants to use once again. (#1)

Food Producers

Food producers don't need to consume other organisms in order to survive. They make their own food. Producers occupy all portions of the planet. Most producers are plants. Plants capture their energy from the sun and produce their own food through the process of photosynthesis. However, scientists have discovered that some organisms don't use sunlight as their energy source, yet they are still food producers. These producers break apart energy-rich molecules to produce their own food. This process of breaking apart simple molecules to harvest the energy is known as **chemosynthesis**. It is a process similar to photosynthesis, however these producers use the energy from chemicals instead of energy from the sun to produce food. (#2)

Sources of Energy for Food

Student Book: Application Lesson 3 41

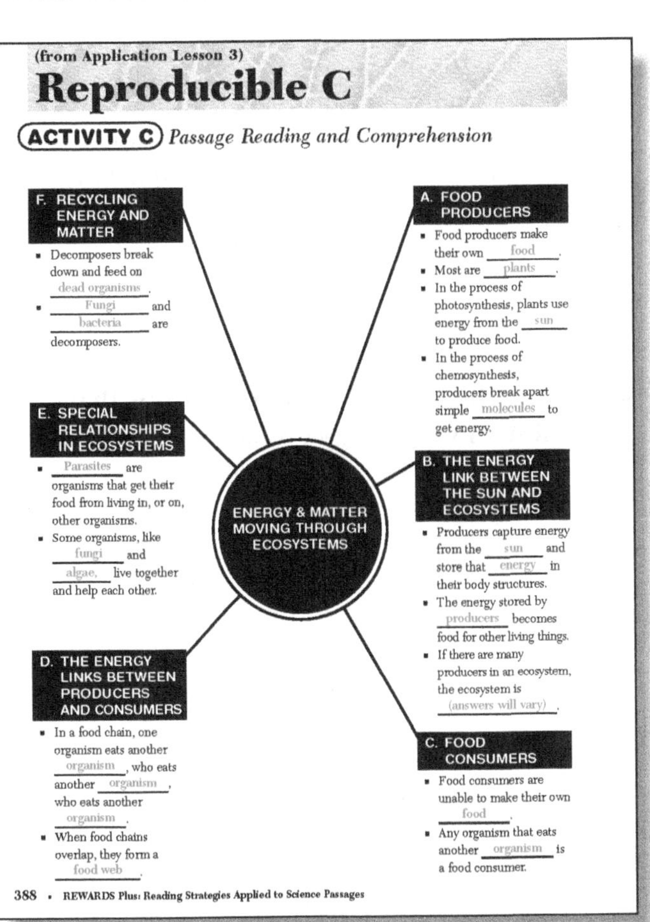

(from Application Lesson 3)

Reproducible C

ACTIVITY C *Passage Reading and Comprehension*

388 • REWARDS Plus: Reading Strategies Applied to Science Passages

4. Find number 1 in the passage. (Pause). Read down to number 1 silently. Look up when you are done._
5. (Wait for students to complete the reading. Then have students reread the part by having them read orally to a partner, read together orally as a group, or read aloud individually.)
6. (Ask the question or questions associated with the number. Provide feedback to students regarding their answers.)
7. (Repeat steps 4–6 for all paragraphs in Section A.)
8. Now, look at your Information Web. Find the section labeled A._ The information you've just read will help you to fill in this section of the Web.
9. With your partner, fill in the blanks for Section A. You can refer back to the passage for information. Look up when you're done._ (Move around the room and monitor students as they complete the section.)
10. (When the majority of students have finished, show Overhead 12.) Look at the overhead and check your work. Fix up or add to any of your answers.
11. Now read down to the next number silently. Look up when you are done._
12. (Repeat steps 5–11 until the students have finished the passage and the Information Web.)
13. Now use your Information Web to retell the important information from the passage to your partner.

Comprehension Questions

#1 Name the three types of organisms that maintain the energy cycles of an ecosystem.
Food producers, food consumers, and decomposers.

#2 What is chemosynthesis?
Breaking apart energy-rich molecules to produce food.

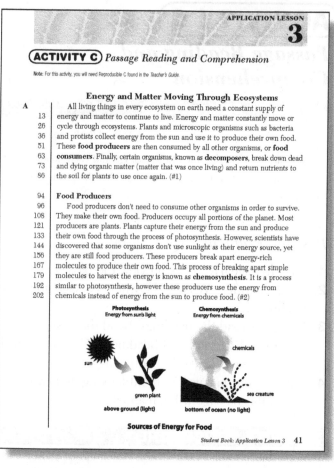

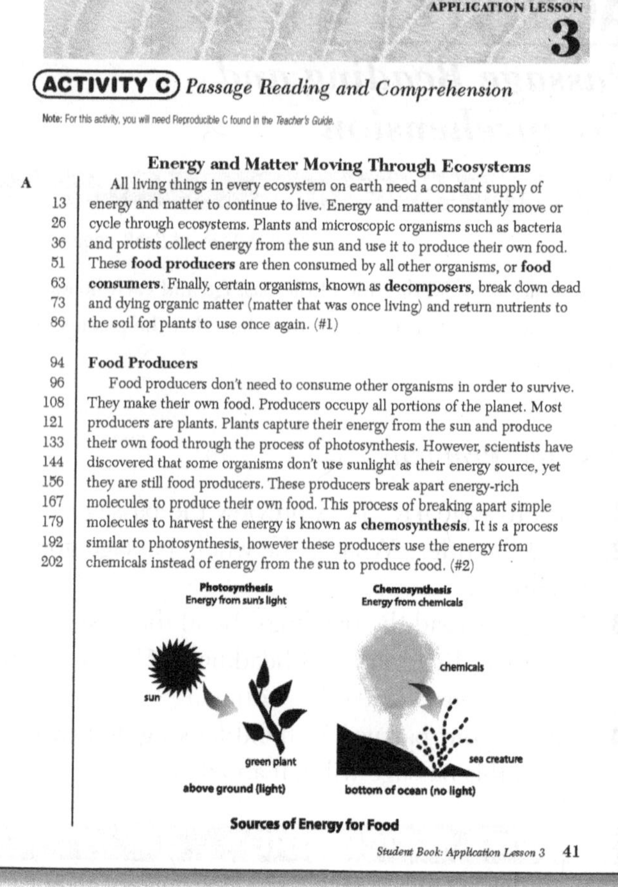

APPLICATION LESSON 3

ACTIVITY C *Passage Reading and Comprehension*

Note: For this activity, you will need Reproducible C found in the *Teacher's Guide*.

Energy and Matter Moving Through Ecosystems

A All living things in every ecosystem on earth need a constant supply of
13 energy and matter to continue to live. Energy and matter constantly move or
26 cycle through ecosystems. Plants and microscopic organisms such as bacteria
36 and protists collect energy from the sun and use it to produce their own food.
51 These **food producers** are then consumed by all other organisms, or **food**
63 **consumers**. Finally, certain organisms, known as **decomposers**, break down dead
73 and dying organic matter (matter that was once living) and return nutrients to
86 the soil for plants to use once again. (#1)

94 **Food Producers**
96 Food producers don't need to consume other organisms in order to survive.
108 They make their own food. Producers occupy all portions of the planet. Most
121 producers are plants. Plants capture their energy from the sun and produce
133 their own food through the process of photosynthesis. However, scientists have
144 discovered that some organisms don't use sunlight as their energy source, yet
156 they are still food producers. These producers break apart energy-rich
167 molecules to produce their own food. This process of breaking apart simple
179 molecules to harvest the energy is known as **chemosynthesis**. It is a process
192 similar to photosynthesis, however these producers use the energy from
202 chemicals instead of energy from the sun to produce food. (#2)

Sources of Energy for Food

Student Book: Application Lesson 3 41

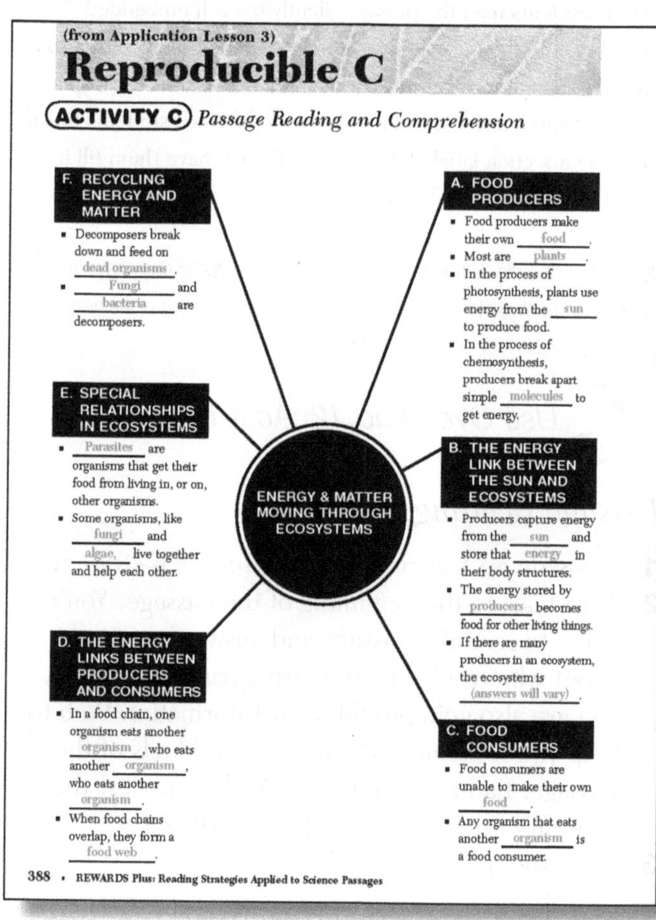

(from Application Lesson 3)

Reproducible C

ACTIVITY C *Passage Reading and Comprehension*

A. FOOD PRODUCERS
- Food producers make their own __food__.
- Most are __plants__.
- In the process of photosynthesis, plants use energy from the __sun__ to produce food.
- In the process of chemosynthesis, producers break apart simple __molecules__ to get energy.

B. THE ENERGY LINK BETWEEN THE SUN AND ECOSYSTEMS
- Producers capture energy from the __sun__ and store that __energy__ in their body structures.
- The energy stored by __producers__ becomes food for other living things.
- If there are many producers in an ecosystem, the ecosystem is __(answers will vary)__.

C. FOOD CONSUMERS
- Food consumers are unable to make their own __food__.
- Any organism that eats another __organism__ is a food consumer.

D. THE ENERGY LINKS BETWEEN PRODUCERS AND CONSUMERS
- In a food chain, one organism eats another __organism__, who eats another __organism__, who eats another __organism__.
- When food chains overlap, they form a __food web__.

E. SPECIAL RELATIONSHIPS IN ECOSYSTEMS
- __Parasites__ are organisms that get their food from living in, or on, other organisms.
- Some organisms, like __fungi__ and __algae,__ live together and help each other.

F. RECYCLING ENERGY AND MATTER
- Decomposers break down and feed on __dead organisms__.
- __Fungi__ and __bacteria__ are decomposers.

388 • REWARDS Plus: Reading Strategies Applied to Science Passages

#3 Why are producers so important to all members of an ecosystem?

Every living thing, including humans, depends on producers for their food energy.

#4 What characteristic differentiates a consumer from a producer? Name three organisms that are consumers.

Consumers cannot produce their own food; to get food they eat other organisms. Consumers include orcas, humans, horses, and bugs among others.

#5 What is the difference between a food chain and a food web?

A food chain is a model that describes the flow of energy and matter through an ecosystem. Food webs describe overlapping food chains.

#6 What are parasites?

Parasites are organisms that get their food from living in or on other organisms and harming them.

#7 What two organisms make up a lichen? How do these two organisms interact?

Fungi and algae; fungi collect water and nutrients and provide the living space algae need; in return, fungi get food from algae.

#8 What is the function of a decomposer? When a decomposer dies, where do its remains go?

Breaks down and feeds on dead organisms; energy and nutrients from its body are released into the ecosystem and quickly taken up from the soil by producers.

APPLICATION LESSON

3

B 212 **The Energy Link Between the Sun and Ecosystems**
220 Food producers have a critical role in all ecosystems. The producers that
232 capture energy from the sun are the energy link between the sun and other
246 living things. Producers capture energy from the sun and store that energy in
259 food molecules in their own body structures. That energy then provides food for
272 all other members of an ecosystem, including humans. Every living thing
283 depends on producers for their food energy. Without producers, there would be
295 no living things. The more producers in an ecosystem, the more the ecosystem
308 is energy-rich, productive, and able to support a variety of living things. When
322 producers are reduced in size and number, the richness and diversity of that
335 ecosystem is also reduced. (#3)

C

339 **Food Consumers**
341 Food consumers are organisms that are unable to produce their own food.
353 Essentially, any organism that eats another organism is a consumer. People are
365 consumers because they consume products made from plants and animals.
375 Birds, whales, spiders, and horses are consumers. Even smaller creatures,
385 including the protists in water and in soil, are consumers. (#4)

D

395 **The Energy Links Between Producers and Consumers**
402 To show the energy links between producers and consumers, scientists
412 created models called **food chains** and **food webs**. A food chain shows the flow
426 of energy from a food producer to one consumer after another. In other words,
440 a plant provides food for an organism, which provides food for another
452 organism, and so on. In one example, a producer provides food for a herring,
466 the herring is consumed by a salmon, the salmon is consumed by a sea lion, and
482 the sea lion is consumed by an orca (killer whale). The illustration below shows
496 another example, with the food producer at the base of the food chain.

509 When food chains overlap, they form a food web. The term food web
522 describes the complex feeding relationships that occur in most ecosystems. For
533 example, in the ecosystem described above, whales consume sea lions and also
545 consume other organisms. Sea lions eat salmon and also other organisms. So,
557 several food chains overlap to create a marine life food web. (#5)

APPLICATION LESSON

3

E 568 **Special Relationships in Ecosystems**
572 The collection and transfer of food energy in an ecosystem does not always
585 require organisms to die. Some energy transfers are relatively harmless.
595 **Parasites** are organisms that get their food from living in, or on other organisms.
609 Many animals, and even people, have parasites living in them. Parasites can be
622 relatively harmless, or deadly. (#6)
626 Some energy transfer relationships are friendly, such as those that occur with
638 lichens. **Lichens** are mossy-looking things that grow on trees and rocks. Lichens
651 are major producers in the food web of the tundra. They are consumed by
665 caribou and lemmings, which are consumed by wolves. Lichens are actually two
677 organisms, fungi and algae, living together and helping each other. The green
689 alga of the lichen is a producer and a photosynthesizer. But, the alga needs
703 water, minerals, and a place to live. The fungus, like mushrooms and mold,
716 cannot produce. The fungus must consume. Fungi act like sponges, collecting
727 water and nutrients and providing the living space that the algae need. In
740 return, the fungi are rewarded with a supply of food from the algae. This special
755 arrangement is a mutual community of two types of organisms. (#7)

F

765 **Recycling Energy and Matter**
769 The last link of any food chain is an organism known as a decomposer.
783 Decomposers break down and feed on dead organisms. Some fungi and bacteria
795 are decomposers.
797 Eventually, decomposers also die. But this isn't the end of the story, because
810 there is no end. When decomposers die, the energy and nutrients contained in
823 their bodies are released into the ecosystem and quickly taken up from the soil
837 by producers (plants). Energy and matter are thus recycled again and again.
849 This recycling is like a bicycle chain; all the links of the chain are connected, and
865 the chain keeps going around and around. The last link connects to the first, and
880 each link is important so that the system functions properly. (#8)
890

ACTIVITY D *Fluency Building*

Cold Timing		Practice 1	
Practice 2		Hot Timing	

ACTIVITY D

Fluency Building

ACTIVITY PROCEDURE

(See the *Student Book*, page 43.)

In this activity, students will be using a repeated reading procedure of the Activity C article to increase their reading fluency. First, have students do a Cold Timing, in which they whisper-read for one minute as you time them. Have them record in their books the number of correct words they read. Then, have students repeat with one or two practice readings to attempt to beat their Cold Timing. Finally, students exchange books in preparation for a Hot Timing. Have students listen to a partner read for one minute, underlining any word errors, and have them determine the number of correct words their partner read. When both students have completed their Hot Timing, they return each other's books and complete their own Fluency Graphs by indicating the number of words they read correctly in the one-minute Cold Timing and the one-minute Hot Timing.

Note D-1: When assigning partners for this activity, have the stronger reader read first. As a result, the other reader will have one additional practice opportunity.

1. Now, it's time for fluency building.
2. Find the beginning of the passage again. (Pause.)
3. Whisper-read. See how many words you can read in one minute. Begin._ (Time students for one minute.) Stop._ Circle the last word that you read._ Count the number of words you read in one minute. (Assist students in determining the number of words by counting from the number at the beginning of the line to the circled word.)_ Record the number of words you read after **Cold Timing.**_
4. Let's practice again. Return to the beginning of the article. Remember to whisper-read. See if you can beat your Cold Timing. Begin._ (Time students for one minute.) Stop._ Put a box around the last word that you read._ Count the number of words you read in one minute._ Find **Practice 1.**_ Record the number of words you read._
5. (Optional) Let's practice one more time before the Hot Timing. Return to the beginning of the article. Remember to whisper-read. See if you can beat your Cold Timing. Begin._ (Time students for one minute.) Stop._ Put a box around the last word that you read._ Count the number of words you read in one minute._ Find **Practice 2.**_ Record the number of words you read._
6. Please exchange books with your partner._ Partner 1, you are going to read first. Partner 2, you are going to listen carefully to your partner as he or she reads. If your partner makes a mistake or leaves out a word, underline that word. Ones, get ready to read quietly to your partner. Begin._ (Time students for one minute.) Stop._ Twos, cross out the last word that your partner read._ Twos, determine the number of words your partner read correctly in one minute._ (Assist students in subtracting the number of mistakes from the number of words read.) Record the number in your partner's book after **Hot Timing.**_
7. Partner 2, you are going to read next. Partner 1, you are going to listen carefully to your partner as he or she reads. If your partner makes a mistake or leaves out a word, underline that word. Twos, get ready to read quietly to your partner. Begin._ (Time students for one minute.) Stop._ Ones, cross out the last word that your partner read._ Ones, determine the number of words your partner read correctly in one minute._ Record the number in your partner's book after **Hot Timing.**_
8. Exchange books._ Turn to the Fluency Graph on the last page of your book, and indicate on the graph the number of Cold Timing and Hot Timing words you read correctly._

765 **Recycling Energy and Matter**
769 The last link of any food chain is an organism known as a decomposer.
783 Decomposers break down and feed on dead organisms. Some fungi and bacteria
795 are decomposers.
797 Eventually, decomposers also die. But this isn't the end of the story, because
810 there is no end. When decomposers die, the energy and nutrients contained in
823 their bodies are released into the ecosystem and quickly taken up from the soil
837 by producers (plants). Energy and matter are thus recycled again and again.
849 This recycling is like a bicycle chain; all the links of the chain are connected, and
865 the chain keeps going around and around. The last link connects to the first, and
880 each link is important so that the system functions properly. (#8)
890

ACTIVITY D *Fluency Building*

Cold Timing		Practice 1	
Practice 2		Hot Timing	

Student Book: Application Lesson 3 43

ACTIVITY E

Comprehension Questions—Multiple Choice

ACTIVITY PROCEDURE

(See the *Student Book*, page 44.)

Review the steps in the Multiple Choice Strategy. Lead students through items #1 and #2, proceeding step-by-step. Have students proceed item by item for the remaining multiple-choice items, reminding them to prepare a rationale for the *best* answer. Have students share their answers and the rationale for their answers. Encourage thoughtful discussion. Provide feedback and have students record points for each correct item.

Note E-1: The correct Multiple Choice answers are circled.

1. Turn to page 44._ Find **Activity E.**_ Let's review the steps in the Multiple Choice Strategy.
2. Read **Step 1.**_
3. Read **Step 2.**_
4. Read **Step 3.**_ Remember, this is the most critical step in the strategy. For each choice, you must really think about why the choice might be correct or incorrect. It may be necessary to look back in the article.
5. Read **Step 4.**_
6. Find question #1. Read it._
7. Read choice **a.**_ Food consumers depend on food producers in order to get the energy and matter they require to live. This is an important fact and may be the correct answer.
8. Read choice **b.**_ This choice focuses on an important difference between producers and consumers and may be the correct answer.
9. Read choice **c.**_ This choice identifies types of organisms that are producers and consumers but does not mention other types of producers such as bacteria and protists. This may not be the best answer to this question.
10. Read choice **d.**_ This choice focuses on comparing the number of producers to the number of consumers. Although there are more producers than consumers, this is probably not the most important difference between them.
11. Which is the best answer?_ Circle it._
12. Let's do the next one. Read item #2.

APPLICATION LESSON

3

ACTIVITY E *Comprehension Questions—Multiple Choice*

Comprehension Strategy—Multiple Choice

Step 1: Read the item.
Step 2: Read all of the choices.
Step 3: Think about why each choice might be correct or incorrect. Check the article as needed.
Step 4: From the possible correct choices, select the best answer.

1. (Compare and contrast) **Select the statement that summarizes the most important difference between food producers and consumers.**
   a. Consumers are dependent on food producers.
   (b.) Food producers make their own food. Consumers must eat other organisms.
   c. Food producers are plants. Animals are consumers.
   d. Food producers are vast in number. Consumers are far fewer in number.
2. (Compare and contrast) **What is the essential difference between the process of photosynthesis and chemosynthesis?**
   (a.) In photosynthesis, energy is captured from the sun. In chemosynthesis, energy comes from the breaking apart of molecules.
   b. Photosynthesis occurs in plants. Chemosynthesis occurs in animals.
   c. Photosynthesis is a much more common process than chemosynthesis.
   d. Photosynthesis and chemosynthesis are both processes of producing food.
3. (Cause and effect) **Which of these is not an example of a food chain?**
   a. plant → bug → robin → cat
   b. plankton → herring → salmon → sea lion → whale
   c. grass → deer → wolf → vulture
   (d.) sheep → wolf → vulture
4. (Vocabulary) **"Microscopic" has two meaningful parts: "micro" and "scopic." What are the meanings of the parts?**
   (a.) small + view or see
   b. small + understanding
   c. loud + view or see
   d. loud + understanding

MULTIPLE CHOICE COMPREHENSION 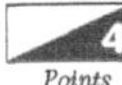 4 Points

13. Read choice **a.**_ Think about why this choice might be correct or incorrect. (Pause. Then, call on individual students.)
14. This is what I was thinking. These statements are true. Each process captures or changes energy from one form to another, but each captures energy from a different source. This is an essential difference between the two processes and may be the correct answer.
15. Read choice **b.**_ Think about why this choice might be correct or incorrect. (Pause. Then, call on individual students.)
16. This is what I was thinking. Photosynthesis does occur in plants but also in some bacteria and protists. Chemosynthesis also occurs in some bacteria but does not occur in animals. This last statement is false, so this could not be the correct answer.
17. Read choice **c.**_ Think about why this choice might be correct or incorrect. (Pause. Then, call on individual students.)
18. This is what I was thinking. Although this statement may be true, it does not talk about an essential difference in the two processes. This is probably not the best answer.

19. Read choice **d.**_ Think about why this choice might be correct or incorrect. (Pause. Then, call on individual students.)

20. This is what I was thinking. Although this statement is true, it identified how the two processes are the same, not how they are different. Therefore, this could not be the right answer.

21. Which is the best answer?_ Circle it._

22. Use the Multiple Choice Strategy to complete item #3. Be ready to explain why you selected your answer. (Wait while students complete the item. Call on individual students. Ask them why they chose their answer and why they eliminated the other choices. Encourage discussion. Provide students with feedback on their choices, focusing on why or why not those choices might be appropriate.)

23. Use the Multiple Choice Strategy to complete item #4. Be ready to explain why you selected your answer. (Wait while students complete the item. Call on individual students. Ask them why they chose their answer and why they eliminated the other choices. Encourage discussion. Provide students with feedback on their choices, focusing on why or why not those choices might be appropriate.)

24. Count the number of items you got correct, and record that number in the blank half of the Multiple Choice Comprehension box._

25. (Distribute Appendix A Reproducible 3: Comprehension Strategy—Multiple Choice. Have students place this in a notebook or a folder for future reference.)

APPLICATION LESSON
3

ACTIVITY E *Comprehension Questions—Multiple Choice*

Comprehension Strategy—Multiple Choice

Step 1: Read the item.
Step 2: Read all of the choices.
Step 3: Think about why each choice might be correct or incorrect. Check the article as needed.
Step 4: From the possible correct choices, select the best answer.

1. (Compare and contrast) **Select the statement that summarizes the most important difference between food producers and consumers.**
   a. Consumers are dependent on food producers.
   (b.) Food producers make their own food. Consumers must eat other organisms.
   c. Food producers are plants. Animals are consumers.
   d. Food producers are vast in number. Consumers are far fewer in number.

2. (Compare and contrast) **What is the essential difference between the process of photosynthesis and chemosynthesis?**
   (a.) In photosynthesis, energy is captured from the sun. In chemosynthesis, energy comes from the breaking apart of molecules.
   b. Photosynthesis occurs in plants. Chemosynthesis occurs in animals.
   c. Photosynthesis is a much more common process than chemosynthesis.
   d. Photosynthesis and chemosynthesis are both processes of producing food.

3. (Cause and effect) **Which of these is not an example of a food chain?**
   a. plant → bug → robin → cat
   b. plankton → herring → salmon → sea lion → whale
   c. grass → deer → wolf → vulture
   (d.) sheep → wolf → vulture

4. (Vocabulary) **"Microscopic" has two meaningful parts: "micro" and "scopic." What are the meanings of the parts?**
   (a.) small + view or see
   b. small + understanding
   c. loud + view or see
   d. loud + understanding

MULTIPLE CHOICE COMPREHENSION

Points

44 *REWARDS Plus: Reading Strategies Applied to Science Passages*

ACTIVITY F

Vocabulary Activities

ACTIVITY PROCEDURE

(See the *Student Book*, page 45–46.)

Have students complete each item orally and provide feedback on their answers. Then have students respond to each question in writing by answering "yes" or "no" and providing a reason for their answers.

Yes/No/Why

1. Turn to page 45. Find **Activity F.** Read item #1. Tell your partner your answer and your reason for it. (Pause. Then call on individual students.)
2. My answer is definitely "No." Orcas are killer whales that hunt and kill other animals in order to get the energy and nutrients they need. Producers are organisms that produce their own food through photosynthesis or chemosynthesis.
3. Write your answer and your reason for it in the space provided. Look up when you are done.
4. Read item #2. Tell your partner your answer and your reason for it. (Pause. Then call on individual students.)
5. My answer is a definite "No." Caribou are a type of reindeer that are certainly big enough to be seen without using a microscope.
6. Write your answer and your reason for it in the space provided. Look up when you are done.
7. Read item #3. Tell your partner your answer and your reason for it. (Pause. Then call on individual students.) I would definitely answer "Yes" to this question. Decomposers are those organisms that break down dead and decaying organisms and release nutrients into the soil where they are quickly used by producers. In this way energy and matter are recycled—made usable again.
8. Write your answer and your reason for it in the space provided. Look up when you are done.

Note F-1: You may wish to do this as an oral task only rather than an oral and a written task.

APPLICATION LESSON 3

ACTIVITY F *Vocabulary Activities*

Yes/No/Why

1. Are **orcas producers**?
Example answer: No. Orcas are killer whales that hunt and kill other animals in order to get the energy and nutrients they need. Producers are organisms that produce their own food through photosynthesis or chemosynthesis.

2. Are **caribou microscopic**?
Example answer: No. Caribou are a type of reindeer that are certainly big enough to be seen without using a microscope.

3. Are **decomposers** necessary for **recycling**?
Example answer: Yes. Decomposers are those organisms that break down dead and decaying organisms and return nutrients to the soil where they are quickly used by producers. In this way, energy and matter are recycled—made usable again.

Student Book: Application Lesson 3 45

ACTIVITY PROCEDURE

Have students read the words and definitions and then complete the sentence stems for each vocabulary word. Have them share answers with partners and with the class. Then, have students give themselves points in the blank half of the Vocabulary box.

Completion Activity

1. Turn to page 46._ Read the first word and its definition._
2. Now, read the sentence stem._
3. Think of how you would complete the sentence stem and write it._ Share your answer with your partner._ (Call on a few students to share answers with the class.)
4. (Repeat Steps 1–3 for the rest of the words.)
5. If you participated in answering all seven questions, give yourself seven points in the blank half of the Vocabulary box.

Note F-2: You may wish to do this as an oral task only rather than an oral task and a written task.

APPLICATION LESSON

3

Completion Activities

1. **relatively:** in relation to something else; comparatively
Name three things you would like for your birthday that are relatively inexpensive.
Answers will vary.

2. **collect:** to put together a group of things
People collect all types of objects, such as
Answers will vary.

3. **requirement:** a need
One of the requirements for getting a driver's license is
Answers will vary.

4. **mutual:** shared
My friend and I have a mutual interest in
Answers will vary.

VOCABULARY 7 *Points*

46 *REWARDS Plus: Reading Strategies Applied to Science Passages*

ACTIVITY G

Expository Writing— Multi-Paragraph Answer

ACTIVITY PROCEDURE, Plan and Write

(See the *Student Book*, page 47–49.)

Review with students the steps in the Multi-Paragraph Writing Strategy. Have students read the prompt and Grace's topics. Explain how Grace made a **LIST** of critical details under each topic. Have students read Grace's details for topic a, b, and c, then look at topic a again. Explain that details that don't go with a topic should be eliminated, and have them **CROSS OUT** the same detail as Grace. Next, explain how details can be combined into one sentence, and have students **CONNECT** details as Grace did in her plan. Have students **NUMBER** their details in the same manner as Grace. Next, have students read the example paragraph a. Guide students in examining and completing the plan for topic b and writing paragraph b. Repeat for topic c. Finally, explain that after they **WRITE**, they should **EDIT** their work, revising for clarity and proofreading for errors in capitalization, punctuation, and spelling.

Use Overheads 13 and 14: Activity G

1. Turn to page 47._ Find **Activity G.**_ Today we are going to work on writing multi-paragraph answers. Study the Writing Strategy. Be sure that you will be able to say the steps._ Say the steps in the strategy with me: **List, cross out, connect, number, write, edit.**_ Ones, say the steps to your partner. Twos, say the steps to your partner._
2. Find the prompt in the middle of the page._ Read the prompt out loud with me: **Explain the roles of producers, consumers, and decomposers in the transfer of energy within an ecosystem.**
3. Turn to page 48._ First, Grace recorded the topics for her paragraphs. Read topic a._ Read topic b._ Read topic c._ These topics will be incorporated into topic sentences.
4. Next, she followed the steps in the Writing Strategy to write her answer. What is **Step 1**?_ Read the details **listed** under topic a._ Grace then listed details for topic b and c.
5. Next, Grace applied **Steps 2 through 5** to each paragraph.
6. What is **Step 2**?_ Grace reread her details and **crossed out** any details that did not go with the

APPLICATION LESSON **3**

ACTIVITY G *Expository Writing—Multi-Paragraph Answer*

Writing Strategy—Multi-Paragraph Answer

Step 1: LIST (List the details that are important enough to include in your answer.)
- **Step 2: CROSS OUT** (Reread the details. Cross out any that don't go with the topic.)
- **Step 3: CONNECT** (Connect any details that could go into one sentence.)
- **Step 4: NUMBER** (Number the details in a logical order.)
- **Step 5: WRITE** (Write the paragraph.)

Step 6: EDIT (Revise and proofread your answer.)

Prompt: Explain the roles of producers, consumers, and decomposers in the transfer of energy within an ecosystem.

Plan: Complete the Planning Box with your teacher.

Student Book: Application Lesson 3 47

APPLICATION LESSON **3**

Example Multi-Paragraph Plan

Planning Box
(topic a) *producers*
① (detail) – *photosynthesis—plants capture energy from sun to make food*
② (detail) – *chemosynthesis—produce food by breaking apart molecules to capture energy*
③ (detail) – *producers provide food for other organisms*
④ (detail) – *energy link between sun and other living things*
⑤ (detail) – *without producers, no life*
(detail) – ~~*consumers eat consumers*~~
(topic b) *consumers*
① { (detail) – *unable to produce their own food by capturing the sun's energy*
(detail) – *an organism that eats another organism is a consumer* }
② { (detail) – *consumers eat producers*
(detail) – *in food webs consumers also eat consumers*
(detail) – *gain energy needed for life* }
(topic c) *decomposers*
(detail) – ~~*plants are producers*~~
① (detail) – *decomposers break down and feed on dead organisms*
② { (detail) – *when decomposers die, energy released into ecosystem*
(detail) – *when decomposers die, nutrients released into ecosystem* }
③ (detail) – *plants can then take energy and nutrients from soil*

Write: Examine paragraph a and write paragraphs b and c on a separate piece of paper.

48 *REWARDS Plus: Reading Strategies Applied to Science Passages*

topic._ Look at the overhead._ What detail did she cross out?_ Why do you think this detail was eliminated?_ Cross out the same detail on your paper._

7. What is **Step 3**?_ Look at the overhead._ Please draw brackets on your paper to **connect** the details that Grace connected._
8. What is **Step 4**?_ Next, Grace **numbered** the details in the order she wished them to occur in the paragraph. Looking at the overhead, number your details as Grace did._
9. What is **Step 5**?_ Next, Grace **wrote** the paragraph. Locate paragraph a on the next page._ (Read paragraph a with your students or to your students.)
10. Grace then repeated these steps for topic b. Look at the overhead._ First, she looked for details to **cross out** that did not go with the topic. Did she cross off any details?_ Next, she **connected** details that could go into one sentence. Please draw brackets on your paper to connect the details that Grace connected._ Next, she **numbered** the details in a logical order. Number your details as Grace did._
11. Take out a blank piece of paper._ Use Grace's plan for paragraph b and **write** paragraph b. If you finish early, please reread and **edit** your paragraph. Don't forget to use the spelling of words in the plan and the article to correct any errors. (Move around the room and monitor your students as they are writing.)
12. (When the majority of students are done, proceed with the lesson.) It's your turn to use the steps for topic c. First, read the details and **cross out** any details that do not go with the topic._ Next, draw brackets to **connect** details that could easily go into one sentence._ Now, **number** the details in a logical order._
13. Now, examine Grace's plan on the overhead. Yours doesn't need to be the same, but it should be similar._
14. Locate your piece of paper._ Using your plan for paragraph c, **write** paragraph c. If you finish early, please **edit** your paragraph._ (Move around the room and monitor your students as they are writing.)
15. (When the majority of students are done, proceed with the lesson.) What is **Step 6**?_ Grace revised paragraph a and proofread for any errors. Please carefully read your paragraphs.

APPLICATION LESSON 3

ACTIVITY G *Expository Writing—Multi-Paragraph Answer*

Writing Strategy—Multi-Paragraph Answer

Step 1: LIST (List the details that are important enough to include in your answer.)
Step 2: CROSS OUT (Reread the details. Cross out any that don't go with the topic.)
Step 3: CONNECT (Connect any details that could go into one sentence.)
Step 4: NUMBER (Number the details in a logical order.)
Step 5: WRITE (Write the paragraph.)
Step 6: EDIT (Revise and proofread your answer.)

Prompt: Explain the roles of producers, consumers, and decomposers in the transfer of energy within an ecosystem.

Plan: Complete the Planning Box with your teacher.

Student Book: Application Lesson 3 47

APPLICATION LESSON 3

Example Multi-Paragraph Plan

Planning Box
(topic a) *producers*
① (detail) – *photosynthesis—plants capture energy from sun to make food*
② (detail) – *chemosynthesis—produce food by breaking apart molecules to capture energy*
③ (detail) – *producers provide food for other organisms*
④ (detail) – *energy link between sun and other living things*
⑤ (detail) – *without producers, no life*
(detail) – ~~*consumers eat consumers*~~
(topic b) *consumers*
① { (detail) – *unable to produce their own food by capturing the sun's energy*
① { (detail) – *an organism that eats another organism is a consumer*
② { (detail) – *consumers eat producers*
② { (detail) – *in food webs consumers also eat consumers*
② { (detail) – *gain energy needed for life*
(topic c) *decomposers*
(detail) – ~~*plants are producers*~~
① (detail) – *decomposers break down and feed on dead organisms*
② { (detail) – *when decomposers die, energy released into ecosystem*
② { (detail) – *when decomposers die, nutrients released into ecosystem*
③ (detail) – *plants can then take energy and nutrients from soil*

Write: Examine paragraph a and write paragraphs b and c on a separate piece of paper.

48 *REWARDS Plus: Reading Strategies Applied to Science Passages*

Revise your paragraphs so that they are easy to understand and clear. Proofread for any errors in capitalization, punctuation, and spelling. (Give students time to proofread their paragraphs.)

ACTIVITY PROCEDURE, Evaluate

Ask students to read each question in the rubric. Guide them in evaluating the paragraphs using the guidelines. Have students total their points and record them in the blank half of the Writing box.

16. Turn to page 49. Grace has already evaluated paragraph a. Let's evaluate your paragraph b.

17. Read question #1 with me. Circle "Yes" for b if your topic sentence includes the topic, consumers.

18. Read question #2 with me. Circle "Yes" for b if all of your details tell about consumers.

19. Read question #3 with me. Circle "Yes" for b if you combined details into one sentence.

20. Now, check paragraph c carefully and answer questions 1 through 3.

21. Read question #4. Reread your paragraphs. Circle "Yes" if your paragraphs are easy to understand.

22. Read question #5. Carefully examine your paragraphs. If you think a word is misspelled, underline it and check back in the plan or article and correct the spelling. Circle "Yes" if you believe that you have very few spelling errors.

23. Read question #6. Carefully examine your sentences. Be sure that each sentence begins with a capital. If all sentences begin with a capital, circle "Yes."

24. Read question #7. Examine your sentences. Be sure that each sentence ends with a period. If all sentences end with a period, circle "Yes."

25. Count up your points and record them in the Writing box.

26. (Show Overhead 14.) Look at the overhead. Let's read Grace's remaining paragraphs. Yours do not have to be the same, but they should be similar. (Read the paragraphs to your students or with your students or call on a student to read the example paragraphs.)

27. In the next lesson, you will be writing more paragraphs.

APPLICATION LESSON **3**

Example Multi-Paragraph Answer

(paragraph a)

The role of producers in the ecosystem is to make food for themselves and other organisms. In the process of photosynthesis, plants capture energy from the sun to produce their own food. In a similar process, chemosynthesis, organisms use energy from the breaking apart of molecules to produce food. Producers provide food for other organisms. As a result, producers are the energy link between the sun and all living organisms. Without producers, there would be no life.

Evaluate: Evaluate the paragraphs using this rubric.

Rubric—Multi-Paragraph Answer	Student or Partner Rating	Teacher Rating
1. Did the author state the topic in the first sentence?	a. (Yes) Fix up b. (Yes) Fix up c. (Yes) Fix up	a. Yes No b. Yes No c. Yes No
2. Did the author include details that go with the topic?	a. (Yes) Fix up b. (Yes) Fix up c. (Yes) Fix up	a. Yes No b. Yes No c. Yes No
3. Did the author combine details in some of the sentences?	a. (Yes) Fix up b. (Yes) Fix up c. (Yes) Fix up	a. Yes No b. Yes No c. Yes No
4. Is the answer easy to understand?	(Yes) Fix up	Yes No
5. Did the author correctly spell words, particularly the words found in the article?	(Yes) Fix up	Yes No
6. Did the author use correct capitalization, capitalizing the first word in the sentence and proper names of people, places, and things?	(Yes) Fix up	Yes No
7. Did the author use correct punctuation, including a period at the end of each sentence?	(Yes) Fix up	Yes No

WRITING 13 Points

Student Book: Application Lesson 3 49

Note G-1: The rubric can be used in a variety of ways. Instead of the students evaluating their own paragraphs, you may wish to have their partners provide feedback. The second column is designed for teacher feedback. If you have a small group, it would be useful to give daily feedback on writing. If the group size is large, you can give feedback to a number of children each day. You may wish to give students bonus points based on your feedback.

ACTIVITY H

Comprehension—Single-Paragraph Answer

ACTIVITY PROCEDURE

(See the *Student Book*, page 50.)

Have students read the *What Is* statement and the *What If* question. Have students turn the question into part of the answer and write down a topic sentence for their answer. Then, have them complete their answer. Encourage them to use evidence from the article and their own experience and background knowledge. Finally, review the discussion behaviors in the "Looks Like/Sounds Like" chart and engage students in a discussion. Award points for writing and participating in the discussion.

Note H-1: To increase the quality of the discussion, the students are asked to think and write about the *What If* before the discussion. However, you may be working with students who have difficulty generating ideas for their paragraph. If that is the case, switch the order of activities: engage the students in a discussion, and then have them write their paragraphs.

1. Turn to page 50._ Find **Activity H.**_

2. Today, you are going to write a paragraph answer to the *What If* question and participate in a discussion. Let's use the strategy to answer the question.

3. Read Step 1._ Find the *What Is* statement in the middle of the page._ Read it out loud with me: **Producers, consumers, and decomposers live together in an ecosystem and use existing resources to keep energy and matter moving through the ecosystem.**

4. Find the *What If* question._ Read it with me: **What would happen if, all of a sudden, decomposers could no longer do their job?**

5. Read **Step 2.**_ Think how you might turn the question into part of the answer._ Tell me your idea for a topic sentence._ (Example sentence: If all of a sudden decomposers could no longer do their job, we could expect a number of things to occur.) Take out a piece of paper and write your topic sentence._ (Move around the room and monitor as students write.)

6. Read **Step 3.**_ After you have created a topic sentence using the wording from the question, you are ready to add ideas. You may think of an answer based on your experience and background knowledge, but you should also include evidence from the article or other materials that you have studied. Take some time to look back in the article and consider how you would respond to this question. Then, add sentences to your paragraph. If you finish early, reread your paragraph and edit it so that it is easy to understand and clear._ (Move around the room and monitor as students write.)

7. Read your paragraph to your partner._

8. You can earn four points for your paragraph: two points for turning the question into part of the answer and two points for using evidence from the article. If you included wording from the question in your answer and added evidence from the article, award yourself four points for writing._ Write them in the Writing box.

9. Before we discuss your answers, reread the discussion guidelines to yourself._

10. (Engage students in a discussion. Award four points to students who are active participants in the discussion, and have them write them in the Discussion box.)

APPLICATION LESSON
3

ACTIVITY H *Comprehension—Single-Paragraph Answer*

Writing Strategy—Single-Paragraph Answer

Step 1: Read the item.
Step 2: Turn the question into part of the answer and write it down.
Step 3: Think of the answer or locate the answer in the article.
Step 4: Complete your answer.

Prompt:

What Is—Producers, consumers, and decomposers live together in an ecosystem and use existing resources to keep energy and matter moving through the ecosystem.

What If—What would happen if, all of a sudden, decomposers could no longer do their job?

Write and Discuss: Write a paragraph. Then share your ideas. Use the Discussion Guidelines.

Discussion Guidelines

Speaker		Listener	
Looks like:	**Sounds like:**	**Looks like:**	**Sounds like:**
• Facing peers • Making eye contact • Participating	• Using pleasant, easy-to-hear voice • Sharing opinions, supporting facts and reasons from the article and from your experience • Staying on the topic	• Facing speaker • Making eye contact • Participating	• Waiting quietly to speak • Giving positive, supportive comments • Disagreeing respectfully

WRITING	DISCUSSION
4 Points	4 Points

50 *REWARDS Plus: Reading Strategies Applied to Science Passages*

Note H-2: If your students are having difficulty writing the *What If* paragraphs, read or show them the following example paragraph:

Example Single-Paragraph Answer

If decomposers could no longer do their job of breaking down and feeding on dead organisms, a number of things would happen in the ecosystem. First, nutrients and energy from the dead organisms would not be returned to the soil. As a result, the soil would become less and less able to support the growth of plants. With the less fertile soil, many plants would die from lack of nutrients. If there were fewer plants, there would be less food for consumers. In turn, consumers who eat consumers would also have less food and would die.

Application Lesson 4

Materials Needed:

- *Student Book*: Application Lesson 4
- Application Overhead Transparencies 15–19
- Appendix A Reproducible 4: Writing Strategy—Single-Paragraph Answer
- Appendix B Reproducible D: Application Lesson 4
- Appendix C Optional Vocabulary Activity: Application Lesson 4
- Paper or cardboard to use when covering the overhead transparency
- Paper or cardboard for each student to use during spelling dictation
- Washable overhead transparency pen

Text Treatment Notes:

- Black text signifies teacher script (exact wording to say to students).
- Green text in parentheses signifies directions or prompts for the teacher.
- Green text signifies answers or examples of answers.
- Green graphics treatment signifies reproduction of Overhead information.
- Green text and green graphics treatment do not appear in the *Student Book*.

ACTIVITY A
Vocabulary

ACTIVITY PROCEDURE, List 1

(See the *Student Book*, page 51.)

Tell students each word in the list. Then, have students repeat the word and read the definition aloud. For each definition, provide any additional information that may be necessary. Then, have students practice reading the words themselves.

Note A-1: If you wish to emphasize the part of speech, have students say the part of speech before reading the definition.

Use Overhead 15: Activity A
List 1: Tell

1. (Show the top half of Overhead 15.) Before we read the passage, let's read the difficult words. (Point to **ancient**.) The first word is **ancient**. What word?_ Now, read the definition._
2. (Point to **dehydration**.) The next word is **dehydration**. What word?_ Now, read the definition._
3. (Pronounce each word in List 1, and then have students repeat each word and read the definition.)
4. Open your *Student Book* to **Application Lesson 4**, page 51._
5. Find **Activity A**, **List 1**, in your book._ Let's read the words again. First word._ Next word._ (Continue for all words in List 1.)

ACTIVITY PROCEDURE, List 2

(See the *Student Book*, page 51.)

Have students circle prefixes and suffixes, then underline the vowels. Using the overhead transparency, assist students in checking their work. Next, have students figure out each word to themselves, then say it aloud. Have them read the definition aloud.

Note A.2-1: Provide additional information for any definitions as needed.

Note A.2-2: If you wish to emphasize the part of speech, have students say the part of speech before reading the definition.

Note A.2-3: If you are teaching older students for whom "thumbs-up" is inappropriate, have students look at you when they can read the word.

APPLICATION LESSON **4**

ACTIVITY A *Vocabulary*

List 1: Tell		
1. **ancient**	*adj.*	▶ (old)
2. **dehydration**	*n.*	▶ (the loss of water from an organism)
3. **elements**	*n.*	▶ (basic parts from which something is made)
4. **ingredients**	*n.*	▶ (the foods or other elements combined to make a mixture)
5. **Louis Pasteur**	*n.*	▶ (the scientist who discovered how to keep foods safe by killing microbes with heat)
6. **pasteurization**	*n.*	▶ (the process of using heat to kill microbes and prevent food from spoiling rapidly)
7. **pathogens**	*n.*	▶ (microorganisms, such as bacteria and viruses, that cause disease)
8. **sodium benzoate**	*n.*	▶ (an odorless white powder used to keep food fresh)
9. **sulfur dioxide**	*n.*	▶ (a colorless liquid used to keep food fresh)
10. **techniques**	*n.*	▶ (particular methods of doing things)
11. **vinegar**	*n.*	▶ (a sour liquid used to keep food from spoiling)

List 2: Strategy Practice		
1. **alternatives**	*n.*	▶ (things used or things done instead of other things)
2. **contaminated**	*v.*	▶ (spoiled)
3. **controversy**	*n.*	▶ (a longstanding disagreement)
4. **deprive**	*v.*	▶ (to take away from)
5. **environments**	*n.*	▶ (the physical surroundings)
6. **nutritional**	*adj.*	▶ (having to do with food so the body functions properly)
7. **poisonous**	*adj.*	▶ (causing death or illness if put into the body)
8. **refrigeration**	*n.*	▶ (the process used to make things cool or cold)
9. **spoilage**	*n.*	▶ (the decay of food)
10. **sterilization**	*n.*	▶ (the act of making something free from bacteria)

TALLY [ ] VOCABULARY 5 Points

Student Book: Application Lesson 4 51

Use Overhead 15: Activity A
List 2: Strategy Practice

1. Find **List 2**. Circle the prefixes and suffixes, and underline the vowels. Look up when you are done._
2. (Show the bottom half of Overhead 15.) Now, check and fix any mistakes._
3. Go back to the first word._ Sound out the word to yourself. Put your thumb up when you can read the word. Be sure that it is a real word._ What word?_ Now, read the definition._
4. (Continue Step 3 with all remaining words in List 2.)

Note A.2-4: You may wish to provide additional practice by having students read words to a partner.

ACTIVITY PROCEDURE, List 1 and 2

(See the *Student Book*, page 51.)

Tell students to look in List 1 or List 2 for a word you are thinking about. Have them circle the number of the word and tell you the word. Explain to students to make a tally mark for each correct word in the Tally box, and then enter the number of tally marks as points in the blank half of the Vocabulary box.

1. Remember, the words I'm thinking about will be in either List 1 or List 2. For every word you correctly identify, make a tally mark in the Tally box. If you don't identify the correct word, don't do anything.
2. I am thinking of a word. Circle the number of the appropriate word.
   - Our physical surroundings are also called this. (Wait.) What word? **environments**
   - You eventually combine all of these when you make a mixture. (Wait.) What word? **ingredients**
   - When you think about doing something one way instead of another way, you are considering these. (Wait.) What word? **alternatives**
   - When people disagree over important issues and this disagreement lasts a long time, it is usually called this. (Wait.) What word? **controversy**
   - When something is spoiled, it is this. (Wait.) What word? **contaminated**
3. Count all the tally marks, and enter that number as points in the blank half of the Vocabulary box.

ACTIVITY PROCEDURE, List 3

(See the *Student Book*, page 52.)

The words in the third list are related. Have students use the *REWARDS* Strategies to figure out the first word in each family. Have them read the definition of the verb and then read nouns and adjectives that are related to that verb.

Note A.3-1: Provide additional information for any definitions as needed.

Note A.3-2: If you wish to emphasize the part of speech, have students say the part of speech before reading the definition.

Note A.3-3: If you are teaching older students for whom "thumbs-up" is inappropriate, have students look at you when they can read the word.

APPLICATION LESSON
4

List 3: Word Families

	Verb	Noun	Adjective
Family 1	preserve (to keep safe or free from harm)	preservation preservative	preservable
Family 2	survive (to live longer than)	survivor survival	
Family 3	research (to study or investigate in a particular field	researcher	researchable
Family 4	moisten (to make or become slightly wet)	moisture	moist
Family 5	conduct (to direct)	conduction conductor	

ACTIVITY B *Spelling Dictation*

1. preserve	4. research
2. preservation	5. researcher
3. preservable	6. researchable

SPELLING 6 Points

52 *REWARDS Plus: Reading Strategies Applied to Science Passages*

Use Overhead 16: Activity A
List 3: Word Families

1. Turn to page 52._ Find **Family 1** in **List 3**. Figure out the first word. Use your pencil if you wish. Put your thumb up when you know the word._ What word?_ Read the definition._
2. Look at the nouns in Family 1. Figure out the first word._ What word?_ Next word._ What word?_
3. Look at the adjective in Family 1. Figure out the word._ What word?_
4. (Repeat Steps 1–3 for all word families in List 3.)

Note A.3-4: You may wish to provide additional practice by having students read a word family to the group or to a partner.

Note A.3-5: An additional vocabulary practice activity called Quick Words is provided in Appendix C of this Teacher's Guide. See Appendix C for information about how this optional activity can be used.

Spelling Dictation

ACTIVITY PROCEDURE

(See the *Student Book*, page 52.)

For each word, tell students the word, then have students say the parts of the word to themselves while they write the word. Using the overhead transparency, assist students in checking their spelling and correcting if they misspelled. Then, have students enter the number of correctly spelled words as points in the blank half of the Spelling box.

Note B-1: Distribute a piece of light cardboard to students so they can cover their page during spelling dictation. Students can also use the cardboard as a bookmark to quickly locate pages at the beginning of lessons.

Use Overhead 16: Activity B

1. Find **Activity B.**
2. The first word is **preserve.** What word?_ Say the parts in **preserve** to yourself as you write the word. (Pause and monitor.)
3. (Show **preserve** on the overhead.) Check **preserve.** If you misspelled it, cross it out and write it correctly.
4. The second word is **preservation.** What word?_ Say the parts in **preservation** to yourself as you write the word. (Pause and monitor.)
5. (Show **preservation** on the overhead.) Check **preservation.** If you misspelled it, cross it out and write it correctly.
6. (Repeat the procedures for the words **preservable**, **research**, **researcher**, and **researchable**.)
7. Count the number of words you spelled correctly, and record that number as points in the blank half of the Spelling box at the bottom of the page.

APPLICATION LESSON
4

List 3: Word Families

	Verb	Noun	Adjective
Family 1	preserve (to keep safe or free from harm)	preservation preservative	preservable
Family 2	survive (to live longer than)	survivor survival	
Family 3	research (to study or investigate in a particular field	researcher	researchable
Family 4	moisten (to make or become slightly wet)	moisture	moist
Family 5	conduct (to direct)	conduction conductor	

ACTIVITY B *Spelling Dictation*

1. preserve	4. research
2. preservation	5. researcher
3. preservable	6. researchable

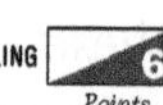

52 *REWARDS Plus: Reading Strategies Applied to Science Passages*

ACTIVITY C

Passage Reading and Comprehension

ACTIVITY PROCEDURE

(See the *Student Book*, pages 53–55.)

Have students read the title of the passage and each heading. Ask them to tell their partners two things that the passage will tell about.

Passage Preview

1. Turn to page 53._ Let's preview the passage.
2. Read the title._ What is the whole passage going to tell about?_
3. Now, let's read the headings. Read the first heading._ Read the next heading._ (Continue until students have read all headings.)
4. Turn to your partner. Without looking, tell two things this passage will tell about._

ACTIVITY PROCEDURE

Provide students with an Information Web from Appendix B. Have students read the passage silently to each embedded number, and then reread the same information orally either to a partner, together as a group, or individually. Ask the corresponding comprehension question or questions. Once students finish reading a section labeled A, B, C, D, E, or F, have them fill in the Information Web before going on to the next section.

Note C-1: If students do not finish reading the passage during class, have them use their Information Webs to review the information at the beginning of the next class.

Use Overhead 17: Activity C

Passage Reading

1. (Provide an Information Web for each student.)
2. Turn back to the beginning of the passage. You're going to read the passage and answer questions about what you've read. During passage reading, you are also going to fill in an Information Web to help you remember the important details of the passage. Later, you'll use this Web to review the content of the passage with your partner.
3. Read the title._

APPLICATION LESSON
4

ACTIVITY C *Passage Reading and Comprehension*

Note: For this activity, you will need Reproducible D found in the *Teacher's Guide.*

Food Preservation

A
Have you ever seen food that has become moldy? Have you ever tasted
13 spoiled milk? Maybe you bit into part of an apple that was mushy and brown.
28 These are some of the examples of what can happen when food spoils.

41 **Spoiled Food**
43 Food spoils because microscopic organisms, or **microbes**, called bacteria and
53 fungi, break down or change the structure of the food. These microbes are the
67 most common cause of food poisoning, a condition that frequently results in
79 mild illness for a short period but occasionally results in extreme illness.
91 In order to avoid spoilage, you must find a way to kill the microbes, to slow
107 down their growth, or to change the composition of the food so microbes can't
121 use it anymore. Many food preservation techniques can be utilized to keep food
134 from spoiling. (#1)

B
136 **Drying and Smoking**
139 The most ancient form of food preservation is simply drying or dehydrating
151 the food. Dehydration deprives the microbes of one of their basic needs, which
164 is water. Just like you and plants, microbes can't live without water. (#2)
176 One way to dry out the food is to add large amounts of salt. Not many
192 organisms can survive living in salty environments. Thus, salt curing of food is an
206 effective way to prevent, or slow, the growth of microbes.
216 Smoking is used to preserve meat and fish. Smoke contains chemicals that
228 are toxic, or poisonous, to microbes. Smoke also creates a sort of waterproofing.
241 When meat is hung over a small, cold, smoky fire for a number of days, the
257 meat dries and takes on a coating of smoke that protects it from moisture and
272 from rotting. (#3)

C
274 **Refrigeration and Freezing**
277 Today, the most widely used forms of food preservation are refrigeration and
289 freezing. Refrigeration slows microbial action. Refrigerated food items might
298 stay good for a week or two, instead of spoiling in a day. Freezing can slow or
315 stop the growth of microbes altogether, which is why things can be stored in a
330 freezer for a long time. Refrigeration and freezing are popular methods for

Student Book: Application Lesson 4 53

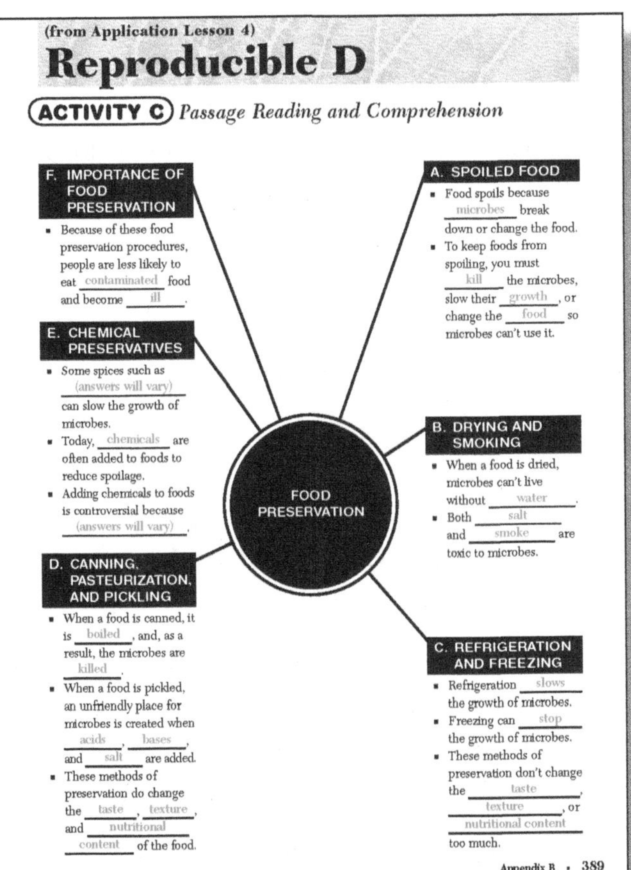

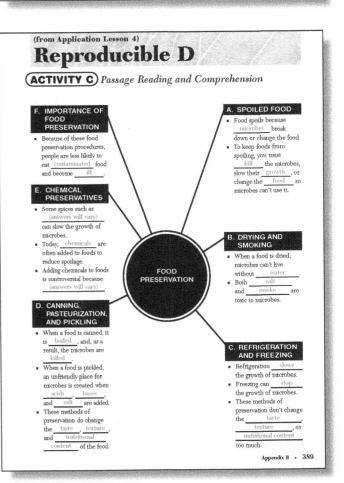

(from Application Lesson 4)

Reproducible D

ACTIVITY C *Passage Reading and Comprehension*

FOOD PRESERVATION

A. SPOILED FOOD
- Food spoils because microbes break down or change the food.
- To keep foods from spoiling, you must kill the microbes, slow their growth, or change the food so microbes can't use it.

B. DRYING AND SMOKING
- When a food is dried, microbes can't live without water.
- Both salt and smoke are toxic to microbes.

C. REFRIGERATION AND FREEZING
- Refrigeration slows the growth of microbes.
- Freezing can stop the growth of microbes.
- These methods of preservation don't change the taste, texture, or nutritional content too much.

D. CANNING, PASTEURIZATION, AND PICKLING
- When a food is canned, it is boiled, and, as a result, the microbes are killed.
- When a food is pickled, an unfriendly place for microbes is created when acids, bases, and salt are added.
- These methods of preservation do change the taste, texture, and nutritional content of the food.

E. CHEMICAL PRESERVATIVES
- Some spices such as (answers will vary) can slow the growth of microbes.
- Today, chemicals are often added to foods to reduce spoilage.
- Adding chemicals to foods is controversial because (answers will vary).

F. IMPORTANCE OF FOOD PRESERVATION
- Because of these food preservation procedures, people are less likely to eat contaminated food and become ill.

Appendix B • 389

4. Find number 1 in the passage. (Pause). Read down to number 1 silently. Look up when you are done._
5. (Wait for students to complete the reading. Then have students reread the part by having them read orally to a partner, read together orally as a group, or read aloud individually.)
6. (Ask the question or questions associated with the number. Provide feedback to students regarding their answers.)
7. (Repeat steps 4–6 for all paragraphs in Section A.)
8. Now, look at your Information Web. Find the section labeled A._ The information you've just read will help you to fill in this section of the Web.
9. With your partner, fill in the blanks for Section A. You can refer back to the passage for information. Look up when you're done._ (Move around the room and monitor students as they complete the section.)
10. (When the majority of students have finished, show Overhead 17). Look at the overhead and check your work. Fix up or add to any of your answers.
11. Now read down to the next number silently. Look up when you are done._
12. (Repeat steps 5–11 until the students have finished the passage and the Information Web.)
13. Now use your Information Web to retell the important information from the passage to your partner.

Comprehension Questions

#1 Why does food spoil?
Microscopic organisms (microbes) called bacteria and fungi break down or change the structure of the food.

#2 What is an ancient form of food preservation? Why does it work?
Drying or dehydrating; microbes can't live without water.

#3 How does smoking food keep it from spoiling?
Smoke contains chemicals that are toxic to microbes; also creates a waterproof coating that protects the meat from moisture and rotting.

APPLICATION LESSON 4

ACTIVITY C *Passage Reading and Comprehension*

Note: For this activity, you will need Reproducible D found in the *Teacher's Guide*.

Food Preservation

A
Have you ever seen food that has become moldy? Have you ever tasted
13 spoiled milk? Maybe you bit into part of an apple that was mushy and brown.
28 These are some of the examples of what can happen when food spoils.

41 **Spoiled Food**
43 Food spoils because microscopic organisms, or **microbes**, called bacteria and
53 fungi, break down or change the structure of the food. These microbes are the
67 most common cause of food poisoning, a condition that frequently results in
79 mild illness for a short period but occasionally results in extreme illness.
91 In order to avoid spoilage, you must find a way to kill the microbes, to slow
107 down their growth, or to change the composition of the food so microbes can't
121 use it anymore. Many food preservation techniques can be utilized to keep food
134 from spoiling. (#1)

B
136 **Drying and Smoking**
139 The most ancient form of food preservation is simply drying or dehydrating
151 the food. Dehydration deprives the microbes of one of their basic needs, which
164 is water. Just like you and plants, microbes can't live without water. (#2)
176 One way to dry out the food is to add large amounts of salt. Not many
192 organisms can survive living in salty environments. Thus, salt curing of food is an
206 effective way to prevent, or slow, the growth of microbes.
216 Smoking is used to preserve meat and fish. Smoke contains chemicals that
228 are toxic, or poisonous, to microbes. Smoke also creates a sort of waterproofing.
241 When meat is hung over a small, cold, smoky fire for a number of days, the
257 meat dries and takes on a coating of smoke that protects it from moisture and
272 from rotting. (#3)

C
274 **Refrigeration and Freezing**
277 Today, the most widely used forms of food preservation are refrigeration and
289 freezing. Refrigeration slows microbial action. Refrigerated food items might
298 stay good for a week or two, instead of spoiling in a day. Freezing can slow or
315 stop the growth of microbes altogether, which is why things can be stored in a
330 freezer for a long time. Refrigeration and freezing are popular methods for

Student Book: Application Lesson 4 53

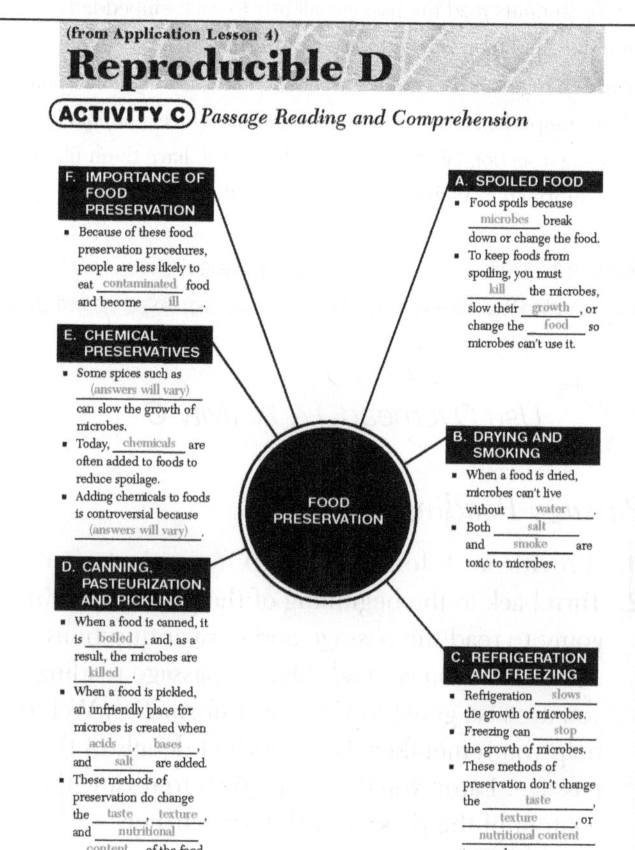
(from Application Lesson 4)

Reproducible D

ACTIVITY C *Passage Reading and Comprehension*

FOOD PRESERVATION

A. SPOILED FOOD
- Food spoils because microbes break down or change the food.
- To keep foods from spoiling, you must kill the microbes, slow their growth, or change the food so microbes can't use it.

B. DRYING AND SMOKING
- When a food is dried, microbes can't live without water.
- Both salt and smoke are toxic to microbes.

C. REFRIGERATION AND FREEZING
- Refrigeration slows the growth of microbes.
- Freezing can stop the growth of microbes.
- These methods of preservation don't change the taste, texture, or nutritional content too much.

D. CANNING, PASTEURIZATION, AND PICKLING
- When a food is canned, it is boiled, and, as a result, the microbes are killed.
- When a food is pickled, an unfriendly place for microbes is created when acids, bases, and salt are added.
- These methods of preservation do change the taste, texture, and nutritional content of the food.

E. CHEMICAL PRESERVATIVES
- Some spices such as (answers will vary) can slow the growth of microbes.
- Today, chemicals are often added to foods to reduce spoilage.
- Adding chemicals to foods is controversial because (answers will vary).

F. IMPORTANCE OF FOOD PRESERVATION
- Because of these food preservation procedures, people are less likely to eat contaminated food and become ill.

Appendix B • 389

#4 Why are refrigeration and freezing popular forms of food preservation?
They slow microbial growth but don't change the taste, texture, or nutritional content of food very much.

#5 How does canning prevent food from spoiling?
The food is boiled before being sealed; boiling kills the microbes; container is sealed so new microbes cannot get in.

#6 Why is pickling not used often today?
Pickling drastically changes the taste of a food.

#7 Why are chemical preservatives being questioned as a preservation technique?
People may be allergic to the preservatives; others believe that adding chemicals diminishes safety and nutrition.

#8 Why is food preservation so important?
Food preservation techniques protect people from food-borne pathogens; some illnesses can be very serious; the techniques help ensure safety and health.

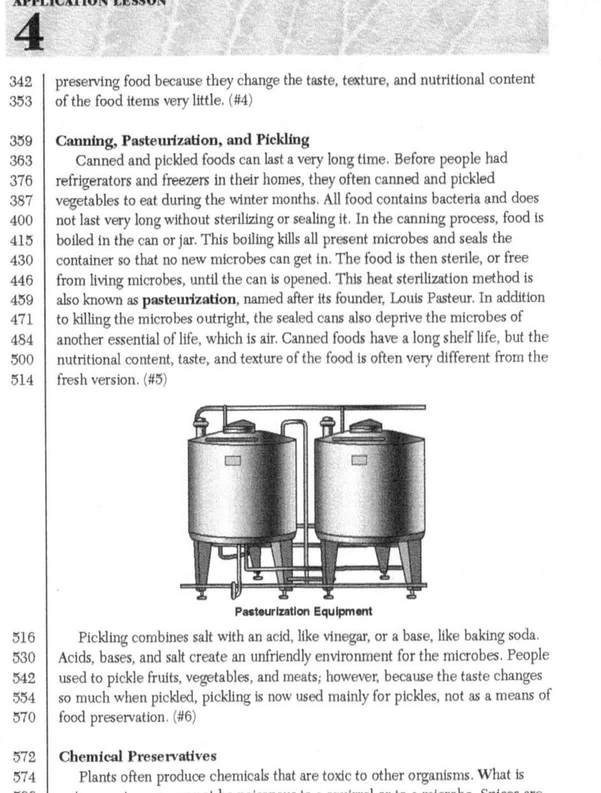

APPLICATION LESSON
4

342 preserving food because they change the taste, texture, and nutritional content
353 of the food items very little. (#4)

D

359 **Canning, Pasteurization, and Pickling**
363 Canned and pickled foods can last a very long time. Before people had
376 refrigerators and freezers in their homes, they often canned and pickled
387 vegetables to eat during the winter months. All food contains bacteria and does
400 not last very long without sterilizing or sealing it. In the canning process, food is
415 boiled in the can or jar. This boiling kills all present microbes and seals the
430 container so that no new microbes can get in. The food is then sterile, or free
446 from living microbes, until the can is opened. This heat sterilization method is
459 also known as **pasteurization**, named after its founder, Louis Pasteur. In addition
471 to killing the microbes outright, the sealed cans also deprive the microbes of
484 another essential of life, which is air. Canned foods have a long shelf life, but the
500 nutritional content, taste, and texture of the food is often very different from the
514 fresh version. (#5)

Pasteurization Equipment

516 Pickling combines salt with an acid, like vinegar, or a base, like baking soda.
530 Acids, bases, and salt create an unfriendly environment for the microbes. People
542 used to pickle fruits, vegetables, and meats; however, because the taste changes
554 so much when pickled, pickling is now used mainly for pickles, not as a means of
570 food preservation. (#6)

E

572 **Chemical Preservatives**
574 Plants often produce chemicals that are toxic to other organisms. What is
586 poisonous to you may not be poisonous to a squirrel or to a microbe. Spices are
602 made from parts of plants. Some spices, used in large amounts, can slow the

54 *REWARDS Plus: Reading Strategies Applied to Science Passages*

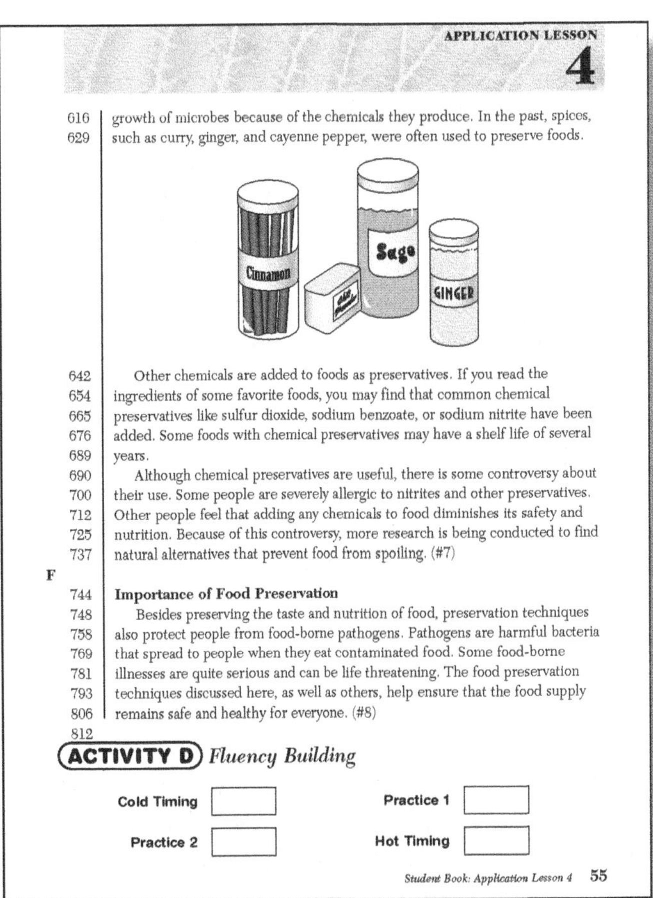

APPLICATION LESSON
4

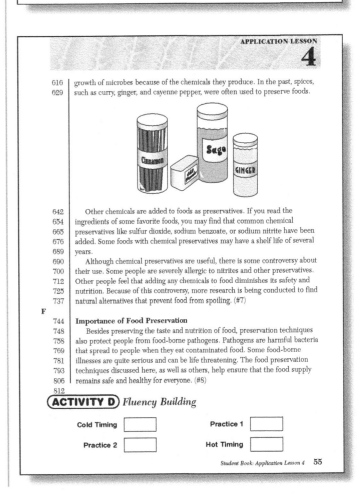

616 growth of microbes because of the chemicals they produce. In the past, spices,
629 such as curry, ginger, and cayenne pepper, were often used to preserve foods.

642 Other chemicals are added to foods as preservatives. If you read the
654 ingredients of some favorite foods, you may find that common chemical
665 preservatives like sulfur dioxide, sodium benzoate, or sodium nitrite have been
676 added. Some foods with chemical preservatives may have a shelf life of several
689 years.
690 Although chemical preservatives are useful, there is some controversy about
700 their use. Some people are severely allergic to nitrites and other preservatives.
712 Other people feel that adding any chemicals to food diminishes its safety and
725 nutrition. Because of this controversy, more research is being conducted to find
737 natural alternatives that prevent food from spoiling. (#7)

F

744 **Importance of Food Preservation**
748 Besides preserving the taste and nutrition of food, preservation techniques
758 also protect people from food-borne pathogens. Pathogens are harmful bacteria
769 that spread to people when they eat contaminated food. Some food-borne
781 illnesses are quite serious and can be life threatening. The food preservation
793 techniques discussed here, as well as others, help ensure that the food supply
806 remains safe and healthy for everyone. (#8)
812

ACTIVITY D *Fluency Building*

Cold Timing		Practice 1	
Practice 2		Hot Timing	

Student Book: Application Lesson 4 55

Fluency Building

ACTIVITY PROCEDURE

(See the *Student Book*, page 55.)

In this activity, students will be using a repeated reading procedure of the Activity C article to increase their reading fluency. First, have students do a Cold Timing, in which they whisper-read for one minute as you time them. Have them record in their books the number of correct words they read. Then, have students repeat with one or two practice readings to attempt to beat their Cold Timing. Finally, students exchange books in preparation for a Hot Timing. Have students listen to a partner read for one minute, underlining any word errors, and have them determine the number of correct words their partner read. When both students have completed their Hot Timing, they return each other's books and complete their own Fluency Graphs by indicating the number of words they read correctly in the one-minute Cold Timing and the one-minute Hot Timing.

Note D-1: When assigning partners for this activity, have the stronger reader read first. As a result, the other reader will have one additional practice opportunity.

1. Now, it's time for fluency building.
2. Find the beginning of the passage again. (Pause.)
3. Whisper-read. See how many words you can read in one minute. Begin._ (Time students for one minute.) Stop._ Circle the last word that you read._ Count the number of words you read in one minute. (Assist students in determining the number of words by counting from the number at the beginning of the line to the circled word.)_ Record the number of words you read after **Cold Timing**._
4. Let's practice again. Return to the beginning of the article. Remember to whisper-read. See if you can beat your Cold Timing. Begin._ (Time students for one minute.) Stop._ Put a box around the last word that you read._ Count the number of words you read in one minute._ Find **Practice 1**._ Record the number of words you read._
5. (Optional) Let's practice one more time before the Hot Timing. Return to the beginning of the article. Remember to whisper-read. See if you can beat your Cold Timing. Begin._ (Time students for one minute.) Stop._ Put a box around the last word that you read._ Count the number of words you read in one minute._ Find **Practice 2**._ Record the number of words you read._
6. Please exchange books with your partner._ Partner 1, you are going to read first. Partner 2, you are going to listen carefully to your partner as he or she reads. If your partner makes a mistake or leaves out a word, underline that word. Ones, get ready to read quietly to your partner. Begin._ (Time students for one minute.) Stop._ Twos, cross out the last word that your partner read._ Twos, determine the number of words your partner read correctly in one minute._ (Assist students in subtracting the number of mistakes from the number of words read.) Record the number in your partner's book after **Hot Timing**._
7. Partner 2, you are going to read next. Partner 1, you are going to listen carefully to your partner as he or she reads. If your partner makes a mistake or leaves out a word, underline that word. Twos, get ready to read quietly to your partner. Begin._ (Time students for one minute.) Stop._ Ones, cross out the last word that your partner read._ Ones, determine the number of words your partner read correctly in one minute._ Record the number in your partner's book after **Hot Timing**._
8. Exchange books._ Turn to the Fluency Graph on the last page of your book, and indicate on the graph the number of Cold Timing and Hot Timing words you read correctly._

689 ye...
690 Although chemical preservatives are useful, there is some controversy about
700 their use. Some people are severely allergic to nitrites and other preservatives.
712 Other people feel that adding any chemicals to food diminishes its safety and
725 nutrition. Because of this controversy, more research is being conducted to find
737 natural alternatives that prevent food from spoiling. (#7)

F

744 **Importance of Food Preservation**
748 Besides preserving the taste and nutrition of food, preservation techniques
758 also protect people from food-borne pathogens. Pathogens are harmful bacteria
769 that spread to people when they eat contaminated food. Some food-borne
781 illnesses are quite serious and can be life threatening. The food preservation
793 techniques discussed here, as well as others, help ensure that the food supply
806 remains safe and healthy for everyone. (#8)
812

ACTIVITY D *Fluency Building*

Cold Timing		Practice 1	
Practice 2		Hot Timing	

Student Book: Application Lesson 4 55

ACTIVITY E

Comprehension Questions—Multiple Choice

ACTIVITY PROCEDURE

(See the *Student Book*, page 56.)

Review the steps in the Multiple Choice Strategy. Lead students through items #1 and #2, proceeding step-by-step. Have students proceed item by item for the remaining multiple-choice items, reminding them to prepare a rationale for the *best* answer. Have students share their answers and the rationale for their answers. Encourage thoughtful discussion. Provide feedback and have students record points for each correct item.

Note E-1: The correct Multiple Choice answers are circled.

APPLICATION LESSON

4

ACTIVITY E *Comprehension Questions—Multiple Choice*

Comprehension Strategy—Multiple Choice

Step 1: Read the item.
Step 2: Read all of the choices.
Step 3: Think about why each choice might be correct or incorrect. Check the article as needed.
Step 4: From the possible correct choices, select the best answer.

1. (Cause and effect) **If you wanted to avoid food spoilage, which of these methods would you NOT use?**
   - (a.) Picking out each microbe from the food.
   - b. Killing the microbes within the food.
   - c. Slowing down the growth of the microbes.
   - d. Changing the composition of the food so microbes can't use it.
2. (Compare and contrast) **How do "drying" and "smoking" methods of preservation <u>differ</u>?**
   - a. Drying is a method of preserving plant foods. Smoking is a method of preserving meat.
   - (b.) Drying removes water from the food, depriving microbes of a necessity. Smoking not only dries the food, but the smoke is toxic to the microbes.
   - c. Drying is an ancient form of preservation. Smoking is a recent development in preservation.
   - d. Drying always requires the use of salt to kill microbes. Smoking requires the use of fire to make the meat or fish poisonous.
3. (Compare and contrast) **How do canning and pickling preservation processes <u>differ</u>?**
   - a. Canned foods have a long shelf life due to the killing of microbes. Pickled foods have a short shelf life due to the growth of microbes in the acid.
   - b. Canned foods taste like fresh vegetables. Pickled foods have an altered flavor.
   - (c.) In the canning process, the food is boiled in a can or jar and the microbes are killed. In pickling, ingredients such as salt or vinegar are added to the foods to create a "hostile" environment for microbes.
   - d. Canned foods are in cans. Pickled foods are in jars.
4. (Main idea) **If you were picking a clever title for this article, which of the following would most accurately convey the article's topic?**
   - a. Spice is NICE
   - b. Don't Preserve—SERVE
   - c. DRY, FRY, Then CRY
   - (d.) Microbes BEWARE!

MULTIPLE CHOICE COMPREHENSION 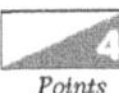 4 Points

56 *REWARDS Plus: Reading Strategies Applied to Science Passages*

1. Turn to page 56._ Find **Activity E.**_ Let's review the steps in the Multiple Choice Strategy.
2. Read **Step 1.**_
3. Read **Step 2.**_
4. Read **Step 3.**_
5. Read **Step 4.**_
6. Find question #1. Read it._
7. Read choice **a.**_ Think about why this choice might be correct or incorrect. (Pause. Then, call on individual students.)
8. Here's what I think. The question asks which is NOT a method used to avoid food spoilage. Picking out each microbe would be impossible. Microbes are very tiny living organisms and are not visible to the human eye. This would definitely not be an efficient method.
9. Read choice **b.**_ Think about why this choice might be correct or incorrect. (Pause. Then, call on individual students.)
10. Here's what I was thinking. This choice focuses on killing microbes, an important type of food preservation.
11. Read choice **c.**_ Think about why this choice might be correct or incorrect. (Pause. Then, call on individual students.)
12. This choice identifies slowing down microbial growth, again helping to slow food spoilage.
13. Read choice **d.**_ Think about why this choice might be correct or incorrect. (Pause. Then, call on individual students.)
14. This is what I was thinking. Microbes are a main cause of food spoilage so if microbes can't use the food, this would avoid spoilage.
15. Which is the best answer?_ Circle it._
16. Let's do the next one. Read item #2._
17. Read choice **a.**_ Think about why this choice might be correct or incorrect. (Pause. Then, call on individual students.)
18. This is what I was thinking. Drying can be used to preserve plant foods, but it can also be used to preserve meat. Because the first statement was false, this cannot be the correct answer.
19. Read choice **b.**_ Think about why this choice might be correct or incorrect. (Pause. Then, call on individual students.)
20. This is what I was thinking. Choice **b** compares drying and smoking and tells how they are different. Choice **b** is probably the best answer.
21. Read choice **c.**_ Think about why this choice might be correct or incorrect. (Pause. Then, call on individual students.)
22. This is what I was thinking. Drying is an ancient form of food preservation, but it is still used today. Smoking is more recent, but it is also used today.

Because both are used today, this tells about how drying and smoking are the same. This may not be the best answer.

23. Read choice **d.** Think about why this choice might be correct or incorrect. (Pause. Then, call on individual students.)

24. This is what I was thinking. Drying doesn't always require the use of salt. Smoking creates toxins for microbes but doesn't make the food poisonous for people. Because both of these statements are false, this could not be the right answer.

25. Which is the best answer? Circle it.

26. Use the Multiple Choice Strategy to complete item #3. Be ready to explain why you selected your answer. (Wait while students complete the item. Call on individual students. Ask them why they chose their answer and why they eliminated the other choices. Encourage discussion. Provide students with feedback on their choices, focusing on why or why not those choices might be appropriate.)

27. Use the Multiple Choice Strategy to complete item #4. Be ready to explain why you selected your answer. (Wait while students complete the item. Call on individual students. Ask them why they chose their answer and why they eliminated the other choices. Encourage discussion. Provide students with feedback on their choices, focusing on why or why not those choices might be appropriate.)

28. Count the number of items you got correct, and record that number in the blank half of the Multiple Choice Comprehension box.

APPLICATION LESSON

4

ACTIVITY E *Comprehension Questions—Multiple Choice*

Comprehension Strategy—Multiple Choice

Step 1: Read the item.
Step 2: Read all of the choices.
Step 3: Think about why each choice might be correct or incorrect. Check the article as needed.
Step 4: From the possible correct choices, select the best answer.

1. (Cause and effect) **If you wanted to avoid food spoilage, which of these methods would you NOT use?**
   - (a.) Picking out each microbe from the food.
   - b. Killing the microbes within the food.
   - c. Slowing down the growth of the microbes.
   - d. Changing the composition of the food so microbes can't use it.

2. (Compare and contrast) **How do "drying" and "smoking" methods of preservation <u>differ</u>?**
   - a. Drying is a method of preserving plant foods. Smoking is a method of preserving meat.
   - (b.) Drying removes water from the food, depriving microbes of a necessity. Smoking not only dries the food, but the smoke is toxic to the microbes.
   - c. Drying is an ancient form of preservation. Smoking is a recent development in preservation.
   - d. Drying always requires the use of salt to kill microbes. Smoking requires the use of fire to make the meat or fish poisonous.

3. (Compare and contrast) **How do canning and pickling preservation processes <u>differ</u>?**
   - a. Canned foods have a long shelf life due to the killing of microbes. Pickled foods have a short shelf life due to the growth of microbes in the acid.
   - b. Canned foods taste like fresh vegetables. Pickled foods have an altered flavor.
   - (c.) In the canning process, the food is boiled in a can or jar and the microbes are killed. In pickling, ingredients such as salt or vinegar are added to the foods to create a "hostile" environment for microbes.
   - d. Canned foods are in cans. Pickled foods are in jars.

4. (Main idea) **If you were picking a clever title for this article, which of the following would most accurately convey the article's topic?**
   - a. Spice is NICE
   - b. Don't Preserve—SERVE
   - c. DRY, FRY, Then CRY
   - (d.) Microbes BEWARE!

MULTIPLE CHOICE COMPREHENSION

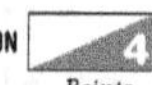

4 Points

56 *REWARDS Plus: Reading Strategies Applied to Science Passages*

ACTIVITY F

Vocabulary Activities

ACTIVITY PROCEDURE

(See the *Student Book*, page 57–58.)

Have students complete each item orally and provide feedback on their answers. Then have students respond to each question in writing by answering "yes" or "no" and providing a reason for their answers.

Yes/No/Why

1. Turn to page 57. Find **Activity F**. Read item #1. Tell your partner your answer and your reason for it. (Pause. Then call on individual students.)
2. My answer is definitely "Yes." Many foods or elements could be poisonous and thus dangerous.
3. Write your answer and your reason for it in the space provided. Look up when you are done.
4. Read item #2. Tell your partner your answer and your reason for it. (Pause. Then call on individual students. Encourage discussion. Provide feedback, especially on the reason for the answer.)
5. Write your answer and your reason for it in the space provided. Look up when you are done.
6. Read item #3. Tell your partner your answer and your reason for it. (Pause. Then call on individual students. Encourage discussion. Provide feedback, especially on the reason for the answer.)
7. Write your answer and your reason for it in the space provided. Look up when you are done.

Note F-1: You may wish to do this as an oral task only rather than an oral and a written task.

APPLICATION LESSON 4

ACTIVITY F *Vocabulary Activities*

Yes/No/Why

1. Could **ingredients** be **poisonous**?
Example answer: Yes. Many foods or elements could be poisonous and thus dangerous.

2. Is **pasteurization** the same process as **refrigeration**?
Example answer: No. When using pasteurization the food is boiled, killing microbes. When refrigeration is used, the growth of microbes is slowed or stopped.

3. Are there good **alternatives** to **controversy**?
Example answer: Yes. One good alternative would be compromise.

Student Book: Application Lesson 4 57

ACTIVITY PROCEDURE

Have students read the words and definitions and then complete the sentence stems for each vocabulary word. Have them share answers with partners and with the class. Then, have students give themselves points in the blank half of the Vocabulary box.

Completion Activity

1. Turn to page 58._ Read the first word and its definition._
2. Now, read the sentence stem._
3. Think of how you would complete the sentence stem and write it._ Share your answer with your partner._ (Call on a few students to share answers with the class.)
4. (Repeat Steps 1–3 for the rest of the words.)
5. If you participated in answering all seven questions, give yourself seven points in the blank half of the Vocabulary box.

Note F-2: You may wish to do this as an oral task only rather than an oral task and a written task.

APPLICATION LESSON
4

Completion Activities

1. **dehydration:** the loss of water from an organism
You might experience dehydration if you
Answers will vary.

2. **research:** to study or investigate in a particular field
During my lifetime, I hope we have research on
Answers will vary.

3. **deprive:** to take away from
If you stay out past your curfew, your parents might deprive you of
Answers will vary.

4. **preserved:** kept safe or free from harm
Berries and other fruits are often preserved by
Answers will vary.

VOCABULARY 7 Points

58 *REWARDS Plus: Reading Strategies Applied to Science Passages*

ACTIVITY G

Expository Writing— Multi-Paragraph Answer

ACTIVITY PROCEDURE, Plan and Write

(See the *Student Book*, pages 59–61.)

Review with students the steps in the Multi-Paragraph Writing Strategy. Have students read the prompt and Roberto's topics. Explain how Roberto made a **LIST** of critical details under each topic. Have students read Roberto's details for topic a, b, and c, then look at topic a again. Explain that details that don't go with a topic should be eliminated, but Roberto did not **CROSS OUT** anything. Next, explain how details can be combined into one sentence, but Roberto did not **CONNECT** anything. Have students **NUMBER** their details in the same manner as Roberto. Next, have students read the example paragraph a. Guide students in examining and completing the plan for topic b, and have them **WRITE** paragraph b. Repeat for topic c. Finally, explain that after the answer is written, they should **EDIT** their work, revising for clarity and proofreading for errors in capitalization, punctuation, and spelling.

Use Overheads 18 and 19: Activity G

1. Turn to page 59._ Find **Activity G**._ Let's work on paragraph writing. Study the steps in the Writing Strategy._ Say the steps with me: **List, cross out, connect, number, write, edit**. Say the steps again._
2. Find the prompt in the middle of the page._ Read the prompt out loud with me: **Describe the three most popular types of food preservation methods used today.**
3. Turn to page 60._ First, Roberto recorded the topics for his paragraphs. Read topic a._ Read topic b._ Read topic c._ These topics will be incorporated into topic sentences.
4. Next, he followed the steps in the Writing Strategy to write his answer. What is **Step 1**?_ Read the details **listed** under topic a._ Roberto then listed details for topic b.
5. Now, it's your turn to add details to topic c. Look back in the article and locate details that tell about the process of chemical preservation. Write the details in the Planning Box._
6. Next, Roberto applied **Steps 2 through 5** to each paragraph.

APPLICATION LESSON **4**

ACTIVITY G *Expository Writing—Multi-Paragraph Answer*

Writing Strategy—Multi-Paragraph Answer

Step 1: LIST (List the details that are important enough to include in your answer.)
Step 2: CROSS OUT (Reread the details. Cross out any that don't go with the topic.)
Step 3: CONNECT (Connect any details that could go into one sentence.)
Step 4: NUMBER (Number the details in a logical order.)
Step 5: WRITE (Write the paragraph.)
Step 6: EDIT (Revise and proofread your answer.)

Prompt: Describe the three most popular types of food preservation methods used today.

Plan: Complete the Planning Box with your teacher.

Student Book: Application Lesson 4 59

APPLICATION LESSON **4**

Example Multi-Paragraph Plan

Planning Box
(topic a) *refrigeration & freezing*
① (detail) – *slows or stops growth of microbes*
② (detail) – *stays good for weeks rather than days*
③ (detail) – *doesn't change taste, texture, or nutritional content*
(topic b) *canning & pasteurization*
① { (detail) – *food boiled in can or jar*
(detail) – *boiling kills microbes*
(detail) – ~~*freezing slows growth of microbes*~~
② (detail) – *container sealed so microbes can't enter*
③ (detail) – *long shelf life*
④ (detail) – *nutritional content, taste, & texture altered*
(topic c) *chemical preservation*
① { (detail) – *chemicals are added to foods*
(detail) – *sulfur dioxide, sodium benzoate, & sodium nitrite*
② (detail) – *shelf life of years*
③ { (detail) – *controversial*
(detail) – *people allergic*
(detail) – *may not be safe*

Write: Examine paragraph a and write paragraphs b and c on a separate piece of paper.

60 *REWARDS Plus: Reading Strategies Applied to Science Passages*

7. What is **Step 2**?_ Roberto reread his details for topic a and looked for details to **cross out**._ Look at the overhead._ Did he cross out any details?_
8. What is **Step 3**?_ Look at the overhead._ In this case, Roberto did NOT **connect** any details. Each detail will be in a separate sentence.
9. What is **Step 4**?_ Next, Roberto **numbered** the details in the order he wished them to occur in the paragraph. Looking at the overhead, number your details as Roberto did._
10. What is **Step 5**?_ Next, Roberto **wrote** the paragraph. Locate paragraph a on the next page._ (Read paragraph a with your students or to your students.)
11. It's your turn to use the steps for topic b. First, read the details and **cross out** any details that do not go with the topic._ Next, draw brackets to **connect** details that could easily go into one sentence._ Now, **number** the details in a logical order._
12. Now, examine Roberto's plan for topic b on the overhead. Yours doesn't need to be the same, but it should be similar._
13. Take out a blank piece of paper._ Using your plan for paragraph b, **write** paragraph b. If you finish early, please reread and **edit** your paragraph. Don't forget to use the spelling of words in the plan and the article to correct any errors._ (Move around the room and monitor your students as they are writing.)
14. (When the majority of students are done, proceed with the lesson.) Now, use the steps for topic c. First, read the details and **cross out** any details that do not go with the topic._ Next, draw brackets to **connect** details that could easily go into one sentence._ Now, **number** the details in a logical order._
15. Examine Roberto's plan for topic c on the overhead. Yours doesn't need to be the same, but it should be similar._
16. Locate your piece of paper._ Using your plan for paragraph c, **write** paragraph c. If you finish early, please **edit** your paragraph._ (Move around the room and monitor your students as they are writing.)
17. (When the majority of students are done, proceed with the lesson.) What is **Step 6**?_ Roberto revised paragraph a and proofread for any errors. Please carefully read your paragraphs. Be

APPLICATION LESSON **4**

ACTIVITY G *Expository Writing—Multi-Paragraph Answer*

Writing Strategy—Multi-Paragraph Answer

Step 1: LIST (List the details that are important enough to include in your answer.)
Step 2: CROSS OUT (Reread the details. Cross out any that don't go with the topic.)
Step 3: CONNECT (Connect any details that could go into one sentence.)
Step 4: NUMBER (Number the details in a logical order.)
Step 5: WRITE (Write the paragraph.)
Step 6: EDIT (Revise and proofread your answer.)

Prompt: Describe the three most popular types of food preservation methods used today.

Plan: Complete the Planning Box with your teacher.

Student Book: Application Lesson 4 59

APPLICATION LESSON

Example Multi-Paragraph Plan

Planning Box
(topic a) *refrigeration & freezing*
① (detail) – *slows or stops growth of microbes*
② (detail) – *stays good for weeks rather than days*
③ (detail) – *doesn't change taste, texture, or nutritional content*
(topic b) *canning & pasteurization*
① (detail) – *food boiled in can or jar*
(detail) – *boiling kills microbes*
(detail) – ~~*freezing slows growth of microbes*~~
② (detail) – *container sealed so microbes can't enter*
③ (detail) – *long shelf life*
④ (detail) – *nutritional content, taste, & texture altered*
(topic c) *chemical preservation*
① (detail) – *chemicals are added to foods*
(detail) – *sulfur dioxide, sodium benzoate, & sodium nitrite*
② (detail) – *shelf life of years*
③ (detail) – *controversial*
(detail) – *people allergic*
(detail) – *may not be safe*

Write: Examine paragraph a and write paragraphs b and c on a separate piece of paper.

60 *REWARDS Plus: Reading Strategies Applied to Science Passages*

sure that your paragraphs are clear. Proofread for any errors in capitalization, punctuation, and spelling._ (Give students time to proofread their paragraphs.)

ACTIVITY PROCEDURE, Evaluate

Ask students to read each question in the rubric. Guide them in evaluating the paragraphs using the guidelines. Have students total their points and record them in the blank half of the Writing box.

18. Turn to page 61._ Roberto has already evaluated paragraph a. Let's evaluate your paragraph b._

19. Read question #1 with me._ Circle "Yes" for b if your topic sentence includes the topic: canning and pasteurization._

20. Read question #2 with me._ Circle "Yes" for b if all of your details tell about canning and pasteurization._

21. Read question #3 with me._ Circle "Yes" for b if you combined details into one sentence._

22. Now, check paragraph c carefully and answer questions 1 through 3._

23. Read question #4._ Reread your paragraphs._ Circle "Yes" if your paragraphs are easy to understand._

24. Read question #5._ Carefully examine your paragraphs. If you think a word is misspelled, underline it and check back in the plan or article and correct the spelling._ Circle "Yes" if you believe that you have very few spelling errors._

25. Read question #6._ Carefully examine your sentences. Be sure that each sentence begins with a capital._ If all sentences begin with a capital, circle "Yes."_

26. Read question #7._ Examine your sentences. Be sure that each sentence ends with a period._ If all sentences end with a period, circle "Yes."_

27. Count up your points and record them in the Writing box._

28. (Show Overhead 19.) Look at the overhead._ Let's read Roberto's remaining paragraphs. Yours do not have to be the same, but they should be similar._ (Read the paragraphs to your students or with your students or call on a student to read the example paragraphs.)

29. In the next lesson, you will be planning and writing more paragraphs independently.

APPLICATION LESSON **4**

Example Multi-Paragraph Answer

(paragraph a)

Refrigeration and freezing are popular modern means of food preservation. These processes result in slowing down or stopping the growth of microbes in food. As a result, the food may last weeks rather than days. These methods are also popular because they don't change the taste, texture, or nutritional value of the food very much.

Evaluate: Evaluate the paragraphs using this rubric.

Rubric—Multi-Paragraph Answer	Student or Partner Rating	Teacher Rating
1. Did the author state the topic in the first sentence?	a. (Yes) Fix up b. (Yes) Fix up c. (Yes) Fix up	a. Yes No b. Yes No c. Yes No
2. Did the author include details that go with the topic?	a. (Yes) Fix up b. (Yes) Fix up c. (Yes) Fix up	a. Yes No b. Yes No c. Yes No
3. Did the author combine details in some of the sentences?	a. (Yes) Fix up b. (Yes) Fix up c. (Yes) Fix up	a. Yes No b. Yes No c. Yes No
4. Is the answer easy to understand?	(Yes) Fix up	Yes No
5. Did the author correctly spell words, particularly the words found in the article?	(Yes) Fix up	Yes No
6. Did the author use correct capitalization, capitalizing the first word in the sentence and proper names of people, places, and things?	(Yes) Fix up	Yes No
7. Did the author use correct punctuation, including a period at the end of each sentence?	(Yes) Fix up	Yes No

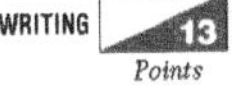

Note G-1: The rubric can be used in a variety of ways. Instead of the students evaluating their own paragraphs, you may wish to have their partners provide feedback. The second column is designed for teacher feedback. If you have a small group, it would be useful to give daily feedback on writing. If the group size is large, you can give feedback to a number of children each day. You may wish to give students bonus points based on your feedback.

ACTIVITY H

Comprehension— Single-Paragraph Answer

ACTIVITY PROCEDURE

(See the *Student Book*, page 62.)

Have students read the *What Is* statement and the *What If* question. Have students turn the question into part of the answer and write down a topic sentence for their answer. Then, have them complete their answer. Encourage them to use evidence from the article and their own experience and background knowledge. Engage students in a discussion. Award points for writing and participating in the discussion.

Note H-1: To increase the quality of the discussion, the students are asked to think and write about the *What If* before the discussion. However, you may be working with students who have difficulty generating ideas for their paragraph. If that is the case, switch the order of activities: engage the students in a discussion, and then have them write their paragraphs.

1. Turn to page 62._ Find **Activity H.**_
2. Today, you are going to write a paragraph answer to the *What If* question and participate in a discussion.
3. Find the *What Is* statement in the middle of the page._ Read it out loud with me: **We depend on our food supply to be available, varied, and fresh.**
4. Find the *What If* question._ Read it with me: **What would happen if all known methods of food preservation were suddenly ineffective in stopping the growth of microbes?**
5. Think how you might turn the question into part of the answer._ Tell me your idea for a topic sentence._ (Example sentence: If all known methods of food preservation were suddenly ineffective in stopping the growth of microbes, a number of things would immediately happen.) Take out a piece of paper and write your topic sentence._ (Move around the room and monitor as students write.)
6. You are ready to add ideas. You may think of an answer based on your experience and background knowledge, but you should also include evidence from the article or other materials that you have studied. Take some time to look back in the article and consider how you would respond to this question. Then, add sentences to your paragraph.

APPLICATION LESSON

4

ACTIVITY H *Comprehension—Single-Paragraph Answer*

Writing Strategy—Single-Paragraph Answer

Step 1: Read the item.
Step 2: Turn the question into part of the answer and write it down.
Step 3: Think of the answer or locate the answer in the article.
Step 4: Complete your answer.

Prompt:
What Is–We depend on our food supply to be available, varied, and fresh.

What If–What would happen if all known methods of food preservation were suddenly ineffective in stopping the growth of microbes?

Write and Discuss: Write a paragraph. Then share your ideas. Use the Discussion Guidelines.

Discussion Guidelines

Speaker		Listener	
Looks like:	**Sounds like:**	**Looks like:**	**Sounds like:**
• Facing peers • Making eye contact • Participating	• Using pleasant, easy-to-hear voice • Sharing opinions, supporting facts and reasons from the article and from your experience • Staying on the topic	• Facing speaker • Making eye contact • Participating	• Waiting quietly to speak • Giving positive, supportive comments • Disagreeing respectfully

WRITING	DISCUSSION
4	4
Points	Points

62 *REWARDS Plus: Reading Strategies Applied to Science Passages*

If you finish early, reread your paragraph and edit it so that it is easy to understand and clear._ (Move around the room and monitor as students write.)

7. Read your paragraph to your partner._
8. If you included wording from the question in your answer and added evidence from the article, award yourself four points for writing._ Write them in the Writing box.
9. Before we discuss your answers, reread the discussion guidelines to yourself._
10. (Engage students in a discussion. Award four points to students who are active participants in the discussion, and have them write them in the Discussion box.)
11. (Distribute Appendix A Reproducible 4: Writing Strategy—Single-Paragraph Answer. Have students place this in a notebook or a folder for future reference.)

Note H-2: If your students are having difficulty writing the *What If* paragraphs, read or show them the following example paragraph:

Example Single-Paragraph Answer

If all known methods of food preservation were suddenly ineffective in stopping the growth of microbes, all food would spoil quickly. We would no longer be able to buy canned or frozen food and would have to eat only fresh food. With no methods of food preservation, fresh food could not travel very far without becoming spoiled so we would only be able to eat food grown or raised near our homes. Food like milk and meat would spoil very quickly, making them available to very few people. Due to spoilage and the unavailability of food, more people would become ill from disease and possibly die.

Application Lesson 5

Materials Needed:

- *Student Book*: Application Lesson 5
- Application Overhead Transparencies 20–24
- Appendix A Reproducible 5: Discussion Guidelines
- Appendix B Reproducible E: Application Lesson 5
- Appendix C Optional Vocabulary Activity: Application Lesson 5
- Paper or cardboard to use when covering the overhead transparency
- Paper or cardboard for each student to use during spelling dictation
- Washable overhead transparency pen

Text Treatment Notes:

- Black text signifies teacher script (exact wording to say to students).
- Green text in parentheses signifies directions or prompts for the teacher.
- Green text signifies answers or examples of answers.
- Green graphics treatment signifies reproduction of Overhead information.
- Green text and green graphics treatment do not appear in the *Student Book*.

ACTIVITY A

Vocabulary

ACTIVITY PROCEDURE, List 1

(See the *Student Book*, page 63.)

Tell students each word in the list. Then, have students repeat the word and read the definition aloud. For each definition, provide any additional information that may be necessary. Then, have students practice reading the words themselves.

Use Overhead 20: Activity A
List 1: Tell

1. (Show the top half of Overhead 20.) Before we read the passage, let's read the difficult words. (Point to **arteries**.) This word is **arteries**. What word?_ Now, read the definition._
2. (Point to **arterioles**.) The next word is **arterioles**. What word?_ Now, read the definition._
3. (Pronounce each word in List 1, and then have students repeat each word and read the definition.)
4. Open your *Student Book* to **Application Lesson 5**, page 63._
5. Find **Activity A**, **List 1**, in your book._ Let's read the words again. First word._ Next word._ (Continue for all words in List 1.)

ACTIVITY PROCEDURE, List 2

(See the *Student Book*, page 63.)

Have students circle prefixes and suffixes, then underline the vowels. Using the overhead transparency, assist students in checking their work. Next, have students figure out each word to themselves, then say it aloud. Have them read the definition aloud.

APPLICATION LESSON 5

ACTIVITY A *Vocabulary*

List 1: Tell

1.	arteries	*n.*	► (large blood vessels that carry blood away from the heart)
2.	arterioles	*n.*	► (small blood vessels that carry blood away from the heart)
3.	arteriosclerosis	*n.*	► (a condition that happens when the walls of the arteries become thick and not as flexible)
4.	plaque	*n.*	► (a hard substance that builds up in blood vessels and limits the flow of blood)
5.	atherosclerosis	*n.*	► (a condition that happens when deposits of plaque build up on the inside of the arteries)
6.	atria	*n.*	► (the two top chambers of the heart)
7.	capillaries	*n.*	► (small blood vessels that connect arteries to venules)
8.	deoxygenated	*v.*	► (having the oxygen removed)
9.	hemoglobin	*n.*	► (a substance in red blood cells that helps carry oxygen throughout the body)
10.	platelets	*n.*	► (pieces of cells that promote blood clotting)
11.	pulmonary	*adj.*	► (relating to or affecting the lungs)
12.	systemic	*adj.*	► (relating to or affecting the body)
13.	ventricles	*n.*	► (the two lower chambers of the heart)
14.	venules	*n.*	► (small blood vessels that connect capillaries to veins)

List 2: Strategy Practice

1.	cardiovascular	*adj.*	► (of the body system that consists of the heart, blood, and blood vessels)
2.	circulates	*v.*	► (moves from place to place in a circular path)
3.	components	*n.*	► (parts)
4.	fragments	*n.*	► (small pieces)
5.	infections	*n.*	► (diseases caused by germs entering part of the body)
6.	multicellular	*adj.*	► (made up of many cells)
7.	particular	*adj.*	► (special)
8.	pressures	*n.*	► (forces made by one thing against another)
9.	responsible for	*adj.*	► (in charge of; charged with being the source for)
10.	trillion	*n.*	► (the number 1 followed by 12 zeroes; a lot)

TALLY ___ VOCABULARY 5 Points

Student Book: Application Lesson 5 63

Use Overhead 20: Activity A
List 2: Strategy Practice

1. Find **List 2**. Circle the prefixes and suffixes, and underline the vowels. Look up when you are done._
2. (Show the bottom half of Overhead 20.) Before you check your work on List 2, look at item #6. (Point to the second example and the **multi** that is circled.) From now on, you can also circle **multi**, which means *many*. The prefix is /multi/. Say it._ Now, go back to item #1. Check and fix any mistakes._
3. Go back to the first word again._ Sound out the word to yourself. Put your thumb up when you can read the word. Be sure that it is a real word._ What word?_ Now, read the definition._
4. (Continue Step 3 with all remaining words in List 2.)

Note A.2-1: You may wish to provide additional practice by having students read words to a partner.

ACTIVITY PROCEDURE, List 1 and 2

(See the *Student Book*, page 63.)

Tell students to look in List 1 or List 2 for a word you are thinking about. Have them circle the number of the word and tell you the word. Explain to students to make a tally mark for each correct word in the Tally box, and then enter the number of tally marks as points in the blank half of the Vocabulary box.

1. Remember, the words I'm thinking about will be in either List 1 or List 2. For every word you correctly identify, make a tally mark in the Tally box. If you don't identify the correct word, don't do anything.
2. Circle the number of the appropriate word.
   - Something that is in small pieces is in this. (Wait.) What word? **fragments**
   - Organisms made up of many, many cells are these types of organisms. (Wait.) What word? **multicellular**
   - The parts of a system are often called these. (Wait.) What word? **components**
   - If you cut yourself and don't cleanse the wound, you may end up with these. (Wait.) What word? **infections**
   - When something moves around and around, it does this. (Wait.) What word? **circulates**
3. Count all the tally marks, and enter that number as points in the blank half of the Vocabulary box.

ACTIVITY PROCEDURE, List 3

(See the *Student Book*, page 64.)

The words in the third list are related. Have students use the *REWARDS* Strategies to figure out the first word in each family. Have them read the definition of the verb and then read nouns and adjectives that are related to that verb.

Use Overhead 21: Activity A
List 3: Word Families

1. Turn to page 64._ Find **Family 1** in **List 3**. Figure out the first word. Use your pencil if you wish. Put your thumb up when you know the word._ What word?_ Read the definition._
2. Look at the nouns in Family 1. Figure out the first word._ What word?_ Next word._ What word?_
3. Look at the adjective in Family 1. Figure out the word._ What word?_
4. (Repeat Steps 1–3 for all word families in List 3.)

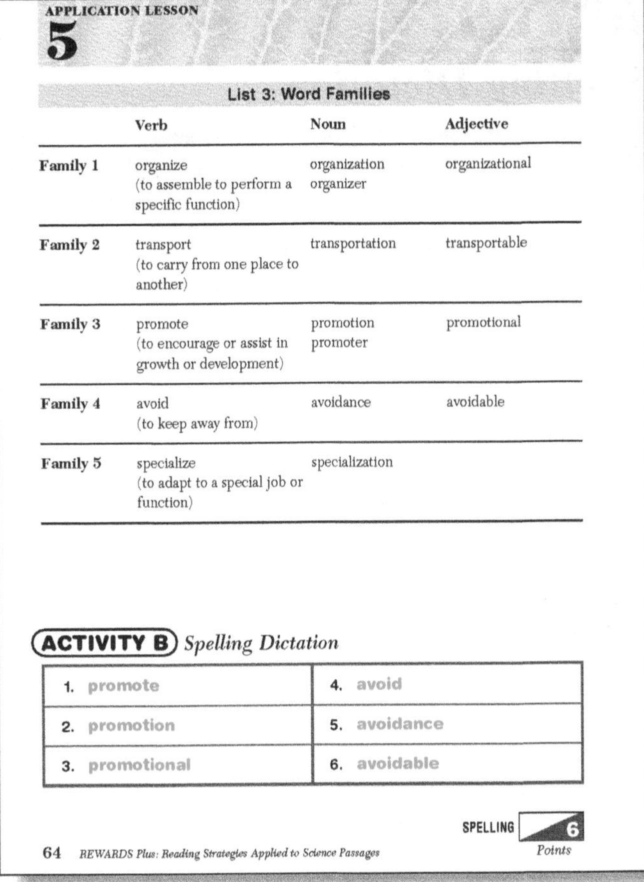

APPLICATION LESSON
5

List 3: Word Families

	Verb	Noun	Adjective
Family 1	organize (to assemble to perform a specific function)	organization organizer	organizational
Family 2	transport (to carry from one place to another)	transportation	transportable
Family 3	promote (to encourage or assist in growth or development)	promotion promoter	promotional
Family 4	avoid (to keep away from)	avoidance	avoidable
Family 5	specialize (to adapt to a special job or function)	specialization	

ACTIVITY B *Spelling Dictation*

1. promote	4. avoid
2. promotion	5. avoidance
3. promotional	6. avoidable

SPELLING 6 Points

64 *REWARDS Plus: Reading Strategies Applied to Science Passages*

Note A.3-1: You may wish to provide additional practice by having students read a word family to the group or to a partner.

Note A.3-2: An additional vocabulary practice activity called Quick Words is provided in Appendix C of this Teacher's Guide. See Appendix C for information about how this optional activity can be used.

ACTIVITY B

Spelling Dictation

ACTIVITY PROCEDURE

(See the *Student Book*, page 64.)

For each word, tell students the word, then have students say the parts of the word to themselves while they write the word. Using the overhead transparency, assist students in checking their spelling and correcting if they misspelled. Then, have students enter the number of correctly spelled words as points in the blank half of the Spelling box.

Note B-1: Distribute a piece of light cardboard to each of the students.

Use Overhead 21: Activity B

1. Find **Activity B**.
2. The first word is **promote**. What word?_ Say the parts in **promote** to yourself as you write the word. (Pause and monitor.)
3. (Show **promote** on the overhead.) Check **promote**. If you misspelled it, cross it out and write it correctly.
4. The second word is **promotion**. What word?_ Say the parts in **promotion** to yourself as you write the word. (Pause and monitor.)
5. (Show **promotion** on the overhead.) Check **promotion**. If you misspelled it, cross it out and write it correctly.
6. (Repeat the procedures for the words **promotional**, **avoid**, **avoidance**, and **avoidable**.)
7. Count the number of words you spelled correctly, and record that number as points in the blank half of the Spelling box at the bottom of the page.

APPLICATION LESSON 5

List 3: Word Families

	Verb	Noun	Adjective
Family 1	organize (to assemble to perform a specific function)	organization organizer	organizational
Family 2	transport (to carry from one place to another)	transportation	transportable
Family 3	promote (to encourage or assist in growth or development)	promotion promoter	promotional
Family 4	avoid (to keep away from)	avoidance	avoidable
Family 5	specialize (to adapt to a special job or function)	specialization	

ACTIVITY B *Spelling Dictation*

1. promote	4. avoid
2. promotion	5. avoidance
3. promotional	6. avoidable

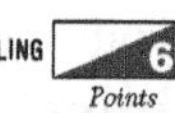
SPELLING 6 *Points*

64 *REWARDS Plus: Reading Strategies Applied to Science Passages*

ACTIVITY C
Passage Reading and Comprehension

ACTIVITY PROCEDURE

(See the *Student Book*, pages 65–67.)

Have students read the title of the passage and each heading. Ask them to tell their partners two things that the passage will tell about.

Passage Preview

1. Turn to page 65._ Let's preview the passage.
2. Read the title._ What is the whole passage going to tell about?_
3. Now, let's read the headings. Read the first heading._ Read the next heading._ (Continue until students have read all headings.)
4. Turn to your partner. Without looking, tell two things this passage will tell about._

ACTIVITY PROCEDURE

Provide students with an Information Web from Appendix B. Have students read the passage silently to each embedded number, and then reread the same information orally either to a partner, together as a group, or individually. Ask the corresponding comprehension question or questions. Once students finish reading a section labeled A, B, C, D, E, or F, have them fill in the Information Web before going on to the next section.

Note C-1: If students do not finish reading the passage during class, have them use their Information Webs to review the information at the beginning of the next class.

Use Overhead 22: Activity C

Passage Reading

1. (Provide an Information Web for each student.)
2. Turn back to the beginning of the passage. You're going to read the passage and answer questions about what you've read. During passage reading, you are also going to fill in an Information Web to help you remember the important details of the passage. Later, you'll use this Web to review the content of the passage with your partner.
3. Read the title._

APPLICATION LESSON **5**

ACTIVITY C *Passage Reading and Comprehension*

Note: For this activity, you will need Reproducible E found in the *Teacher's Guide*.

The Cardiovascular System

A

All living things are made up of cells, the basic units of life. Most organisms
15 are made up of many, many cells (multicellular organisms). In fact, humans have
28 over a trillion cells. In multicellular organisms, various life functions are
39 performed by specialized groups of cells. In humans, there are five levels of
52 organization: cells, tissues, organs, organ systems, and the whole organism. **Cells**
63 group together to form **tissues**. Similar tissues group together to form **organs**,
75 and organs group together with other organs to form **organ systems**. Each organ
88 system performs a particular function. (#1)
93 One organ system is the **cardiovascular system**, which includes your heart,
104 blood, and blood vessels. This system is a type of transportation system that
117 delivers oxygen and nutrients throughout the body and then removes waste
128 products from the body. The cardiovascular system is one of several organ
140 systems that are central to the human body's functioning. For a person's body to
154 function smoothly, all organ systems, including the cardiovascular system, must
164 run smoothly. (#2)

B

166 **The Heart**
168 Make a fist. Your **heart** is a muscle about the same size as your closed fist. It
185 is hollow on the inside and divided into four chambers, or parts. The top
199 chambers are the atria. The lower chambers are the ventricles. The atria pump
212 blood into the heart and down into the ventricles. The ventricles pump the
225 blood out of the heart and toward the rest of the body. When the blood goes
241 from the atria to the ventricles, it passes through valves that prevent the blood
255 from flowing backwards. (#3)

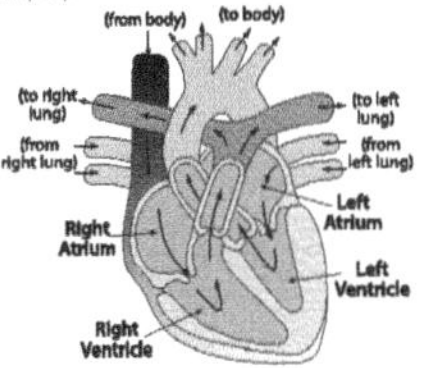

Student Book: Application Lesson 5 65

(from Application Lesson 5)

Reproducible E

ACTIVITY C *Passage Reading and Comprehension*

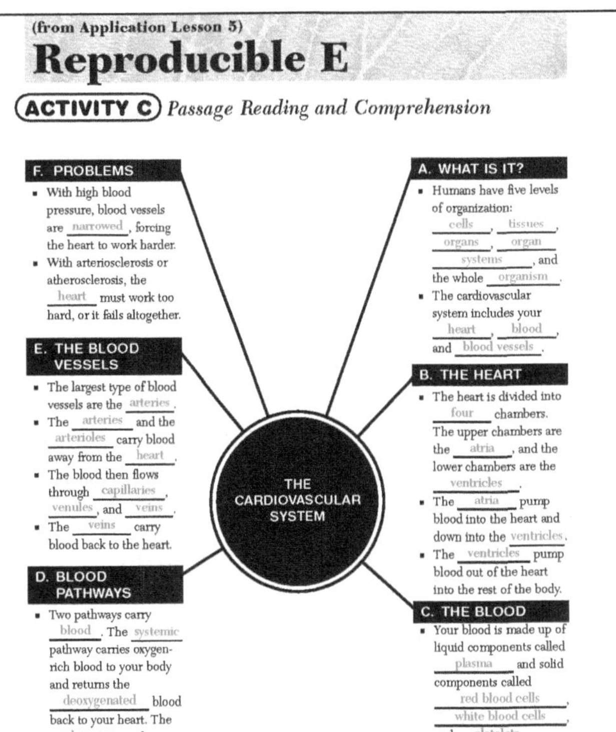

THE CARDIOVASCULAR SYSTEM

A. WHAT IS IT?
- Humans have five levels of organization: cells, tissues, organs, organ systems, and the whole organism.
- The cardiovascular system includes your heart, blood, and blood vessels.

B. THE HEART
- The heart is divided into four chambers. The upper chambers are the atria, and the lower chambers are the ventricles.
- The atria pump blood into the heart and down into the ventricles.
- The ventricles pump blood out of the heart into the rest of the body.

C. THE BLOOD
- Your blood is made up of liquid components called plasma and solid components called red blood cells, white blood cells, and platelets.
- Red blood cells carry oxygen to the body. White blood cells work hard to fight infections and diseases.
- Platelets promote clotting.

D. BLOOD PATHWAYS
- Two pathways carry blood. The systemic pathway carries oxygen-rich blood to your body and returns the deoxygenated blood back to your heart. The pulmonary pathway carries the deoxygenated blood from your heart to your lungs, where carbon dioxide is released and oxygen is picked up.

E. THE BLOOD VESSELS
- The largest type of blood vessels are the arteries.
- The arteries and the arterioles carry blood away from the heart.
- The blood then flows through capillaries, venules, and veins.
- The veins carry blood back to the heart.

F. PROBLEMS
- With high blood pressure, blood vessels are narrowed, forcing the heart to work harder.
- With arteriosclerosis or atherosclerosis, the heart must work too hard, or it fails altogether.

390 • REWARDS Plus: Reading Strategies Applied to Science Passages

4. Find number 1 in the passage. (Pause). Read down to number 1 silently. Look up when you are done._
5. (Wait for students to complete the reading. Then have students reread the part by having them read orally to a partner, read together orally as a group, or read aloud individually.)
6. (Ask the question or questions associated with the number. Provide feedback to students regarding their answers.)
7. (Repeat steps 4–6 for all paragraphs in Section A.)
8. Now, look at your Information Web. Find the section labeled A._ The information you've just read will help you to fill in this section of the Web.
9. With your partner, fill in the blanks for Section A. You can refer back to the passage for information. Look up when you're done._ (Move around the room and monitor students as they complete the section.)
10. (When the majority of students have finished, show Overhead 22). Look at the overhead and check your work. Fix up or add to any of your answers.
11. Now read down to the next number silently. Look up when you are done._
12. (Repeat steps 5–11 until the students have finished the passage and the Information Web.)
13. Now use your Information Web to retell the important information from the passage to your partner.

Comprehension Questions

#1 What are the five levels of organization in the human body?

Cells, tissues, organs, organ systems, and the whole organism.

#2 What three parts of the body make up the cardiovascular system? What important functions does this system perform?

Made up of heart, blood, and blood vessels; delivers oxygen and nutrients throughout the body and removes waste products from the body.

#3 Name the chambers of the heart. What are their functions?

Atria and ventricles; atria pump blood into the heart and ventricles; ventricles pump blood out of the heart and toward the rest of the body.

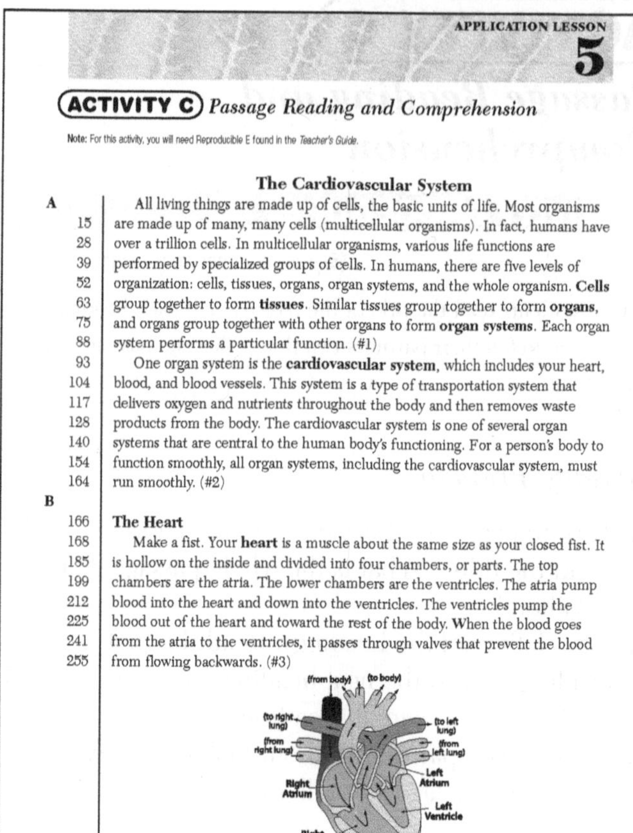

APPLICATION LESSON 5

ACTIVITY C *Passage Reading and Comprehension*

Note: For this activity, you will need Reproducible E found in the *Teacher's Guide*.

The Cardiovascular System

A

All living things are made up of cells, the basic units of life. Most organisms are made up of many, many cells (multicellular organisms). In fact, humans have over a trillion cells. In multicellular organisms, various life functions are performed by specialized groups of cells. In humans, there are five levels of organization: cells, tissues, organs, organ systems, and the whole organism. **Cells** group together to form **tissues**. Similar tissues group together to form **organs**, and organs group together with other organs to form **organ systems**. Each organ system performs a particular function. (#1)

One organ system is the **cardiovascular system**, which includes your heart, blood, and blood vessels. This system is a type of transportation system that delivers oxygen and nutrients throughout the body and then removes waste products from the body. The cardiovascular system is one of several organ systems that are central to the human body's functioning. For a person's body to function smoothly, all organ systems, including the cardiovascular system, must run smoothly. (#2)

B

The Heart

Make a fist. Your **heart** is a muscle about the same size as your closed fist. It is hollow on the inside and divided into four chambers, or parts. The top chambers are the atria. The lower chambers are the ventricles. The atria pump blood into the heart and down into the ventricles. The ventricles pump the blood out of the heart and toward the rest of the body. When the blood goes from the atria to the ventricles, it passes through valves that prevent the blood from flowing backwards. (#3)

Student Book: Application Lesson 5 65

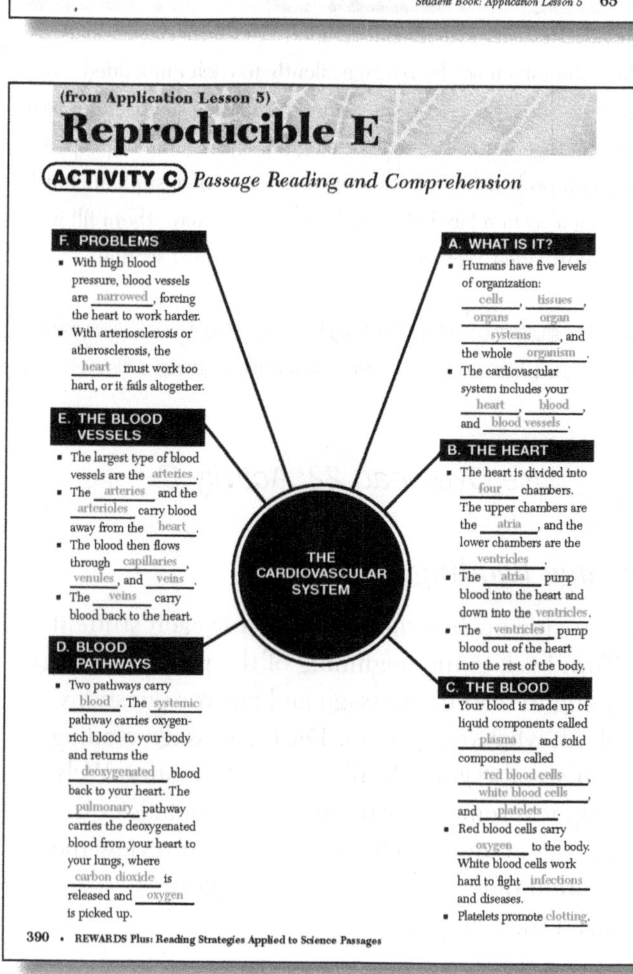

(from Application Lesson 5)

Reproducible E

ACTIVITY C *Passage Reading and Comprehension*

THE CARDIOVASCULAR SYSTEM

A. WHAT IS IT?

- Humans have five levels of organization: cells, tissues, organs, organ systems, and the whole organism.
- The cardiovascular system includes your heart, blood, and blood vessels.

B. THE HEART

- The heart is divided into four chambers. The upper chambers are the atria, and the lower chambers are the ventricles.
- The atria pump blood into the heart and down into the ventricles.
- The ventricles pump blood out of the heart into the rest of the body.

C. THE BLOOD

- Your blood is made up of liquid components called plasma and solid components called red blood cells, white blood cells, and platelets.
- Red blood cells carry oxygen to the body. White blood cells work hard to fight infections and diseases.
- Platelets promote clotting.

D. BLOOD PATHWAYS

- Two pathways carry blood. The systemic pathway carries oxygen-rich blood to your body and returns the deoxygenated blood back to your heart. The pulmonary pathway carries the deoxygenated blood from your heart to your lungs, where carbon dioxide is released and oxygen is picked up.

E. THE BLOOD VESSELS

- The largest type of blood vessels are the arteries.
- The arteries and the arterioles carry blood away from the heart.
- The blood then flows through capillaries, venules, and veins.
- The veins carry blood back to the heart.

F. PROBLEMS

- With high blood pressure, blood vessels are narrowed, forcing the heart to work harder.
- With arteriosclerosis or atherosclerosis, the heart must work too hard, or it fails altogether.

390 • REWARDS Plus: Reading Strategies Applied to Science Passages

#4 What components make up your blood?
Liquid components (plasma) and solid components, including white and red blood cells and platelets.

#5 How does hemoglobin help red blood cells function?
Hemoglobin helps red blood cells hold oxygen until it is delivered to places in the body that need it.

#6 Why are white blood cells important to the human body?
They work to destroy viruses and bacteria that can cause illnesses; travel to the site of an infection.

#7 How do platelets help people stop bleeding?
They stick to the walls of the blood vessels and promote clotting when a blood vessel is damaged.

#8 What is the difference between the systemic and the pulmonary pathways?
Systemic carries oxygen-rich blood from the heart to all parts of body except the lungs and returns deoxygenated blood back to the heart; pulmonary carries deoxygenated blood from the heart to the lungs and returns oxygenated blood back to the heart.

#9 Name the five types of blood vessels and their functions.
Arteries and arterioles carry blood away from the heart; capillaries help exchange nutrients and waste; veins and venules carry blood toward the heart.

#10 What measures can you take to maintain a healthy and strong cardiovascular system?
Eat a nutritional diet, avoid smoking, and exercise daily.

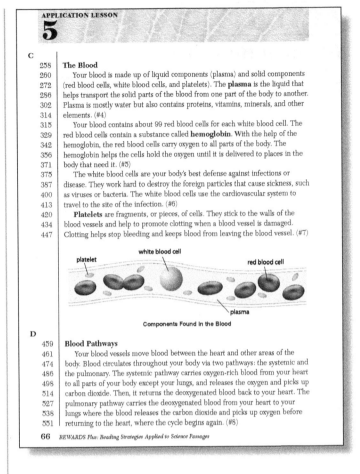

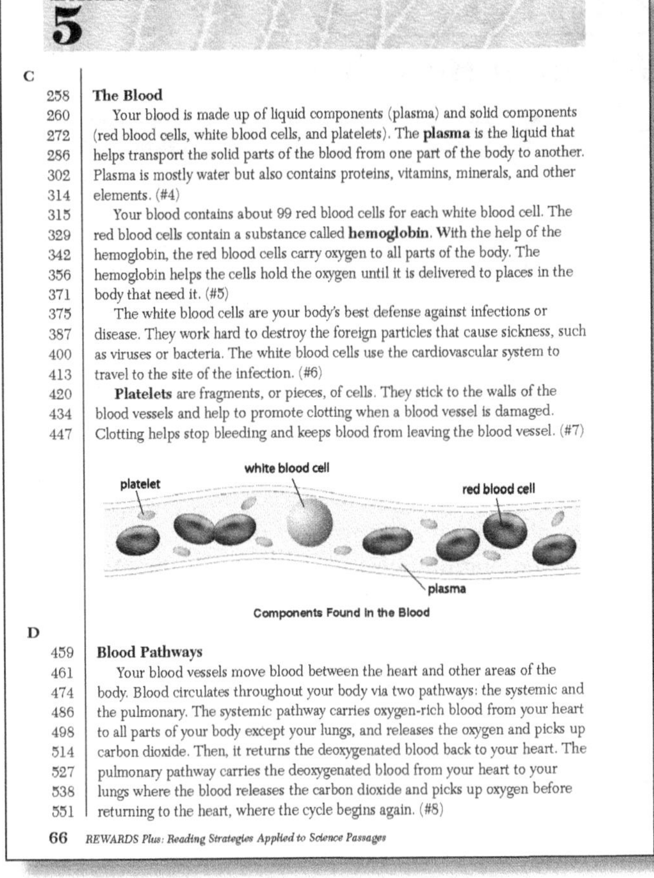

APPLICATION LESSON
5

C

The Blood

Your blood is made up of liquid components (plasma) and solid components (red blood cells, white blood cells, and platelets). The **plasma** is the liquid that helps transport the solid parts of the blood from one part of the body to another. Plasma is mostly water but also contains proteins, vitamins, minerals, and other elements. (#4)

Your blood contains about 99 red blood cells for each white blood cell. The red blood cells contain a substance called **hemoglobin**. With the help of the hemoglobin, the red blood cells carry oxygen to all parts of the body. The hemoglobin helps the cells hold the oxygen until it is delivered to places in the body that need it. (#5)

The white blood cells are your body's best defense against infections or disease. They work hard to destroy the foreign particles that cause sickness, such as viruses or bacteria. The white blood cells use the cardiovascular system to travel to the site of the infection. (#6)

Platelets are fragments, or pieces, of cells. They stick to the walls of the blood vessels and help to promote clotting when a blood vessel is damaged. Clotting helps stop bleeding and keeps blood from leaving the blood vessel. (#7)

Components Found in the Blood

D

Blood Pathways

Your blood vessels move blood between the heart and other areas of the body. Blood circulates throughout your body via two pathways: the systemic and the pulmonary. The systemic pathway carries oxygen-rich blood from your heart to all parts of your body except your lungs, and releases the oxygen and picks up carbon dioxide. Then, it returns the deoxygenated blood back to your heart. The pulmonary pathway carries the deoxygenated blood from your heart to your lungs where the blood releases the carbon dioxide and picks up oxygen before returning to the heart, where the cycle begins again. (#8)

66 *REWARDS Plus: Reading Strategies Applied to Science Passages*

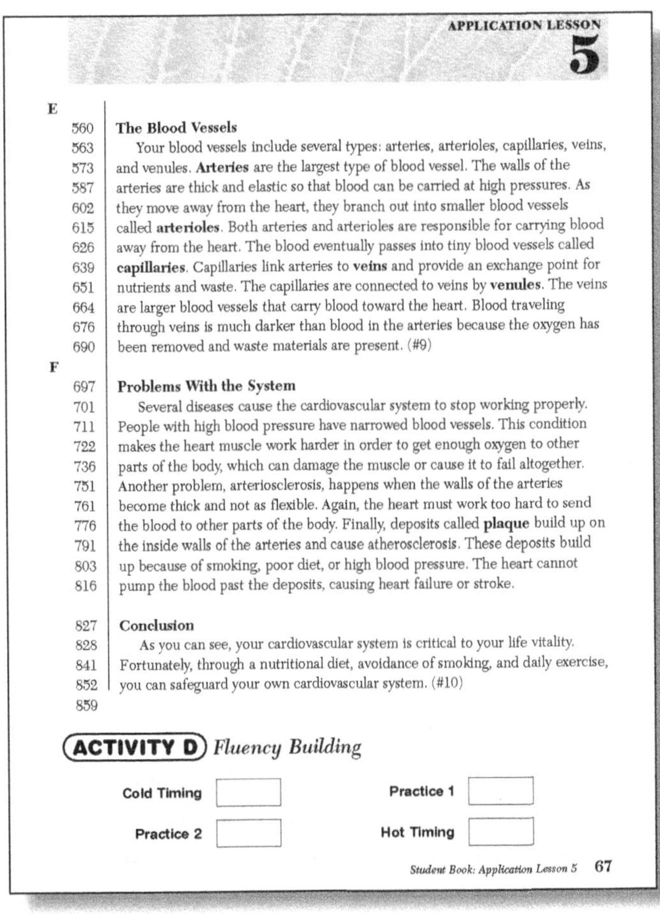

APPLICATION LESSON
5

E

The Blood Vessels

Your blood vessels include several types: arteries, arterioles, capillaries, veins, and venules. **Arteries** are the largest type of blood vessel. The walls of the arteries are thick and elastic so that blood can be carried at high pressures. As they move away from the heart, they branch out into smaller blood vessels called **arterioles**. Both arteries and arterioles are responsible for carrying blood away from the heart. The blood eventually passes into tiny blood vessels called **capillaries**. Capillaries link arteries to **veins** and provide an exchange point for nutrients and waste. The capillaries are connected to veins by **venules**. The veins are larger blood vessels that carry blood toward the heart. Blood traveling through veins is much darker than blood in the arteries because the oxygen has been removed and waste materials are present. (#9)

F

Problems With the System

Several diseases cause the cardiovascular system to stop working properly. People with high blood pressure have narrowed blood vessels. This condition makes the heart muscle work harder in order to get enough oxygen to other parts of the body, which can damage the muscle or cause it to fail altogether. Another problem, arteriosclerosis, happens when the walls of the arteries become thick and not as flexible. Again, the heart must work too hard to send the blood to other parts of the body. Finally, deposits called **plaque** build up on the inside walls of the arteries and cause atherosclerosis. These deposits build up because of smoking, poor diet, or high blood pressure. The heart cannot pump the blood past the deposits, causing heart failure or stroke.

Conclusion

As you can see, your cardiovascular system is critical to your life vitality. Fortunately, through a nutritional diet, avoidance of smoking, and daily exercise, you can safeguard your own cardiovascular system. (#10)

ACTIVITY D *Fluency Building*

Cold Timing		Practice 1	
Practice 2		Hot Timing	

Student Book: Application Lesson 5 67

Fluency Building

ACTIVITY PROCEDURE

(See the *Student Book,* page 67.)

Have students complete a Cold Timing, one or two practices, and a Hot Timing of the Activity C article. For each timing, have students record the number of correct words read. Finally, have students complete their Fluency Graphs.

Note D-1: When assigning partners for this activity, have the stronger reader read first. As a result, the other reader will have one additional practice opportunity.

1. Now, it's time for fluency building.
2. Find the beginning of the passage again. (Pause.)
3. Whisper-read. See how many words you can read in one minute. Begin._ (Time students for one minute.) Stop._ Circle the last word that you read._ Record the number of words you read after **Cold Timing**._
4. Let's practice again. Begin._ (Time students for one minute.) Stop._ Put a box around the last word that you read._ Record the number of words you read after **Practice 1**._
5. (Optional) Let's practice one more time before the Hot Timing. Begin._ (Time students for one minute.) Stop._ Put a box around the last word that you read._ Record the number of words you read after **Practice 2**._
6. Please exchange books with your partner._ Partner 1, you are going to read first. Partner 2, listen carefully and underline any mistakes or words left out. Ones, begin._ (Time students for one minute.) Stop._ Twos, cross out the last word that your partner read._ (Assist students in subtracting the number of mistakes from the number of words read.) Twos, record the number of correct words in your partner's book after **Hot Timing**._
7. Partner 2, you are going to read next. Partner 1, listen carefully and underline any mistakes or words left out. Twos, begin. (Time students for one minute.) Stop._ Ones, cross out the last word that your partner read._ Ones, record the number of correct words in your partner's book after **Hot Timing**._
8. Exchange books._ Turn to the Fluency Graph on the last page of your book, and indicate on the graph the number of Cold Timing and Hot Timing words you read correctly._

APPLICATION LESSON **5**

E

560 **The Blood Vessels**
563 Your blood vessels include several types: arteries, arterioles, capillaries, veins,
573 and venules. **Arteries** are the largest type of blood vessel. The walls of the
587 arteries are thick and elastic so that blood can be carried at high pressures. As
602 they move away from the heart, they branch out into smaller blood vessels
615 called **arterioles**. Both arteries and arterioles are responsible for carrying blood
626 away from the heart. The blood eventually passes into tiny blood vessels called
639 **capillaries**. Capillaries link arteries to **veins** and provide an exchange point for
651 nutrients and waste. The capillaries are connected to veins by **venules**. The veins
664 are larger blood vessels that carry blood toward the heart. Blood traveling
676 through veins is much darker than blood in the arteries because the oxygen has
690 been removed and waste materials are present. (#9)

F

697 **Problems With the System**
701 Several diseases cause the cardiovascular system to stop working properly.
711 People with high blood pressure have narrowed blood vessels. This condition
722 makes the heart muscle work harder in order to get enough oxygen to other
736 parts of the body, which can damage the muscle or cause it to fail altogether.
751 Another problem, arteriosclerosis, happens when the walls of the arteries
761 become thick and not as flexible. Again, the heart must work too hard to send
776 the blood to other parts of the body. Finally, deposits called **plaque** build up on
791 the inside walls of the arteries and cause atherosclerosis. These deposits build
803 up because of smoking, poor diet, or high blood pressure. The heart cannot
816 pump the blood past the deposits, causing heart failure or stroke.

827 **Conclusion**
828 As you can see, your cardiovascular system is critical to your life vitality.
841 Fortunately, through a nutritional diet, avoidance of smoking, and daily exercise,
852 you can safeguard your own cardiovascular system. (#10)
859

ACTIVITY D *Fluency Building*

Cold Timing		**Practice 1**	
Practice 2		**Hot Timing**	

Student Book: Application Lesson 5 67

ACTIVITY E

Comprehension Questions—Multiple Choice

ACTIVITY PROCEDURE

(See the *Student Book*, page 68.)

Review the steps in the Multiple Choice Strategy. Have students complete item #1. Then, have students share the rationale for their answers. Encourage thoughtful discussion. Proceed item by item, emphasizing the rationale for the *best* answer. Have students record points for each correct item.

Note E-1: The correct Multiple Choice answers are circled.

APPLICATION LESSON

5

ACTIVITY E *Comprehension Questions—Multiple Choice*

Comprehension Strategy—Multiple Choice

Step 1: Read the item.
Step 2: Read all of the choices.
Step 3: Think about why each choice might be correct or incorrect. Check the article as needed.
Step 4: From the possible correct choices, select the best answer.

1. (Main idea) **Which list best represents the levels of organization of human cells?**
   a. cells, organs, organ systems, tissue, whole human
   b. tissues, organs, organ systems, whole human
   (c.) cells, tissues, organs, organ systems, whole human
   d. heart, blood, blood vessels, arteries

2. (Vocabulary) **In the article, the author calls the cardiovascular system a "transportation system" because**
   (a.) like other transportation systems, it carries things from place to place.
   b. blood vessels and arteries are like the tunnels that trains pass through.
   c. like other transportation systems, it has a number of critical parts.
   d. the blood flows similarly to cars moving down a freeway.

3. (Cause and effect) **Determine which relationship is NOT true.**
   a. If you had an absence of hemoglobin, your body would have difficulty carrying oxygen to all parts of your body.
   (b.) If your body had an infection, red blood cells (the body's defense against infection) would travel to the infection.
   c. If your body had a reduced number of platelets in the blood, clotting would be impaired.
   d. If your blood vessels became narrow, you would have high blood pressure.

4. (Compare and contrast) **If you were comparing red and white blood cells, which of the following would be true of BOTH?**
   a. We have about the same number of red and white blood cells.
   b. Red and white blood cells work to destroy particles causing illness.
   (c.) Plasma carries red and white blood cells from one part of your body to another.
   d. Red and white blood cells contain hemoglobin which helps them deliver oxygen to all parts of the body.

MULTIPLE CHOICE COMPREHENSION 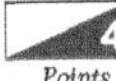 4 Points

68 *REWARDS Plus: Reading Strategies Applied to Science Passages*

1. Find **Activity E.** Let's review the steps in the Multiple Choice Strategy.
2. Read **Step 1.**
3. Read **Step 2.**
4. Read **Step 3.**
5. Read **Step 4.**
6. Find item #1. Read it. This question asks about levels and implies that you look for the correct order of organization.
7. Read choice **a.**
8. Read choice **b.**
9. Read choice **c.**
10. Read choice **d.**
11. Which is the best answer? (Call on individual students. Ask them why they chose their answer and why they eliminated the other choices. Encourage discussion. Provide students with feedback on their choices, focusing on why or why not those choices might be appropriate.)
12. Let's do the next one. Read item #2. This question asks you to figure out why the author compares the cardiovascular system to a "transportation system."
13. Use the Multiple Choice Strategy to complete item #2. Be ready to explain why you selected your answer. (Wait while students complete the item. Call on individual students. Ask them why they chose their answer and why they eliminated the other choices. Encourage discussion. Provide students with feedback on their choices, focusing on why or why not those choices might be appropriate.)
14. Use the Multiple Choice Strategy to complete item #3. Be ready to explain why you selected your answer. (Wait while students complete the item. Call on individual students. Ask them why they chose their answer and why they eliminated the other choices. Encourage discussion. Provide students with feedback on their choices, focusing on why or why not those choices might be appropriate.)
15. Use the Multiple Choice Strategy to complete item #4. Be ready to explain why you selected your answer. (Wait while students complete the item. Call on individual students. Ask them why they chose their answer and why they eliminated the other choices. Encourage discussion. Provide students with feedback on their choices, focusing on why or why not those choices might be appropriate.)
16. Count the number of items you got correct, and record that number in the blank half of the Multiple Choice Comprehension box.

ACTIVITY F

Vocabulary Activities

ACTIVITY PROCEDURE

(See the *Student Book*, pages 69–70.)

Have students complete each item orally and provide feedback on their answers. Then have students respond to each question in writing by answering "yes" or "no" and providing a reason for their answers.

Yes/No/Why

1. Turn to page 69._ Find **Activity F.**_ Read item 1. Tell your partner your answer and your reason for it. (Pause. Then call on individual students.)
2. My answer would be "No." The pulmonary pathway relates to the lungs. The ventricles are the two lower chambers of the heart and thus are not part of the pulmonary pathway.
3. Write your answer and your reason for it in the space provided. Look up when you are done._
4. Read item #2. Tell your partner your answer and your reason for it. (Pause. Then call on individual students. Encourage discussion. Provide students with feedback on their choices, focusing on their explanations for their answer.)
5. Write your answer and your reason for it in the space provided. Look up when you are done._
6. Read item #3. Tell your partner your answer and your reason for it. (Pause. Then call on individual students. Encourage discussion. Provide students with feedback on their choices focusing their explanations for their answer.)
7. Write your answer and your reason for it in the space provided. Look up when you are done._

Note F-1: You may wish to do this as an oral task only rather than an oral and a written task.

APPLICATION LESSON **5**

ACTIVITY F *Vocabulary Activities*

Yes/No/Why

1. Does the **pulmonary** pathway include **ventricles**?
Example answer: No. The pulmonary pathway relates to the lungs. The ventricles are the two lower chambers of the heart and thus are not part of the pulmonary pathway.

2. Do **arteries** lead to **infections**?
Example answer: No. Arteries are the largest type of blood vessel. Arteries carry blood away from the heart. They are not related to infection.

3. Can **plaque** be **responsible for** disease?
Example answer: Yes. Plaque builds up inside of arteries and causes atherosclerosis, a serious disease.

Student Book: Application Lesson 5 69

ACTIVITY PROCEDURE

Have students read the definitions and then complete the sentence stems for each vocabulary word. Have them share answers with partners and with the class. Then, have students give themselves points in the blank half of the Vocabulary box.

Completion Activity

1. Turn to page 70. Read the first word and its definition.
2. Now, read the sentence stem.
3. Think of how you would complete the sentence stem and write it. Share your answer with your partner. (Call on a few students to share answers with the class.)
4. (Repeat Steps 1–3 for the rest of the words.)
5. If you participated in answering all seven questions, give yourself seven points in the blank half of the Vocabulary box.

Note F-2: You may wish to do this as an oral task only rather than an oral task and a written task.

APPLICATION LESSON

5

Completion Activities

1. **avoidance:** the act of keeping away from
   Things that you have an avoidance for include
   Answers will vary.

2. **components:** parts
   The components of the perfect sound system include
   Answers will vary.

3. **promotional:** having to do with encouragement or assistance in growth or development
   Businesses may have a promotional offer for their products. Some of these offers might be
   Answers will vary.

4. **transportation:** something that carries things from one place to another
   Name six methods of transportation.
   Answers will vary.

VOCABULARY 7 *Points*

70 *REWARDS Plus: Reading Strategies Applied to Science Passages*

ACTIVITY G

Expository Writing—Multi-Paragraph Answer

ACTIVITY PROCEDURE, Plan and Write

(See the *Student Book*, pages 71–73.)

Review with students the steps in the Multi-Paragraph Writing Strategy. Have students read the prompt and Andrew's topics. Explain how Andrew made a **LIST** of critical details under each topic. Have students read Andrew's details for topic a and b, then guide them in adding details for topic c. Have students look at topic a again. Explain that details that don't go with a topic should be eliminated, and have them **CROSS OUT** the same detail as Andrew. Next, explain how details can be combined into one sentence, and have students **CONNECT** details as Andrew did in his plan. Have students **NUMBER** their details in the same manner as Andrew. Next, have students read example paragraph a. Guide students in examining and completing the plan for topic b and have them **WRITE** paragraph b. Have students complete the plan for topic c and write paragraph c. Finally, explain that after the answer is written, they should **EDIT** their work, revising for clarity and proofreading for errors in capitalization, punctuation, and spelling.

Use Overheads 23 and 24: Activity G

1. Turn to page 71._ Find **Activity G.**_ Let's work on paragraph writing. Study the steps in the Writing Strategy._ Ones, tell your partner the steps in the strategy._ Twos, tell your partner the steps in the strategy._
2. Find the prompt in the middle of the page._ Read the prompt out loud with me: **Describe the structure and function of the three main parts of the cardiovascular system.**
3. Turn to page 72._ Read topic a._ Read topic b._ Read topic c._ These topics will be incorporated into topic sentences.
4. What is **Step 1**?_ Read the details **listed** under topic a._ Andrew then listed details for topic b.
5. Now, it's your turn to add details to topic c. Look back in the article and locate details that describe the structure and function of the blood vessels. Write the details in the Planning Box._
6. Next, Andrew applied **Steps 2 through 5** to each paragraph.

APPLICATION LESSON 5

ACTIVITY G *Expository Writing—Multi-Paragraph Answer*

Writing Strategy—Multi-Paragraph Answer

- **Step 1: LIST** (List the details that are important enough to include in your answer.)
  - **Step 2: CROSS OUT** (Reread the details. Cross out any that don't go with the topic.)
  - **Step 3: CONNECT** (Connect any details that could go into one sentence.)
  - **Step 4: NUMBER** (Number the details in a logical order.)
  - **Step 5: WRITE** (Write the paragraph.)
- **Step 6: EDIT** (Revise and proofread your answer.)

Prompt: Describe the structure and function of the three main parts of the cardiovascular system.

Plan: Complete the Planning Box with your teacher.

Student Book: Application Lesson 5 71

APPLICATION LESSON 5

Example Multi-Paragraph Plan

Planning Box		
(topic a)		*heart*
①	(detail)	– *4 chambers*
	(detail)	– *top chambers—atria*
	(detail)	– *bottom chambers—ventricles*
②	(detail)	– *atria pumps blood into heart and down into ventricles*
③	(detail)	– *ventricles pump blood out of the heart to rest of body*
(topic b)		*blood*
①	(detail)	– *made of liquid and solid components*
②	(detail)	– *liquid component called plasma*
③	(detail)	– *solid components include red blood cells, white blood cells, & platelets*
	(detail)	– *plasma mostly water with proteins, vitamins, & minerals*
④	(detail)	– *red blood cells carry oxygen to all parts of body*
⑤	(detail)	– *white blood cells fight infection and diseases*
⑥	(detail)	– *platelets help promote blood clotting*
(topic c)		*blood vessels*
①	(detail)	– *arteries—largest type of blood vessel*
②	(detail)	– *arterioles—smaller blood vessels that arteries flow into*
③	(detail)	– *arteries & arterioles carry blood from heart*
④	(detail)	– *capillaries link arteries to veins*
⑤	(detail)	– *at this point nutrients are exchanged for waste*
⑥	(detail)	– *veins carry blood back to heart*
⑦	(detail)	– *blood going back to heart is darker because of waste and lack of oxygen*

Write: Examine paragraph a and write paragraphs b and c on a separate piece of paper.

72 *REWARDS Plus: Reading Strategies Applied to Science Passages*

7. What is **Step 2**? Andrew reread his details for topic a and looked for details to **cross out**. Look at the overhead. Did he cross out any details?
8. What is **Step 3**? Look at the overhead. Please add brackets to **connect** the details that Andrew connected.
9. What is **Step 4**? Next, Andrew **numbered** the details in the order he wished them to occur in the paragraph. Looking at the overhead, number your details as Andrew did.
10. What is **Step 5**? Next, Andrew **wrote** the paragraph. Locate paragraph a on the next page. (Read paragraph a with your students or to your students.)
11. It's your turn to use the steps for topic b. First, read the details and **cross out** any details that do not go with the topic. Next, draw brackets to **connect** details that could easily go into one sentence. Now, **number** the details in a logical order.
12. Now, examine Andrew's plan for topic b on the overhead. Yours doesn't need to be the same, but it should be similar.
13. Take out a blank piece of paper. Using your plan for paragraph b, **write** paragraph b. If you finish early, please reread and **edit** your paragraph. Don't forget to use the spelling of words in the plan and the article to correct any errors. (Move around the room and monitor your students as they are writing.)
14. (When the majority of students are done, proceed with the lesson.) Now, use the steps for topic c. First, read the details and **cross out** any details that do not go with the topic. Next, draw brackets to **connect** details that could easily go into one sentence. Now, **number** the details in a logical order.
15. Examine Andrew's plan for topic c on the overhead. Yours doesn't need to be the same, but it should be similar.
16. Locate your piece of paper. Using your plan for paragraph c, **write** paragraph c. If you finish early, please **edit** your paragraph. (Move around the room and monitor your students as they are writing.)
17. (When the majority of students are done, proceed with the lesson.) What is **Step 6**? Andrew revised paragraph a and proofread for any errors. Please carefully read your paragraphs. Be sure that your paragraphs are easy to understand and clear. Proofread for any errors in capitalization, punctuation, and spelling. (Give students time to proofread their paragraphs.)

APPLICATION LESSON **5**

Example Multi-Paragraph Answer

(paragraph a)

The heart is one part of the cardiovascular system. The heart has four chambers: two chambers on the top called the atria and two chambers on the bottom called the ventricles. The atria pump blood into the heart and then into the ventricles. Then, the ventricles pump blood out of the heart into the rest of the body.

Evaluate: Evaluate the paragraphs using this rubric.

Rubric— Multi-Paragraph Answer	Student or Partner Rating	Teacher Rating
1. Did the author state the topic in the first sentence?	a. (Yes) Fix up b. (Yes) Fix up c. (Yes) Fix up	a. Yes No b. Yes No c. Yes No
2. Did the author include details that go with the topic?	a. (Yes) Fix up b. (Yes) Fix up c. (Yes) Fix up	a. Yes No b. Yes No c. Yes No
3. Did the author combine details in some of the sentences?	a. (Yes) Fix up b. (Yes) Fix up c. (Yes) Fix up	a. Yes No b. Yes No c. Yes No
4. Is the answer easy to understand?	(Yes) Fix up	Yes No
5. Did the author correctly spell words, particularly the words found in the article?	(Yes) Fix up	Yes No
6. Did the author use correct capitalization, capitalizing the first word in the sentence and proper names of people, places, and things?	(Yes) Fix up	Yes No
7. Did the author use correct punctuation, including a period at the end of each sentence?	(Yes) Fix up	Yes No

WRITING 13 Points

Student Book: Application Lesson 5 73

ACTIVITY PROCEDURE, Evaluate

Ask students to read each question in the rubric. Guide them in evaluating the paragraphs using the guidelines. Have students total their points and record them in the blank half of the Writing box.

18. Turn to page 73. Paragraph a has been evaluated. Let's evaluate paragraph b.
19. Read question #1 with me. Circle "Yes" for b if your topic sentence includes the topic: blood.
20. Read question #2 with me. Circle "Yes" for b if all of your details tell about blood.
21. Read question #3 with me. Circle "Yes" for b if you combined details into one sentence.
22. Now, check paragraph c carefully and answer questions 1 through 3.
23. Read question #4. Reread your paragraphs. Circle "Yes" if your paragraphs are easy to understand.

24. Read question #5._ Carefully examine your paragraphs. If you think a word is misspelled, underline it and check back in the plan or article and correct the spelling._ Circle "Yes" if you believe that you have very few spelling errors._

25. Read question #6._ Carefully examine your sentences. Be sure that each sentence begins with a capital._ If all sentences begin with a capital, circle "Yes."_

26. Read question #7._ Examine your sentences. Be sure that each sentence ends with a period._ If all sentences end with a period, circle "Yes."_

27. Count up your points and record them in the Writing box._

28. (Show Overhead 24.) Look at the overhead._ Let's read Andrew's remaining paragraphs. Yours do not have to be the same, but they should be similar. (Read the paragraphs to your students or with your students or call on a student to read the example paragraph.)

29. In the next lesson, you will do more of the writing on your own.

Note G-1: The rubric can be used in a variety of ways. Instead of the students evaluating their own paragraphs, you may wish to have their partners provide feedback. The second column is designed for teacher feedback. If you have a small group, it would be useful to give daily feedback on writing. If the group size is large, you can give feedback to a number of children each day. You may wish to give students bonus points based on your feedback.

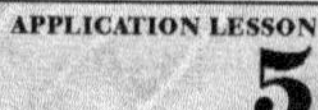

Example Multi-Paragraph Answer

(paragraph a)

The heart is one part of the cardiovascular system. The heart has four chambers: two chambers on the top called the atria and two chambers on the bottom called the ventricles. The atria pump blood into the heart and then into the ventricles. Then, the ventricles pump blood out of the heart into the rest of the body.

Evaluate: Evaluate the paragraphs using this rubric.

Rubric—Multi-Paragraph Answer	Student or Partner Rating	Teacher Rating
1. Did the author state the topic in the first sentence?	a. (Yes) Fix up b. (Yes) Fix up c. (Yes) Fix up	a. Yes No b. Yes No c. Yes No
2. Did the author include details that go with the topic?	a. (Yes) Fix up b. (Yes) Fix up c. (Yes) Fix up	a. Yes No b. Yes No c. Yes No
3. Did the author combine details in some of the sentences?	a. (Yes) Fix up b. (Yes) Fix up c. (Yes) Fix up	a. Yes No b. Yes No c. Yes No
4. Is the answer easy to understand?	(Yes) Fix up	Yes No
5. Did the author correctly spell words, particularly the words found in the article?	(Yes) Fix up	Yes No
6. Did the author use correct capitalization, capitalizing the first word in the sentence and proper names of people, places, and things?	(Yes) Fix up	Yes No
7. Did the author use correct punctuation, including a period at the end of each sentence?	(Yes) Fix up	Yes No

WRITING 

Points

Student Book: Application Lesson 5 73

ACTIVITY H

Comprehension—Single-Paragraph Answer

ACTIVITY PROCEDURE

(See the *Student Book*, page 74.)

Have students read the *What Is* statement and the *What If* question. Have students turn the question into part of the answer and write down a topic sentence for their answer. Then, have them complete their answer. Encourage them to use evidence from the article and their own experience and background knowledge. Engage students in a discussion. Award points for writing and participating in the discussion.

Note H-1: To increase the quality of the discussion, the students are asked to think and write about the *What If* before the discussion. However, you may be working with students who have difficulty generating ideas for their paragraph. If that is the case, switch the order of activities: engage the students in a discussion, and then have them write their paragraphs.

1. Turn to page 74._ Find **Activity H.**_
2. Find the *What Is* statement in the middle of the page._ Read it out loud with me: **A healthy cardiovascular system is critical to a person's overall health.**
3. Find the *What If* question._ Read it with me: **What would happen to you and your daily activities if your white blood cells were weakened or destroyed?**
4. Think how you might turn the question into part of the answer._ Tell me your idea for a topic sentence._ (Example sentence: A number of things would happen to you and your daily activities if your white blood cells were weakened or destroyed.) Take out a piece of paper and write your topic sentence._ (Move around the room and monitor as students write.)
5. You are ready to add ideas to your paragraph. Use evidence from the article as well as your own experience and background knowledge. If you finish early, reread your paragraph and edit it so that it is easy to understand and clear._ (Move around the room and monitor as students write.)
6. Read your paragraph to your partner._
7. If you included wording from the question in your answer and added evidence from the article, award yourself four points for writing._

APPLICATION LESSON
5

ACTIVITY H *Comprehension—Single-Paragraph Answer*

Writing Strategy—Single-Paragraph Answer

Step 1: Read the item.
Step 2: Turn the question into part of the answer and write it down.
Step 3: Think of the answer or locate the answer in the article.
Step 4: Complete your answer.

Prompt:
What Is–A healthy cardiovascular system is critical to a person's overall health.

What If–What would happen to you and your daily activities if your white blood cells were weakened or destroyed?

Write and Discuss: Write a paragraph. Then share your ideas. Use the Discussion Guidelines.

Discussion Guidelines

Speaker		Listener	
Looks like:	**Sounds like:**	**Looks like:**	**Sounds like:**
• Facing peers • Making eye contact • Participating	• Using pleasant, easy-to-hear voice • Sharing opinions, supporting facts and reasons from the article and from your experience • Staying on the topic	• Facing speaker • Making eye contact • Participating	• Waiting quietly to speak • Giving positive, supportive comments • Disagreeing respectfully

74 *REWARDS Plus: Reading Strategies Applied to Science Passages*

8. (Engage students in a discussion. Award four points to students who are active participants in the discussion.)
9. (Distribute Appendix A Reproducible 5: Discussion Guidelines. Have students place this in a notebook or a folder for future reference.)

Note H-2: If your students are having difficulty writing the *What If* paragraphs, read or show them the following example paragraph:

Example Single-Paragraph Answer

If your white blood cells were weakened or destroyed, a number of things could happen to you and your daily activities. First, your body would be unable to fight infection effectively. You would be much more likely to contract colds and the flu, as well as more serious diseases. In addition, cuts and other injuries would have a more difficult time healing. As a result, you would have to change your life activities. You might have to limit your contact with other people, especially people that were ill, and terminate your participation in public activities such as attending school or sporting events. You might even have to live in a sterile environment where there was no chance of exposure to bacteria.

Application Lesson 6

Materials Needed:

- *Student Book*: Application Lesson 6
- Application Overhead Transparencies 25–29
- Appendix A Reproducible 6: Writing Strategy—Multi-Paragraph Answer
- Appendix B Reproducible F: Application Lesson 6
- Appendix C Optional Vocabulary Activity: Application Lesson 6
- Paper or cardboard to use when covering the overhead transparency
- Paper or cardboard for each student to use during spelling dictation
- Washable overhead transparency pen

Text Treatment Notes:

- Black text signifies teacher script (exact wording to say to students).
- Green text in parentheses signifies directions or prompts for the teacher.
- Green text signifies answers or examples of answers.
- Green graphics treatment signifies reproduction of Overhead information.
- Green text and green graphics treatment do not appear in the *Student Book*.

ACTIVITY A
Vocabulary

ACTIVITY PROCEDURE, List 1

(See the *Student Book*, page 75.)

Tell students each word in the list. Then, have students repeat the word and read the definition aloud. For each definition, provide any additional information that may be necessary. Then, have students practice reading the words themselves.

Use Overhead 25: Activity A
List 1: Tell

1. (Show the top half of Overhead 25.) Before we read the passage, let's read the difficult words. (Point to **patients**.) The first word is **patients**. What word?_ Now, read the definition._
2. (Point to **medicines**.) The next word is **medicines**. What word?_ Now, read the definition._
3. (Pronounce each word in List 1, and then have students repeat each word and read the definition.)
4. Open your *Student Book* to **Application Lesson 6**, page 75._
5. Find **Activity A**, **List 1**, in your book._ Let's read the words again. First word._ Next word._ (Continue for all words in List 1.)

ACTIVITY PROCEDURE, List 2

(See the *Student Book*, page 75.)

Have students circle prefixes and suffixes, then underline the vowels. Using the overhead transparency, assist students in checking their work. Next, have students figure out each word to themselves, then say it aloud. Have them read the definition aloud.

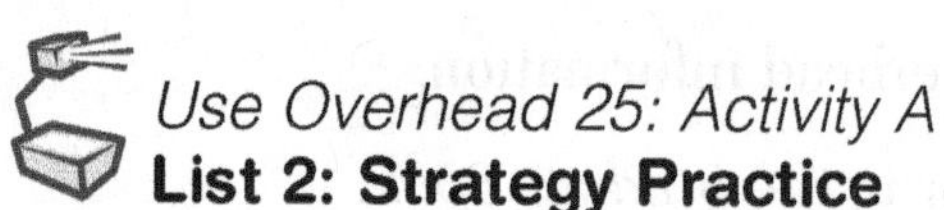

Use Overhead 25: Activity A
List 2: Strategy Practice

1. Find **List 2**. Circle the prefixes and suffixes, and underline the vowels. Look up when you are done._
2. (Show the bottom half of Overhead 25.) Now, check and fix any mistakes._
3. Go back to the first word._ Sound out the word to yourself. Put your thumb up when you can read the

APPLICATION LESSON **6**

ACTIVITY A *Vocabulary*

List 1: Tell

1.	patients	*n.*	▶ (people under a doctor's care)
2.	medicines	*n.*	▶ (drugs or other substances used to treat disease or to relieve pain)
3.	procedure	*n.*	▶ (a course of action with steps in a definite order)
4.	recipient	*n.*	▶ (a person who receives)
5.	anesthetic	*n.*	▶ (a drug or other substance that causes loss of feeling, especially pain)
6.	efficiently	*adv.*	▶ (getting the desired result with as little effort as possible)
7.	foreign	*adj.*	▶ (not belonging to)

List 2: Strategy Practice

1.	generosity	*n.*	▶ (willingness to give or share freely)
2.	incompatible	*adj.*	▶ (not able to work together or get along with)
3.	suitable	*adj.*	▶ (meets the requirements of)
4.	surgery	*n.*	▶ (the removal or repair of injured or diseased parts of the body)
5.	suture	*v.*	▶ (to stitch together the edges of a cut or wound)
6.	consciousness	*n.*	▶ (the state of being awake)
7.	susceptible	*adj.*	▶ (easily affected)
8.	immune	*adj.*	▶ (protected from a disease or infection)
9.	medications	*n.*	▶ (substances used to treat diseases)
10.	gradually	*adv.*	▶ (little by little; slowly)

TALLY [ ] VOCABULARY 5 *Points*

Student Book: Application Lesson 6 75

word. Be sure that it is a real word._ What word?_ Now, read the definition._

4. (Continue Step 3 with all remaining words in List 2.)

Note A.2-1: You may wish to provide additional practice by having students read words to a partner.

ACTIVITY PROCEDURE, List 1 and 2

(See the *Student Book*, page 75.)

Tell students to look in List 1 or List 2 for a word you are thinking about. Have them circle the number of the word and tell you the word. Explain to students to make a tally mark for each correct word in the Tally box, and then enter the number of tally marks as points in the blank half of the Vocabulary box.

1. Remember, the words I'm thinking about will be in either List 1 or List 2. For every word you correctly identify, make a tally mark in the Tally box. If you don't identify the correct word, don't do anything.
2. Circle the number of the appropriate word.
   - If you are willing to give and to share freely with other people, you are said to have this. (Wait.) What word? **generosity**

- When two people cannot get along or work together they are said to be this. (Wait.) What word? **incompatible**
- When something happens slowly over time, it happens like this. (Wait.) What word? **gradually**
- People who are under the care of a doctor are these. (Wait.) What word? **patients**
- If you get the desired result with as little effort as possible, you are working in this way. (Wait.) What word? **efficiently**

3. Count all the tally marks, and enter that number as points in the blank half of the Vocabulary box.

ACTIVITY PROCEDURE, List 3

(See the *Student Book*, page 76.)

The words in the third list are related. Have students use the *REWARDS* Strategies to figure out the first word in each family. Have them read the definition of the verb and then read nouns and adjectives that are related to that verb.

Use Overhead 26: Activity A
List 3: Word Families

1. Turn to page 76._ Find **Family 1** in **List 3**. Figure out the first word. Use your pencil if you wish. Put your thumb up when you know the word._ What word?_ Read the definition._
2. Look at the noun in Family 1. Figure out the word._ What word?_
3. Look at the adjective in Family 1. Figure out the word._ What word?_
4. (Repeat Steps 1–3 for all word families in List 3.)

Note A.3-1: You may wish to provide additional practice by having students read a word family to the group or to a partner.

Note A.3-2: An additional vocabulary practice activity called Quick Words is provided in Appendix C of this Teacher's Guide. See Appendix C for information about how this optional activity can be used.

APPLICATION LESSON
6

List 3: Word Families

	Verb	Noun	Adjective
Family 1	incorporate (to make part of another thing)	incorporation	incorporated
Family 2	designate (to indicate)	designation	
Family 3	permit (to allow)	permission	permissible
Family 4	donate (to give)	donor donation	
Family 5	commune (to come together)	community	communal

ACTIVITY B *Spelling Dictation*

1. incorporate	4. permit
2. incorporation	5. permission
3. incorporated	6. permissible

SPELLING 6 *Points*

76 *REWARDS Plus: Reading Strategies Applied to Science Passages*

Spelling Dictation

ACTIVITY PROCEDURE

(See the *Student Book*, page 76.)

For each word, tell students the word, then have students say the parts of the word to themselves while they write the word. Using the overhead transparency, assist students in checking their spelling and correcting if they misspelled. Then, have students enter the number of correctly spelled words as points in the blank half of the Spelling box.

Note B-1: Distribute a piece of light cardboard to each of the students.

Use Overhead 26: Activity B

1. Find **Activity B**.
2. The first word is **incorporate**. What word?_ Say the parts in **incorporate** to yourself as you write the word. (Pause and monitor.)
3. (Show **incorporate** on the overhead.) Check **incorporate**. If you misspelled it, cross it out and write it correctly.
4. The second word is **incorporation**. What word?_ Say the parts in **incorporation** to yourself as you write the word. (Pause and monitor.)
5. (Show **incorporation** on the overhead.) Check **incorporation**. If you misspelled it, cross it out and write it correctly.
6. (Repeat the procedures for the words **incorporated**, **permit**, **permission**, and **permissible**.)
7. Count the number of words you spelled correctly, and record that number as points in the blank half of the Spelling box at the bottom of the page.

APPLICATION LESSON

6

List 3: Word Families

	Verb	Noun	Adjective
Family 1	incorporate (to make part of another thing)	incorporation	incorporated
Family 2	designate (to indicate)	designation	
Family 3	permit (to allow)	permission	permissible
Family 4	donate (to give)	donor donation	
Family 5	commune (to come together)	community	communal

ACTIVITY B *Spelling Dictation*

1. incorporate	4. permit
2. incorporation	5. permission
3. incorporated	6. permissible

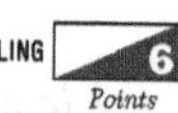

SPELLING 6 Points

76 *REWARDS Plus: Reading Strategies Applied to Science Passages*

ACTIVITY C

Passage Reading and Comprehension

ACTIVITY PROCEDURE

(See the *Student Book,* pages 77–79.)

Have students read the title of the passage and each heading. Ask them to tell their partners two things that the passage will tell about.

Passage Preview

1. Turn to page 77._ Let's preview the passage.
2. Read the title._ What is the whole passage going to tell about?_
3. Now, let's read the headings. Read the first heading._ Read the next heading._ (Continue until students have read all headings.)
4. Turn to your partner. Without looking, tell two things this passage will tell about._

ACTIVITY PROCEDURE

Provide students with an Information Web from Appendix B. Have students read the passage silently to each embedded number, and then reread the same information orally either to a partner, together as a group, or individually. Ask the corresponding comprehension question or questions. Once students finish reading a section labeled A, B, C, or D, have them fill in the Information Web before going on to the next section.

Note C-1: If students do not finish reading the passage during class, have them use their Information Webs to review the information at the beginning of the next class.

Use Overhead 27: Activity C

Passage Reading

1. (Provide an Information Web for each student.)
2. Turn back to the beginning of the passage. You're going to read the passage and answer questions about what you've read. During passage reading, you are also going to fill in an Information Web to help you remember the important details of the passage. Later, you'll use this Web to review the content of the passage with your partner.
3. Read the title._

APPLICATION LESSON 6

ACTIVITY C *Passage Reading and Comprehension*

Note: For this activity, you will need Reproducible F found in the *Teacher's Guide.*

Heart Transplants

A
In the last lesson, you read about the cardiovascular system. This organ
12 system is one of several systems that perform specific life functions. Organ
24 systems consist of organs and tissues that work together to perform specific jobs.
37 However, organs such as the heart, liver, kidneys, or lungs can become diseased
50 and unable to perform their job efficiently, leading to life-threatening illnesses.
62 When a person's life is threatened because of a weakened or damaged organ, an
76 organ transplant can be performed. In this article, you will read about one type
90 of organ transplant, the **heart transplant**, the first of which was completed in
103 December 1967. At that time, it was an extremely experimental procedure.
114 Today, however, heart transplants save thousands of lives each year. (#1)

124 **Who Is Eligible for a New Heart?**
131 Heart disease is one of the leading causes of death among both men and
145 women. Doctors prescribe many types of medicines to people who have heart
157 disease; however, when a person's heart is failing in spite of all other therapies,
171 that person may become a candidate for a heart transplant. Generally, the
183 patients should be under 60 and in good health other than having advanced
196 heart disease. People who have other health problems may not be eligible for a
210 transplant. Because their immune system is weakened during the transplant
220 procedure, people with an already weak immune system or other health
231 problems would be too susceptible to, or too likely to get, an infection. (#2)

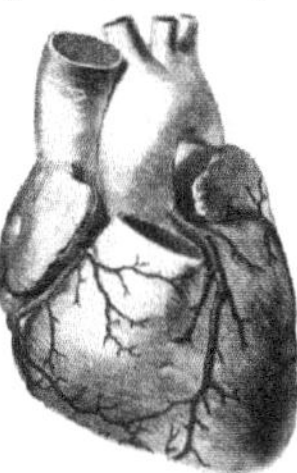

Student Book: Application Lesson 6 77

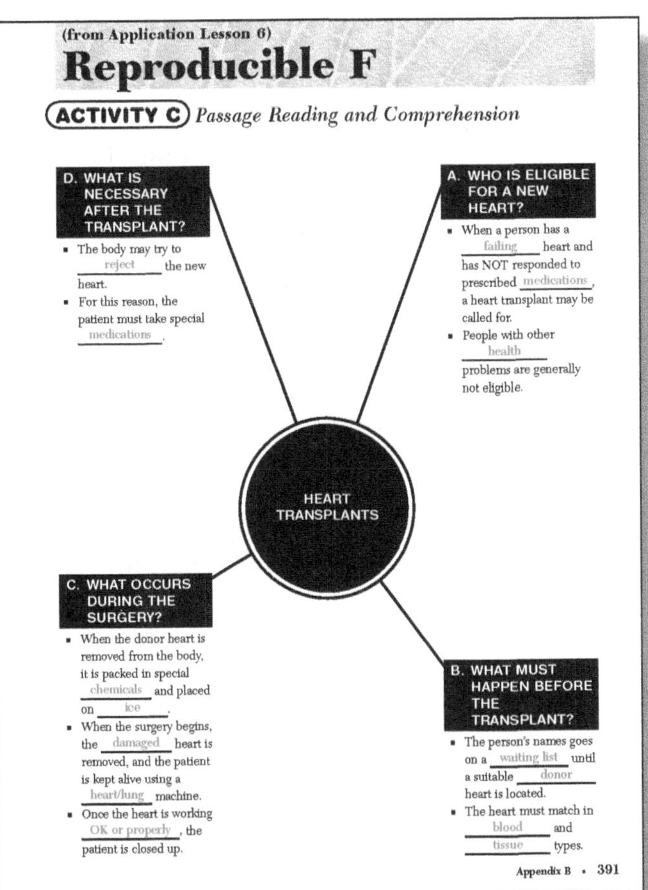

(from Application Lesson 6)

Reproducible F

ACTIVITY C *Passage Reading and Comprehension*

HEART TRANSPLANTS

A. WHO IS ELIGIBLE FOR A NEW HEART?
- When a person has a failing heart and has NOT responded to prescribed medications, a heart transplant may be called for.
- People with other health problems are generally not eligible.

B. WHAT MUST HAPPEN BEFORE THE TRANSPLANT?
- The person's names goes on a waiting list until a suitable donor heart is located.
- The heart must match in blood and tissue types.

C. WHAT OCCURS DURING THE SURGERY?
- When the donor heart is removed from the body, it is packed in special chemicals and placed on ice.
- When the surgery begins, the damaged heart is removed, and the patient is kept alive using a heart/lung machine.
- Once the heart is working OK or properly, the patient is closed up.

D. WHAT IS NECESSARY AFTER THE TRANSPLANT?
- The body may try to reject the new heart.
- For this reason, the patient must take special medications.

Appendix B • 391

4. Find number 1 in the passage. (Pause). Read down to number 1 silently. Look up when you are done.
5. (Wait for students to complete the reading. Then have students reread the part by having them read orally to a partner, read together orally as a group, or read aloud individually.)
6. (Ask the question or questions associated with the number. Provide feedback to students regarding their answers.)
7. (Repeat steps 4–6 for all paragraphs in Section A.)
8. Now, look at your Information Web. Find the section labeled A. The information you've just read will help you to fill in this Web.
9. With your partner, fill in the blanks for Section A. You can refer back to the passage for information. Look up when you're done. (Move around the room and monitor students as they complete the section.)
10. (When the majority of students have finished, show Overhead 27). Look at the overhead and check your work. Fix up or add to any of your answers.
11. Now read down to the next number silently. Look up when you are done.
12. (Repeat steps 5–11 until the students have finished the passage and the Information Web.)
13. Now use your Information Web to retell the important information from the passage to your partner.

Comprehension Questions

#1 When would doctors consider performing an organ transplant?

When a person's life is threatened because of a weakened or damaged organ.

#2 Who is a good candidate for a heart transplant? Who may not be eligible?

Good candidates are people whose hearts are failing despite trying all other therapies, in good health, and under 60 years of age. Individuals may not be eligible who have other health problems or weak immune systems, leaving them more susceptible to infections.

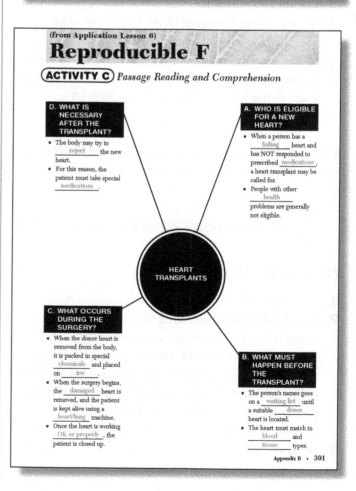

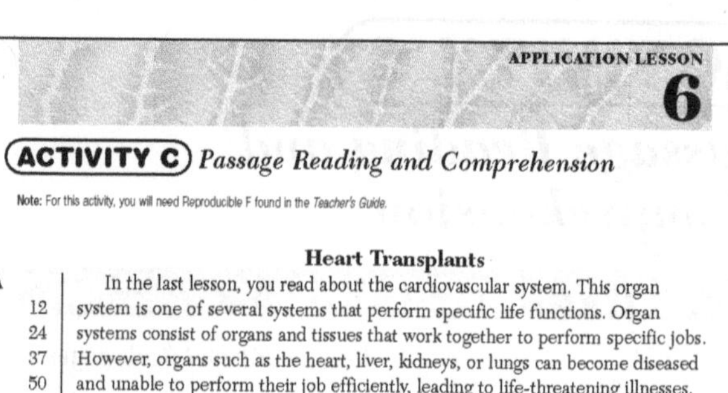
APPLICATION LESSON 6

ACTIVITY C *Passage Reading and Comprehension*

Note: For this activity, you will need Reproducible F found in the *Teacher's Guide.*

Heart Transplants

A
In the last lesson, you read about the cardiovascular system. This organ
12 system is one of several systems that perform specific life functions. Organ
24 systems consist of organs and tissues that work together to perform specific jobs.
37 However, organs such as the heart, liver, kidneys, or lungs can become diseased
50 and unable to perform their job efficiently, leading to life-threatening illnesses.
62 When a person's life is threatened because of a weakened or damaged organ, an
76 organ transplant can be performed. In this article, you will read about one type
90 of organ transplant, the **heart transplant**, the first of which was completed in
103 December 1967. At that time, it was an extremely experimental procedure.
114 Today, however, heart transplants save thousands of lives each year. (#1)

124 **Who Is Eligible for a New Heart?**
131 Heart disease is one of the leading causes of death among both men and
145 women. Doctors prescribe many types of medicines to people who have heart
157 disease; however, when a person's heart is failing in spite of all other therapies,
171 that person may become a candidate for a heart transplant. Generally, the
183 patients should be under 60 and in good health other than having advanced
196 heart disease. People who have other health problems may not be eligible for a
210 transplant. Because their immune system is weakened during the transplant
220 procedure, people with an already weak immune system or other health
231 problems would be too susceptible to, or too likely to get, an infection. (#2)

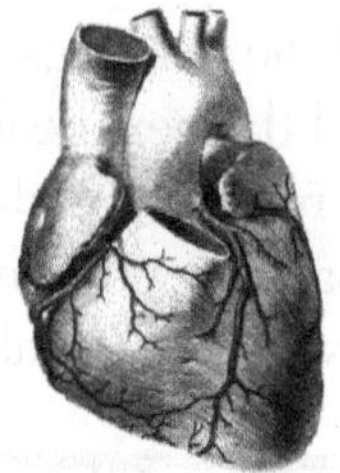

Student Book: Application Lesson 6 77

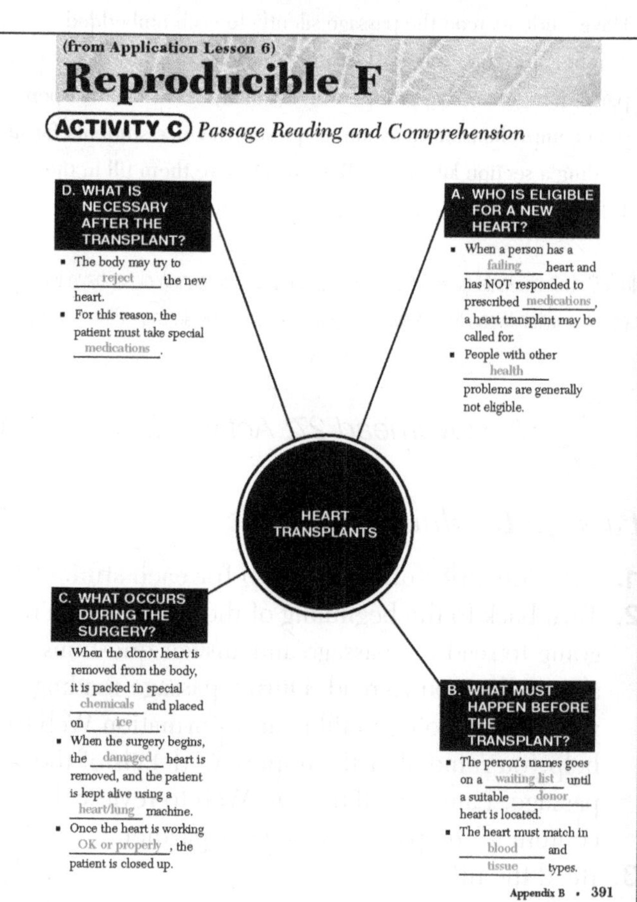
(from Application Lesson 6)

Reproducible F

ACTIVITY C *Passage Reading and Comprehension*

HEART TRANSPLANTS

A. WHO IS ELIGIBLE FOR A NEW HEART?
- When a person has a failing heart and has NOT responded to prescribed medications, a heart transplant may be called for.
- People with other health problems are generally not eligible.

B. WHAT MUST HAPPEN BEFORE THE TRANSPLANT?
- The person's names goes on a waiting list until a suitable donor heart is located.
- The heart must match in blood and tissue types.

C. WHAT OCCURS DURING THE SURGERY?
- When the donor heart is removed from the body, it is packed in special chemicals and placed on ice.
- When the surgery begins, the damaged heart is removed, and the patient is kept alive using a heart/lung machine.
- Once the heart is working OK or properly, the patient is closed up.

D. WHAT IS NECESSARY AFTER THE TRANSPLANT?
- The body may try to reject the new heart.
- For this reason, the patient must take special medications.

Appendix B • 391

#3 From where do donor hearts come?
Most often from people who are brain dead and who have specified to their family and friends that they will donate if they die.

#4 Why do people have to wait a long time for a transplant?
Have to wait for a heart that matches their tissue and blood types; there also aren't as many designated donors as needed.

#5 Once a donor heart is removed, how do the doctors help preserve it before surgery?
Pack it in special chemicals and pack it in an ice cooler for transport.

#6 How do doctors keep the recipient's blood flowing through the body while the heart is removed during surgery?
Connect the recipient to a heart-lung machine that allows oxygen and blood to continue to flow through the body during surgery.

#7 What do recipients take to help their body accept the new organ?
Special medications to prevent the body from rejecting the heart.

APPLICATION LESSON
6

B

244 **What Must Happen Before the Transplant?**
250 Once a patient is accepted for a transplant, their name goes on a waiting list.
265 They must wait until a suitable donor heart is located. Donor hearts usually
278 come from people who are brain dead. This means that their brains no longer
292 function, but their bodies do. Their organs, including their heart, are still
304 healthy. **Donors** are people who have specified to their family and friends that
317 they are willing to donate organs when they die. Doctors must have this
330 permission in order to use donor organs for transplants. (#3)
339 People on the waiting list must wait until a heart becomes available that
352 matches their blood and tissue type. Except when organs are donated from an
365 identical twin, donor organs will be somewhat incompatible with those of the
377 recipient. Nevertheless, it is important to find a heart that is as similar to the
392 recipient's blood and tissue type as possible.
399 Unfortunately, the waiting list is a major barrier to people receiving needed
411 transplants. The list is long, and not enough donor organs are available. The
424 medical community is trying to educate people about how important it is to
437 designate themselves as organ donors before they die so that more people will
450 choose to be organ donors. (#4)

C

455 **What Occurs During the Surgery?**
460 When a suitable donor is found, the donor heart is removed from the body
474 and packed in special chemicals that will help to preserve the heart while in
488 transport. It is then packed in a cooler of ice and quickly brought to the hospital
504 where the transplant patient is prepared for surgery. As soon as the new heart
518 arrives, the surgery begins. (#5)
522 The surgery takes about five hours. First, doctors put the patient to sleep
535 with an anesthetic. Next, they open the patient's chest and remove the diseased
548 heart. Meanwhile, the patient is hooked up to a heart-lung machine. This
561 machine functions as the patient's heart and lungs during surgery, allowing
572 oxygen and blood to continue flowing through the body. It also cools the blood,
586 which protects the other organs. The doctors sew the new heart's blood vessels
599 into the blood vessels in the patient's chest. Once the heart is connected
612 properly, the blood is warmed gradually. The new heart starts to beat. Once the
626 doctors are sure it is working properly, they suture (sew or close up) the patient's
641 chest and bring him or her to the recovery room. Most patients regain
654 consciousness in a few hours, and leave the hospital within a week. (#6)

78 *REWARDS Plus: Reading Strategies Applied to Science Passages*

APPLICATION LESSON
6

D

666 **What Is Necessary After the Transplant?**
672 Heart transplant patients generally return to normal lives. It is, however, very
684 important that they incorporate special medications into their routine. These
694 medications ensure that the body accepts the new heart. Normally, the body's
706 immune system gets rid of or rejects foreign material. Doctors need to prevent the
720 body from rejecting the new heart, which the body experiences as foreign material.
733 Special drugs suppress, or restrain, the patient's immune system. Otherwise, the
744 body might see the new heart as foreign and reject it. As long as these drugs are
761 successful, heart transplant patients are able to continue their lives, thanks to the
774 generosity of people who were willing to share their organs. (#7)
784

Prescription for heart transplant patient

ACTIVITY D *Fluency Building*

Cold Timing		Practice 1	
Practice 2		Hot Timing	

Student Book: Application Lesson 6 79

ACTIVITY D

Fluency Building

ACTIVITY PROCEDURE

(See the *Student Book*, page 79.)

Have students complete a Cold Timing, one or two practices, and a Hot Timing of the Activity C article. For each timing, have students record the number of correct words read. Finally, have students complete their Fluency Graphs.

Note D-1: When assigning partners for this activity, have the stronger reader read first. As a result, the other reader will have one additional practice opportunity.

1. Now, it's time for fluency building.
2. Find the beginning of the passage again. (Pause.)
3. Whisper-read. See how many words you can read in one minute. Begin._ (Time students for one minute.) Stop._ Circle the last word that you read._ Record the number of words you read after **Cold Timing**._
4. Let's practice again. Begin._ (Time students for one minute.) Stop._ Put a box around the last word that you read._ Record the number of words you read after **Practice 1**._
5. (Optional) Let's practice one more time before the Hot Timing. Begin._ (Time students for one minute.) Stop._ Put a box around the last word that you read._ Record the number of words you read after **Practice 2**._
6. Please exchange books with your partner._ Partner 1, you are going to read first. Partner 2, listen carefully and underline any mistakes or words left out. Ones, begin._ (Time students for one minute.) Stop._ Twos, cross out the last word that your partner read._ (Assist students in subtracting the number of mistakes from the number of words read.) Twos, record the number of correct words in your partner's book after **Hot Timing**._
7. Partner 2, you are going to read next. Partner 1, listen carefully and underline any mistakes or words left out. Twos, begin. (Time students for one minute.) Stop._ Ones, cross out the last word that your partner read._ Ones, record the number of correct words in your partner's book after **Hot Timing**._
8. Exchange books._ Turn to the Fluency Graph on the inside back cover, and indicate on the graph the number of Cold Timing and Hot Timing words you read correctly._

D

666 **What Is Necessary After the Transplant?**
672 Heart transplant patients generally return to normal lives. It is, however, very
684 important that they incorporate special medications into their routine. These
694 medications ensure that the body accepts the new heart. Normally, the body's
706 immune system gets rid of or rejects foreign material. Doctors need to prevent the
720 body from rejecting the new heart, which the body experiences as foreign material.
733 Special drugs suppress, or restrain, the patient's immune system. Otherwise, the
744 body might see the new heart as foreign and reject it. As long as these drugs are
761 successful, heart transplant patients are able to continue their lives, thanks to the
774 generosity of people who were willing to share their organs. (#7)
784

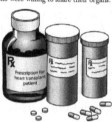

ACTIVITY D *Fluency Building*

Cold Timing		Practice 1	
Practice 2		Hot Timing	

ACTIVITY E

Comprehension Questions—Multiple Choice

ACTIVITY PROCEDURE

(See the *Student Book*, page 80.)

Have students complete item #1. Then, have students share the rationale for their answers. Encourage thoughtful discussion. Proceed item-by-item, emphasizing the rationale for the *best* answer. Have students record points for each correct item.

Note E-1: The correct Multiple Choice answers are circled.

1. Turn to page 80. Find **Activity E**.
2. Use the Multiple Choice Strategy to complete item #1. Be ready to explain why you selected your answer. (Wait while students complete the item. Call on individual students. Ask them why they chose their answer and why they eliminated the other choices. Encourage discussion. Provide students with feedback on their choices, focusing on why or why not those choices might be appropriate.)
3. (Repeat Step 2 for items 2–4, pausing after each item to confirm student responses and provide feedback.)
4. Count the number of items you got correct, and record that number in the blank half of the Multiple Choice Comprehension box.

APPLICATION LESSON

6

ACTIVITY E *Comprehension Questions—Multiple Choice*

Comprehension Strategy—Multiple Choice

Step 1: Read the item.
Step 2: Read all of the choices.
Step 3: Think about why each choice might be correct or incorrect. Check the article as needed.
Step 4: From the possible correct choices, select the best answer.

1. (Cause and effect) **Which person is most likely to be eligible for a heart transplant?**
   a. Pete—a wealthy 80-year-old with lung cancer and a defective heart.
   b. Harry—a 45-year-old with a defective heart and a poor immune system.
   (c.) Rita—a 50-year-old former professional tennis player with advanced heart disease.
   d. Martha—a 52-year-old with high blood pressure who has just started a diet and exercise program.

2. (Compare and contrast) **Which of the following would be an unnecessary requirement for a person to be a heart donor?**
   a. The individual must be brain-dead with organs that are still healthy.
   b. The individual must have blood and tissue types that match closely that of the recipient.
   c. Prior to death, the organ donor must have told friends and family members that he or she wished to be an organ donor.
   (d.) Prior to death, the individual must specify to his or her minister, rabbi, or priest his or her desires.

3. (Vocabulary) **Which of these words is related to the word recipient?**
   a. repent
   (b.) receive
   c. recent
   d. recipe

4. (Main idea) **What is the main idea of this passage?**
   a. The first heart transplants in 1967 were very experimental.
   (b.) Many people with heart disease can live normal lives if they have the benefit of a donated heart and surgery.
   c. A heart donor must be brain-dead and still have a healthy heart that closely matches the blood and tissue types of the recipient.
   d. One of the perils of heart transplants is the possibility that the body might reject an incompatible heart.

MULTIPLE CHOICE COMPREHENSION

4 Points

80 *REWARDS Plus: Reading Strategies Applied to Science Passages*

ACTIVITY F

Vocabulary Activities

ACTIVITY PROCEDURE

(See the *Student Book*, page 81.)

Have students complete each item orally and provide feedback on their answers. Then have students respond to each question in writing by answering "yes" or "no" and providing a reason for their answers.

Yes/No/Why

1. Turn to page 81._ Find **Activity F**._ Read item #1. Tell your partner your answer and your reason for it. (Pause. Then call on individual students. Encourage discussion. Provide students with feedback on their choices, focusing on their explanations for their answer.)
2. Write your answer and your reason for it in the space provided. Look up when you are done._
3. Read item #2. Tell your partner your answer and your reason for it. (Pause. Then call on individual students. Encourage discussion. Provide students with feedback on their choices, focusing on their explanations for their answer.)
4. Write your answer and your reason for it in the space provided. Look up when you are done._
5. Read item #3. Tell your partner your answer and your reason for it. (Pause. Then call on individual students. Encourage discussion. Provide students with feedback on their choices, focusing on their explanations for their answer.)
6. Write your answer and your reason for it in the space provided. Look up when you are done._

Note F-1: You may wish to do this as an oral task only rather than an oral and a written task.

APPLICATION LESSON **6**

ACTIVITY F *Vocabulary Activities*

Yes/No/Why

1. Is **surgery suitable** for most **patients**?
Example answer: No. Most patients do not need surgery when they are ill.

2. If you are **susceptible** to a disease, are you **immune** to it?
Example answer: No. These are opposites. If you are susceptible to a disease, you are easily affected. If you are immune, you are protected from the disease.

3. Is **anesthetic incompatible** with **consciousness**?
Example answer: Yes. If you are under an anesthetic, you are asleep, so you will not be conscious at the same time.

Student Book: Application Lesson 6 81

ACTIVITY PROCEDURE

Have students read the words and definitions and then complete the sentence stems for each vocabulary word. Have them share answers with partners and with the class. Then, have students give themselves points in the blank half of the Vocabulary box.

Completion Activity

1. Turn to page 82. Read the first word and its definition.
2. Now, read the sentence stem.
3. Think of how you would complete the sentence stem and write it. Share your answer with your partner. (Call on a few students to share answers with the class.)
4. (Repeat Steps 1–3 for the rest of the words.)
5. If you participated in answering all seven questions, give yourself seven points in the blank half of the Vocabulary box.

Note F-2: You may wish to do this as an oral task only rather than an oral task and a written task.

APPLICATION LESSON
6

Completion Activities

1. **donation:** something you give
   Some organizations that accept donations are
   Answers will vary.

2. **permitted:** allowed to
   Special events that you are permitted to attend include
   Answers will vary.

3. **gradually:** little by little; slowly
   Some things happen very quickly in life, but these things happen gradually:
   Answers will vary.

4. **generosity:** willingness to give or share freely
   People demonstrate their generosity by
   Answers will vary.

VOCABULARY 7 Points

82 *REWARDS Plus: Reading Strategies Applied to Science Passages*

ACTIVITY G

Expository Writing—Multi-Paragraph Answer

ACTIVITY PROCEDURE, Plan and Write

(See the *Student Book*, pages 83–85.)

Have students read the prompt and the three topics. Have students read the **LIST** of details under topic a, then guide them in adding details for topics b and c. Have students look at topic a again. Explain that details that don't go with a topic should be **CROSSED OUT**. Have students **CONNECT** details as shown in the example plan. Have students **NUMBER** their details in the same manner as in the example plan for topic a. Next, have students **WRITE** paragraph a. Guide students in completing the plan for topic b and writing paragraph b. Repeat for topic c. Finally, explain that after the answer is written, they should **EDIT** their work, revising for clarity and proofreading for errors in capitalization, punctuation, and spelling.

Use Overheads 28 and 29: Activity G

1. Turn to page 83._ Find **Activity G.**_ Today you will write all three paragraphs.
2. Find the prompt in the middle of the page._ Read the prompt out loud with me: **Describe what occurs during each stage of a heart transplant: before surgery, during surgery, and after surgery.**
3. Turn to page 84._ Read topic a._ Read topic b._ Read topic c._
4. Read the details **listed** under topic a._
5. Now, it's your turn to add details to topic b. Look back in the article and locate details that describe what happens during heart transplant surgery. Write the details in the Planning Box._
6. Add details to topic c. Look back in the article and locate details that describe what happens after heart surgery. Write the details in the Planning Box._
7. Let's use the steps for topic a. First, read the details and **cross out** any details that do not go with the topic._ Next, draw brackets to **connect** details that could easily go into one sentence._ Now, **number** the details in a logical order._
8. (Show Overhead 28). Now, look at the example plan for topic a on the overhead. Yours doesn't need to be the same, but it should be similar._

APPLICATION LESSON 6

ACTIVITY G *Expository Writing—Multi-Paragraph Answer*

Writing Strategy—Multi-Paragraph Answer

Step 1: LIST (List the details that are important enough to include in your answer.)
Step 2: CROSS OUT (Reread the details. Cross out any that don't go with the topic.)
Step 3: CONNECT (Connect any details that could go into one sentence.)
Step 4: NUMBER (Number the details in a logical order.)
Step 5: WRITE (Write the paragraph.)
Step 6: EDIT (Revise and proofread your answer.)

Prompt: Describe what occurs during each stage of a heart transplant: before surgery, during surgery, and after surgery.

Plan: Complete the Planning Box with your teacher.

Student Book: Application Lesson 6 83

APPLICATION LESSON 6

Example Multi-Paragraph Plan

Planning Box
(topic a) *before surgery*
① (detail) – *must be eligible*
② (detail) – *eligible—under 60 and otherwise healthy*
③ (detail) – *goes on waiting list*
(detail) – *wait for suitable donor heart*
④ (detail) – *must match blood and tissue type of recipient*
(topic b) *during surgery*
① (detail) – *donor heart removed from body*
② (detail) – *donor heart packed in special chemicals and packed in ice*
(detail) – *transported quickly*
③ (detail) – *recipient is put to sleep*
(detail) – *diseased heart removed*
(detail) – *recipient put on heart-lung machine*
④ (detail) – *new heart is connected to blood vessels*
(detail) – *blood is warmed and heart begins to beat*
⑤ (detail) – *incision is sutured*
(topic c) *after surgery*
① (detail) – *resume a normal life*
(detail) – *must take special medications so his or her body won't reject the heart*
② (detail) – *these drugs suppress the immune system so it won't reject the heart as a foreign material*
(detail) – ~~*wait for a suitable donor*~~

Write: Write paragraphs a, b, and c on a separate piece of paper.

84 *REWARDS Plus: Reading Strategies Applied to Science Passages*

9. Take out a blank piece of paper. Using your plan for paragraph a, **write** paragraph a. If you finish early, please reread and **edit** your paragraph. Don't forget to use the spelling of words in the plan and the article to correct your errors. (Move around the room and monitor your students as they are writing.)
10. (When the majority of students are done, proceed with the lesson.) Now, use the steps for topic b. First, read the details and **cross out** any details that do not go with the topic. Next, draw brackets to **connect** details that could easily go into one sentence. Now, **number** the details in a logical order.
11. Now, look at the example plan for topic b on the overhead. Yours doesn't need to be the same, but it should be similar.
12. Locate your piece of paper. Using your plan for paragraph b, **write** paragraph b. If you finish early, please **edit** your paragraph. (Move around the room and monitor your students as they are writing.)
13. (When the majority of students are done, proceed with the lesson.) Now, use the steps for topic c. First, read the details and **cross out** any details that do not go with the topic. Next, draw brackets to **connect** details that could easily go into one sentence. Now, **number** the details in a logical order.
14. Look at the example plan for topic c on the overhead. Yours doesn't need to be the same, but it should be similar.
15. Locate your piece of paper. Using your plan for paragraph c, **write** paragraph c. If you finish early, please **edit** your paragraph. (Move around the room and monitor your students as they are writing.)
16. (When the majority of students are done, proceed with the lesson.) Now, edit your paragraphs. Please carefully read your paragraphs. Be sure that your paragraphs are clear. Proofread for any errors in capitalization, punctuation, and spelling. (Give students time to proofread their paragraphs.)

APPLICATION LESSON **6**

Evaluate: Evaluate the paragraphs using this rubric.

Rubric—Multi-Paragraph Answer	Student or Partner Rating	Teacher Rating
1. Did the author state the topic in the first sentence?	a. Yes Fix up b. Yes Fix up c. Yes Fix up	a. Yes No b. Yes No c. Yes No
2. Did the author include details that go with the topic?	a. Yes Fix up b. Yes Fix up c. Yes Fix up	a. Yes No b. Yes No c. Yes No
3. Did the author combine details in some of the sentences?	a. Yes Fix up b. Yes Fix up c. Yes Fix up	a. Yes No b. Yes No c. Yes No
4. Is the answer easy to understand?	Yes Fix up	Yes No
5. Did the author correctly spell words, particularly the words found in the article?	Yes Fix up	Yes No
6. Did the author use correct capitalization, capitalizing the first word in the sentence and proper names of people, places, and things?	Yes Fix up	Yes No
7. Did the author use correct punctuation, including a period at the end of each sentence?	Yes Fix up	Yes No

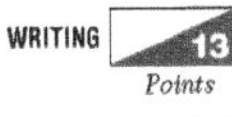

Student Book: Application Lesson 6 85

ACTIVITY PROCEDURE: Evaluate

Ask students to read each question in the rubric. Guide them in evaluating the paragraphs using the guidelines. Have students total their points and record them in the blank half of the Writing box.

17. Turn to page 85. Let's evaluate paragraph a.
18. Read question #1 with me. Circle "Yes" for a if your topic sentence includes the topic, before surgery.
19. Read question #2 with me. Circle "Yes" for a if all of your details tell about what occurs before surgery.
20. Read question #3 with me. Circle "Yes" for a if you combined details into one sentence.
21. Now, check paragraphs b and c carefully and answer questions 1 through 3.
22. Read question #4. Reread your paragraphs. Circle "Yes" if your paragraphs are easy to understand.
23. Read question #5. Carefully examine your paragraphs. If you think a word is misspelled, underline it and check back in the plan or article

and correct the spelling. Circle "Yes" if you believe that you have very few spelling errors.

24. Read question #6. Carefully examine your sentences. Be sure that each sentence begins with a capital. If all sentences begin with a capital, circle "Yes."
25. Read question #7. Examine your sentences. Be sure that each sentence ends with a period. If all sentences end with a period, circle "Yes."
26. Count up your points and record them in the Writing box.
27. (Show Overhead 29). Look at the overhead. Let's read the three example paragraphs. Yours do not have to be the same, but they should be similar. (Read the paragraphs to your students or with your students or call on a student to read the example paragraph.)
28. (Distribute Appendix A Reproducible 6: Writing Strategy—Multi-Paragraph Answer. Have students place this in a notebook or a folder for future reference.)
29. In the next lesson, you will do more of the writing on your own.

Note G-1: The rubric can be used in a variety of ways. Instead of the students evaluating their own paragraphs, you may wish to have their partners provide feedback. The second column is designed for teacher feedback. If you have a small group, it would be useful to give daily feedback on writing. If the group size is large, you can give feedback to a number of children each day. You may wish to give students bonus points based on your feedback.

APPLICATION LESSON **6**

Evaluate: Evaluate the paragraphs using this rubric.

Rubric—Multi-Paragraph Answer	Student or Partner Rating	Teacher Rating
1. Did the author state the topic in the first sentence?	a. (Yes) Fix up b. (Yes) Fix up c. (Yes) Fix up	a. Yes No b. Yes No c. Yes No
2. Did the author include details that go with the topic?	a. (Yes) Fix up b. (Yes) Fix up c. (Yes) Fix up	a. Yes No b. Yes No c. Yes No
3. Did the author combine details in some of the sentences?	a. (Yes) Fix up b. (Yes) Fix up c. (Yes) Fix up	a. Yes No b. Yes No c. Yes No
4. Is the answer easy to understand?	(Yes) Fix up	Yes No
5. Did the author correctly spell words, particularly the words found in the article?	(Yes) Fix up	Yes No
6. Did the author use correct capitalization, capitalizing the first word in the sentence and proper names of people, places, and things?	(Yes) Fix up	Yes No
7. Did the author use correct punctuation, including a period at the end of each sentence?	(Yes) Fix up	Yes No

Student Book: Application Lesson 6 85

ACTIVITY H

Comprehension— Single-Paragraph Answer

ACTIVITY PROCEDURE

(See the *Student Book*, page 86.)

Have students read the *What Is* statement and the *What If* question. Have students turn the question into part of the answer and write down a topic sentence for their answer. Then, have them complete their answer. Encourage them to use evidence from the article and their own experience and background knowledge. Engage students in a discussion. Award points for writing and participating in the discussion.

Note H-1: To increase the quality of the discussion, the students are asked to think and write about the *What If* before the discussion. However, you may be working with students who have difficulty generating ideas for their paragraph. If that is the case, switch the order of activities: engage the students in a discussion, and then have them write their paragraphs.

1. Turn to page 86. Find **Activity H.**
2. Find the *What Is* statement in the middle of the page. Read it out loud with me: **Heart transplants can significantly improve an individual's length and quality of life.**
3. Find the *What If* question. Read it with me: **What would your chances be of being on a heart transplant waiting list IF you smoked, did not exercise, and were overweight? Explain your answer.**
4. Think how you might turn the question into part of the answer. Tell me your idea for a topic sentence. (Example sentence: If you smoked, did not exercise, and were overweight, you would NEVER be on a waiting list for a heart.) Take out a piece of paper and write your topic sentence. (Move around the room and monitor as students write.)
5. You are ready to add ideas to your paragraph. Use evidence from the article, as well as your own experience and background knowledge. If you finish early, reread your paragraph and edit it so that it is easy to understand and clear. (Move around the room and monitor as students write.)
6. Read your paragraph to your partner.
7. If you included wording from the question in your answer and added evidence from the article, award yourself four points for writing.

APPLICATION LESSON
6

ACTIVITY H *Comprehension—Single-Paragraph Answer*

Writing Strategy—Single-Paragraph Answer

Step 1: Read the item.
Step 2: Turn the question into part of the answer and write it down.
Step 3: Think of the answer or locate the answer in the article.
Step 4: Complete your answer.

Prompt:
What Is—Heart transplants can significantly improve an individual's length and quality of life.

What If—What would your chances be of being on a heart transplant waiting list IF you smoked, did not exercise, and were overweight? Explain your answer.

Write and Discuss: Write a paragraph. Then share your ideas. Use the Discussion Guidelines.

Discussion Guidelines

Speaker		Listener	
Looks like:	**Sounds like:**	**Looks like:**	**Sounds like:**
• Facing peers • Making eye contact • Participating	• Using pleasant, easy-to-hear voice • Sharing opinions, supporting facts and reasons from the article and from your experience • Staying on the topic	• Facing speaker • Making eye contact • Participating	• Waiting quietly to speak • Giving positive, supportive comments • Disagreeing respectfully

WRITING 4 Points DISCUSSION 4 Points

86 *REWARDS Plus: Reading Strategies Applied to Science Passages*

8. (Engage students in a discussion. Award four points to students who are active participants in the discussion.)

Note H-2: If your students are having difficulty writing the *What If* paragraphs, read or show them the following example paragraph:

Example Single-Paragraph Answer

If you smoked, did not exercise, and were overweight, you certainly would be more likely to suffer from heart disease. However, you would never find your name on a heart waiting list because you must be healthy in other ways to make the success of the transplant more probable. If you were a stationary, overweight person who smokes, you would be very unlikely to be healthy in all other ways, making you ineligible for a transplant.

Application Lesson 7

Materials Needed:

- *Student Book*: Application Lesson 7
- Application Overhead Transparencies 30–34
- Appendix A Reproducible 7: Rubric—Multi-Paragraph Answer
- Appendix B Reproducible G: Application Lesson 7
- Appendix C Optional Vocabulary Activity: Application Lesson 7
- Paper or cardboard to use when covering the overhead transparency
- Paper or cardboard for each student to use during spelling dictation
- Washable overhead transparency pen

Text Treatment Notes:

- Black text signifies teacher script (exact wording to say to students).
- Green text in parentheses signifies directions or prompts for the teacher.
- Green text signifies answers or examples of answers.
- Green graphics treatment signifies reproduction of Overhead information.
- Green text and green graphics treatment do not appear in the *Student Book*.

ACTIVITY A

Vocabulary

ACTIVITY PROCEDURE, List 1

(See the *Student Book*, page 87.)

Tell students each word in the list. Then, have students repeat the word and read the definition aloud. For each definition, provide any additional information that may be necessary. Then, have students practice reading the words themselves.

Use Overhead 30: Activity A
List 1: Tell

1. (Show the top half of Overhead 30.) Before we read the passage, let's read the difficult words. (Point to **virus**.) The first word is **virus**. What word?_ Now, read the definition._
2. (Point to **polyhedral**.) The next word is **polyhedral**. What word?_ Now, read the definition._
3. (Pronounce each word in List 1, and then have students repeat each word and read the definition.)
4. Open your *Student Book* to **Application Lesson 7**, page 87._
5. Find **Activity A**, **List 1**, in your book._ Let's read the words again. First word._ Next word._ (Continue for all words in List 1.)

ACTIVITY PROCEDURE, List 2

(See the *Student Book*, page 87.)

Have students circle prefixes and suffixes, then underline the vowels. Using the overhead transparency, assist students in checking their work. Next, have students figure out each word to themselves, then say it aloud. Have them read the definition aloud.

Use Overhead 30: Activity A
List 2: Strategy Practice

1. Find **List 2**. Circle the prefixes and suffixes, and underline the vowels. Look up when you are done._
2. (Show the bottom half of Overhead 30.) Before you check your work on List 2, look at item #6. (Point to the second example and the **as** that is circled.) From now on, you can circle **as**. The prefix is /as/. Say it._ Now, go back to item #1. Check and fix any mistakes._
3. Go back to the first word again._ Sound out the word to yourself. Put your thumb up when you can read the word. Be sure that it is a real word._ What word?_ Now, read the definition._
4. (Continue Step 3 with all remaining words in List 2.)

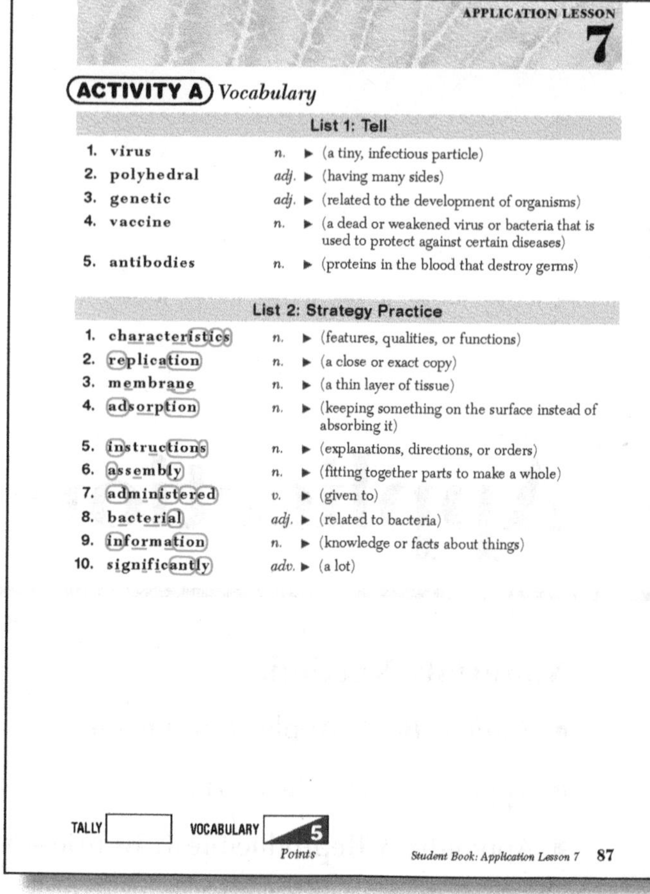

APPLICATION LESSON 7

ACTIVITY A Vocabulary

List 1: Tell

1.	virus	n.	▶ (a tiny, infectious particle)
2.	polyhedral	adj.	▶ (having many sides)
3.	genetic	adj.	▶ (related to the development of organisms)
4.	vaccine	n.	▶ (a dead or weakened virus or bacteria that is used to protect against certain diseases)
5.	antibodies	n.	▶ (proteins in the blood that destroy germs)

List 2: Strategy Practice

1.	characteristics	n.	▶ (features, qualities, or functions)
2.	replication	n.	▶ (a close or exact copy)
3.	membrane	n.	▶ (a thin layer of tissue)
4.	adsorption	n.	▶ (keeping something on the surface instead of absorbing it)
5.	instructions	n.	▶ (explanations, directions, or orders)
6.	assembly	n.	▶ (fitting together parts to make a whole)
7.	administered	v.	▶ (given to)
8.	bacterial	adj.	▶ (related to bacteria)
9.	information	n.	▶ (knowledge or facts about things)
10.	significantly	adv.	▶ (a lot)

TALLY VOCABULARY 5 Points

Student Book: Application Lesson 7 87

Note A.2-1: You may wish to provide additional practice by having students read words to a partner.

ACTIVITY PROCEDURE, List 1 and 2

(See the *Student Book*, page 87.)

Tell students to look in List 1 or List 2 for a word you are thinking about. Have them circle the number of the word and tell you the word. Explain to students to make a tally mark for each correct word in the Tally box, and then enter the number of tally marks as points in the blank half of the Vocabulary box.

1. Remember, the words I'm thinking about will be in either List 1 or List 2. For every word you correctly identify, make a tally mark in the Tally box. If you don't identify the correct word, don't do anything.
2. Circle the number of the appropriate word.
   - The features or qualities of things are known as these. (Wait.) What word? **characteristics**
   - When someone gives directions or explanations, they are giving you these. (Wait.) What word? **instructions**
   - If you were to make an exact copy of a picture, you would be making this. (Wait.) What word? **replication**
   - If a situation changes a lot, it is said to change in this way. (Wait.) What word? **significantly**
   - If you have a lot of knowledge or facts about things, you have this. (Wait.) What word? **information**
3. Count all the tally marks, and enter that number as points in the blank half of the Vocabulary box.

ACTIVITY PROCEDURE, List 3

(See the *Student Book*, page 88.)

The words in the third list are related. Have students use the *REWARDS* Strategies to figure out the first word in each family. Have them read the definition of the verb and then read nouns and adjectives that are related to that verb.

Use Overhead 31: Activity A
List 3: Word Families

1. Turn to page 88._ Find **Family 1** in **List 3**. Figure out the first word. Use your pencil if you wish. Put your thumb up when you know the word._ What word?_ Read the definition._
2. Look at the nouns in Family 1. Figure out the first word._ What word?_ Next word._ What word?_
3. Look at the adjective in Family 1. Figure out the word._ What word?_
4. (Repeat Steps 1–3 for all word families in List 3.)

APPLICATION LESSON
7

List 3: Word Families

	Verb	Noun	Adjective
Family 1	develop (to grow and change)	development developer	developmental
Family 2	reproduce (to produce others of the same kind)	reproduction	reproducible
Family 3	infect (to cause disease in)	infection	infectious
Family 4	invade (to enter and overrun)	invasion invader	
Family 5	detect (to find out or discover)	detection detective	detectable

ACTIVITY B *Spelling Dictation*

1. reproduce	4. infect
2. reproduction	5. infection
3. reproducible	6. infectious

SPELLING 6 *Points*

88 *REWARDS Plus: Reading Strategies Applied to Science Passages*

Note A.3-1: You may wish to provide additional practice by having students read a word family to the group or to a partner.

Note A.3-2: An additional vocabulary practice activity called Quick Words is provided in Appendix C of this Teacher's Guide. See Appendix C for information about how this optional activity can be used.

ACTIVITY B

Spelling Dictation

ACTIVITY PROCEDURE

(See the *Student Book*, page 88.)

For each word, tell students the word, then have students say the parts of the word to themselves while they write the word. Using the overhead transparency, assist students in checking their spelling and correcting if they misspelled. Then, have students enter the number of correctly spelled words as points in the blank half of the Spelling box.

Note B-1: Distribute a piece of light cardboard to each of the students.

Use Overhead 31: Activity B

1. Find **Activity B**.
2. The first word is **reproduce**. What word?_ Say the parts in **reproduce** to yourself as you write the word. (Pause and monitor.)
3. (Show **reproduce** on the overhead.) Check **reproduce**. If you misspelled it, cross it out and write it correctly.
4. The second word is **reproduction**. What word?_ Say the parts in **reproduction** to yourself as you write the word. (Pause and monitor.)
5. (Show **reproduction** on the overhead.) Check **reproduction**. If you misspelled it, cross it out and write it correctly.
6. (Repeat the procedures for the words **reproducible**, **infect**, **infection,** and **infectious**.)
7. Count the number of words you spelled correctly, and record that number as points in the blank half of the Spelling box at the bottom of the page.

APPLICATION LESSON **7**

List 3: Word Families

	Verb	Noun	Adjective
Family 1	develop (to grow and change)	development developer	developmental
Family 2	reproduce (to produce others of the same kind)	reproduction	reproducible
Family 3	infect (to cause disease in)	infection	infectious
Family 4	invade (to enter and overrun)	invasion invader	
Family 5	detect (to find out or discover)	detection detective	detectable

ACTIVITY B *Spelling Dictation*

1. reproduce	4. infect
2. reproduction	5. infection
3. reproducible	6. infectious

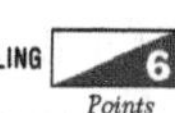

SPELLING 6 *Points*

88 *REWARDS Plus: Reading Strategies Applied to Science Passages*

ACTIVITY C

Passage Reading and Comprehension

ACTIVITY PROCEDURE

(See the *Student Book*, pages 89–91.)

Have students read the title of the passage and each heading. Ask them to tell their partners two things that the passage will tell about.

Passage Preview

1. Turn to page 89._ Let's preview the passage.
2. Read the title._ What is the whole passage going to tell about?_
3. Now, let's read the headings. Read the first heading._ Read the next heading._ (Continue until students have read all headings.)
4. Turn to your partner. Without looking, tell two things this passage will tell about._

ACTIVITY PROCEDURE

Provide students with an Information Web from Appendix B. Have students read the passage silently to each embedded number, and then reread the same information orally either to a partner, together as a group, or individually. Ask the corresponding comprehension question or questions. Once students finish reading a section labeled A, B, C, or D, have them fill in the Information Web before going on to the next section.

Note C-1: If students do not finish reading the passage during class, have them use their Information Webs to review the information at the beginning of the next class.

Use Overhead 32: Activity C

Passage Reading

1. (Provide an Information Web for each student.)
2. Turn back to the beginning of the passage. You're going to read the passage and answer questions about what you've read. During passage reading, you are also going to fill in an Information Web to help you remember the important details of the passage. Later, you'll use this Web to review the content of the passage with your partner.
3. Read the title._

APPLICATION LESSON **7**

ACTIVITY C *Passage Reading and Comprehension*

Note: For this activity, you will need Reproducible G found in the *Teacher's Guide*.

Viruses

A
Have you ever had a cold or the flu? The coughing and sneezing, aches and
15 fevers are all the work of a tiny virus living inside some of your body's cells. How
32 can such a tiny thing cause you to feel so awful?

43 **What Are Viruses?**
46 All living things, like plants and animals, share common behaviors that
57 include growing, developing, reproducing, and responding to surroundings.
65 Things that do not share these behaviors are nonliving things such as air, metal,
79 and sand. Perched between the boundary of living and nonliving things are
91 **viruses**, which are tiny, infectious particles that are considered by some scientists
103 to be living things and by others to be nonliving things. If viruses are floating
118 around in the air or sitting on a kitchen counter, they are inert, having as much
134 life as a rock. However, unlike nonliving things, viruses can live and reproduce.
147 When they attach to a suitable plant, animal, or bacterial cell, referred to as a
162 **host cell**, they infect and take over the cell. To live and to reproduce, they must
178 invade a host cell and use it. (#1)
185 Viruses are not cells even though they have some substances also found in cells.
199 Viruses are particles that are about a thousand times smaller than bacteria. These
212 tiny particles contain genetic instructions that give the virus its characteristics,
223 such as shape and how to reproduce. Viruses are wrapped in a protein coat. Some
238 types of viruses also have a membrane around the protein. (#2)

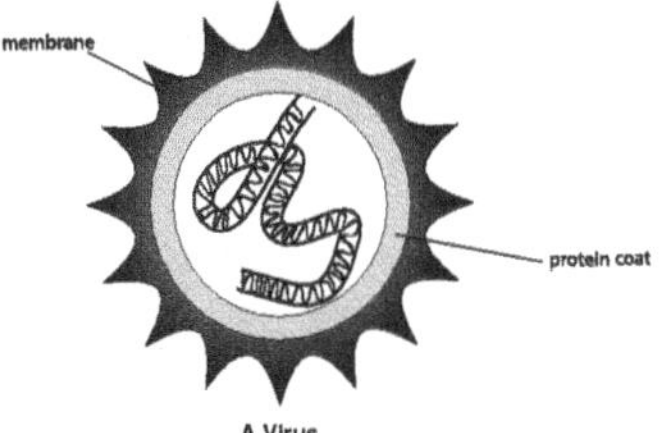

A Virus

Student Book: Application Lesson 7 89

(from Application Lesson 7)

Reproducible G

ACTIVITY C *Passage Reading and Comprehension*

VIRUSES

A. WHAT ARE VIRUSES?
- Viruses have some characteristics of living things and nonliving things.
- In some cases, viruses are inert, but they can live and reproduce.
- To live and reproduce, viruses must invade a host cell and use it.
- Viruses are NOT cells but have genetic instructions.

B. HOW DO YOU GET INFECTED?
- Different viruses need different host cells.
- The protein coat helps the virus detect the right kind of host cell.
- In adsorption, the virus attaches to the outside of a host cell.
- In entry, the virus injects genetic information into the host cell.
- During replication and assembly, the host cell's enzymes obey the virus's genetic instructions.
- During release, new virus particles leave the host cell in search of new host cells.

C. WHAT DO VIRUSES LOOK LIKE?
- Viruses are smaller than most bacteria cells.
- Viruses can only be observed using electron microscopes.
- Viruses have different shapes.
- One common virus is shaped like a spaceship.

D. HOW CAN WE BE PROTECTED FROM VIRUSES?
- To reduce the spread of viruses, individuals should cover their mouths with a tissue when coughing, and they should wash their hands.
- In some cases, a vaccine can prevent the virus from infecting individuals.
- Vaccines promote the production of antibodies within the body.
- Because the genetic code in viruses can change, vaccines also have to be altered.

392 • REWARDS Plus: Reading Strategies Applied to Science Passages

4. Find number 1 in the passage. (Pause). Read down to number 1 silently. Look up when you are done._
5. (Wait for students to complete the reading. Then have students reread the part by having them read orally to a partner, read together orally as a group, or read aloud individually.)
6. (Ask the question or questions associated with the number. Provide feedback to students regarding their answers.)
7. (Repeat steps 4–6 for all paragraphs in Section A.)
8. Now, look at your Information Web. Find the section labeled A._ The information you've just read will help you to fill in this Web.
9. With your partner, fill in the blanks for Section A. You can refer back to the passage for information. Look up when you're done._ (Move around the room and monitor students as they complete the section.)
10. (When the majority of students have finished, show Overhead 32.) Look at the overhead and check your work. Fix up or add to any of your answers.
11. Now read down to the next number silently. Look up when you are done._
12. (Repeat steps 5–11 until the students have finished the passage and the Information Web.)
13. Now use your Information Web to retell the important information from the passage to your partner.

Comprehension Questions

#1 Do scientists consider viruses living or nonliving things? Why?

Both living and nonliving; if viruses are floating around in the air, they are inert, thus nonliving; if they attach to a suitable plant or animal (host), they invade it and use it, and thus they are living.

#2 What do the genetic instructions tell the virus?

What shape to have and how to reproduce.

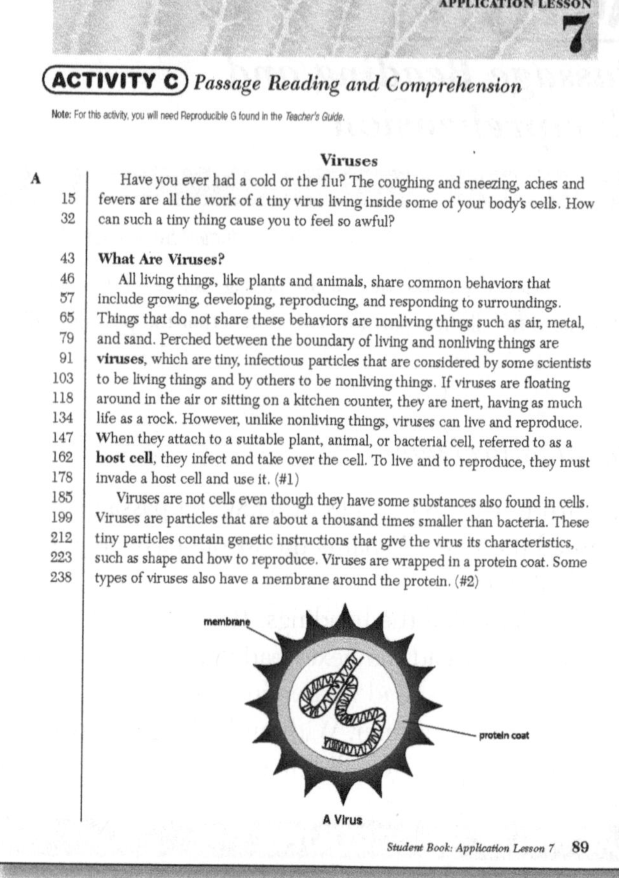

APPLICATION LESSON 7

ACTIVITY C *Passage Reading and Comprehension*

Note: For this activity, you will need Reproducible G found in the *Teacher's Guide*.

Viruses

A

Have you ever had a cold or the flu? The coughing and sneezing, aches and fevers are all the work of a tiny virus living inside some of your body's cells. How can such a tiny thing cause you to feel so awful?

What Are Viruses?

All living things, like plants and animals, share common behaviors that include growing, developing, reproducing, and responding to surroundings. Things that do not share these behaviors are nonliving things such as air, metal, and sand. Perched between the boundary of living and nonliving things are **viruses**, which are tiny, infectious particles that are considered by some scientists to be living things and by others to be nonliving things. If viruses are floating around in the air or sitting on a kitchen counter, they are inert, having as much life as a rock. However, unlike nonliving things, viruses can live and reproduce. When they attach to a suitable plant, animal, or bacterial cell, referred to as a **host cell**, they infect and take over the cell. To live and to reproduce, they must invade a host cell and use it. (#1)

Viruses are not cells even though they have some substances also found in cells. Viruses are particles that are about a thousand times smaller than bacteria. These tiny particles contain genetic instructions that give the virus its characteristics, such as shape and how to reproduce. Viruses are wrapped in a protein coat. Some types of viruses also have a membrane around the protein. (#2)

A Virus

Student Book: Application Lesson 7 89

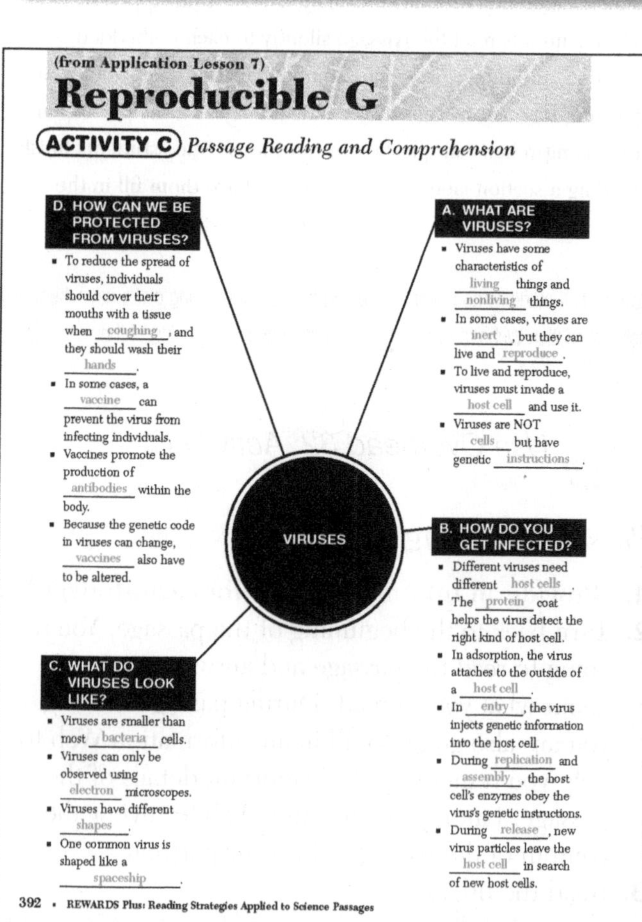

(from Application Lesson 7)

Reproducible G

ACTIVITY C *Passage Reading and Comprehension*

A. WHAT ARE VIRUSES?
- Viruses have some characteristics of living things and nonliving things.
- In some cases, viruses are inert, but they can live and reproduce.
- To live and reproduce, viruses must invade a host cell and use it.
- Viruses are NOT cells but have genetic instructions.

B. HOW DO YOU GET INFECTED?
- Different viruses need different host cells.
- The protein coat helps the virus detect the right kind of host cell.
- In adsorption, the virus attaches to the outside of a host cell.
- In entry, the virus injects genetic information into the host cell.
- During replication and assembly, the host cell's enzymes obey the virus's genetic instructions.
- During release, new virus particles leave the host cell in search of new host cells.

C. WHAT DO VIRUSES LOOK LIKE?
- Viruses are smaller than most bacteria cells.
- Viruses can only be observed using electron microscopes.
- Viruses have different shapes.
- One common virus is shaped like a spaceship.

D. HOW CAN WE BE PROTECTED FROM VIRUSES?
- To reduce the spread of viruses, individuals should cover their mouths with a tissue when coughing, and they should wash their hands.
- In some cases, a vaccine can prevent the virus from infecting individuals.
- Vaccines promote the production of antibodies within the body.
- Because the genetic code in viruses can change, vaccines also have to be altered.

392 • REWARDS Plus: Reading Strategies Applied to Science Passages

#3 How do viruses invade our bodies?
They enter through our mouths, noses, and/or breaks in our skin.

#4 Use the flow chart to describe the steps in virus reproduction.
See chart in the passage for the answer.

#5 Why do scientists need a special type of microscope to look at viruses?
Because viruses are many times smaller than bacteria.

#6 What steps can be taken to reduce the spread of a virus?
People who are sick can cover their mouths with a tissue when coughing or sneezing; they should also wash their hands before having contact with food or people.

#7 How does a vaccine work? Can it cure someone who is already sick?
Vaccines teach the body to produce antibodies, which intercept a virus in the bloodstream and prevent the virus from infecting the person. No, a vaccine cannot cure a person; it can only prevent infection.

#8 What can be done to try to stop the spread of new strains of viruses?
Vaccines need to be updated frequently to try to prevent new waves of infections.

APPLICATION LESSON
7

B

248 **How Do You Get Infected?**
253 Viruses are around you all the time. They enter your body through your
266 mouth or nose or through breaks in your skin. Different types of viruses require
280 different types of host cells. The protein coat on the virus helps it detect the
295 right kind of host cell. For example, a virus that causes a respiratory infection
309 would detect and attack cells that line the lungs. (#3)
318 Once the host cell is detected, the virus attaches itself to the outside of the
333 cell (*adsorption*). It then injects its genetic information through the cell
344 membrane and into the host cell (*entry*). The host cell's enzymes obey the virus's
358 genetic instructions, creating new virus particles (*replication* and *assembly*).
367 New particles leave the host cell in search of other host cells, where the cycle
382 then continues (*release*). The host cell may be destroyed during this process. As
395 the virus spreads, you begin to feel more and more sick. Carefully examine the
409 flowchart below to better understand how viruses work. (#4)

Adsorption → Entry → Replication → Assembly → Release

C

417 **What Do Viruses Look Like?**
422 In order to look at a virus, you would have to look through an electron
437 microscope. Electron microscopes are much more powerful than those you use
448 at school, which may only be able to see bacteria. Remember that viruses are
462 many times smaller than most bacteria cells. Scientists use electron microscopes
473 to see the tiniest of particles.
479 Different kinds of viruses have different shapes. Some viruses are polyhedral,
490 meaning that they have many sides, while some are stick-shaped. Others look
503 like they have pieces of string looped around them. One very common virus is
517 shaped like a spaceship. (#5)

Rotavirus   Ebola Virus

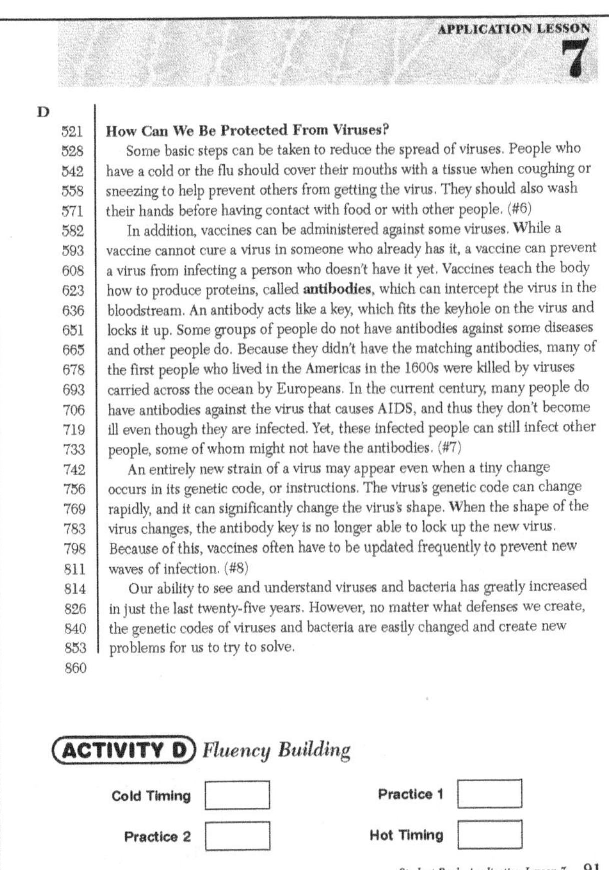

APPLICATION LESSON
7

D

521 **How Can We Be Protected From Viruses?**
528 Some basic steps can be taken to reduce the spread of viruses. People who
542 have a cold or the flu should cover their mouths with a tissue when coughing or
558 sneezing to help prevent others from getting the virus. They should also wash
571 their hands before having contact with food or with other people. (#6)
582 In addition, vaccines can be administered against some viruses. While a
593 vaccine cannot cure a virus in someone who already has it, a vaccine can prevent
608 a virus from infecting a person who doesn't have it yet. Vaccines teach the body
623 how to produce proteins, called **antibodies**, which can intercept the virus in the
636 bloodstream. An antibody acts like a key, which fits the keyhole on the virus and
651 locks it up. Some groups of people do not have antibodies against some diseases
665 and other people do. Because they didn't have the matching antibodies, many of
678 the first people who lived in the Americas in the 1600s were killed by viruses
693 carried across the ocean by Europeans. In the current century, many people do
706 have antibodies against the virus that causes AIDS, and thus they don't become
719 ill even though they are infected. Yet, these infected people can still infect other
733 people, some of whom might not have the antibodies. (#7)
742 An entirely new strain of a virus may appear even when a tiny change
756 occurs in its genetic code, or instructions. The virus's genetic code can change
769 rapidly, and it can significantly change the virus's shape. When the shape of the
783 virus changes, the antibody key is no longer able to lock up the new virus.
798 Because of this, vaccines often have to be updated frequently to prevent new
811 waves of infection. (#8)
814 Our ability to see and understand viruses and bacteria has greatly increased
826 in just the last twenty-five years. However, no matter what defenses we create,
840 the genetic codes of viruses and bacteria are easily changed and create new
853 problems for us to try to solve.
860

ACTIVITY D *Fluency Building*

Cold Timing		Practice 1	
Practice 2		Hot Timing	

Student Book: Application Lesson 7 91

ACTIVITY D

Fluency Building

ACTIVITY PROCEDURE

(See the *Student Book*, page 91.)

Have students complete a Cold Timing, one or two practices, and a Hot Timing of the Activity C article. For each timing, have students record the number of correct words read. Finally, have students complete their Fluency Graphs.

Note D-1: When assigning partners for this activity, have the stronger reader read first. As a result, the other reader will have one additional practice opportunity.

1. Now, it's time for fluency building.
2. Find the beginning of the passage again. (Pause.)
3. Whisper-read. See how many words you can read in one minute. Begin._ (Time students for one minute.) Stop._ Circle the last word that you read._ Record the number of words you read after **Cold Timing**._
4. Let's practice again. Begin._ (Time students for one minute.) Stop._ Put a box around the last word that you read._ Record the number of words you read after **Practice 1**._
5. (Optional) Let's practice one more time before the Hot Timing. Begin._ (Time students for one minute.) Stop._ Put a box around the last word that you read._ Record the number of words you read after **Practice 2**._
6. Please exchange books with your partner._ Partner 1, you are going to read first. Partner 2, listen carefully and underline any mistakes or words left out. Ones, begin._ (Time students for one minute.) Stop._ Twos, cross out the last word that your partner read._ (Assist students in subtracting the number of mistakes from the number of words read.) Twos, record the number of correct words in your partner's book after **Hot Timing**._
7. Partner 2, you are going to read next. Partner 1, listen carefully and underline any mistakes or words left out. Twos, begin. (Time students for one minute.) Stop._ Ones, cross out the last word that your partner read._ Ones, record the number of correct words in your partner's book after **Hot Timing**._
8. Exchange books._ Turn to the Fluency Graph on the inside back cover, and indicate on the graph the number of Cold Timing and Hot Timing words you read correctly._

APPLICATION LESSON 7

D

521 **How Can We Be Protected From Viruses?**
528 Some basic steps can be taken to reduce the spread of viruses. People who
542 have a cold or the flu should cover their mouths with a tissue when coughing or
558 sneezing to help prevent others from getting the virus. They should also wash
571 their hands before having contact with food or with other people. (#6)
582 In addition, vaccines can be administered against some viruses. While a
593 vaccine cannot cure a virus in someone who already has it, a vaccine can prevent
608 a virus from infecting a person who doesn't have it yet. Vaccines teach the body
623 how to produce proteins, called **antibodies**, which can intercept the virus in the
636 bloodstream. An antibody acts like a key, which fits the keyhole on the virus and
651 locks it up. Some groups of people do not have antibodies against some diseases
665 and other people do. Because they didn't have the matching antibodies, many of
678 the first people who lived in the Americas in the 1600s were killed by viruses
693 carried across the ocean by Europeans. In the current century, many people do
706 have antibodies against the virus that causes AIDS, and thus they don't become
719 ill even though they are infected. Yet, these infected people can still infect other
733 people, some of whom might not have the antibodies. (#7)
742 An entirely new strain of a virus may appear even when a tiny change
756 occurs in its genetic code, or instructions. The virus's genetic code can change
769 rapidly, and it can significantly change the virus's shape. When the shape of the
783 virus changes, the antibody key is no longer able to lock up the new virus.
798 Because of this, vaccines often have to be updated frequently to prevent new
811 waves of infection. (#8)
814 Our ability to see and understand viruses and bacteria has greatly increased
826 in just the last twenty-five years. However, no matter what defenses we create,
840 the genetic codes of viruses and bacteria are easily changed and create new
853 problems for us to try to solve.
860

ACTIVITY D *Fluency Building*

Cold Timing		Practice 1	
Practice 2		Hot Timing	

Student Book: Application Lesson 7 91

ACTIVITY E

Comprehension Questions—Multiple Choice

ACTIVITY PROCEDURE

(See the *Student Book*, page 92.)

Have students complete item #1. Then, have students share the rationale for their answers. Encourage thoughtful discussion. Proceed item-by-item, emphasizing the rationale for the *best* answer. Have students record points for each correct item.

Note E-1: The correct Multiple Choice answers are circled.

1. Turn to page 92. Find **Activity E.**
2. Use the Multiple Choice Strategy to complete item #1. Be ready to explain why you selected your answer. (Wait while students complete the item. Call on individual students. Ask them why they chose their answer and why they eliminated the other choices. Encourage discussion. Provide students with feedback on their choices, focusing on why or why not those choices might be appropriate.)
3. (Repeat Step 2 for items 2–4, pausing after each item to confirm student responses and provide feedback.)
4. Count the number of items you got correct, and record that number in the blank half of the Multiple Choice Comprehension box.

APPLICATION LESSON **7**

ACTIVITY E *Comprehension Questions—Multiple Choice*

Comprehension Strategy—Multiple Choice

Step 1: Read the item.
Step 2: Read all of the choices.
Step 3: Think about why each choice might be correct or incorrect. Check the article as needed.
Step 4: From the possible correct choices, select the best answer.

1. (Vocabulary) **In the article, the author says that a virus can be inert, having as much life as a rock. This statement means that a virus:**
   a. can experience erosion.
   ⓑ can have no life at times.
   c. can be shaped like a variety of rocks.
   d. can reproduce and grow at any time.
2. (Compare and contrast) **How are viruses DIFFERENT from living things?**
   a. Living things grow and develop. Viruses do not.
   b. Living things reproduce. Viruses do not.
   ⓒ Living things are never inert. In some cases, viruses are inert.
   d. Living things can change. Viruses do not.
3. (Cause and effect) **In order for a virus to live and produce, it must:**
   a. be invaded by a host cell.
   ⓑ invade the right kind of host cell.
   c. be invaded by the right kind of host cell.
   d. be detected by the right kind of host cell using a protein coat.
4. (Main idea) **Which of the following might be a better title for this article?**
   a. Viruses & Bacteria
   ⓑ Viruses—What They Are and How They Work
   c. Vaccines—A Cure?
   d. Viruses—Secret in the DNA

MULTIPLE CHOICE COMPREHENSION 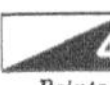
Points

92 *REWARDS Plus: Reading Strategies Applied to Science Passages*

ACTIVITY F

Vocabulary Activities

ACTIVITY PROCEDURE

(See the *Student Book*, pages 93–94.)

Have students complete each item orally and provide feedback on their answers. Then have students respond to each question in writing by answering "yes" or "no" and providing a reason for their answers.

Yes/No/Why

1. Turn to page 93._ Find **Activity F.**_ Read item #1. Tell your partner your answer and your reason for it. (Pause. Then call on individual students. Encourage discussion. Provide students with feedback on their choices, focusing on their explanations for their answer.)
2. Write your answer and your reason for it in the space provided. Look up when you are done._
3. Read item #2. Tell your partner your answer and your reason for it. (Pause. Then call on individual students. Encourage discussion. Provide students with feedback on their choices, focusing on their explanations for their answer.)
4. Write your answer and your reason for it in the space provided. Look up when you are done._
5. Read item #3. Tell your partner your answer and your reason for it. (Pause. Then call on individual students. Encourage discussion. Provide students with feedback on their choices, focusing on their explanations for their answer.)
6. Write your answer and your reason for it in the space provided. Look up when you are done._

Note F-1: You may wish to do this as an oral task only rather than an oral and a written task.

APPLICATION LESSON **7**

ACTIVITY F *Vocabulary Activities*

Yes/No/Why

1. Does a **virus** carry **information**?
   Example answer: Yes. A virus contains genetic instructions that tell the virus about itself.
2. Do **genetic instructions** influence **characteristics**?
   Example answer: Yes. Genetic instructions tell all organisms what to look like and how to behave.
3. Is **adsorption** part of **replication**?
   Example answer: No. Adsorption and replication are steps that a virus goes through. First, the virus attaches to the outside of a cell (adsorption). Later, the host cell will create new virus particles (replication).

Student Book: Application Lesson 7 93

ACTIVITY PROCEDURE

Have students read the words and definitions and then complete the sentence stems for each vocabulary word. Have them share answers with partners and with the class. Then, have students give themselves points in the blank half of the Vocabulary box.

Completion Activity

1. Turn to page 94. Read the first word and its definition.
2. Now, read the sentence stem.
3. Think of how you would complete the sentence stem and write it. Share your answer with your partner. (Call on a few students to share answers with the class.)
4. (Repeat Steps 1–3 for the rest of the words.)
5. If you participated in answering all seven questions, give yourself seven points in the blank half of the Vocabulary box.

Note F-2: You may wish to do this as an oral task only rather than an oral task and a written task.

APPLICATION LESSON

7

Completion Activities

1. **significantly:** a lot
   Your ability to get good grades increases significantly when you
   Answers will vary.

2. **reproduce:** to produce others of the same kind
   Ways to reproduce music include
   Answers will vary.

3. **assembly:** fitting together parts to make a whole
   Several things require assembly when you bring them home from the store. Name five of those things.
   Answers will vary.

4. **developing:** growing and changing
   Some signs that a neighborhood is developing are
   Answers will vary.

VOCABULARY 7 Points

94 *REWARDS Plus: Reading Strategies Applied to Science Passages*

ACTIVITY G

Expository Writing— Multi-Paragraph Answer

ACTIVITY PROCEDURE, Plan and Write

(See the *Student Book*, pages 95–97.)

Have students read the prompt and the three topics. Have students read the **LIST** of details under topic a, then guide them in adding details for topics b and c. Have students look at topic a again. Explain that details that don't go with a topic should be **CROSSED OUT**. Have students **CONNECT** details as shown in the example plan. Have students **NUMBER** their details in the same manner as in the example plan for topic a. Next, have students **WRITE** paragraph a. Guide students in completing the plan for topic b and writing paragraph b. Repeat for topic c. Finally, explain that after the answer is written, they should **EDIT** their work, revising for clarity and proofreading for errors in capitalization, punctuation, and spelling.

Use Overheads 33 and 34: Activity G

1. Turn to page 95._ Find **Activity G.**_ Today you will write three paragraphs.
2. Find the prompt in the middle of the page._ Read the prompt out loud with me: **Explain each big idea in this article about viruses: what they are like, how they reproduce, and how we can protect ourselves and others from infection.**
3. Turn to page 96._ Read topic a._ Read topic b._ Read topic c._
4. Read the details **listed** under topic a._
5. Now, it's your turn to add details to topic b. Look back in the article and locate details that explain how viruses reproduce. Write the details in the Planning Box._
6. Add details to topic c. Look back in the article and locate details that explain how we can protect ourselves and others from infection. Write the details in the Planning Box._
7. Let's use the steps for topic a. First, read the details and **cross out** any details that do not go with the topic._ Next, draw brackets to **connect** details that could easily go into one sentence._ Now, **number** the details in a logical order._

APPLICATION LESSON 7

ACTIVITY G *Expository Writing—Multi-Paragraph Answer*

Writing Strategy—Multi-Paragraph Answer

Step 1: **LIST** (List the details that are important enough to include in your answer.)
Step 2: **CROSS OUT** (Reread the details. Cross out any that don't go with the topic.)
Step 3: **CONNECT** (Connect any details that could go into one sentence.)
Step 4: **NUMBER** (Number the details in a logical order.)
Step 5: **WRITE** (Write the paragraph.)
Step 6: **EDIT** (Revise and proofread your answer.)

Prompt: Explain each big idea in this article about viruses: what they are like, how they reproduce, and how we can protect ourselves and others from infection.

Plan: Complete the Planning Box with your teacher.

Student Book: Application Lesson 7 95

APPLICATION LESSON 7

Example Multi-Paragraph Plan

Planning Box
(topic a) *viruses—what they are like*
① (detail) – *very tiny, infectious particles*
① (detail) – *considered by some as living*
① ② (detail) – *can live and reproduce if they invade host cells*
① (detail) – *considered by some as nonliving*
③ (detail) – *in air or on surface, inert*
④ (detail) – *much smaller than bacteria*
⑤ (detail) – *not cells*
⑤ (detail) – *contain genetic instructions*
(topic b) *viruses—how they reproduce*
① (detail) – *detect appropriate host cells*
① (detail) – *attach themselves to host cells*
② (detail) – *inject genetic information into host cells*
③ (detail) – *host cell follows genetic instructions*
③ (detail) – *host cell creates new virus particles*
④ (detail) – *new virus particles search out new host cells*
⑤ (detail) – *virus spreads*
(topic c) *viruses—how we can protect ourselves and others from infection*
① (detail) – *cover mouth to limit spread of virus*
(detail) – ~~*viruses tiny infectious particles*~~
② (detail) – *wash hands before contact with food or people*
③ (detail) – *take vaccines that stop viruses from infecting people*
④ (detail) – *vaccines produce antibodies that matches virus*

Write: Write paragraphs a, b, and c on a separate piece of paper.

96 *REWARDS Plus: Reading Strategies Applied to Science Passages*

8. (Show Overhead 34.) Now, look at the example plan for topic a on the overhead. Yours doesn't need to be the same, but it should be similar.
9. Take out a blank piece of paper. Using your plan for paragraph a, **write** paragraph a. If you finish early, please reread and **edit** your paragraph. Don't forget to use the spelling of words in the plan and article to correct any errors. (Move around the room and monitor your students as they are writing.)
10. (When the majority of students are done, proceed with the lesson.) Now, use the steps for topic b. First, read the details and **cross out** any details that do not go with the topic. Next, draw brackets to **connect** details that could easily go into one sentence. Now, **number** the details in a logical order.
11. Now, look at the example plan for topic b on the overhead. Yours doesn't need to be the same, but it should be similar.
12. Locate your piece of paper. Using your plan for paragraph b, **write** paragraph b. If you finish early, please **edit** your paragraph. (Move around the room and monitor your students as they are writing.)
13. (When the majority of students are done, proceed with the lesson.) Now, use the steps for topic c. First, read the details and **cross out** any details that do not go with the topic. Next, draw brackets to **connect** details that could easily go into one sentence. Now, **number** the details in a logical order.
14. Look at the example plan for topic c on the overhead. Yours doesn't need to be the same, but it should be similar.
15. Locate your piece of paper. Using your plan for paragraph c, **write** paragraph c. If you finish early, please **edit** your paragraph. (Move around the room and monitor your students as they are writing.)
16. (When the majority of students are done, proceed with the lesson.) Now, edit your paragraphs. Please carefully read your paragraphs. Be sure that your paragraphs are easy to understand and clear. Proofread for any errors in capitalization, punctuation, and spelling. (Give students time to proofread their paragraphs.)

APPLICATION LESSON **7**

Evaluate: Evaluate the paragraphs using this rubric.

Rubric—Multi-Paragraph Answer	Student or Partner Rating	Teacher Rating
1. Did the author state the topic in the first sentence?	a. Yes Fix up b. Yes Fix up c. Yes Fix up	a. Yes No b. Yes No c. Yes No
2. Did the author include details that go with the topic?	a. Yes Fix up b. Yes Fix up c. Yes Fix up	a. Yes No b. Yes No c. Yes No
3. Did the author combine details in some of the sentences?	a. Yes Fix up b. Yes Fix up c. Yes Fix up	a. Yes No b. Yes No c. Yes No
4. Is the answer easy to understand?	Yes Fix up	Yes No
5. Did the author correctly spell words, particularly the words found in the article?	Yes Fix up	Yes No
6. Did the author use correct capitalization, capitalizing the first word in the sentence and proper names of people, places, and things?	Yes Fix up	Yes No
7. Did the author use correct punctuation, including a period at the end of each sentence?	Yes Fix up	Yes No

WRITING 13 Points

Student Book: Application Lesson 7 97

ACTIVITY PROCEDURE, Evaluate

Ask students to read each question in the rubric. Guide them in evaluating the paragraphs using the guidelines. Have students total their points and record them in the blank half of the Writing box.

17. Turn to page 97. Let's evaluate paragraph a.
18. Read question #1 with me. Circle "Yes" for a if your topic sentence includes the topic: what viruses are like.
19. Read question #2 with me. Circle "Yes" for a if all of your details tell what viruses are like.
20. Read question #3 with me. Circle "Yes" for a if you combined details into one sentence.
21. Now, check paragraphs b and c carefully and answer questions 1 through 3.
22. Read question #4. Reread your paragraphs. Circle "Yes" if your paragraphs are easy to understand.
23. Read question #5. Carefully examine your paragraphs. If you think a word is misspelled, underline it and check back in the plan or article and correct the spelling. Circle "Yes" if you believe that you have very few spelling errors.

24. Read question #6._ Carefully examine your sentences. Be sure that each sentence begins with a capital._ If all sentences begin with a capital, circle "Yes."_

25. Read question #7._ Examine your sentences. Be sure that each sentence ends with a period._ If all sentences end with a period, circle "Yes."_

26. Count up your points and record them in the Writing box._

27. (Show Overhead 35.) Look at the overhead._ Let's read the three example paragraphs. Yours do not have to be the same, but they should be similar._ (Read the paragraphs to your students or with your students or call on a student to read the example paragraph.)

28. (Distribute Appendix A Reproducible 7: Rubric—Multi-Paragraph Answer. Have students place this in a notebook or a folder for future reference.)

Note G-1: The rubric can be used in a variety of ways. Instead of the students evaluating their own paragraphs, you may wish to have their partners provide feedback. The second column is designed for teacher feedback. If you have a small group, it would be useful to give daily feedback on writing. If the group size is large, you can give feedback to a number of children each day. You may wish to give students bonus points based on your feedback.

APPLICATION LESSON
7

Evaluate: Evaluate the paragraphs using this rubric.

Rubric— Multi-Paragraph Answer	Student or Partner Rating	Teacher Rating
1. Did the author state the topic in the first sentence?	a. (Yes) Fix up b. (Yes) Fix up c. (Yes) Fix up	a. Yes No b. Yes No c. Yes No
2. Did the author include details that go with the topic?	a. (Yes) Fix up b. (Yes) Fix up c. (Yes) Fix up	a. Yes No b. Yes No c. Yes No
3. Did the author combine details in some of the sentences?	a. (Yes) Fix up b. (Yes) Fix up c. (Yes) Fix up	a. Yes No b. Yes No c. Yes No
4. Is the answer easy to understand?	(Yes) Fix up	Yes No
5. Did the author correctly spell words, particularly the words found in the article?	(Yes) Fix up	Yes No
6. Did the author use correct capitalization, capitalizing the first word in the sentence and proper names of people, places, and things?	(Yes) Fix up	Yes No
7. Did the author use correct punctuation, including a period at the end of each sentence?	(Yes) Fix up	Yes No

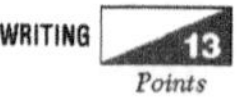

Student Book: Application Lesson 7 97

ACTIVITY H

Comprehension—Single-Paragraph Answer

ACTIVITY PROCEDURE

(See the *Student Book*, page 98.)

Have students read the *What Is* statement and the *What If* question. Have students turn the question into part of the answer and write down a topic sentence for their answer. Then, have them complete their answer. Encourage them to use evidence from the article and their own experience and background knowledge. Engage students in a discussion. Award points for writing and participating in the discussion

Note H-1: To increase the quality of the discussion, the students are asked to think and write about the *What If* before the discussion. However, you may be working with students who have difficulty generating ideas for their paragraph. If that is the case, switch the order of activities: engage the students in a discussion, and then have them write their paragraphs.

1. Turn to page 98. Find **Activity H.**
2. Find the *What Is* statement in the middle of the page. Read it out loud with me: **In order for a virus to reproduce, it must attach itself to a specific type of host cell. Thus, viruses cannot attach to all cells.**
3. Find the *What If* question. Read it with me: **What if viruses could attach to any plant or animal cell and reproduce in all situations?**
4. Think how you might turn the question into part of the answer. Tell me your idea for a topic sentence. (Example sentence: If viruses could attach to any plant or animal cell, the results would be catastrophic.) Take out a piece of paper and write your topic sentence. (Move around the room and monitor as students write.)
5. You are ready to add ideas to your paragraph. Use evidence from the article as well as your own experience and background knowledge. If you finish early, reread your paragraph and edit it so that it is easy to understand and clear. (Move around the room and monitor as students write.)
6. Read your paragraph to your partner.
7. If you included wording from the question in your answer and added evidence from the article, award yourself four points for writing.

APPLICATION LESSON

7

ACTIVITY H *Comprehension—Single-Paragraph Answer*

Writing Strategy—Single-Paragraph Answer

Step 1: Read the item.
Step 2: Turn the question into part of the answer and write it down.
Step 3: Think of the answer or locate the answer in the article.
Step 4: Complete your answer.

Prompt:

What Is—In order for a virus to reproduce, it must attach itself to a specific type of host cell. Thus, viruses cannot attach to all cells.

What If—What if viruses could attach to any plant or animal cell and reproduce in all situations?

Write and Discuss: Write a paragraph. Then share your ideas. Use the Discussion Guidelines.

Discussion Guidelines

Speaker		Listener	
Looks like:	**Sounds like:**	**Looks like:**	**Sounds like:**
• Facing peers • Making eye contact • Participating	• Using pleasant, easy-to-hear voice • Sharing opinions, supporting facts and reasons from the article and from your experience • Staying on the topic	• Facing speaker • Making eye contact • Participating	• Waiting quietly to speak • Giving positive, supportive comments • Disagreeing respectfully

WRITING DISCUSSION

Points Points

98 *REWARDS Plus: Reading Strategies Applied to Science Passages*

8. (Engage students in a discussion. Award four points to students who are active participants in the discussion.)

Note H-2: If your students are having difficulty writing the *What If* paragraphs, read or show them the following example paragraph:

Example Single-Paragraph Answer

If viruses could attach to any plant or animal cell, the results would be catastrophic. Because they would not be limited to certain cells, all cells would be potential host cells. The viruses could attach to, inject genetic information into, and reproduce with all cells. Thus, viruses would spread instantaneously. There wouldn't be any time to develop a vaccine or to put people in protective sterile environments. As a result, people and other organisms would become ill and die.

Application Lesson 8

Materials Needed:

- *Student Book*: Application Lesson 8
- Application Overhead Transparencies 35–39
- Appendix B Reproducible H: Application Lesson 8
- Appendix C Optional Vocabulary Activity: Application Lesson 8
- Paper or cardboard to use when covering the overhead transparency
- Paper or cardboard for each student to use during spelling dictation
- Washable overhead transparency pen

Text Treatment Notes:

- Black text signifies teacher script (exact wording to say to students).
- Green text in parentheses signifies directions or prompts for the teacher.
- Green text signifies answers or examples of answers.
- Green graphics treatment signifies reproduction of Overhead information.
- Green text and green graphics treatment do not appear in the *Student Book*.

ACTIVITY A

Vocabulary

ACTIVITY PROCEDURE, List 1

(See the *Student Book*, page 99.)

Tell students each word in the list. Then, have students repeat the word and read the definition aloud. For each definition, provide any additional information that may be necessary. Then, have students practice reading the words themselves.

Use Overhead 35: Activity A
List 1: Tell

1. (Show the top half of Overhead 35.) Before we read the passage, let's read the difficult words. The first words are someone's name. (Point to **Antoni van Leeuwenhoek**.) The name is **Antoni van Leeuwenhoek**. What name?_ Now, read the definition._
2. (Point to ***Micrographia***.) The next word is the name of a book, ***Micrographia***. What word?_ Now, read the definition._
3. (Pronounce each word in List 1, and then have students repeat each word and read the definition.)
4. Open your *Student Book* to **Application Lesson 8**, page 99._
5. Find **Activity A**, **List 1**, in your book._ Let's read the words again. First words._ Next word._ (Continue for all words in List 1.)

ACTIVITY PROCEDURE, List 2

(See the *Student Book*, page 99.)

Have students circle prefixes and suffixes, then underline the vowels. Using the overhead transparency, assist students in checking their work. Next, have students figure out each word to themselves, then say it aloud. Have them read the definition aloud.

Use Overhead 35: Activity A
List 2: Strategy Practice

1. Find **List 2**. Circle the prefixes and suffixes, and underline the vowels. Remember, you can circle the prefix **micro**. Look up when you are done._
2. (Show the bottom half of Overhead 35.). Now, check and fix any mistakes._

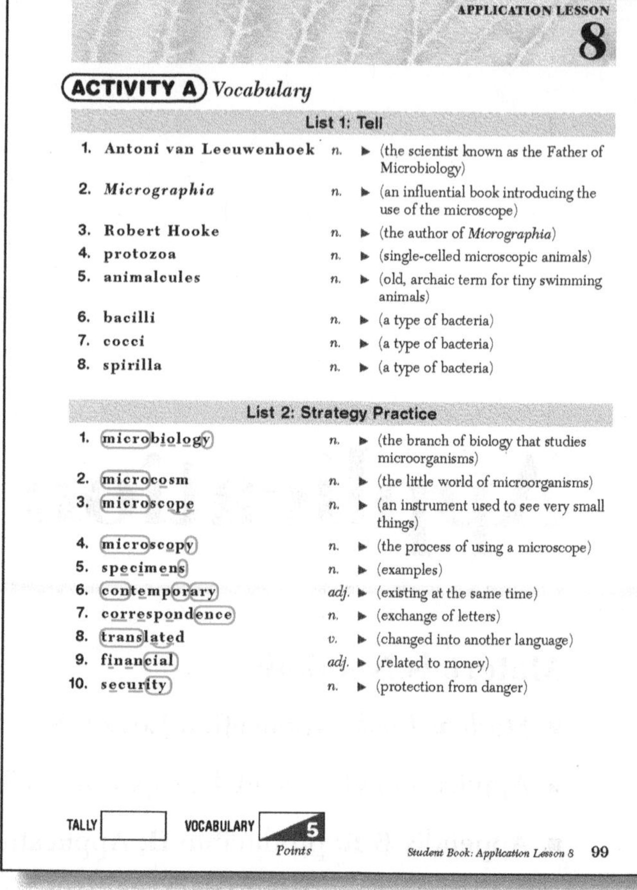

APPLICATION LESSON 8

ACTIVITY A *Vocabulary*

List 1: Tell

1. **Antoni van Leeuwenhoek** *n.* ▶ (the scientist known as the Father of Microbiology)
2. ***Micrographia*** *n.* ▶ (an influential book introducing the use of the microscope)
3. **Robert Hooke** *n.* ▶ (the author of *Micrographia*)
4. **protozoa** *n.* ▶ (single-celled microscopic animals)
5. **animalcules** *n.* ▶ (old, archaic term for tiny swimming animals)
6. **bacilli** *n.* ▶ (a type of bacteria)
7. **cocci** *n.* ▶ (a type of bacteria)
8. **spirilla** *n.* ▶ (a type of bacteria)

List 2: Strategy Practice

1. **microbiology** *n.* ▶ (the branch of biology that studies microorganisms)
2. **microcosm** *n.* ▶ (the little world of microorganisms)
3. **microscope** *n.* ▶ (an instrument used to see very small things)
4. **microscopy** *n.* ▶ (the process of using a microscope)
5. **specimens** *n.* ▶ (examples)
6. **contemporary** *adj.* ▶ (existing at the same time)
7. **correspondence** *n.* ▶ (exchange of letters)
8. **translated** *v.* ▶ (changed into another language)
9. **financial** *adj.* ▶ (related to money)
10. **security** *n.* ▶ (protection from danger)

TALLY VOCABULARY 5 Points

Student Book: Application Lesson 8 99

3. Go back to the first word._ Sound out the word to yourself. Put your thumb up when you can read the word. Be sure that it is a real word._ What word?_ Now, read the definition._
4. (Continue Step 3 with all remaining words in List 2.)

Note A.2-1: You may wish to provide additional practice by having students read words to a partner.

ACTIVITY PROCEDURE, List 1 and 2

(See the *Student Book*, page 99.)

Tell students to look in List 1 or List 2 for a word you are thinking about. Have them circle the number of the word and tell you the word. Explain to students to make a tally mark for each correct word in the Tally box, and then enter the number of tally marks as points in the blank half of the Vocabulary box.

1. Remember, the words I'm thinking about will be in either List 1 or List 2. Make a tally mark for every correctly identified word.
2. Circle the number of the appropriate word.
   - When you exchange letters or emails with someone you are engaging in this. (Wait.) What word? **correspondence**
   - If money is involved in a transaction, it is said to be this type of transaction. (Wait.) What word? **financial**
   - Because of threats of danger, these types of measures have been increased, especially at airports. (Wait.) What word? **security**
   - When a book written in one language is changed into a different language, the book is said to have been this. (Wait.) What word? **translated**
   - This object is used to see very small things. (Wait.) What word? **microscope**
3. Count all the tally marks, and enter that number as points in the blank half of the Vocabulary box.

ACTIVITY PROCEDURE, List 3

(See the *Student Book*, page 100.)

The words in the third list are related. Have students use the *REWARDS* Strategies to figure out the first word in each family. Have them read the definition of the verb and then read nouns and adjectives that are related to that verb.

Use Overhead 36: Activity A
List 3: Word Families

1. Turn to page 100._ Find **Family 1** in **List 3**. Figure out the first word. Use your pencil if you wish. Put your thumb up when you know the word._ What word?_ Read the definition._
2. Look at the nouns in Family 1. Figure out the first word._ What word?_ Next word._ What word?_
3. Look at the adjective in Family 1. Figure out the word._ What word?_
4. (Repeat Steps 1–3 for all word families in List 3.)

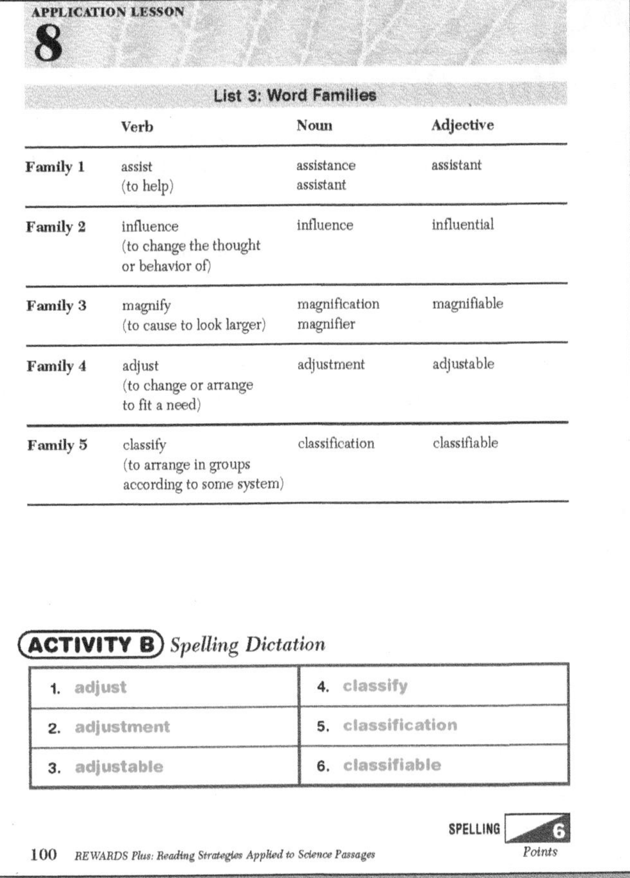

APPLICATION LESSON
8

List 3: Word Families

	Verb	Noun	Adjective
Family 1	assist (to help)	assistance assistant	assistant
Family 2	influence (to change the thought or behavior of)	influence	influential
Family 3	magnify (to cause to look larger)	magnification magnifier	magnifiable
Family 4	adjust (to change or arrange to fit a need)	adjustment	adjustable
Family 5	classify (to arrange in groups according to some system)	classification	classifiable

ACTIVITY B *Spelling Dictation*

1. adjust	4. classify
2. adjustment	5. classification
3. adjustable	6. classifiable

SPELLING 6 Points

100 *REWARDS Plus: Reading Strategies Applied to Science Passages*

Note A.3-1: You may wish to provide additional practice by having students read a word family to the group or to a partner.

Note A.3-2: An additional vocabulary practice activity called Quick Words is provided in Appendix C of this Teacher's Guide. See Appendix C for information about how this optional activity can be used.

ACTIVITY B

Spelling Dictation

ACTIVITY PROCEDURE

(See the *Student Book*, page 100.)

For each word, tell students the word, then have students say the parts of the word to themselves while they write the word. Using the overhead transparency, assist students in checking their spelling and correcting if they misspelled. Then, have students enter the number of correctly spelled words as points in the blank half of the Spelling box.

Note B-1: Distribute a piece of light cardboard to each of the students.

Use Overhead 36: Activity B

1. Find **Activity B.**
2. The first word is **adjust**. What word?_ Say the parts in **adjust** to yourself as you write the word. (Pause and monitor.)
3. (Show **adjust** on the overhead.) Check **adjust**. If you misspelled it, cross it out and write it correctly.
4. The second word is **adjustment**. What word?_ Say the parts in **adjustment** to yourself as you write the word. (Pause and monitor.)
5. (Show **adjustment** on the overhead.) Check **adjustment**. If you misspelled it, cross it out and write it correctly.
6. (Repeat the procedures for the words **adjustable**, **classify**, **classification**, and **classifiable**.)
7. Count the number of words you spelled correctly, and record that number as points in the blank half of the Spelling box at the bottom of the page.

APPLICATION LESSON 8

List 3: Word Families

	Verb	Noun	Adjective
Family 1	assist (to help)	assistance assistant	assistant
Family 2	influence (to change the thought or behavior of)	influence	influential
Family 3	magnify (to cause to look larger)	magnification magnifier	magnifiable
Family 4	adjust (to change or arrange to fit a need)	adjustment	adjustable
Family 5	classify (to arrange in groups according to some system)	classification	classifiable

ACTIVITY B *Spelling Dictation*

1. adjust	4. classify
2. adjustment	5. classification
3. adjustable	6. classifiable

100 *REWARDS Plus: Reading Strategies Applied to Science Passages*

SPELLING 6 *Points*

ACTIVITY C

Passage Reading and Comprehension

ACTIVITY PROCEDURE

(See the *Student Book*, pages 101–103.)

Have students read the title of the passage and each heading. Ask them to tell their partners two things that the passage will tell about.

Passage Preview

1. Turn to page 101. Let's preview the passage.
2. Read the title. What is the whole passage going to tell about?
3. Now, let's read the headings. Read the first heading. Read the next heading. (Continue until students have read all headings.)
4. Turn to your partner. Without looking, tell two things this passage will tell about.

ACTIVITY PROCEDURE

Provide students with an Information Web from Appendix B. Have students read the passage silently to each embedded number, and then reread the same information orally either to a partner, together as a group, or individually. Ask the corresponding comprehension question or questions. Once students finish reading a section labeled A, B, C, D, or E, have them fill in the Information Web before going on to the next section.

Note C-1: If students do not finish reading the passage during class, have them use their Information Webs to review the information at the beginning of the next class.

Use Overhead 37: Activity C

Passage Reading

1. (Provide an Information Web for each student.)
2. Turn back to the beginning of the passage. You're going to read the passage and answer questions about what you've read. During passage reading, you are also going to fill in an Information Web to help you remember the important details of the passage. Later, you'll use this Web to review the content of the passage with your partner.
3. Read the title.

APPLICATION LESSON **8**

ACTIVITY C *Passage Reading and Comprehension*

Note: For this activity, you will need Reproducible H found in the *Teacher's Guide*.

Antoni van Leeuwenhoek—The Father of Microbiology

A
Whom do you think of when you think of an important scientist? Someone
13 who studies science in school for many years and then applies what he or she
28 learns? Someone who works in a scientific field? Antoni van Leeuwenhoek did
40 none of these things, but he became one of the best-known scientists in history.
55 He is often referred to as the Father of Microbiology, the branch of biology that
70 studies living things that are too small to be seen with the unaided eye.
84 Van Leeuwenhoek worked in his native country of Holland, first as a fabric
97 merchant and later as a chamberlain (assistant) to the town's sheriffs. Because
109 working as a chamberlain gave him a great deal of financial security and free
123 time, he had time to read many books. In the late 1660s, he was introduced to
139 microscopes through a book titled *Micrographia* by Robert Hooke. This book
150 was highly influential and introduced the public to microscopy, the use of the
163 microscope to investigate tiny living things. (#1)

B
169 **An Unusual Hobby**
172 This field of study fascinated van Leeuwenhoek. He began to practice
183 microscopy and developed an unusual hobby. He learned how to grind his own
196 lenses, and he created his own microscope that differed from the compound
208 microscopes of that day. Unlike compound microscopes that used more than one
220 lens, van Leeuwenhoek's microscopes were simple devices that used only one
231 lens. While the contemporary microscopes of his day magnified a specimen 20 to
244 30 times, van Leeuwenhoek's microscopes magnified a specimen 200 to 300
255 times. This difference was due chiefly to Leeuwenhoek's skill at lens grinding and
268 his patience in adjusting the light source when viewing tiny specimens. (#2)

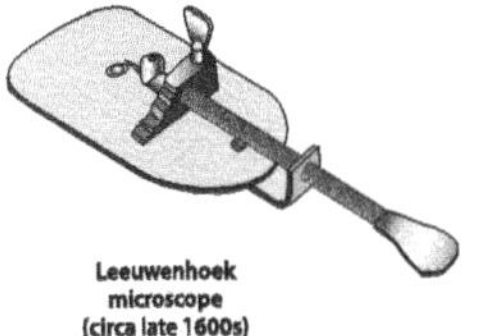

Leeuwenhoek microscope (circa late 1600s)

Student Book: Application Lesson 8 101

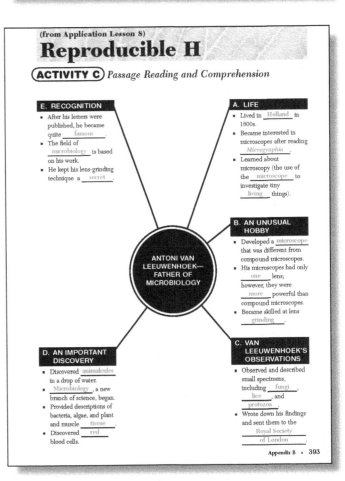

(from Application Lesson 8)

Reproducible H

ACTIVITY C *Passage Reading and Comprehension*

ANTONI VAN LEEUWENHOEK—FATHER OF MICROBIOLOGY

A. LIFE

- Lived in Holland in 1600s.
- Became interested in microscopes after reading *Micrographia*.
- Learned about microscopy (the use of the microscope to investigate tiny living things).

B. AN UNUSUAL HOBBY

- Developed a microscope that was different from compound microscopes.
- His microscopes had only one lens; however, they were more powerful than compound microscopes.
- Became skilled at lens grinding.

C. VAN LEEUWENHOEK'S OBSERVATIONS

- Observed and described small specimens, including fungi, lice, and protozoa.
- Wrote down his findings and sent them to the Royal Society of London.

D. AN IMPORTANT DISCOVERY

- Discovered animalcules in a drop of water.
- Microbiology, a new branch of science, began.
- Provided descriptions of bacteria, algae, and plant and muscle tissue.
- Discovered red blood cells.

E. RECOGNITION

- After his letters were published, he became quite famous.
- The field of microbiology is based on his work.
- He kept his lens-grinding technique a secret.

Appendix B • 393

4. Find number 1 in the passage. (Pause). Read down to number 1 silently. Look up when you are done._
5. (Wait for students to complete the reading. Then have students reread the part by having them read orally to a partner, read together orally as a group, or read aloud individually.)
6. (Ask the question or questions associated with the number. Provide feedback to students regarding their answers.)
7. (Repeat steps 4–6 for all paragraphs in Section A.)
8. Now, look at your Information Web. Find the section labeled A._ The information you've just read will help you to fill in this Web.
9. With your partner, fill in the blanks for Section A. You can refer back to the passage for information. Look up when you're done._ (Move around the room and monitor students as they complete the section.)
10. (When the majority of students have finished, show Overhead 37.) Look at the overhead and check your work. Fix up or add to any of your answers.
11. Now read down to the next number silently. Look up when you are done._
12. (Repeat steps 5–11 until the students have finished the passage and the Information Web.)
13. Now use your Information Web to retell the important information from the passage to your partner.

Comprehension Questions

#1 How did Antoni van Leeuwenhoek first become interested in microbiology?

He read a book called *Micrographia* that introduced the use of microscopes to investigate tiny things.

#2 How were van Leeuwenhoek's microscopes different from the compound microscopes of the day?

His microscope used only one lens while the compound microscope used more than one lens; his microscope could magnify a specimen 200 to 300 times versus the 20 to 30 times of the compound microscope.

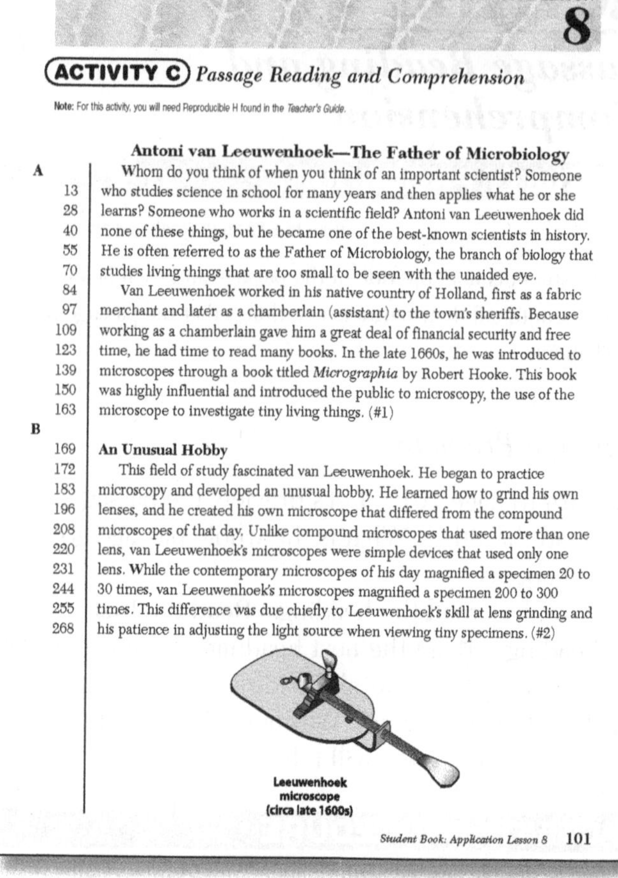

APPLICATION LESSON 8

ACTIVITY C *Passage Reading and Comprehension*

Note: For this activity, you will need Reproducible H found in the *Teacher's Guide*.

Antoni van Leeuwenhoek—The Father of Microbiology

A
Whom do you think of when you think of an important scientist? Someone
13 who studies science in school for many years and then applies what he or she
28 learns? Someone who works in a scientific field? Antoni van Leeuwenhoek did
40 none of these things, but he became one of the best-known scientists in history.
55 He is often referred to as the Father of Microbiology, the branch of biology that
70 studies living things that are too small to be seen with the unaided eye.
84 Van Leeuwenhoek worked in his native country of Holland, first as a fabric
97 merchant and later as a chamberlain (assistant) to the town's sheriffs. Because
109 working as a chamberlain gave him a great deal of financial security and free
123 time, he had time to read many books. In the late 1660s, he was introduced to
139 microscopes through a book titled *Micrographia* by Robert Hooke. This book
150 was highly influential and introduced the public to microscopy, the use of the
163 microscope to investigate tiny living things. (#1)

B
169 **An Unusual Hobby**
172 This field of study fascinated van Leeuwenhoek. He began to practice
183 microscopy and developed an unusual hobby. He learned how to grind his own
196 lenses, and he created his own microscope that differed from the compound
208 microscopes of that day. Unlike compound microscopes that used more than one
220 lens, van Leeuwenhoek's microscopes were simple devices that used only one
231 lens. While the contemporary microscopes of his day magnified a specimen 20 to
244 30 times, van Leeuwenhoek's microscopes magnified a specimen 200 to 300
255 times. This difference was due chiefly to Leeuwenhoek's skill at lens grinding and
268 his patience in adjusting the light source when viewing tiny specimens. (#2)

Leeuwenhoek microscope (circa late 1600s)

Student Book: Application Lesson 8 101

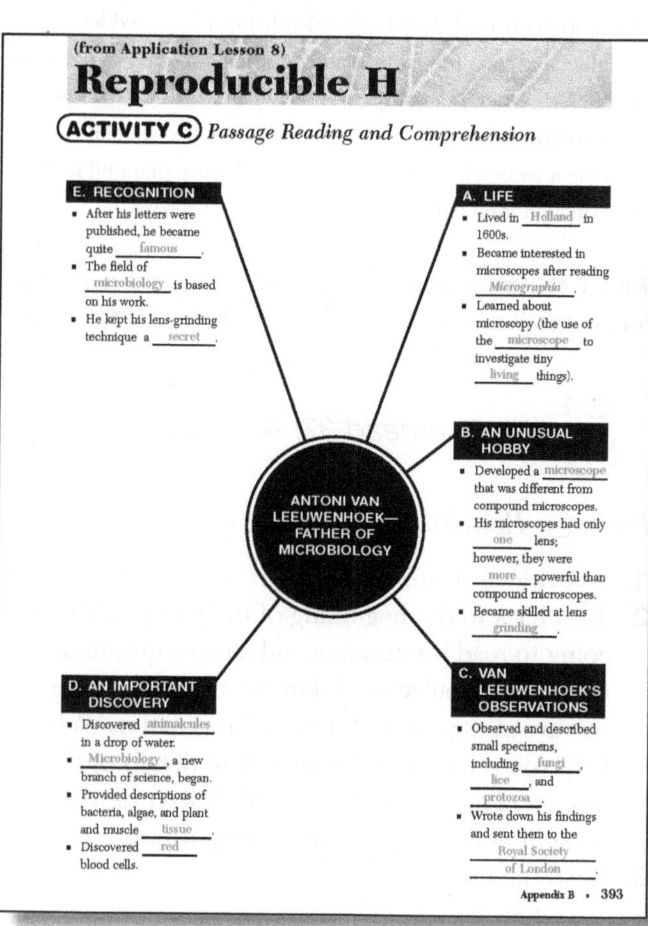

(from Application Lesson 8)

Reproducible H

ACTIVITY C *Passage Reading and Comprehension*

ANTONI VAN LEEUWENHOEK—FATHER OF MICROBIOLOGY

A. LIFE
- Lived in Holland in 1600s.
- Became interested in microscopes after reading *Micrographia*.
- Learned about microscopy (the use of the microscope to investigate tiny living things).

B. AN UNUSUAL HOBBY
- Developed a microscope that was different from compound microscopes.
- His microscopes had only one lens; however, they were more powerful than compound microscopes.
- Became skilled at lens grinding.

C. VAN LEEUWENHOEK'S OBSERVATIONS
- Observed and described small specimens, including fungi, lice, and protozoa.
- Wrote down his findings and sent them to the Royal Society of London.

D. AN IMPORTANT DISCOVERY
- Discovered animalcules in a drop of water.
- Microbiology, a new branch of science, began.
- Provided descriptions of bacteria, algae, and plant and muscle tissue.
- Discovered red blood cells.

E. RECOGNITION
- After his letters were published, he became quite famous.
- The field of microbiology is based on his work.
- He kept his lens-grinding technique a secret.

Appendix B • 393

#3 What are protozoa?

Protozoa are single-celled microscopic animals that are too small for the human eye to observe.

#4 With whom did van Leeuwenhoek correspond?

The Royal Society of London—a scientific group in England.

#5 What did van Leeuwenhoek find in a tiny drop of water? Why was this important to the world of science?

A world of tiny swimming creatures; this discovery, along with the discovery of protozoa, led to a new branch of science—microbiology.

#6 Name at least one other contribution van Leeuwenhoek made to science.

Classified three types of bacteria: bacilli, cocci, and spirilla; discovered red blood cells.

#7 How has van Leeuwenhoek's work influenced microbiology?

Provided a basis for other experiments; set the stage for future advances in technology, medicine, and general research.

#8 Why did it take until the 19th century for more advances to be made in microbiology?

Van Leeuwenhoek kept his lens grinding technique a secret; the compound microscope was improved a great deal in the 19th century.

APPLICATION LESSON

8

C

Van Leeuwenhoek's Observations

Once van Leeuwenhoek had developed his powerful, one-lens microscope, his observations expanded and focused on a range of specimens. He observed and described fungi, bee stingers, and lice. He even described creatures that were too small for the human eye to observe unaided. He called these creatures **protozoa**. Protozoa are single-celled microscopic animals. (#3)

In 1673, van Leeuwenhoek began a correspondence with the Royal Society of London, a scientific group in England. He sent regular letters that were filled with a jumble of observations about various subjects. Each letter described his experiments and findings. But it wasn't until he described the world he saw in a drop of water that the Royal Society began to take real notice of his work. (#4)

D

An Important Discovery

Van Leeuwenhoek discovered that the drop of water was host to many tiny, swimming creatures, which he called **animalcules**. This news caused a great stir in the Royal Society of London. They realized that he must have made an important discovery. He had found a whole new world that is much smaller than anything humans can see with their eyes. The Society set out to reproduce the experiment. Once they had seen the tiny creatures for themselves, they were convinced. This discovery, coupled with van Leeuwenhoek's discovery of protozoa, formed the basis for a new branch of science: **microbiology**. (#5)

animalcules

drop of water

Van Leeuwenhoek did not stop making his observations. He continued his experiments and provided descriptions of many types of bacteria, algae, and other single-celled organisms that scientists are familiar with today. He even discovered that bacteria are present in the mouth. He eventually classified the bacteria he witnessed into three types: bacilli, cocci, and spirilla. He observed

APPLICATION LESSON

8

plant and muscle tissue. He also discovered red blood cells. Throughout his lifetime, he continued to write to the Royal Society of London, describing his findings and observations. (#6)

E

Recognition

As his letters were translated and published, van Leeuwenhoek became quite famous. He was elected to be part of the Royal Society, though he never actually attended a meeting in London. His discoveries provided a basis for many other types of experiments in the decades to come. Van Leeuwenhoek's exploration of the microcosm set the stage for future advances in technology, medicine, and general research. Our current understandings in microbiology are based upon his work. (#7)

Despite his importance to the field of microbiology, he kept his lens-grinding technique a secret. It wasn't until the 19th century, when the compound microscope was improved significantly, that more advances could be made in microbiology. (#8)

ACTIVITY D *Fluency Building*

Cold Timing		Practice 1	
Practice 2		Hot Timing	

ACTIVITY D

Fluency Building

ACTIVITY PROCEDURE

(See the *Student Book*, page 103.)

Have students complete a Cold Timing, one or two practices, and a Hot Timing of the Activity C article. For each timing, have students record the number of correct words read. Finally, have students complete their Fluency Graphs.

Note D-1: When assigning partners for this activity, have the stronger reader read first. As a result, the other reader will have one additional practice opportunity.

1. Now, it's time for fluency building.
2. Find the beginning of the passage again. (Pause.)
3. Whisper-read. See how many words you can read in one minute. Begin._ (Time students for one minute.) Stop._ Circle the last word that you read._ Record the number of words you read after **Cold Timing**._
4. Let's practice again. Begin._ (Time students for one minute.) Stop._ Put a box around the last word that you read._ Record the number of words you read after **Practice 1**._
5. (Optional) Let's practice one more time before the Hot Timing. Begin._ (Time students for one minute.) Stop._ Put a box around the last word that you read._ Record the number of words you read after **Practice 2**._
6. Please exchange books with your partner._ Partner 1, you are going to read first. Partner 2, listen carefully and underline any mistakes or words left out. Ones, begin._ (Time students for one minute.) Stop._ Twos, cross out the last word that your partner read._ (Assist students in subtracting the number of mistakes from the number of words read.) Twos, record the number of correct words in your partner's book after **Hot Timing**._
7. Partner 2, you are going to read next. Partner 1, listen carefully and underline any mistakes or words left out. Twos, begin. (Time students for one minute.) Stop._ Ones, cross out the last word that your partner read._ Ones, record the number of correct words in your partner's book after **Hot Timing**._
8. Exchange books._ Turn to the Fluency Graph on the inside back cover, and indicate on the graph the number of Cold Timing and Hot Timing words you read correctly._

564 plant and muscle tissue. He also discovered red blood cells. Throughout his
576 lifetime, he continued to write to the Royal Society of London, describing his
589 findings and observations. (#6)

E

592 **Recognition**
593 As his letters were translated and published, van Leeuwenhoek became quite
604 famous. He was elected to be part of the Royal Society, though he never actually
619 attended a meeting in London. His discoveries provided a basis for many other
632 types of experiments in the decades to come. Van Leeuwenhoek's exploration of
644 the microcosm set the stage for future advances in technology, medicine, and
656 general research. Our current understandings in microbiology are based upon
666 his work. (#7)
668 Despite his importance to the field of microbiology, he kept his lens-grinding
681 technique a secret. It wasn't until the 19th century, when the compound
693 microscope was improved significantly, that more advances could be made in
704 microbiology. (#8)
705

ACTIVITY D *Fluency Building*

Cold Timing		Practice 1	
Practice 2		Hot Timing	

ACTIVITY E

Comprehension Questions—Multiple Choice

ACTIVITY PROCEDURE

(See the *Student Book*, page 104.)

Have students complete item #1. Then, have students share the rationale for their answers. Encourage thoughtful discussion. Proceed item-by-item, emphasizing the rationale for the *best* answer. Have students record points for each correct item.

Note E-1: The correct Multiple Choice answers are circled.

1. Turn to page 104. Find **Activity E.**
2. Use the Multiple Choice Strategy to complete item #1. Be ready to explain why you selected your answer. (Wait while students complete the item. Call on individual students. Ask them why they chose their answer and why they eliminated the other choices. Encourage discussion. Provide students with feedback on their choices, focusing on why or why not those choices might be appropriate.)
3. (Repeat Step 2 for items 2–4, pausing after each item to confirm student responses and provide feedback.)
4. Count the number of items you got correct, and record that number in the blank half of the Multiple Choice Comprehension box.

APPLICATION LESSON

8

ACTIVITY E *Comprehension Questions—Multiple Choice*

Comprehension Strategy—Multiple Choice

Step 1: Read the item.
Step 2: Read all of the choices.
Step 3: Think about why each choice might be correct or incorrect. Check the article as needed.
Step 4: From the possible correct choices, select the best answer.

1. (Vocabulary) **You could conclude that "micro" in <u>micro</u>biology means:**
   a. living things.
   (b.) small.
   c. hot.
   d. microscope.
2. (Cause and effect) **One of the major things that led to Antoni Van Leeuwenhoek's success was:**
   a. the level of education that he received through the Royal Society of London.
   b. his background working as an assistant to the town's sheriff.
   (c.) his skill at developing powerful microscopes.
   d. his election to the Royal Society of London so he could attend meetings and enhance his scientific knowledge.
3. (Compare and contrast) **When comparing Van Leeuwenhoek's microscopes to compound microscopes of that day, which of the following is NOT a correct statement?**
   a. Van Leeuwenhoek's microscope had one lens while compound microscopes had more than one lens.
   b. Van Leeuwenhoek's microscope magnified a 200 to 300 times while compound microscopes magnified 20 to 30 times.
   c. Van Leeuwenhoek's microscope was simple while compound microscopes were more complex.
   (d.) Van Leeuwenhoek's microscope was designed to observe small specimens while compound microscopes were designed to examine large items.
4. (Cause and effect) **When Van Leeuwenhoek discovered "tiny swimming creatures" in a drop of water, which of the following did NOT result?**
   a. A new branch of science was formed.
   b. The Royal Society of London knew an important discovery had been made.
   (c.) He shared his lens-grinding techniques so that other scientists could verify his results.
   d. Van Leeuwenhoek continued his experiments and described many small specimens.

MULTIPLE CHOICE COMPREHENSION 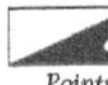 Points

104 *REWARDS Plus: Reading Strategies Applied to Science Passages*

Vocabulary Activities

ACTIVITY PROCEDURE

(See the *Student Book*, page 105–106.)

Have students complete each item orally and provide feedback on their answers. Then have students respond to each question in writing by answering "yes" or "no" and providing a reason for their answers.

Yes/No/Why

1. Turn to page 105._ Find **Activity F**._ Read item 1. Tell your partner your answer and your reason for it. (Pause. Then call on individual students. Encourage discussion. Provide students with feedback on their choices, focusing on their explanations for their answer.)
2. Write your answer and your reason for it in the space provided. Look up when you are done._
3. Read item #2. Tell your partner your answer and your reason for it. (Pause. Then call on individual students. Encourage discussion. Provide students with feedback on their choices, focusing on their explanations for their answer.)
4. Write your answer and your reason for it in the space provided. Look up when you are done._
5. Read item #3. Tell your partner your answer and your reason for it. (Pause. Then call on individual students. Encourage discussion. Provide students with feedback on their choices, focusing on their explanations for their answer.)
6. Write your answer and your reason for it in the space provided. Look up when you are done._

Note F-1: You may wish to do this as an oral task only rather than an oral and a written task.

APPLICATION LESSON 8

ACTIVITY F *Vocabulary Activities*

Yes/No/Why

1. Would **microbiology** include the study of **microcosms**?
Example answer: Yes. Microbiology is the branch of science that studies microorganisms, which are found in microcosms.

2. Would you require a **microscope** to study **bacilli specimens**?
Example answer: Yes. Bacilli specimens are too small to be seen with the naked eye, so a microscope would be needed.

3. Could ***Micrographia*** have provided **Robert Hooke** with **financial security**?
Example answer: Yes. As the author, Hooke would receive royalties for the sale of each book. If they sold a lot of books, he would have plenty of money to live on.

Student Book: Application Lesson 8 105

ACTIVITY PROCEDURE

Have students read the words and definitions and then complete the sentence stems for each vocabulary word. Have them share answers with partners and with the class. Then, have students give themselves points in the blank half of the Vocabulary box.

Completion Activity

1. Turn to page 106. Read the first word and its definition.
2. Now, read the sentence stem.
3. Think of how you would complete the sentence stem and write it. Share your answer with your partner. (Call on a few students to share answers with the class.)
4. (Repeat Steps 1–3 for the rest of the words.)
5. If you participated in answering all seven questions, give yourself seven points in the blank half of the Vocabulary box.

Note F-2: You may wish to do this as an oral task only rather than an oral task and a written task.

APPLICATION LESSON

8

Completion Activities

1. **influence:** to change the thought or behavior of
   Some things in life we have little influence over, but these things we can greatly influence:
   Answers will vary.

2. **assistant:** one who helps
   Although some jobs can be completed by one person, assistants are required for these jobs:
   Answers will vary.

3. **correspondence:** exchange of letters
   In the past, correspondence was difficult because the process was slow. Correspondence is easier now because
   Answers will vary.

4. **translated:** changed into another language
   In order to be read by people in Spain, France, and Italy, books written in English need to be translated into
   Answers will vary.

VOCABULARY 7 Points

106 *REWARDS Plus: Reading Strategies Applied to Science Passages*

ACTIVITY G

Expository Writing— Multi-Paragraph Answer

ACTIVITY PROCEDURE, Plan and Write

(See the *Student Book*, pages 107–109.)

Have students read the prompt and the three topics. Have students read the **LIST** of details under topic a, then guide them in adding details for topics b and c. Have students look at topic a again. Explain that details that don't go with a topic should be **CROSSED OUT**. Have students **CONNECT** details as shown in the example plan. Have students **NUMBER** their details in the same manner as in the example plan for topic a. Next, have students **WRITE** paragraph a. Guide students in completing the plan for topic b and writing paragraph b. Repeat for topic c. Finally, explain that after the answer is written, they should **EDIT** their work, revising for clarity and proofreading for errors in capitalization, punctuation, and spelling.

Use Overheads 38 and 39: Activity G

1. Turn to page 107._ Find **Activity G.**_
2. Find the prompt in the middle of the page._ Read the prompt out loud with me: **Summarize the information presented on van Leeuwenhoek's hobby, his discoveries, and the recognition of his contributions to science.**
3. Turn to page 108._ Read topic a._ Read topic b._ Read topic c._
4. Read the details **listed** under topic a._
5. Add details to topic b. Look back in the article and locate details that tell about van Leeuwenhoek's discoveries. Write the details in the Planning Box._
6. Add details to topic c. Look back in the article and locate details that tell about the recognition of Leeuwenhoek's scientific contributions. Write the details in the Planning Box._
7. Use the steps for topic a. Read the details and **cross out** any details that do not go with the topic._ Next, draw brackets to **connect** details that could easily go into one sentence._ Now, **number** the details in a logical order._
8. (Show Overhead 38.) Now, look at the example plan for topic a on the overhead. Yours doesn't need to be the same, but it should be similar._

APPLICATION LESSON 8

ACTIVITY G *Expository Writing—Multi-Paragraph Answer*

Writing Strategy—Multi-Paragraph Answer

Step 1: **LIST** (List the details that are important enough to include in your answer.)
Step 2: **CROSS OUT** (Reread the details. Cross out any that don't go with the topic.)
Step 3: **CONNECT** (Connect any details that could go into one sentence.)
Step 4: **NUMBER** (Number the details in a logical order.)
Step 5: **WRITE** (Write the paragraph.)
Step 6: **EDIT** (Revise and proofread your answer.)

Prompt: Summarize the information presented on van Leeuwenhoek's hobby, his discoveries, and the recognition of his contributions to science.

Plan: Complete the Planning Box with your teacher.

Student Book: Application Lesson 8 107

APPLICATION LESSON 8

Example Multi-Paragraph Plan

Planning Box
(topic a) *van Leeuwenhoek—hobby*
① (detail) – *read Micrographia*
① (detail) – *became interested in the study of small things using microscopes*
② (detail) – *created his own microscope*
② (detail) – *much more powerful than microscopes of the time*
③ (detail) – *observed many small things such as fungi, bee stingers, & lice*
(topic b) *van Leeuwenhoek's discoveries*
(detail) – ~~*shared discoveries with Royal Society of London*~~
① (detail) – *protozoa—single-celled microscopic animals*
② (detail) – *animalcules—tiny creatures in water*
③ (detail) – *described microscopic organisms such as algae and bacteria*
④ (detail) – *classified bacteria: bacilli, cocci, spirilla*
⑤ (detail) – *discovered red blood cells*
(topic c) *van Leeuwenhoek—recognition of scientific contributions*
① (detail) – *communicated with Royal Society of London*
② (detail) – *in the beginning they took little notice of his findings*
② (detail) – *discovery of small creatures in water was recognized as important finding*
③ (detail) – *his letters were translated and printed*
③ (detail) – *became famous*
④ (detail) – *invited to join Royal Society of London*
⑤ (detail) – *founder of microbiology*

Write: Write paragraphs a, b, and c on a separate piece of paper.

108 *REWARDS Plus: Reading Strategies Applied to Science Passages*

9. Take out a blank piece of paper. Using your plan for paragraph a, **write** paragraph a. If you finish early, please reread and **edit** your paragraph. (Move around the room and monitor your students as they are writing.)

10. (When the majority of students are done, proceed with the lesson.) Now, use the steps for topic b. First, read the details and **cross out** any details that do not go with the topic. Next, draw brackets to **connect** details that could easily go into one sentence. Now, **number** the details in a logical order.

11. Now, look at the example plan for topic b on the overhead. Yours doesn't need to be the same, but it should be similar.

12. Locate your piece of paper. Using your plan for paragraph b, **write** paragraph b. If you finish early, please **edit** your paragraph. (Move around the room and monitor your students as they are writing.)

13. (When the majority of students are done, proceed with the lesson.) Now, use the steps for topic c. First, read the details and **cross out** any details that do not go with the topic. Next, draw brackets to **connect** details that could easily go into one sentence. Now, **number** the details in a logical order.

14. Look at the example plan for topic c on the overhead. Yours doesn't need to be the same, but it should be similar.

15. Locate your piece of paper. Using your plan for paragraph c, **write** paragraph c. If you finish early, please **edit** your paragraph. (Move around the room and monitor your students as they are writing.)

16. (When the majority of students are done, proceed with the lesson.) Now, edit your paragraphs. Please carefully read your paragraphs. Be sure that your paragraphs are easy to understand and clear. Proofread for any errors in capitalization, punctuation, and spelling. (Give students time to proofread their paragraphs.)

ACTIVITY PROCEDURE, Evaluate

Ask students to read each question in the rubric. Guide them in evaluating the paragraphs using the guidelines. Have students total their points and record them in the blank half of the Writing box.

APPLICATION LESSON **8**

Evaluate: Evaluate the paragraphs using this rubric.

Rubric—Multi-Paragraph Answer	Student or Partner Rating	Teacher Rating
1. Did the author state the topic in the first sentence?	a. Yes Fix up b. Yes Fix up c. Yes Fix up	a. Yes No b. Yes No c. Yes No
2. Did the author include details that go with the topic?	a. Yes Fix up b. Yes Fix up c. Yes Fix up	a. Yes No b. Yes No c. Yes No
3. Did the author combine details in some of the sentences?	a. Yes Fix up b. Yes Fix up c. Yes Fix up	a. Yes No b. Yes No c. Yes No
4. Is the answer easy to understand?	Yes Fix up	Yes No
5. Did the author correctly spell words, particularly the words found in the article?	Yes Fix up	Yes No
6. Did the author use correct capitalization, capitalizing the first word in the sentence and proper names of people, places, and things?	Yes Fix up	Yes No
7. Did the author use correct punctuation, including a period at the end of each sentence?	Yes Fix up	Yes No

WRITING 13 Points

Student Book: Application Lesson 8 109

17. Turn to page 109. Let's evaluate paragraph a.

18. Read question #1 with me. Circle "Yes" for a if your topic sentence includes the topic: van Leeuwenhoek's hobby.

19. Read question #2 with me. Circle "Yes" for a if all of your details tell about van Leeuwenhoek's hobby.

20. Read question #3 with me. Circle "Yes" for a if you combined details into one sentence.

21. Now, check paragraphs b and c carefully and answer questions 1 through 3.

22. Read question #4. Reread your paragraphs. Circle "Yes" if your paragraphs are easy to understand.

23. Read question #5. Carefully examine your paragraphs. If you think a word is misspelled, underline it and check back in the plan or article and correct the spelling. Circle "Yes" if you believe that you have very few spelling errors.

24. Read question #6. Carefully examine your sentences. Be sure that each sentence begins with a capital. If all sentences begin with a capital, circle "Yes."

25. Read question #7._ Examine your sentences. Be sure that each sentence ends with a period._ If all sentences end with a period, circle "Yes."_

26. Count up your points and record them in the Writing box._

27. (Show Overhead 39.) Look at the overhead._ Let's read the three example paragraphs. Yours do not have to be the same, but they should be similar. (Read the paragraphs to your students or with your students or call on a student to read the example paragraph.)

Note G-1: The rubric can be used in a variety of ways. Instead of the students evaluating their own paragraphs, you may wish to have their partners provide feedback. The second column is designed for teacher feedback. If you have a small group, it would be useful to give daily feedback on writing. If the group size is large, you can give feedback to a number of children each day. You may wish to give students bonus points based on your feedback.

APPLICATION LESSON 8

Evaluate: Evaluate the paragraphs using this rubric.

Rubric— Multi-Paragraph Answer	Student or Partner Rating	Teacher Rating
1. Did the author state the topic in the first sentence?	a. (Yes) Fix up b. (Yes) Fix up c. (Yes) Fix up	a. Yes No b. Yes No c. Yes No
2. Did the author include details that go with the topic?	a. (Yes) Fix up b. (Yes) Fix up c. (Yes) Fix up	a. Yes No b. Yes No c. Yes No
3. Did the author combine details in some of the sentences?	a. (Yes) Fix up b. (Yes) Fix up c. (Yes) Fix up	a. Yes No b. Yes No c. Yes No
4. Is the answer easy to understand?	(Yes) Fix up	Yes No
5. Did the author correctly spell words, particularly the words found in the article?	(Yes) Fix up	Yes No
6. Did the author use correct capitalization, capitalizing the first word in the sentence and proper names of people, places, and things?	(Yes) Fix up	Yes No
7. Did the author use correct punctuation, including a period at the end of each sentence?	(Yes) Fix up	Yes No

WRITING 13 Points

Student Book: Application Lesson 8 109

ACTIVITY H

Comprehension—Single-Paragraph Answer

ACTIVITY PROCEDURE

(See the *Student Book*, page 110.)

Have students read the *What Is* statement and the *What If* question. Have students turn the question into part of the answer and write down a topic sentence for their answer. Then, have them complete their answer. Encourage them to use evidence from the article and their own experience and background knowledge. Engage students in a discussion. Award points for writing and participating in the discussion.

Note H-1: To increase the quality of the discussion, the students are asked to think and write about the *What If* before the discussion. However, you may be working with students who have difficulty generating ideas for their paragraph. If that is the case, switch the order of activities: engage the students in a discussion, and then have them write their paragraphs.

1. Turn to page 110._ Find **Activity H.**_
2. Find the *What Is* statement in the middle of the page._ Read it out loud with me: **Because the Royal Society of London recognized the importance of van Leeuwenhoek's discoveries, they repeated and expanded on many of his studies and distributed his findings.**
3. Find the *What If* question._ Read it with me: **If the Royal Society of London had not recognized the importance of van Leeuwenhoek's discoveries, what might have resulted?**
4. Think how you might turn the question into part of the answer._ Tell me your idea for a topic sentence._ (Example sentence: A number of things could have happened if the Royal Society of London had not recognized the importance of van Leeuwenhoek's discoveries.) Take out a piece of paper and write your topic sentence._ (Move around the room and monitor as students write.)
5. You are ready to add ideas to your paragraph. Use evidence from the article as well as your own experience and background knowledge. If you finish early, reread your paragraph and edit it so that it is easy to understand and clear._ (Move around the room and monitor as students write.)
6. Read your paragraph to your partner._
7. If you included wording from the question in your answer and added evidence from the article, award yourself four points for writing._

APPLICATION LESSON

8

ACTIVITY H *Comprehension—Single-Paragraph Answer*

Writing Strategy—Single-Paragraph Answer

Step 1: Read the item.
Step 2: Turn the question into part of the answer and write it down.
Step 3: Think of the answer or locate the answer in the article.
Step 4: Complete your answer.

Prompt:

What Is—Because the Royal Society of London recognized the importance of van Leeuwenhoek's discoveries, they repeated and expanded on many of his studies and distributed his findings.

What If—If the Royal Society of London had not recognized the importance of van Leeuwenhoek's discoveries, what might have resulted?

Write and Discuss: Write a paragraph. Then share your ideas. Use the Discussion Guidelines.

Discussion Guidelines

Speaker		Listener	
Looks like:	**Sounds like:**	**Looks like:**	**Sounds like:**
• Facing peers • Making eye contact • Participating	• Using pleasant, easy-to-hear voice • Sharing opinions, supporting facts and reasons from the article and from your experience • Staying on the topic	• Facing speaker • Making eye contact • Participating	• Waiting quietly to speak • Giving positive, supportive comments • Disagreeing respectfully

WRITING DISCUSSION

4 Points 4 Points

110 *REWARDS Plus: Reading Strategies Applied to Science Passages*

8. (Engage students in a discussion. Award four points to students who are active participants in the discussion.)

Note H-2: If your students are having difficulty writing the *What If* paragraphs, read or show them the following example paragraph:

Example Single-Paragraph Answer

A number of things could have happened if the Royal Society of London had not recognized the importance of van Leeuwenhoek's discoveries. First, the members of the society would not have reproduced van Leeuwenhoek's experiments. Thus, there would have been less evidence supporting his discoveries. Second, the development of microbiology might have been slowed significantly. Other scientists might have made similar discoveries, but these discoveries might have happened decades later. It is even possible that another scientist might have been labeled the "Father of Microbiology" had van Leeuwenhoek's contributions not been recognized.

Application Lesson 9

Materials Needed:

- *Student Book*: Application Lesson 9
- Application Overhead Transparencies 40–44
- Appendix B Reproducible I: Application Lesson 9
- Appendix C Optional Vocabulary Activity: Application Lesson 9
- Paper or cardboard to use when covering the overhead transparency
- Paper or cardboard for each student to use during spelling dictation
- Washable overhead transparency pen

Text Treatment Notes:

- Black text signifies teacher script (exact wording to say to students).
- Green text in parentheses signifies directions or prompts for the teacher.
- Green text signifies answers or examples of answers.
- Green graphics treatment signifies reproduction of Overhead information.
- Green text and green graphics treatment do not appear in the *Student Book*.

ACTIVITY A

Vocabulary

ACTIVITY PROCEDURE, List 1

(See the *Student Book*, page 111.)

Tell students each word in the list. Then, have students repeat the word and read the definition aloud. For each definition, provide any additional information that may be necessary. Then, have students practice reading the words themselves.

Use Overhead 40: Activity A
List 1: Tell

1. (Show the top half of Overhead 40.) Before we read the passage, let's read the difficult words. The first two items are names. (Point to **Democritus**.) The first name is **Democritus**. What name?_ Now, read the definition._
2. (Point to **John Dalton**.) The next name is **John Dalton**. What name?_ Now, read the definition._
3. (Pronounce each word in List 1, and then have students repeat each word and read the definition.)
4. Open your *Student Book* to **Application Lesson 9**, page 111._
5. Find **Activity A**, **List 1**, in your book._ Let's read the words again. First word._ Next words._ (Continue for all words in List 1.)

ACTIVITY PROCEDURE, List 2

(See the *Student Book*, page 111.)

Have students circle prefixes and suffixes, then underline the vowels. Using the overhead transparency, assist students in checking their work. Next, have students figure out each word to themselves, then say it aloud. Have them read the definition aloud.

Use Overhead 40: Activity A
List 2: Strategy Practice

1. Find **List 2**. Circle the prefixes and suffixes, and underline the vowels. Look up when you are done._
2. (Show the bottom half of Overhead 40.) Before you check your work on List 2, look at item #2. (Point to the second example and the **hydro** that is circled.) From now on, you can also circle **hydro**, which means *water*. The prefix is /hydro/. Say it._ Look at item #5. (Point to the second example and the **sub** that is circled.) From now on, you can also circle **sub**. The prefix is /sub/. Say it._ Look at item #9. (Point to the second example and the **at** that is circled.) From now on, you can also circle **at**. The prefix is /at/. Say it._ Now, go back to item #1. Check and fix any mistakes._
3. Go back to the first word again._ Sound out the word to yourself. Put your thumb up when you can read the word. Be sure that it is a real word._ What word?_ Now, read the definition._
4. (Continue Step 3 with all remaining words in List 2.)

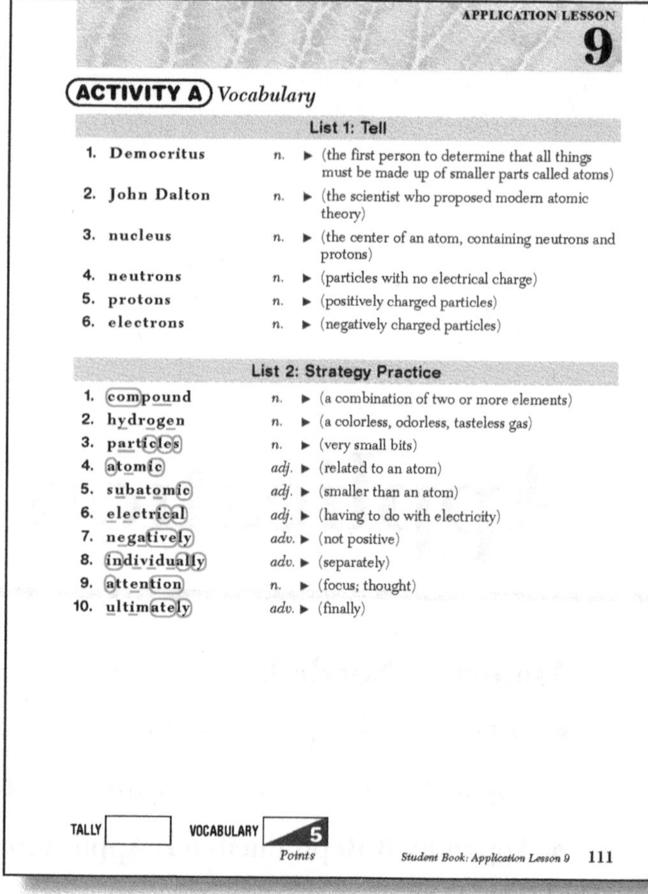

APPLICATION LESSON 9

ACTIVITY A *Vocabulary*

List 1: Tell

1.	Democritus	n.	▶ (the first person to determine that all things must be made up of smaller parts called atoms)
2.	John Dalton	n.	▶ (the scientist who proposed modern atomic theory)
3.	nucleus	n.	▶ (the center of an atom, containing neutrons and protons)
4.	neutrons	n.	▶ (particles with no electrical charge)
5.	protons	n.	▶ (positively charged particles)
6.	electrons	n.	▶ (negatively charged particles)

List 2: Strategy Practice

1.	compound	n.	▶ (a combination of two or more elements)
2.	hydrogen	n.	▶ (a colorless, odorless, tasteless gas)
3.	particles	n.	▶ (very small bits)
4.	atomic	adj.	▶ (related to an atom)
5.	subatomic	adj.	▶ (smaller than an atom)
6.	electrical	adj.	▶ (having to do with electricity)
7.	negatively	adv.	▶ (not positive)
8.	individually	adv.	▶ (separately)
9.	attention	n.	▶ (focus; thought)
10.	ultimately	adv.	▶ (finally)

TALLY VOCABULARY 5 Points

Student Book: Application Lesson 9 111

Note A.2-1: You may wish to provide additional practice by having students read words to a partner.

ACTIVITY PROCEDURE, List 1 and 2

(See the *Student Book*, page 111.)

Tell students to look in List 1 or List 2 for a word you are thinking about. Have them circle the number of the word and tell you the word. Explain to students to make a tally mark for each correct word in the Tally box, and then enter the number of tally marks as points in the blank half of the Vocabulary box.

1. Remember, the words I'm thinking about will be in either List 1 or List 2. Make a tally mark for every correctly identified word.
2. Circle the number of the appropriate word.
   - If you are focusing on an idea and giving it careful thought, you are giving it this. (Wait.) What word? **attention**
   - Very small bits of things are called these. (Wait.) What word? **particles**
   - These negatively charged particles are part of atoms. (Wait) What word? **electrons**
   - This is the center of an atom. (Wait.) What word? **nucleus**
   - When parcels are wrapped separately, they are said to be wrapped in this way. (Wait.) What word? **individually**
3. Count all the tally marks, and enter that number as points in the blank half of the Vocabulary box.

ACTIVITY PROCEDURE, List 3

(See the *Student Book*, page 112.)

The words in the third list are related. Have students use the *REWARDS* Strategies to figure out the first word in each family. Have them read the definition of the verb and then read nouns and adjectives that are related to that verb.

1. Turn to page 112._ Find **Family 1** in **List 3.** Figure out the first word. Use your pencil if you wish. Put your thumb up when you know the word._ What word?_ Read the definition._
2. Look at the nouns in Family 1. Figure out the first word._ What word?_ Next word._ What word?_
3. Look at the adjective in Family 1. Figure out the word._ What word?_
4. (Repeat Steps 1–3 for all word families in List 3.)

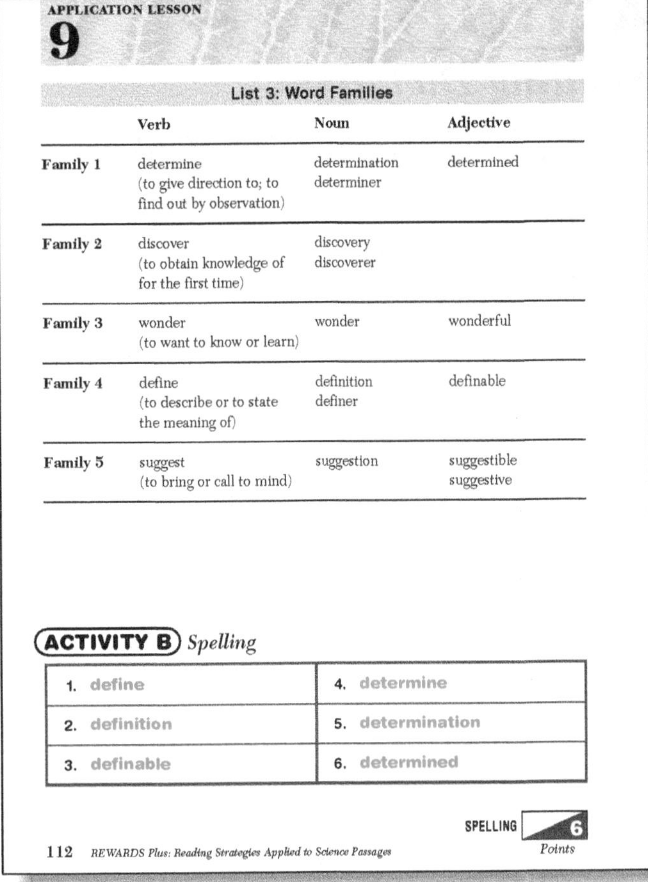

APPLICATION LESSON
9

List 3: Word Families

	Verb	Noun	Adjective
Family 1	determine (to give direction to; to find out by observation)	determination determiner	determined
Family 2	discover (to obtain knowledge of for the first time)	discovery discoverer	
Family 3	wonder (to want to know or learn)	wonder	wonderful
Family 4	define (to describe or to state the meaning of)	definition definer	definable
Family 5	suggest (to bring or call to mind)	suggestion	suggestible suggestive

ACTIVITY B *Spelling*

1. define	4. determine
2. definition	5. determination
3. definable	6. determined

SPELLING 6 *Points*

112 *REWARDS Plus: Reading Strategies Applied to Science Passages*

Note A.3-1: You may wish to provide additional practice by having students read a word family to the group or to a partner.

Note A.3-2: An additional vocabulary practice activity called Quick Words is provided in Appendix C of this Teacher's Guide. See Appendix C for information about how this optional activity can be used.

ACTIVITY B

Spelling Dictation

ACTIVITY PROCEDURE

(See the *Student Book*, page 112.)

For each word, tell students the word, then have students say the parts of the word to themselves while they write the word. Using the overhead transparency, assist students in checking their spelling and correcting if they misspelled. Then, have students enter the number of correctly spelled words as points in the blank half of the Spelling box.

Note B-1: Distribute a piece of light cardboard to each of the students.

 *Use Overhead 41: Activity B*

1. Find **Activity B**.
2. The first word is **define**. What word?_ Say the parts in **define** to yourself as you write the word. (Pause and monitor.)
3. (Show **define** on the overhead.) Check **define**. If you misspelled it, cross it out and write it correctly.
4. The second word is **definition**. What word?_ Say the parts in **definition** to yourself as you write the word. (Pause and monitor.)
5. (Show **definition** on the overhead.) Check **definition**. If you misspelled it, cross it out and write it correctly.
6. (Repeat the procedures for the words **definable**, **determine**, **determination**, and **determined**.)
7. Count the number of words you spelled correctly, and record that number as points in the blank half of the Spelling box at the bottom of the page.

APPLICATION LESSON
9

List 3: Word Families

	Verb	Noun	Adjective
Family 1	determine (to give direction to; to find out by observation)	determination determiner	determined
Family 2	discover (to obtain knowledge of for the first time)	discovery discoverer	
Family 3	wonder (to want to know or learn)	wonder	wonderful
Family 4	define (to describe or to state the meaning of)	definition definer	definable
Family 5	suggest (to bring or call to mind)	suggestion	suggestible suggestive

ACTIVITY B *Spelling*

1. define	4. determine
2. definition	5. determination
3. definable	6. determined

112 *REWARDS Plus: Reading Strategies Applied to Science Passages*

SPELLING 6 *Points*

ACTIVITY C

Passage Reading and Comprehension

ACTIVITY PROCEDURE

(See the *Student Book*, pages 113–115.)

Have students read the title of the passage and each heading. Ask them to tell their partners two things that the passage will tell about.

Passage Preview

1. Turn to page 113._ Let's preview the passage.
2. Read the title._ What is the whole passage going to tell about?_
3. Now, let's read the headings. Read the first heading._ Read the next heading._ (Continue until students have read all headings.)
4. Turn to your partner. Without looking, tell two things this passage will tell about._

ACTIVITY PROCEDURE

Provide students with an Information Web from Appendix B. Have students read the passage silently to each embedded number, and then reread the same information orally either to a partner, together as a group, or individually. Ask the corresponding comprehension question or questions. Once students finish reading a section labeled A, B, C, D, or E, have them fill in the Information Web before going on to the next section.

Note C-1: If students do not finish reading the passage during class, have them use their Information Webs to review the information at the beginning of the next class.

Use Overhead 42: Activity C

Passage Reading

1. (Provide an Information Web for each student.)
2. Turn back to the beginning of the passage. You're going to read the passage and answer questions about what you've read. During passage reading, you are also going to fill in an Information Web to help you remember the important details of the passage. Later, you'll use this Web to review the content of the passage with your partner.
3. Read the title._

APPLICATION LESSON **9**

ACTIVITY C *Passage Reading and Comprehension*

Note: For this activity, you will need Reproducible I found in the *Teacher's Guide.*

Atoms

A
Your table may be made of wood. Your toothbrush may be made of plastic.
14 Have you ever stopped to wonder what the plastic and wood are made of? They
29 are made up of elements, like carbon and hydrogen, all arranged in specific
42 ways. But what are these elements made of? If you break down an element into
57 the smallest part of itself that still behaves like that element, you have an atom.
72 An **atom** is the smallest particle of an element that can exist alone. Atoms are
87 the building blocks of all matter. (#1)

B
93 **History**
94 The first person to define an atom was Democritus in 530 B.C. He
107 determined that all things must be made up of smaller parts, and that ultimately
121 they could be broken down into atoms, or that which cannot be divided. His
135 theory suggested that these atoms would make up all substances, even though
147 they were too small to see individually. (#2)
154 In 1808, John Dalton added to the work of Democritus. Dalton stated the
167 following principles:
169 • Every element is made of atoms.
175 • All atoms of any element are the same.
183 • Atoms of different elements are different.
189 • Atoms of different elements can combine to form compounds.
198 • In any compound, the numbers and kinds of atoms remain the same.
210 These principles formed modern atomic theory until the discovery of the
221 electron in 1897. (#3)

C
224 **Simple Atomic Structure**
227 Each atom contains a nucleus at its center. The **nucleus** is a tightly packed
241 cluster of protons (which carry a positive electrical charge) and neutrons (which
253 carry no electrical charge). The protons determine how an atom behaves. Each
265 type of element is defined by the number of protons it contains. This is called
280 the element's **atomic number**. The higher the atomic number, the more the
292 atom weighs. (#4)
294 There is more to an atom than its center. A series of smaller, negatively
308 charged particles, called **electrons**, orbit the nucleus. The electrons are

Student Book: Application Lesson 9 113

(from Application Lesson 9)

Reproducible I

ACTIVITY C *Passage Reading and Comprehension*

ATOMS

A. WHAT ARE ATOMS?
- Atoms are the building blocks of all _matter_.
- Atoms are the smallest part of an _element_ that behaves like the _element_.
- Thus, elements such as carbon and hydrogen are made up of _atoms_.

B. HISTORY
- In 530 B.C., Democritus theorized that all things could be broken into _smaller_ parts and ultimately into _atoms_.
- In 1808, _Dalton_ added to the work of Democritus by stating:
  - Every element has _atoms_.
  - All _atoms_ in an element are the same.
  - Atoms of different elements are _different_.
  - Atoms of different elements can combine to form _compounds_.
  - In a compound, the number and kind of _atoms_ remain the same.
- These principles formed atomic theory until 1897 when the _electron_ was discovered.

C. SIMPLE ATOMIC STRUCTURE
- At the center of an atom is the _nucleus_.
- The nucleus contains _protons_ (positive electrical charge) and _neutrons_ (no electrical charge).
- The _protons_ determine how an atom behaves.
- _Electrons_ (negative electrical charge) orbit the nucleus.
- If the number of _protons_ (+) and the number of _electrons_ (–) are equal, the atom is electrically _neutral_.
- If the number of _protons_ and _electrons_ are NOT the same, it is called an _ion_.
- Atoms are hooked together to form _molecules_.

D. HOW DO WE KNOW ATOMS EXIST?
- Atoms can't be seen by the naked _eye_ even when aided by a _microscope_.
- A special microscope called a _Scanning Tunneling Microscope_ creates pictures of atoms.

E. IS THERE ANYTHING SMALLER THAN ATOMS?
- _Subatomic_ particles are smaller than atoms.
- Many subatomic particles exist.
- One such particle is the _quark_.

394 • REWARDS Plus: Reading Strategies Applied to Science Passages

4. Find number 1 in the passage. (Pause). Read down to number 1 silently. Look up when you are done._
5. (Wait for students to complete the reading. Then have students reread the part by having them read orally to a partner, read together orally as a group, or read aloud individually.)
6. (Ask the question or questions associated with the number. Provide feedback to students regarding their answers.)
7. (Repeat steps 4–6 for all paragraphs in Section A.)
8. Now, look at your Information Web. Find the section labeled A._ The information you've just read will help you to fill in this Web.
9. With your partner, fill in the blanks for Section A. You can refer back to the passage for information. Look up when you're done._ (Move around the room and monitor students as they complete the section.)
10. (When the majority of students have finished, show Overhead 42). Look at the overhead and check your work. Fix up or add to any of your answers.
11. Now read down to the next number silently. Look up when you are done._
12. (Repeat steps 5–11 until the students have finished the passage and the Information Web.)
13. Now use your Information Web to retell the important information from the passage to your partner.

Comprehension Questions

#1 What is an atom?

The smallest particle of an element that can exist alone; the building block of all matter.

#2 What did Democritus' theory claim?

That all things are made up of smaller parts and could be broken down into atoms; these atoms would make up all substances.

#3 What are the five principles of Dalton's modern atomic theory?

Elements are made of atoms; atoms of any element are the same; atoms of different elements are different; atoms of different elements can combine to form compounds; in any compound the numbers and kinds of atoms remain the same.

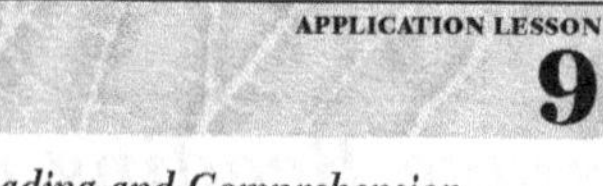

ACTIVITY C *Passage Reading and Comprehension*

Note: For this activity, you will need Reproducible I found in the *Teacher's Guide.*

Atoms

A

Your table may be made of wood. Your toothbrush may be made of plastic. Have you ever stopped to wonder what the plastic and wood are made of? They are made up of elements, like carbon and hydrogen, all arranged in specific ways. But what are these elements made of? If you break down an element into the smallest part of itself that still behaves like that element, you have an atom. An **atom** is the smallest particle of an element that can exist alone. Atoms are the building blocks of all matter. (#1)

B

History

The first person to define an atom was Democritus in 530 B.C. He determined that all things must be made up of smaller parts, and that ultimately they could be broken down into atoms, or that which cannot be divided. His theory suggested that these atoms would make up all substances, even though they were too small to see individually. (#2)

In 1808, John Dalton added to the work of Democritus. Dalton stated the following principles:

- Every element is made of atoms.
- All atoms of any element are the same.
- Atoms of different elements are different.
- Atoms of different elements can combine to form compounds.
- In any compound, the numbers and kinds of atoms remain the same.

These principles formed modern atomic theory until the discovery of the electron in 1897. (#3)

C

Simple Atomic Structure

Each atom contains a nucleus at its center. The **nucleus** is a tightly packed cluster of protons (which carry a positive electrical charge) and neutrons (which carry no electrical charge). The protons determine how an atom behaves. Each type of element is defined by the number of protons it contains. This is called the element's **atomic number**. The higher the atomic number, the more the atom weighs. (#4)

There is more to an atom than its center. A series of smaller, negatively charged particles, called **electrons**, orbit the nucleus. The electrons are

Student Book: Application Lesson 9 113

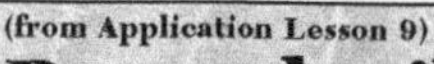

Reproducible I

ACTIVITY C *Passage Reading and Comprehension*

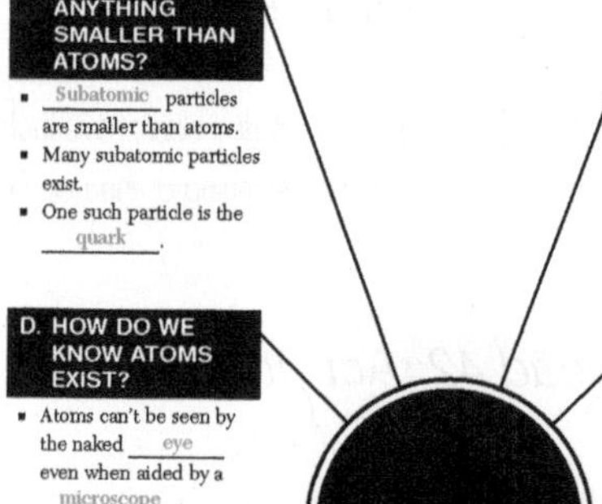

A. WHAT ARE ATOMS?
- Atoms are the building blocks of all _matter_.
- Atoms are the smallest part of an _element_ that behaves like the _element_.
- Thus, elements such as carbon and hydrogen are made up of _atoms_.

B. HISTORY
- In 530 B.C., Democritus theorized that all things could be broken into _smaller_ parts and ultimately into _atoms_.
- In 1808, _Dalton_ added to the work of Democritus by stating:
  - Every element has _atoms_.
  - All _atoms_ in an element are the same.
  - Atoms of different elements are _different_.
  - Atoms of different elements can combine to form _compounds_.
  - In a compound, the number and kind of _atoms_ remain the same.
- These principles formed atomic theory until 1897 when the _electron_ was discovered.

C. SIMPLE ATOMIC STRUCTURE
- At the center of an atom is the _nucleus_.
- The nucleus contains _protons_ (positive electrical charge) and _neutrons_ (no electrical charge).
- The _protons_ determine how an atom behaves.
- _Electrons_ (negative electrical charge) orbit the nucleus.
- If the number of _protons_ (+) and the number of _electrons_ (–) are equal, the atom is electrically _neutral_.
- If the number of _protons_ and _electrons_ are NOT the same, it is called an _ion_.
- Atoms are hooked together to form _molecules_.

D. HOW DO WE KNOW ATOMS EXIST?
- Atoms can't be seen by the naked _eye_ even when aided by a _microscope_.
- A special microscope called a _Scanning Tunneling Microscope_ creates pictures of atoms.

E. IS THERE ANYTHING SMALLER THAN ATOMS?
- _Subatomic_ particles are smaller than atoms.
- Many subatomic particles exist.
- One such particle is the _quark_.

394 • REWARDS Plus: Reading Strategies Applied to Science Passages

#4 What is a nucleus? What does it contain?
The center of an atom; contains protons and neutrons.

#5 What are electrons?
Smaller, negatively charged particles that orbit the nucleus; significantly smaller than a proton.

#6 When electrons move very fast, what do they create? Are they really clouds?
Energy clouds; these energy clouds are actually force fields.

#7 What is an STM? How does it differ from a regular light microscope?
Scanning Tunneling Microscope; uses tiny electrical currents that interact with the electrical charges of atoms on the surface.

#8 Why are scientists trying to find particles smaller than atoms?
To try to understand how everything in the universe works.

318 significantly smaller, about 1/1860th the size of a proton. If the number of
331 electrons (negatively charged particles) equals the number of protons (positively
341 charged particles), then the atom is electrically neutral. However, if the numbers
353 are not the same, because of a collision or other event, then the atom is called
369 an **ion**. Ions have an electrical charge, either positive or negative. (#5)

neutron
proton
electron

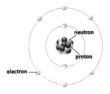

An Oxygen Atom

380 The electrons move very fast and create clouds of energy. These clouds may
393 look much the same as when you wave a sparkler around very fast in the dark.
409 These energy clouds are actually force fields that make specific shapes. The
421 larger an atom is, the more electrons and force fields it has, giving that atom a
437 more complex shape. Atoms are hooked to one another with these electron
449 clouds to form **molecules**. When atoms combine, it's like twisting a bunch of
462 balloons together, creating some really cool, 3D molecules.

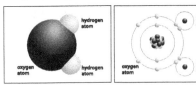

hydrogen atom
hydrogen atom
oxygen atom
hydrogen atom
hydrogen atom
oxygen atom

Two Models of a Water Molecule (H_2O)

470 Consider this: Because the outside of an atom is just an energy field and not
485 solid, you aren't really touching this page; your energy fields are bumping into
498 the energy fields of the paper. (#6)

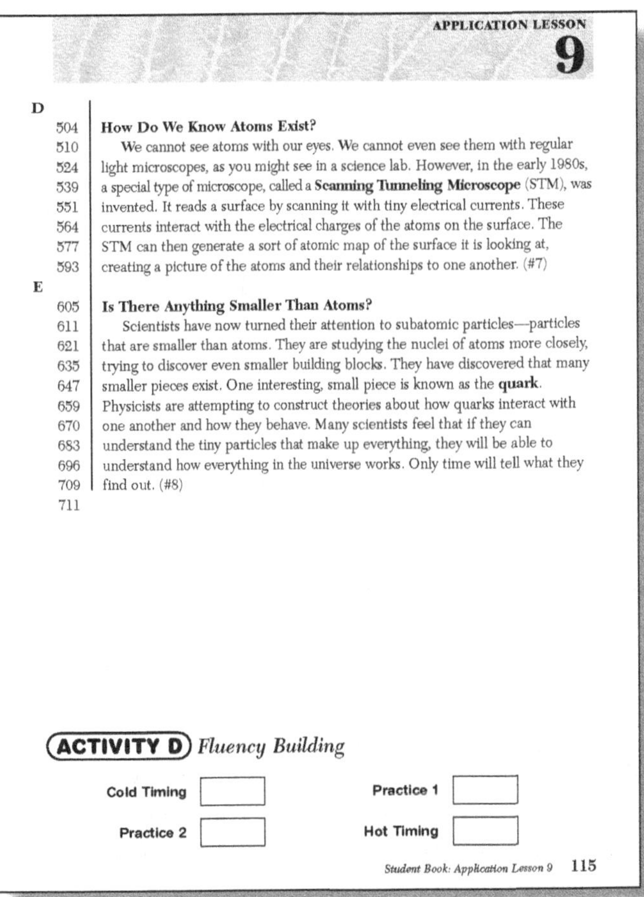

D
504 **How Do We Know Atoms Exist?**
510 We cannot see atoms with our eyes. We cannot even see them with regular
524 light microscopes, as you might see in a science lab. However, in the early 1980s,
539 a special type of microscope, called a **Scanning Tunneling Microscope** (STM), was
551 invented. It reads a surface by scanning it with tiny electrical currents. These
564 currents interact with the electrical charges of the atoms on the surface. The
577 STM can then generate a sort of atomic map of the surface it is looking at,
593 creating a picture of the atoms and their relationships to one another. (#7)

E
605 **Is There Anything Smaller Than Atoms?**
611 Scientists have now turned their attention to subatomic particles—particles
621 that are smaller than atoms. They are studying the nuclei of atoms more closely,
635 trying to discover even smaller building blocks. They have discovered that many
647 smaller pieces exist. One interesting, small piece is known as the **quark**.
659 Physicists are attempting to construct theories about how quarks interact with
670 one another and how they behave. Many scientists feel that if they can
683 understand the tiny particles that make up everything, they will be able to
696 understand how everything in the universe works. Only time will tell what they
709 find out. (#8)
711

ACTIVITY D *Fluency Building*

Cold Timing		Practice 1	
Practice 2		Hot Timing	

Fluency Building

ACTIVITY PROCEDURE

(See the *Student Book*, page 115.)

Have students complete a Cold Timing, one or two practices, and a Hot Timing of the Activity C article. For each timing, have students record the number of correct words read. Finally, have students complete their Fluency Graphs.

Note D-1: When assigning partners for this activity, have the stronger reader read first. As a result, the other reader will have one additional practice opportunity.

1. Now, it's time for fluency building.
2. Find the beginning of the passage again. (Pause.)
3. Whisper-read. See how many words you can read in one minute. Begin._ (Time students for one minute.) Stop._ Circle the last word that you read._ Record the number of words you read after **Cold Timing**._
4. Let's practice again. Begin._ (Time students for one minute.) Stop._ Put a box around the last word that you read._ Record the number of words you read after **Practice 1**._
5. (Optional) Let's practice one more time before the Hot Timing. Begin._ (Time students for one minute.) Stop._ Put a box around the last word that you read._ Record the number of words you read after **Practice 2**._
6. Please exchange books with your partner._ Partner 1, you are going to read first. Partner 2, listen carefully and underline any mistakes or words left out. Ones, begin._ (Time students for one minute.) Stop._ Twos, cross out the last word that your partner read._ (Assist students in subtracting the number of mistakes from the number of words read.) Twos, record the number of correct words in your partner's book after **Hot Timing**._
7. Partner 2, you are going to read next. Partner 1, listen carefully and underline any mistakes or words left out. Twos, begin. (Time students for one minute.) Stop._ Ones, cross out the last word that your partner read._ Ones, record the number of correct words in your partner's book after **Hot Timing**._
8. Exchange books._ Turn to the Fluency Graph on the inside back cover, and indicate on the graph the number of Cold Timing and Hot Timing words you read correctly._

APPLICATION LESSON **9**

D

504 **How Do We Know Atoms Exist?**
510 We cannot see atoms with our eyes. We cannot even see them with regular
524 light microscopes, as you might see in a science lab. However, in the early 1980s,
539 a special type of microscope, called a **Scanning Tunneling Microscope** (STM), was
551 invented. It reads a surface by scanning it with tiny electrical currents. These
564 currents interact with the electrical charges of the atoms on the surface. The
577 STM can then generate a sort of atomic map of the surface it is looking at,
593 creating a picture of the atoms and their relationships to one another. (#7)

E

605 **Is There Anything Smaller Than Atoms?**
611 Scientists have now turned their attention to subatomic particles—particles
621 that are smaller than atoms. They are studying the nuclei of atoms more closely,
635 trying to discover even smaller building blocks. They have discovered that many
647 smaller pieces exist. One interesting, small piece is known as the **quark**.
659 Physicists are attempting to construct theories about how quarks interact with
670 one another and how they behave. Many scientists feel that if they can
683 understand the tiny particles that make up everything, they will be able to
696 understand how everything in the universe works. Only time will tell what they
709 find out. (#8)
711

ACTIVITY D *Fluency Building*

Cold Timing		Practice 1	
Practice 2		Hot Timing	

ACTIVITY E

Comprehension Questions—Multiple Choice

ACTIVITY PROCEDURE

(See the *Student Book*, page 116.)

Have students complete item #1. Then, have students share the rationale for their answers. Encourage thoughtful discussion. Proceed item-by-item, emphasizing the rationale for the *best* answer. Have students record points for each correct item.

Note E-1: The correct Multiple Choice answers are circled.

1. Turn to page 116. Find **Activity E.**
2. Use the Multiple Choice Strategy to complete item #1. Be ready to explain why you selected your answer. (Wait while students complete the item. Call on individual students. Ask them why they chose their answer and why they eliminated the other choices. Encourage discussion. Provide students with feedback on their choices, focusing on why or why not those choices might be appropriate.)
3. (Repeat Step 2 for items 2–4, pausing after each item to confirm student responses and provide feedback.)
4. Count the number of items you got correct, and record that number in the blank half of the Multiple Choice Comprehension box.

APPLICATION LESSON

9

ACTIVITY E *Comprehension Questions—Multiple Choice*

Comprehension Strategy—Multiple Choice

Step 1: Read the item.
Step 2: Read all of the choices.
Step 3: Think about why each choice might be correct or incorrect. Check the article as needed.
Step 4: From the possible correct choices, select the best answer.

1. (Vocabulary) **If you were defining an atom, which of the following would you NOT include as a definition?**
   a. Smallest part of an element that can exist alone.
   b. Smallest part of an element that acts like the element.
   c. Building blocks of all matter.
   (d.) Smallest element in a substance.
2. (Main idea) **What was the major accomplishment of John Dalton?**
   a. He was the first person to define an atom and explain that all things are made up of atoms.
   (b.) He stated principles that formed modern atomic theory for almost 100 years.
   c. He was the first scientist to suggest that a substance contained smaller substances.
   d. He determined that all things could be broken down into atoms.
3. (Compare and contrast) **Which of the following comparisons is true?**
   a. Protons carry a positive electrical charge while electrons have a neutral charge.
   b. Protons and electrons are found in the nucleus of an atom.
   (c.) Protons are found in the nucleus of the atom while electrons orbit the nucleus.
   d. Protons carry a positive electrical charge while neutrons have an opposing negative charge.
4. (Main idea) **The author suggests that "you aren't really touching this page" because:**
   (a.) the outside of an atom is just an energy field.
   b. all life is an illusion.
   c. an atom cannot be seen by the naked eye.
   d. we cannot detect the protons and electrons.

MULTIPLE CHOICE COMPREHENSION 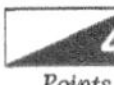 4 Points

116 *REWARDS Plus: Reading Strategies Applied to Science Passages*

ACTIVITY F

Vocabulary Activities

ACTIVITY PROCEDURE

(See the *Student Book*, pages 117–118.)

Have students complete each item orally and provide feedback on their answers. Then have students respond to each question in writing by answering "yes" or "no" and providing a reason for their answers.

Yes/No/Why

1. Turn to page 117._ Find **Activity F.**_ Read item #1. Tell your partner your answer and your reason for it. (Pause. Then call on individual students. Encourage discussion. Provide students with feedback on their choices, focusing on their explanations for their answer.)
2. Write your answer and your reason for it in the space provided. Look up when you are done._
3. Read item #2. Tell your partner your answer and your reason for it. (Pause. Then call on individual students. Encourage discussion. Provide students with feedback on their choices, focusing on their explanations for their answer.)
4. Write your answer and your reason for it in the space provided. Look up when you are done._
5. Read item #3. Tell your partner your answer and your reason for it. (Pause. Then call on individual students. Encourage discussion. Provide students with feedback on their choices, focusing on their explanations for their answer.)
6. Write your answer and your reason for it in the space provided. Look up when you are done._

Note F-1: You may wish to do this as an oral task only rather than an oral and a written task.

APPLICATION LESSON 9

ACTIVITY F *Vocabulary Activities*

Yes/No/Why

1. Can **subatomic particles** be viewed **individually**?
Example answer: No. At this time we can't view subatomic particles such as quarks.

2. Would **protons**, **electrons**, and **neutrons** be found in the **nucleus**?
Example answer: No. Only protons (+) and neutrons are found in the nucleus. Electrons (–) orbit the nucleus.

3. Does **John Dalton's atomic** theory still receive **attention**?
Example answer: Yes. Dalton's atomic theory is still important even though new discoveries have added to the theory.

Student Book: Application Lesson 9 117

ACTIVITY PROCEDURE

Have students read the words and definitions and then complete the sentence stems for each vocabulary word. Have them share answers with partners and with the class. Then, have students give themselves points in the blank half of the Vocabulary box.

Completion Activity

1. Turn to page 118. Read the first word and its definition.
2. Now, read the sentence stem.
3. Think of how you would complete the sentence stem and write it. Share your answer with your partner. (Call on a few students to share answers with the class.)
4. (Repeat Steps 1–3 for the rest of the words.)
5. If you participated in answering all seven questions, give yourself seven points in the blank half of the Vocabulary box.

Note F-2: You may wish to do this as an oral task only rather than an oral task and a written task.

APPLICATION LESSON

9

Completion Activities

1. **individually:** separately
   If I were working in a department store, I would wrap these things individually:
   Answers will vary.
2. **determine:** to give direction to; to find out by observation
   If I were a scientist, I would want to determine
   Answers will vary.
3. **ultimately:** finally
   Ultimately in life we all have to decide these three things:
   Answers will vary.
4. **attention:** focus; thought
   I must give my full attention in these situations:
   Answers will vary.

VOCABULARY 7 Points

118 *REWARDS Plus: Reading Strategies Applied to Science Passages*

ACTIVITY G

Expository Writing—Multi-Paragraph Answer

ACTIVITY PROCEDURE, Plan and Write

(See the *Student Book*, pages 119–121.)

Have students read the prompt and the three topics. Guide students as they **LIST** details for topics a, b, and c. Have students look at topic a again. Have students **CROSS OUT** details that don't go with the topic. Have students **CONNECT** details as shown in the example plan. Have students **NUMBER** their details, and then compare with the example plan for topic a. Next, have students **WRITE** paragraph a. Repeat for topics b and c. Finally, explain that after the answer is written, they should **EDIT** their work, revising for clarity and proofreading for errors in capitalization, punctuation, and spelling.

Use Overheads 43 and 44: Activity G

1. Turn to page 119._ Find **Activity G.**_
2. Find the prompt in the middle of the page._ Read the prompt out loud with me: **Explain and provide information on the following statements: (1) All matter is made of atoms. (2) All atoms have a nucleus. (3) Electrons orbit the nucleus.**
3. Turn to page 120._ Read topic a._ Read topic b._ Read topic c._
4. Add details to topic a. Look back in the article and locate details that explain the statement: All matter is made of atoms. Write the details in the Planning Box._
5. Add details to topic b. Look back in the article and locate details that explain the statement: All atoms have a nucleus. Write the details in the Planning Box._
6. Add details to topic c. Look back in the article and locate details that explain the statement: Electrons orbit the nucleus. Write the details in the Planning Box._
7. Use the steps for topic a. Read the details and **cross out** any details that do not go with the topic._ Next, draw brackets to **connect** details that could easily go into one sentence._ Now, **number** the details in a logical order._
8. Now, look at the example plan for topic a on the overhead. Yours should be similar._

APPLICATION LESSON **9**

ACTIVITY G *Expository Writing—Multi-Paragraph Answer*

Writing Strategy—Multi-Paragraph Answer

Step 1: LIST (List the details that are important enough to include in your answer.)
Step 2: CROSS OUT (Reread the details. Cross out any that don't go with the topic.)
Step 3: CONNECT (Connect any details that could go into one sentence.)
Step 4: NUMBER (Number the details in a logical order.)
Step 5: WRITE (Write the paragraph.)
Step 6: EDIT (Revise and proofread your answer.)

Prompt: Explain and provide information on the following statements: (1) All matter is made of atoms. (2) All atoms have a nucleus. (3) Electrons orbit the nucleus.

Plan: Complete the Planning Box.

Student Book: Application Lesson 9 119

APPLICATION LESSON

Example Multi-Paragraph Plan

Planning Box
(topic a) ***All matter is made of atoms.***
① (detail) – *all things are made of elements*
② (detail) – *if you break element into smallest part that acts like an element—an atom*
③ (detail) – *atom—smallest particle of an element that can exist alone*
(topic b) ***All atoms have a nucleus.***
① (detail) – *the nucleus is at the center of the atom*
② { (detail) – *contains protons with a positive charge*
(detail) – *contains neutrons with no electrical charge* }
③ (detail) – *protons determine how the atom acts*
(topic c) ***Electrons orbit the nucleus.***
① (detail) – *electrons—smaller, negatively charged particles*
② (detail) – *if number of electrons and number of protons same—atom electrically neutral*
③ (detail) – *if number of electrons and number of protons not same—atom called ion*
④ (detail) – *ion—either positive or negative*

Write: Write paragraphs a, b, and c on a separate piece of paper.

120 *REWARDS Plus: Reading Strategies Applied to Science Passages*

9. Take out a blank piece of paper. Using your plan for paragraph a, **write** paragraph a. If you finish early, please reread and **edit** your paragraph. (Move around the room and monitor your students as they are writing.)
10. (When the majority of students are done, proceed with the lesson.) Now, use the steps for topic b.
11. (Show Overhead 43.) Now, look at the example plan for topic b on the overhead. Yours should be similar.
12. Locate your piece of paper. Using your plan for paragraph b, **write** paragraph b. If you finish early, please **edit** your paragraph. (Move around the room and monitor your students as they are writing.)
13. (When the majority of students are done, proceed with the lesson.) Now, use the steps for topic c.
14. Look at the example plan for topic c on the overhead. Yours should be similar.
15. Locate your piece of paper. Using your plan for paragraph c, **write** paragraph c. If you finish early, please **edit** your paragraph. (Move around the room and monitor your students as they are writing.)
16. (When the majority of students are done, proceed with the lesson.) Please carefully read your paragraphs. Be sure that your paragraphs are clear. Proofread for any errors in capitalization, punctuation, and spelling. (Give students time to proofread their paragraphs.)

ACTIVITY PROCEDURE, Evaluate

Ask students to read each question in the rubric. Guide them in evaluating the paragraphs using the guidelines. Have students total their points and record them in the blank half of the Writing box.

17. Turn to page 121. Let's evaluate paragraph a.
18. Circle "Yes" for a if your topic sentence includes the topic: All matter is made of atoms.
19. Circle "Yes" for a if all of your details tell about how matter is made of atoms.
20. Circle "Yes" for a if you combined details into one sentence.
21. Now, check paragraphs b and c carefully and answer questions 1 through 3.
22. Reread your paragraphs. Circle "Yes" if your paragraphs are easy to understand.
23. Carefully examine your paragraphs. If you think a word is misspelled, underline it and check back in the plan or article and correct the spelling. Circle "Yes" if you believe that you have very few spelling errors.
24. Carefully examine your sentences. Be sure that each sentence begins with a capital. If all sentences begin with a capital, circle "Yes."
25. Examine your sentences. Be sure that each sentence ends with a period. If all sentences end with a period, circle "Yes."
26. Count up your points and record them in the Writing box.
27. (Show Overhead 44.) Look at the overhead. Let's read the three example paragraphs. Yours should be similar. (Read the paragraphs to your students or with your students or call on a student to read the example paragraph.)

9

Evaluate: Evaluate the paragraphs using this rubric.

Rubric—Multi-Paragraph Answer	Student or Partner Rating	Teacher Rating
1. Did the author state the topic in the first sentence?	a. Yes Fix up b. Yes Fix up c. Yes Fix up	a. Yes No b. Yes No c. Yes No
2. Did the author include details that go with the topic?	a. Yes Fix up b. Yes Fix up c. Yes Fix up	a. Yes No b. Yes No c. Yes No
3. Did the author combine details in some of the sentences?	a. Yes Fix up b. Yes Fix up c. Yes Fix up	a. Yes No b. Yes No c. Yes No
4. Is the answer easy to understand?	Yes Fix up	Yes No
5. Did the author correctly spell words, particularly the words found in the article?	Yes Fix up	Yes No
6. Did the author use correct capitalization, capitalizing the first word in the sentence and proper names of people, places, and things?	Yes Fix up	Yes No
7. Did the author use correct punctuation, including a period at the end of each sentence?	Yes Fix up	Yes No

WRITING 13 Points

Student Book: Application Lesson 9 121

Note G-1: The rubric can be used in a variety of ways. Instead of the students evaluating their own paragraphs, you may wish to have their partners provide feedback. The second column is designed for teacher feedback. If you have a small group, it would be useful to give daily feedback on writing. If the group size is large, you can give feedback to a number of children each day. You may wish to give students bonus points based on your feedback.

ACTIVITY H

Comprehension—Single-Paragraph Answer

ACTIVITY PROCEDURE

(See the *Student Book*, page 122.)

Have students read the *What Is* statement and the *What If* question. Have students turn the question into part of the answer and write down a topic sentence for their answer. Then, have them complete their answer. Encourage them to use evidence from the article and their own experience and background knowledge. Engage students in a discussion. Award points for writing and participating in the discussion.

Note H-1: To increase the quality of the discussion, the students are asked to think and write about the *What If* before the discussion. However, you may be working with students who have difficulty generating ideas for their paragraph. If that is the case, switch the order of activities: engage the students in a discussion, and then have them write their paragraphs.

1. Turn to page 122._ Find **Activity H.**_
2. Find the *What Is* statement in the middle of the page._ Read it out loud with me: **A special type of microscope, the Scanning Tunneling Microscope, allows us to create a picture of atoms and their relationships to one another.**
3. Find the *What If* question._ Read it with me: **What would have happened if we had never developed the Scanning Tunneling Microscope?**
4. Think how you might turn the question into part of the answer._ Tell me your idea for a topic sentence._ (Example sentence: A number of things would have resulted if the Scanning Tunneling Microscope had not been developed.) Take out a piece of paper and write your topic sentence._ (Move around the room and monitor as students write.)
5. You are ready to add ideas to your paragraph. Use evidence from the article as well as your own experience and background knowledge. If you finish early, reread your paragraph and edit it so that it is easy to understand and clear._ (Move around the room and monitor as students write.)
6. Read your paragraph to your partner._
7. If you included wording from the question in your answer and added evidence from the article, award yourself four points for writing._

APPLICATION LESSON

9

ACTIVITY H *Comprehension—Single-Paragraph Answer*

Writing Strategy—Single-Paragraph Answer

Step 1: Read the item.
Step 2: Turn the question into part of the answer and write it down.
Step 3: Think of the answer or locate the answer in the article.
Step 4: Complete your answer.

Prompt:

What Is—A special type of microscope, the Scanning Tunneling Microscope, allows us to create a picture of atoms and their relationships to one another.

What If—What would have happened if we had never developed the Scanning Tunneling Microscope?

Write and Discuss: Write a paragraph. Then share your ideas. Use the Discussion Guidelines.

Discussion Guidelines

Speaker		Listener	
Looks like:	**Sounds like:**	**Looks like:**	**Sounds like:**
• Facing peers • Making eye contact • Participating	• Using pleasant, easy-to-hear voice • Sharing opinions, supporting facts and reasons from the article and from your experience • Staying on the topic	• Facing speaker • Making eye contact • Participating	• Waiting quietly to speak • Giving positive, supportive comments • Disagreeing respectfully

WRITING 4 Points DISCUSSION 4 Points

122 *REWARDS Plus: Reading Strategies Applied to Science Passages*

8. (Engage students in a discussion. Award four points to students who are active participants in the discussion.)

Note H-2: If your students are having difficulty writing the *What If* paragraphs, read or show them the following example paragraph:

Example Single-Paragraph Answer

Scientific knowledge would not be what it is today if the Scanning Tunneling Microscope had not been developed. We would have been unable to create a picture of atoms and their relationship to one another. Because this knowledge is critical to scientific study, progress in many areas of science would have been halted or delayed. Not only that, we would have to rely on a theory concerning atoms without firsthand knowledge of atoms.

Application Lesson 10

Materials Needed:

- *Student Book*: Application Lesson 10
- Application Overhead Transparencies 45–49
- Appendix B Reproducible J: Application Lesson 10
- Appendix C Optional Vocabulary Activity: Application Lesson 10
- Paper or cardboard to use when covering the overhead transparency
- Paper or cardboard for each student to use during spelling dictation
- Washable overhead transparency pen

Text Treatment Notes:

- Black text signifies teacher script (exact wording to say to students).
- Green text in parentheses signifies directions or prompts for the teacher.
- Green text signifies answers or examples of answers.
- Green graphics treatment signifies reproduction of Overhead information.
- Green text and green graphics treatment do not appear in the *Student Book*.

ACTIVITY A

Vocabulary

ACTIVITY PROCEDURE, List 1

(See the *Student Book*, page 123.)

Tell students each word in the list. Then, have students repeat the word and read the definition aloud For each definition, provide any additional information that may be necessary. Then, have students practice reading the words themselves.

1. (Show the top half of Overhead 45.) Before we read the passage, let's read the difficult words. The first words are someone's name. (Point to **Rachel Carson**.) The name is **Rachel Carson**. What name?_ Now, read the definition._
2. (Point to **biology**.) The next word is **biology**. What word?_ Now, read the definition._
3. (Pronounce each word in List 1, and then have students repeat each word and read the definition.)
4. Open your *Student Book* to **Application Lesson 10**, page 123._
5. Find **Activity A**, **List 1**, in your book._ Let's read the words again. First words._ Next word._ (Continue for all words in List 1.)

ACTIVITY PROCEDURE, List 2

(See the *Student Book*, page 123.)

Have students circle prefixes and suffixes, then underline the vowels. Using the overhead transparency, assist students in checking their work. Next, have students figure out each word to themselves, then say it aloud. Have them read the definition aloud.

Use Overhead 45: Activity A
List 2: Strategy Practice

1. Find **List 2**. Circle the prefixes and suffixes, and underline the vowels. Look up when you are done._
2. (Show the bottom half of Overhead 45.) Before you check your work on List 2, look at item #9. (Point to the second example and the **ir** that is circled.) From now on, you can also circle **ir**. The prefix is /ir/. Say it._ Now, go back to item #1. Check and fix any mistakes._
3. Go back to the first word again._ Sound out the word to yourself. Put your thumb up when you can read the word. Be sure that it is a real word._ What word?_ Now, read the definition._
4. (Continue Step 3 with all remaining words in List 2.)

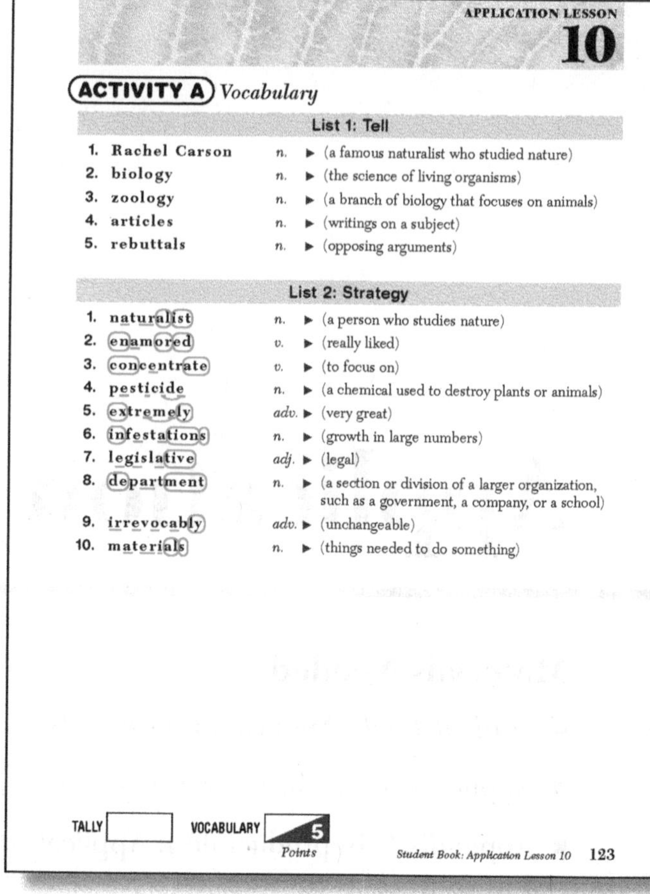

APPLICATION LESSON **10**

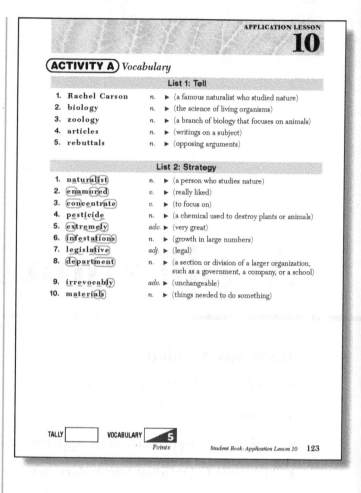

ACTIVITY A *Vocabulary*

List 1: Tell

1.	Rachel Carson	*n.*	► (a famous naturalist who studied nature)
2.	biology	*n.*	► (the science of living organisms)
3.	zoology	*n.*	► (a branch of biology that focuses on animals)
4.	articles	*n.*	► (writings on a subject)
5.	rebuttals	*n.*	► (opposing arguments)

List 2: Strategy

1.	naturalist	*n.*	► (a person who studies nature)
2.	enamored	*v.*	► (really liked)
3.	concentrate	*v.*	► (to focus on)
4.	pesticide	*n.*	► (a chemical used to destroy plants or animals)
5.	extremely	*adv.*	► (very great)
6.	infestations	*n.*	► (growth in large numbers)
7.	legislative	*adj.*	► (legal)
8.	department	*n.*	► (a section or division of a larger organization, such as a government, a company, or a school)
9.	irrevocably	*adv.*	► (unchangeable)
10.	materials	*n.*	► (things needed to do something)

TALLY VOCABULARY 5 Points

Student Book: Application Lesson 10 123

Note A.2-1: You may wish to provide additional practice by having students read words to a partner.

ACTIVITY PROCEDURE, List 1 and 2

(See the *Student Book*, page 123.)

Tell students to look in List 1 or List 2 for a word you are thinking about. Have them circle the number of the word and tell you the word. Explain to students to make a tally mark for each correct word in the Tally box, and then enter the number of tally marks as points in the blank half of the Vocabulary box.

1. Remember, the words I'm thinking about will be in either List 1 or List 2. Make a tally mark for every correctly identified word.
2. Circle the number of the appropriate word.
   - This branch of biology focuses on animals. (Wait.) What word? **zoology**
   - If you really like something, you are said to be this of that thing. (Wait.) What word? **enamored**
   - Magazines contain different writings on subjects. These writings are called these. (Wait.) What word? **articles**
   - This is a chemical used to destroy plants or animals. (Wait.) What word? **pesticide**
   - Opposing arguments are called these. (Wait.) What word? **rebuttals**
3. Count all the tally marks, and enter that number as points in the blank half of the Vocabulary box.

ACTIVITY PROCEDURE, List 3

(See the *Student Book*, page 124.)

The words in the third list are related. Have students use the *REWARDS* Strategies to figure out the first word in each family. Have them read the definition of the verb and then read nouns and adjectives that are related to that verb.

Use Overhead 46: Activity A
List 3: Word Families

1. Turn to page 124._ Find **Family 1** in **List 3.** Figure out the first word. Use your pencil if you wish. Put your thumb up when you know the word._ What word?_ Read the definition._
2. Look at the nouns in Family 1. Figure out the first word._ What word?_ Next word._ What word?_
3. Look at the adjective in Family 1. Figure out the word._ What word?_
4. (Repeat Steps 1–3 for all word families in List 3.)

APPLICATION LESSON
10

List 3: Word Families

	Verb	Noun	Adjective
Family 1	conserve (to protect from loss, harm, or waste)	conservation conservationist	conservative
Family 2	realize (to understand completely)	realization	realistic
Family 3	produce (to make)	production producer	productive
Family 4	publish (to produce and sell a book or other written material)	publication publisher	publishable
Family 5	represent (to speak for)	representation representative	representative

ACTIVITY B *Spelling Dictation*

1. represent	4. conserve
2. representation	5. conservation
3. representative	6. conservative

SPELLING 6 Points

124 *REWARDS Plus: Reading Strategies Applied to Science Passages*

Note A.3-1: You may wish to provide additional practice by having students read a word family to the group or to a partner.

Note A.3-2: An additional vocabulary practice activity called Quick Words is provided in Appendix C of this Teacher's Guide. See Appendix C for information about how this optional activity can be used.

ACTIVITY B

Spelling Dictation

ACTIVITY PROCEDURE

(See the *Student Book*, page 124.)

For each word, tell students the word, then have students say the parts of the word to themselves while they write the word. Using the overhead transparency, assist students in checking their spelling and correcting if they misspelled. Then, have students enter the number of correctly spelled words as points in the blank half of the Spelling box.

Note B-1: Distribute a piece of light cardboard to each of the students.

Use Overhead 46: Activity B

1. Find **Activity B.**
2. The first word is **represent**. What word?_ Say the parts in **represent** to yourself as you write the word. (Pause and monitor.)
3. (Show **represent** on the overhead.) Check **represent**. If you misspelled it, cross it out and write it correctly.
4. The second word is **representation**. What word?_ Say the parts in **representation** to yourself as you write the word. (Pause and monitor.)
5. (Show **representation** on the overhead.) Check **representation**. If you misspelled it, cross it out and write it correctly.
6. (Repeat the procedures for the words **representative**, **conserve**, **conservation**, and **conservative**.)
7. Count the number of words you spelled correctly, and record that number as points in the blank half of the Spelling box at the bottom of the page.

APPLICATION LESSON **10**

List 3: Word Families

	Verb	Noun	Adjective
Family 1	conserve (to protect from loss, harm, or waste)	conservation conservationist	conservative
Family 2	realize (to understand completely)	realization	realistic
Family 3	produce (to make)	production producer	productive
Family 4	publish (to produce and sell a book or other written material)	publication publisher	publishable
Family 5	represent (to speak for)	representation representative	representative

ACTIVITY B *Spelling Dictation*

1. represent	4. conserve
2. representation	5. conservation
3. representative	6. conservative

SPELLING 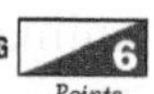 Points

124 *REWARDS Plus: Reading Strategies Applied to Science Passages*

ACTIVITY C

Passage Reading and Comprehension

ACTIVITY PROCEDURE

(See the *Student Book*, pages 125–127.)

Have students read the title of the passage and each heading. Ask them to tell their partners two things that the passage will tell about.

Passage Preview

1. Turn to page 125._ Let's preview the passage.
2. Read the title._ What is the whole passage going to tell about?_
3. Now, let's read the headings. Read the first heading._ Read the next heading._ (Continue until students have read all headings.)
4. Turn to your partner. Without looking, tell two things this passage will tell about._

ACTIVITY PROCEDURE

Provide students with an Information Web from Appendix B. Have students read the passage silently to each embedded number, and then reread the same information orally either to a partner, together as a group, or individually. Ask the corresponding comprehension question or questions. Once students finish reading a section labeled A, B, C, D, E, or F, have them fill in the Information Web before going on to the next section.

Note C-1: If students do not finish reading the passage during class, have them use their Information Webs to review the information at the beginning of the next class.

Use Overhead 47: Activity C

Passage Reading

1. (Provide an Information Web for each student.)
2. Turn back to the beginning of the passage. You're going to read the passage and answer questions about what you've read. During passage reading, you are also going to fill in an Information Web to help you remember the important details of the passage. Later, you'll use this Web to review the content of the passage with your partner.
3. Read the title._

APPLICATION LESSON **10**

ACTIVITY C *Passage Reading and Comprehension*

Note: For this activity, you will need Reproducible J found in the *Teacher's Guide*.

Rachel Carson, Famous Naturalist

A
Born in 1907 in Springdale, Pennsylvania, Rachel Carson was always
10 enamored with nature. As a child, she played by the river that ran through her
25 hometown. When she got older, she studied biology and zoology, a branch of
38 biology that focuses on animals, at the Pennsylvania College for Women and
50 Johns Hopkins University. (#1)

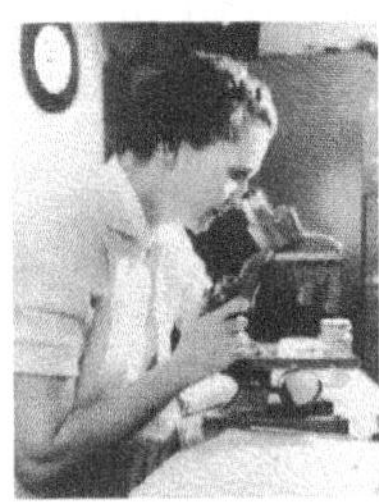

B
53 Following five years of teaching zoology at the University of Maryland,
64 Rachel Carson worked for the next seventeen years with the Fish and Wildlife
77 Service, an agency of the United States' government. There, she wrote
88 conservation materials and scientific articles based on her research. She also
99 wrote books concerning studies of nature. In 1951, she published a book she
112 had written as a study of the ocean called *The Sea Around Us*, which became a
128 bestseller in the fall of 1952. She followed this in 1955 with a book called *The*
144 *Edge of the Sea*. These books made her a famous naturalist. She became known
158 as a science writer for the public. In 1952, she left the Fish and Wildlife Service
174 to write full time. (#2)

C
178 **Her Beliefs**
180 All of Carson's writings shared a similar theme. She believed that human
192 beings were part of nature, not in charge of it. The difference between other

Student Book: Application Lesson 10 125

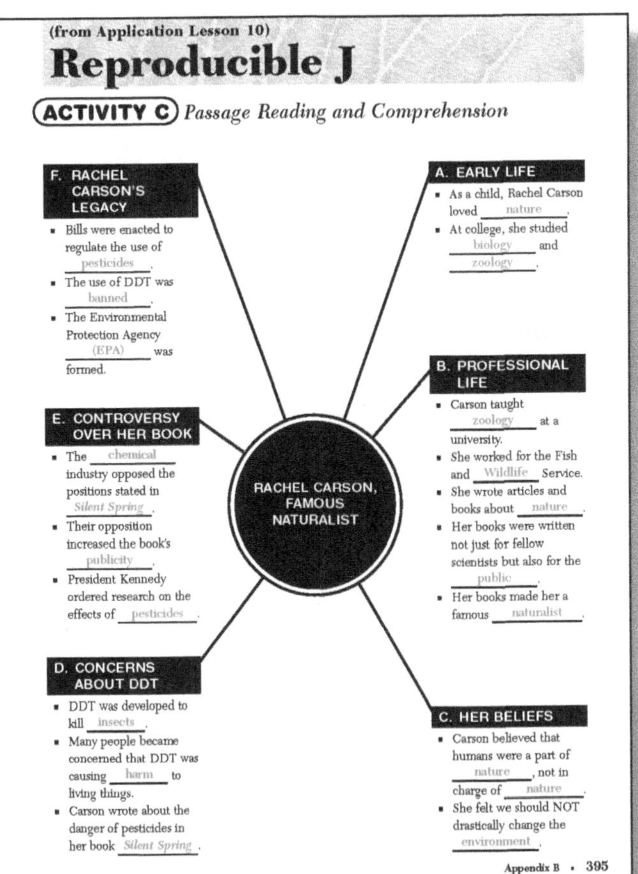

(from Application Lesson 10)

Reproducible J

ACTIVITY C *Passage Reading and Comprehension*

RACHEL CARSON, FAMOUS NATURALIST

A. EARLY LIFE
- As a child, Rachel Carson loved nature.
- At college, she studied biology and zoology.

B. PROFESSIONAL LIFE
- Carson taught zoology at a university.
- She worked for the Fish and Wildlife Service.
- She wrote articles and books about nature.
- Her books were written not just for fellow scientists but also for the public.
- Her books made her a famous naturalist.

C. HER BELIEFS
- Carson believed that humans were a part of nature, not in charge of nature.
- She felt we should NOT drastically change the environment.

D. CONCERNS ABOUT DDT
- DDT was developed to kill insects.
- Many people became concerned that DDT was causing harm to living things.
- Carson wrote about the danger of pesticides in her book *Silent Spring*.

E. CONTROVERSY OVER HER BOOK
- The chemical industry opposed the positions stated in *Silent Spring*.
- Their opposition increased the book's publicity.
- President Kennedy ordered research on the effects of pesticides.

F. RACHEL CARSON'S LEGACY
- Bills were enacted to regulate the use of pesticides.
- The use of DDT was banned.
- The Environmental Protection Agency (EPA) was formed.

Appendix B • 395

4. Find number 1 in the passage. (Pause). Read down to number 1 silently. Look up when you are done._
5. (Wait for students to complete the reading. Then have students reread the part by having them read orally to a partner, read together orally as a group, or read aloud individually.)
6. (Ask the question or questions associated with the number. Provide feedback to students regarding their answers.)
7. (Repeat steps 4–6 for all paragraphs in Section A.)
8. Now, look at your Information Web. Find the section labeled A._ The information you've just read will help you to fill in this Web.
9. With your partner, fill in the blanks for Section A. You can refer back to the passage for information. Look up when you're done._ (Move around the room and monitor students as they complete the section.)
10. (When the majority of students have finished, show Overhead 47). Look at the overhead and check your work. Fix up or add to any of your answers.
11. Now read down to the next number silently. Look up when you are done._
12. (Repeat steps 5–11 until the students have finished the passage and the Information Web.)
13. Now use your Information Web to retell the important information from the passage to your partner.

Comprehension Questions

#1 What subjects did Rachel Carson study at Johns Hopkins University?

Biology and zoology.

#2 What two books did Rachel Carson author while working for the Fish and Wildlife Service?

The Sea Around Us and *The Edge of the Sea*.

#3 What was the common theme of all of Carson's writings?

That humans are a part of nature, not in charge of it.

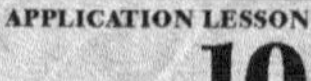

ACTIVITY C *Passage Reading and Comprehension*

Note: For this activity, you will need Reproducible J found in the *Teacher's Guide*.

Rachel Carson, Famous Naturalist

A Born in 1907 in Springdale, Pennsylvania, Rachel Carson was always enamored with nature. As a child, she played by the river that ran through her hometown. When she got older, she studied biology and zoology, a branch of biology that focuses on animals, at the Pennsylvania College for Women and Johns Hopkins University. (#1)

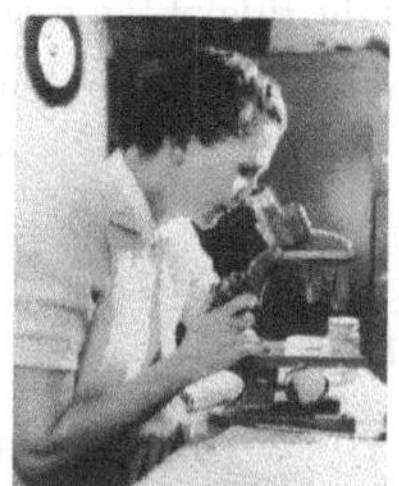

B Following five years of teaching zoology at the University of Maryland, Rachel Carson worked for the next seventeen years with the Fish and Wildlife Service, an agency of the United States' government. There, she wrote conservation materials and scientific articles based on her research. She also wrote books concerning studies of nature. In 1951, she published a book she had written as a study of the ocean called *The Sea Around Us*, which became a bestseller in the fall of 1952. She followed this in 1955 with a book called *The Edge of the Sea*. These books made her a famous naturalist. She became known as a science writer for the public. In 1952, she left the Fish and Wildlife Service to write full time. (#2)

C **Her Beliefs**

All of Carson's writings shared a similar theme. She believed that human beings were part of nature, not in charge of it. The difference between other

Student Book: Application Lesson 10 125

(from Application Lesson 10)

Reproducible J

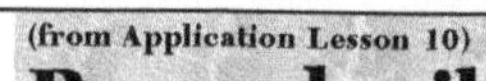

Passage Reading and Comprehension

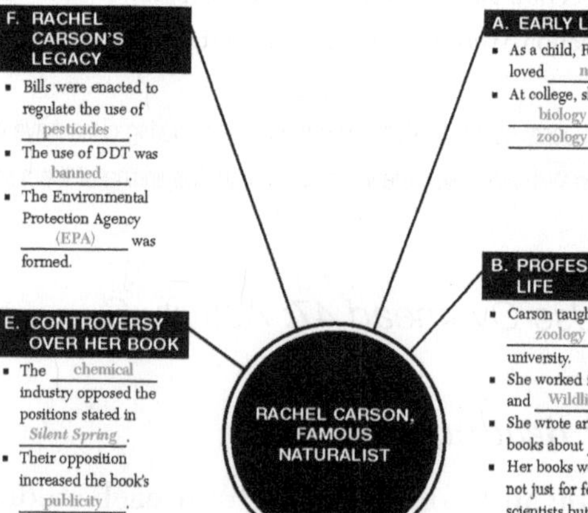

RACHEL CARSON, FAMOUS NATURALIST

A. EARLY LIFE
- As a child, Rachel Carson loved nature.
- At college, she studied biology and zoology.

B. PROFESSIONAL LIFE
- Carson taught zoology at a university.
- She worked for the Fish and Wildlife Service.
- She wrote articles and books about nature.
- Her books were written not just for fellow scientists but also for the public.
- Her books made her a famous naturalist.

C. HER BELIEFS
- Carson believed that humans were a part of nature, not in charge of nature.
- She felt we should NOT drastically change the environment.

D. CONCERNS ABOUT DDT
- DDT was developed to kill insects.
- Many people became concerned that DDT was causing harm to living things.
- Carson wrote about the danger of pesticides in her book *Silent Spring*.

E. CONTROVERSY OVER HER BOOK
- The chemical industry opposed the positions stated in *Silent Spring*.
- Their opposition increased the book's publicity.
- President Kennedy ordered research on the effects of pesticides.

F. RACHEL CARSON'S LEGACY
- Bills were enacted to regulate the use of pesticides.
- The use of DDT was banned.
- The Environmental Protection Agency (EPA) was formed.

Appendix B • 395

#4 What was DDT designed to do?
To kill insects; to control insect infestations.

#5 What negative effects did DDT have on the environment and its inhabitants?
Fish were being killed by DDT; mammals and fish had significant levels in their system; infected worms were poisoning robins.

#6 What issues did Carson focus on in her book *Silent Spring*?
On humans and ecology and on the damage done to the environment by pesticides.

#7 How did the chemical industry react to the publication of *Silent Spring*?
They attacked Carson and her research through articles, press releases, and letters.

#8 How did the government respond to the use of pesticides at that time?
Forty legislative bills were passed to regulate pesticide use; DDT was banned; and the Environmental Protection Agency (EPA) was formed.

206 creatures and ourselves is that we have the power to change nature at will,
220 sometimes irrevocably, allowing no return to nature's original state. However,
230 Carson believed that human beings should not use their power to enact drastic
243 change on their environment. She realized that this is exactly what was
255 occurring, and she set out to write the truth. (#3)

D

264 **Concerns About DDT**
267 At the time, DDT was an extremely popular, widely used chemical pesticide
279 designed to kill insects. People considered it a "miracle" substance, capable of
291 controlling many insect infestations. Between 1946 and 1955, the production of
302 DDT increased by nearly 500 million pounds. The chemical industry, the
313 government, and the Public Health Department endorsed its use. (#4)

322 However, not everyone believed DDT was amazing stuff. As early as 1946,
334 naturalists and scientists wrote about the dangers of DDT to fish, mammals, and
347 birds. They described how DDT-laden earthworms were poisoning robins. They
358 observed that mammals and fish had significant levels of DDT in their fatty
371 tissues. Even the U.S. Congress kept track of the numbers of fish killed by
385 DDT. Yet, the public did not hear about these effects of their miracle substance.
399 They only knew that DDT was easy to use and produced quick benefits. (#5)
412 Rachel Carson was familiar with the early studies of the effects of DDT from
426 her work with the Fish and Wildlife Service. She had proposed an article on the
441 dangers of the pesticide to *Reader's Digest*, but they turned it down. Carson
454 already knew she wanted to write another book about humans and ecology, so she
468 decided to concentrate on the damage done to the environment by pesticides.

480 The book would be called *Silent Spring*, because of the death of the birds that
495 were ingesting (eating) the DDT, making their songs absent in springtime. (#6)

Effects of DDT

E

506 **Controversy Over Her Book**
510 Even before the book was published, *Silent Spring* caused an uproar. The
522 chemical industry could lose a lot of money if people stopped buying their
535 products in large quantities. Representatives of the industry attacked Rachel
545 Carson and her research through articles, press releases, and letters. But all of
558 the rebuttals (opposing arguments) generated by the chemical industry only
568 caused the book to have more publicity. President Kennedy ordered further
579 research into the effects of pesticides. (#7)

F

585 **Rachel Carson's Legacy**
588 Because of the attention that *Silent Spring* brought to the use of pesticides in
602 America, many legislative bills were introduced to regulate the use of pesticides. In
615 1972, DDT was banned. Since that time, some of the wildlife threatened by the
629 chemical has made progress towards recovery, although the pesticide is still present
641 in the environment. In the United States, the Environmental Protection Agency
652 (EPA) was formed in response to heightened awareness of human effects on the
665 environment. People are more aware of the effects pesticides might have on life.
678 Many are choosing pesticide-free farming, gardening, and organic produce. (#8)
688

ACTIVITY D *Fluency Building*

Cold Timing		Practice 1	
Practice 2		Hot Timing	

ACTIVITY D

Fluency Building

ACTIVITY PROCEDURE

(See the *Student Book*, page 127.)

Have students complete a Cold Timing, one or two practices, and a Hot Timing of the Activity C article. For each timing, have students record the number of correct words read. Finally, have students complete their Fluency Graphs.

Note D-1: When assigning partners for this activity, have the stronger reader read first. As a result, the other reader will have one additional practice opportunity.

1. Now, it's time for fluency building.
2. Find the beginning of the passage again. (Pause.)
3. Whisper-read. See how many words you can read in one minute. Begin._ (Time students for one minute.) Stop._ Circle the last word that you read._ Record the number of words you read after **Cold Timing.**_
4. Let's practice again. Begin._ (Time students for one minute.) Stop._ Put a box around the last word that you read._ Record the number of words you read after **Practice 1.**_
5. (Optional) Let's practice one more time before the Hot Timing. Begin._ (Time students for one minute.) Stop._ Put a box around the last word that you read._ Record the number of words you read after **Practice 2.**_
6. Please exchange books with your partner._ Partner 1, you are going to read first. Partner 2, listen carefully and underline any mistakes or words left out. Ones, begin._ (Time students for one minute.) Stop._ Twos, cross out the last word that your partner read._ (Assist students in subtracting the number of mistakes from the number of words read.) Twos, record the number of correct words in your partner's book after **Hot Timing.**_
7. Partner 2, you are going to read next. Partner 1, listen carefully and underline any mistakes or words left out. Twos, begin. (Time students for one minute.) Stop._ Ones, cross out the last word that your partner read._ Ones, record the number of correct words in your partner's book after **Hot Timing.**_
8. Exchange books._ Turn to the Fluency Graph on the inside back cover, and indicate on the graph the number of Cold Timing and Hot Timing words you read correctly._

---

480 The book would be called *Silent Spring*, because of the death of the birds that
495 were ingesting (eating) the DDT, making their songs absent in springtime. (#6)

Effects of DDT

E

506 **Controversy Over Her Book**
510 Even before the book was published, *Silent Spring* caused an uproar. The
522 chemical industry could lose a lot of money if people stopped buying their
535 products in large quantities. Representatives of the industry attacked Rachel
545 Carson and her research through articles, press releases, and letters. But all of
558 the rebuttals (opposing arguments) generated by the chemical industry only
568 caused the book to have more publicity. President Kennedy ordered further
579 research into the effects of pesticides. (#7)

F

585 **Rachel Carson's Legacy**
588 Because of the attention that *Silent Spring* brought to the use of pesticides in
602 America, many legislative bills were introduced to regulate the use of pesticides. In
615 1972, DDT was banned. Since that time, some of the wildlife threatened by the
629 chemical has made progress towards recovery, although the pesticide is still present
641 in the environment. In the United States, the Environmental Protection Agency
652 (EPA) was formed in response to heightened awareness of human effects on the
665 environment. People are more aware of the effects pesticides might have on life.
678 Many are choosing pesticide-free farming, gardening, and organic produce. (#8)
688

ACTIVITY D *Fluency Building*

Cold Timing		**Practice 1**	
Practice 2		**Hot Timing**	

ACTIVITY E

Comprehension Questions—Multiple Choice

ACTIVITY PROCEDURE

(See the *Student Book*, page 128.)

Have students complete item #1. Then, have students share the rationale for their answers. Encourage thoughtful discussion. Proceed item-by-item, emphasizing the rationale for the *best* answer. Have students record points for each correct item.

Note E-1: The correct Multiple Choice answers are circled.

1. Turn to page 128. Find **Activity E**.
2. Use the Multiple Choice Strategy to complete item #1. Be ready to explain why you selected your answer. (Wait while students complete the item. Call on individual students. Ask them why they chose their answer and why they eliminated the other choices. Encourage discussion. Provide students with feedback on their choices, focusing on why or why not those choices might be appropriate.)
3. (Repeat Step 2 for items 2–4, pausing after each item to confirm student responses and provide feedback.)
4. Count the number of items you got correct, and record that number in the blank half of the Multiple Choice Comprehension box.

APPLICATION LESSON

10

ACTIVITY E *Comprehension Questions—Multiple Choice*

Comprehension Strategy—Multiple Choice

Step 1: Read the item.
Step 2: Read all of the choices.
Step 3: Think about why each choice might be correct or incorrect. Check the article as needed.
Step 4: From the possible correct choices, select the best answer.

1. (Vocabulary) **When the author states that Rachel Carson was "enamored with nature," she means:**
   a. Rachel wanted to armor herself against the dangers of nature.
   b. Rachel wanted to get her teeth's enamel into nature.
   (c.) Rachel was fascinated by nature.
   d. Rachel knew since childhood that she wanted to study nature.
2. (Main idea) **Which of the following statements would best summarize Rachel Carson's primary beliefs?**
   (a.) All creatures, including humans, are part of nature, and humans should proceed with care in changing the environment.
   b. All creatures, including humans, are part of nature, but humans have the ability to control nature and should use that power.
   c. All creatures are part of nature and experience growth, development, and reproduction.
   d. All creatures are part of nature and thus affected by the environment.
3. (Vocabulary) **Rachel Carson titled her book *Silent Spring* because:**
   a. she often wrote by a river spring that ran through her hometown.
   b. animals such as frogs and fish that would normally be found in a spring would be killed by DDT, making the spring silent.
   (c.) birds that ate things sprayed with DDT often died and, as a result, in the spring their songs were no longer heard.
   d. by the spring of 1951, Rachel Carson no longer wanted to be silent about DDT.
4. (Cause and effect) **Who probably disagreed the most with the ideas presented in *Silent Spring*?**
   a. Industrial leaders in the publishing field.
   b. President Kennedy's environmental advisors.
   c. Republicans opposing President Kennedy.
   (d.) Industrial leaders in the chemical field.

MULTIPLE CHOICE COMPREHENSION 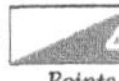
Points

128 *REWARDS Plus: Reading Strategies Applied to Science Passages*

ACTIVITY F

Vocabulary Activities

ACTIVITY PROCEDURE

(See the *Student Book*, pages 129–130.)

Have students complete each item orally and provide feedback on their answers. Then have students respond to each question in writing by answering "yes" or "no" and providing a reason for their answers.

Yes/No/Why

1. Turn to page 129._ Find **Activity F.**_ Read item 1. Tell your partner your answer and your reason for it. (Pause. Then call on individual students. Encourage discussion. Provide students with feedback on their choices, focusing on their explanations for their answer.)
2. Write your answer and your reason for it in the space provided. Look up when you are done._
3. Read item #2. Tell your partner your answer and your reason for it. (Pause. Then call on individual students. Encourage discussion. Provide students with feedback on their choices, focusing on their explanations for their answer.)
4. Write your answer and your reason for it in the space provided. Look up when you are done._
5. Read item #3. Tell your partner your answer and your reason for it. (Pause. Then call on individual students. Encourage discussion. Provide students with feedback on their choices, focusing on their explanations for their answer.)
6. Write your answer and your reason for it in the space provided. Look up when you are done._

Note F-1: You may wish to do this as an oral task only rather than an oral and a written task.

APPLICATION LESSON **10**

ACTIVITY F *Vocabulary Activities*

Yes/No/Why

1. Would a **naturalist** generally be **enamored** with **legislative** issues?
Example answer: No. A naturalist would be very interested in elements of nature: animals, birds, plants, etc. Generally, they would be less interested in laws.

2. Could insect **infestations** be reduced by use of **pesticides?**
Example answer: Yes. If you had an insect infestation that involved an increased number of insects, you could kill them with pesticides.

3. Could **articles** present **rebuttals**?
Example answer: Yes. Articles are often written to convey opposing arguments.

Student Book: Application Lesson 10 129

ACTIVITY PROCEDURE

Have students read the words and definitions and then complete the sentence stems for each vocabulary word. Have them share answers with partners and with the class. Then, have students give themselves points in the blank half of the Vocabulary box.

Completion Activity

1. Turn to page 130. Read the first word and its definition.
2. Now, read the sentence stem.
3. Think of how you would complete the sentence stem and write it. Share your answer with your partner. (Call on a few students to share answers with the class.)
4. (Repeat Steps 1–3 for the rest of the words.)
5. If you participated in answering all seven questions, give yourself seven points in the blank half of the Vocabulary box.

Note F-2: You may wish to do this as an oral task only rather than an oral task and a written task.

APPLICATION LESSON

10

Completion Activities

1. **realize:** to understand completely
   Recently, I came to realize that
   Answers will vary.
2. **enamored:** really liked
   When I was in fourth grade, I was enamored with
   Answers will vary.
3. **produce:** to make
   These are some of the things that I can produce:
   Answers will vary.
4. **materials:** things needed to do something
   To produce a birthday card for a friend, I would need the following materials:
   Answers will vary.

VOCABULARY 7 Points

130 *REWARDS Plus: Reading Strategies Applied to Science Passages*

ACTIVITY G

Expository Writing— Multi-Paragraph Answer

ACTIVITY PROCEDURE, Plan and Write

(See the *Student Book*, pages 131–133.)

Have students read the prompt. Guide students as they determine the three topics and **LIST** details for topics a, b, and c. Have students look at topic a again. Have students **CROSS OUT** details that don't go with the topic. Have students **CONNECT** details as shown in the example plan. Have students **NUMBER** their details, and then compare with the example plan for topic a. Next, have students **WRITE** paragraph a. Repeat for topics b and c. Finally, explain that after the answer is written, they should **EDIT** their work, revising for clarity and proofreading for errors in capitalization, punctuation, and spelling.

Use Overheads 48 and 49: Activity G

1. Turn to page 131._ Find **Activity G.**_
2. Find the prompt in the middle of the page._ Read the prompt out loud with me: **Rachel Carson was a fascinating person. Describe her professional life, her beliefs and environmental concerns, and her legacy (outcomes of her work).**
3. It is your turn to determine the topics. Reread the prompt and locate three topics. Record the topics in your Planning Box._ Compare your topics with your partner. (Move around the room and assist students in determining the topics.)
4. Look back in the article and locate details that go with each of your topics. Record the details in the Planning Box._
5. Use the steps for topic a. Read the details and **cross out** any details that do not go with the topic._ Next, draw brackets to **connect** details that could easily go into one sentence._ Now, **number** the details in a logical order._
6. (Show Overhead 48.) Now, look at the example plan for topic a on the overhead. Yours should be similar._
7. Take out a blank piece of paper._ Using your plan for paragraph a, **write** paragraph a. If you finish early, please reread and **edit** your paragraph._ (Move around the room and monitor your students as they are writing.)

APPLICATION LESSON **10**

ACTIVITY G *Expository Writing—Multi-Paragraph Answer*

Writing Strategy—Multi-Paragraph Answer

Step 1: LIST (List the details that are important enough to include in your answer.)
- **Step 2: CROSS OUT** (Reread the details. Cross out any that don't go with the topic.)
- **Step 3: CONNECT** (Connect any details that could go into one sentence.)
- **Step 4: NUMBER** (Number the details in a logical order.)
- **Step 5: WRITE** (Write the paragraph.)

Step 6: EDIT (Revise and proofread your answer.)

Prompt: Rachel Carson was a fascinating person. Describe her professional life, her beliefs and environmental concerns, and her legacy (outcomes of her work).

Plan: Complete the Planning Box.

Student Book: Application Lesson 10 131

APPLICATION LESSON **10**

Example Multi-Paragraph Plan

Planning Box
(topic a) *Rachel Carson—professional life as a naturalist*
① (detail) – *studied biology and zoology in college*
① (detail) – *taught zoology at a university*
② (detail) – *worked for Fish and Wildlife Service*
③ (detail) – *published books concerning the sea*
④ (detail) – *became a famous naturalist*
⑤ (detail) – *became a full-time writer*
⑥ (detail) – *concerned about pesticides*
⑥ (detail) – *wrote her famous book, Silent Spring*
(topic b) *Rachel Carson—beliefs and environmental concerns*
① (detail) – *humans shouldn't make drastic changes in the environment*
② (detail) – *believed that DDT was dangerous*
③ (detail) – *wrote about danger to environment by pesticides*
(detail) ~~*wrote Silent Spring*~~
(topic c) *Rachel Carson—legacy (outcomes of her work)*
① (detail) – *her book brought attention to the use of pesticides*
② (detail) – *legislation was enacted to regulate pesticides*
② (detail) – *use of DDT was banned*
③ (detail) – *since DDT was banned, wildlife recovering*
④ (detail) – *because of concern, EPA established*
⑤ (detail) – *people more aware of effects of pesticides*
⑤ (detail) – *people more environmentally aware*

Write: Write paragraphs a, b, and c on a separate piece of paper.

132 *REWARDS Plus: Reading Strategies Applied to Science Passages*

8. (When the majority of students are done, proceed with the lesson.) Now, use the steps for topic b.
9. Now, look at the example plan for topic b on the overhead. Yours should be similar.
10. Locate your piece of paper. Using your plan for paragraph b, **write** paragraph b. If you finish early, please **edit** your paragraph. (Move around the room and monitor your students as they are writing.)
11. (When the majority of students are done, proceed with the lesson.) Now, use the steps for topic c.
12. Look at the example plan for topic c on the overhead. Yours should be similar.
13. Locate your piece of paper. Using your plan for paragraph c, **write** paragraph c. If you finish early, please **edit** your paragraph. (Move around the room and monitor your students as they are writing.)
14. (When the majority of students are done, proceed with the lesson.) Please carefully read your paragraphs. Be sure that your paragraphs are clear. Proofread for any errors in capitalization, punctuation, and spelling. (Give students time to proofread their paragraphs.)

ACTIVITY PROCEDURE, Evaluate

Ask students to read each question in the rubric. Guide them in evaluating the paragraphs using the guidelines. Have students total their points and record them in the blank half of the Writing box.

15. Turn to page 133. Let's evaluate paragraphs a, b, and c.
16. Check paragraphs a, b, and c carefully and answer questions 1 through 3.
17. Reread your paragraphs. Circle "Yes" if your paragraphs are easy to understand.
18. Carefully examine your paragraphs. If you think a word is misspelled, underline it and check back in the plan or article and correct the spelling. Circle "Yes" if you believe that you have very few spelling errors.
19. Carefully examine your sentences. Be sure that each sentence begins with a capital. If all sentences begin with a capital, circle "Yes."
20. Examine your sentences. Be sure that each sentence ends with a period. If all sentences end with a period, circle "Yes."

APPLICATION LESSON **10**

Evaluate: Evaluate the paragraphs using this rubric.

Rubric—Multi-Paragraph Answer	Student or Partner Rating	Teacher Rating
1. Did the author state the topic in the first sentence?	a. (Yes) Fix up b. (Yes) Fix up c. (Yes) Fix up	a. Yes No b. Yes No c. Yes No
2. Did the author include details that go with the topic?	a. (Yes) Fix up b. (Yes) Fix up c. (Yes) Fix up	a. Yes No b. Yes No c. Yes No
3. Did the author combine details in some of the sentences?	a. (Yes) Fix up b. (Yes) Fix up c. (Yes) Fix up	a. Yes No b. Yes No c. Yes No
4. Is the answer easy to understand?	(Yes) Fix up	Yes No
5. Did the author correctly spell words, particularly the words found in the article?	(Yes) Fix up	Yes No
6. Did the author use correct capitalization, capitalizing the first word in the sentence and proper names of people, places, and things?	(Yes) Fix up	Yes No
7. Did the author use correct punctuation, including a period at the end of each sentence?	(Yes) Fix up	Yes No

WRITING 13 Points

Student Book: Application Lesson 10 133

21. Count up your points and record them in the Writing box.
22. (Show Overhead 49.) Look at the overhead. Let's read the three example paragraphs. Yours should be similar. (Read the paragraphs to your students or with your students or call on a student to read the example paragraphs.)

Note G-1: The rubric can be used in a variety of ways. You may wish to have students evaluate their own paragraphs or have partners provide feedback, and then use the second column of the rubric for teacher feedback. You may wish to give students bonus points based on your feedback.

ACTIVITY H

Comprehension— Single-Paragraph Answer

ACTIVITY PROCEDURE

(See the *Student Book*, page 134.)

Have students read the *What Is* statement and the *What If* question. Have students turn the question into part of the answer and write down a topic sentence for their answer. Then, have them complete their answer. Encourage them to use evidence from the article and their own experience and background knowledge. Engage students in a discussion. Award points for writing and participating in the discussion.

Note H-1: If you are working with students who have difficulty generating ideas for writing their paragraph, switch the order of activities: engage the students in a discussion, and then have them write their paragraphs.

1. Turn to page 134._ Find **Activity H.**_
2. Find the *What Is* statement in the middle of the page._ Read it out loud with me: **When Rachel Carson wrote *Silent Spring*, DDT was widely used as a pesticide.**
3. Find the *What If* question._ Read it with me: **What if Rachel Carson had not written *Silent Spring?***
4. Think how you might turn the question into part of the answer._ Tell me your idea for a topic sentence._ (Example sentence: It is quite interesting to guess what would have happened if Rachel Carson had not written *Silent Spring*.) Take out a piece of paper and write your topic sentence._ (Move around the room and monitor as students write.)
5. You are ready to add ideas to your paragraph. Use evidence from the article as well as your own experience and background knowledge. If you finish early, reread your paragraph and edit it so that it is easy to understand and clear._ (Move around the room and monitor as students write.)
6. Read your paragraph to your partner._
7. If you included wording from the question in your answer and added evidence from the article, award yourself four points for writing._
8. (Engage students in a discussion. Award four points to students who are active participants in the discussion.)

APPLICATION LESSON

10

ACTIVITY H *Comprehension—Single-Paragraph Answer*

Writing Strategy—Single-Paragraph Answer

Step 1: Read the item.
Step 2: Turn the question into part of the answer and write it down.
Step 3: Think of the answer or locate the answer in the article.
Step 4: Complete your answer.

Prompt:

What Is—When Rachel Carson wrote *Silent Spring*, DDT was widely used as a pesticide.

What If—What if Rachel Carson had not written *Silent Spring*?

Write and Discuss: Write a paragraph. Then share your ideas. Use the Discussion Guidelines.

Discussion Guidelines

Speaker		Listener	
Looks like:	**Sounds like:**	**Looks like:**	**Sounds like:**
• Facing peers • Making eye contact • Participating	• Using pleasant, easy-to-hear voice • Sharing opinions, supporting facts and reasons from the article and from your experience • Staying on the topic	• Facing speaker • Making eye contact • Participating	• Waiting quietly to speak • Giving positive, supportive comments • Disagreeing respectfully

WRITING DISCUSSION
4 Points 4 Points

134 *REWARDS Plus: Reading Strategies Applied to Science Passages*

Note H-2: If your students are having difficulty writing the *What If* paragraphs, read or show them the following example paragraph:

Example Single-Paragraph Answer

It is quite interesting to speculate on what would have happened if Rachel Carson had not written *Silent Spring*. First, because the publication of the book led to legislation that regulated use of pesticides, it is very possible that legislation would not have ever been passed or would have been delayed for decades. Second, the banning of DDT would also not have occurred or would have been delayed. As a result, DDT would have continued to damage birds and other wildlife as well as our soil and water. Finally, if the book had not been published, it is possible that the EPA would not have been established and people's awareness of environmental issues would be lower.

Application Lesson 11

Materials Needed:

- *Student Book*: Application Lesson 11
- Application Overhead Transparencies 50–54
- Appendix B Reproducible K: Application Lesson 11
- Appendix C Optional Vocabulary Activity: Application Lesson 11
- Paper or cardboard to use when covering the overhead transparency
- Paper or cardboard for each student to use during spelling dictation
- Washable overhead transparency pen

Text Treatment Notes:

- Black text signifies teacher script (exact wording to say to students).
- Green text in parentheses signifies directions or prompts for the teacher.
- Green text signifies answers or examples of answers.
- Green graphics treatment signifies reproduction of Overhead information.
- Green text and green graphics treatment do not appear in the *Student Book*.

ACTIVITY A

Vocabulary

ACTIVITY PROCEDURE, List 1

(See the *Student Book*, page 135.)

Tell students each word in the list. Then, have students repeat the word and read the definition aloud For each definition, provide any additional information that may be necessary. Then, have students practice reading the words themselves.

Use Overhead 50: Activity A
List 1: Tell

1. (Show the top half of Overhead 50.) Before we read the passage, let's read the difficult words. (Point to **fissures**.) The first word is **fissures**. What word?_ Now, read the definition._
2. (Point to **volcanoes**.) The next word is **volcanoes**. What word?_ Now, read the definition._
3. (Pronounce each word in List 1, and then have students repeat each word and read the definition.)
4. Open your *Student Book* to **Application Lesson 11**, page 135._
5. Find **Activity A**, **List 1**, in your book._ Let's read the words again. First word._ Next word._ (Continue for all words in List 1.)

ACTIVITY PROCEDURE, List 2

(See the *Student Book*, page 135.)

Have students circle prefixes and suffixes, then underline the vowels. Using the overhead transparency, assist students in checking their work. Next, have students figure out each word to themselves, then say it aloud. Have them read the definition aloud.

Use Overhead 50: Activity A
List 2: Strategy Practice

1. Find **List 2**. Circle the prefixes and suffixes, and underline the vowels. Remember, you can circle the prefixes **sub** and **hydro**. Look up when you are done._
2. (Show the bottom half of Overhead 50.) Now, check and fix any mistakes._

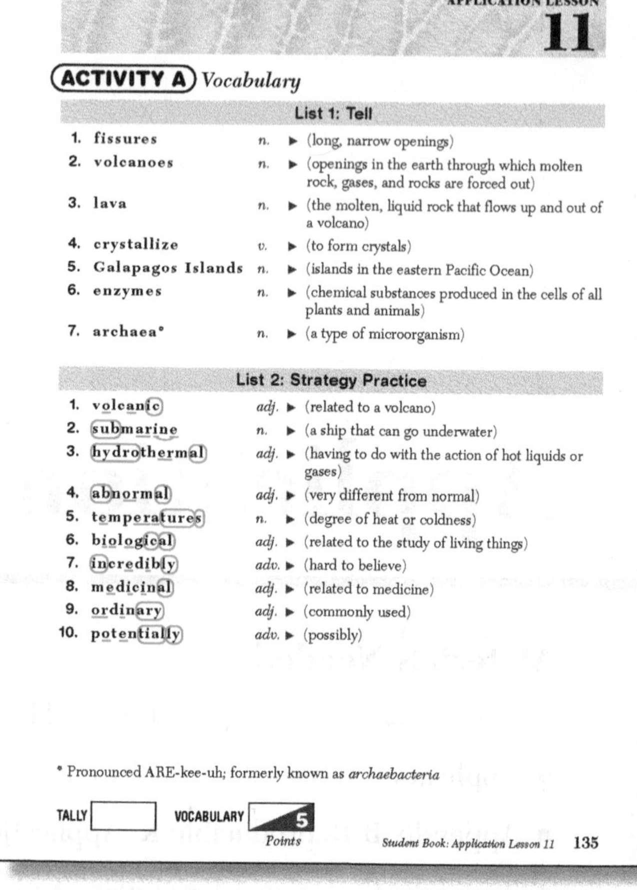

APPLICATION LESSON
11

ACTIVITY A *Vocabulary*

List 1: Tell

1.	**fissures**	*n.*	► (long, narrow openings)
2.	**volcanoes**	*n.*	► (openings in the earth through which molten rock, gases, and rocks are forced out)
3.	**lava**	*n.*	► (the molten, liquid rock that flows up and out of a volcano)
4.	**crystallize**	*v.*	► (to form crystals)
5.	**Galapagos Islands**	*n.*	► (islands in the eastern Pacific Ocean)
6.	**enzymes**	*n.*	► (chemical substances produced in the cells of all plants and animals)
7.	**archaea***	*n.*	► (a type of microorganism)

List 2: Strategy Practice

1.	**volcanic**	*adj.*	► (related to a volcano)
2.	**submarine**	*n.*	► (a ship that can go underwater)
3.	**hydrothermal**	*adj.*	► (having to do with the action of hot liquids or gases)
4.	**abnormal**	*adj.*	► (very different from normal)
5.	**temperatures**	*n.*	► (degree of heat or coldness)
6.	**biological**	*adj.*	► (related to the study of living things)
7.	**incredibly**	*adv.*	► (hard to believe)
8.	**medicinal**	*adj.*	► (related to medicine)
9.	**ordinary**	*adj.*	► (commonly used)
10.	**potentially**	*adv.*	► (possibly)

* Pronounced ARE-kee-uh; formerly known as *archaebacteria*

TALLY | VOCABULARY 5 *Points*

Student Book: Application Lesson 11 135

3. Go back to the first word._ Sound out the word to yourself. Put your thumb up when you can read the word. Be sure that it is a real word._ What word?_ Now, read the definition._
4. (Continue Step 3 with all remaining words in List 2.)

Note A.2-1: You may wish to provide additional practice by having students read words to a partner.

ACTIVITY PROCEDURE, List 1 and 2

(See the *Student Book*, page 135.)

Tell students to look in List 1 or List 2 for a word you are thinking about. Have them circle the number of the word and tell you the word. Explain to students to make a tally mark for each correct word in the Tally box, and then enter the number of tally marks as points in the blank half of the Vocabulary box.

1. Remember, the words I'm thinking about will be in either List 1 or List 2. Make a tally mark for every correctly identified word.
2. Circle the number of the appropriate word.
   - If something is very different from normal, it is said to be this. (Wait.) What word? **abnormal**
   - If something is commonly used, it is this. (Wait.) What word? **ordinary**
   - These are long, narrow openings. (Wait.) What word? **fissures**
   - These are degrees of heat or coldness in the air or in objects. (Wait.) What word? **temperatures**
   - These are chemical substances produced in the cells of plants and animals. (Wait.) What word? **enzymes**
3. Count all the tally marks, and enter that number as points in the blank half of the Vocabulary box.

ACTIVITY PROCEDURE, List 3

(See the *Student Book*, page 136.)

The words in the third list are related. Have students use the *REWARDS* Strategies to figure out the first word in each family. Have them read the definition of the verb and then read nouns and adjectives that are related to that verb.

Use Overhead 51: Activity A
List 3: Word Families

1. Turn to page 136._ Find **Family 1** in **List 3.** Figure out the first word. Use your pencil if you wish. Put your thumb up when you know the word._ What word?_ Read the definition._
2. Look at the noun in Family 1. Figure out the word._ What word?_
3. Look at the adjective in Family 1. Figure out the word._ What word?_
4. (Repeat Steps 1–3 for all word families in List 3.)

APPLICATION LESSON
11

List 3: Word Families

	Verb	Noun	Adjective
Family 1	solidify (to make solid or hard)	solid	solid-state
Family 2	document (to furnish evidence)	document documentary documentation	documentary
Family 3	react (to respond to something)	reaction reactants reactionary	reactionary reactive
Family 4	surround (to enclose on all sides)	surrounding	surrounding
Family 5	descend (to go down)	descent	descendant

ACTIVITY B *Spelling Dictation*

1. react	4. document
2. reaction	5. documentation
3. reactive	6. documentary

SPELLING 6 *Points*

136 *REWARDS Plus: Reading Strategies Applied to Science Passages*

Note A.3-1: You may wish to provide additional practice by having students read a word family to the group or to a partner.

Note A.3-2: An additional vocabulary practice activity called Quick Words is provided in Appendix C of this Teacher's Guide. See Appendix C for information about how this optional activity can be used.

ACTIVITY B

Spelling Dictation

ACTIVITY PROCEDURE

(See the *Student Book*, page 136.)

For each word, tell students the word, then have students say the parts of the word to themselves while they write the word. Using the overhead transparency, assist students in checking their spelling and correcting if they misspelled. Then, have students enter the number of correctly spelled words as points in the blank half of the Spelling box.

Note B-1: Distribute a piece of light cardboard to each of the students.

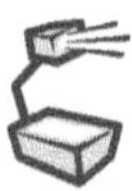

Use Overhead 51: Activity B

1. Find **Activity B.**
2. The first word is **react**. What word?_ Say the parts in **react** to yourself as you write the word. (Pause and monitor.)
3. (Show **react** on the overhead.) Check **react**. If you misspelled it, cross it out and write it correctly.
4. The second word is **reaction**. What word?_ Say the parts in **reaction** to yourself as you write the word. (Pause and monitor.)
5. (Show **reaction** on the overhead.) Check **reaction**. If you misspelled it, cross it out and write it correctly.
6. (Repeat the procedures for the words **reactive**, **document**, **documentation**, and **documentary**.)
7. Count the number of words you spelled correctly, and record that number as points in the blank half of the Spelling box at the bottom of the page.

APPLICATION LESSON
11

List 3: Word Families

	Verb	Noun	Adjective
Family 1	solidify (to make solid or hard)	solid	solid-state
Family 2	document (to furnish evidence)	document documentary documentation	documentary
Family 3	react (to respond to something)	reaction reactants reactionary	reactionary reactive
Family 4	surround (to enclose on all sides)	surrounding	surrounding
Family 5	descend (to go down)	descent	descendant

ACTIVITY B *Spelling Dictation*

1. react	4. document
2. reaction	5. documentation
3. reactive	6. documentary

SPELLING

Points

136 *REWARDS Plus: Reading Strategies Applied to Science Passages*

ACTIVITY C

Passage Reading and Comprehension

ACTIVITY PROCEDURE

(See the *Student Book*, pages 137–139.)

Have students read the title of the passage and each heading. Ask them to tell their partners two things that the passage will tell about.

Passage Preview

1. Turn to page 137._ Let's preview the passage.
2. Read the title._ What is the whole passage going to tell about?_
3. Now, let's read the headings. Read the first heading._ Read the next heading._ (Continue until students have read all headings.)
4. Turn to your partner. Without looking, tell two things this passage will tell about._

ACTIVITY PROCEDURE

Provide students with an Information Web from Appendix B. Have students read the passage silently to each embedded number, and then reread the same information orally either to a partner, together as a group, or individually. Ask the corresponding comprehension question or questions. Once students finish reading a section labeled A, B, C, D, or E, have them fill in the Information Web before going on to the next section.

Note C-1: If students do not finish reading the passage during class, have them use their Information Webs to review the information at the beginning of the next class.

Use Overhead 52: Activity C

Passage Reading

1. (Provide an Information Web for each student.)
2. Turn back to the beginning of the passage. You're going to read the passage and answer questions about what you've read. During passage reading, you are also going to fill in an Information Web to help you remember the important details of the passage. Later, you'll use this Web to review the content of the passage with your partner.
3. Read the title._

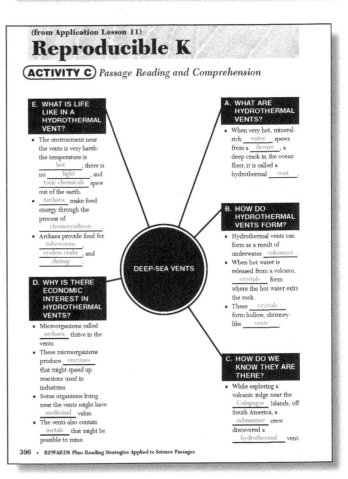

APPLICATION LESSON **11**

ACTIVITY C *Passage Reading and Comprehension*

Note: For this activity, you will need Reproducible K found in the *Teacher's Guide.*

Deep-Sea Vents

A

What Are Hydrothermal Vents?

4 A mile under the ocean's surface, scientists have discovered a strange, foreign
16 world. They found deep cracks, called **fissures**, in the ocean floor. Some of these
30 fissures are small—only half an inch wide. Some are as large as a football
45 stadium. Some fissures spew very hot, mineral-rich water, so scientists call them
58 **hydrothermal vents**. (#1)

B

60 **How Do Hydrothermal Vents Form?**
65 Just as there are active volcanoes among our land-based mountain ranges,
77 volcanoes are also found underwater. Many of these underwater volcanoes are
88 active, releasing lava and hot water filled with many types of minerals. When
101 this hot water flows onto the ocean floor, some of the minerals solidify and form
116 crystals. They crystallize around the area where the hot water is exiting the rock.
130 Gradually, these crystals form hollow, chimney-like vents through which the hot
142 water flows. Some vents are long and narrow, like tubes, while others are short
156 and wide. (#2)

C

158 **How Do We Know They Are There?**
165 In 1977, a special three-person submarine called **Alvin** made a very deep dive
179 near the Galapagos Islands off the western coast of South America. At those
192 depths, the pressure is great enough to crush ordinary vessels. Alvin is one of only
207 a few submarines in the world that descends deep enough to see things at the
222 bottom of the ocean. The submarine has thick portholes for viewing and has
235 cameras mounted on its outside. While exploring a volcanic ridge at the bottom of
249 the ocean, Alvin's crew discovered a hydrothermal vent. Since then, Alvin's crews
261 have gone on to document numerous deep-sea vents around the world. (#3)

Student Book: Application Lesson 11 137

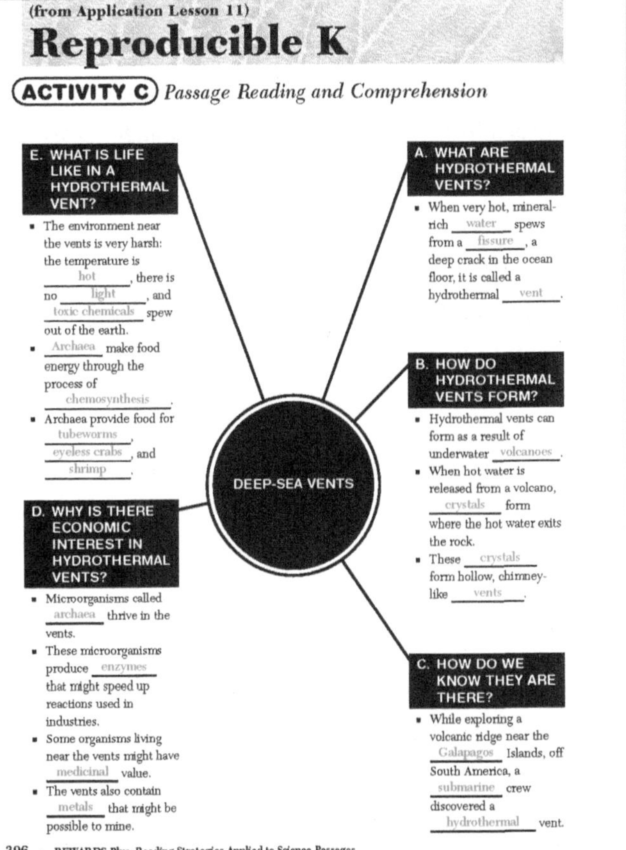

4. Find number 1 in the passage. (Pause.) Read down to number 1 silently. Look up when you are done._
5. (Wait for students to complete the reading. Then have students reread the part by having them read orally to a partner, read together orally as a group, or read aloud individually.)
6. (Ask the question or questions associated with the number. Provide feedback to students regarding their answers.)
7. (Repeat steps 4–6 for all paragraphs in Section A.)
8. Now, look at your Information Web. Find the section labeled A._ The information you've just read will help you to fill in this Web.
9. With your partner, fill in the blanks for Section A. You can refer back to the passage for information. Look up when you're done._ (Move around the room and monitor students as they complete the section.)
10. (When the majority of students have finished, show Overhead 52.) Look at the overhead and check your work. Fix up or add to any of your answers.
11. Now read down to the next number silently. Look up when you are done._
12. (Repeat steps 5–11 until the students have finished the passage and the Information Web.)
13. Now use your Information Web to retell the important information from the passage to your partner.

Comprehension Questions

#1 What are hydrothermal vents?
Deep cracks called fissures that spew very hot, mineral-rich water.

#2 How do hydrothermal vents form?
Underwater volcanoes release lava and hot water; the minerals in the water form crystals, the crystals form chimney-like vents through which the water flows.

#3 Who first discovered deep-sea vents?
The crew of a specially designed submarine named Alvin.

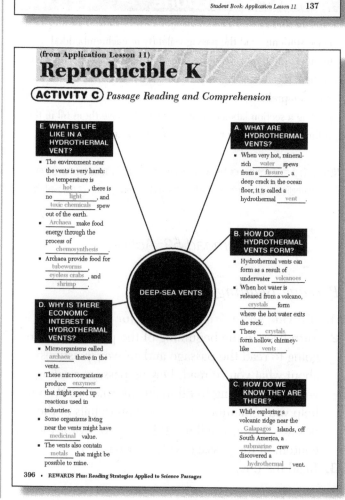

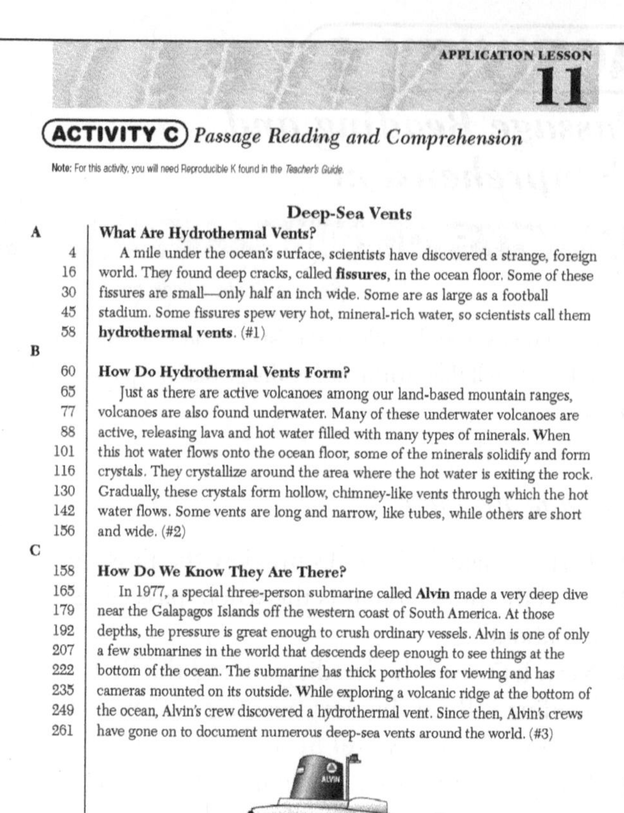

APPLICATION LESSON 11

ACTIVITY C *Passage Reading and Comprehension*

Note: For this activity, you will need Reproducible K found in the *Teacher's Guide*.

Deep-Sea Vents

A
What Are Hydrothermal Vents?
4 A mile under the ocean's surface, scientists have discovered a strange, foreign
16 world. They found deep cracks, called **fissures**, in the ocean floor. Some of these
30 fissures are small—only half an inch wide. Some are as large as a football
45 stadium. Some fissures spew very hot, mineral-rich water, so scientists call them
58 **hydrothermal vents**. (#1)

B
60 **How Do Hydrothermal Vents Form?**
65 Just as there are active volcanoes among our land-based mountain ranges,
77 volcanoes are also found underwater. Many of these underwater volcanoes are
88 active, releasing lava and hot water filled with many types of minerals. When
101 this hot water flows onto the ocean floor, some of the minerals solidify and form
116 crystals. They crystallize around the area where the hot water is exiting the rock.
130 Gradually, these crystals form hollow, chimney-like vents through which the hot
142 water flows. Some vents are long and narrow, like tubes, while others are short
156 and wide. (#2)

C
158 **How Do We Know They Are There?**
165 In 1977, a special three-person submarine called **Alvin** made a very deep dive
179 near the Galapagos Islands off the western coast of South America. At those
192 depths, the pressure is great enough to crush ordinary vessels. Alvin is one of only
207 a few submarines in the world that descends deep enough to see things at the
222 bottom of the ocean. The submarine has thick portholes for viewing and has
235 cameras mounted on its outside. While exploring a volcanic ridge at the bottom of
249 the ocean, Alvin's crew discovered a hydrothermal vent. Since then, Alvin's crews
261 have gone on to document numerous deep-sea vents around the world. (#3)

Student Book: Application Lesson 11 137

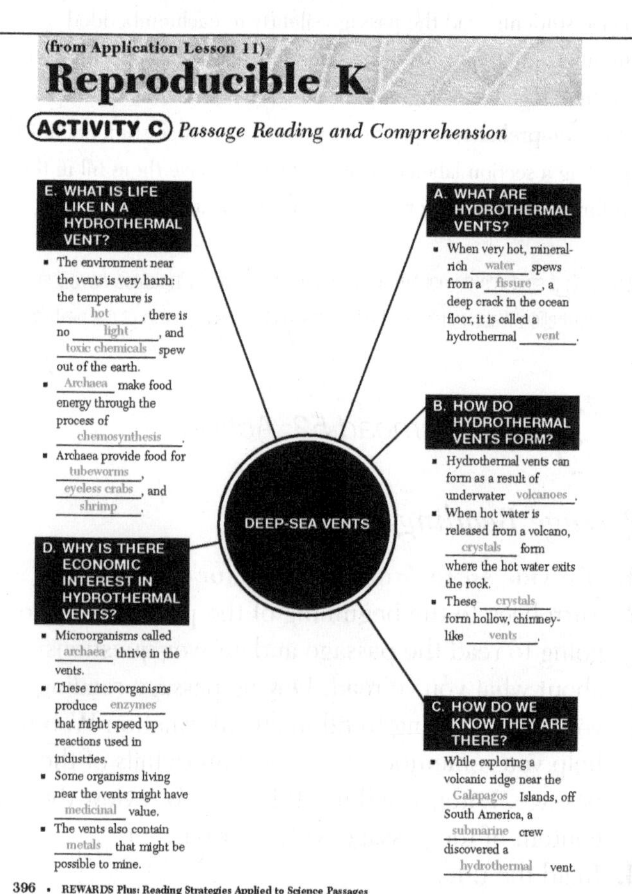

(from Application Lesson 11)

Reproducible K

ACTIVITY C *Passage Reading and Comprehension*

DEEP-SEA VENTS

A. WHAT ARE HYDROTHERMAL VENTS?
- When very hot, mineral-rich __water__ spews from a __fissure__, a deep crack in the ocean floor, it is called a hydrothermal __vent__.

B. HOW DO HYDROTHERMAL VENTS FORM?
- Hydrothermal vents can form as a result of underwater __volcanoes__.
- When hot water is released from a volcano, __crystals__ form where the hot water exits the rock.
- These __crystals__ form hollow, chimney-like __vents__.

C. HOW DO WE KNOW THEY ARE THERE?
- While exploring a volcanic ridge near the __Galapagos__ Islands, off South America, a __submarine__ crew discovered a __hydrothermal__ vent.

D. WHY IS THERE ECONOMIC INTEREST IN HYDROTHERMAL VENTS?
- Microorganisms called __archaea__ thrive in the vents.
- These microorganisms produce __enzymes__ that might speed up reactions used in industries.
- Some organisms living near the vents might have __medicinal__ value.
- The vents also contain __metals__ that might be possible to mine.

E. WHAT IS LIFE LIKE IN A HYDROTHERMAL VENT?
- The environment near the vents is very harsh: the temperature is __hot__, there is no __light__, and __toxic chemicals__ spew out of the earth.
- __Archaea__ make food energy through the process of __chemosynthesis__.
- Archaea provide food for __tubeworms__, __eyeless crabs__, and __shrimp__.

396 • REWARDS Plus: Reading Strategies Applied to Science Passages

#4 Why are scientists interested in hydrothermal vents?
Microorganisms that live in this hot environment could be useful to many of our own industries including medicine; also, vents contain large amounts of important metals.

#5 How do archaea meet their energy needs while living in hydrothermal vents?
Through chemosynthesis.

#6 What other organisms live in the hot temperatures surrounding a vent?
Eyeless crabs, shrimp, giant clams, sea sponges, brittle stars.

#7 What information do scientists hope the vents will provide?
How life first appeared on earth.

APPLICATION LESSON
11

D

Why Is There Economic Interest in Hydrothermal Vents?

Scientists are interested in hydrothermal vents for many reasons. They have discovered that a microorganism called **archaea** thrive in that hot, unfriendly environment. These microorganisms produce enzymes that could potentially be very useful to many of our own industries. These microorganisms might be able to speed up common chemical and biological reactions that are used in industrial processes.

Secondly, other forms of life exist in and around these vents. Scientists believe that these life forms might contain compounds that could have medicinal value. Scientists also want to discover how these organisms can exist in such harsh conditions.

In addition, the hot water and the vent chimneys contain vast amounts of important metals such as copper, zinc, gold, and iron. People are researching whether it might be possible to mine these resources without harming the hydrothermal vent systems. (#4)

E

What Is Life Like in a Hydrothermal Vent?

Most of the creatures we think of would not be able to survive the incredibly high temperatures surrounding a vent. Because these vents are located in the depths of the ocean, there is no light. Toxic chemicals spew out of the earth. You might think that nothing could live in such an environment. But in reality, many varieties of creatures are suited to live and thrive in these difficult conditions. Archaea are the base of the deep-sea food chain. Instead of using sunlight to photosynthesize like surface-dwelling organisms, these microorganisms collect the energy they need from the minerals coming out of the hydrothermal vents. The archaea use this chemical energy in a process called chemosynthesis to make their food energy and carry out life processes. (#5)

Archaea are the prime food source for giant tubeworms and other creatures living near deep-sea vents. Tubeworms that live near hydrothermal vents can grow to be 12 feet tall. Smaller creatures such as eyeless crabs and shrimp crawl around the vents. In such a dark, hostile environment, "abnormal" creatures born with no eyes may actually have a better chance of survival than if they had eyes. These sightless creatures are sensitive to heat and know when they are close to or distant from the vent. In addition, giant clams and other types of mollusks, as well as small fish, sea sponges, and even brittle stars (a type of starfish) live in this hostile, dark place. (#6)

138 *REWARDS Plus: Reading Strategies Applied to Science Passages*

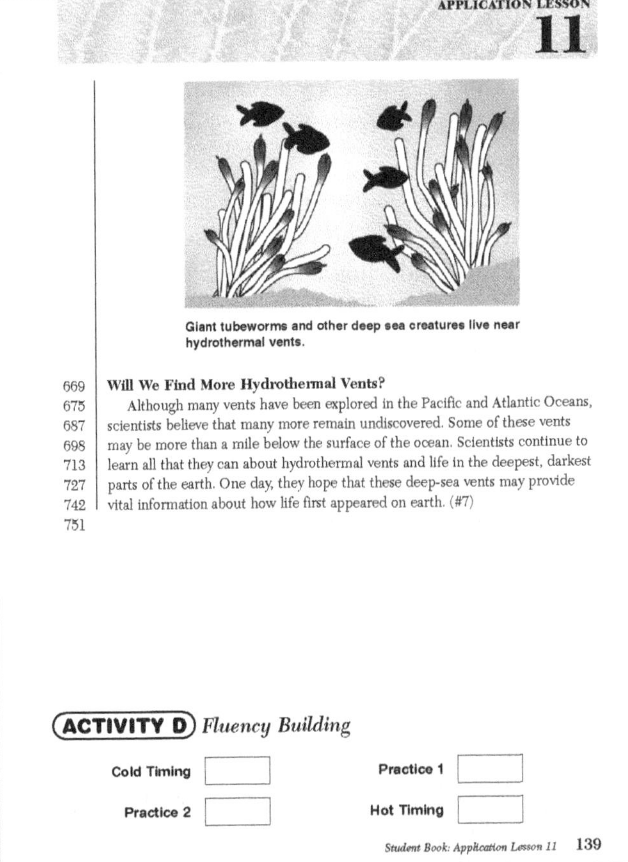

APPLICATION LESSON
11

Giant tubeworms and other deep sea creatures live near hydrothermal vents.

Will We Find More Hydrothermal Vents?

Although many vents have been explored in the Pacific and Atlantic Oceans, scientists believe that many more remain undiscovered. Some of these vents may be more than a mile below the surface of the ocean. Scientists continue to learn all that they can about hydrothermal vents and life in the deepest, darkest parts of the earth. One day, they hope that these deep-sea vents may provide vital information about how life first appeared on earth. (#7)

ACTIVITY D *Fluency Building*

Cold Timing		Practice 1	
Practice 2		Hot Timing	

Student Book: Application Lesson 11 139

ACTIVITY D

Fluency Building

ACTIVITY PROCEDURE

(See the *Student Book*, page 139.)

Have students complete a Cold Timing, one or two practices, and a Hot Timing of the Activity C article. For each timing, have students record the number of correct words read. Finally, have students complete their Fluency Graphs.

Note D-1: When assigning partners for this activity, have the stronger reader read first. As a result, the other reader will have one additional practice opportunity.

1. Now, it's time for fluency building.
2. Find the beginning of the passage again. (Pause.)
3. Whisper-read. See how many words you can read in one minute. Begin._ (Time students for one minute.) Stop._ Circle the last word that you read._ Record the number of words you read after **Cold Timing**._
4. Let's practice again. Begin._ (Time students for one minute.) Stop._ Put a box around the last word that you read._ Record the number of words you read after **Practice 1**._
5. (Optional) Let's practice one more time before the Hot Timing. Begin._ (Time students for one minute.) Stop._ Put a box around the last word that you read._ Record the number of words you read after **Practice 2**._
6. Please exchange books with your partner._ Partner 1, you are going to read first. Partner 2, listen carefully and underline any mistakes or words left out. Ones, begin._ (Time students for one minute.) Stop._ Twos, cross out the last word that your partner read._ (Assist students in subtracting the number of mistakes from the number of words read.) Twos, record the number of correct words in your partner's book after **Hot Timing**._
7. Partner 2, you are going to read next. Partner 1, listen carefully and underline any mistakes or words left out. Twos, begin. (Time students for one minute.) Stop._ Ones, cross out the last word that your partner read._ Ones, record the number of correct words in your partner's book after **Hot Timing**._
8. Exchange books._ Turn to the Fluency Graph on the inside back cover, and indicate on the graph the number of Cold Timing and Hot Timing words you read correctly._

APPLICATION LESSON **11**

Giant tubeworms and other deep sea creatures live near hydrothermal vents.

669 **Will We Find More Hydrothermal Vents?**
675 Although many vents have been explored in the Pacific and Atlantic Oceans,
687 scientists believe that many more remain undiscovered. Some of these vents
698 may be more than a mile below the surface of the ocean. Scientists continue to
713 learn all that they can about hydrothermal vents and life in the deepest, darkest
727 parts of the earth. One day, they hope that these deep-sea vents may provide
742 vital information about how life first appeared on earth. (#7)
751

ACTIVITY D *Fluency Building*

Cold Timing		Practice 1	
Practice 2		Hot Timing	

Student Book: Application Lesson 11 139

ACTIVITY E

Comprehension Questions—Multiple Choice

ACTIVITY PROCEDURE

(See the *Student Book*, page 140.)

Have students complete item #1. Then, have students share the rationale for their answers. Encourage thoughtful discussion. Proceed item by item, emphasizing the rationale for the *best* answer. Have students record points for each correct item.

Note E-1: The correct Multiple Choice answers are circled.

1. Turn to page 140. Find **Activity E**.
2. Use the Multiple Choice Strategy to complete item #1. Be ready to explain why you selected your answer. (Wait while students complete the item. Call on individual students. Ask them why they chose their answer and why they eliminated the other choices. Encourage discussion. Provide students with feedback on their choices, focusing on why or why not those choices might be appropriate.)
3. (Repeat Step 2 for items #2–4, pausing after each item to confirm student responses and provide feedback.)
4. Count the number of items you got correct, and record that number in the blank half of the Multiple Choice Comprehension box.

APPLICATION LESSON

11

ACTIVITY E *Comprehension Questions—Multiple Choice*

Comprehension Strategy—Multiple Choice

Step 1: Read the item.
Step 2: Read all of the choices.
Step 3: Think about why each choice might be correct or incorrect. Check the article as needed.
Step 4: From the possible correct choices, select the best answer.

1. (Vocabulary) **The word "hydrothermal" has two meaningful parts. The parts mean:**
   a. hydrogen + sea
   b. hydrogen + thermos
   c. water + mineral
   (d.) water + hot
2. (Cause and effect) **Which is NOT true of hydrothermal vents?**
   a. Hot, mineral-rich water spews out of hydrothermal vents.
   b. Hydrothermal vents are found on the ocean floor.
   c. Hydrothermal vents are one type of fissure found in the ocean floor.
   (d.) Hydrothermal vents are found deep within underwater volcanoes.
3. (Cause and effect) **When underwater volcanoes release lava and mineral-rich water:**
   (a.) some of the minerals become solid and form crystals and gradually form a vent.
   b. the mixtures runs out over the surface of the ocean, creating the base of new volcanoes.
   c. some of the water turns into lava, creating the walls of a volcano.
   d. vent chimneys are formed from the fossil remains of shells and fish.
4. (Cause and effect) **Which statement would be false?**
   a. Most creatures found in the ocean would not be able to survive life in a hydrothermal vent because of the heat.
   b. Most ocean creatures could not survive in the toxic chemicals found at a vent.
   c. Most creatures found in the ocean could not survive without light, which is absent at the vents.
   (d.) Most ocean creatures would not be able to survive life in or around the hydrothermal vents because of the minerals.

MULTIPLE CHOICE COMPREHENSION

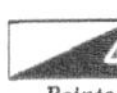

4 Points

140 *REWARDS Plus: Reading Strategies Applied to Science Passages*

Vocabulary Activities

ACTIVITY PROCEDURE

(See the *Student Book*, pages 141–142.)

Have students complete each item orally and provide feedback on their answers. Then have students respond to each question in writing by answering "yes" or "no" and providing a reason for their answers.

Yes/No/Why

1. Turn to page 141._ Find **Activity F**._ Read item #1. Tell your partner your answer and your reason for it. (Pause. Then call on individual students. Encourage discussion. Provide students with feedback on their choices, focusing on their explanations for their answer.)
2. Write your answer and your reason for it in the space provided. Look up when you are done._
3. Read item #2. Tell your partner your answer and your reason for it. (Pause. Then call on individual students. Encourage discussion. Provide students with feedback on their choices, focusing on their explanations for their answer.)
4. Write your answer and your reason for it in the space provided. Look up when you are done._
5. Read item #3. Tell your partner your answer and your reason for it. (Pause. Then call on individual students. Encourage discussion. Provide students with feedback on their choices, focusing on their explanations for their answer.)
6. Write your answer and your reason for it in the space provided. Look up when you are done._

Note F-1: You may wish to do this as an oral task only rather than an oral and a written task.

APPLICATION LESSON **11**

ACTIVITY F *Vocabulary Activities*

Yes/No/Why

1. **Potentially**, could a **submarine** explore a **volcano**?
Example answer: Yes. There are volcanoes in the ocean that submarines could explore.

2. Is it possible to have **abnormal temperatures** at a **hydrothermal** vent?
Example answer: Yes. The temperatures at a hydrothermal vent are so hot that we could say they are abnormal.

3. Could something very **ordinary** turn out to be **medicinal**?
Example answer: Yes. There are some very ordinary plants that have proven medicinal value.

Student Book: Application Lesson 11 141

ACTIVITY PROCEDURE

Have students read the words and definitions and then complete the sentence stems for each vocabulary word. Have them share answers with partners and with the class. Then, have students give themselves points in the blank half of the Vocabulary box.

Completion Activity

1. Turn to page 142. Read the first word and its definition.
2. Now, read the sentence stem.
3. Think of how you would complete the sentence stem and write it. Share your answer with your partner. (Call on a few students to share answers with the class.)
4. (Repeat Steps 1–3 for the rest of the words.)
5. If you participated in answering all seven questions, give yourself seven points in the blank half of the Vocabulary box.

Note F-2: You may wish to do this as an oral task only rather than an oral task and a written task.

APPLICATION LESSON

11

Completion Activities

1. **descend:** to go down
If I were to descend from the top floor of a building, I might use
Answers will vary.

2. **react:** to respond to something
Sometimes we react kindly to others. Other ways that we might react include
Answers will vary.

3. **surrounded:** enclosed on all sides
I would hate to be surrounded by water for very long. You would hate to be surrounded by
Answers will vary.

4. **incredibly:** hard to believe
An incredibly wonderful meal would include
Answers will vary.

VOCABULARY 7 Points

142 *REWARDS Plus: Reading Strategies Applied to Science Passages*

ACTIVITY G

Expository Writing—Multi-Paragraph Answer

ACTIVITY PROCEDURE, Plan and Write

(See the *Student Book*, pages 143–145.)

Have students read the prompt. Guide students as they determine the three topics and **LIST** details for topics a, b, and c. Have students look at topic a again. Have students **CROSS OUT** details that don't go with the topic. Have students **CONNECT** details as shown in the example plan. Have students **NUMBER** their details, and then compare with the example plan for topic a. Next, have students **WRITE** paragraph a. Repeat for topics b and c. Finally, explain that after the answer is written, they should **EDIT** their work, revising for clarity and proofreading for errors in capitalization, punctuation, and spelling.

Use Overheads 53 and 54: Activity G

1. Turn to page 143._ Find **Activity G.**_
2. Find the prompt in the middle of the page._ Read the prompt out loud with me: **Summarize the information on hydrothermal vents using the following topics: (1) What are hydrothermal vents and how are they formed? (2) What is life like in hydrothermal vents? (3) What might be the value in hydrothermal vents?**
3. Reread the prompt and determine three topics. Record the topics in your Planning Box._ Compare your topics with your partner._ (Move around the room and assist students in determining the topics.)
4. Look back in the article and locate details that go with each of your topics. Record the details in the Planning Box._
5. Use the steps for topic a. Read the details and **cross out** any details that do not go with the topic._ Next, draw brackets to **connect** details that could easily go into one sentence._ Now, **number** the details in a logical order._
6. (Show Overhead 53.) Now, look at the example plan for topic a on the overhead. Yours should be similar._
7. Take out a blank piece of paper._ Using your plan for paragraph a, **write** paragraph a. If you finish early, please reread and **edit** your paragraph._ (Move around the room and monitor your students as they are writing.)

APPLICATION LESSON **11**

ACTIVITY G *Expository Writing—Multi-Paragraph Answer*

Writing Strategy—Multi-Paragraph Answer

Step 1: LIST (List the details that are important enough to include in your answer.)
Step 2: CROSS OUT (Reread the details. Cross out any that don't go with the topic.)
Step 3: CONNECT (Connect any details that could go into one sentence.)
Step 4: NUMBER (Number the details in a logical order.)
Step 5: WRITE (Write the paragraph.)
Step 6: EDIT (Revise and proofread your answer.)

Prompt: Summarize the information on hydrothermal vents using the following topics: (1) What are hydrothermal vents and how are they formed? (2) What is life like in hydrothermal vents? (3) What might be the value in hydrothermal vents?

Plan: Complete the Planning Box.

Student Book: Application Lesson 11 143

APPLICATION LESSON **11**

Example Multi-Paragraph Plan

Planning Box		
(topic a)		*hydrothermal vents—what they are and how they are formed*
①	(detail)	– *fissures that spew very hot, mineral-rich water*
	(detail)	– *fissures are deep cracks in ocean floor*
②	(detail)	– *underwater volcanoes release lava and hot water filled w/ minerals*
③	(detail)	– *some minerals solidify and form crystals*
④	(detail)	– *this may occur where hot water is exiting rock*
⑤	(detail)	– *crystals can form hollow, chimney-like vents*
⑥	(detail)	– *hot water flows out of vents*
(topic b)		*hydrothermal vents—life in them*
①	(detail)	– *very high temperatures*
	(detail)	– *no light*
	(detail)	– *toxic chemicals*
②	(detail)	– *archaea—base of food chain*
	(detail)	– *archaea use chemosynthesis to make their food*
③	(detail)	– *giant tubeworms and other creatures eat archaea*
④	(detail)	– *other creatures—eyeless crabs, shrimp, giant clams, small fish, sea sponges, brittle stars (a type of starfish)*
(topic c)		*hydrothermal vents—value*
①	(detail)	– *scientists interested in archaea*
	(detail)	– *produce enzymes that might speed up chemical and biological reactions in industrial processes*
②	(detail)	– *some organisms might be useful in medicine*
③	(detail)	– *vast amounts of copper, zinc, gold, iron*

Write: Write paragraphs a, b, and c on a separate piece of paper.

144 *REWARDS Plus: Reading Strategies Applied to Science Passages*

8. (When the majority of students are done, proceed with the lesson.) Now, use the steps for topic b.
9. Now, look at the example plan for topic b on the overhead. Yours should be similar.
10. Locate your piece of paper. Using your plan for paragraph b, **write** paragraph b. If you finish early, please **edit** your paragraph. (Move around the room and monitor your students as they are writing.)
11. (When the majority of students are done, proceed with the lesson.) Now, use the steps for topic c.
12. Look at the example plan for topic c on the overhead. Yours should be similar.
13. Locate your piece of paper. Using your plan for paragraph c, **write** paragraph c. If you finish early, please **edit** your paragraph. (Move around the room and monitor your students as they are writing.)
14. (When the majority of students are done, proceed with the lesson.) Please carefully read your paragraphs. Be sure that your paragraphs are clear. Proofread for any errors in capitalization, punctuation, and spelling. (Give students time to proofread their paragraphs.)

ACTIVITY PROCEDURE, Evaluate

Ask students to read each question in the rubric. Guide them in evaluating the paragraphs using the guidelines. Have students total their points and record them in the blank half of the Writing box.

15. Turn to page 145. Let's evaluate paragraphs a, b, and c.
16. Check paragraphs a, b, and c carefully and answer questions 1 through 3.
17. Reread your paragraphs. Circle "Yes" if your paragraphs are easy to understand.
18. Carefully examine your paragraphs. If you think a word is misspelled, underline it and check back in the plan or article and correct the spelling. Circle "Yes" if you believe that you have very few spelling errors.
19. Carefully examine your sentences. Be sure that each sentence begins with a capital. If all sentences begin with a capital, circle "Yes."
20. Examine your sentences. Be sure that each sentence ends with a period. If all sentences end with a period, circle "Yes."

APPLICATION LESSON **11**

Evaluate: Evaluate the paragraphs using this rubric.

Rubric— Multi-Paragraph Answer	Student or Partner Rating	Teacher Rating
1. Did the author state the topic in the first sentence?	a. Yes Fix up b. Yes Fix up c. Yes Fix up	a. Yes No b. Yes No c. Yes No
2. Did the author include details that go with the topic?	a. Yes Fix up b. Yes Fix up c. Yes Fix up	a. Yes No b. Yes No c. Yes No
3. Did the author combine details in some of the sentences?	a. Yes Fix up b. Yes Fix up c. Yes Fix up	a. Yes No b. Yes No c. Yes No
4. Is the answer easy to understand?	Yes Fix up	Yes No
5. Did the author correctly spell words, particularly the words found in the article?	Yes Fix up	Yes No
6. Did the author use correct capitalization, capitalizing the first word in the sentence and proper names of people, places, and things?	Yes Fix up	Yes No
7. Did the author use correct punctuation, including a period at the end of each sentence?	Yes Fix up	Yes No

WRITING 13 Points

Student Book: Application Lesson 11 145

21. Count up your points and record them in the Writing box.
22. (Show Overhead 54.) Look at the overhead. Let's read the three example paragraphs. Yours should be similar. (Read the paragraphs to your students or with your students or call on a student to read the example paragraph.)

Note G-1: The rubric can be used in a variety of ways. You may wish to have students evaluate their own paragraphs or have partners provide feedback, and then use the second column of the rubric for teacher feedback. You may wish to give students bonus points based on your feedback.

ACTIVITY H

Comprehension—Single-Paragraph Answer

ACTIVITY PROCEDURE

(See the *Student Book*, page 146.)

Have students read the *What Is* statement and the *What If* question. Have students turn the question into part of the answer and write down a topic sentence for their answer. Then, have them complete their answer. Encourage them to use evidence from the article and their own experience and background knowledge. Engage students in a discussion. Award points for writing and participating in the discussion.

Note H-1: If you are working with students who have difficulty generating ideas for their paragraphs, switch the order of activities: engage the students in a discussion, and then have them write their paragraphs.

1. Turn to page 146._ Find **Activity H.**_
2. Find the *What Is* statement in the middle of the page._ Read it out loud with me: **Scientists believe that some of the organisms found in hydrothermal vents may have medicinal value and could be used to cure some diseases.**
3. Find the *What If* question._ Read it with me: **What would happen if scientists discovered that the strange organisms living in or near deep-sea vents were REALLY valuable to medical research or as a cure to a disease such as cancer?**
4. Think how you might turn the question into part of the answer._ Tell me your idea for a topic sentence._ (Example sentence: If scientists discovered that the strange organisms living in or near deep-sea vents were really valuable to medical research or as a cure to a disease, a number of things would happen.) Take out a piece of paper and write your topic sentence._ (Move around the room and monitor as students write.)
5. You are ready to add ideas to your paragraph. Use evidence from the article as well as your own experience and background knowledge. If you finish early, reread your paragraph and edit it so that it is easy to understand and clear._ (Move around the room and monitor as students write.)
6. Read your paragraph to your partner._
7. If you included wording from the question in your answer and added evidence from the article, award yourself four points for writing._

APPLICATION LESSON

11

ACTIVITY H *Comprehension—Single-Paragraph Answer*

Writing Strategy—Single-Paragraph Answer

Step 1: Read the item.
Step 2: Turn the question into part of the answer and write it down.
Step 3: Think of the answer or locate the answer in the article.
Step 4: Complete your answer.

Prompt:

What Is—Scientists believe that some of the organisms found in hydrothermal vents may have medicinal value and could be used to cure some diseases.

What If—What would happen if scientists discovered that the strange organisms living in or near deep-sea vents were REALLY valuable to medical research or as a cure to a disease such as cancer?

Write and Discuss: Write a paragraph. Then share your ideas. Use the Discussion Guidelines.

Discussion Guidelines

Speaker		Listener	
Looks like:	**Sounds like:**	**Looks like:**	**Sounds like:**
• Facing peers • Making eye contact • Participating	• Using pleasant, easy-to-hear voice • Sharing opinions, supporting facts and reasons from the article and from your experience • Staying on the topic	• Facing speaker • Making eye contact • Participating	• Waiting quietly to speak • Giving positive, supportive comments • Disagreeing respectfully

WRITING DISCUSSION

4 Points 4 Points

146 *REWARDS Plus: Reading Strategies Applied to Science Passages*

8. (Engage students in a discussion. Award four points to students who are active participants in the discussion.)

Note H-2: If your students are having difficulty writing the *What If* paragraphs, read or show them the following example paragraph:

Example Single-Paragraph Answer

If scientists discovered that the strange organisms living in or near deep-sea vents were really valuable to medical research or as a cure to a disease, a number of things would happen. First, there would be a demand for the organisms. This is a challenge because most submarines cannot descend that deep. In fact, most vessels would be destroyed if they tried. So, new ways would have to be developed just to get access to the vents. We would also have to develop procedures for removing and transporting the organisms. Given that the organisms are currently surviving in a hostile environment, we would have difficulty creating a similar environment so that the organisms could survive when removed.

Application Lesson 12

Materials Needed:

- *Student Book*: Application Lesson 12
- Application Overhead Transparencies 55–59
- Appendix B Reproducible L: Application Lesson 12
- Appendix C Optional Vocabulary Activity: Application Lesson 12
- Paper or cardboard to use when covering the overhead transparency
- Paper or cardboard for each student to use during spelling dictation
- Washable overhead transparency pen

Text Treatment Notes:

- Black text signifies teacher script (exact wording to say to students).
- Green text in parentheses signifies directions or prompts for the teacher.
- Green text signifies answers or examples of answers.
- Green graphics treatment signifies reproduction of Overhead information.
- Green text and green graphics treatment do not appear in the *Student Book*.

ACTIVITY A
Vocabulary

ACTIVITY PROCEDURE, List 1

(See the *Student Book*, page 147.)

Tell students each word in the list. Then, have students repeat the word and read the definition aloud For each definition, provide any additional information that may be necessary. Then, have students practice reading the words themselves.

Use Overhead 55: Activity A
List 1: Tell

1. (Show the top half of Overhead 55.) Before we read the passage, let's read the difficult words. (Point to **earthquakes**.) The first word is **earthquakes**. What word?_ Now, read the definition._
2. (Point to **seismologists**.) The next word is **seismologists**. What word?_ Now, read the definition._
3. (Pronounce each word in List 1, and then have students repeat each word and read the definition.)
4. Open your *Student Book* to **Application Lesson 12**, page 147._
5. Find **Activity A**, **List 1**, in your book._ Let's read the words again. First word._ Next word._ (Continue for all words in List 1.)

ACTIVITY PROCEDURE, List 2

(See the *Student Book*, page 147.)

Have students circle prefixes and suffixes, then underline the vowels. Using the overhead transparency, assist students in checking their work. Next, have students figure out each word to themselves, then say it aloud. Have them read the definition aloud.

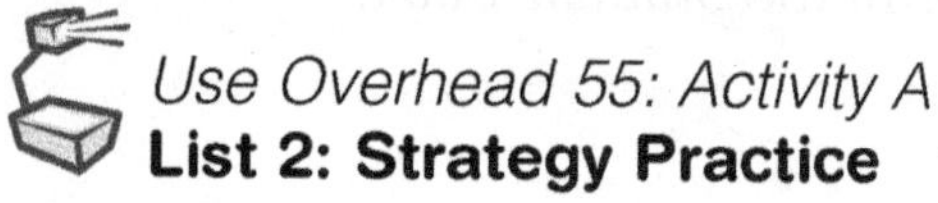

Use Overhead 55: Activity A
List 2: Strategy Practice

1. Find **List 2**. Circle the prefixes and suffixes, and underline the vowels. Look up when you are done._
2. (Show the bottom half of Overhead 55.) Now, check and fix any mistakes._

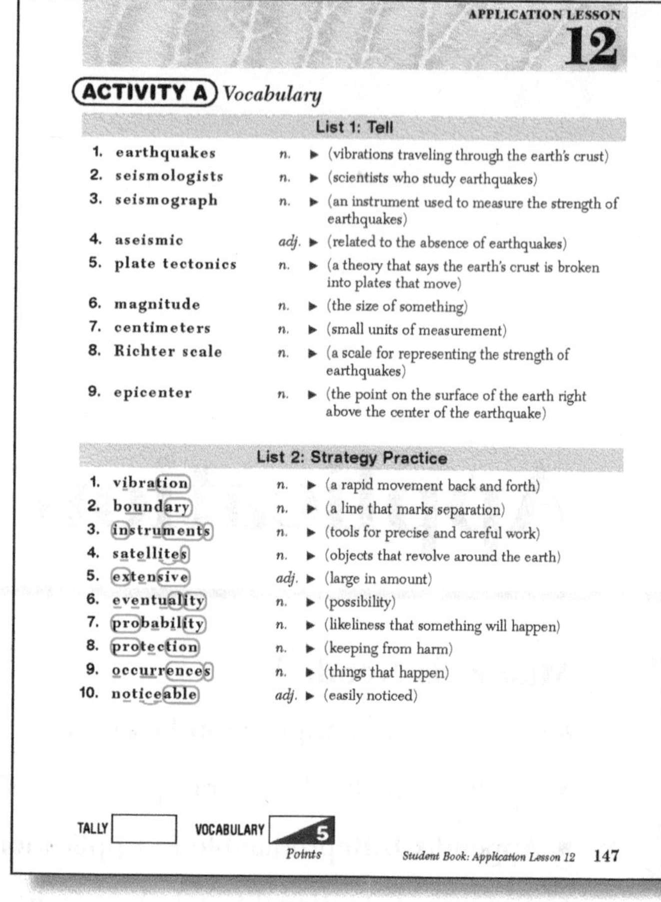

APPLICATION LESSON **12**

ACTIVITY A *Vocabulary*

List 1: Tell

1.	**earthquakes**	*n.*	► (vibrations traveling through the earth's crust)
2.	**seismologists**	*n.*	► (scientists who study earthquakes)
3.	**seismograph**	*n.*	► (an instrument used to measure the strength of earthquakes)
4.	**aseismic**	*adj.*	► (related to the absence of earthquakes)
5.	**plate tectonics**	*n.*	► (a theory that says the earth's crust is broken into plates that move)
6.	**magnitude**	*n.*	► (the size of something)
7.	**centimeters**	*n.*	► (small units of measurement)
8.	**Richter scale**	*n.*	► (a scale for representing the strength of earthquakes)
9.	**epicenter**	*n.*	► (the point on the surface of the earth right above the center of the earthquake)

List 2: Strategy Practice

1.	**vibration**	*n.*	► (a rapid movement back and forth)
2.	**boundary**	*n.*	► (a line that marks separation)
3.	**instruments**	*n.*	► (tools for precise and careful work)
4.	**satellites**	*n.*	► (objects that revolve around the earth)
5.	**extensive**	*adj.*	► (large in amount)
6.	**eventuality**	*n.*	► (possibility)
7.	**probability**	*n.*	► (likeliness that something will happen)
8.	**protection**	*n.*	► (keeping from harm)
9.	**occurrences**	*n.*	► (things that happen)
10.	**noticeable**	*adj.*	► (easily noticed)

TALLY ☐ VOCABULARY 5 Points

Student Book: Application Lesson 12 147

3. Go back to the first word._ Sound out the word to yourself. Put your thumb up when you can read the word. Be sure that it is a real word._ What word?_ Now, read the definition._
4. (Continue Step 3 with all remaining words in List 2.)

Note A.2-1: You may wish to provide additional practice by having students read words to a partner.

ACTIVITY PROCEDURE, List 1 and 2

(See the *Student Book*, page 147.)

Tell students to look in List 1 or List 2 for a word you are thinking about. Have them circle the number of the word and tell you the word. Explain to students to make a tally mark for each correct word in the Tally box, and then enter the number of tally marks as points in the blank half of the Vocabulary box.

1. Remember, the words I'm thinking about will be in either List 1 or List 2. Make a tally mark for every correctly identified word.
2. Circle the number of the appropriate word.
   - A line that marks separation of things is this. (Wait.) What word? **boundary**
   - If something is easy to notice, it is said to be this. (Wait.) What word? **noticeable**
   - This is a rapid back and forth movement. (Wait.) What word? **vibration**
   - When we talk about the size of something, we talk about this. (Wait.) What word? **magnitude**
   - These tools are used for precise and careful work. (Wait.) What word? **instruments**
3. Count all the tally marks, and enter that number as points in the blank half of the Vocabulary box.

ACTIVITY PROCEDURE, List 3

(See the *Student Book*, page 148.)

The words in the third list are related. Have students use the *REWARDS* Strategies to figure out the first word in each family. Have them read the definition of the verb and then read nouns and adjectives that are related to the verb.

Use Overhead 56: Activity A
List 3: Word Families

1. Turn to page 148. Find **Family 1** in **List 3**. Figure out the first word. Use your pencil if you wish. Put your thumb up when you know the word. What word? Read the definition.
2. Look at the noun in Family 1. Figure out the word. What word?
3. Look at the adjective in Family 1. Figure out the word. What word?
4. (Repeat Steps 1–3 for all word families in List 3.)

Note A.3-1: You may wish to provide additional practice by having students read a word family to the group or to a partner.

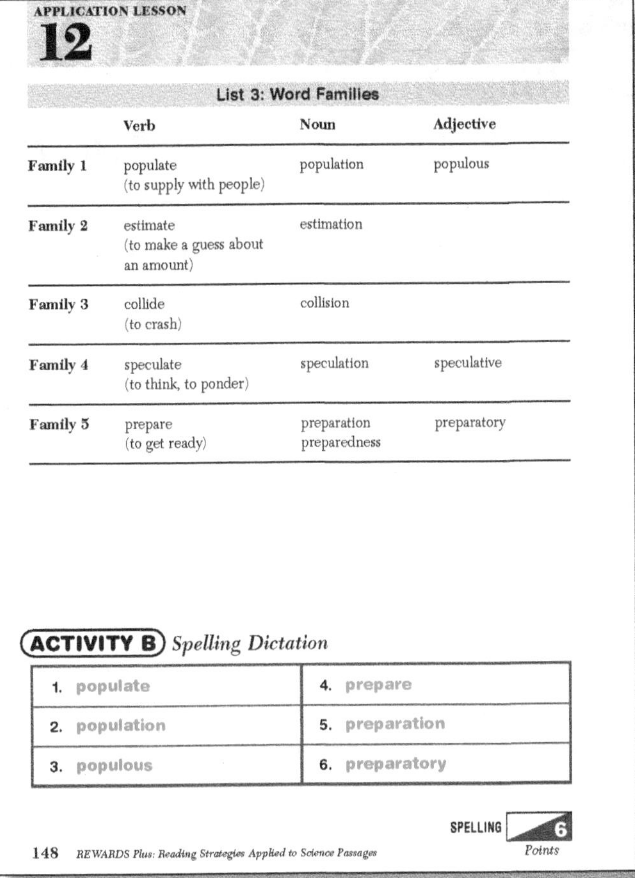

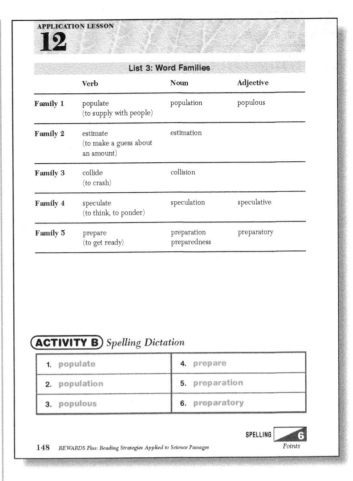

APPLICATION LESSON
12

List 3: Word Families

	Verb	Noun	Adjective
Family 1	populate (to supply with people)	population	populous
Family 2	estimate (to make a guess about an amount)	estimation	
Family 3	collide (to crash)	collision	
Family 4	speculate (to think, to ponder)	speculation	speculative
Family 5	prepare (to get ready)	preparation preparedness	preparatory

ACTIVITY B *Spelling Dictation*

1. populate	4. prepare
2. population	5. preparation
3. populous	6. preparatory

SPELLING 6 Points

148 *REWARDS Plus: Reading Strategies Applied to Science Passages*

Note A.3-2: An additional vocabulary practice activity called Quick Words is provided in Appendix C of this Teacher's Guide. See Appendix C for information about how this optional activity can be used.

Spelling Dictation

ACTIVITY PROCEDURE

(See the *Student Book*, page 148.)

For each word, tell students the word, then have students say the parts of the word to themselves while they write the word. Using the overhead transparency, assist students in checking their spelling and correcting if they misspelled. Then, have students enter the number of correctly spelled words as points in the blank half of the Spelling box.

Note B-1: Distribute a piece of light cardboard to each of the students.

Use Overhead 56: Activity B

1. Find **Activity B**.
2. The first word is **populate**. What word?_ Say the parts in **populate** to yourself as you write the word. (Pause and monitor.)
3. (Show **populate** on the overhead.) Check **populate**. If you misspelled it, cross it out and write it correctly.
4. The second word is **population**. What word?_ Say the parts in **population** to yourself as you write the word. (Pause and monitor.)
5. (Show **population** on the overhead.) Check **population**. If you misspelled it, cross it out and write it correctly.
6. (Repeat the procedures for the words **populous**, **prepare**, **preparation**, and **preparatory**.)
7. Count the number of words you spelled correctly, and record that number as points in the blank half of the Spelling box at the bottom of the page.

APPLICATION LESSON
12

List 3: Word Families

	Verb	Noun	Adjective
Family 1	populate (to supply with people)	population	populous
Family 2	estimate (to make a guess about an amount)	estimation	
Family 3	collide (to crash)	collision	
Family 4	speculate (to think, to ponder)	speculation	speculative
Family 5	prepare (to get ready)	preparation preparedness	preparatory

ACTIVITY B *Spelling Dictation*

1. populate	4. prepare
2. population	5. preparation
3. populous	6. preparatory

148 *REWARDS Plus: Reading Strategies Applied to Science Passages*

SPELLING  *Points*

ACTIVITY C

Passage Reading and Comprehension

ACTIVITY PROCEDURE

(See the *Student Book*, pages 149–151.)

Have students read the title of the passage and each heading. Ask them to tell their partners two things that the passage will tell about.

Passage Preview

1. Turn to page 149._ Let's preview the passage.
2. Read the title._ What is the whole passage going to tell about?_
3. Now, let's read the headings. Read the first heading._ Read the next heading._ (Continue until students have read all headings.)
4. Turn to your partner. Without looking, tell two things this passage will tell about._

ACTIVITY PROCEDURE

Provide students with an Information Web from Appendix B. Have students read the passage silently to each embedded number, and then reread the same information orally either to a partner, together as a group, or individually. Ask the corresponding comprehension question or questions. Once students finish reading a section labeled A, B, C, or D, have them fill in the Information Web before going on to the next section.

Note C-1: If students do not finish reading the passage during class, have them use their Information Webs to review the information at the beginning of the next class.

Use Overhead 57: Activity C

Passage Reading

1. (Provide an Information Web for each student.)
2. Turn back to the beginning of the passage. You're going to read the passage and answer questions about what you've read. During passage reading, you are also going to fill in an Information Web to help you remember the important details of the passage. Later, you'll use this Web to review the content of the passage with your partner.
3. Read the title._

APPLICATION LESSON **12**

ACTIVITY C *Passage Reading and Comprehension*

Note: For this activity, you will need Reproducible L found in the *Teacher's Guide*.

Earthquakes

A

Earthquakes occur worldwide on a daily basis even though we only hear about large quakes that occur where people live. It has been estimated that more than three million earthquakes occur yearly with the vast majority being very weak. Stronger earthquakes that have happened in populated areas have caused extensive property damage and loss of life. (#1)

What Is an Earthquake?

To understand earthquakes, first you must understand the structure of the earth. Picture a model of the eath with one section removed so you could see all the layers. At the center of the earth is an **inner core** of solid nickel and iron, surrounded by an **outer core** of molten metals. Around the layer of metals is a layer of rock that is called the earth's **mantle**. The coolest, top-most layer is called the earth's **crust**. When a vibration travels through the earth's crust, it is called an **earthquake**. (#2)

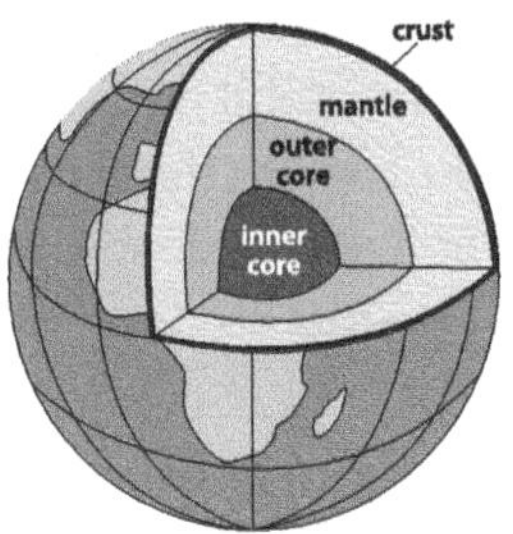
crust
mantle
outer core
inner core

B

What Is the Origin of Earthquakes?

The field of seismology, or the study of earthquakes, changed greatly in the middle of the 20th century when seismologists developed the theory of plate

Student Book: Application Lesson 12 149

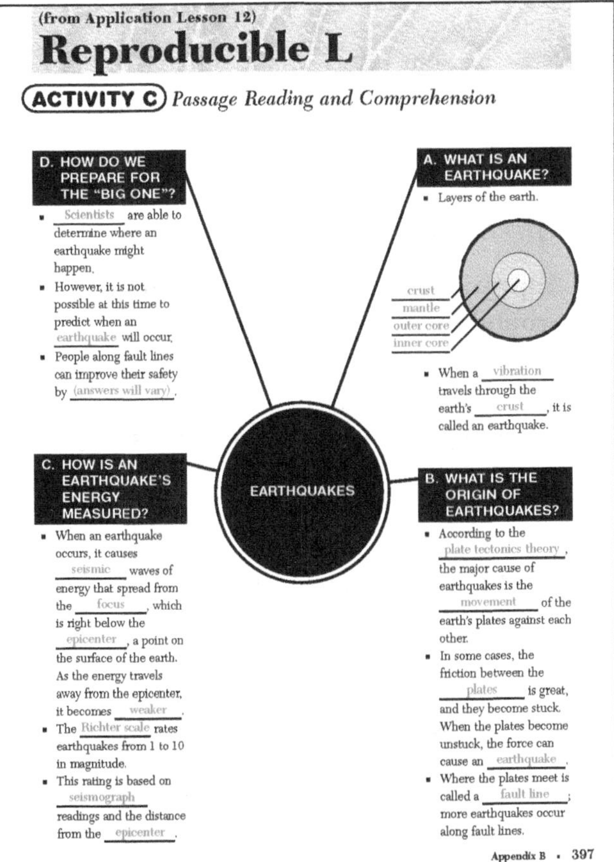
(from Application Lesson 12)

Reproducible L

ACTIVITY C *Passage Reading and Comprehension*

EARTHQUAKES
A. WHAT IS AN EARTHQUAKE?
Layers of the earth.
crust
mantle
outer core
inner core
When a vibration travels through the earth's crust, it is called an earthquake.
B. WHAT IS THE ORIGIN OF EARTHQUAKES?
According to the plate tectonics theory, the major cause of earthquakes is the movement of the earth's plates against each other.
In some cases, the friction between the plates is great, and they become stuck. When the plates become unstuck, the force can cause an earthquake.
Where the plates meet is called a fault line; more earthquakes occur along fault lines.
C. HOW IS AN EARTHQUAKE'S ENERGY MEASURED?
When an earthquake occurs, it causes seismic waves of energy that spread from the focus, which is right below the epicenter, a point on the surface of the earth. As the energy travels away from the epicenter, it becomes weaker.
The Richter scale rates earthquakes from 1 to 10 in magnitude.
This rating is based on seismograph readings and the distance from the epicenter.
D. HOW DO WE PREPARE FOR THE "BIG ONE"?
Scientists are able to determine where an earthquake might happen.
However, it is not possible at this time to predict when an earthquake will occur.
People along fault lines can improve their safety by (answers will vary).

Appendix B • 397

4. Find number 1 in the passage. (Pause). Read down to number 1 silently. Look up when you are done.
5. (Wait for students to complete the reading. Then have students reread the part by having them read orally to a partner, read together orally as a group, or read aloud individually.)
6. (Ask the question or questions associated with the number. Provide feedback to students regarding their answers.)
7. (Repeat steps 4–6 for all paragraphs in Section A.)
8. Now, look at your Information Web. Find the section labeled A. The information you've just read will help you to fill in this Web.
9. With your partner, fill in the blanks for Section A. You can refer back to the passage for information. Look up when you're done. (Move around the room and monitor students as they complete the section.)
10. (When the majority of students have finished, show Overhead 57.) Look at the overhead and check your work. Fix up or add to any of your answers.
11. Now read down to the next number silently. Look up when you are done.
12. (Repeat steps 5–11 until the students have finished the passage and the Information Web.)
13. Now use your Information Web to retell the important information from the passage to your partner.

Comprehension Questions

#1 Approximately how many earthquakes occur around the world annually?
3 million.

#2 What are the layers of the earth in order, starting from the center?
Inner core, outer core, mantle, and crust.

#3 What does the theory of plate tectonics describe?
The movement of the earth's plates as they drift and slide.

APPLICATION LESSON
12

ACTIVITY C *Passage Reading and Comprehension*

Note: For this activity, you will need Reproducible L found in the *Teacher's Guide*.

Earthquakes

A
Earthquakes occur worldwide on a daily basis even though we only hear
12 about large quakes that occur where people live. It has been estimated that
25 more than three million earthquakes occur yearly with the vast majority being
37 very weak. Stronger earthquakes that have happened in populated areas have
48 caused extensive property damage and loss of life. (#1)

56 **What Is an Earthquake?**
60 To understand earthquakes, first you must understand the structure of the
71 earth. Picture a model of the eath with one section removed so you could see all
87 the layers. At the center of the earth is an **inner core** of solid nickel and iron,
104 surrounded by an **outer core** of molten metals. Around the layer of metals is a
119 layer of rock that is called the earth's **mantle**. The coolest, top-most layer is
134 called the earth's **crust**. When a vibration travels through the earth's crust, it is
148 called an **earthquake**. (#2)

crust
mantle
outer core
inner core

B
151 **What Is the Origin of Earthquakes?**
157 The field of seismology, or the study of earthquakes, changed greatly in the
170 middle of the 20th century when seismologists developed the theory of plate

Student Book: Application Lesson 12 149

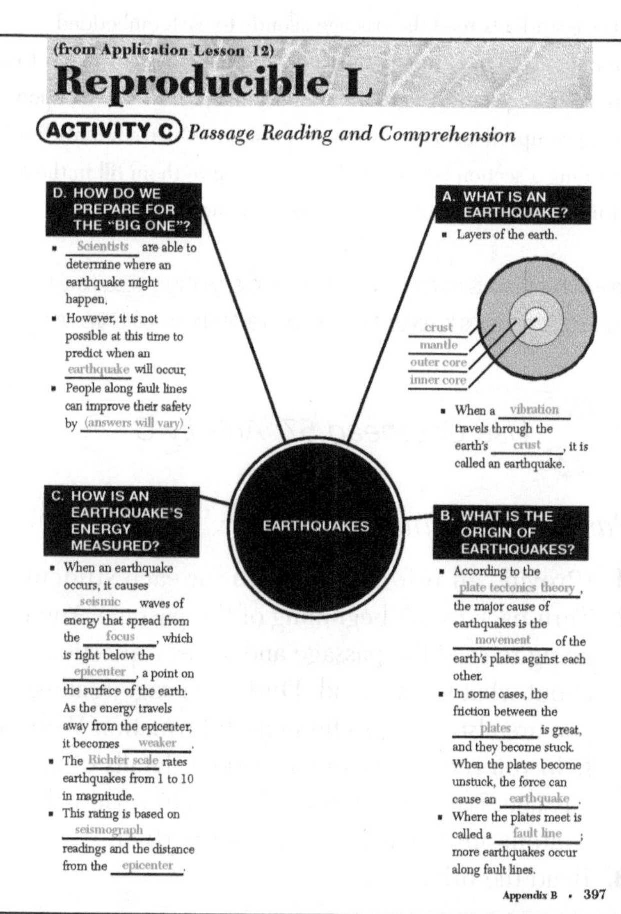
(from Application Lesson 12)
Reproducible L
ACTIVITY C *Passage Reading and Comprehension*

EARTHQUAKES

A. WHAT IS AN EARTHQUAKE?
- Layers of the earth.
  - crust
  - mantle
  - outer core
  - inner core
- When a vibration travels through the earth's crust, it is called an earthquake.

B. WHAT IS THE ORIGIN OF EARTHQUAKES?
- According to the plate tectonics theory, the major cause of earthquakes is the movement of the earth's plates against each other.
- In some cases, the friction between the plates is great, and they become stuck. When the plates become unstuck, the force can cause an earthquake.
- Where the plates meet is called a fault line; more earthquakes occur along fault lines.

C. HOW IS AN EARTHQUAKE'S ENERGY MEASURED?
- When an earthquake occurs, it causes seismic waves of energy that spread from the focus, which is right below the epicenter, a point on the surface of the earth. As the energy travels away from the epicenter, it becomes weaker.
- The Richter scale rates earthquakes from 1 to 10 in magnitude.
- This rating is based on seismograph readings and the distance from the epicenter.

D. HOW DO WE PREPARE FOR THE "BIG ONE"?
- Scientists are able to determine where an earthquake might happen.
- However, it is not possible at this time to predict when an earthquake will occur.
- People along fault lines can improve their safety by (answers will vary).

Appendix B • 397

#4 What causes a major earthquake?

Large sections of rock stick together; when they become unstuck in a sudden jerk, it causes an earthquake.

#5 Where do humans feel seismic waves the most?

Felt by humans the most at the epicenter—a point on the surface of the earth above where seismic waves are released.

#6 Describe the uses of a seismograph and Richter scale. What is the rating of a major earthquake?

Seismographs measure the vibrations of the earth during an earthquake; those readings and the distance from the epicenter are used to determine a rating on the Richter scale; a major earthquake is rated 7 or above.

#7 Can a scientist predict an earthquake? Why or why not?

No; their instruments allow them to see the patterns that the faults are forming; they can determine the probability of an earthquake but cannot predict when an earthquake will occur.

#8 What steps can be taken to ensure safety during an earthquake?

Earthquake drills in schools, build earthquake-proof buildings and other structures, and be prepared.

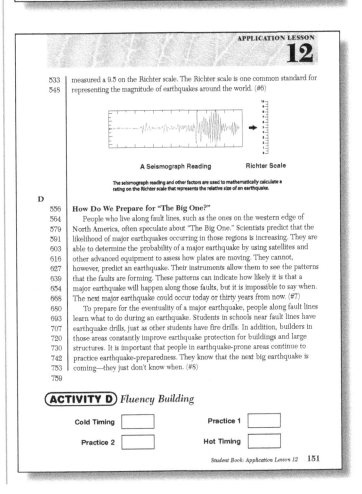

182 tectonics. According to the plate tectonics theory, the earth's crust is broken
194 into about 7 large and 12 smaller plates, or sections, that slide past or over each
210 other. They drift constantly at very, very slow rates of speed. Plates are like the
225 bumper cars at the fair; plates are in a constant struggle, pulling apart and
239 crashing into each other. Although earthquakes have other causes, the cause of
251 most earthquakes is now attributed to the movement of the earth's plates. (#3)
263 Normally, plates slide past each other at a steady, slow pace of only a few
278 centimeters a year. Scientists call this motion **aseismic creep**. In some instances,
290 however, the friction between the plates is very great, and large sections of rock
304 become stuck against one another. As one section continues moving, the
315 pressure builds until finally the plates become unstuck in one sudden jerk of
328 motion and the force causes a major earthquake to occur. The boundary where
341 two plates met and collided is called a **fault line** or a fault. More earthquakes are
357 highly likely to occur along a fault line. (#4)

fault line / fault line / fault line

Pressure begins to build. / Vibration travels through the earth's crust. / Some earthquakes leave damage.

C

365 **How Is an Earthquake's Energy Measured?**
371 When an earthquake occurs, the force of its vibration creates seismic waves of
384 energy. The release of these seismic waves begins at a point inside the earth called
399 the **focus**. These waves of energy are most felt by humans directly above the focus
414 on the surface at a point called the **epicenter**. The further the energy travels from
429 the epicenter, the weaker it becomes. People who live further away from the
442 epicenter of an earthquake feel less vibration than those who live close by. (#5)
455 Seismologists use instruments called **seismographs** to measure the vibration of
465 the earth during an earthquake. The resulting seismograph readings and the
476 distance from the epicenter are used to determine a rating on a special scale called
491 the **Richter scale**. The ratings on the Richter scale range from 1 to 10. Earthquakes
506 below a 4 aren't very noticeable and do not generally cause much damage. Major
520 earthquakes are rated at 7 and above. The strongest earthquake currently on record

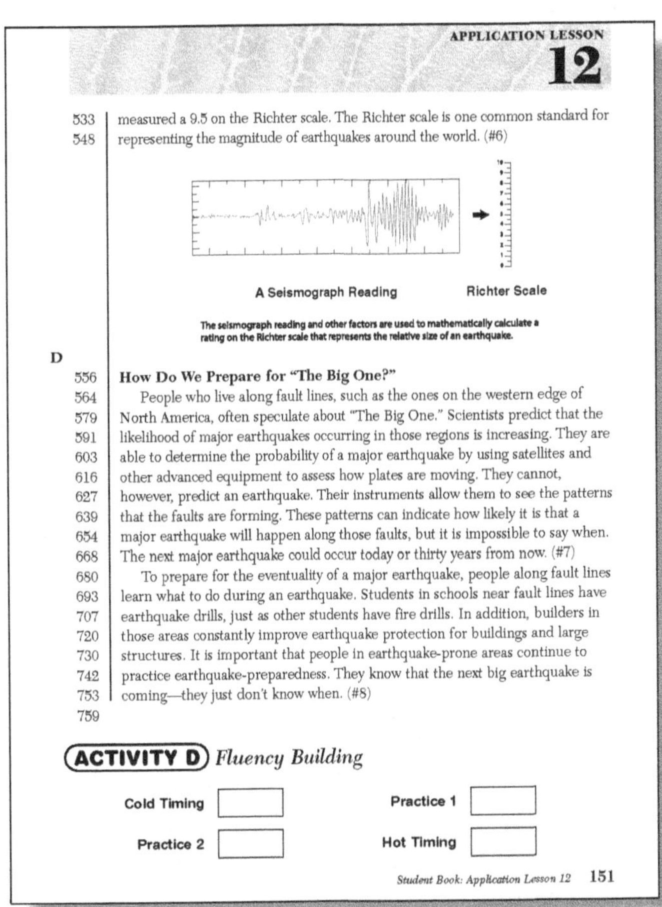

533 measured a 9.5 on the Richter scale. The Richter scale is one common standard for
548 representing the magnitude of earthquakes around the world. (#6)

The seismograph reading and other factors are used to mathematically calculate a rating on the Richter scale that represents the relative size of an earthquake.

D

556 **How Do We Prepare for "The Big One?"**
564 People who live along fault lines, such as the ones on the western edge of
579 North America, often speculate about "The Big One." Scientists predict that the
591 likelihood of major earthquakes occurring in those regions is increasing. They are
603 able to determine the probability of a major earthquake by using satellites and
616 other advanced equipment to assess how plates are moving. They cannot,
627 however, predict an earthquake. Their instruments allow them to see the patterns
639 that the faults are forming. These patterns can indicate how likely it is that a
654 major earthquake will happen along those faults, but it is impossible to say when.
668 The next major earthquake could occur today or thirty years from now. (#7)
680 To prepare for the eventuality of a major earthquake, people along fault lines
693 learn what to do during an earthquake. Students in schools near fault lines have
707 earthquake drills, just as other students have fire drills. In addition, builders in
720 those areas constantly improve earthquake protection for buildings and large
730 structures. It is important that people in earthquake-prone areas continue to
742 practice earthquake-preparedness. They know that the next big earthquake is
753 coming—they just don't know when. (#8)
759

ACTIVITY D *Fluency Building*

Cold Timing		Practice 1	
Practice 2		Hot Timing	

ACTIVITY D

Fluency Building

ACTIVITY PROCEDURE

(See the *Student Book*, page 151.)

Have students complete a Cold Timing, one or two practices, and a Hot Timing of the Activity C article. For each timing, have students record the number of correct words read. Finally, have students complete their Fluency Graphs.

Note D-1: When assigning partners for this activity, have the stronger reader read first. As a result, the other reader will have one additional practice opportunity.

1. Now, it's time for fluency building.
2. Find the beginning of the passage again. (Pause.)
3. Whisper-read. See how many words you can read in one minute. Begin._ (Time students for one minute.) Stop._ Circle the last word that you read._ Record the number of words you read after **Cold Timing**._
4. Let's practice again. Begin._ (Time students for one minute.) Stop._ Put a box around the last word that you read._ Record the number of words you read after **Practice 1**._
5. (Optional) Let's practice one more time before the Hot Timing. Begin._ (Time students for one minute.) Stop._ Put a box around the last word that you read._ Record the number of words you read after **Practice 2**._
6. Please exchange books with your partner._ Partner 1, you are going to read first. Partner 2, listen carefully and underline any mistakes or words left out. Ones, begin._ (Time students for one minute.) Stop._ Twos, cross out the last word that your partner read._ (Assist students in subtracting the number of mistakes from the number of words read.) Twos, record the number of correct words in your partner's book after **Hot Timing**._
7. Partner 2, you are going to read next. Partner 1, listen carefully and underline any mistakes or words left out. Twos, begin. (Time students for one minute.) Stop._ Ones, cross out the last word that your partner read._ Ones, record the number of correct words in your partner's book after **Hot Timing**._
8. Exchange books._ Turn to the Fluency Graph on the inside back cover, and indicate on the graph the number of Cold Timing and Hot Timing words you read correctly._

APPLICATION LESSON **12**

533 measured a 9.5 on the Richter scale. The Richter scale is one common standard for
548 representing the magnitude of earthquakes around the world. (#6)

A Seismograph Reading — Richter Scale

The seismograph reading and other factors are used to mathematically calculate a rating on the Richter scale that represents the relative size of an earthquake.

D

556 **How Do We Prepare for "The Big One?"**
564 People who live along fault lines, such as the ones on the western edge of
579 North America, often speculate about "The Big One." Scientists predict that the
591 likelihood of major earthquakes occurring in those regions is increasing. They are
603 able to determine the probability of a major earthquake by using satellites and
616 other advanced equipment to assess how plates are moving. They cannot,
627 however, predict an earthquake. Their instruments allow them to see the patterns
639 that the faults are forming. These patterns can indicate how likely it is that a
654 major earthquake will happen along those faults, but it is impossible to say when.
668 The next major earthquake could occur today or thirty years from now. (#7)
680 To prepare for the eventuality of a major earthquake, people along fault lines
693 learn what to do during an earthquake. Students in schools near fault lines have
707 earthquake drills, just as other students have fire drills. In addition, builders in
720 those areas constantly improve earthquake protection for buildings and large
730 structures. It is important that people in earthquake-prone areas continue to
742 practice earthquake-preparedness. They know that the next big earthquake is
753 coming—they just don't know when. (#8)
759

ACTIVITY D *Fluency Building*

Cold Timing		Practice 1	
Practice 2		Hot Timing	

ACTIVITY E

Comprehension Questions—Multiple Choice

ACTIVITY PROCEDURE

(See the *Student Book*, page 152.)

Have students complete item #1. Then, have students share the rationale for their answers. Encourage thoughtful discussion. Proceed item-by-item, emphasizing the rationale for the *best* answer. Have students record points for each correct item.

Note E-1: The correct Multiple Choice answers are circled.

1. Turn to page 152. Find **Activity E.**
2. Use the Multiple Choice Strategy to complete item #1. Be ready to explain why you selected your answer. (Wait while students complete the item. Call on individual students. Ask them why they chose their answer and why they eliminated the other choices. Encourage discussion. Provide students with feedback on their choices, focusing on why or why not those choices might be appropriate.)
3. (Repeat Step 2 for items 2–4, pausing after each item to confirm student responses and provide feedback.)
4. Count the number of items you got correct, and record that number in the blank half of the Multiple Choice Comprehension box.

APPLICATION LESSON
12

ACTIVITY E *Comprehension Questions—Multiple Choice*

Comprehension Strategy—Multiple Choice

Step 1: Read the item.
Step 2: Read all of the choices.
Step 3: Think about why each choice might be correct or incorrect. Check the article as needed.
Step 4: From the possible correct choices, select the best answer.

1. (Vocabulary) **Which set of words best represents the layers of the earth?**
   (a.) inner core – outer core — mantle – crust
   b. inner core – crust — outer core — mantle
   c. mantle – crust — inner core — outer core
   d. molten rock — metals — nickel — core
2. (Cause and effect) **According to plate tectonics theory, most earthquakes occur when:**
   a. two large plates slide over each other very slowly.
   (b.) large sections of rock that have become stuck against one another become unstuck in one sudden jerk.
   c. a plate moves too quickly and collides with another plate.
   d. a volcano erupts and an earthquake soon follows.
3. (Cause and effect) **The force of an earthquake is most likely to be felt by human beings at:**
   a. the focus of the earthquake.
   (b.) the epicenter.
   c. the earth's core.
   d. a distance of 100 miles from the epicenter.
4. (Compare and contrast) **Which of these would best represent the Richter scale?**

(a.) 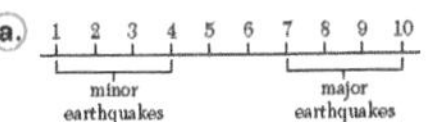

c. 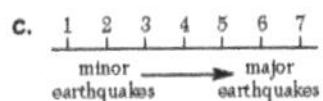

b. 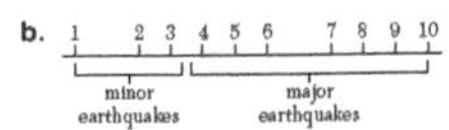

d. 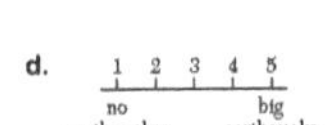

MULTIPLE CHOICE COMPREHENSION 

Points

152 *REWARDS Plus: Reading Strategies Applied to Science Passages*

Vocabulary Activities

ACTIVITY PROCEDURE

(See the *Student Book*, pages 153–154.)

Have students complete each item orally and provide feedback on their answers. Then have students respond to each question in writing by answering "yes" or "no" and providing a reason for their answers.

Yes/No/Why

1. Turn to page 153._ Find **Activity F**._ Read item #1. Tell your partner your answer and your reason for it. (Pause. Then call on individual students. Encourage discussion. Provide students with feedback on their choices, focusing on their explanations for their answer.)
2. Write your answer and your reason for it in the space provided. Look up when you are done._
3. Read item #2. Tell your partner your answer and your reason for it. (Pause. Then call on individual students. Encourage discussion. Provide students with feedback on their choices, focusing on their explanations for their answer.)
4. Write your answer and your reason for it in the space provided. Look up when you are done._
5. Read item #3. Tell your partner your answer and your reason for it. (Pause. Then call on individual students. Encourage discussion. Provide students with feedback on their choices, focusing on their explanations for their answer.)
6. Write your answer and your reason for it in the space provided. Look up when you are done._

Note F-1: You may wish to do this as an oral task only rather than an oral and a written task.

APPLICATION LESSON **12**

ACTIVITY F *Vocabulary*

Yes/No/Why

1. Are **earthquakes** generally represented in **centimeters**?
Example answer: No. The strength of an earthquake is represented by the Richter scale.

2. Is there a high **probability** that there will be more **satellites**?
Example answer: Yes. As time passes, it is highly likely that more and more objects will be orbiting the earth.

3. Can an **epicenter** be **aseismic**?
Example answer: No. The epicenter is right above the center of the earthquake, thus it is VERY related to having an earthquake.

Student Book: Application Lesson 12 153

ACTIVITY PROCEDURE

Have students read the words and definitions and then complete the sentence stems for each vocabulary word. Have them share answers with partners and with the class. Then, have students give themselves points in the blank half of the Vocabulary box.

Completion Activity

1. Turn to page 154. Read the first word and its definition.
2. Now, read the sentence stem.
3. Think of how you would complete the sentence stem and write it. Share your answer with your partner. (Call on a few students to share answers with the class.)
4. (Repeat Steps 1–3 for the rest of the words.)
5. If you participated in answering all seven questions, give yourself seven points in the blank half of the Vocabulary box.

Note F-2: You may wish to do this as an oral task only rather than an oral and a written task.

APPLICATION LESSON

12

Completion Activities

1. **speculate:** to think, to ponder
   When you think of your future, you might speculate about
   Answers will vary.
2. **probability:** likeliness that something will happen
   During the school day, there is a high probability that
   Answers will vary.
3. **occurrences:** things that happen
   Some common occurrences in the morning include
   Answers will vary.
4. **prepare:** to get ready
   To prepare for writing a paper, you might have to
   Answers will vary.

VOCABULARY 7 Points

154 *REWARDS Plus: Reading Strategies Applied to Science Passages*

ACTIVITY G

Expository Writing—Multi-Paragraph Answer

ACTIVITY PROCEDURE, Plan and Write

(See the *Student Book*, pages 155–157.)

Have students read the prompt. Guide students as they determine the three topics and **LIST** details for topics a, b, and c. Have students look at topic a again. Have students **CROSS OUT** details that don't go with the topic. Have students **CONNECT** details as shown in the example plan. Have students **NUMBER** their details, and then compare with the example plan for topic a. Next, have students **WRITE** paragraph a. Repeat for topics b and c. Finally, explain that after the answer is written, they should **EDIT** their work, revising for clarity and proofreading for errors in capitalization, punctuation, and spelling.

Use Overheads 58 and 59: Activity G

1. Turn to page 155._ Find **Activity G.**_
2. Find the prompt in the middle of the page._ Read the prompt out loud with me: **Summarize the information provided on the structure of the earth and location of earthquakes; the cause or origin of earthquakes; and the measurement of earthquakes.**
3. Reread the prompt and determine three topics. Record the topics in your Planning Box on the next page._ Compare your topics with your partner._ (Move around the room and assist students in determining the topics.)
4. Look back in the article and locate details that go with each of your topics. Record the details in the Planning Box._
5. Use the steps for topic a. Read the details and **cross out** any details that do not go with the topic._ Next, draw brackets to **connect** details that could easily go into one sentence._ Now, **number** the details in a logical order._
6. (Show Overhead 58.) Look at the example plan for topic a on the overhead. Yours should be similar._
7. Take out a blank piece of paper._ **Write** paragraph a. If you finish early, please reread and **edit** your paragraph._ (Move around the room and monitor your students as they are writing.)
8. (When the majority of students are done, proceed with the lesson.) Now, use the steps for topic b._

APPLICATION LESSON **12**

ACTIVITY G *Expository Writing—Multi-Paragraph Answer*

Writing Strategy—Multi-Paragraph Answer

Step 1: LIST (List the details that are important enough to include in your answer.)
- **Step 2: CROSS OUT** (Reread the details. Cross out any that don't go with the topic.)
- **Step 3: CONNECT** (Connect any details that could go into one sentence.)
- **Step 4: NUMBER** (Number the details in a logical order.)
- **Step 5: WRITE** (Write the paragraph.)

Step 6: EDIT (Revise and proofread your answer.)

Prompt: Summarize the information provided on the structure of the earth and location of earthquakes; the cause or origin of earthquakes; and the measurement of earthquakes.

Plan: Complete the Planning Box.

Student Book: Application Lesson 12 155

APPLICATION LESSON **12**

Example Multi-Paragraph Plan

Planning Box
(topic a) *structure of the earth and location of earthquakes*
① (detail) – *core—solid nickel and iron (inner) surrounded by molten*
metals (outer)
② (detail) – *mantle—layer of rock*
③ (detail) – *crust—coolest, top layer*
④ (detail) – *earthquake—when vibration travels through earth's crust*
(topic b) *earthquakes—cause/origin*
① (detail) – *explained through theory of plate tectonics*
② { (detail) – *earth's plates move*
(detail) – *plates drift at very slow rates* }
③ (detail) – *normally plates slide past each other*
④ (detail) – *when friction great, sections of rock can get stuck*
⑤ (detail) – *if become unstuck in sudden jerk, force causes earthquake*
(topic c) *earthquakes—measurement*
① (detail) – *seismographs measure vibration of earth during earthquake*
② { (detail) – *using seismograph readings and the distance from the*
epicenter, Richter scale rating determined
(detail) – *Richter scale rating between 1 and 10* }
③ (detail) – *major earthquake above 7*

Write: Write paragraphs a, b, and c on a separate piece of paper.

156 *REWARDS Plus: Reading Strategies Applied to Science Passages*

9. Look at the example plan for topic b on the overhead. Yours should be similar.
10. Locate your piece of paper. **Write** paragraph b. If you finish early, please **edit** your paragraph. (Move around the room and monitor your students as they are writing.)
11. (When the majority of students are done, proceed with the lesson.) Now, use the steps for topic c.
12. Look at the example plan for topic c on the overhead. Yours should be similar.
13. **Write** paragraph c. Please **edit** your paragraph when you are done. (Move around the room and monitor your students as they are writing.)
14. (When the majority of students are done, proceed with the lesson.) Please carefully read your paragraphs. Be sure that your paragraphs are easy to understand and clear. Proofread for any errors in capitalization, punctuation, and spelling. (Give students time to proofread their paragraphs.)

ACTIVITY PROCEDURE, Evaluate

Ask students to read each question in the rubric. Guide them in evaluating the paragraphs using the guidelines. Have students total their points and record them in the blank half of the Writing box.

15. Turn to page 157. Let's evaluate paragraphs a, b, and c.
16. Check paragraphs a, b, and c carefully and answer questions 1 through 3.
17. Reread your paragraphs. Circle "Yes" if your paragraphs are easy to understand.
18. Carefully examine your paragraphs. If you think a word is misspelled, underline it and check back in the plan or article and correct the spelling. Circle "Yes" if you believe that you have very few spelling errors.
19. Carefully examine your sentences. Be sure that each sentence begins with a capital. If all sentences begin with a capital, circle "Yes."
20. Examine your sentences. Be sure that each sentence ends with a period. If all sentences end with a period, circle "Yes."
21. Count up your points and record them in the Writing box.
22. (Show Overhead 59.) Look at the overhead. Let's read the three example paragraphs. Yours should be similar. (Read the paragraphs to your students or with your students or call on a student to read the example paragraph.)

APPLICATION LESSON **12**

Evaluate: Evaluate the paragraphs using this rubric.

Rubric—Multi-Paragraph Answer	Student or Partner Rating	Teacher Rating
1. Did the author state the topic in the first sentence?	a. Yes Fix up b. Yes Fix up c. Yes Fix up	a. Yes No b. Yes No c. Yes No
2. Did the author include details that go with the topic?	a. Yes Fix up b. Yes Fix up c. Yes Fix up	a. Yes No b. Yes No c. Yes No
3. Did the author combine details in some of the sentences?	a. Yes Fix up b. Yes Fix up c. Yes Fix up	a. Yes No b. Yes No c. Yes No
4. Is the answer easy to understand?	Yes Fix up	Yes No
5. Did the author correctly spell words, particularly the words found in the article?	Yes Fix up	Yes No
6. Did the author use correct capitalization, capitalizing the first word in the sentence and proper names of people, places, and things?	Yes Fix up	Yes No
7. Did the author use correct punctuation, including a period at the end of each sentence?	Yes Fix up	Yes No

WRITING 13 Points

Student Book: Application Lesson 12 157

Note G-1: The rubric can be used in a variety of ways. You may wish to have students evaluate their own paragraphs or have partners provide feedback, and then use the second column of the rubric for teacher feedback. You may wish to give students bonus points based on your feedback.

ACTIVITY H

Comprehension—Single-Paragraph Answer

ACTIVITY PROCEDURE

(See the *Student Book*, page 158.)

Have students read the *What Is* statement and the *What If* question. Have students turn the question into part of the answer and write down a topic sentence for their answer. Then, have them complete their answer. Encourage them to use evidence from the article and their own experience and background knowledge. Engage students in a discussion. Award points for writing and participating in the discussion.

Note H-1: If you are working with students who have difficulty generating ideas for their paragraph, switch the order of activities: engage the students in a discussion, and then have them write their paragraphs.

1. Turn to page 158._ Find **Activity H.**_
2. Find the *What Is* statement in the middle of the page._ Read it out loud with me: **Earthquakes are highly likely to occur along a fault line where two plates have met and collided.**
3. Find the *What If* question._ Read it with me: **What if you were living in an earthquake area right on a fault line? What precautions could you take?**
4. Think how you might turn the question into part of the answer._ Tell me your idea for a topic sentence._ (Example sentence: If I lived in an earthquake area right on a fault line, here are some of the precautions that I would take.) Take out a piece of paper and write your topic sentence._ (Move around the room and monitor as students write.)
5. Add ideas to your paragraph. Use evidence from the article as well as your own experience and background knowledge. If you finish early, reread your paragraph and edit it so that it is easy to understand and clear._ (Move around the room and monitor as students write.)
6. Read your paragraph to your partner._
7. If you included wording from the question in your answer and added evidence from the article, award yourself four points for writing._
8. (Engage students in a discussion. Award four points to students who are active participants in the discussion.)

APPLICATION LESSON **12**

ACTIVITY H *Comprehension—Single-Paragraph Answer*

Writing Strategy—Single-Paragraph Answer

Step 1: Read the item.
Step 2: Turn the question into part of the answer and write it down.
Step 3: Think of the answer or locate the answer in the article.
Step 4: Complete your answer.

Prompt:

What Is—Earthquakes are highly likely to occur along a fault line where two plates have met and collided.

What if—What if you were living in an earthquake area right on a fault line? What precautions could you take?

Write and Discuss: Write a paragraph. Then share your ideas. Use the Discussion Guidelines.

Discussion Guidelines

Speaker		Listener	
Looks like:	**Sounds like:**	**Looks like:**	**Sounds like:**
• Facing peers • Making eye contact • Participating	• Using pleasant, easy-to-hear voice • Sharing opinions, supporting facts and reasons from the article and from your experience • Staying on the topic	• Facing speaker • Making eye contact • Participating	• Waiting quietly to speak • Giving positive, supportive comments • Disagreeing respectfully

158 *REWARDS Plus: Reading Strategies Applied to Science Passages*

Note H-2: If your students are having difficulty writing the *What If* paragraphs, read or show them the following example paragraph:

Example Single-Paragraph Answer

If I lived in an earthquake area right on a fault line, I could take a number of precautions. First, I would ensure that buildings I lived in and worked in were designed to withstand the force of an earthquake. Second, I would have supplies available at home and school. I would make sure I have water and food and other necessities (toilet paper). Because services would be wiped out for a period of time, I would have a way to create light and heat. In addition, I would make sure I knew how to turn off the gas, water, and electricity to avoid additional damage. I would want a working cell phone so I could communicate with my family and friends. I would also want a battery-operated radio so I could get needed information concerning the effects of the earthquake and any directions from the government. Our family would also need a plan for what to do in the event of an earthquake and how to connect with each other. Or perhaps my best precaution would be to MOVE.

Application Lesson 13

Materials Needed:

- *Student Book*: Application Lesson 13
- Application Overhead Transparencies 60–64
- Appendix B Reproducible M: Application Lesson 13
- Appendix C Optional Vocabulary Activity: Application Lesson 13
- Paper or cardboard to use when covering the overhead transparency
- Paper or cardboard for each student to use during spelling dictation
- Washable overhead transparency pen

Text Treatment Notes:

- Black text signifies teacher script (exact wording to say to students).
- Green text in parentheses signifies directions or prompts for the teacher.
- Green text signifies answers or examples of answers.
- Green graphics treatment signifies reproduction of Overhead information.
- Green text and green graphics treatment do not appear in the *Student Book*.

ACTIVITY A

Vocabulary

ACTIVITY PROCEDURE, List 1

(See the *Student Book,* page 159.)

Tell students each word in the list. Then, have students repeat the word and read the definition aloud For each definition, provide any additional information that may be necessary. Then, have students practice reading the words themselves.

Use Overhead 60: Activity A
List 1: Tell

1. (Show the top half of Overhead 60.) Before we read the passage, let's read the difficult words. (Point to **meteorologists**.) The first word is **meteorologists**. What word?_ Now, read the definition._
2. (Point to **atmosphere**.) The next word is **atmosphere**. What word?_ Now, read the definition._
3. (Pronounce each word in List 1, and then have students repeat each word and read the definition.)
4. Open your *Student Book* to **Application Lesson 13**, page 159._
5. Find **Activity A**, **List 1**, in your book._ Let's read the words again. First word._ Next word._ (Continue for all words in List 1.)

ACTIVITY PROCEDURE, List 2

(See the *Student Book,* page 159.)

Have students circle prefixes and suffixes, then underline the vowels. Using the overhead transparency, assist students in checking their work. Next, have students figure out each word to themselves, then say it aloud. Have them read the definition aloud.

Use Overhead 60: Activity A
List 2: Strategy Practice

1. Find **List 2**. Circle the prefixes and suffixes, and underline the vowels. Look up when you are done._
2. (Show the bottom half of Overhead 60.) Now, check and fix any mistakes._

APPLICATION LESSON
13

ACTIVITY A *Vocabulary*

List 1: Tell

1.	**meteorologists**	*n.*	► (people who study the atmosphere and changes within it—especially the weather)
2.	**atmosphere**	*n.*	► (the mass of gases surrounding the earth)
3.	**climatologists**	*n.*	► (people who study climate)
4.	**associated**	*v.*	► (connected in one's mind)
5.	**phenomenon**	*n.*	► (an event that can be observed)
6.	**chemistry**	*n.*	► (the science that deals with how things are made up and how they change when they react with other things)
7.	**hurricanes**	*n.*	► (storms with violent winds)
8.	**tornadoes**	*n.*	► (dark columns of fast-moving air shaped like a funnel)
9.	**glaciers**	*n.*	► (large, slow-moving masses of ice)
10.	**supercomputers**	*n.*	► (very large and fast computers)
11.	**typically**	*adv.*	► (usually)
12.	**frequently**	*adv.*	► (often)

List 2: Strategy Practice

1.	**conversation**	*n.*	► (friendly talk between people)
2.	**climatic**	*adj.*	► (related to typical weather)
3.	**conditions**	*n.*	► (the way things are)
4.	**density**	*n.*	► (thickness)
5.	**condensation**	*n.*	► (the change of a gas to a liquid)
6.	**precipitation**	*n.*	► (any form of water falling to earth)
7.	**accompanying**	*v.*	► (going along with)
8.	**alternatively**	*adv.*	► (on the other hand)
9.	**completion**	*n.*	► (the end; the state of being finished)
10.	**productivity**	*n.*	► (the ability to produce a lot)

TALL Y ☐ VOCABULARY 5 Points

Student Book: Application Lesson 13 159

3. Go back to the first word._ Sound out the word to yourself. Put your thumb up when you can read the word. Be sure that it is a real word._ What word?_ Now, read the definition._
4. (Continue Step 3 with all remaining words in List 2.)

Note A.1: You may wish to provide additional practice by having students read words to a partner.

ACTIVITY PROCEDURE, List 1 and 2

(See the *Student Book*, page 159.)

Tell students to look in List 1 or List 2 for a word you are thinking about. Have them circle the number of the word and tell you the word. Explain to students to make a tally mark for each correct word in the Tally box, and then enter the number of tally marks as points in the blank half of the Vocabulary box.

1. Remember, the words I'm thinking about will be in either List 1 or List 2. Make a tally mark for every correctly identified word.
2. Circle the number of the appropriate word.
   - An event that can be observed is called this. (Wait.) What word? **phenomenon**
   - Things that are connected in one's mind are this. (Wait.) What word? **associated**
   - People often engage in friendly talk, which we call this. (Wait.) What word? **conversation**
   - If you are going somewhere with a person, you are doing this. (Wait.) What word? **accompanying**
   - Sleet, rain, hail, and snow are all types of this. (Wait.) What word? **precipitation**
3. Count all the tally marks, and enter that number as points in the blank half of the Vocabulary box.

ACTIVITY PROCEDURE, List 3

(See the *Student Book*, page 160.)

The words in the third list are related. Have students use the *REWARDS* Strategies to figure out the first word in each family. Have them read the definition of the verb and then read nouns and adjectives that are related to that verb.

Use Overhead 61: Activity A
List 3: Word Families

1. Turn to page 160._ Find **Family 1** in **List 3**. Figure out the first word. Use your pencil if you wish. Put your thumb up when you know the word._ What word?_ Read the definition._
2. Look at the noun in Family 1. Figure out the word._ What word?_
3. Look at the adjective in Family 1. Figure out the word._ What word?_
4. (Repeat Steps 1–3 for all word families in List 3.)

Note A.3-1: You may wish to provide additional practice by having students read a word family to the group or to a partner.

APPLICATION LESSON
13

List 3: Word Families

	Verb	Noun	Adjective
Family 1	complete (to end; to finish)	completion	complete
Family 2	predict (to declare beforehand)	prediction	predictable
Family 3	direct (to manage or control the course)	direction director	directional
Family 4	create (to cause to exist)	creation creator	creative
Family 5	evaporate (to change a liquid into a gas)	evaporation	evaporable

ACTIVITY B *Spelling Dictation*

1. predict	4. create
2. prediction	5. creation
3. predictable	6. creative

SPELLING 6 *Points*

160 *REWARDS Plus: Reading Strategies Applied to Science Passages*

Note A.3-2: An additional vocabulary practice activity called Quick Words is provided in Appendix C of this Teacher's Guide. See Appendix C for information about how this optional activity can be used.

ACTIVITY B

Spelling Dictation

ACTIVITY PROCEDURE

(See the *Student Book*, page 160.)

For each word, tell students the word, then have students say the parts of the word to themselves while they write the word. Using the overhead transparency, assist students in checking their spelling and correcting if they misspelled. Then, have students enter the number of correctly spelled words as points in the blank half of the Spelling box.

Note B-1: Distribute a piece of light cardboard to each of the students.

Use Overhead 61: Activity B

1. Find **Activity B**.
2. The first word is **predict**. What word?_ Say the parts in **predict** to yourself as you write the word. (Pause and monitor.)
3. (Show **predict** on the overhead.) Check **predict**. If you misspelled it, cross it out and write it correctly.
4. The second word is **prediction**. What word?_ Say the parts in **prediction** to yourself as you write the word. (Pause and monitor.)
5. (Show **prediction** on the overhead.) Check **prediction**. If you misspelled it, cross it out and write it correctly.
6. (Repeat the procedures for the words **predictable**, **create**, **creation**, and **creative**.)
7. Count the number of words you spelled correctly, and record that number as points in the blank half of the Spelling box at the bottom of the page.

APPLICATION LESSON **13**

List 3: Word Families

	Verb	Noun	Adjective
Family 1	complete (to end; to finish)	completion	complete
Family 2	predict (to declare beforehand)	prediction	predictable
Family 3	direct (to manage or control the course)	direction director	directional
Family 4	create (to cause to exist)	creation creator	creative
Family 5	evaporate (to change a liquid into a gas)	evaporation	evaporable

ACTIVITY B *Spelling Dictation*

1. predict	4. create
2. prediction	5. creation
3. predictable	6. creative

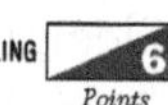

160 *REWARDS Plus: Reading Strategies Applied to Science Passages*

ACTIVITY C

Passage Reading and Comprehension

ACTIVITY PROCEDURE

(See the *Student Book*, pages 161–163.)

Have students read the title of the passage and each heading. Ask them to tell their partners two things that the passage will tell about.

Passage Preview

1. Turn to page 161._ Let's preview the passage.
2. Read the title._ What is the whole passage going to tell about?_
3. Now, let's read the headings. Read the first heading._ Read the next heading._ (Continue until students have read all headings.)
4. Turn to your partner. Without looking, tell two things this passage will tell about._

ACTIVITY PROCEDURE

Provide students with an Information Web from Appendix B. Have students read the passage silently to each embedded number, and then reread the same information orally either to a partner, together as a group, or individually. Ask the corresponding comprehension question or questions. Once students finish reading a section labeled A, B, C, D, E, F, G, or H, have them fill in the Information Web before going on to the next section.

Note C-1: If students do not finish reading the passage during class, have them use their Information Webs to review the information at the beginning of the next class.

Use Overhead 62: Activity C

Passage Reading

1. (Provide an Information Web for each student.)
2. Turn back to the beginning of the passage. You're going to read the passage and answer questions about what you've read. During passage reading, you are also going to fill in an Information Web to help you remember the important details of the passage. Later, you'll use this Web to review the content of the passage with your partner.
3. Read the title._

APPLICATION LESSON **13**

ACTIVITY C *Passage Reading and Comprehension*

Note: For this activity, you will need Reproducible M found in the *Teacher's Guide.*

Weather

A
The weather is frequently a topic of conversation, but few people other than
13 meteorologists (people who study weather) understand how it happens. Rain,
23 snow, and even violent storms happen because of the movement of air masses,
36 the land, the sun's energy, and the jet stream. Before you can understand how
50 these factors interact to cause weather, you need to understand the rising and
63 falling of air masses. (#1)

67 **What Is an Air Mass?**
72 An **air mass** is a large chunk of air in the earth's atmosphere. It can be
88 anywhere from ten miles to hundreds or thousands of miles wide, and it can be
103 warm or cold. Warm and cold air masses are full of moisture. The sun is
118 constantly causing evaporation of water from the earth's surface and changing
129 the water (a liquid) into water vapor (a gas consisting of very small drops of
144 water). The warm air masses contain this water vapor. In cold air masses, the
158 water vapor has cooled and squeezed together, or condensed, into much larger
170 drops of water. (#2)
173 When things get warm, they expand and become less dense, and when things
186 cool, they condense and become denser. When an air mass becomes warmer
198 and less dense, it rises. Alternatively, when an air mass becomes cooler and
211 denser, it falls. (#3)

B
214 **The Movement of Air Masses as a Factor in the Weather**
225 Air masses are constantly moving. This constant movement causes weather. As
236 a warm air mass rises, it carries water vapor up into the atmosphere. Then, the
251 water vapor in the air begins to cool and drops of water condense into bigger
266 drops of water, eventually forming clouds. This process is called **condensation**.
277 Once condensation has been completed, and the clouds have become heavier and
289 heavier, the clouds produce precipitation (e.g., rain, snow, hail). (#4)
298 When warm air masses and cold air masses collide with each other, they
311 create a weather front and various kinds of weather happen. The nature of the
325 weather depends upon where the air masses are located, which direction they
337 are moving, and many other characteristics.

Student Book: Application Lesson 13 161

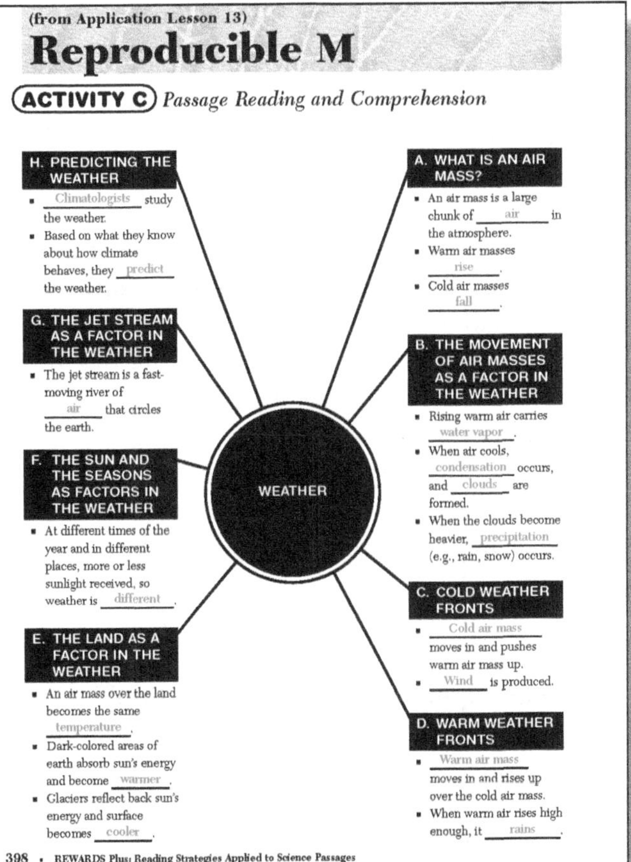
(from Application Lesson 13)

Reproducible M

ACTIVITY C *Passage Reading and Comprehension*

WEATHER

A. WHAT IS AN AIR MASS?
- An air mass is a large chunk of ___air___ in the atmosphere.
- Warm air masses ___rise___.
- Cold air masses ___fall___.

B. THE MOVEMENT OF AIR MASSES AS A FACTOR IN THE WEATHER
- Rising warm air carries ___water vapor___.
- When air cools, ___condensation___ occurs, and ___clouds___ are formed.
- When the clouds become heavier, ___precipitation___ (e.g., rain, snow) occurs.

C. COLD WEATHER FRONTS
- ___Cold air mass___ moves in and pushes warm air mass up.
- ___Wind___ is produced.

D. WARM WEATHER FRONTS
- ___Warm air mass___ moves in and rises up over the cold air mass.
- When warm air rises high enough, it ___rains___.

E. THE LAND AS A FACTOR IN THE WEATHER
- An air mass over the land becomes the same ___temperature___.
- Dark-colored areas of earth absorb sun's energy and become ___warmer___.
- Glaciers reflect back sun's energy and surface becomes ___cooler___.

F. THE SUN AND THE SEASONS AS FACTORS IN THE WEATHER
- At different times of the year and in different places, more or less sunlight received, so weather is ___different___.

G. THE JET STREAM AS A FACTOR IN THE WEATHER
- The jet stream is a fast-moving river of ___air___ that circles the earth.

H. PREDICTING THE WEATHER
- ___Climatologists___ study the weather.
- Based on what they know about how climate behaves, they ___predict___ the weather.

398 • REWARDS Plus: Reading Strategies Applied to Science Passages

4. Read down to number 1 silently. Look up when you are done._
5. (Wait for students to complete the reading. Then have students reread the part orally.)
6. (Ask the question or questions associated with the number. Provide feedback to students regarding their answers.)
7. (Repeat steps 4–6 for all paragraphs in Section A.)
8. Now, look at your Information Web.
9. With your partner, fill in the blanks for Section A. You can refer back to the passage for information. Look up when you're done._ (Move around the room and monitor students as they complete the section.)
10. (When the majority of students have finished, show Overhead 62.) Look at the overhead and check your work. Fix up or add to your answers.
11. Now read down to the next number silently. Look up when you are done._
12. (Repeat steps 5–11 until the students have finished the passage and the Information Web.)
13. Use your Information Web to retell the important information to your partner.

Comprehension Questions

#1 What causes rain, snow, and violent storms to occur?

The movement of air masses, the land, the sun's energy, and the jet stream.

#2 What are the two types of air masses? How are they the same? How are they different?

Cold and warm air masses; both full of moisture; warm air masses contain water vapor that was formed through evaporation; in cold air masses, the water vapor has cooled and squeezed together into larger drops of water.

#3 What happens when an air mass becomes warmer?

It expands and becomes less dense; it rises.

#4 What happens during condensation?

Warm air mass rises, carries water vapor up into atmosphere, water vapor begins to cool, and drops of water condense into bigger drops of water, which then form clouds.

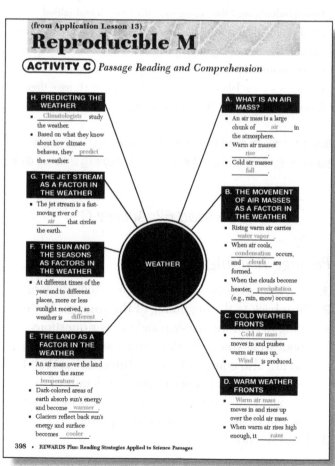

APPLICATION LESSON **13**

ACTIVITY C *Passage Reading and Comprehension*

Note: For this activity, you will need Reproducible M found in the *Teacher's Guide.*

Weather

A
The weather is frequently a topic of conversation, but few people other than
13 meteorologists (people who study weather) understand how it happens. Rain,
23 snow, and even violent storms happen because of the movement of air masses,
36 the land, the sun's energy, and the jet stream. Before you can understand how
50 these factors interact to cause weather, you need to understand the rising and
63 falling of air masses. (#1)

67 **What Is an Air Mass?**
72 An **air mass** is a large chunk of air in the earth's atmosphere. It can be
88 anywhere from ten miles to hundreds or thousands of miles wide, and it can be
103 warm or cold. Warm and cold air masses are full of moisture. The sun is
118 constantly causing evaporation of water from the earth's surface and changing
129 the water (a liquid) into water vapor (a gas consisting of very small drops of
144 water). The warm air masses contain this water vapor. In cold air masses, the
158 water vapor has cooled and squeezed together, or condensed, into much larger
170 drops of water. (#2)
173 When things get warm, they expand and become less dense, and when things
186 cool, they condense and become denser. When an air mass becomes warmer
198 and less dense, it rises. Alternatively, when an air mass becomes cooler and
211 denser, it falls. (#3)

B
214 **The Movement of Air Masses as a Factor in the Weather**
225 Air masses are constantly moving. This constant movement causes weather. As
236 a warm air mass rises, it carries water vapor up into the atmosphere. Then, the
251 water vapor in the air begins to cool and drops of water condense into bigger
266 drops of water, eventually forming clouds. This process is called **condensation.**
277 Once condensation has been completed, and the clouds have become heavier and
289 heavier, the clouds produce precipitation (e.g., rain, snow, hail). (#4)
298 When warm air masses and cold air masses collide with each other, they
311 create a weather front and various kinds of weather happen. The nature of the
325 weather depends upon where the air masses are located, which direction they
337 are moving, and many other characteristics.

Student Book: Application Lesson 13 **161**

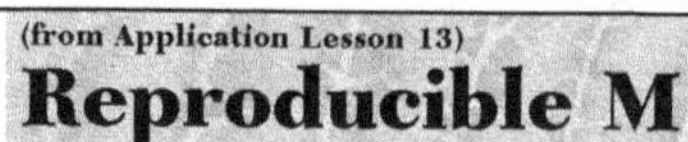

(from Application Lesson 13)

Reproducible M

ACTIVITY C *Passage Reading and Comprehension*

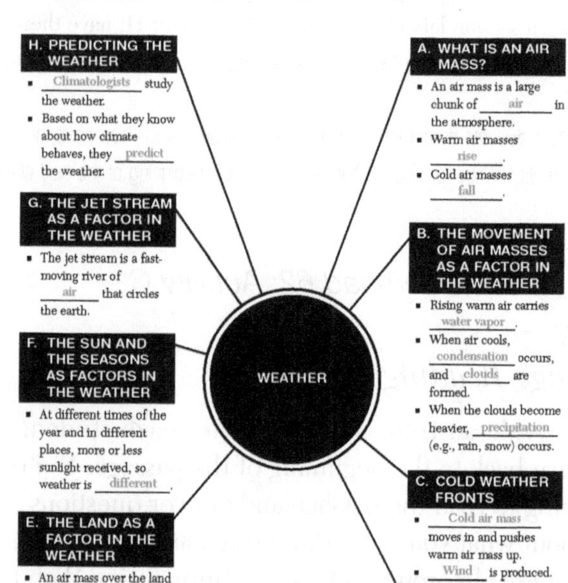

398 • REWARDS Plus: Reading Strategies Applied to Science Passages

#5 When does a cold weather front occur? What can a cold front lead to?

When a cold air mass moves quickly into a region and pushes a warm air mass upward; can lead to hurricanes or tornadoes.

#6 When does a warm weather front occur?

Warm air mass moves quickly into a region, bumps into a cold air mass, and rises up over the top of the cold air mass.

#7 What happens to an air mass above a particular piece of land? Give an example of this phenomenon.

Becomes the same temperature as the land; glaciers reflect the sun's energy back into space so the glaciers' surfaces are cooler, and the air masses above them are cooler as well.

#8 How do seasons affect weather patterns?

Earth receives more or less sunlight depending on the season, and this change leads to differences in temperature, how much water evaporates, and the nature and direction of the winds.

#9 What is the jet stream?

The jet stream is a fast-flowing river of air that circles the planet from west to east at speeds of 100 to 200 miles per hour.

#10 What do climatologists study? What technological advances have improved their studies?

Climatologists study weather and climatic conditions over many, many years; supercomputers help create a complex model of how the climate behaves; and climatologists use this model to predict the weather.

APPLICATION LESSON

13

C

343 **Cold Weather Fronts**
346 A **cold weather front** occurs when a cold air mass moves quickly into a region
361 and pushes a warm air mass upward. When the colder, denser air rushes in to
376 take the place of the warmer, moisture-filled air, wind is produced, and tall,
390 puffy clouds are formed. Sometimes the characteristics (such as temperature
400 and density of water vapor) of the cold and warm air masses are greatly
414 different. As a result, stronger winds occur. The greater the differences, the
426 more violent the weather will be. Sometimes, the cold front factors even lead to
440 hurricanes or tornadoes. Usually, this bad weather doesn't last very long. (#5)

D

451 **Warm Weather Fronts**
454 A **warm weather front** occurs when a warm air mass moves quickly into a
468 region, bumps into a cold air mass, and rises up over the top of the cold air
485 mass. When the warm air rises high enough, clouds form and rain begins to fall.
500 The rain can last for many days. Typically, however, the warm front is associated
514 with less violent weather than that caused by a cold front. (#6)

E

525 **The Land as a Factor in the Weather**
533 An air mass above a particular piece of land becomes the same temperature
546 as that land. Dark-colored areas of the earth, including mountains, plowed
558 fields, and pavement, tend to absorb more of the sun's energy, so these surfaces
572 are warmer, and the air masses above these surfaces are warmer. Glaciers,
584 snowfields, and even plants tend to reflect the sun's energy back into space, so
598 these surfaces are cooler, and the air masses above them are cooler. Because
611 cities and farmlands are dark-colored areas, they tend to heat up and create
625 drying winds. These winds dry the land further. This phenomenon might even
637 harm the farmland's productivity. Careful planning can make a big difference in
649 the kind of weather the land creates. (#7)

F

656 **The Sun and the Seasons as Factors in the Weather**
666 Although the sun affects the temperature of the land and the accompanying
678 air masses, seasons cause changes in weather patterns, too. During different

162 *REWARDS Plus: Reading Strategies Applied to Science Passages*

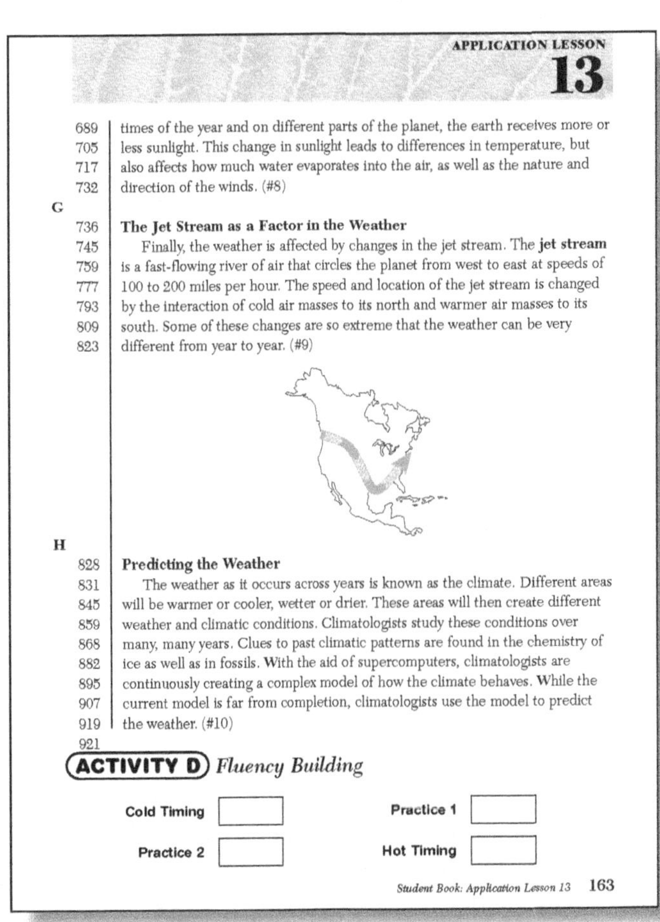
APPLICATION LESSON

13

689 times of the year and on different parts of the planet, the earth receives more or
705 less sunlight. This change in sunlight leads to differences in temperature, but
717 also affects how much water evaporates into the air, as well as the nature and
732 direction of the winds. (#8)

G

736 **The Jet Stream as a Factor in the Weather**
745 Finally, the weather is affected by changes in the jet stream. The **jet stream**
759 is a fast-flowing river of air that circles the planet from west to east at speeds of
777 100 to 200 miles per hour. The speed and location of the jet stream is changed
793 by the interaction of cold air masses to its north and warmer air masses to its
809 south. Some of these changes are so extreme that the weather can be very
823 different from year to year. (#9)

H

828 **Predicting the Weather**
831 The weather as it occurs across years is known as the climate. Different areas
845 will be warmer or cooler, wetter or drier. These areas will then create different
859 weather and climatic conditions. Climatologists study these conditions over
868 many, many years. Clues to past climatic patterns are found in the chemistry of
882 ice as well as in fossils. With the aid of supercomputers, climatologists are
895 continuously creating a complex model of how the climate behaves. While the
907 current model is far from completion, climatologists use the model to predict
919 the weather. (#10)
921

ACTIVITY D *Fluency Building*

Cold Timing		Practice 1	
Practice 2		Hot Timing	

Student Book: Application Lesson 13 163

ACTIVITY D

Fluency Building

ACTIVITY PROCEDURE

(See the *Student Book*, page 163.)

Have students complete a Cold Timing, one or two practices, and a Hot Timing of the Activity C article. For each timing, have students record the number of correct words read. Finally, have students complete their Fluency Graphs.

Note D-1: When assigning partners for this activity, have the stronger reader read first. As a result, the other reader will have one additional practice opportunity.

1. Now, it's time for fluency building.
2. Find the beginning of the passage again. (Pause.)
3. Whisper-read. See how many words you can read in one minute. Begin._ (Time students for one minute.) Stop._ Circle the last word that you read._ Record the number of words you read after **Cold Timing.**_
4. Let's practice again. Begin._ (Time students for one minute.) Stop._ Put a box around the last word that you read._ Record the number of words you read after **Practice 1.**_
5. (Optional) Let's practice one more time before the Hot Timing. Begin._ (Time students for one minute.) Stop._ Put a box around the last word that you read._ Record the number of words you read after **Practice 2.**_
6. Please exchange books with your partner._ Partner 1, you are going to read first. Partner 2, listen carefully and underline any mistakes or words left out. Ones, begin._ (Time students for one minute.) Stop._ Twos, cross out the last word that your partner read._ (Assist students in subtracting the number of mistakes from the number of words read.) Twos, record the number of correct words in your partner's book after **Hot Timing.**_
7. Partner 2, you are going to read next. Partner 1, listen carefully and underline any mistakes or words left out. Twos, begin. (Time students for one minute.) Stop._ Ones, cross out the last word that your partner read._ Ones, record the number of correct words in your partner's book after **Hot Timing.**_
8. Exchange books._ Turn to the Fluency Graph on the inside back cover, and indicate on the graph the number of Cold Timing and Hot Timing words you read correctly._

689 times of the year and on different parts of the planet, the earth receives more or
705 less sunlight. This change in sunlight leads to differences in temperature, but
717 also affects how much water evaporates into the air, as well as the nature and
732 direction of the winds. (#8)

G

736 **The Jet Stream as a Factor in the Weather**
745 Finally, the weather is affected by changes in the jet stream. The **jet stream**
759 is a fast-flowing river of air that circles the planet from west to east at speeds of
777 100 to 200 miles per hour. The speed and location of the jet stream is changed
793 by the interaction of cold air masses to its north and warmer air masses to its
809 south. Some of these changes are so extreme that the weather can be very
823 different from year to year. (#9)

H

828 **Predicting the Weather**
831 The weather as it occurs across years is known as the climate. Different areas
845 will be warmer or cooler, wetter or drier. These areas will then create different
859 weather and climatic conditions. Climatologists study these conditions over
868 many, many years. Clues to past climatic patterns are found in the chemistry of
882 ice as well as in fossils. With the aid of supercomputers, climatologists are
895 continuously creating a complex model of how the climate behaves. While the
907 current model is far from completion, climatologists use the model to predict
919 the weather. (#10)
921

ACTIVITY D *Fluency Building*

Cold Timing		Practice 1	
Practice 2		Hot Timing	

ACTIVITY E

Comprehension Questions—Multiple Choice

ACTIVITY PROCEDURE

(See the *Student Book*, page 164.)

Have students complete item #1. Then, have students share the rationale for their answers. Encourage thoughtful discussion. Proceed item-by-item, emphasizing the rationale for the *best* answer. Have students record points for each correct item.

Note E-1: The correct Multiple Choice answers are circled.

1. Turn to page 164._ Find **Activity E.**
2. Use the Multiple Choice Strategy to complete item #1. Be ready to explain why you selected your answer. (Wait while students complete the item. Call on individual students. Ask them why they chose their answer and why they eliminated the other choices. Encourage discussion. Provide students with feedback on their choices, focusing on why or why not those choices might be appropriate.)
3. (Repeat Step 2 for items 2–4, pausing after each item to confirm student responses and provide feedback.)
4. Count the number of items you got correct, and record that number in the blank half of the Multiple Choice Comprehension box._

APPLICATION LESSON
13

ACTIVITY E *Comprehension Questions—Multiple Choice*

Comprehension Strategy—Multiple Choice

Step 1: Read the item.
Step 2: Read all of the choices.
Step 3: Think about why each choice might be correct or incorrect. Check the article as needed.
Step 4: From the possible correct choices, select the best answer.

1. (Vocabulary) **The word "meteorologist" has two meaningful parts: "meteor" and "ologist." These parts mean:**
   - (a.) atmosphere + people who study
   - b. meteorites + people who study
   - c. people who study + measurement
   - d. meteor + scientists
2. (Cause and effect) **Which of these relationships is NOT true?**
   - a. Dark-colored areas of the earth absorb more of the sun's energy and, as a result, these surfaces are warmer.
   - (b.) When a warm front occurs, violent weather conditions such as hurricanes occur.
   - c. When condensation is completed, clouds become heavier, and precipitation is produced.
   - d. Changes in sunlight lead to changes in temperatures.
3. (Compare and contrast) **Which diagram best represents a cold front?**

a. 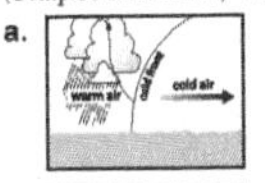

b. 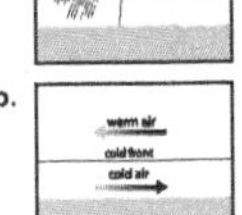

(c.) 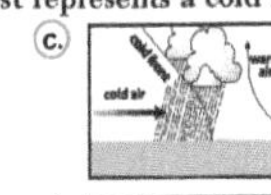

d. 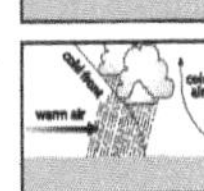

4. (Main Idea) **The main idea of this article is best stated as:**
   - a. The sun affects temperature, evaporation, and the direction of winds.
   - (b.) Weather is affected by many factors, including the movement of air masses, the land, the energy of the sun, seasons, and the jet stream.
   - c. To understand changes in weather you only need to understand cold and warm weather fronts.
   - d. Climatologists have studied different weather patterns for many years.

MULTIPLE CHOICE COMPREHENSION 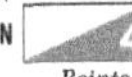 4 *Points*

164 *REWARDS Plus: Reading Strategies Applied to Science Passages*

ACTIVITY F

Vocabulary Activities

ACTIVITY PROCEDURE

(See the *Student Book*, pages 165–166.)

Have students complete each item orally and provide feedback on their answers. Then have students respond to each question in writing by answering "yes" or "no" and providing a reason for their answers.

Yes/No/Why

1. Turn to page 165._ Find **Activity F.**_ Read item #1. Tell your partner your answer and your reason for it. (Pause. Then call on individual students. Encourage discussion. Provide students with feedback on their choices, focusing on their explanations for their answer.)
2. Write your answer and your reason for it in the space provided. Look up when you are done._
3. (Repeat Steps 1–2 for the rest of the items.)

Note F-1: You may wish to do this as an oral task only rather than an oral and a written task.

APPLICATION LESSON **13**

ACTIVITY F *Vocabulary*

Yes/No/Why

1. Does **condensation accompany precipitation?**
Example answer: Yes. When condensation occurs, drops of water become larger and larger, clouds become heavier, and precipitation results.

2. Would **meteorologists frequently** study viruses?
Example answer: No. Meteorologists study the atmosphere and weather—not viruses.

3. Would the work of **meteorologists** and **climatologists** be **associated?**
Example answer: Yes. Both groups of people are interested in weather and climate.

Student Book: Application Lesson 13 165

ACTIVITY PROCEDURE

Have students read the words and definitions and then complete the sentence stems for each vocabulary word. Have them share answers with partners and with the class. Then, have students give themselves points in the blank half of the Vocabulary box.

Completion Activity

1. Turn to page 166._ Read the first word and its definition._
2. Now, read the sentence stem._
3. Think of how you would complete the sentence stem and write it._ Share your answer with your partner._ (Call on a few students to share answers with the class.)
4. (Repeat Steps 1–3 for the rest of the words.)
5. If you participated in answering all seven questions, give yourself seven points in the blank half of the Vocabulary box.

Note F-2: You may wish to do this as an oral task only rather than an oral task and a written task.

APPLICATION LESSON **13**

Completion Activities

1. **direct:** to manage or control the course
Some of the things that a person could direct include
Answers will vary.

2. **predict:** to declare beforehand
If you were going to predict the winner of a football game, you might want to know
Answers will vary.

3. **productivity:** the ability to produce a lot
The productivity of a factory could be improved by
Answers will vary.

4. **completion:** the end; the state of being finished
Projects that you have seen through to completion include
Answers will vary.

VOCABULARY 7 *Points*

166 *REWARDS Plus: Reading Strategies Applied to Science Passages*

ACTIVITY G

Expository Writing—Multi-Paragraph Answer

ACTIVITY PROCEDURE, Plan and Write

(See the *Student Book*, pages 167–169.)

Have students read the prompt. Guide students as they determine the three topics and **LIST** details for topics a, b, and c. Have students look at topic a again. Have students **CROSS OUT** details that don't go with the topic. Have students **CONNECT** details as shown in the example plan. Have students **NUMBER** their details, and then compare with the example plan for topic a. Next, have students **WRITE** paragraph a. Repeat for topics b and c. Finally, explain that after the answer is written, they should **EDIT** their work, revising for clarity and proofreading for errors in capitalization, punctuation, and spelling.

Use Overheads 63 and 64: Activity G

1. Turn to page 167. Find **Activity G.**
2. Find the prompt in the middle of the page. Read the prompt out loud with me: **Describe how the movement of air masses, the land, and the sun affect weather on the earth.**
3. Reread the prompt and determine three topics. Record the topics in your Planning Box. Compare your topics with your partner. (Move around the room and assist students in determining the topics.)
4. Look back in the article and locate details that go with each topic. Record the details in the Planning Box.
5. Use the steps for topic a. **Cross out** any details that do not go with the topic, draw brackets to **connect** details that could easily go into one sentence, and **number** the details in a logical order.
6. (Show Overhead 63.) Look at the example plan for topic a on the overhead. Yours should be similar.
7. Take out a blank piece of paper. **Write** paragraph a. Please reread and **edit** your paragraph. (Move around the room and monitor your students as they are writing.)
8. (When the majority of students are done, proceed with the lesson.) Now, use the steps for topic b.
9. Look at the example plan for topic b on the overhead. Yours should be similar.

APPLICATION LESSON **13**

ACTIVITY G *Expository Writing—Multi-Paragraph Answer*

Writing Strategy—Multi-Paragraph Answer

Step 1: LIST (List the details that are important enough to include in your answer.)
Step 2: CROSS OUT (Reread the details. Cross out any that don't go with the topic.)
Step 3: CONNECT (Connect any details that could go into one sentence.)
Step 4: NUMBER (Number the details in a logical order.)
Step 5: WRITE (Write the paragraph.)
Step 6: EDIT (Revise and proofread your answer.)

Prompt: Describe how the movement of air masses, the land, and the sun affect weather on the earth.

Plan: Complete the Planning Box.

Student Book: Application Lesson 13 167

APPLICATION LESSON **13**

Example Multi-Paragraph Plan

Planning Box
(topic a) *effects on weather—movement of air masses*
① (detail) – *air masses are always moving*
② (detail) – *when warm air mass rises, carries water vapor up*
③ (detail) – *water vapor cools and condensation occurs*
④ { (detail) – *when condensation completed, clouds become heavier*
(detail) – *precipitation results*
⑤ { (detail) – *warm air masses and cold air masses collide*
(detail) – *various kinds of weather develop*
(topic b) *effects on weather—land*
① (detail) – *air mass above earth becomes same temperature as land*
② (detail) – *dark-colored areas of earth (e.g., mountains) absorb sunlight*
and heat up
③ (detail) – *air above dark-colored areas becomes warmer*
④ (detail) – *dark-colored areas heat up and create drying winds*
⑤ (detail) – *glaciers and snowfields reflect sunlight back into atmosphere*
⑥ (detail) – *surface and air becomes cooler*
(topic c) *effects on weather—sun*
① (detail) – *at different times of the year, different parts of the earth*
receive more or less sunlight
② (detail) – *changes in sunlight lead to different temperatures*
③ { (detail) – *amount of sunlight also affects how much water evaporates*
into air
(detail) – *affects the nature and direction of winds*

Write: Write paragraphs a, b, and c on a separate piece of paper.

168 *REWARDS Plus: Reading Strategies Applied to Science Passages*

10. Locate your piece of paper._ **Write** paragraph b. **Edit** your paragraph. (Move around the room and monitor your students as they are writing.)

11. (When the majority of students are done, proceed with the lesson.) Use the steps for topic c._

12. Look at the example plan for topic c on the overhead. Yours should be similar._

13. **Write** paragraph c. **Edit** your paragraph._ (Move around the room and monitor your students as they are writing.)

14. (When the majority of students are done, proceed with the lesson.) Please carefully read your paragraphs. Be sure that your paragraphs are clear. Proofread for any errors in capitalization, punctuation, and spelling. (Give students time to proofread their paragraphs.)

ACTIVITY PROCEDURE, Evaluate

Ask students to read each question in the rubric. Guide them in evaluating the paragraphs using the guidelines. Have students total their points and record them in the blank half of the Writing box.

15. Turn to page 169._ Let's evaluate paragraphs a, b, and c.

16. Check paragraphs a, b, and c carefully and answer questions 1 through 3._

17. Reread your paragraphs._ Circle "Yes" if your paragraphs are easy to understand._

18. Carefully examine your paragraphs. If you think a word is misspelled, underline it and check back in the plan or article and correct the spelling._ Circle "Yes" if you believe that you have very few spelling errors.

19. Carefully examine your sentences. Be sure that each sentence begins with a capital._ If all sentences begin with a capital, circle "Yes."

20. Examine your sentences. Be sure that each sentence ends with a period._ If all sentences end with a period, circle "Yes."

21. Count up your points and record them in the Writing box._

22. (Show Overhead 64.) Look at the overhead._ Let's read the three example paragraphs. Yours should be similar. (Read the paragraphs to your students or with your students or call on a student to read the example paragraph.)

Note G-1: The rubric can be used in a variety of ways. You may wish to have students evaluate their own paragraphs or have partners provide feedback, and then use the second column of the rubric for teacher feedback. You may wish to give students bonus points based on your feedback.

APPLICATION LESSON

13

Example Multi-Paragraph Plan

Planning Box
(topic a) *effects on weather—movement of air masses*
① (detail) – *air masses are always moving*
② (detail) – *when warm air mass rises, carries water vapor up*
③ (detail) – *water vapor cools and condensation occurs*
④ (detail) – *when condensation completed, clouds become heavier*
(detail) – *precipitation results*
⑤ (detail) – *warm air masses and cold air masses collide*
(detail) – *various kinds of weather develop*
(topic b) *effects on weather—land*
① (detail) – *air mass above earth becomes same temperature as land*
② (detail) – *dark-colored areas of earth (e.g., mountains) absorb sunlight and heat up*
③ (detail) – *air above dark-colored areas becomes warmer*
④ (detail) – *dark-colored areas heat up and create drying winds*
⑤ (detail) – *glaciers and snowfields reflect sunlight back into atmosphere*
⑥ (detail) – *surface and air becomes cooler*
(topic c) *effects on weather—sun*
① (detail) – *at different times of the year, different parts of the earth receive more or less sunlight*
② (detail) – *changes in sunlight lead to different temperatures*
③ (detail) – *amount of sunlight also affects how much water evaporates into air*
(detail) – *affects the nature and direction of winds*

Write: Write paragraphs a, b, and c on a separate piece of paper.

APPLICATION LESSON

13

Evaluate: Evaluate the paragraphs using this rubric.

Rubric—Multi-Paragraph Answer	Student or Partner Rating	Teacher Rating
1. Did the author state the topic in the first sentence?	a. Yes Fix up b. Yes Fix up c. Yes Fix up	a. Yes No b. Yes No c. Yes No
2. Did the author include details that go with the topic?	a. Yes Fix up b. Yes Fix up c. Yes Fix up	a. Yes No b. Yes No c. Yes No
3. Did the author combine details in some of the sentences?	a. Yes Fix up b. Yes Fix up c. Yes Fix up	a. Yes No b. Yes No c. Yes No
4. Is the answer easy to understand?	Yes Fix up	Yes No
5. Did the author correctly spell words, particularly the words found in the article?	Yes Fix up	Yes No
6. Did the author use correct capitalization, capitalizing the first word in the sentence and proper names of people, places, and things?	Yes Fix up	Yes No
7. Did the author use correct punctuation, including a period at the end of each sentence?	Yes Fix up	Yes No

WRITING 13 Points

ACTIVITY H

Comprehension—Single-Paragraph Answer

ACTIVITY PROCEDURE

(See the *Student Book*, page 170.)

Have students read the *What Is* statement and the *What If* question. Have students turn the question into part of the answer and write down a topic sentence for their answer. Then, have them complete their answer. Encourage them to use evidence from the article and their own experience and background knowledge. Engage students in a discussion. Award points for writing and participating in the discussion.

Note H-1: If you are working with students who have difficulty generating ideas for their paragraphs, switch the order of activities: engage the students in a discussion, and then have them write their paragraphs.

1. Turn to page 170._ Find **Activity H.**_
2. Find the *What Is* statement in the middle of the page._ Read it out loud with me: **The land affects weather.**
3. Find the *What If* question._ Read it with me: **What would happen to the weather if more and more cities were built in a particular area?**
4. Think how you might turn the question into part of the answer._ Tell me your idea for a topic sentence._ (Example sentence: It is possible to hypothesize about the effects that building more and more cities might have on the weather.) Take out a piece of paper and write your topic sentence._ (Move around the room and monitor as students write.)
5. Add ideas to your paragraph. Use evidence from the article as well as your own experience and background knowledge. If you finish early, reread your paragraph and edit it so that it is easy to understand and clear._ (Move around the room and monitor as students write.)
6. Read your paragraph to your partner._
7. If you included wording from the question in your answer and added evidence from the article, award yourself four points for writing._
8. (Engage students in a discussion. Award four points to students who are active participants in the discussion.)

APPLICATION LESSON
13

ACTIVITY H *Comprehension—Single-Paragraph Answer*

Writing Strategy—Single-Paragraph Answer

Step 1: Read the item.
Step 2: Turn the question into part of the answer and write it down.
Step 3: Think of the answer or locate the answer in the article.
Step 4: Complete your answer.

Prompt:
What Is—The land affects weather.

What If—What would happen to the weather if more and more cities were built in a particular area?

Write and Discuss: Write a paragraph. Then share your ideas. Use the Discussion Guidelines.

Discussion Guidelines

Speaker		Listener	
Looks like:	**Sounds like:**	**Looks like:**	**Sounds like:**
• Facing peers • Making eye contact • Participating	• Using pleasant, easy-to-hear voice • Sharing opinions, supporting facts and reasons from the article and from your experience • Staying on the topic	• Facing speaker • Making eye contact • Participating	• Waiting quietly to speak • Giving positive, supportive comments • Disagreeing respectfully

WRITING 4 Points — DISCUSSION 4 Points

170 *REWARDS Plus: Reading Strategies Applied to Science Passages*

Note H-2: If your students are having difficulty writing the *What If* paragraphs, read or show them the following example paragraph:

Example Single-Paragraph Answer

It is possible to hypothesize about the effects that building more and more cities might have on the weather. Because the cities would contain many buildings, roads, and parking lots, the cities would absorb more sunlight. The cities would then become warmer. Of course, the air above the cities would also become warmer. If the cities were widespread, the air above the earth would rise in temperature. As a result, the building of cities would contribute to overall global warming.

Application Lesson 14

Materials Needed:

- *Student Book*: Application Lesson 14
- Application Overhead Transparencies 65–69
- Appendix B Reproducible N: Application Lesson 14
- Appendix C Optional Vocabulary Activity: Application Lesson 14
- Paper or cardboard to use when covering the overhead transparency
- Paper or cardboard for each student to use during spelling dictation
- Washable overhead transparency pen

Text Treatment Notes:

- Black text signifies teacher script (exact wording to say to students).
- Green text in parentheses signifies directions or prompts for the teacher.
- Green text signifies answers or examples of answers.
- Green graphics treatment signifies reproduction of Overhead information.
- Green text and green graphics treatment do not appear in the *Student Book*.

ACTIVITY A
Vocabulary

ACTIVITY PROCEDURE, List 1

(See the *Student Book*, page 171.)

Tell students each word in the list. Then, have students repeat the word and read the definition aloud For each definition, provide any additional information that may be necessary. Then, have students practice reading the words themselves.

1. (Show the top half of Overhead 65.) Before we read the passage, let's read the difficult words. (Point to **canopy**.) The first word is **canopy**. What word?_ Now, read the definition._
2. (Point to **emergent**.) The next word is **emergent**. What word?_ Now, read the definition._
3. (Point to **understory.**) The last word is **understory.** What word?_ Now, read the definition._
4. Open your *Student Book* to **Application Lesson 14**, page 171._
5. Find **Activity A**, **List 1**, in your book._ Let's read the words again. First word._ Next word._ Next word._

ACTIVITY PROCEDURE, List 2

(See the *Student Book*, page 171.)

Have students circle prefixes and suffixes, then underline the vowels. Using the overhead transparency, assist students in checking their work. Next, have students figure out each word to themselves, then say it aloud. Have them read the definition aloud.

1. Find **List 2**. Circle the prefixes and suffixes, and underline the vowels. Look up when you are done._
2. (Show the bottom half of Overhead 65.) Now, check and fix any mistakes._

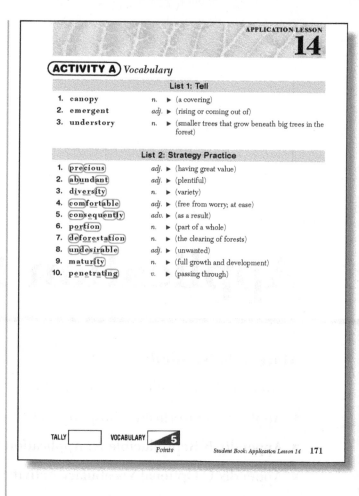

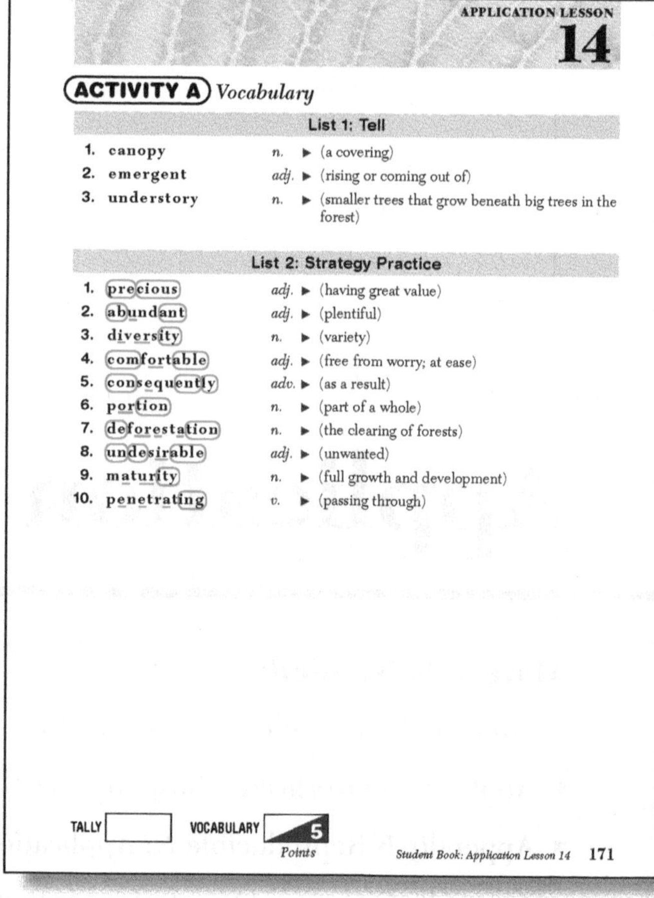

APPLICATION LESSON 14

ACTIVITY A *Vocabulary*

List 1: Tell

1. canopy *n.* ▸ (a covering)
2. emergent *adj.* ▸ (rising or coming out of)
3. understory *n.* ▸ (smaller trees that grow beneath big trees in the forest)

List 2: Strategy Practice

1. precious *adj.* ▸ (having great value)
2. abundant *adj.* ▸ (plentiful)
3. diversity *n.* ▸ (variety)
4. comfortable *adj.* ▸ (free from worry; at ease)
5. consequently *adv.* ▸ (as a result)
6. portion *n.* ▸ (part of a whole)
7. deforestation *n.* ▸ (the clearing of forests)
8. undesirable *adj.* ▸ (unwanted)
9. maturity *n.* ▸ (full growth and development)
10. penetrating *v.* ▸ (passing through)

TALLY [ ] VOCABULARY 5 Points

Student Book: Application Lesson 14 171

3. Go back to the first word._ Sound out the word to yourself. Put your thumb up when you can read the word. Be sure that it is a real word._ What word?_ Now, read the definition._
4. (Continue Step 3 with all remaining words in List 2.)

Note A.2-1: You may wish to provide additional practice by having students read words to a partner.

ACTIVITY PROCEDURE, List 1 and 2

(See the *Student Book*, page 171.)

Tell students to look in List 1 or List 2 for a word you are thinking about. Have them circle the number of the word and tell you the word. Explain to students to make a tally mark for each correct word in the Tally box, and then enter the number of tally marks as points in the blank half of the Vocabulary box.

1. Remember, the words I'm thinking about will be in either List 1 or List 2. Make a tally mark for every correctly identified word.
2. Circle the number of the appropriate word.
   - If water is plentiful, it is said to be this. (Wait.) What word? **abundant**
   - Something that is unwanted is this. (Wait.) What word? **undesirable**
   - A part of something is this. (Wait.) What word? **portion**
   - When something happens as a result of something else, it happens in this way. (Wait.) What word? **consequently**
   - Something that has great value is said to be this. (Wait.) What word? **precious**
3. Count all the tally marks, and enter that number as points in the blank half of the Vocabulary box.

ACTIVITY PROCEDURE, List 3

(See the *Student Book*, page 172.)

The words in the third list are related. Have students use the *REWARDS* Strategies to figure out the first word in each family. Have them read the definition of the verb and then read nouns and adjectives that are related to that verb.

Use Overhead 66: Activity A
List 3: Word Families

1. Turn to page 172._ Find **Family 1** in **List 3**. Figure out the first word. Use your pencil if you wish. Put your thumb up when you know the word._ What word?_ Read the definition._
2. Look at the noun in Family 1. Figure out the word._ What word?_
3. Look at the adjective in Family 1. Figure out the word._ What word?_
4. (Repeat Steps 1–3 for all word families in List 3.)

Note A.3-1: You may wish to provide additional practice by having students read a word family to the group or to a partner.

APPLICATION LESSON
14

List 3: Word Families

	Verb	Noun	Adjective
Family 1	prefer (to like better)	preference	preferable
Family 2	decompose (to rot)	decomposition decomposer	decomposable
Family 3	destroy (to ruin completely; to cause to go away; to end)	destruction	destructive destructible
Family 4	contribute (to give)	contribution contributor	contributable
Family 5	inhabit (to live in a place)	inhabitant	inhabitable

ACTIVITY B *Spelling Dictation*

1. prefer	4. contribute
2. preference	5. contribution
3. preferable	6. contributor

SPELLING 6 Points

172 *REWARDS Plus: Reading Strategies Applied to Science Passages*

Note A.3-2: An additional vocabulary practice activity called Quick Words is provided in Appendix C of this Teacher's Guide. See Appendix C for information about how this optional activity can be used.

Spelling Dictation

ACTIVITY PROCEDURE

(See the *Student Book*, page 172.)

For each word, tell students the word, then have students say the parts of the word to themselves while they write the word. Using the overhead transparency, assist students in checking their spelling and correcting if they misspelled. Then, have students enter the number of correctly spelled words as points in the blank half of the Spelling box.

Note B-1: Distribute a piece of light cardboard to each of the students.

Use Overhead 66: Activity B

1. Find **Activity B.**
2. The first word is **prefer.** What word?_ Say the parts in **prefer** to yourself as you write the word. (Pause and monitor.)
3. (Show **prefer** on the overhead.) Check **prefer.** If you misspelled it, cross it out and write it correctly.
4. The second word is **preference.** What word?_ Say the parts in **preference** to yourself as you write the word. (Pause and monitor.)
5. (Show **preference** on the overhead.) Check **preference.** If you misspelled it, cross it out and write it correctly.
6. (Repeat the procedures for the words **preferable, contribute, contribution,** and **contributor.**)
7. Count the number of words you spelled correctly, and record that number as points in the blank half of the Spelling box at the bottom of the page.

APPLICATION LESSON
14

List 3: Word Families

	Verb	Noun	Adjective
Family 1	prefer (to like better)	preference	preferable
Family 2	decompose (to rot)	decomposition decomposer	decomposable
Family 3	destroy (to ruin completely; to cause to go away; to end)	destruction	destructive destructible
Family 4	contribute (to give)	contribution contributor	contributable
Family 5	inhabit (to live in a place)	inhabitant	inhabitable

ACTIVITY B *Spelling Dictation*

1. prefer	4. contribute
2. preference	5. contribution
3. preferable	6. contributor

172 *REWARDS Plus: Reading Strategies Applied to Science Passages*

SPELLING 6 *Points*

ACTIVITY C

Passage Reading and Comprehension

ACTIVITY PROCEDURE

(See the *Student Book*, pages 173–175.)

Have students read the title of the passage and each heading. Ask them to tell their partners two things that the passage will tell about.

Passage Preview

1. Turn to page 173. Let's preview the passage.
2. Read the title. What is the whole passage going to tell about?
3. Now, let's read the headings. Read the first heading. Read the next heading. (Continue until students have read all headings.)
4. Turn to your partner. Without looking, tell two things this passage will tell about.

ACTIVITY PROCEDURE

Provide students with an Information Web from Appendix B. Have students read the passage silently to each embedded number, and then reread the same information orally either to a partner, together as a group, or individually. Ask the corresponding comprehension question or questions. Once students finish reading a section labeled A, B, C, D, E, or F, have them fill in the Information Web before going on to the next section.

Note C-1: If students do not finish reading the passage during class, have them use their Information Webs to review the information at the beginning of the next class.

Use Overhead 67: Activity C

Passage Reading

1. (Provide an Information Web for each student.)
2. Turn back to the beginning of the passage. You're going to read the passage and answer questions about what you've read. During passage reading, you are also going to fill in an Information Web to help you remember the important details of the passage. Later, you'll use this Web to review the content of the passage with your partner.
3. Read the title.

APPLICATION LESSON 14

ACTIVITY C *Passage Reading and Comprehension*

Note: For this activity, you will need Reproducible N found in the *Teacher's Guide*.

Tropical Rainforests

A
Tropical rainforests are ecosystems located near the equator. They cover about
11 7% of the earth's total land area. These rainforests grow near the equator in
25 more than 85 countries in Africa, Southeast Asia, and Central and South
37 America. Even though they cover a relatively small portion of the earth, tropical
50 rainforests contain between 50% and 90% of the world's species. (#1)

B
60 **Rainforest Layers**
62 Tropical rainforests are divided into four layers. Each layer has specific
73 characteristics that provide unique food and shelter not found in the other
85 layers. Therefore, each layer has its own diverse and unique group of species.

98 The **emergent layer** is the topmost layer. Here is where the tops of the
112 tallest trees emerge from the canopy below. These trees are some of the tallest
126 in the forest, often reaching a height of 200 feet or more. Many of them have

Student Book: Application Lesson 14 173

(from Application Lesson 14)

Reproducible N

ACTIVITY C *Passage Reading and Comprehension*

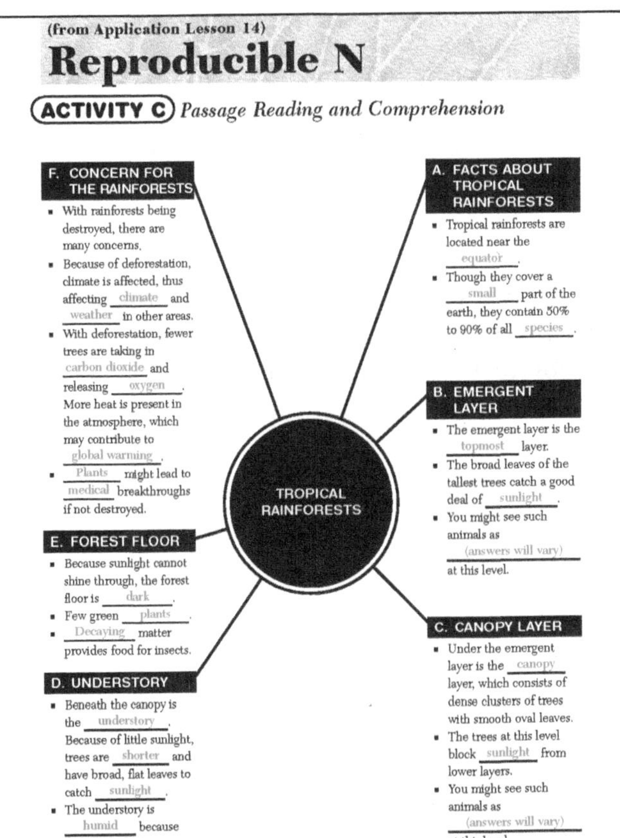

TROPICAL RAINFORESTS

A. FACTS ABOUT TROPICAL RAINFORESTS
- Tropical rainforests are located near the equator.
- Though they cover a small part of the earth, they contain 50% to 90% of all species.

B. EMERGENT LAYER
- The emergent layer is the topmost layer.
- The broad leaves of the tallest trees catch a good deal of sunlight.
- You might see such animals as (answers will vary) at this level.

C. CANOPY LAYER
- Under the emergent layer is the canopy layer, which consists of dense clusters of trees with smooth oval leaves.
- The trees at this level block sunlight from lower layers.
- You might see such animals as (answers will vary) at this level.

D. UNDERSTORY
- Beneath the canopy is the understory. Because of little sunlight, trees are shorter and have broad, flat leaves to catch sunlight.
- The understory is humid because moisture collects.

E. FOREST FLOOR
- Because sunlight cannot shine through, the forest floor is dark.
- Few green plants.
- Decaying matter provides food for insects.

F. CONCERN FOR THE RAINFORESTS
- With rainforests being destroyed, there are many concerns.
- Because of deforestation, climate is affected, thus affecting climate and weather in other areas.
- With deforestation, fewer trees are taking in carbon dioxide and releasing oxygen. More heat is present in the atmosphere, which may contribute to global warming.
- Plants might lead to medical breakthroughs if not destroyed.

Appendix B • 399

4. Read down to number 1 silently. Look up when you are done._
5. (Wait for students to complete the reading. Then have students reread the part orally.)
6. (Ask the question or questions associated with the number. Provide feedback to students regarding their answers.)
7. (Repeat steps 4–6 for all paragraphs in Section A.)
8. Now, look at your Information Web.
9. With your partner, fill in the blanks for Section A. You can refer back to the passage for information. Look up when you're done._ (Move around the room and monitor students as they complete the section.)
10. (When the majority of students have finished, show Overhead 67.) Look at the overhead and check your work. Fix up or add to your answers.
11. Now read down to the next number silently. Look up when you are done._
12. (Repeat steps 5–11 until the students have finished the passage and the Information Web.)
13. Use your Information Web to retell the important information to your partner.

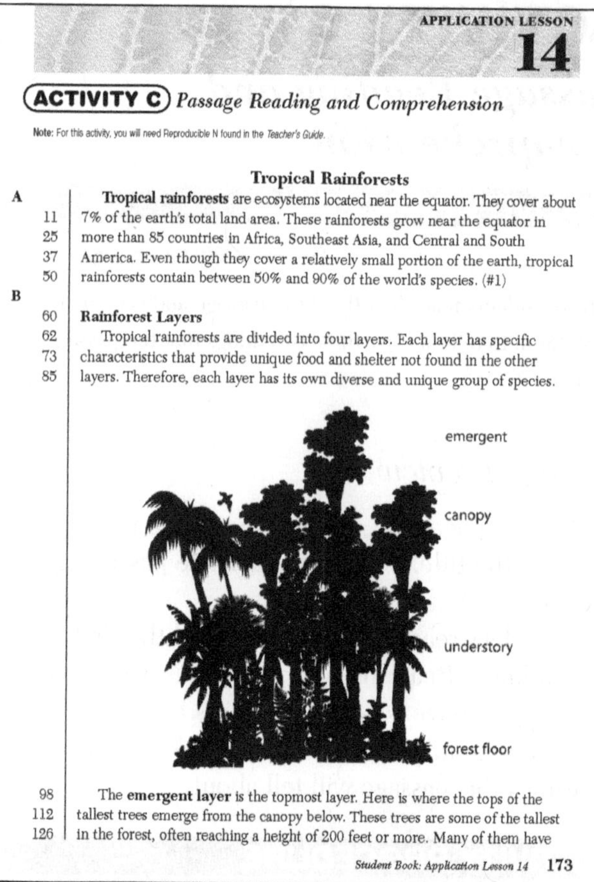

APPLICATION LESSON
14

ACTIVITY C *Passage Reading and Comprehension*

Note: For this activity, you will need Reproducible N found in the *Teacher's Guide.*

Tropical Rainforests

A
Tropical rainforests are ecosystems located near the equator. They cover about
11 7% of the earth's total land area. These rainforests grow near the equator in
25 more than 85 countries in Africa, Southeast Asia, and Central and South
37 America. Even though they cover a relatively small portion of the earth, tropical
50 rainforests contain between 50% and 90% of the world's species. (#1)

B
60 **Rainforest Layers**
62 Tropical rainforests are divided into four layers. Each layer has specific
73 characteristics that provide unique food and shelter not found in the other
85 layers. Therefore, each layer has its own diverse and unique group of species.

98 The **emergent layer** is the topmost layer. Here is where the tops of the
112 tallest trees emerge from the canopy below. These trees are some of the tallest
126 in the forest, often reaching a height of 200 feet or more. Many of them have

Student Book: Application Lesson 14 **173**

Comprehension Questions

#1 What percentage of the earth do tropical rainforests cover? Where are they located?
7%; located near the equator in more than 85 countries in Africa, Southeast Asia, and Central and South America.

#2 What is the topmost layer of a rainforest called? What types of animals are comfortable living at that height?
The emergent layer; butterflies, eagles, bats, some types of monkeys, lizards, and flying squirrels.

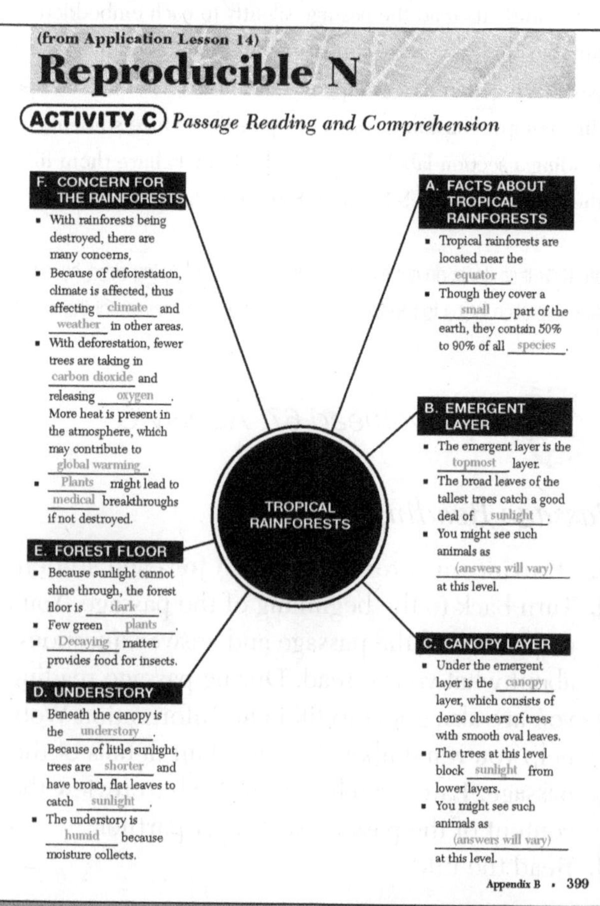

(from Application Lesson 14)

Reproducible N

ACTIVITY C *Passage Reading and Comprehension*

TROPICAL RAINFORESTS

A. FACTS ABOUT TROPICAL RAINFORESTS
- Tropical rainforests are located near the equator.
- Though they cover a small part of the earth, they contain 50% to 90% of all species.

B. EMERGENT LAYER
- The emergent layer is the topmost layer.
- The broad leaves of the tallest trees catch a good deal of sunlight.
- You might see such animals as (answers will vary) at this level.

C. CANOPY LAYER
- Under the emergent layer is the canopy layer, which consists of dense clusters of trees with smooth oval leaves.
- The trees at this level block sunlight from lower layers.
- You might see such animals as (answers will vary) at this level.

D. UNDERSTORY
- Beneath the canopy is the understory. Because of little sunlight, trees are shorter and have broad, flat leaves to catch sunlight.
- The understory is humid because moisture collects.

E. FOREST FLOOR
- Because sunlight cannot shine through, the forest floor is dark.
- Few green plants.
- Decaying matter provides food for insects.

F. CONCERN FOR THE RAINFORESTS
- With rainforests being destroyed, there are many concerns,
- Because of deforestation, climate is affected, thus affecting climate and weather in other areas.
- With deforestation, fewer trees are taking in carbon dioxide and releasing oxygen. More heat is present in the atmosphere, which may contribute to global warming.
- Plants might lead to medical breakthroughs if not destroyed.

Appendix B • 399

#3 How does the canopy layer affect the lower levels?
Blocks most of the sunlight from penetrating below.

#4 What is a major difference between the understory and the two higher layers?
Humid (moist) and quite still rather than dry and windy; trees are shorter.

#5 What does the forest floor consist of? What types of organisms live there?
Made up of decaying matter from the three layers above; insects and some animals that feed off the insects live there.

#6 Why should people be concerned about the destruction of the earth's rainforests?
All organisms that make up the rainforest ecosystem affect and create the weather and climate of that region as well as other parts of the world.

#7 Why do many scientists believe that the destruction of rainforests may contribute to global warming?
Trees take in carbon dioxide, which contributes to global warming; leaves reflect heat back into space—fewer trees equals more carbon dioxide and more heat in the atmosphere.

#8 How else might tropical rainforests benefit humankind?
Rich diversity of plant life may contribute to major medical breakthroughs.

142 broad green leaves, which catch a great deal of sunlight. Animals also live at this
157 highest layer of the forest. Butterflies, eagles, and bats are comfortable flying at
170 these heights. Some types of monkeys prefer the tops of the trees. Other tree-
184 dwellers, such as lizards and flying squirrels, may also be found at the emergent
198 layer. (#2)
C 199 Traveling downwards from the emergent layer, we find the **canopy layer**.
210 The canopy is a dense cluster of trees with smooth oval leaves. These trees block
225 most of the sunlight and keep it from penetrating to lower levels. The trees in
240 the canopy layer are not as tall as the trees of the emergent layer. Trees in the
257 canopy layer reach maturity at 75 to 90 feet. Food is abundant in these smaller,
272 mature trees. Monkeys, snakes, treefrogs, and birds populate this layer. (#3)
D 282 Below the canopy layer is the **understory**. Very little sunlight reaches the
294 plants found in the understory layer because of the dense canopy layer above.
307 Unlike the higher layers, which are drier, hot, and very windy, the understory layer
321 is humid (moist) and quite still. Moisture collects at these lower levels and does
335 not evaporate easily. The trees in this layer do not grow very tall at all, seldom
351 reaching 12 feet. They often have broad, flat leaves that catch as much light as
366 possible in this shadowy layer. Even though little light shines into the understory, a
380 lot of life exists there. Many animals feed on fruits and leaves from shrubs or small
396 trees. Some animals, such as leopards and jaguars, feed on smaller animals. Many
409 types of insects favor this layer of the tropical rainforest. (#4)
E 419 At the bottom of the tropical rainforest, we find the **forest floor**. Here, the
433 ground is made up of decaying matter from the upper layers. The sunlight
446 cannot shine easily through the three layers above, so it is very dark at this
461 lowest layer. Few green plants can thrive here. Consequently, the forest floor
473 has poor soil. Many insects live on the floor, feeding on the dead and
487 decomposing wood, leaves, and other matter. Some larger animals, such as the
499 giant anteater, feed on the insects that live in this layer. (#5)
F

510 **Concern for the Rainforests**
514 People have good reason to be concerned about destruction of the
525 rainforests. Many of the world's tropical rainforests are rapidly disappearing.
535 Rainforests are being chopped down for wood and farmland. Scientists have said
547 that deforestation, or removal of the forests' trees, may have a greater impact on
561 the rest of the world than anyone realizes. All organisms that make up the
575 rainforest ecosystem affect and create the weather and climate of that region.
587 The climate created by a rainforest also affects the weather and climate in other
601 parts of the world. (#6)

605 Many scientists believe that tropical rainforests are essential for preventing
615 serious global warming. Trees take in carbon dioxide (a harmful gas which
627 contributes to global warming) and release oxygen into the atmosphere. Their
638 leaves reflect heat energy back into space. As the rainforests are destroyed,
650 fewer trees are available to take in carbon dioxide and to release oxygen, and
664 more heat is present in our atmosphere. The destruction of rainforests will upset
677 weather patterns and alter the amounts of certain gasses in the air, thus
690 increasing the rate of global warming. As a result, the overall temperatures on
703 the earth may rise and produce undesirable changes in the earth's weather
715 patterns. The graph below shows how much warmer or colder than normal it
728 has been when measurements from thousands of meteorological stations are
738 combined. (#7)

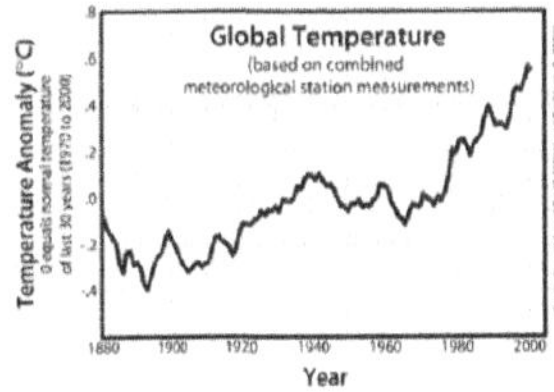

739 In addition, many scientists feel that the rich diversity of plant life in the
753 tropical rainforests may hold the key to major medical breakthroughs.
763 Nevertheless, these plants are being destroyed before we have the chance to
775 understand their potential. Tropical rainforests and their inhabitants are
784 disappearing at an alarming rate. It is important to conserve these precious and
797 vital resources. (#8)
799

ACTIVITY D *Fluency Building*

Cold Timing		Practice 1	
Practice 2		Hot Timing	

ACTIVITY D

Fluency Building

ACTIVITY PROCEDURE

(See the *Student Book*, page 175.)

Have students complete a Cold Timing, one or two practices, and a Hot Timing of the Activity C article. For each timing, have students record the number of correct words read. Finally, have students complete their Fluency Graphs.

Note D-1: When assigning partners for this activity, have the stronger reader read first. As a result, the other reader will have one additional practice opportunity.

1. Now, it's time for fluency building.
2. Find the beginning of the passage again. (Pause.)
3. Whisper-read. See how many words you can read in one minute. Begin._ (Time students for one minute.) Stop._ Circle the last word that you read._ Record the number of words you read after **Cold Timing**._
4. Let's practice again. Begin._ (Time students for one minute.) Stop._ Put a box around the last word that you read._ Record the number of words you read after **Practice 1**._
5. (Optional) Let's practice one more time before the Hot Timing. Begin._ (Time students for one minute.) Stop._ Put a box around the last word that you read._ Record the number of words you read after **Practice 2**._
6. Please exchange books with your partner._ Partner 1, you are going to read first. Partner 2, listen carefully and underline any mistakes or words left out. Ones, begin._ (Time students for one minute.) Stop._ Twos, cross out the last word that your partner read._ (Assist students in subtracting the number of mistakes from the number of words read.) Twos, record the number of correct words in your partner's book after **Hot Timing**._
7. Partner 2, you are going to read next. Partner 1, listen carefully and underline any mistakes or words left out. Twos, begin. (Time students for one minute.) Stop._ Ones, cross out the last word that your partner read._ Ones, record the number of correct words in your partner's book after **Hot Timing**._
8. Exchange books._ Turn to the Fluency Graph on the inside back cover, and indicate on the graph the number of Cold Timing and Hot Timing words you read correctly._

---

605 Many scientists believe that tropical rainforests are essential for preventing
615 serious global warming. Trees take in carbon dioxide (a harmful gas which
627 contributes to global warming) and release oxygen into the atmosphere. Their
638 leaves reflect heat energy back into space. As the rainforests are destroyed,
650 fewer trees are available to take in carbon dioxide and to release oxygen, and
664 more heat is present in our atmosphere. The destruction of rainforests will upset
677 weather patterns and alter the amounts of certain gasses in the air, thus
690 increasing the rate of global warming. As a result, the overall temperatures on
703 the earth may rise and produce undesirable changes in the earth's weather
715 patterns. The graph below shows how much warmer or colder than normal it
728 has been when measurements from thousands of meteorological stations are
738 combined. (#7)

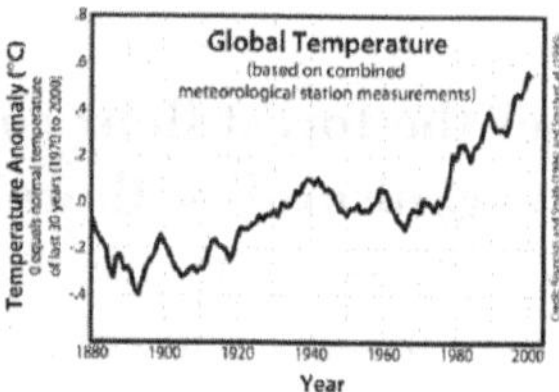

739 In addition, many scientists feel that the rich diversity of plant life in the
753 tropical rainforests may hold the key to major medical breakthroughs.
763 Nevertheless, these plants are being destroyed before we have the chance to
775 understand their potential. Tropical rainforests and their inhabitants are
784 disappearing at an alarming rate. It is important to conserve these precious and
797 vital resources. (#8)
799

ACTIVITY D *Fluency Building*

Cold Timing		Practice 1	
Practice 2		Hot Timing	

ACTIVITY E

Comprehension Questions—Multiple Choice

ACTIVITY PROCEDURE

(See the *Student Book*, page 170.)

Have students complete item #1. Then, have students share the rationale for their answers. Encourage thoughtful discussion. Proceed item-by-item, emphasizing the rationale for the *best* answer. Have students record points for each correct item.

Note E-1: The correct Multiple Choice answers are circled.

1. Turn to page 176. Find **Activity E.**
2. Use the Multiple Choice Strategy to complete item #1. Be ready to explain why you selected your answer. (Wait while students complete the item. Call on individual students. Ask them why they chose their answer and why they eliminated the other choices. Encourage discussion. Provide students with feedback on their choices, focusing on why or why not those choices might be appropriate.)
3. (Repeat Step 2 for items 2–4, pausing after each item to confirm student responses and provide feedback.)
4. Count the number of items you got correct, and record that number in the blank half of the Multiple Choice Comprehension box.

APPLICATION LESSON

14

ACTIVITY E *Comprehension Questions—Multiple Choice*

Comprehension Strategy—Multiple Choice

Step 1: Read the item.
Step 2: Read all of the choices.
Step 3: Think about why each choice might be correct or incorrect. Check the article as needed.
Step 4: From the possible correct choices, select the best answer.

1. (Vocabulary) **Which set of words would best represent tropical rain forests?**
   a. canopy layer, emergent layer, understory, forest floor
   (b.) forest floor, understory, canopy layer, emergent layer
   c. emergent layer, canopy layer, forest floor, understory
   d. tallest trees, humid layer, cluster of trees, decaying matter
2. (Cause and effect) **Many scientists are concerned about deforestation of rainforests because:**
   a. rainforests could be used for farmlands if preserved.
   b. rainforests are one of the few pristine vacation spots available.
   (c.) rainforests have a rich diversity of plants and animals that will be lost.
   d. rainforests currently cover 50 to 90% of the land.
3. (Cause and effect) **Which of these relationships is false?**
   a. Because the emergent layer has the tallest trees, it is inhabited with eagles, bats, and monkeys.
   b. Because the canopy layer has mature trees, food is abundant.
   c. Because the understory has little sunlight, moisture collects, and it is very humid.
   (d.) Because sunlight cannot penetrate the forest floor, green plants thrive.
4. (Main Idea) **Tropical rainforests might hold the "key to major medical breakthroughs" because:**
   (a.) medicines are often developed from plants.
   b. cures might come from the animals that feed on the plants.
   c. the study of the plants' cells could let us know about the cells of humans.
   d. plants in rainforests may contain viruses.

MULTIPLE CHOICE COMPREHENSION 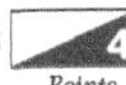
Points

176 *REWARDS Plus: Reading Strategies Applied to Science Passages*

Vocabulary Activities

ACTIVITY PROCEDURE

(See the *Student Book*, pages 177–178.)

Have students complete each item orally and provide feedback on their answers. Then have students respond to each question in writing by answering "yes" or "no" and providing a reason for their answers.

Yes/No/Why

1. Turn to page 177._ Find **Activity F**._ Read item #1. Tell your partner your answer and your reason for it._ (Pause. Then call on individual students. Encourage discussion. Provide students with feedback on their choices, focusing on their explanations for their answer.)
2. Write your answer and your reason for it in the space provided. Look up when you are done._
3. (Repeat Steps 1–2 for the rest of the items.)

Note F-1: You may wish to do this as an oral task only rather than an oral and a written task.

APPLICATION LESSON 14

ACTIVITY F *Vocabulary Activities*

Yes/No/Why

1. Are there **abundant** trees in the **understory**?
Example answer: No. Because little sunlight gets to the understory, there are NOT many trees.

2. Is **deforestation undesirable**?
Example answer: Yes. Deforestation may have many negative outcomes, including extinction of species and global warming.

3. Is it possible that **emergent** values could result from reaching **maturity**?
Example answer: Yes. As a person reaches full growth and development, new values might come from it.

Student Book: Application Lesson 14 177

ACTIVITY PROCEDURE

Have students read the words and definitions and then complete the sentence stems for each vocabulary word. Have them share answers with partners and with the class. Then, have students give themselves points in the blank half of the Vocabulary box.

Completion Activity

1. Turn to page 178._ Read the first word and its definition._
2. Now, read the sentence stem._
3. Think of how you would complete the sentence stem and write it._ Share your answer with your partner._ (Call on a few students to share answers with the class.)
4. (Repeat Steps 1–3 for the rest of the words.)
5. If you participated in answering all seven questions, give yourself seven points in the blank half of the Vocabulary box.

Note F-2: You may wish to do this as an oral task only rather than an oral task and a written task.

APPLICATION LESSON 14

Completion Activities

1. **precious:** having great value
Some of the things that a person considers to be precious may include
Answers will vary.

2. **contribute:** to give
The best way that you could contribute to the world would be to
Answers will vary.

3. **penetrating:** passing through
Penetrating light could pass through
Answers will vary.

4. **comfortable:** free from worry; at ease
In a new situation, I would feel more comfortable if
Answers will vary.

VOCABULARY 7 *Points*

178 *REWARDS Plus: Reading Strategies Applied to Science Passages*

ACTIVITY G

Expository Writing— Multi-Paragraph Answer

ACTIVITY PROCEDURE, Plan and Write

(See the *Student Book*, pages 179–181.)

Have students read the prompt. Guide students as they determine the two topics and **LIST** details for topics a and b. Have students look at topic a again. Have students **CROSS OUT** details that don't go with the topic. Have students **CONNECT** details as shown in the example plan. Have students **NUMBER** their details, and then compare with the example plan for topic a. Next, have students **WRITE** paragraph a. Repeat for topic b. Finally, explain that after the answer is written, they should **EDIT** their work, revising for clarity and proofreading for errors in capitalization, punctuation, and spelling.

Use Overheads 68 and 69: Activity G

1. Turn to page 179._ Find **Activity G.**_
2. Find the prompt in the middle of the page._ Read the prompt out loud with me: **Write one paragraph summarizing information about the four layers of the rainforest and one paragraph about scientists' concerns about the destruction of the rainforests.**
3. Reread the prompt and determine two topics. Record the topics in your Planning Box._ Compare your topics with your partner._ (Move around the room and assist students in determining the topics.)
4. Look back in the article and locate details that go with each topic. Record the details in the Planning Box._
5. Use the steps for topic a. **Cross out** any details that do not go with the topic, draw brackets to **connect** details that could go into one sentence, and **number** the details in a logical order._
6. (Show Overhead 68.) Look at the example plan for topic a on the overhead. Yours should be similar._
7. Take out a blank piece of paper._ **Write** paragraph a. Please reread and **edit** your paragraph._ (Move around the room and monitor your students as they are writing.)
8. (When the majority of students are done, proceed with the lesson.) Use the steps for topic b._

APPLICATION LESSON **14**

ACTIVITY G *Expository Writing—Multi-Paragraph Answer*

Writing Strategy—Multi-Paragraph Answer

Step 1: LIST (List the details that are important enough to include in your answer.)
Step 2: CROSS OUT (Reread the details. Cross out any that don't go with the topic.)
Step 3: CONNECT (Connect any details that could go into one sentence.)
Step 4: NUMBER (Number the details in a logical order.)
Step 5: WRITE (Write the paragraph.)
Step 6: EDIT (Revise and proofread your answer.)

Prompt: Write one paragraph summarizing information about the four layers of the rainforest and one paragraph about scientists' concerns about the destruction of the rainforests.

Plan: Complete the Planning Box.

Student Book: Application Lesson 14 179

APPLICATION LESSON **14**

Example Multi-Paragraph Plan

Planning Box		
	(topic a)	*rainforests—four layers*
①	(detail)	– *emergent layer—topmost layer*
①	(detail)	– *emergent layer—tall trees with broad leaves*
②	(detail)	– *emergent layer—butterflies, eagles, monkeys*
③	(detail)	– *canopy layer—shorter trees with smooth oval leaves*
④	(detail)	– *canopy layer—abundant food for monkeys, snakes, birds*
⑤	(detail)	– *understory—below canopy*
⑤	(detail)	– *understory—little sunlight reaches plants*
⑥	(detail)	– *understory—shorter trees, few animals, many insects*
⑦	(detail)	– *forest floor—bottom of rainforest*
⑧	(detail)	– *forest floor—decaying matter on ground*
⑧	(detail)	– *forest floor—insects thrive by eating decaying matter*
⑨	(detail)	– *forest floor—few green plants*
	(topic b)	*rainforests—scientists concerned about destruction of rainforests*
①	(detail)	– *chopped down for wood and farmland*
②	(detail)	– *fewer trees available to take in carbon dioxide and release oxygen into atmosphere*
③	(detail)	– *result—more heat in our atmosphere*
④	(detail)	– *change in gases released into air and changes in weather patterns will increase global warming*
⑤	(detail)	– *plants that could have medicinal use are being destroyed*
⑤	(detail)	– *inhabitants of rainforests disappearing*

Write: Write paragraphs a and b on a separate piece of paper.

180 *REWARDS Plus: Reading Strategies Applied to Science Passages*

9. Look at the example plan for topic b on the overhead. Yours should be similar.
10. **Write** paragraph b. When you are done, **edit** your paragraph. (Move around the room and monitor your students as they are writing.)
11. (When the majority of students are done, proceed with the lesson.) Please carefully read your paragraphs. Be sure that your paragraphs are easy to understand and clear. Proofread for any errors in capitalization, punctuation, and spelling. (Give students time to proofread their paragraphs.)

ACTIVITY PROCEDURE, Evaluate

Ask students to read each question in the rubric. Guide them in evaluating the paragraphs using the guidelines. Have students total their points and record them in the blank half of the Writing box.

12. Turn to page 181. Let's evaluate paragraphs a and b.
13. Check paragraphs a and b carefully and answer questions 1 through 3.
14. Reread your paragraphs. Circle "Yes" if your paragraphs are easy to understand.
15. Carefully examine your paragraphs. If you think a word is misspelled, underline it and check back in the plan or article and correct the spelling. Circle "Yes" if you believe that you have very few spelling errors.
16. Carefully examine your sentences. Be sure that each sentence begins with a capital. If all sentences begin with a capital, circle "Yes."
17. Examine your sentences. Be sure that each sentence ends with a period. If all sentences end with a period, circle "Yes."
18. Count up your points and record them in the box.
19. (Show Overhead 69.) Look at the overhead. Let's read the two example paragraphs. Yours should be similar. (Read the paragraphs to your students or with your students or call on a student to read the example paragraph.)

Note G-1: The rubric can be used in a variety of ways. You may wish to have students evaluate their own paragraphs or have partners provide feedback, and then use the second column of the rubric for teacher feedback. You may wish to give students bonus points based on your feedback.

APPLICATION LESSON **14**

Example Multi-Paragraph Plan

Planning Box
(topic a) *rainforests—four layers*
① (detail) – *emergent layer—topmost layer*
(detail) – *emergent layer—tall trees with broad leaves*
② (detail) – *emergent layer—butterflies, eagles, monkeys*
③ (detail) – *canopy layer—shorter trees with smooth oval leaves*
④ (detail) – *canopy layer—abundant food for monkeys, snakes, birds*
⑤ (detail) – *understory—below canopy*
(detail) – *understory—little sunlight reaches plants*
⑥ (detail) – *understory—shorter trees, few animals, many insects*
⑦ (detail) – *forest floor—bottom of rainforest*
⑧ (detail) – *forest floor—decaying matter on ground*
(detail) – *forest floor—insects thrive by eating decaying matter*
⑨ (detail) – *forest floor—few green plants*
(topic b) *rainforests—scientists concerned about destruction of rainforests*
① (detail) – *chopped down for wood and farmland*
② (detail) – *fewer trees available to take in carbon dioxide and release oxygen into atmosphere*
③ (detail) – *result—more heat in our atmosphere*
④ (detail) – *change in gases released into air and changes in weather patterns will increase global warming*
⑤ (detail) – *plants that could have medicinal use are being destroyed*
(detail) – *inhabitants of rainforests disappearing*

Write: Write paragraphs a and b on a separate piece of paper.

APPLICATION LESSON **14**

Evaluate: Evaluate the paragraphs using this rubric.

Rubric—Multi-Paragraph Answer	Student or Partner Rating	Teacher Rating
1. Did the author state the topic in the first sentence?	a. (Yes) Fix up b. (Yes) Fix up c. (Yes) Fix up	a. Yes No b. Yes No c. Yes No
2. Did the author include details that go with the topic?	a. (Yes) Fix up b. (Yes) Fix up c. (Yes) Fix up	a. Yes No b. Yes No c. Yes No
3. Did the author combine details in some of the sentences?	a. (Yes) Fix up b. (Yes) Fix up c. (Yes) Fix up	a. Yes No b. Yes No c. Yes No
4. Is the answer easy to understand?	(Yes) Fix up	Yes No
5. Did the author correctly spell words, particularly the words found in the article?	(Yes) Fix up	Yes No
6. Did the author use correct capitalization, capitalizing the first word in the sentence and proper names of people, places, and things?	(Yes) Fix up	Yes No
7. Did the author use correct punctuation, including a period at the end of each sentence?	(Yes) Fix up	Yes No

WRITING 13 Points

ACTIVITY H

Comprehension—Single-Paragraph Answer

ACTIVITY PROCEDURE

(See the *Student Book*, page 182.)

Have students read the *What Is* statement and the *What If* question. Have students turn the question into part of the answer and write down a topic sentence for their answer. Then, have them complete their answer. Encourage them to use evidence from the article and their own experience and background knowledge. Engage students in a discussion. Award points for writing and participating in the discussion.

Note H-1: If you are working with students who have difficulty generating ideas for their paragraphs, switch the order of activities: engage the students in a discussion and then have them write their paragraphs.

1. Turn to page 182._ Find **Activity H**._
2. Find the *What Is* statement in the middle of the page._ Read it out loud with me: **Rainforests are being cut down at an alarming rate.**
3. Find the *What If* question._ Read it with me: **What would happen if most of the earth's rainforests were cut down?** Read the Hint._
4. Think how you might turn the question into part of the answer._ Tell me your idea for a topic sentence._ (Example sentence: Many perhaps irreversible changes would happen to the earth if most of the earth's rainforests were cut down.) Take out a piece of paper and write your topic sentence._ (Move around the room and monitor as students write.)
5. Add ideas to your paragraph. Use evidence from the article as well as your own experience and background knowledge. If you finish early, reread your paragraph and edit it so that it is easy to understand and clear._ (Move around the room and monitor as students write.)
6. Read your paragraph to your partner._
7. If you included wording from the question in your answer and added evidence from the article, award yourself four points for writing._
8. (Engage students in a discussion. Award four points to students who are active participants in the discussion.)

APPLICATION LESSON

14

ACTIVITY H *Comprehension—Single-Paragraph Answer*

Writing Strategy—Single-Paragraph Answer

Step 1: Read the item.
Step 2: Turn the question into part of the answer and write it down.
Step 3: Think of the answer or locate the answer in the article.
Step 4: Complete your answer.

Prompt:

What Is—Rainforests are being cut down at an alarming rate.

What If—What would happen if most of the earth's rainforests were cut down? (Hint: Think about ecosystems, energy and matter, and weather.)

Write and Discuss: Write a paragraph. Then share your ideas. Use the Discussion Guidelines.

Discussion Guidelines

Speaker		Listener	
Looks like:	**Sounds like:**	**Looks like:**	**Sounds like:**
• Facing peers • Making eye contact • Participating	• Using pleasant, easy-to-hear voice • Sharing opinions, supporting facts and reasons from the article and from your experience • Staying on the topic	• Facing speaker • Making eye contact • Participating	• Waiting quietly to speak • Giving positive, supportive comments • Disagreeing respectfully

WRITING DISCUSSION

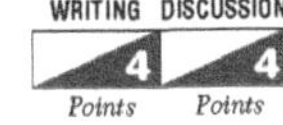

Points Points

182 *REWARDS Plus: Reading Strategies Applied to Science Passages*

Note H-2: If your students are having difficulty writing the *What If* paragraphs, read or show them the following example paragraph:

Example Single-Paragraph Answer

Many startling and perhaps irreversible changes would happen to the earth if most of the earth's rainforests were cut down. First, if the rainforests were cut down, that ecosystem would be affected. There would be no plants to complete the critical processes of photosynthesis and cellular respiration. Without food and oxygen in the air, animals in the ecosystem would not be able to survive. However, the results of deforestation would go way beyond the ecosystem if the destruction were widespread. Deforestation would result in a change in the gases put into the atmosphere and in the earth's temperature. These factors, in turn, would affect the earth's climate and contribute to global warming. Taken to its full extent, deforestation could have an effect on the weather in all ecosystems and on their plants and animals.

Application Lesson 15

Materials Needed:

- *Student Book*: Application Lesson 15
- Application Overhead Transparencies 70–74
- Appendix B Reproducible O: Application Lesson 15
- Appendix C Optional Vocabulary Activity: Application Lesson 15
- Paper or cardboard to use when covering the overhead transparency
- Paper or cardboard for each student to use during spelling dictation
- Washable overhead transparency pen

Text Treatment Notes:

- Black text signifies teacher script (exact wording to say to students).
- Green text in parentheses signifies directions or prompts for the teacher.
- Green text signifies answers or examples of answers.
- Green graphics treatment signifies reproduction of Overhead information.
- Green text and green graphics treatment do not appear in the *Student Book*.

ACTIVITY A

Vocabulary

ACTIVITY PROCEDURE, List 1

(See the *Student Book*, page 183.)

Tell students each word in the list. Then, have students repeat the word and read the definition aloud For each definition, provide any additional information that may be necessary. Then, have students practice reading the words themselves.

Use Overhead 70: Activity A
List 1: Tell

1. (Show the top half of Overhead 70.) Before we read the passage, let's read the difficult words. (Point to **industrialized**.) The first word is **industrialized**. What word?_ Now, read the definition._
2. (Point to **Exxon Valdez**) The next words are **Exxon Valdez**. What words?_ Now, read the definition._
3. (Pronounce each word in List 1, and then have students repeat each word and read the definition.)
4. Open your *Student Book* to **Application Lesson 15**, page 183._
5. Find **Activity A**, **List 1**, in your book._ Let's read the words again. First word._ Next words._ (Continue for all words in List 1.)

ACTIVITY PROCEDURE, List 2

(See the *Student Book*, page 183.)

Have students circle prefixes and suffixes, then underline the vowels. Using the overhead transparency, assist students in checking their work. Next, have students figure out each word to themselves, then say it aloud. Have them read the definition aloud.

Use Overhead 70: Activity A
List 2: Strategy Practice

1. Find **List 2**. Circle the prefixes and suffixes, and underline the vowels. Look up when you are done._
2. (Show the bottom half of Overhead 70.) Before you check your work on List 2, look at item #6. (Point to the second example and the **ize** that is circled.) From now on, you can also circle **ize**. The suffix is /ize/. Say it._ Now, go back to item #1. Check and fix any mistakes._
3. Go back to the first word again._ Sound out the word to yourself. Put your thumb up when you can read the word. Be sure that it is a real word._ What word?_ Now, read the definition._
4. (Continue Step 3 with all remaining words in List 2.)

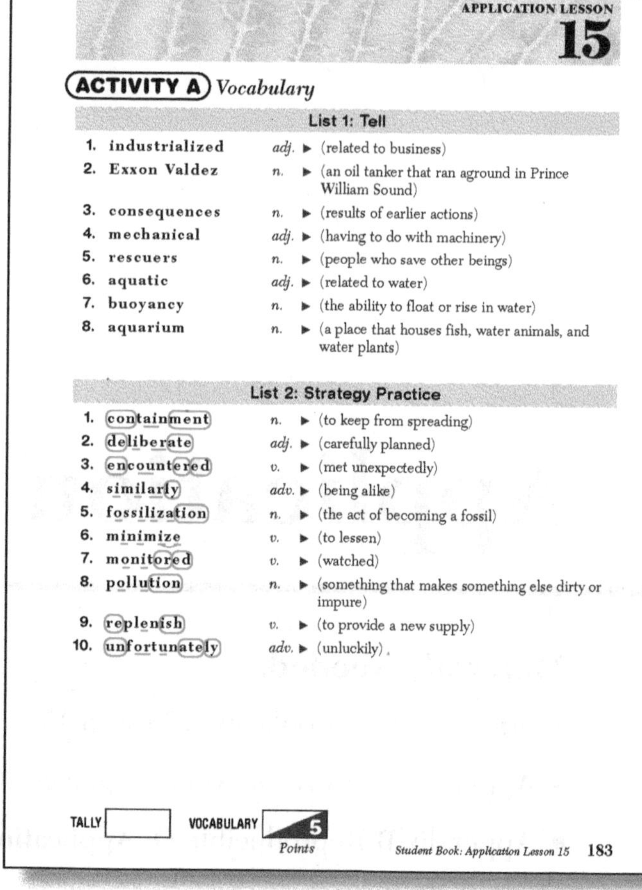

APPLICATION LESSON **15**

ACTIVITY A *Vocabulary*

List 1: Tell

1.	**industrialized**	*adj.*	► (related to business)
2.	**Exxon Valdez**	*n.*	► (an oil tanker that ran aground in Prince William Sound)
3.	**consequences**	*n.*	► (results of earlier actions)
4.	**mechanical**	*adj.*	► (having to do with machinery)
5.	**rescuers**	*n.*	► (people who save other beings)
6.	**aquatic**	*adj.*	► (related to water)
7.	**buoyancy**	*n.*	► (the ability to float or rise in water)
8.	**aquarium**	*n.*	► (a place that houses fish, water animals, and water plants)

List 2: Strategy Practice

1.	**containment**	*n.*	► (to keep from spreading)
2.	**deliberate**	*adj.*	► (carefully planned)
3.	**encountered**	*v.*	► (met unexpectedly)
4.	**similarly**	*adv.*	► (being alike)
5.	**fossilization**	*n.*	► (the act of becoming a fossil)
6.	**minimize**	*v.*	► (to lessen)
7.	**monitored**	*v.*	► (watched)
8.	**pollution**	*n.*	► (something that makes something else dirty or impure)
9.	**replenish**	*v.*	► (to provide a new supply)
10.	**unfortunately**	*adv.*	► (unluckily)

TALLY VOCABULARY 5 Points

Student Book: Application Lesson 15 183

Note A.2-1: You may wish to provide additional practice by having students read words to a partner.

ACTIVITY PROCEDURE, List 1 and 2

(See the *Student Book*, page 183.)

Tell students to look in List 1 or List 2 for a word you are thinking about. Have them circle the number of the word and tell you the word. Explain to students to make a tally mark for each correct word in the Tally box, and then enter the number of tally marks as points in the blank half of the Vocabulary box.

1. Remember, the words I'm thinking about will be in either List 1 or List 2. Make a tally mark for every correctly identified word.
2. Circle the number of the appropriate word.
   - Actions that are carefully planned are these kinds of actions. (Wait.) What word? **deliberate**
   - If you met someone unexpectedly, you did this to that person. (Wait.) What word? **encountered**
   - Someone's actions that are watched closely are this. (Wait.) What word? **monitored**
   - The ability to float or rise in water is called this. (Wait.) What word? **buoyancy**
   - When you provide a new supply of something, you do this to that thing. (Wait.) What word? **replenish**
3. Count all the tally marks, and enter that number as points in the blank half of the Vocabulary box.

ACTIVITY PROCEDURE, List 3

(See the *Student Book*, page 184.)

The words in the third list are related. Have students use the *REWARDS* Strategies to figure out the first word in each family. Have them read the definition of the verb and then read nouns and adjectives that are related to that verb.

Use Overhead 71: Activity A
List 3: Word Families

1. Turn to page 184._ Find **Family 1** in **List 3.** Figure out the first word. Use your pencil if you wish. Put your thumb up when you know the word._ What word?_ Read the definition._
2. Look at the noun in Family 1. Figure out the word._ What word?_
3. Look at the adjective in Family 1. Figure out the word._ What word?_
4. (Repeat Steps 1–3 for all word families in List 3.)

Note A.3-1: You may wish to provide additional practice by having students read a word family to the group or to a partner.

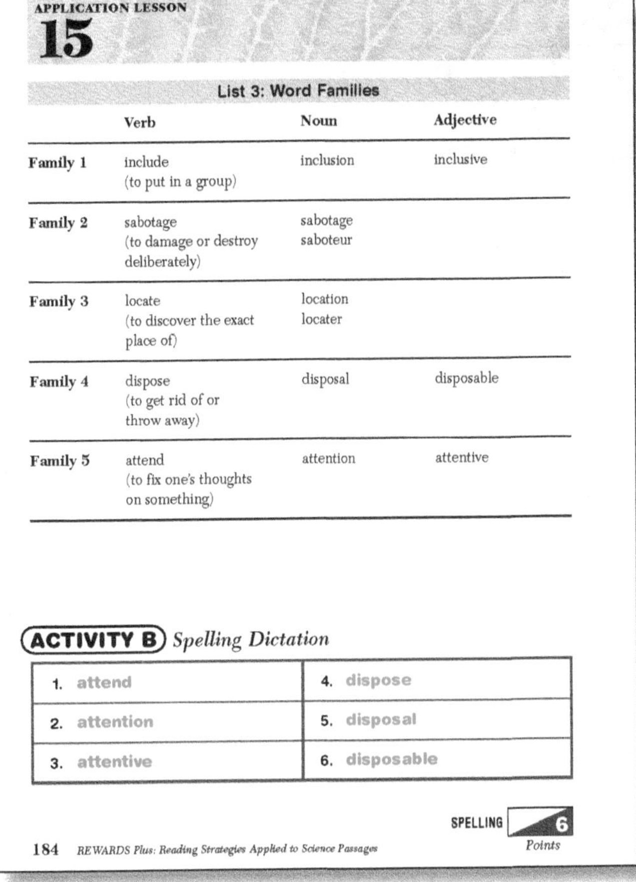

APPLICATION LESSON
15

List 3: Word Families

	Verb	Noun	Adjective
Family 1	include (to put in a group)	inclusion	inclusive
Family 2	sabotage (to damage or destroy deliberately)	sabotage saboteur	
Family 3	locate (to discover the exact place of)	location locater	
Family 4	dispose (to get rid of or throw away)	disposal	disposable
Family 5	attend (to fix one's thoughts on something)	attention	attentive

ACTIVITY B *Spelling Dictation*

1. attend	4. dispose
2. attention	5. disposal
3. attentive	6. disposable

SPELLING 6 Points

184 *REWARDS Plus: Reading Strategies Applied to Science Passages*

Note A.3-2: An additional vocabulary practice activity called Quick Words is provided in Appendix C of this Teacher's Guide. See Appendix C for information about how this optional activity can be used.

ACTIVITY B

Spelling Dictation

ACTIVITY PROCEDURE

(See the *Student Book*, page 184.)

For each word, tell students the word, then have students say the parts of the word to themselves while they write the word. Using the overhead transparency, assist students in checking their spelling and correcting if they misspelled. Then, have students enter the number of correctly spelled words as points in the blank half of the Spelling box.

Note B-1: Distribute a piece of light cardboard to each of the students.

Use Overhead 71: Activity B

1. Find **Activity B.**
2. The first word is **attend**. What word?_ Say the parts in **attend** to yourself as you write the word. (Pause and monitor.)
3. (Show **attend** on the overhead.) Check **attend**. If you misspelled it, cross it out and write it correctly.
4. The second word is **attention**. What word?_ Say the parts in **attention** to yourself as you write the word. (Pause and monitor.)
5. (Show **attention** on the overhead.) Check **attention**. If you misspelled it, cross it out and write it correctly.
6. (Repeat the procedures for the words **attentive**, **dispose**, **disposal**, and **disposable**.)
7. Count the number of words you spelled correctly, and record that number as points in the blank half of the Spelling box at the bottom of the page.

APPLICATION LESSON

15

List 3: Word Families

	Verb	Noun	Adjective
Family 1	include (to put in a group)	inclusion	inclusive
Family 2	sabotage (to damage or destroy deliberately)	sabotage saboteur	
Family 3	locate (to discover the exact place of)	location locater	
Family 4	dispose (to get rid of or throw away)	disposal	disposable
Family 5	attend (to fix one's thoughts on something)	attention	attentive

ACTIVITY B *Spelling Dictation*

1. attend	4. dispose
2. attention	5. disposal
3. attentive	6. disposable

184 *REWARDS Plus: Reading Strategies Applied to Science Passages*

SPELLING

6

Points

ACTIVITY C

Passage Reading and Comprehension

ACTIVITY PROCEDURE

(See the *Student Book*, pages 185–187.)

Have students read the title of the passage and each heading. Have them tell their partners two things the passage will tell about.

Passage Preview

1. Turn to page 185._ Let's preview the passage.
2. Read the title._ What is the whole passage going to tell about?_
3. Now, let's read the headings. Read the first heading._ Read the next heading._ (Continue until students have read all headings.)
4. Turn to your partner. Without looking, tell two things this passage will tell about._

ACTIVITY PROCEDURE

Provide students with an Information Web from Appendix B. Have students read the passage silently to each embedded number, and then reread the same information orally either to a partner, together as a group, or individually. Ask the corresponding comprehension question or questions. Once students finish reading a section labeled A, B, C, D, E, or F, have them fill in the Information Web before going on to the next section.

Note C-1: If students do not finish reading the passage during class, have them use their Information Webs to review the information at the beginning of the next class.

Use Overhead 72: Activity C

Passage Reading

1. (Provide an Information Web for each student.)
2. Turn back to the beginning of the passage. You are going to read the passage and answer questions about what you have read. During passage reading, you are also going to fill in an Information Web to help you remember the important details of the passage. Later, you will use this Web to review the content of the passage with your partner.
3. Read the title._

APPLICATION LESSON **15**

ACTIVITY C *Passage Reading and Comprehension*

Note: For this activity, you will need Reproducible O found in the *Teacher's Guide*.

Oil Spills

A
Oil is a resource that is used by most people in the world to some extent.
16 The United States, Canada, Australia, Great Britain, Germany, and other
26 industrialized countries, however, use great quantities of oil. Because oil is the
38 end result of a long natural process called **fossilization**, it takes many years for oil
53 to be formed. Oil is found only in certain areas of the world, including the
68 bottoms of oceans. It can be very expensive to remove the oil from the ground
83 and from under the ocean floor. (#1)

B
89 **Causes of Oil Spills**
93 Once oil is removed, it must be transported to the country where it is going
108 to be used. Huge ships, called **oil tankers**, transport oil over the world's
121 waterways. Unfortunately, accidents occur, and oil is spilled into the seas and
133 waterways. In March of 1989, the Exxon Valdez oil tanker ran aground in Prince
147 William Sound, Alaska. Almost 11 million gallons of oil spilled out of the tanker
161 and into the water. That's enough oil to fill up 430 classrooms! Although that was
176 the largest tanker spill in the waters of the United States, nearly 14,000 oil spills
191 occur worldwide each year. (#2)
195 Sometimes the spills are caused by mistakes on the part of people. For
208 example, the Exxon Valdez ran aground because the man steering the boat did
221 not follow an order to change his course. Sometimes spills are a result of bad
236 equipment or old ships. Poor weather conditions can cause a ship to run
249 aground and spill oil. Oil spills can also be the result of deliberate sabotage or
264 illegal dumping. (#3)

C
266 **Consequences of Oil Spills**
270 The spilled oil spreads out across the surface of the water, where it floats in a
286 thin layer called an **oil slick**. As it spreads more and more thinly, it resembles a
302 rainbow on the surface of the water. This rainbow is called a **sheen**.
315 Oil spills can be extremely dangerous for marine animals. Marine mammals
326 and birds depend on their fur and feathers to keep them warm and dry. When
341 their fur or feathers become oiled, they lose the ability to repel water. The
355 animals can no longer keep warm or float as easily. Animals and birds may also
370 ingest (swallow) the oil when they try to clean themselves. The oil can poison

Student Book: Application Lesson 15 185

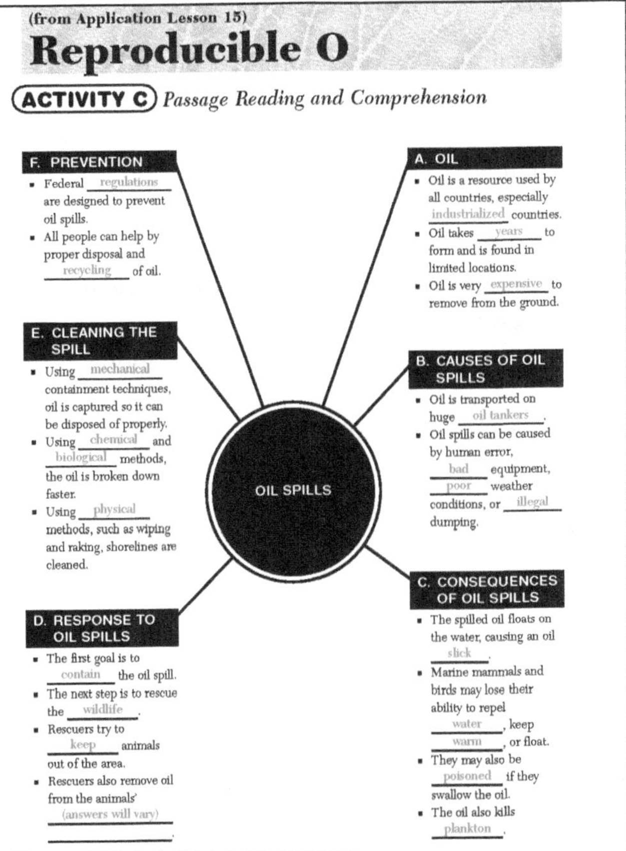
(from Application Lesson 15)

Reproducible O

ACTIVITY C *Passage Reading and Comprehension*

OIL SPILLS

A. OIL
- Oil is a resource used by all countries, especially industrialized countries.
- Oil takes years to form and is found in limited locations.
- Oil is very expensive to remove from the ground.

B. CAUSES OF OIL SPILLS
- Oil is transported on huge oil tankers.
- Oil spills can be caused by human error, bad equipment, poor weather conditions, or illegal dumping.

C. CONSEQUENCES OF OIL SPILLS
- The spilled oil floats on the water, causing an oil slick.
- Marine mammals and birds may lose their ability to repel water, keep warm, or float.
- They may also be poisoned if they swallow the oil.
- The oil also kills plankton.

D. RESPONSE TO OIL SPILLS
- The first goal is to contain the oil spill.
- The next step is to rescue the wildlife.
- Rescuers try to keep animals out of the area.
- Rescuers also remove oil from the animals' (answers will vary)

E. CLEANING THE SPILL
- Using mechanical containment techniques, oil is captured so it can be disposed of properly.
- Using chemical and biological methods, the oil is broken down faster.
- Using physical methods, such as wiping and raking, shorelines are cleaned.

F. PREVENTION
- Federal regulations are designed to prevent oil spills.
- All people can help by proper disposal and recycling of oil.

400 • REWARDS Plus: Reading Strategies Applied to Science Passages

4. Read down to number 1 silently. Look up when you are done._
5. (Wait for students to complete the reading. Then have students reread the part orally.)
6. (Ask the question or questions associated with the number. Provide feedback to students regarding their answers.)
7. (Repeat Steps 4–6 for all paragraphs in Section A.)
8. Now, look at your Information Web.
9. With your partner, fill in the blanks for Section A. You can refer back to the passage for information. Look up when you are done._ (Move around the room and monitor students as they complete the section.)
10. (When the majority of students have finished, show Overhead 72.) Look at the overhead and check your work. Fix up or add to your answers.
11. Now read down to the next number silently. Look up when you are done._
12. (Repeat steps 5–11 until the students have finished the passage and the Information Web.)
13. Use your Information Web to retell the important information to your partner.

Comprehension Questions

#1 Why does it take so long for oil to be formed?

Because it is the end result of fossilization, which is a long process.

#2 What was the largest tanker spill in U.S. waters? How many gallons of oil were spilled?

The Exxon Valdez in Alaska; 11 million gallons.

#3 What are some of the causes of oil spills?

Bad equipment, old ships, human error, poor weather conditions, illegal dumping, and/or deliberate sabotage.

APPLICATION LESSON **15**

ACTIVITY C *Passage Reading and Comprehension*

Note: For this activity, you will need Reproducible O found in the *Teacher's Guide.*

Oil Spills

A

Oil is a resource that is used by most people in the world to some extent. The United States, Canada, Australia, Great Britain, Germany, and other industrialized countries, however, use great quantities of oil. Because oil is the end result of a long natural process called **fossilization**, it takes many years for oil to be formed. Oil is found only in certain areas of the world, including the bottoms of oceans. It can be very expensive to remove the oil from the ground and from under the ocean floor. (#1)

B

Causes of Oil Spills

Once oil is removed, it must be transported to the country where it is going to be used. Huge ships, called **oil tankers**, transport oil over the world's waterways. Unfortunately, accidents occur, and oil is spilled into the seas and waterways. In March of 1989, the Exxon Valdez oil tanker ran aground in Prince William Sound, Alaska. Almost 11 million gallons of oil spilled out of the tanker and into the water. That's enough oil to fill up 430 classrooms! Although that was the largest tanker spill in the waters of the United States, nearly 14,000 oil spills occur worldwide each year. (#2)

Sometimes the spills are caused by mistakes on the part of people. For example, the Exxon Valdez ran aground because the man steering the boat did not follow an order to change his course. Sometimes spills are a result of bad equipment or old ships. Poor weather conditions can cause a ship to run aground and spill oil. Oil spills can also be the result of deliberate sabotage or illegal dumping. (#3)

C

Consequences of Oil Spills

The spilled oil spreads out across the surface of the water, where it floats in a thin layer called an **oil slick**. As it spreads more and more thinly, it resembles a rainbow on the surface of the water. This rainbow is called a **sheen**.

Oil spills can be extremely dangerous for marine animals. Marine mammals and birds depend on their fur and feathers to keep them warm and dry. When their fur or feathers become oiled, they lose the ability to repel water. The animals can no longer keep warm or float as easily. Animals and birds may also ingest (swallow) the oil when they try to clean themselves. The oil can poison

Student Book: Application Lesson 15 185

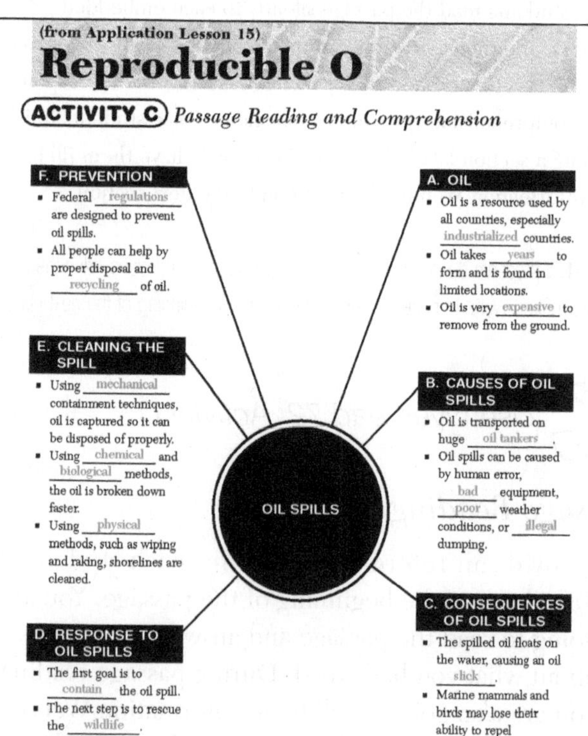
(from Application Lesson 15)

Reproducible O

ACTIVITY C *Passage Reading and Comprehension*

OIL SPILLS

A. OIL
- Oil is a resource used by all countries, especially industrialized countries.
- Oil takes years to form and is found in limited locations.
- Oil is very expensive to remove from the ground.

B. CAUSES OF OIL SPILLS
- Oil is transported on huge oil tankers.
- Oil spills can be caused by human error, bad equipment, poor weather conditions, or illegal dumping.

C. CONSEQUENCES OF OIL SPILLS
- The spilled oil floats on the water, causing an oil slick.
- Marine mammals and birds may lose their ability to repel water, keep warm, or float.
- They may also be poisoned if they swallow the oil.
- The oil also kills plankton.

D. RESPONSE TO OIL SPILLS
- The first goal is to contain the oil spill.
- The next step is to rescue the wildlife.
- Rescuers try to keep animals out of the area.
- Rescuers also remove oil from the animals' (answers will vary)

E. CLEANING THE SPILL
- Using mechanical containment techniques, oil is captured so it can be disposed of properly.
- Using chemical and biological methods, the oil is broken down faster.
- Using physical methods, such as wiping and raking, shorelines are cleaned.

F. PREVENTION
- Federal regulations are designed to prevent oil spills.
- All people can help by proper disposal and recycling of oil.

400 ▪ REWARDS Plus: Reading Strategies Applied to Science Passages

#4 How does an oil spill affect marine animals and birds?
Oil gets on their fur and feathers and makes it so they cannot repel water; they cannot keep warm or float easily; can poison them; can cause reproductive problems.

#5 How does containment of contaminated areas help the efforts to clean up?
Limits the amount of damage.

#6 What do rescuers do to keep animals away from a contaminated area? How do they help those animals that are affected?
Use devices designed to scare wildlife away from a given area; capture affected animals; flush oil from eyes and intestines, wash feathers or fur.

#7 What happens to the animals after they've received care?
Some are tagged and released; some are too young or still sick and cannot be released on their own and are often sent to an aquarium or wildlife center for more care.

#8 What methods are used to clean up a contaminated area after an oil spill?
Mechanical containment, chemical and biological methods to change composition of oil so it breaks down faster, and physical methods such as wiping, washing, scrubbing, and raking.

#9 Where does most oil pollution of water come from?
From mishandling oil products, such as pouring oil down drains.

384 them. Similarly, fish and bottom-dwellers may experience the oil as toxic and
397 may develop long-term diseases or reproductive problems. An even more
408 serious consequence results when oil kills the plankton. **Plankton** are tiny
419 organisms that produce much of our oxygen and serve as the base of aquatic
433 food webs. (#4)

D

435 **Response to Oil Spills**
439 The first step in reducing the impact of an oil spill is to contain the spill at its
457 source. Containment helps to limit the amount of damage the spill causes.
469 Local, state, and federal agencies as well as volunteers move into the area
482 immediately. The next step is to begin wildlife rescue and clean-up efforts. (#5)
495 Rescuers begin by trying to keep unharmed wildlife away from contaminated
506 areas. They use devices designed to scare wildlife away from a given area. Then
520 rescuers turn their attention to the wildlife that has already encountered the oil.
533 Birds and marine mammals are captured by wildlife experts and taken to nearby
546 treatment centers. At these centers, officials and volunteers do their best to
558 flush oil from the animals' eyes and intestines and to minimize the stress such a
573 crisis can cause. Special procedures are used for gradually washing the oil out of
587 animals' feathers or fur and allowing their bodies to replenish the natural oils
600 necessary to provide warmth and buoyancy. (#6)
606 The animals' health and nutrition are carefully monitored to help the natural
618 healing process. After they have regained their health and their body coverings
630 have returned to normal, the animals may be tagged for tracking, and then
643 released into an appropriate habitat. Sometimes, if animals are very sick, or too
656 young to be released on their own, they may be given to an aquarium or a
672 wildlife center for care. (#7)

E

676 **Cleaning the Spill**
679 Depending on the location and conditions of the spill, several techniques can
691 be used to clean it up. Mechanical containment techniques include equipment
702 designed to capture the spilled oil so that it can be disposed of properly.
716 Chemical and biological methods are used to change the composition of the oil
729 and help it break down faster. Physical methods are used to clean up shorelines.
743 These methods include wiping, washing, scrubbing, and raking the oil. (#8)

F

753 **Prevention**
754 Federal regulations are designed to help prevent large-scale spills like that of
767 the Exxon Valdez. Most oil pollution of water, however, comes from the
779 mishandling of oil products. Although 37 million gallons of oil are spilled into
792 the ocean each year, regular people pour over 360 million gallons of oil down
806 drains that lead to waterways. Proper disposal and recycling of used oils can go a
821 long way toward helping to prevent oil pollution in the water. (#9)
832

ACTIVITY D *Fluency Building*

Cold Timing		Practice 1	
Practice 2		Hot Timing	

ACTIVITY D

Fluency Building

ACTIVITY PROCEDURE

(See the *Student Book*, page 187.)

Have students complete a Cold Timing, one or two practices, and a Hot Timing of the Activity C article. For each timing, have students record the number of correct words read. Finally, have students complete their Fluency Graphs.

Note D-1: When assigning partners for this activity, have the stronger reader read first. As a result, the other reader will have one additional practice opportunity.

1. Now, it's time for fluency building.
2. Find the beginning of the passage again. (Pause.)
3. Whisper-read. See how many words you can read in one minute. Begin._ (Time students for one minute.) Stop._ Circle the last word that you read._ Record the number of words you read after **Cold Timing** in **Activity D** at the bottom of page 187._
4. Let's practice again. Begin._ (Time students for one minute.) Stop._ Put a box around the last word that you read._ Record the number of words you read after **Practice 1**._
5. (Optional) Let's practice one more time before the Hot Timing. Begin._ (Time students for one minute.) Stop._ Put a box around the last word that you read._ Record the number of words you read after **Practice 2**._
6. Please exchange books with your partner._ Partner 1, you are going to read first. Partner 2, listen carefully and underline any mistakes or words left out. Ones, begin._ (Time students for one minute.) Stop._ Twos, cross out the last word that your partner read._ (Assist students in subtracting the number of mistakes from the number of words read.) Twos, record the number of correct words in your partner's book after **Hot Timing**._
7. Partner 2, you are going to read next. Partner 1, listen carefully and underline any mistakes or words left out. Twos, begin._ (Time students for one minute.) Stop._ Ones, cross out the last word that your partner read._ Ones, record the number of correct words in your partner's book after **Hot Timing**._
8. Exchange books._ Turn to the Fluency Graph on the inside back cover, and indicate on the graph the number of Cold Timing and Hot Timing words you read correctly._

APPLICATION LESSON **15**

E

676 **Cleaning the Spill**
679 Depending on the location and conditions of the spill, several techniques can
691 be used to clean it up. Mechanical containment techniques include equipment
702 designed to capture the spilled oil so that it can be disposed of properly.
716 Chemical and biological methods are used to change the composition of the oil
729 and help it break down faster. Physical methods are used to clean up shorelines.
743 These methods include wiping, washing, scrubbing, and raking the oil. (#8)

F

753 **Prevention**
754 Federal regulations are designed to help prevent large-scale spills like that of
767 the Exxon Valdez. Most oil pollution of water, however, comes from the
779 mishandling of oil products. Although 37 million gallons of oil are spilled into
792 the ocean each year, regular people pour over 360 million gallons of oil down
806 drains that lead to waterways. Proper disposal and recycling of used oils can go a
821 long way toward helping to prevent oil pollution in the water. (#9)
832

ACTIVITY D *Fluency Building*

Cold Timing		**Practice 1**	
Practice 2		**Hot Timing**	

Student Book: Application Lesson 15 **187**

ACTIVITY E

Comprehension Questions—Multiple Choice

ACTIVITY PROCEDURE

(See the *Student Book*, page 188.)

Have students complete item #1. Then, have students share the rationale for their answers. Encourage thoughtful discussion. Proceed item-by-item, emphasizing the rationale for the *best* answer. Have students record points for each correct item.

Note E-1: The correct Multiple Choice answers are circled.

1. Turn to page 188._ Find **Activity E**.
2. Use the Multiple Choice Strategy to complete item #1. Be ready to explain why you selected your answer. (Wait while students complete the item. Call on individual students. Ask them why they chose their answer and why they eliminated the other choices. Encourage discussion. Provide students with feedback on their choices, focusing on why or why not those choices might be appropriate.)
3. (Repeat Step 2 for items 2–4, pausing after each item to confirm student responses and provide feedback.)
4. Count the number of items you got correct, and record that number in the blank half of the Multiple Choice Comprehension box._

APPLICATION LESSON
15

ACTIVITY E *Comprehension Questions—Multiple Choice*

Comprehension Strategy—Multiple Choice

Step 1: Read the item.
Step 2: Read all of the choices.
Step 3: Think about why each choice might be correct or incorrect. Check the article as needed.
Step 4: From the possible correct choices, select the best answer.

1. (Cause and effect) **Which of these relationships is NOT accurate?**
   a. oil spill → oil on birds' feathers thus birds can't repel water thus can't keep warm.
   b. oil spill → oil on birds' feathers thus birds swallow oil when cleaning thus oil poisons them.
   c. oil spill → oil kills plankton thus food for ocean fish limited.
   (d.) oil spill → air is filled with oil thus birds can't breath air thus birds die of fumes.
2. (Cause and effect) **Oil spills are NOT caused by:**
   a. weather conditions that cause a ship to run aground.
   (b.) oil seeping out of the floor of the ocean.
   c. human mistakes on oil carriers.
   d. illegal dumping of oil from a ship.
3. (Main idea) **Which of these titles would best indicate the content covered in this article?**
   a. Oil Spills: Value and Danger
   b. Oil Spills: Whose Fault Is It?
   (c.) Oil Spills: Causes, Results, Solutions
   d. Oil Spills: Consequences to the Environment
4. (Cause and effect) **Which one of these would probably be the best plan for reducing the damage done by oil?**
   a. Try to reduce oil spills by improving the ships that carry oil, the weather information available to ships, and the quality of their crew.
   b. Improve the procedures for containing an oil spill at its source.
   c. Train rescuers to use a variety of devices to keep wildlife out of the contaminated area.
   (d.) Try to get people to stop pouring oil down drains that lead to waterways.

MULTIPLE CHOICE COMPREHENSION 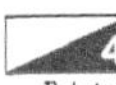
Points

188 *REWARDS Plus: Reading Strategies Applied to Science Passages*

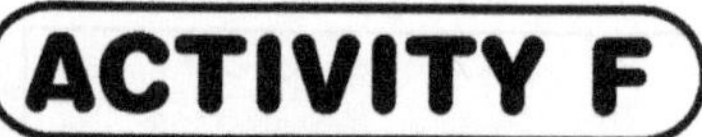

Vocabulary Activities

ACTIVITY PROCEDURE

(See the *Student Book*, pages 189–190.)

Have students complete each item orally and provide feedback on their answers. Then have students respond to each question in writing by answering "yes" or "no" and providing a reason for their answers.

Yes/No/Why

1. Turn to page 189._ Find **Activity F.**_ Read item #1. Tell your partner your answer and your reason for it._ (Wait. Call on individual students. Provide students with feedback, focusing on the reasons they give for their answers. Encourage discussion.)
2. Write your answer and your reason for it in the space provided._
3. (Repeat Steps 1–2 for the rest of the items.)

Note F-1: You may wish to do this as an oral task only rather than an oral and a written task.

APPLICATION LESSON 15

ACTIVITY F *Vocabulary*

Yes/No/Why

1. Would **containment** of **industrialized** nations **minimize** resource usage?
Example answer: Yes. Industrialized nations tend to use more resources than other nations.

2. Would **deliberate monitoring** of the **Exxon Valdez** have reduced the **consequences?**
Example answer: Yes. Someone monitoring the Exxon Valdez would have noticed that the man steering the boat was not following an order.

3. Does **pollution replenish aquariums?**
Example answer: No. Pollution is something that makes another thing dirty. It does not provide anything new to aquariums.

Student Book: Application Lesson 15 189

ACTIVITY PROCEDURE

Have students read the words and definitions and then complete the sentence stems for each vocabulary word. Have them share answers with partners and with the class. Then, have students give themselves points in the blank half of the Vocabulary box.

Completion Activity

1. Turn to page 190._ Read the first word and its definition._
2. Now, read the sentence stem._
3. Think of how you would complete the sentence stem and write it._ Share your answer with your partner._ (Call on a few students to share answers with the class.)
4. (Repeat Steps 1–3 for the rest of the words.)
5. If you participated in answering all seven questions, give yourself seven points in the blank half of the Vocabulary box.

Note F-2: You may wish to do this as an oral task only rather than an oral task and a written task.

APPLICATION LESSON 15

Completion Activities

1. **sabotage:** to damage or destroy deliberately
Some ways that you could sabotage getting a good grade in a class would include
Answers will vary

2. **locate:** to discover the exact place of
When trying to locate a specific fact, you might
Answers will vary

3. **dispose:** to get rid of or throw away
Some things that you should <u>never</u> dispose of include
Answers will vary

4. **monitored:** watched
One thing that would need to be carefully monitored is
Answers will vary

VOCABULARY 7 Points

190 *REWARDS Plus: Reading Strategies Applied to Science Passages*

ACTIVITY G

Expository Writing—Multi-Paragraph Answer

ACTIVITY PROCEDURE, Plan and Write

(See the *Student Book*, pages 191–193.)

Have students read the prompt. Guide students as they determine the three topics and **LIST** details for topics a, b, and c. Have students look at topic a again. Have students **CROSS OUT** details that don't go with the topic. Have students **CONNECT** details as shown in the example plan. Have students **NUMBER** their details, and then compare with the example plan for topic a. Next, have students **WRITE** paragraph a. Repeat for topics b and c. Finally, explain that after the answer is written, they should **EDIT** their work, revising for clarity and proofreading for errors in capitalization, punctuation, and spelling.

Use Overheads 73 and 74: Activity G

1. Turn to page 191. Find **Activity G.**
2. Find the prompt in the middle of the page. Read the prompt out loud with me: **Describe the causes, consequences, and responses to oil spills.**
3. Reread the prompt and determine three topics. Record the topics in your Planning Box. Compare your topics with your partner. (Move around the room and assist students in determining the topics.)
4. Look back in the article and locate details that go with each topic. Record the details in the Planning Box.
5. Use the steps for topic a. **Cross out** any details that do not go with the topic, draw brackets to **connect** details that could go into one sentence, and **number** the details in a logical order.
6. (Show Overhead 73.) Look at the example plan for topic a on the overhead. Yours should be similar.
7. Take out a blank piece of paper. **Write** paragraph a. Please reread and **edit** your paragraph. (Move around the room and monitor your students as they are writing.)
8. (When the majority of students are done, proceed with the lesson.) Use the steps for topic b.
9. Look at the example plan for topic b on the overhead. Yours should be similar.

APPLICATION LESSON **15**

ACTIVITY G *Expository Writing—Multi-Paragraph Answer*

Writing Strategy—Multi-Paragraph Answer

Step 1: LIST (List the details that are important enough to include in your answer.)
Step 2: CROSS OUT (Reread the details. Cross out any that don't go with the topic.)
Step 3: CONNECT (Connect any details that could go into one sentence.)
Step 4: NUMBER (Number the details in a logical order.)
Step 5: WRITE (Write the paragraph.)
Step 6: EDIT (Revise and proofread your answer.)

Prompt: Describe the causes, consequences, and responses to oil spills.

Plan: Complete the Planning Box.

Student Book: Application Lesson 15 191

APPLICATION LESSON **15**

Example Multi-Paragraph Plan

Planning Box	
(topic a)	*oil spills—causes*
① (detail)	– *oil must be transported to the country where it will be used*
① (detail)	– *when being transported, accidents may happen*
② (detail)	– *caused by mistakes of people*
② (detail)	– *caused by inadequate equipment*
② (detail)	– *caused by poor weather conditions*
③ (detail)	– *deliberate dumping of oil*
(topic b)	*oil spills—consequences*
(detail)	– ~~*caused by people's actions*~~
① (detail)	– *spilled oil spreads out over water—oil slick*
② (detail)	– *gets on the feathers and fur of animals*
② (detail)	– *animals can't stay warm or float*
③ (detail)	– *ingested oil can poison fish*
④ (detail)	– *kills plankton—food for other organisms*
(topic c)	*oil spills—responses*
① (detail)	– *contain spill*
② (detail)	– *keep wildlife away from contaminated area*
③ (detail)	– *capture and treat birds and marine mammals that have been affected by oil*
④ (detail)	– *flush oil from eyes and intestines*
④ (detail)	– *wash fur and feathers*
⑤ (detail)	– *release when health regained*

Write: Write paragraphs a, b, and c on a separate piece of paper.

192 *REWARDS Plus: Reading Strategies Applied to Science Passages*

10. **Write** paragraph b. When you finish, **edit** your paragraph._ (Move around the room and monitor your students as they are writing.)
11. (When the majority of students are done, proceed with the lesson.) Use the steps for topic c._
12. Look at the example plan for topic c on the overhead. Yours should be similar._
13. **Write** paragraph c. When you finish, **edit** your paragraph._ (Move around the room and monitor your students as they are writing.)
14. (When the majority of students are done, proceed with the lesson.) Please carefully read your paragraphs. Be sure that your paragraphs are easy to understand and clear. Proofread for any errors in capitalization, punctuation, and spelling._ (Give students time to proofread their paragraphs.)

ACTIVITY PROCEDURE, Evaluate

Ask students to read each question in the rubric. Guide them in evaluating the paragraphs using the guidelines. Have students total their points and record them in the blank half of the Writing box.

15. Turn to page 193._ Let's evaluate paragraphs a, b, and c.
16. Check paragraphs a, b, and c carefully and answer questions 1 through 3._
17. Reread your paragraphs._ Circle "Yes" if your paragraphs are easy to understand._
18. Carefully examine your paragraphs. If you think a word is misspelled, underline it and check back in the plan or article and correct the spelling._ Circle "Yes" if you believe that you have very few spelling errors._
19. Carefully examine your sentences. Be sure that each sentence begins with a capital._ If all sentences begin with a capital, circle "Yes."_
20. Examine your sentences. Be sure that each sentence ends with a period._ If all sentences end with a period, circle "Yes."_
21. Count up your points and record them in the Writing box._
22. (Show Overhead 74.) Look at the overhead._ Let's read the three example paragraphs. Yours should be similar. (Read the paragraphs to your students or with your students or call on a student to read the example paragraph.)

Note G-1: The rubric can be used in a variety of ways. You may wish to have students evaluate their own paragraphs or have partners provide feedback, and then use the second column of the rubric for teacher feedback. You may wish to give students bonus points based on your feedback.

APPLICATION LESSON
15

Example Multi-Paragraph Plan

Planning Box
(topic a) *oil spills—causes*
① (detail) – *oil must be transported to the country where it will be used*
(detail) – *when being transported, accidents may happen*
② (detail) – *caused by mistakes of people*
(detail) – *caused by inadequate equipment*
(detail) – *caused by poor weather conditions*
③ (detail) – *deliberate dumping of oil*
(topic b) *oil spills—consequences*
(detail) ~~*caused by people's actions*~~
① (detail) – *spilled oil spreads out over water—oil slick*
② (detail) – *gets on the feathers and fur of animals*
(detail) – *animals can't stay warm or float*
③ (detail) – *ingested oil can poison fish*
④ (detail) – *kills plankton—food for other organisms*
(topic c) *oil spills—responses*
① (detail) – *contain spill*
② (detail) – *keep wildlife away from contaminated area*
③ (detail) – *capture and treat birds and marine mammals that have been affected by oil*
④ (detail) – *flush oil from eyes and intestines*
(detail) – *wash fur and feathers*
⑤ (detail) – *release when health regained*

Write: Write paragraphs a, b, and c on a separate piece of paper.

APPLICATION LESSON
15

Evaluate: Evaluate the paragraphs using this rubric.

Rubric—Multi-Paragraph Answer	Student or Partner Rating	Teacher Rating
1. Did the author state the topic in the first sentence?	a. (Yes) Fix up b. (Yes) Fix up c. (Yes) Fix up	a. Yes No b. Yes No c. Yes No
2. Did the author include details that go with the topic?	a. (Yes) Fix up b. (Yes) Fix up c. (Yes) Fix up	a. Yes No b. Yes No c. Yes No
3. Did the author combine details in some of the sentences?	a. (Yes) Fix up b. (Yes) Fix up c. (Yes) Fix up	a. Yes No b. Yes No c. Yes No
4. Is the answer easy to understand?	(Yes) Fix up	Yes No
5. Did the author correctly spell words, particularly the words found in the article?	(Yes) Fix up	Yes No
6. Did the author use correct capitalization, capitalizing the first word in the sentence and proper names of people, places, and things?	(Yes) Fix up	Yes No
7. Did the author use correct punctuation, including a period at the end of each sentence?	(Yes) Fix up	Yes No

WRITING 13 Points

Comprehension—Single-Paragraph Answer

ACTIVITY PROCEDURE

(See the *Student Book*, page 194.)

Have students read the *What Is* statement and the *What If* question. Have students turn the question into part of the answer and write down a topic sentence for their answer. Then, have them complete their answer. Encourage them to use evidence from the article and their own experience and background knowledge. Engage students in a discussion. Award points for writing and participating in the discussion.

Note H-1: If you are working with students who have difficulty generating ideas for their paragraphs, switch the order of activities: engage the students in a discussion and then have them write their paragraphs.

1. Turn to page 194. Find **Activity H.**
2. Find the *What Is* statement in the middle of the page. Read it out loud with me: **In the movement of oil from one country to another, oil spills are a fairly frequent occurrence.**
3. Find the *What If* question. Read it with me: **What if you were asked to outline a plan to keep future oil spills from happening? What would you suggest?**
4. Think how you might turn the question into part of the answer. Tell me your idea for a topic sentence. (Example sentence: There are a number of things I would suggest to prevent future oil spills.) Take out a piece of paper and write your topic sentence. (Move around the room and monitor as students write.)
5. Add ideas to your paragraph. Use evidence from the article as well as your own experience and background knowledge. If you finish early, reread your paragraph and edit it so that it is easy to understand and clear. (Move around the room and monitor as students write.)
6. Read your paragraph to your partner. Look at the overhead. Let's read an example paragraph. Yours should be similar. (Read the paragraph to your students, with your students, or call on a student to read the paragraph.)
7. If you included wording from the question in your answer and added evidence from the article, award yourself four points for writing.

APPLICATION LESSON
15

ACTIVITY H *Comprehension—Single-Paragraph Answer*

Writing Strategy—Single-Paragraph Answer

Step 1: Read the item.
Step 2: Turn the question into part of the answer and write it down.
Step 3: Think of the answer or locate the answer in the article.
Step 4: Complete your answer.

Prompt:

What Is—In the movement of oil from one country to another, oil spills are a fairly frequent occurrence.

What if—What if you were asked to outline a plan to prevent future oil spills from happening? What would you suggest?

Write and Discuss: Write a paragraph. Then share your ideas. Use the Discussion Guidelines.

Discussion Guidelines

Speaker		Listener	
Looks like:	**Sounds like:**	**Looks like:**	**Sounds like:**
• Facing peers • Making eye contact • Participating	• Using pleasant, easy-to-hear voice • Sharing opinions, supporting facts and reasons from the article and from your experience • Staying on the topic	• Facing speaker • Making eye contact • Participating	• Waiting quietly to speak • Giving positive, supportive comments • Disagreeing respectfully

194 *REWARDS Plus: Reading Strategies Applied to Science Passages*

8. (Engage students in a discussion. Award four points to students who are active participants in the discussion.)

Note H-2: If your students are having difficulty writing the *What If* paragraphs, read or show them the following example paragraph:

Example Single-Paragraph Answer

To prevent future oil spills, I would suggest a number of things to do. One thing I would do is to have very careful inspections of the ships to insure that the equipment is adequate for such precarious trips. Second, I would have special certification for the sailors on board to guarantee their competency. Next, I would require that ships causing oil spills pay HUGE fines, thus making them more careful. However, the best way to prevent oil spills is to reduce the need for oil in certain countries. If oil-using countries switched to other methods of producing energy, less oil would need to be shipped, and oil spills would be reduced, if not stopped.

Blackline Masters for Overhead Transparencies

Review Lessons

(from Review Lesson 1)

Overhead A

ACTIVITY D *Strategy Instruction*

1. abstract	insist	impact
2. distraught	misfit	admit

ACTIVITY E *Strategy Practice*

1. birthday	misplay	discard
2. maintain	disband	indistinct
3. modern	addict	imprint
4. absurd	insert	railway

Overhead B

ACTIVITY D *Strategy Instruction*

1.	beside	readjust	prepay
2.	combine	provide	defraud

ACTIVITY E *Strategy Practice*

1.	backbone	reprint	costume
2.	mistake	promote	prescribe
3.	obsolete	propose	sunstroke
4.	decode	holiday	subscribe

(from Review Lesson 3)

Overhead C

ACTIVITY D *Strategy Practice*

1.	perturb	uncurl	confess
2.	afraid	expert	engrave

ACTIVITY E *Independent Strategy Practice*

1.	misinform	disagree	spellbound
2.	sweepstake	reproduce	protect
3.	turmoil	bemoan	discontent
4.	imperfect	boycott	reconstruct

(from Review Lesson 4)

Overhead D

ACTIVITY D Strategy Practice

1.	regardless	softness	unfortunate
2.	programmer	slowest	historical
3.	organism	inventor	personal

ACTIVITY E Independent Strategy Practice

1.	abnormal	respectful	proposal
2.	exaggerate	exhaust	untruthful
3.	careless	unfaithful	astonish
4.	alarmist	energetic	exclude

(from Review Lesson 5)

Overhead E

ACTIVITY D *Strategy Practice*

1.	advertisement	delightful	disinfectant
2.	intentionally	property	expressionless
3.	personality	admittance	incoherence

ACTIVITY E *Independent Strategy Practice*

1.	perfectionist	independently	dictionary
2.	contaminate	precautionary	deductive
3.	inconsistently	excitement	repulsive
4.	opinion	hoodwink	imperfect

(from Review Lesson 6)

Overhead F

ACTIVITY D *Strategy Practice*

1.	official	substantial	delicious
2.	pretentious	impressionable	incombustible
3.	conjecture	inconspicuous	disadvantage

ACTIVITY E *Independent Strategy Practice*

1.	administrative	performance	threadbare
2.	circumstantial	investigation	professionalism
3.	precipitation	environmentally	communication
4.	unconventional	consolidate	misconception

Blackline Masters for Overhead Transparencies

Application Lessons

(from Application Lesson 1)

Overhead 1

ACTIVITY A *Vocabulary*

List 1: Tell

1.	**scientists**	*n.*	▶ (people with expert knowledge of science)
2.	**universe**	*n.*	▶ (all things that exist, including our solar system and beyond)
3.	**organisms**	*n.*	▶ (all living things, including all plants and animals)
4.	**ecosystem**	*n.*	▶ (a living community of organisms and their physical environment)
5.	**climate**	*n.*	▶ (the pattern of weather conditions in an area or region)
6.	**bacteria**	*n.*	▶ (very tiny single-celled organisms)
7.	**fungus**	*n.*	▶ (a plant-like organism without leaves, flowers, or green coloring)
8.	**fungi**	*n.*	▶ (more than one fungus; the plural of fungus)
9.	**protists**	*n.*	▶ (usually single-celled organisms that have both plant and animal characteristics)

List 2: Strategy Practice

1.	**interactions**	*n.*	▶ (actions or influences on each other)
2.	**population**	*n.*	▶ (the number of organisms living in an area)
3.	**function**	*v.*	▶ (to act or operate normally; to perform)
4.	**tropical**	*adj.*	▶ (very humid and hot or having to do with the tropics)
5.	**available**	*adj.*	▶ (ready to be used)
6.	**requirements**	*n.*	▶ (things that are needed or depended upon)
7.	**nutrients**	*n.*	▶ (matter needed by plants and animals so they can live)
8.	**predator**	*n.*	▶ (an animal that hunts or kills another for food)
9.	**eventually**	*adv.*	▶ (finally)
10.	**extinction**	*n.*	▶ (the end of or the dying out of a type of plant or animal)

(from Application Lesson 1)

Overhead 2

ACTIVITY A *Vocabulary*

List 3: Word Families

	Verb	Noun	Adjective
Family 1	energize (to give energy)	energy energizer	energetic
Family 2	consume (to eat)	consumer consumption	consumable
Family 3	transform (to change)	transformation transformer	
Family 4	capture (to catch or attract)	captive captor	
Family 5	compose (to make or create)	composition composer	composite

ACTIVITY B *Spelling Dictation*

1. **energize**	4. **consume**
2. **energy**	5. **consumer**
3. **energetic**	6. **consumable**

(from Application Lesson 1)

Overhead 3

ACTIVITY C *Passage Reading and Comprehension*

A. ENERGY AND MATTER IN ECOSYSTEMS

- Organisms need energy and matter to carry out life processes such as growing (answers will vary).
- Plants and tiny organisms capture the sun's energy and transform it into food energy (matter).
- Organisms that cannot make their own food then eat these plants and tiny organisms.
- When organisms die, the energy and matter in their bodies become food for fungi and bacteria.

B. INTERACTIONS WITHIN ECOSYSTEMS

- Organisms interact with other organisms within their ecosystem.
- Some of these interactions are mutually beneficial. For example, as bees get their food from plants, they distribute pollen so flowers can make seeds.

C. CHANGES IN ECOSYSTEMS

- Since every species has special life requirements, species vary across ecosystems.
- When parts of an ecosystem are changed or altered, the ecosystem may be changed.
- Large changes in climate will create major changes in an ecosystem. For example, the extinction of dinosaurs has been connected to global warming.

(from Application Lesson 1)

Overhead 4

ACTIVITY G *Expository Writing—Multi-Paragraph Answer*

Prompt: What are three important things about ecosystems?

Example Multi-Paragraph Plan

Planning Box
(topic a) *organisms need energy and matter*
① (detail) – *necessary for all life processes*
(detail) – *for growing, developing, reproducing, and responding to environment*
② (detail) – *plants capture energy from sun and make into food for themselves and other organisms*
(detail) ~~*ecosystems can be very large or very small*~~
(topic b) *organisms interact with other organisms and with nonliving things*
① (detail) – *friendly interactions benefit both organisms*
② (detail) – *some interactions less friendly*
(topic c) *changes in ecosystem can affect how ecosystem functions*
① (detail) – *may not function properly*
(detail) – *may cease to function at all*
② (detail) – *extinction of organisms possible, especially if change in climate*

(from Application Lesson 2)

Overhead 5

ACTIVITY A Vocabulary

List 1: Tell

1. **photosynthesis** *n.* ▶ (the process by which green plants use the sun's energy to make food)
2. **synthesis** *n.* ▶ (putting things together)
3. **chlorophyll** *n.* ▶ (the green substance found in most plants)
4. **chloroplasts** *n.* ▶ (parts of the leaf in which photosynthesis takes place)
5. **glucose** *n.* ▶ (a simple sugar)
6. **molecule** *n.* ▶ (a very small amount, formed by combining atoms)
7. **carbon dioxide** *n.* ▶ (a colorless, odorless gas occurring naturally)
8. **cellular** *adj.* ▶ (related to cells)
9. **microbes** *n.* ▶ (very tiny living organisms)
10. **uniquely** *adv.* ▶ (unusually)
11. **integral** *adj.* ▶ (necessary for something to be whole)
12. **resources** *n.* ▶ (things that are ready to use to meet needs)

List 2: Strategy Practice

1. **respiration** *n.* ▶ (the action of breathing)
2. **essential** *adj.* ▶ (absolutely necessary)
3. **chemical** *adj.* ▶ (related to the properties of substances)
4. **properly** *or* **properly** *adv.* ▶ (correctly)
5. **presence** *n.* ▶ (the state of being in a place, of being present)
6. **pigment** *n.* ▶ (a substance that gives color to plant or animal tissues)
7. **release** *v.* ▶ (to let go)
8. **recombine** *v.* ▶ (to join together differently)
9. **continuously** *adv.* ▶ (without end)
10. **existence** *n.* ▶ (the state of existing or being)

(from Application Lesson 2)

Overhead 6

ACTIVITY A *Vocabulary*

List 3: Word Families

	Verb	Noun	Adjective
Family 1	use (to employ for a purpose)	user usage	usable
Family 2	contain (to hold inside itself)	container	
Family 3	reverse (to change to the opposite)	reversal	reversible
Family 4	combine (to join together)	combination	
Family 5	structure (to arrange or to build)	structure	structural

ACTIVITY B *Spelling Dictation*

1. **reverse**	4. **use**
2. **reversal**	5. **user**
3. **reversible**	6. **usable**

(from Application Lesson 2)

Overhead 7

ACTIVITY C *Passage Reading and Comprehension*

PLANTS

A. FACTS ON PLANTS

- Plants cover much of the earth's **surface**.
- Plants use the sun's **energy** to make food that is useable to the plant and other organisms.

B. PHOTOSYNTHESIS IN PLANTS

- Leaves contain **chloroplasts** that collect the sun's **energy**.
- This light energy is used to split water (H_2O) in the plant into **hydrogen** and **oxygen**.
- The plant recombines the **hydrogen** molecules (H_2) with **carbon dioxide** (CO_2) from the air to form a sugar called **glucose**.
- **Oxygen** is released into the air.

C. CELLULAR RESPIRATION IN PLANTS

- During **cellular respiration**, plants take in oxygen.
- By combining the **oxygen** and the **glucose**, they release **carbon dioxide**, **water**, and **energy**.

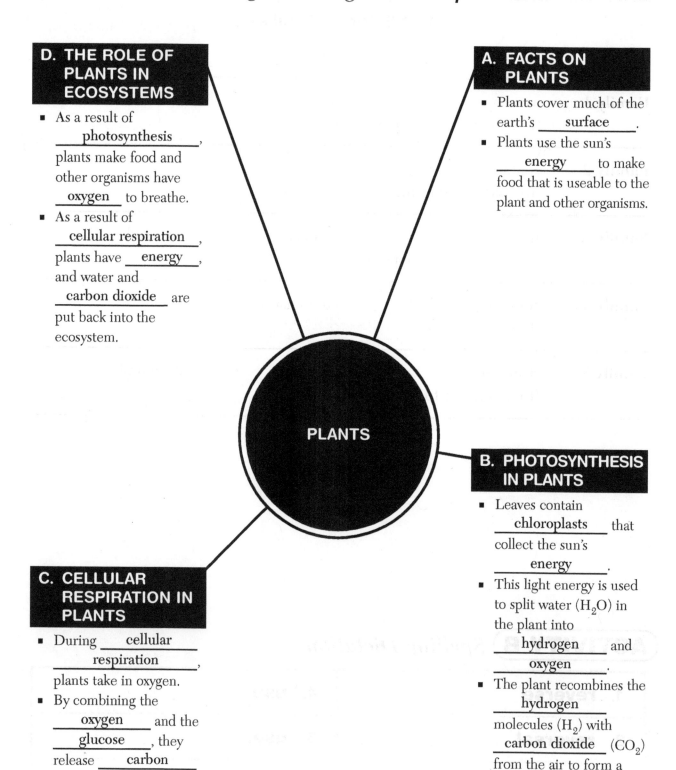

D. THE ROLE OF PLANTS IN ECOSYSTEMS

- As a result of **photosynthesis**, plants make food and other organisms have **oxygen** to breathe.
- As a result of **cellular respiration**, plants have **energy**, and water and **carbon dioxide** are put back into the ecosystem.

(from Application Lesson 2)

Overhead 8

ACTIVITY G *Expository Writing—Multi-Paragraph Answer*

Prompt: Describe the two processes that plants perform to keep the life cycle in ecosystems functioning.

Example Multi-Paragraph Plan

Planning Box		
(topic a)		*photosynthesis*
	(detail)	~~*much of earth covered with plants*~~
①	(detail)	– *process for making food*
②	(detail)	– *leaves contain chloroplasts, which contain chlorophyll*
③	(detail)	– *chloroplasts collect sun's energy*
	(detail)	– *light energy used to split water into hydrogen & oxygen*
④	(detail)	– *hydrogen stays in plant*
	(detail)	– *oxygen leaves plant*
⑤	(detail)	– *plant combines hydrogen with carbon dioxide from air to form glucose*
	(detail)	– *glucose is an energy-rich food*
(topic b)		*cellular respiration*
①	(detail)	– *process of releasing energy*
②	(detail)	– *plants take in oxygen from air*
	(detail)	– *combine oxygen with glucose*
③	(detail)	– *release energy & carbon dioxide & water*
④	(detail)	– *stored energy powers the plant*
	(detail)	– *helps plants live and grow*

(from Application Lesson 2)

Overhead 9

ACTIVITY G *Expository Writing—Multi-Paragraph Answer*

Example Multi-Paragraph Answer

(paragraph b)

The second process is cellular respiration. In this process, energy within the plant is released. This occurs when plants take in oxygen from the air and combine that oxygen with the glucose they have produced. As a result, energy, carbon dioxide, and water are released. The stored energy that is released within the plant powers the plant, helping it to live and grow.

(from Application Lesson 3)

Overhead 10

ACTIVITY A Vocabulary

List 1: Tell

1. **chemosynthesis** *n.* ▶ (the process by which certain organisms break down energy-rich molecules in order to make their own food)
2. **orca** *n.* ▶ (a killer whale)
3. **alga** *n.* ▶ (a simple, nonflowering plant that is usually found in or around water)
4. **algae** *n.* ▶ (more than one alga; the plural of alga)
5. **lichens** *n.* ▶ (slow-growing plants composed of algae and fungi)
6. **caribou** *n.* ▶ (a type of reindeer living in northern Canada and in Alaska)

List 2: Strategy Practice

1. **producers** *n.* ▶ (organisms that produce their own food)
2. **consumers** *n.* ▶ (organisms that eat other organisms)
3. **decomposers** *n.* ▶ (organisms that break down dead organisms)
4. **microscope** *or* **microscope** *n.* ▶ (an instrument used to see very small things)
5. **microscopic** *or* **microscopic** *adj.* ▶ (so small as to be seen only with a microscope)
6. **recycling** *v.* ▶ (changing waste to reusable items)
7. **arrangement** *or* **arrangement** *n.* ▶ (the result of being placed, or arranged, in a certain way)
8. **relatively** *adv.* ▶ (in relation to something else; comparatively)
9. **mutual** *adj.* ▶ (shared)
10. **parasite** *n.* ▶ (an organism that lives in or on another organism and receives benefits while harming the other organism)

(from Application Lesson 3)

Overhead 11

ACTIVITY A *Vocabulary*

List 3: Word Families

	Verb	Noun	Adjective
Family 1	cycle (to occur over and over again in a definite order)	cycle	cyclic
Family 2	collect (to put together a group of things)	collection collector	collective
Family 3	reduce (to make smaller in number or size)	reduction reducer	reduced
Family 4	process (to go through a series of actions leading to an end, or to take a course of action)	process processor	
Family 5	require (to have need of)	requirement	

ACTIVITY B *Spelling Dictation*

1. **collect**	4. **reduce**
2. **collection**	5. **reduction**
3. **collective**	6. **reduced**

(from Application Lesson 3)

Overhead 12

ACTIVITY C *Passage Reading and Comprehension*

ENERGY & MATTER MOVING THROUGH ECOSYSTEMS

A. FOOD PRODUCERS

- Food producers make their own ___food___.
- Most are ___plants___.
- In the process of photosynthesis, plants use energy from the ___sun___ to produce food.
- In the process of chemosynthesis, producers break apart simple ___molecules___ to get energy.

B. THE ENERGY LINK BETWEEN THE SUN AND ECOSYSTEMS

- Producers capture energy from the ___sun___ and store that ___energy___ in their body structures.
- The energy stored by ___producers___ becomes food for other living things.
- If there are many producers in an ecosystem, the ecosystem is ___(answers will vary)___.

C. FOOD CONSUMERS

- Food consumers are unable to make their own ___food___.
- Any organism that eats another ___organism___ is a food consumer.

D. THE ENERGY LINKS BETWEEN PRODUCERS AND CONSUMERS

- In a food chain, one organism eats another ___organism___, which eats another ___organism___, which eats another ___organism___.
- When food chains overlap, they form a ___food web___.

E. SPECIAL RELATIONSHIPS IN ECOSYSTEMS

- ___Parasites___ are organisms that get their food from living in, or on, other organisms.
- Some organisms, like ___fungi___ and ___algae,___ live together and help each other.

F. RECYCLING ENERGY AND MATTER

- Decomposers break down and feed on ___dead organisms___.
- ___Fungi___ and ___bacteria___ are decomposers.

(from Application Lesson 3)

Overhead 13

ACTIVITY G *Expository Writing—Multi-Paragraph Answer*

Prompt: Explain the roles of producers, consumers, and decomposers in the transfer of energy within an ecosystem.

Example Multi-Paragraph Plan

Planning Box
(topic a) *producers*
① (detail) – *photosynthesis—plants capture energy from sun to make food*
② (detail) – *chemosynthesis—produce food by breaking apart molecules to*
capture energy
③ (detail) – *producers provide food for other organisms*
④ (detail) – *energy link between sun and other living things*
⑤ (detail) – *without producers, no life*
(detail) ~~*consumers eat consumers*~~
(topic b) *consumers*
① (detail) – *unable to produce their own food by capturing the sun's energy*
① (detail) – *an organism that eats another organism is a consumer*
② (detail) – *consumers eat producers*
② (detail) – *in food webs consumers also eat consumers*
② (detail) – *gain energy needed for life*
(topic c) *decomposers*
(detail) ~~*plants are producers*~~
① (detail) – *decomposers break down and feed on dead organisms*
② (detail) – *when decomposers die, energy released into ecosystem*
② (detail) – *when decomposers die, nutrients released into ecosystem*
③ (detail) – *plants can then take energy and nutrients from soil*

(from Application Lesson 3)

Overhead 14

ACTIVITY G *Expository Writing—Multi-Paragraph Answer*

Example Multi-Paragraph Answer

(paragraph b)

Consumers also have a critical role in the transfer of energy within an ecosystem. Consumers are unable to produce their own food by capturing the sun's energy and must instead eat other organisms. In food webs, consumers eat producers or other consumers in order to gain the energy that they need for life.

(paragraph c)

Decomposers also have a critical role in the transfer of energy within an ecosystem. The decomposers break down and feed on dead organisms. When the decomposers die, their energy and nutrients are released into the ecosystem. Plants can then utilize the energy and nutrients from the soil.

(from Application Lesson 4)

Overhead 15

ACTIVITY A *Vocabulary*

List 1: Tell

1. **ancient** *adj.* ▶ (old)
2. **dehydration** *n.* ▶ (the loss of water from an organism)
3. **elements** *n.* ▶ (basic parts from which something is made)
4. **ingredients** *n.* ▶ (the foods or other elements combined to make a mixture)
5. **Louis Pasteur** *n.* ▶ (the scientist who discovered how to keep foods safe by killing microbes with heat)
6. **pasteurization** *n.* ▶ (the process of using heat to kill microbes and prevent food from spoiling rapidly)
7. **pathogens** *n.* ▶ (microorganisms, such as bacteria and viruses, that cause disease)
8. **sodium benzoate** *n.* ▶ (an odorless white powder used to keep food fresh)
9. **sulfur dioxide** *n.* ▶ (a colorless liquid used to keep food fresh)
10. **techniques** *n.* ▶ (particular methods of doing things)
11. **vinegar** *n.* ▶ (a sour liquid used to keep food from spoiling)

List 2: Strategy Practice

1. **alternatives** *n.* ▶ (things used or things done instead of other things)
2. **contaminated** *or* **contaminated** *v.* ▶ (spoiled)
3. **controversy** *n.* ▶ (a longstanding disagreement)
4. **deprive** *v.* ▶ (to take away from)
5. **environments** *n.* ▶ (the physical surroundings)
6. **nutritional** *adj.* ▶ (having to do with food so the body functions properly)
7. **poisonous** *adj.* ▶ (causing death or illness if put into the body)
8. **refrigeration** *n.* ▶ (the process used to make things cool or cold)
9. **spoilage** *n.* ▶ (the decay of food)
10. **sterilization** *n.* ▶ (the act of making something free from bacteria)

(from Application Lesson 4)

Overhead 16

ACTIVITY A *Vocabulary*

List 3: Word Families

	Verb	Noun	Adjective
Family 1	preserve (to keep safe or free from harm)	preservation preservative	preservable
Family 2	survive (to live longer than)	survivor survival	
Family 3	research (to study or investigate in a particular field	researcher	researchable
Family 4	moisten (to make or become slightly wet)	moisture	moist
Family 5	conduct (to direct)	conduction conductor	

ACTIVITY B *Spelling Dictation*

1. **preserve**	4. **research**
2. **preservation**	5. **researcher**
3. **preservable**	6. **researchable**

(from Application Lesson 4)

Overhead 17

ACTIVITY C *Passage Reading and Comprehension*

FOOD PRESERVATION

A. SPOILED FOOD

- Food spoils because microbes break down or change the food.
- To keep foods from spoiling, you must kill the microbes, slow their growth, or change the food so microbes can't use it.

B. DRYING AND SMOKING

- When a food is dried, microbes can't live without water.
- Both salt and smoke are toxic to microbes.

C. REFRIGERATION AND FREEZING

- Refrigeration slows the growth of microbes.
- Freezing can stop the growth of microbes.
- These methods of preservation don't change the taste, texture, or nutritional content too much.

D. CANNING, PASTEURIZATION, AND PICKLING

- When a food is canned, it is boiled, and, as a result, the microbes are killed.
- When a food is pickled, an unfriendly place for microbes is created when acids, bases, and salt are added.
- These methods of preservation do change the taste, texture, and nutritional content of the food.

E. CHEMICAL PRESERVATIVES

- Some spices such as (answers will vary) can slow the growth of microbes.
- Today, chemicals are often added to foods to reduce spoilage.
- Adding chemicals to foods is controversial because (answers will vary).

F. IMPORTANCE OF FOOD PRESERVATION

- Because of these food preservation procedures, people are less likely to eat contaminated food and become ill.

(from Application Lesson 4)

Overhead 18

ACTIVITY G *Expository Writing—Multi-Paragraph Answer*

Prompt: Describe the three most popular types of food preservation methods used today.

Example Multi-Paragraph Plan

Planning Box
(topic a) *refrigeration & freezing*
① (detail) – *slows or stops growth of microbes*
② (detail) – *stays good for weeks rather than days*
③ (detail) – *doesn't change taste, texture, or nutritional content*
(topic b) *canning & pasteurization*
① (detail) – *food boiled in can or jar*
① (detail) – *boiling kills microbes*
(detail) ~~– *freezing slows growth of microbes*~~
② (detail) – *container sealed so microbes can't enter*
③ (detail) – *long shelf life*
④ (detail) – *nutritional content, taste, & texture altered*
(topic c) *chemical preservation*
① (detail) – *chemicals are added to foods*
① (detail) – *sulfur dioxide, sodium benzoate, & sodium nitrite*
② (detail) – *shelf life of years*
③ (detail) – *controversial*
③ (detail) – *people allergic*
③ (detail) – *may not be safe*

(from Application Lesson 4)

Overhead 19

ACTIVITY G *Expository Writing—Multi-Paragraph Answer*

Example Multi-Paragraph Answer

(paragraph b)

Canning and pasteurization are also used as food preservation procedures today. In these processes, food is boiled in a can or jar and, as a result, microbes in the food are killed. The container is also sealed so microbes can't enter. Canned foods have a long shelf life. However, their nutritional content, taste, and texture are altered.

(paragraph c)

Another way to make food last longer is through the use of chemical preservatives. In this case, chemicals such as sulfur dioxide, sodium benzoate, and sodium nitrite are added to the food. As a result of adding these chemicals, the foods may have a shelf life of years. This method is controversial as it may cause an allergic response in some people or in other ways harm people.

(from Application Lesson 5)

Overhead 20

ACTIVITY A Vocabulary

List 1: Tell

1. **arteries** *n.* ▶ (large blood vessels that carry blood away from the heart)
2. **arterioles** *n.* ▶ (small blood vessels that carry blood away from the heart)
3. **arteriosclerosis** *n.* ▶ (a condition that happens when the walls of the arteries become thick and not as flexible)
4. **plaque** *n.* ▶ (a hard substance that builds up in blood vessels and limits the flow of blood)
5. **atherosclerosis** *n.* ▶ (a condition that happens when deposits of plaque build up on the inside of the arteries)
6. **atria** *n.* ▶ (the two top chambers of the heart)
7. **capillaries** *n.* ▶ (small blood vessels that connect arteries to venules)
8. **deoxygenated** *v.* ▶ (having the oxygen removed)
9. **hemoglobin** *n.* ▶ (a substance in red blood cells that helps carry oxygen throughout the body)
10. **platelets** *n.* ▶ (pieces of cells that prevent blood clotting)
11. **pulmonary** *adj.* ▶ (relating to or affecting the lungs)
12. **systemic** *adj.* ▶ (relating to or affecting the body)
13. **ventricles** *n.* ▶ (the two lower chambers of the heart)
14. **venules** *n.* ▶ (small blood vessels that connect capillaries to veins)

List 2: Strategy Practice

1. **cardiovascular** *adj.* ▶ (of the body system that consists of the heart, blood, and blood vessels)
2. **circulates** *v.* ▶ (moves from place to place in a circular path)
3. **components** *n.* ▶ (parts)
4. **fragments** *n.* ▶ (small pieces)
5. **infections** *n.* ▶ (diseases caused by germs entering part of the body)
6. **multicellular** *or* **multicellular** *adj.* ▶ (made up of many cells)
7. **particular** *adj.* ▶ (special)
8. **pressures** *n.* ▶ (forces made by one thing against another)
9. **responsible for** *adj.* ▶ (in charge of; charged with being the source for)
10. **trillion** *n.* ▶ (the number 1 followed by 12 zeroes; a lot)

(from Application Lesson 5)

Overhead 21

ACTIVITY A *Vocabulary*

List 3: Word Families

	Verb	Noun	Adjective
Family 1	organize (to assemble to perform a specific function)	organization organizer	organizational
Family 2	transport (to carry from one place to another)	transportation	transportable
Family 3	promote (to encourage or assist in growth or development)	promotion promoter	promotional
Family 4	avoid (to keep away from)	avoidance	avoidable
Family 5	specialize (to adapt to a special job or function)	specialization	

ACTIVITY B *Spelling Dictation*

1. **promote**	4. **avoid**
2. **promotion**	5. **avoidance**
3. **promotional**	6. **avoidable**

(from Application Lesson 5)

Overhead 22

ACTIVITY C *Passage Reading and Comprehension*

THE CARDIOVASCULAR SYSTEM

A. WHAT IS IT?

- Humans have five levels of organization: cells, tissues, organs, organ systems, and the whole organism.
- The cardiovascular system includes your heart, blood, and blood vessels.

B. THE HEART

- The heart is divided into four chambers. The upper chambers are the atria, and the lower chambers are the ventricles.
- The atria pump blood into the heart and down into the ventricles.
- The ventricles pump blood out of the heart into the rest of the body.

C. THE BLOOD

- Your blood is made up of liquid components called plasma and solid components called red blood cells, white blood cells, and platelets.
- Red blood cells carry oxygen to the body. White blood cells work hard to fight infections and diseases.
- Platelets promote clotting.

D. BLOOD PATHWAYS

- Two pathways carry blood. The systemic pathway carries oxygen-rich blood to your body and returns the deoxygenated blood back to your heart. The pulmonary pathway carries the deoxygenated blood from your heart to your lungs, where carbon dioxide is released and oxygen is picked up.

E. THE BLOOD VESSELS

- The largest type of blood vessels are the arteries.
- The arteries and the arterioles carry blood away from the heart.
- The blood then flows through capillaries, venules, and veins.
- The veins carry blood back to the heart.

F. PROBLEMS

- With high blood pressure, blood vessels are narrowed, forcing the heart to work harder.
- With arteriosclerosis or atherosclerosis, the heart must work too hard, or it fails altogether.

(from Application Lesson 5)

Overhead 23

ACTIVITY G *Expository Writing—Multi-Paragraph Answer*

Prompt: Describe the structure and function of the three main parts of the cardiovascular system.

Example Multi-Paragraph Plan

Planning Box
(topic a) *heart*
① (detail) – *4 chambers*
(detail) – *top chambers—atria*
(detail) – *bottom chambers—ventricles*
② (detail) – *atria pumps blood into heart and down into ventricles*
③ (detail) – *ventricles pump blood out of the heart to rest of body*
(topic b) *blood*
① (detail) – *made of liquid and solid components*
② (detail) – *liquid component called plasma*
③ (detail) – *solid components include red blood cells, white blood cells, & platelets*
(detail) – *plasma mostly water with proteins, vitamins, & minerals*
④ (detail) – *red blood cells carry oxygen to all parts of body*
⑤ (detail) – *white blood cells fight infection and diseases*
⑥ (detail) – *platelets help promote blood clotting*
(topic c) *blood vessels*
① (detail) – *arteries—largest type of blood vessel*
② (detail) – *arterioles—smaller blood vessels that arteries flow into*
③ (detail) – *arteries & arterioles carry blood from heart*
④ (detail) – *capillaries link arteries to veins*
⑤ (detail) – *at this point nutrients are exchanged for waste*
⑥ (detail) – *veins carry blood back to heart*
⑦ (detail) – *blood going back to heart is darker because of waste and lack of oxygen*

(from Application Lesson 5)

Overhead 24

ACTIVITY G *Expository Writing—Multi-Paragraph Answer*

Example Multi-Paragraph Answer

(paragraph b)

Another critical part of the cardiovascular system is blood. Blood is made of both liquid and solid components. The liquid component called plasma consists mostly of water, but also contains proteins, vitamins, and minerals. The solid components of blood include red blood cells, white blood cells, and platelets. The red blood cells carry oxygen to all parts of the body. On the other hand, white blood cells fight infection and disease. The final solid component, platelets, help promote blood clotting.

(paragraph c)

The third part of the cardiovascular system is the blood vessels. Arteries are the largest type of blood vessel. The arteries flow into the arterioles, smaller blood vessels. Together the arteries and arterioles carry blood away from the heart. Another type of blood vessel, capillaries, connect arteries to veins. At this point, nutrients are exchanged for waste. The veins carry the blood, including waste products, back to the heart. Because the blood going back to the heart is carrying waste and lacks oxygen, it is a darker color.

(from Application Lesson 6)

Overhead 25

ACTIVITY A *Vocabulary*

List 1: Tell

1. **patients** *n.* ▶ (people under a doctor's care)
2. **medicines** *n.* ▶ (drugs or other substances used to treat disease or to relieve pain)
3. **procedure** *n.* ▶ (a course of action with steps in a definite order)
4. **recipient** *n.* ▶ (a person who receives)
5. **anesthetic** *n.* ▶ (a drug or other substance that causes loss of feeling, especially pain)
6. **efficiently** *adv.* ▶ (getting the desired result with as little effort as possible)
7. **foreign** *adj.* ▶ (not belonging to)

List 2: Strategy Practice

1. **generosity** *n.* ▶ (willingness to give or share freely)
2. **incompatible** *adj.* ▶ (not able to work together or get along with)
3. **suitable** *adj.* ▶ (meets the requirements of)
4. **surgery** *n.* ▶ (the removal or repair of injured or diseased parts of the body)
5. **suture** *v.* ▶ (to stitch together the edges of a cut or wound)
6. **consciousness** *n.* ▶ (the state of being awake)
7. **susceptible** *adj.* ▶ (easily affected)
8. **immune** *adj.* ▶ (protected from a disease or infection)
9. **medications** *n.* ▶ (substances used to treat diseases)
10. **gradually** *adv.* ▶ (little by little; slowly)

(from Application Lesson 6)

Overhead 26

ACTIVITY A *Vocabulary*

List 3: Word Families

	Verb	Noun	Adjective
Family 1	incorporate (to make part of another thing)	incorporation	incorporated
Family 2	designate (to indicate)	designation	
Family 3	permit (to allow)	permission	permissible
Family 4	donate (to give)	donor donation	
Family 5	commune (to come together)	community	communal

ACTIVITY B *Spelling Dictation*

1. **incorporate**	4. **permit**
2. **incorporation**	5. **permission**
3. **incorporated**	6. **permissible**

(from Application Lesson 6)

Overhead 27

ACTIVITY C Passage Reading and Comprehension

HEART TRANSPLANTS

A. WHO IS ELIGIBLE FOR A NEW HEART?

- When a person has a __failing__ heart and has NOT responded to prescribed __medications__, a heart transplant may be called for.
- People with other __health__ problems are generally not eligible.

B. WHAT MUST HAPPEN BEFORE THE TRANSPLANT?

- The person's names goes on a __waiting list__ until a suitable __donor__ heart is located.
- The heart must match in __blood__ and __tissue__ types.

C. WHAT OCCURS DURING THE SURGERY?

- When the donor heart is removed from the body, it is packed in special __chemicals__ and placed on __ice__.
- When the surgery begins, the __damaged__ heart is removed, and the patient is kept alive using a __heart/lung__ machine.
- Once the heart is working __OK or properly__, the patient is closed up.

D. WHAT IS NECESSARY AFTER THE TRANSPLANT?

- The body may try to __reject__ the new heart.
- For this reason, the patient must take special __medications__.

(from Application Lesson 6)

Overhead 28

ACTIVITY G *Expository Writing—Multi-Paragraph Answer*

Prompt: Describe what occurs during each stage of a heart transplant: before surgery, during surgery, and after surgery.

Example Multi-Paragraph Plan

Planning Box	
(topic a)	*before surgery*
① (detail)	– *must be eligible*
② (detail)	– *eligible—under 60 and otherwise healthy*
③ (detail)	– *goes on waiting list*
(detail)	– *wait for suitable donor heart*
④ (detail)	– *must match blood and tissue type of recipient*
(topic b)	*during surgery*
① (detail)	– *donor heart removed from body*
② (detail)	– *donor heart packed in special chemicals and packed in ice*
(detail)	– *transported quickly*
③ (detail)	– *recipient is put to sleep*
(detail)	– *diseased heart removed*
(detail)	– *recipient put on heart-lung machine*
④ (detail)	– *new heart is connected to blood vessels*
(detail)	– *blood is warmed and heart begins to beat*
⑤ (detail)	– *incision is sutured*
(topic c)	*after surgery*
① (detail)	– *resume a normal life*
(detail)	– *must take special medications so his or her body won't reject*
	the heart
② (detail)	– *these drugs suppress the immune system so it won't reject the*
	heart as a foreign material
(detail)	~~*wait for a suitable donor*~~

(from Application Lesson 6)

Overhead 29

ACTIVITY G *Expository Writing—Multi-Paragraph Answer*

Example Multi-Paragraph Answer

(paragraph a)

A number of things must occur before a heart transplant can occur. First, the recipient must be found eligible for a heart transplant. To be eligible, the individual must be younger than 60 and be healthy other than having heart disease. When the recipient is determined eligible, his or her name is placed on a waiting list until a suitable donor heart is located. After it is located, it must match the blood and tissue type of the recipient for the surgery to proceed.

(paragraph b)

The actual heart transplant surgery involves a number of critical steps. First, the donor heart is removed from the body of the deceased person. To preserve the heart, it is placed in special chemicals and packed in ice and immediately transported to the hospital where the recipient waits. Next, the recipient is put to sleep and the diseased heart is removed and the patient is put on a heart-lung machine to support his or her life. The new heart is then connected to the blood vessels and the blood is gradually warmed until the heart begins to beat. At that point, the surgical incision is sutured.

(paragraph c)

A heart transplant patient must take specific precautions after surgery. Though a normal life can be resumed, the patient must take special medications so that his or her body won't reject the heart. Normally, the individual's immune system would reject the heart as a foreign material, making these drugs essential.

(from Application Lesson 7)

Overhead 30

ACTIVITY A *Vocabulary*

List 1: Tell

1. **virus** *n.* ▶ (a tiny, infectious particle)
2. **polyhedral** *adj.* ▶ (having many sides)
3. **genetic** *adj.* ▶ (related to the development of organisms)
4. **vaccine** *n.* ▶ (a dead or weakened virus or bacteria that is used to protect against certain diseases)
5. **antibodies** *n.* ▶ (proteins in the blood that destroy germs)

List 2: Strategy Practice

1. **characteristics** *n.* ▶ (features, qualities, or functions)
2. **replication** *n.* ▶ (a close or exact copy)
3. **membrane** *n.* ▶ (a thin layer of tissue)
4. **adsorption** *n.* ▶ (keeping something on the surface instead of absorbing it)
5. **instructions** *n.* ▶ (explanations, directions, or orders)
6. **assembly** *or* **assembly** *n.* ▶ (fitting together parts to make a whole)
7. **administered** *v.* ▶ (given to)
8. **bacterial** *adj.* ▶ (related to bacteria)
9. **information** *n.* ▶ (knowledge or facts about things)
10. **significantly** *adv.* ▶ (a lot)

(from Application Lesson 7)

Overhead 31

List 3: Word Families

	Verb	Noun	Adjective
Family 1	develop (to grow and change)	development developer	developmental
Family 2	reproduce (to produce others of the same kind)	reproduction	reproducible
Family 3	infect (to cause disease in)	infection	infectious
Family 4	invade (to enter and overrun)	invasion invader	
Family 5	detect (to find out or discover)	detection detective	detectable

ACTIVITY B *Spelling Dictation*

1. **reproduce**	4. **infect**
2. **reproduction**	5. **infection**
3. **reproducible**	6. **infectious**

(from Application Lesson 7)

Overhead 32

ACTIVITY C *Passage Reading and Comprehension*

VIRUSES

A. WHAT ARE VIRUSES?

- Viruses have some characteristics of living things and nonliving things.
- In some cases, viruses are inert, but they can live and reproduce.
- To live and reproduce, viruses must invade a host cell and use it.
- Viruses are NOT cells but have genetic instructions.

B. HOW DO YOU GET INFECTED?

- Different viruses need different host cells.
- The protein coat helps the virus detect the right kind of host cell.
- In adsorption, the virus attaches to the outside of a host cell.
- In entry, the virus injects genetic information into the host cell.
- During replication and assembly, the host cell's enzymes obey the virus's genetic instructions.
- During release, new virus particles leave the host cell in search of new host cells.

C. WHAT DO VIRUSES LOOK LIKE?

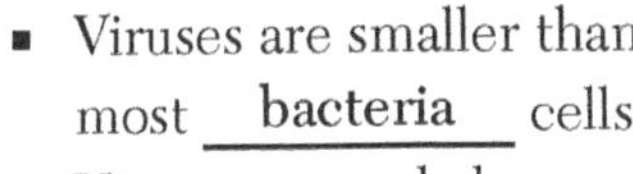

- Viruses are smaller than most bacteria cells.
- Viruses can only be observed using electron microscopes.
- Viruses have different shapes.
- One common virus is shaped like a spaceship.

D. HOW CAN WE BE PROTECTED FROM VIRUSES?

- To reduce the spread of viruses, individuals should cover their mouths with a tissue when coughing, and they should wash their hands.
- In some cases, a vaccine can prevent the virus from infecting individuals.
- Vaccines promote the production of antibodies within the body.
- Because the genetic code in viruses can change, vaccines also have to be altered.

(from Application Lesson 7)

Overhead 33

ACTIVITY G *Expository Writing—Multi-Paragraph Answer*

Prompt: Explain each big idea in this article about viruses: what they are like, how they reproduce, and how we can protect ourselves and others from infection.

Example Multi-Paragraph Plan

Planning Box
(topic a) *viruses—what they are like*
① (detail) – *very tiny, infectious particles*
① (detail) – *considered by some as living*
① ② (detail) – *can live and reproduce if they invade host cells*
① (detail) – *considered by some as nonliving*
③ (detail) – *in air or on surface, inert*
④ (detail) – *much smaller than bacteria*
⑤ (detail) – *not cells*
⑤ (detail) – *contain genetic instructions*
(topic b) *viruses—how they reproduce*
① (detail) – *detect appropriate host cells*
① (detail) – *attach themselves to host cells*
② (detail) – *inject genetic information into host cells*
③ (detail) – *host cell follows genetic instructions*
③ (detail) – *host cell creates new virus particles*
④ (detail) – *new virus particles search out new host cells*
⑤ (detail) – *virus spreads*
(topic c) *viruses—how we can protect ourselves and others from infection*
① (detail) – *cover mouth to limit spread of virus*
(detail) ~~– *viruses tiny infectious particles*~~
② (detail) – *wash hands before contact with food or people*
③ (detail) – *take vaccines that stop viruses from infecting people*
④ (detail) – *vaccines produce antibodies that matches virus*

(from Application Lesson 7)

Overhead 34

ACTIVITY G *Expository Writing—Multi-Paragraph Answer*

Example Multi-Paragraph Answer

(paragraph a)

Viruses are very unique particles. They are very tiny, infectious particles that are considered living by some scientists and nonliving by others. Viruses can live and reproduce if they invade host cells, thus giving them characteristics of living organisms. However, like nonliving organisms, they are totally inert in the air or on a surface. Viruses are much smaller than bacteria. Unlike bacteria, they are not cells though they contain genetic instructions.

(paragraph b)

Reproduction in viruses is quite different from reproduction in other organisms. First, the virus must detect an appropriate host cell and attach to that cell. Next, the virus will inject genetic information into the host cell. The host cell follows the genetic instructions and creates new virus particles. These new virus particles then search out new host cells. As a result, the virus spreads.

(paragraph c)

People can take many actions to protect themselves and others from infections caused by viruses. Of course, we can follow the advice of our mothers. When we are ill, we can cover our mouths with a tissue when we cough to limit the spread of the viruses. We can also wash our hands carefully to reduce the spread of viruses. In some cases, we might take a vaccine to stop the virus from infecting us. The vaccine produces antibodies that match certain viruses and prevents their reproduction.

(from Application Lesson 8)

Overhead 35

ACTIVITY A *Vocabulary*

List 1: Tell

1. **Antoni van Leeuwenhoek** *n.* ▶ (the scientist known as the Father of Microbiology)
2. ***Micrographia*** *n.* ▶ (an influential book introducing the use of the microscope)
3. **Robert Hooke** *n.* ▶ (the author of *Micrographia*)
4. **protozoa** *n.* ▶ (single-celled microscopic animals)
5. **animalcules** *n.* ▶ (old, archaic term for tiny swimming animals)
6. **bacilli** *n.* ▶ (a type of bacteria)
7. **cocci** *n.* ▶ (a type of bacteria)
8. **spirilla** *n.* ▶ (a type of bacteria)

List 2: Strategy Practice

1. **microbiology** *n.* ▶ (the branch of biology that studies microorganisms)
2. **microcosm** *n.* ▶ (the little world of microorganisms)
3. **microscope** *n.* ▶ (an instrument used to see very small things)
4. **microscopy** *n.* ▶ (the process of using a microscope)
5. **specimens** *n.* ▶ (examples)
6. **contemporary** *adj.* ▶ (existing at the same time)
7. **correspondence** *n.* ▶ (exchange of letters)
8. **translated** *v.* ▶ (changed into another language)
9. **financial** *adj.* ▶ (related to money)
10. **security** *n.* ▶ (protection from danger)

(from Application Lesson 8)

Overhead 36

ACTIVITY A *Vocabulary*

List 3: Word Families

	Verb	Noun	Adjective
Family 1	assist (to help)	assistance assistant	assistant
Family 2	influence (to change the thought or behavior of)	influence	influential
Family 3	magnify (to cause to look larger)	magnification magnifier	magnifiable
Family 4	adjust (to change or arrange to fit a need)	adjustment	adjustable
Family 5	classify (to arrange in groups according to some system)	classification	classifiable

ACTIVITY B *Spelling Dictation*

1. **adjust**	4. **classify**
2. **adjustment**	5. **classification**
3. **adjustable**	6. **classifiable**

(from Application Lesson 8)

Overhead 37

ACTIVITY C *Passage Reading and Comprehension*

ANTONI VAN LEEUWENHOEK—FATHER OF MICROBIOLOGY

A. LIFE

- Lived in Holland in 1600s.
- Became interested in microscopes after reading *Micrographia*.
- Learned about microscopy (the use of the microscope to investigate tiny living things).

B. AN UNUSUAL HOBBY

- Developed a microscope that was different from compound microscopes.
- His microscopes had only one lens; however, they were more powerful than compound microscopes.
- Became skilled at lens grinding.

C. VAN LEEUWENHOEK'S OBSERVATIONS

- Observed and described small specimens, including fungi, lice, and protozoa.
- Wrote down his findings and sent them to the Royal Society of London.

D. AN IMPORTANT DISCOVERY

- Discovered animalcules in a drop of water.
- Microbiology, a new branch of science, began.
- Provided descriptions of bacteria, algae, and plant and muscle tissue.
- Discovered red blood cells.

E. RECOGNITION

- After his letters were published, he became quite famous.
- The field of microbiology is based on his work.
- He kept his lens-grinding technique a secret.

(from Application Lesson 8)

Overhead 38

ACTIVITY G *Expository Writing—Multi-Paragraph Answer*

Prompt: Summarize the information presented on van Leeuwenhoek's hobby, his discoveries, and the recognition of his contributions to science.

Example Multi-Paragraph Plan

Planning Box
(topic a) *van Leeuwenhoek—hobby*
① (detail) – *read* Micrographia
(detail) – *became interested in the study of small things using microscopes*
② (detail) – *created his own microscope*
(detail) – *much more powerful than microscopes of the time*
③ (detail) – *observed many small things such as fungi, bee stingers, & lice*
(topic b) *van Leeuwenhoek's discoveries*
(detail) ~~– *shared discoveries with Royal Society of London*~~
① (detail) – *protozoa—single-celled microscopic animals*
② (detail) – *animalcules—tiny creatures in water*
③ (detail) – *described microscopic organisms such as algae and bacteria*
④ (detail) – *classified bacteria: bacilli, cocci, spirilla*
⑤ (detail) – *discovered red blood cells*
(topic c) *van Leeuwenhoek—recognition of scientific contributions*
① (detail) – *communicated with Royal Society of London*
② (detail) – *in the beginning they took little notice of his findings*
(detail) – *discovery of small creatures in water was recognized as*
important finding
③ (detail) – *his letters were translated and printed*
(detail) – *became famous*
④ (detail) – *invited to join Royal Society of London*
⑤ (detail) – *founder of microbiology*

(from Application Lesson 8)

Overhead 39

ACTIVITY G *Expository Writing—Multi-Paragraph Answer*

Example Multi-Paragraph Answer

(paragraph a)

Van Leeuwenhoek's entry into microbiology began with a hobby. After reading the book Micrographia, *he became interested in using microscopes to study small things. Van Leeuwenhoek created his own microscope, which was much more powerful than microscopes of that time. Using his microscope, he observed such small things as fungi, bee stingers, and lice.*

(paragraph b)

Because of his microscope's power and his interest in microscopic organisms, van Leeuwenhoek made many discoveries. Among his first discoveries were protozoa, single-celled microscopic animals. Later, he found tiny creatures in water, which he called animalcules. He also observed and described tiny organisms such as algae and bacteria. After careful observation, he classified bacteria into three types: bacilli, cocci, and spirilla. Van Leeuwenhoek is also credited with discovering red blood cells.

(paragraph c)

Although Van Leeuwenhoek would eventually be recognized as the Father of Microbiology, other scientists did not recognize his initial works. He sent notes about his initial experiments to the scientists of the Royal Society of London. They took little notice of his findings until he discovered small creatures in water. Later, his letters, filled with observations and discoveries, were translated and printed, making him rather famous. He was invited to join the prestigious Royal Society of London, though he never attended a meeting. Certainly, his contributions as the founder of microbiology are recognized by the entire scientific world today.

(from Application Lesson 9)

Overhead 40

ACTIVITY A *Vocabulary*

List 1: Tell

1. **Democritus** *n.* ► (the first person to determine that all things must be made up of smaller parts called atoms)
2. **John Dalton** *n.* ► (the scientist who proposed modern atomic theory)
3. **nucleus** *n.* ► (the center of an atom, containing neutrons and protons)
4. **neutrons** *n.* ► (particles with no electrical charge)
5. **protons** *n.* ► (positively charged particles)
6. **electrons** *n.* ► (negatively charged particles)

List 2: Strategy Practice

1. **compound** *n.* ► (a combination of two or more elements)
2. **hydrogen** *or* **hydrogen** *n.* ► (a colorless, odorless, tasteless gas)
3. **particles** *n.* ► (very small bits)
4. **atomic** *adj.* ► (related to an atom)
5. **subatomic** *or* **subatomic** *adj.* ► (smaller than an atom)
6. **electrical** *adj.* ► (having to do with electricity)
7. **negatively** *adv.* ► (not positive)
8. **individually** *adv.* ► (separately)
9. **attention** *or* **attention** *n.* ► (focus; thought)
10. **ultimately** *adv.* ► (finally)

(from Application Lesson 9)

Overhead 41

ACTIVITY A Vocabulary

List 3: Word Families

	Verb	Noun	Adjective
Family 1	determine (to give direction to; to find out by observation)	determination determiner	determined
Family 2	discover (to obtain knowledge of for the first time)	discovery discoverer	
Family 3	wonder (to want to know or learn)	wonder	wonderful
Family 4	define (to describe or to state the meaning of)	definition definer	definable
Family 5	suggest (to bring or call to mind)	suggestion	suggestible suggestive

ACTIVITY B Spelling

1. **define**	4. **determine**
2. **definition**	5. **determination**
3. **definable**	6. **determined**

(from Application Lesson 9)

Overhead 42

ACTIVITY C Passage Reading and Comprehension

ATOMS

A. WHAT ARE ATOMS?

- Atoms are the building blocks of all matter.
- Atoms are the smallest part of an element that behaves like the element.
- Thus, elements such as carbon and hydrogen are made up of atoms.

B. HISTORY

- In 530 B.C., Democritus theorized that all things could be broken into smaller parts and ultimately into atoms.
- In 1808, Dalton added to the work of Democritus by stating:
  - Every element has atoms.
  - All atoms in an element are the same.
  - Atoms of different elements are different.
  - Atoms of different elements can combine to form compounds.
  - In a compound, the number and kind of atoms remain the same.
- These principles formed atomic theory until 1897 when the electron was discovered.

C. SIMPLE ATOMIC STRUCTURE

- At the center of an atom is the nucleus.
- The nucleus contains protons (positive electrical charge) and neutrons (no electrical charge).
- The protons determine how an atom behaves.
- Electrons (negative electrical charge) orbit the nucleus.
- If the number of protons (+) and the number of electrons (–) are equal, the atom is electrically neutral.
- If the number of protons and electrons are NOT the same, it is called an ion.
- Atoms are hooked together to form molecules.

D. HOW DO WE KNOW ATOMS EXIST?

- Atoms can't be seen by the naked eye even when aided by a microscope.
- A special microscope called a Scanning Tunneling Microscope creates pictures of atoms.

E. IS THERE ANYTHING SMALLER THAN ATOMS?

- Subatomic particles are smaller than atoms.
- Many subatomic particles exist.
- One such particle is the quark.

(from Application Lesson 9)

Overhead 43

ACTIVITY G *Expository Writing—Multi-Paragraph Answer*

Prompt: Explain and provide information on the following statements: (1) All matter is made of atoms. (2) All atoms have a nucleus. (3) Electrons orbit the nucleus.

Example Multi-Paragraph Plan

Planning Box
(topic a) *All matter is made of atoms.*
① (detail) – *all things are made of elements*
② (detail) – *if you break element into smallest part that acts like an*
element—an atom
③ (detail) – *atom—smallest particle of an element that can exist alone*
(topic b) *All atoms have a nucleus.*
① (detail) – *the nucleus is at the center of the atom*
② (detail) – *contains protons with a positive charge*
(detail) – *contains neutrons with no electrical charge*
③ (detail) – *protons determine how the atom acts*
(topic c) *Electrons orbit the nucleus.*
① (detail) – *electrons—smaller, negatively charged particles*
② (detail) – *if number of electrons and number of protons same—atom*
electrically neutral
③ (detail) – *if number of electrons and number of protons not same—atom*
called ion
④ (detail) – *ion—either positive or negative*

(from Application Lesson 9)

Overhead 44

ACTIVITY G *Expository Writing—Multi-Paragraph Answer*

Example Multi-Paragraph Answer

(paragraph a)

All matter is made of atoms. First, all things are made of elements. If you break down the element into its smallest part that still acts like the element, you have an atom. An atom is the smallest particle of an element that can exist alone.

(paragraph b)

All atoms have a nucleus. The nucleus is located at the center of the atom. The nucleus contains protons that have a positive charge and neutrons that have no electrical charge. The protons determine how the atom will act.

(paragraph c)

Electrons orbit the nucleus. Electrons are smaller, negatively charged particles. If the number of electrons and number of protons are the same, the atom will be electrically neutral. If the number of electrons and number of protons are different, the atom is called an ion. The ion can be either positive or negative.

(from Application Lesson 10)

Overhead 45

ACTIVITY A *Vocabulary*

List 1: Tell

1.	**Rachel Carson**	*n.*	▶ (a famous naturalist who studied nature)
2.	**biology**	*n.*	▶ (the science of living organisms)
3.	**zoology**	*n.*	▶ (a branch of biology that focuses on animals)
4.	**articles**	*n.*	▶ (writings on a subject)
5.	**rebuttals**	*n.*	▶ (opposing arguments)

List 2: Strategy

1.	**naturalist**	*n.*	▶ (a person who studies nature)
2.	**enamored**	*v.*	▶ (really liked)
3.	**concentrate**	*v.*	▶ (to focus on)
4.	**pesticide**	*n.*	▶ (a chemical used to destroy plants or animals)
5.	**extremely**	*adv.*	▶ (very great)
6.	**infestations**	*n.*	▶ (growth in large numbers)
7.	**legislative**	*adj.*	▶ (legal)
8.	**department**	*n.*	▶ (a section or division of a larger organization, such as a government, a company, or a school)
9.	**irrevocably** *or* **irrevocably**	*adv.*	▶ (unchangeable)
10.	**materials**	*n.*	▶ (things needed to do something)

(from Application Lesson 10)

Overhead 46

ACTIVITY A *Vocabulary*

List 3: Word Families

	Verb	Noun	Adjective
Family 1	conserve (to protect from loss, harm, or waste)	conservation conservationist	conservative
Family 2	realize (to understand completely)	realization	realistic
Family 3	produce (to make)	production producer	productive
Family 4	publish (to produce and sell a book or other written material)	publication publisher	publishable
Family 5	represent (to speak for)	representation representative	representative

ACTIVITY B *Spelling Dictation*

1. **represent**	4. **conserve**
2. **representation**	5. **conservation**
3. **representative**	6. **conservative**

(from Application Lesson 10)

Overhead 47

ACTIVITY C *Passage Reading and Comprehension*

RACHEL CARSON, FAMOUS NATURALIST

A. EARLY LIFE

- As a child, Rachel Carson loved __nature__.
- At college, she studied __biology__ and __zoology__.

B. PROFESSIONAL LIFE

- Carson taught __zoology__ at a university.
- She worked for the Fish and __Wildlife__ Service.
- She wrote articles and books about __nature__.
- Her books were written not just for fellow scientists but also for the __public__.
- Her books made her a famous __naturalist__.

C. HER BELIEFS

- Carson believed that humans were a part of __nature__, not in charge of __nature__.
- She felt we should NOT drastically change the __environment__.

D. CONCERNS ABOUT DDT

- DDT was developed to kill __insects__.
- Many people became concerned that DDT was causing __harm__ to living things.
- Carson wrote about the danger of pesticides in her book __*Silent Spring*__.

E. CONTROVERSY OVER HER BOOK

- The __chemical__ industry opposed the positions stated in __*Silent Spring*__.
- Their opposition increased the book's __publicity__.
- President Kennedy ordered research on the effects of __pesticides__.

F. RACHEL CARSON'S LEGACY

- Bills were enacted to regulate the use of __pesticides__.
- The use of DDT was __banned__.
- The Environmental Protection Agency __(EPA)__ was formed.

(from Application Lesson 10)

Overhead 48

ACTIVITY G *Expository Writing—Multi-Paragraph Answer*

Prompt: Rachel Carson was a fascinating person. Describe her professional life, her beliefs and environmental concerns, and her legacy (outcomes of her work).

Example Multi-Paragraph Plan

Planning Box		
(topic a)		*Rachel Carson—professional life as a naturalist*
①	(detail)	– *studied biology and zoology in college*
	(detail)	– *taught zoology at a university*
②	(detail)	– *worked for Fish and Wildlife Service*
③	(detail)	– *published books concerning the sea*
④	(detail)	– *became a famous naturalist*
⑤	(detail)	– *became a full-time writer*
⑥	(detail)	– *concerned about pesticides*
	(detail)	– *wrote her famous book,* Silent Spring
(topic b)		*Rachel Carson—beliefs and environmental concerns*
①	(detail)	– *humans shouldn't make drastic changes in the environment*
②	(detail)	– *believed that DDT was dangerous*
③	(detail)	– *wrote about danger to environment by pesticides*
	(detail)	~~– *wrote* Silent Spring~~
(topic c)		*Rachel Carson—legacy (outcomes of her work)*
①	(detail)	– *her book brought attention to the use of pesticides*
②	(detail)	– *legislation was enacted to regulate pesticides*
	(detail)	– *use of DDT was banned*
③	(detail)	– *since DDT was banned, wildlife recovering*
④	(detail)	– *because of concern, EPA established*
⑤	(detail)	– *people more aware of effects of pesticides*
	(detail)	– *people more environmentally aware*

(from Application Lesson 10)

Overhead 49

ACTIVITY G *Expository Writing—Multi-Paragraph Answer*

Example Multi-Paragraph Answer

(paragraph a)

Rachel Carson had a long career as a naturalist. In college, she studied biology and zoology and later taught zoology at a university. For many years, she worked for the Fish and Wildlife Service. During that time, she published many books concerning the sea. As a result of these very readable publications, she became a famous naturalist. Carson spent the rest of her career as a full-time writer. Her concern over the dangers of pesticides led to the writing of her most famous book, Silent Spring.

(paragraph b)

Rachel Carson had very strong beliefs and concerns about our environment. First, she thought that humans should not make drastic changes in the environment. She believed that the use of the pesticide DDT would drastically change the environment and was very dangerous. She wrote about the dangers of DDT to the environment.

(paragraph c)

The work of Rachel Carson had many outcomes. Her book brought much attention to the issue of pesticide use. As a result of that attention, legislation was enacted to regulate pesticides, including the banning of DDT. Since the banning of DDT use, some of the wildlife that was put in danger is beginning to recover. One major outcome of increased environmental concern was the establishment of the EPA, the Environmental Protection Agency. As a result of Carson's work and writing, more people are concerned about the effects of pesticides and other dangers to our environment.

(from Application Lesson 11)

Overhead 50

ACTIVITY A *Vocabulary*

List 1: Tell

1. **fissures** *n.* ▶ (long, narrow openings)
2. **volcanoes** *n.* ▶ (openings in the earth through which molten rock, gases, and rocks are forced out)
3. **lava** *n.* ▶ (the molten, liquid rock that flows up and out of a volcano)
4. **crystallize** *v.* ▶ (to form crystals)
5. **Galapagos Islands** *n.* ▶ (islands in the eastern Pacific Ocean)
6. **enzymes** *n.* ▶ (chemical substances produced in the cells of all plants and animals)
7. **archaea*** *n.* ▶ (a type of microorganism)

List 2: Strategy Practice

1. **volcanic** *adj.* ▶ (related to a volcano)
2. **submarine** *n.* ▶ (a ship that can go underwater)
3. **hydrothermal** *adj.* ▶ (having to do with the action of hot liquids or gases)
4. **abnormal** *adj.* ▶ (very different from normal)
5. **temperatures** *n.* ▶ (degree of heat or coldness)
6. **biological** *adj.* ▶ (related to the study of living things)
7. **incredibly** *adv.* ▶ (hard to believe)
8. **medicinal** *adj.* ▶ (related to medicine)
9. **ordinary** *adj.* ▶ (commonly used)
10. **potentially** *adv.* ▶ (possibly)

* Pronounced ARE-kee-uh; formerly known as *archaebacteria*

(from Application Lesson 11)

Overhead 51

ACTIVITY A *Vocabulary*

List 3: Word Families

	Verb	Noun	Adjective
Family 1	solidify (to make solid or hard)	solid	solid-state
Family 2	document (to furnish evidence)	document documentary documentation	documentary
Family 3	react (to respond to something)	reaction reactants reactionary	reactionary reactive
Family 4	surround (to enclose on all sides)	surrounding	surrounding
Family 5	descend (to go down)	descent	descendant

ACTIVITY B *Spelling Dictation*

1. **react**	4. **document**
2. **reaction**	5. **documentation**
3. **reactive**	6. **documentary**

(from Application Lesson 11)

Overhead 52

ACTIVITY C *Passage Reading and Comprehension*

DEEP-SEA VENTS

A. WHAT ARE HYDROTHERMAL VENTS?

- When very hot, mineral-rich **water** spews from a **fissure**, a deep crack in the ocean floor, it is called a hydrothermal **vent**.

B. HOW DO HYDROTHERMAL VENTS FORM?

- Hydrothermal vents can form as a result of underwater **volcanoes**.
- When hot water is released from a volcano, **crystals** form where the hot water exits the rock.
- These **crystals** form hollow, chimney-like **vents**.

C. HOW DO WE KNOW THEY ARE THERE?

- While exploring a volcanic ridge near the **Galapagos** Islands, off South America, a **submarine** crew discovered a **hydrothermal** vent.

D. WHY IS THERE ECONOMIC INTEREST IN HYDROTHERMAL VENTS?

- Microorganisms called **archaea** thrive in the vents.
- These microorganisms produce **enzymes** that might speed up reactions used in industries.
- Some organisms living near the vents might have **medicinal** value.
- The vents also contain **metals** that it might be possible to mine.

E. WHAT IS LIFE LIKE IN A HYDROTHERMAL VENT?

- The environment near the vents is very harsh: the temperature is **hot**, there is no **light**, and **toxic chemicals** spew out of the earth.
- **Archaea** make food energy through the process of **chemosynthesis**.
- Archaea provide food for **tubeworms**, **eyeless crabs**, and **shrimp**.

(from Application Lesson 11)

Overhead 53

ACTIVITY G *Expository Writing—Multi-Paragraph Answer*

Prompt: Summarize the information on hydrothermal vents using the following topics: (1) What are hydrothermal vents and how are they formed? (2) What is life like in hydrothermal vents? (3) What might be the value in hydrothermal vents?

Example Multi-Paragraph Plan

Planning Box		
	(topic a)	*hydrothermal vents—what they are and how they are formed*
①	(detail)	– *fissures that spew very hot, mineral-rich water*
	(detail)	– *fissures are deep cracks in ocean floor*
②	(detail)	– *underwater volcanoes release lava and hot water filled w/ minerals*
③	(detail)	– *some minerals solidify and form crystals*
④	(detail)	– *this may occur where hot water is exiting rock*
⑤	(detail)	– *crystals can form hollow, chimney-like vents*
⑥	(detail)	– *hot water flows out of vents*
	(topic b)	*hydrothermal vents—life in them*
①	(detail)	– *very high temperatures*
	(detail)	– *no light*
	(detail)	– *toxic chemicals*
②	(detail)	– *archaea—base of food chain*
	(detail)	– *archaea use chemosynthesis to make their food*
③	(detail)	– *giant tubeworms and other creatures eat archaea*
④	(detail)	– *other creatures—eyeless crabs, shrimp, giant clams, small fish, sea sponges, brittle stars (a type of starfish)*
	(topic c)	*hydrothermal vents—value*
①	(detail)	– *scientists interested in archaea*
	(detail)	– *produce enzymes that might speed up chemical and biological reactions in industrial processes*
②	(detail)	– *some organisms might be useful in medicine*
③	(detail)	– *vast amounts of copper, zinc, gold, iron*

(from Application Lesson 11)

Overhead 54

ACTIVITY G Expository Writing—Multi-Paragraph Answer

Example Multi-Paragraph Answer

(paragraph a)

The creation of hydrothermal vents is fascinating. Hydrothermal vents refer to fissures, deep cracks in the ocean floor, that spew very hot, mineral-rich water. Their formation begins when underwater volcanoes release lava and hot water filled with minerals. Some of the minerals solidify and form crystals. The crystal formation may happen at a location where the hot water is exiting rock. In this case, the crystals form hollow, chimney-like vents. Hot water will flow out of these vents.

(paragraph b)

Despite the harsh environment of hydrothermal vents, a number of species do live there. Because of the extreme temperatures, toxic chemicals, and absence of light, the organisms are ones that are unfamiliar to us. At the base of the food chain are archaea, which use chemosynthesis to make their food. Giant tubeworms and other creatures eat archaea. Other creatures such as eyeless crabs, shrimp, giant clams, small fish, sea sponges, and brittle stars (a type of starfish) have been found living in or near hydrothermal vents.

(paragraph c)

The hydrothermal vents have potential value in a number of ways. First, the archaea found in the hydrothermal vents produce enzymes that scientists think might be able to speed up chemical and biological reactions in industrial processes. Second, scientists believe that some of the organisms in the vents might be useful in medicine. Finally, the vents include vast amounts of copper, zinc, gold, and iron that could be a highly valuable resource.

(from Application Lesson 12)

Overhead 55

ACTIVITY A *Vocabulary*

List 1: Tell

1. **earthquakes** *n.* ▶ (vibrations traveling through the earth's crust)
2. **seismologists** *n.* ▶ (scientists who study earthquakes)
3. **seismograph** *n.* ▶ (an instrument used to measure the strength of earthquakes)
4. **aseismic** *adj.* ▶ (related to the absence of earthquakes)
5. **plate tectonics** *n.* ▶ (a theory that says the earth's crust is broken into plates that move)
6. **magnitude** *n.* ▶ (the size of something)
7. **centimeters** *n.* ▶ (small units of measurement)
8. **Richter scale** *n.* ▶ (a scale for representing the strength of earthquakes)
9. **epicenter** *n.* ▶ (the point on the surface of the earth right above the center of the earthquake)

List 2: Strategy Practice

1. **vibration** *n.* ▶ (a rapid movement back and forth)
2. **boundary** *n.* ▶ (a line that marks separation)
3. **instruments** *n.* ▶ (tools for precise and careful work)
4. **satellites** *n.* ▶ (objects that revolve around the earth)
5. **extensive** *adj.* ▶ (large in amount)
6. **eventuality** *n.* ▶ (possibility)
7. **probability** *n.* ▶ (likeliness that something will happen)
8. **protection** *n.* ▶ (keeping from harm)
9. **occurrences** *n.* ▶ (things that happen)
10. **noticeable** *adj.* ▶ (easily noticed)

(from Application Lesson 12)

Overhead 56

ACTIVITY A *Vocabulary*

List 3: Word Families

	Verb	Noun	Adjective
Family 1	populate (to supply with people)	population	populous
Family 2	estimate (to make a guess about an amount)	estimation	
Family 3	collide (to crash)	collision	
Family 4	speculate (to think, to ponder)	speculation	speculative
Family 5	prepare (to get ready)	preparation preparedness	preparatory

ACTIVITY B *Spelling Dictation*

1. **populate**	4. **prepare**
2. **population**	5. **preparation**
3. **populous**	6. **preparatory**

(from Application Lesson 12)

Overhead 57

ACTIVITY C *Passage Reading and Comprehension*

A. WHAT IS AN EARTHQUAKE?

- Layers of the earth.

crust
mantle
outer core
inner core

- When a vibration travels through the earth's crust, it is called an earthquake.

B. WHAT IS THE ORIGIN OF EARTHQUAKES?

- According to the plate tectonics theory, the major cause of earthquakes is the movement of the earth's plates against each other.
- In some cases, the friction between the plates is great, and they become stuck. When the plates become unstuck, the force can cause an earthquake.
- Where the plates meet is called a fault line; more earthquakes occur along fault lines.

C. HOW IS AN EARTHQUAKE'S ENERGY MEASURED?

- When an earthquake occurs, it causes seismic waves of energy that spread from the focus, which is right below the epicenter, a point on the surface of the earth. As the energy travels away from the epicenter, it becomes weaker.
- The Richter scale rates earthquakes from 1 to 10 in magnitude.
- This rating is based on seismograph readings and the distance from the epicenter.

D. HOW DO WE PREPARE FOR THE "BIG ONE"?

- Scientists are able to determine where an earthquake might happen.
- However, it is not possible at this time to predict when an earthquake will occur.
- People along fault lines can improve their safety by (answers will vary).

(from Application Lesson 12)

Overhead 58

ACTIVITY G *Expository Writing—Multi-Paragraph Answer*

Prompt: Summarize the information provided on the structure of the earth and location of earthquakes; the cause or origin of earthquakes; and the measurement of earthquakes.

Example Multi-Paragraph Plan

Planning Box
(topic a) *structure of the earth and location of earthquakes*
① (detail) – *core—solid nickel and iron (inner) surrounded by molten*
metals (outer)
② (detail) – *mantle—layer of rock*
③ (detail) – *crust—coolest, top layer*
④ (detail) – *earthquake—when vibration travels through earth's crust*
(topic b) *earthquakes—cause/origin*
① (detail) – *explained through theory of plate tectonics*
② { (detail) – *earth's plates move*
(detail) – *plates drift at very slow rates*
③ (detail) – *normally plates slide past each other*
④ (detail) – *when friction great, sections of rock can get stuck*
⑤ (detail) – *if become unstuck in sudden jerk, force causes earthquake*
(topic c) *earthquakes—measurement*
① (detail) – *seismographs measure vibration of earth during earthquake*
② { (detail) – *using seismograph readings and the distance from the*
epicenter, Richter scale rating determined
(detail) – *Richter scale rating between 1 and 10*
③ (detail) – *major earthquake above 7*

(from Application Lesson 12)

Overhead 59

ACTIVITY G *Expository Writing—Multi-Paragraph Answer*

Example Multi-Paragraph Answer

(paragraph a)

To understand earthquakes, it is important to understand the structure of the earth and the location of earthquakes. At the center of the earth is the core, which is made of solid nickel and iron (the inner core), surrounded by molten metals (the outer core). The next layer is the mantle, a layer of rock. The coolest, top layer is the crust. When a vibration travels through the earth's crust, it is called an earthquake.

(paragraph b)

The cause of earthquakes is explained using the theory of plate tectonics. According to this theory, the earth has a number of plates that drift at very slow rates. Normally, these plates slide past each other. However, sometimes the friction between the plates is great, and sections of the rock get stuck. If the sections of rock get unstuck in a sudden jerk, the force causes an earthquake.

(paragraph c)

The measurement of the strength of earthquakes is done in the same way around the world. Seismographs are used to measure such things as the vibration of the earth during an earthquake. Using seismograph readings and the distance from the epicenter, a Richter scale rating between 1 and 10 is determined. A Richter scale rating above 7 indicates a major earthquake.

(from Application Lesson 13)

Overhead 60

ACTIVITY A *Vocabulary*

List 1: Tell

1. **meteorologists** *n.* ▶ (people who study the atmosphere and changes within it—especially the weather)
2. **atmosphere** *n.* ▶ (the mass of gases surrounding the earth)
3. **climatologists** *n.* ▶ (people who study climate)
4. **associated** *v.* ▶ (connected in one's mind)
5. **phenomenon** *n.* ▶ (an event that can be observed)
6. **chemistry** *n.* ▶ (the science that deals with how things are made up and how they change when they react with other things)
7. **hurricanes** *n.* ▶ (storms with violent winds)
8. **tornadoes** *n.* ▶ (dark columns of fast-moving air shaped like a funnel)
9. **glaciers** *n.* ▶ (large, slow-moving masses of ice)
10. **supercomputers** *n.* ▶ (very large and fast computers)
11. **typically** *adv.* ▶ (usually)
12. **frequently** *adv.* ▶ (often)

List 2: Strategy Practice

1. **conversation** *n.* ▶ (friendly talk between people)
2. **climatic** *adj.* ▶ (related to typical weather)
3. **conditions** *n.* ▶ (the way things are)
4. **density** *n.* ▶ (thickness)
5. **condensation** *n.* ▶ (the change of a gas to a liquid)
6. **precipitation** *n.* ▶ (any form of water falling to earth)
7. **accompanying** *v.* ▶ (going along with)
8. **alternatively** *adv.* ▶ (on the other hand)
9. **completion** *n.* ▶ (the end; the state of being finished)
10. **productivity** *n.* ▶ (the ability to produce a lot)

(from Application Lesson 13)

Overhead 61

List 3: Word Families

	Verb	Noun	Adjective
Family 1	complete (to end; to finish)	completion	complete
Family 2	predict (to declare beforehand)	prediction	predictable
Family 3	direct (to manage or control the course)	direction director	directional
Family 4	create (to cause to exist)	creation creator	creative
Family 5	evaporate (to change a liquid into a gas)	evaporation	evaporable

ACTIVITY B *Spelling Dictation*

1. **predict**	4. **create**
2. **prediction**	5. **creation**
3. **predictable**	6. **creative**

(from Application Lesson 13)

Overhead 62

ACTIVITY C *Passage Reading and Comprehension*

WEATHER

A. WHAT IS AN AIR MASS?

- An air mass is a large chunk of ___air___ in the atmosphere.
- Warm air masses ___rise___.
- Cold air masses ___fall___.

B. THE MOVEMENT OF AIR MASSES AS A FACTOR IN THE WEATHER

- Rising warm air carries ___water vapor___.
- When air cools, ___condensation___ occurs, and ___clouds___ are formed.
- When the clouds become heavier, ___precipitation___ (e.g., rain, snow) occurs.

C. COLD WEATHER FRONTS

- ___Cold air mass___ moves in and pushes warm air mass up.
- ___Wind___ is produced.

D. WARM WEATHER FRONTS

- ___Warm air mass___ moves in and rises up over the cold air mass.
- When warm air rises high enough, it ___rains___.

E. THE LAND AS A FACTOR IN THE WEATHER

- An air mass over the land becomes the same ___temperature___.
- Dark-colored areas of earth absorb sun's energy and become ___warmer___.
- Glaciers reflect back sun's energy and surface becomes ___cooler___.

F. THE SUN AND THE SEASONS AS FACTORS IN THE WEATHER

- At different times of the year and in different places, more or less sunlight received, so weather is ___different___.

G. THE JET STREAM AS A FACTOR IN THE WEATHER

- The jet stream is a fast-moving river of ___air___ that circles the earth.

H. PREDICTING THE WEATHER

- ___Climatologists___ study the weather.
- Based on what they know about how climate behaves, they ___predict___ the weather.

(from Application Lesson 13)

Overhead 63

ACTIVITY G *Expository Writing—Multi-Paragraph Answer*

Prompt: Describe how the movement of air masses, the land, and the sun affect weather on the earth.

Example Multi-Paragraph Plan

Planning Box
(topic a) *effects on weather—movement of air masses*
① (detail) – *air masses are always moving*
② (detail) – *when warm air mass rises, carries water vapor up*
③ (detail) – *water vapor cools and condensation occurs*
④ (detail) – *when condensation completed, clouds become heavier*
(detail) – *precipitation results*
⑤ (detail) – *warm air masses and cold air masses collide*
(detail) – *various kinds of weather develop*
(topic b) *effects on weather—land*
① (detail) – *air mass above earth becomes same temperature as land*
② (detail) – *dark-colored areas of earth (e.g., mountains) absorb sunlight*
and heat up
③ (detail) – *air above dark-colored areas becomes warmer*
④ (detail) – *dark-colored areas heat up and create drying winds*
⑤ (detail) – *glaciers and snowfields reflect sunlight back into atmosphere*
⑥ (detail) – *surface and air becomes cooler*
(topic c) *effects on weather—sun*
① (detail) – *at different times of the year, different parts of the earth*
receive more or less sunlight
② (detail) – *changes in sunlight lead to different temperatures*
③ (detail) – *amount of sunlight also affects how much water evaporates*
into air
(detail) – *affects the nature and direction of winds*

(from Application Lesson 13)

Overhead 64

ACTIVITY G *Expository Writing—Multi-Paragraph Answer*

Example Multi-Paragraph Answer

(paragraph a)

One thing that affects the weather is the movement of air masses. Air masses are always moving. When a warm air mass rises, it carries water vapor up into the atmosphere. The water vapor then cools, and condensation occurs. When condensation is complete, the clouds become heavier, and precipitation results. Sometimes warm air masses and cold air masses collide, creating a variety of weather conditions.

(paragraph b)

Land also affects the weather. An air mass above the earth becomes the same temperature as the land. Dark-colored areas of the earth (e.g., mountains) absorb sunlight and heat up. As a result, the air above the dark-colored areas also becomes warm. This warming may even cause drying winds. On the other hand, glaciers and snowfields reflect sunlight back into the atmosphere. Here the surface and the air above the land are cooler.

(paragraph c)

A third variable that affects weather is the sun. At different times of the year, different parts of the earth receive more or less sunlight. It is obvious that changes in the amount of sunlight lead to different temperatures. However, that is not the only effect the sun has on weather. The amount of sunlight also affects how much water evaporates into the air and the nature and direction of winds.

(from Application Lesson 14)

Overhead 65

ACTIVITY A *Vocabulary*

List 1: Tell

1.	canopy	*n.*	▶ (a covering)
2.	emergent	*adj.*	▶ (rising or coming out of)
3.	understory	*n.*	▶ (smaller trees that grow beneath big trees in the forest)

List 2: Strategy Practice

1.	precious	*adj.*	▶ (having great value)
2.	abundant	*adj.*	▶ (plentiful)
3.	diversity	*n.*	▶ (variety)
4.	comfortable	*adj.*	▶ (free from worry; at ease)
5.	consequently	*adv.*	▶ (as a result)
6.	portion	*n.*	▶ (part of a whole)
7.	deforestation	*n.*	▶ (the clearing of forests)
8.	undesirable	*adj.*	▶ (unwanted)
9.	maturity	*n.*	▶ (full growth and development)
10.	penetrating	*v.*	▶ (passing through)

(from Application Lesson 14)

Overhead 66

List 3: Word Families

	Verb	Noun	Adjective
Family 1	prefer (to like better)	preference	preferable
Family 2	decompose (to rot)	decomposition decomposer	decomposable
Family 3	destroy (to ruin completely; to cause to go away; to end)	destruction	destructive destructible
Family 4	contribute (to give)	contribution contributor	contributable
Family 5	inhabit (to live in a place)	inhabitant	inhabitable

ACTIVITY B *Spelling Dictation*

1. **prefer**	4. **contribute**
2. **preference**	5. **contribution**
3. **preferable**	6. **contributor**

(from Application Lesson 14)

Overhead 67

ACTIVITY C *Passage Reading and Comprehension*

TROPICAL RAINFORESTS

A. FACTS ABOUT TROPICAL RAINFORESTS

- Tropical rainforests are located near the **equator**.
- Though they cover a **small** part of the earth, they contain 50% to 90% of all **species**.

B. EMERGENT LAYER

- The emergent layer is the **topmost** layer.
- The broad leaves of the tallest trees catch a good deal of **sunlight**.
- You might see such animals as **(answers will vary)** at this level.

C. CANOPY LAYER

- Under the emergent layer is the **canopy** layer, which consists of dense clusters of trees with smooth oval leaves.
- The trees at this level block **sunlight** from lower layers.
- You might see such animals as **(answers will vary)** at this level.

D. UNDERSTORY

- Beneath the canopy is the **understory**. Because of little sunlight, trees are **shorter** and have broad, flat leaves to catch **sunlight**.
- The understory is **humid** because moisture collects.

E. FOREST FLOOR

- Because sunlight cannot shine through, the forest floor is **dark**.
- Few green **plants**.
- **Decaying** matter provides food for insects.

F. CONCERN FOR THE RAINFORESTS

- With rainforests being destroyed, there are many concerns.
- Because of deforestation, climate is affected, thus affecting **climate** and **weather** in other areas.
- With deforestation, fewer trees are taking in **carbon dioxide** and releasing **oxygen**. More heat is present in the atmosphere, which may contribute to **global warming**.
- **Plants** might lead to **medical** breakthroughs if not destroyed.

(from Application Lesson 14)

Overhead 68

ACTIVITY G *Expository Writing—Multi-Paragraph Answer*

Prompt: Write one paragraph summarizing information about the four layers of the rainforest and one paragraph about scientists' concerns about the destruction of the rainforests.

Example Multi-Paragraph Plan

	Planning Box
(topic a)	*rainforests—four layers*
① (detail)	– *emergent layer—topmost layer*
(detail)	– *emergent layer—tall trees with broad leaves*
② (detail)	– *emergent layer—butterflies, eagles, monkeys*
③ (detail)	– *canopy layer—shorter trees with smooth oval leaves*
④ (detail)	– *canopy layer—abundant food for monkeys, snakes, birds*
⑤ (detail)	– *understory—below canopy*
(detail)	– *understory—little sunlight reaches plants*
⑥ (detail)	– *understory—shorter trees, few animals, many insects*
⑦ (detail)	– *forest floor—bottom of rainforest*
⑧ (detail)	– *forest floor—decaying matter on ground*
(detail)	– *forest floor—insects thrive by eating decaying matter*
⑨ (detail)	– *forest floor—few green plants*
(topic b)	*rainforests—scientists concerned about destruction of rainforests*
① (detail)	– *chopped down for wood and farmland*
② (detail)	– *fewer trees available to take in carbon dioxide and release*
	oxygen into atmosphere
③ (detail)	– *result—more heat in our atmosphere*
④ (detail)	– *change in gases released into air and changes in weather*
	patterns will increase global warming
⑤ (detail)	– *plants that could have medicinal use are being destroyed*
(detail)	– *inhabitants of rainforests disappearing*

(from Application Lesson 14)

Overhead 69

ACTIVITY G *Expository Writing—Multi-Paragraph Answer*

Example Multi-Paragraph Answer

(paragraph a)

The rainforest has four layers. The topmost layer, the emergent layer, has many tall trees with broad leaves. Butterflies, eagles, and monkeys find their homes in these trees. The next layer, the canopy layer, has shorter trees with smooth oval leaves. This layer has abundant food for a variety of monkeys, snakes, and birds. The layer below the canopy, the understory, has little sunlight that can reach its plants. At this layer, the trees are even shorter and the animals are fewer in number, but there are a vast number of insects. At the bottom of the rainforest, you find the forest floor. The forest floor is covered with decaying matter, a perfect home for many insects. There are few green plants on the forest floor.

(paragraph b)

Scientists are very concerned about the destruction of rainforests. Currently, many rainforests are being cut down for wood and farmland. When the forests are destroyed, fewer trees are available to take in carbon dioxide and release oxygen into the atmosphere. One result is that more heat is released into our atmosphere. Changes in the gases released into the air and the changes in weather patterns resulting from deforestation will increase global warming. Not only will climate changes emerge, but many plants that could potentially be used for medicine will be destroyed, and other inhabitants of the rainforests will disappear and become extinct.

(from Application Lesson 15)

Overhead 70

ACTIVITY A *Vocabulary*

List 1: Tell

1. **industrialized** *adj.* ▶ (related to business)
2. **Exxon Valdez** *n.* ▶ (an oil tanker that ran aground in Prince William Sound)
3. **consequences** *n.* ▶ (results of earlier actions)
4. **mechanical** *adj.* ▶ (having to do with machinery)
5. **rescuers** *n.* ▶ (people who save other beings)
6. **aquatic** *adj.* ▶ (related to water)
7. **buoyancy** *n.* ▶ (the ability to float or rise in water)
8. **aquarium** *n.* ▶ (a place that houses fish, water animals, and water plants)

List 2: Strategy Practice

1. **containment** *n.* ▶ (to keep from spreading)
2. **deliberate** *adj.* ▶ (carefully planned)
3. **encountered** *v.* ▶ (met unexpectedly)
4. **similarly** *adv.* ▶ (being alike)
5. **fossilization** *n.* ▶ (the act of becoming a fossil)
6. **minimize** *or* **minimize** *v.* ▶ (to lessen)
7. **monitored** *v.* ▶ (watched)
8. **pollution** *n.* ▶ (something that makes something else dirty or impure)
9. **replenish** *v.* ▶ (to provide a new supply)
10. **unfortunately** *adv.* ▶ (unluckily)

(from Application Lesson 15)

Overhead 71

ACTIVITY A *Vocabulary*

List 3: Word Families

	Verb	Noun	Adjective
Family 1	include (to put in a group)	inclusion	inclusive
Family 2	sabotage (to damage or destroy deliberately)	sabotage saboteur	
Family 3	locate (to discover the exact place of)	location locater	
Family 4	dispose (to get rid of or throw away)	disposal	disposable
Family 5	attend (to fix one's thoughts on something)	attention	attentive

ACTIVITY B *Spelling Dictation*

1. **attend**	4. **dispose**
2. **attention**	5. **disposal**
3. **attentive**	6. **disposable**

(from Application Lesson 15)

Overhead 72

ACTIVITY C Passage Reading and Comprehension

OIL SPILLS

A. OIL

- Oil is a resource used by all countries, especially **industrialized** countries.
- Oil takes **years** to form and is found in limited locations.
- Oil is very **expensive** to remove from the ground.

B. CAUSES OF OIL SPILLS

- Oil is transported on huge **oil tankers**.
- Oil spills can be caused by human error, **bad** equipment, **poor** weather conditions, or **illegal** dumping.

C. CONSEQUENCES OF OIL SPILLS

- The spilled oil floats on the water, causing an oil **slick**.
- Marine mammals and birds may lose their ability to repel **water**, keep **warm**, or float.
- They may also be **poisoned** if they swallow the oil.
- The oil also kills **plankton**.

D. RESPONSE TO OIL SPILLS

- The first goal is to **contain** the oil spill.
- The next step is to rescue the **wildlife**.
- Rescuers try to **keep** animals out of the area.
- Rescuers also remove oil from the animals' **(answers will vary)** ______.

E. CLEANING THE SPILL

- Using **mechanical** containment techniques, oil is captured so it can be disposed of properly.
- Using **chemical** and **biological** methods, the oil is broken down faster.
- Using **physical** methods, such as wiping and raking, shorelines are cleaned.

F. PREVENTION

- Federal **regulations** are designed to prevent oil spills.
- All people can help by proper disposal and **recycling** of oil.

(from Application Lesson 15)

Overhead 73

ACTIVITY G *Expository Writing—Multi-Paragraph Answer*

Prompt: Describe the causes, consequences, and responses to oil spills.

Example Multi-Paragraph Plan

Planning Box
(topic a) *oil spills—causes*
① (detail) – *oil must be transported to the country where it will be used*
(detail) – *when being transported, accidents may happen*
② (detail) – *caused by mistakes of people*
(detail) – *caused by inadequate equipment*
(detail) – *caused by poor weather conditions*
③ (detail) – *deliberate dumping of oil*
(topic b) *oil spills—consequences*
(detail) ~~*caused by people's actions*~~
① (detail) – *spilled oil spreads out over water—oil slick*
② (detail) – *gets on the feathers and fur of animals*
(detail) – *animals can't stay warm or float*
③ (detail) – *ingested oil can poison fish*
④ (detail) – *kills plankton—food for other organisms*
(topic c) *oil spills—responses*
① (detail) – *contain spill*
② (detail) – *keep wildlife away from contaminated area*
③ (detail) – *capture and treat birds and marine mammals that have been*
affected by oil
④ (detail) – *flush oil from eyes and intestines*
(detail) – *wash fur and feathers*
⑤ (detail) – *release when health regained*

(from Application Lesson 15)

Overhead 74

ACTIVITY G *Expository Writing—Multi-Paragraph Answer*

Example Multi-Paragraph Answer

(paragraph a)

Oil spills are caused in a number of ways. Since oil must be transported to the country where it will be used, accidents can occur in the transport. These accidents can result from human error, inadequate equipment, or poor weather conditions. In some cases, an oil spill may be even caused by deliberate dumping of oil.

(paragraph b)

The consequences of an oil spill can be enormous and long lasting. When the oil spill occurs, the oil spreads out over the water, creating an oil slick. This oil can get on the feathers and fur of animals, making staying warm and floating very difficult for them. Fish may also ingest or swallow the poisonous oil. One of most devastating consequences of an oil spill is the death of plankton, food for many ocean organisms.

(paragraph c)

The response to oil spills must be very quick to minimize the impact on wildlife. First, an effort must be made to contain the oil spill so that it does not spread even further over the ocean surface. Next, every effort must be made to keep wildlife away from the contaminated area. At the same time, birds and marine mammals that have been affected by the oil spill are captured and treated. Workers flush oil from their eyes and intestines, and wash their fur or feathers carefully. When the animals regain their health, they are released back into nature.

Appendix A

Reproducibles

Reproduce the following student strategies and reference chart. Distribute the copies to students during the indicated lessons.

Reproducible	Lesson
Reproducible 1 *REWARDS* Strategies for Reading Long Words	Review Lesson 1 *or* Application Lesson 1
Reproducible 2 Prefixes, Suffixes, and Vowel Combinations Reference Chart	Review Lesson 1 *or* Application Lesson 1
Reproducible 3 Comprehension Strategy—Multiple Choice	Application Lesson 3
Reproducible 4 Writing Strategy—Single-Paragraph Answer	Application Lesson 4
Reproducible 5 Discussion Guidelines	Application Lesson 5
Reproducible 6 Writing Strategy—Multi-Paragraph Answer	Application Lesson 6
Reproducible 7 Rubric—Multi-Paragraph Answer	Application Lesson 7

Reproducible 1

REWARDS *Strategies for Reading Long Words*

Overt Strategy

1. Circle the prefixes.
2. Circle the suffixes.
3. Underline the vowels.
4. Say the parts of the word.
5. Say the whole word.
6. Make it a real word.

Example:

(re)(con)struc(tion)

Covert Strategy

1. Look for prefixes, suffixes, and vowels.
2. Say the parts of the word.
3. Say the whole word.
4. Make it a real word.

Reproducible 2

Prefixes, Suffixes, and Vowel Combinations Reference Chart

	Decoding Element	Key Word	Decoding Element	Key Word	Decoding Element	Key Word
Prefixes	**a**	above	**com**	compare	**mis**	mistaken
	ab	abdomen	**con**	continue	**multi**	multiage
	ac	accommodate	**de**	depart	**over**	overpopulate
	ad	advertise	**dis**	discover	**per**	permit
	af	afford	**en**	entail	**pre**	prevent
	ap	appreciate	**ex**	example	**pro**	protect
	ar	arrange	**hydro**	hydrothermal	**re**	return
	as	associate	**im**	immediate	**sub**	submarine
	at	attention	**in**	insert	**trans**	translate
	auto	automatic	**ir**	irregular	**un**	uncover
	be	belong	**micro**	microscope		
Suffixes	**able**	disposable	**ful**	careful	**ness**	kindness
	age	courage	**ible**	reversible	**or**	tailor
	al	final	**ic**	frantic	**ous**	nervous
	ance	disturbance	**ing**	running	**s**	birds
	ant	dormant	**ion**	million	**ship**	ownership
	ary	military	**ish**	selfish	**sion**	mission
	ate	regulate	**ism**	realism	**sive**	expensive
	cial	special	**ist**	artist	**tial**	partial
	cious	precious	**ity**	oddity	**tion**	action
	ed	landed	**ize**	criticize	**tious**	cautious
	ence	essence	**le**	cradle	**tive**	attentive
	ent	consistent	**less**	useless	**ture**	picture
	er	farmer	**ly**	safely	**y**	industry
	est	biggest	**ment**	argument		
Vowel Combinations	**ai**	rain	**ou**	loud	**a–e**	make
	au	sauce	**ow**	low, down	**e–e**	Pete
	ay	say	**oy**	boy	**i–e**	side
	ea	meat, thread	**ar**	farm	**o–e**	hope
	ee	deep	**er**	her	**u–e**	use
	oa	foam	**ir**	bird		
	oi	void	**or**	torn		
	oo	moon, book	**ur**	turn		

Reproducible 3

Comprehension Strategy—Multiple Choice

Step 1: Read the item.

Step 2: Read all of the choices.

Step 3: Think about why each choice might be correct or incorrect. Check the article as needed.

Step 4: From the possible correct choices, select the best answer.

Reproducible 4

Writing Strategy—Single-Paragraph Answer

Step 1: Read the item.

Step 2: Turn the question into part of the answer and write it down.

Step 3: Think of the answer or locate the answer in the article.

Step 4: Complete your answer.

Reproducible 5

Discussion Guidelines

Speaker		Listener	
Looks like:	**Sounds like:**	**Looks like:**	**Sounds like:**
• Facing peers • Making eye contact • Participating	• Using pleasant, easy-to-hear voice • Sharing opinions, supporting facts and reasons from the article and from your experience • Staying on the topic	• Facing speaker • Making eye contact • Participating	• Waiting quietly to speak • Giving positive, supportive comments • Disagreeing respectfully

Reproducible 6

Writing Strategy—Multi-Paragraph Answer

Step 1: LIST (List the details that are important enough to include in your answer.)

Step 2: CROSS OUT (Reread the details. Cross out any that don't go with the topic.)

Step 3: CONNECT (Connect any details that could go into one sentence.)

Step 4: NUMBER (Number the details in a logical order.)

Step 5: WRITE (Write the paragraph.)

Step 6: EDIT (Revise and proofread your answer.)

Reproducible 7

Rubric—Multi-Paragraph Answer

Rubric— Multi-Paragraph Answer	Student or Partner Rating	Teacher Rating
1. Did the author state the topic in the first sentence?	a. Yes Fix up b. Yes Fix up c. Yes Fix up	a. Yes No b. Yes No c. Yes No
2. Did the author include details that go with the topic?	a. Yes Fix up b. Yes Fix up c. Yes Fix up	a. Yes No b. Yes No c. Yes No
3. Did the author combine details in some of the sentences?	a. Yes Fix up b. Yes Fix up c. Yes Fix up	a. Yes No b. Yes No c. Yes No
4. Is the answer easy to understand?	Yes Fix up	Yes No
5. Did the author correctly spell words, particularly the words found in the article?	Yes Fix up	Yes No
6. Did the author use correct capitalization, capitalizing the first word in the sentence and proper names of people, places, and things?	Yes Fix up	Yes No
7. Did the author use correct punctuation, including a period at the end of each sentence?	Yes Fix up	Yes No

Appendix B

Reproducible Information Webs

Description: For each of the lessons, an **Information Web** (graphic organizer) is provided. After reading a section of an article, students will be asked to stop and add facts to their **Information Web**. Subsequently, they will use the Web to teach information to their partners, to review with the class, and to study independently. The answers are found on the Information Web overheads provided for each lesson.

Preparation: Before beginning each lesson, reproduce the corresponding **Information Web** for each student.

(from Application Lesson 1)

Reproducible A

ACTIVITY C *Passage Reading and Comprehension*

ECOSYSTEMS

A. ENERGY AND MATTER IN ECOSYSTEMS

- Organisms need ______________ and ______________ to carry out life processes such as ______________ ______________.
- ______________ and tiny organisms capture the sun's ______________ and transform it into food energy (______________).
- Organisms that cannot make their own food then eat these plants and tiny ______________.
- When organisms die, the ______________ and ______________ in their bodies become food for ______________ and bacteria.

B. INTERACTIONS WITHIN ECOSYSTEMS

- Organisms interact with other organisms within their ______________.
- Some of these interactions are mutually beneficial. For example, as bees get their food from plants, they distribute ______________ so flowers can make ______________.

C. CHANGES IN ECOSYSTEMS

- Since every ______________ has special life requirements, species vary across ecosystems.
- When parts of an ______________ are changed or altered, the ______________ may be changed.
- Large changes in ______________ will create major changes in an ecosystem. For example, the extinction of dinosaurs has been connected to ______________.

(from Application Lesson 2)

Reproducible B

ACTIVITY C *Passage Reading and Comprehension*

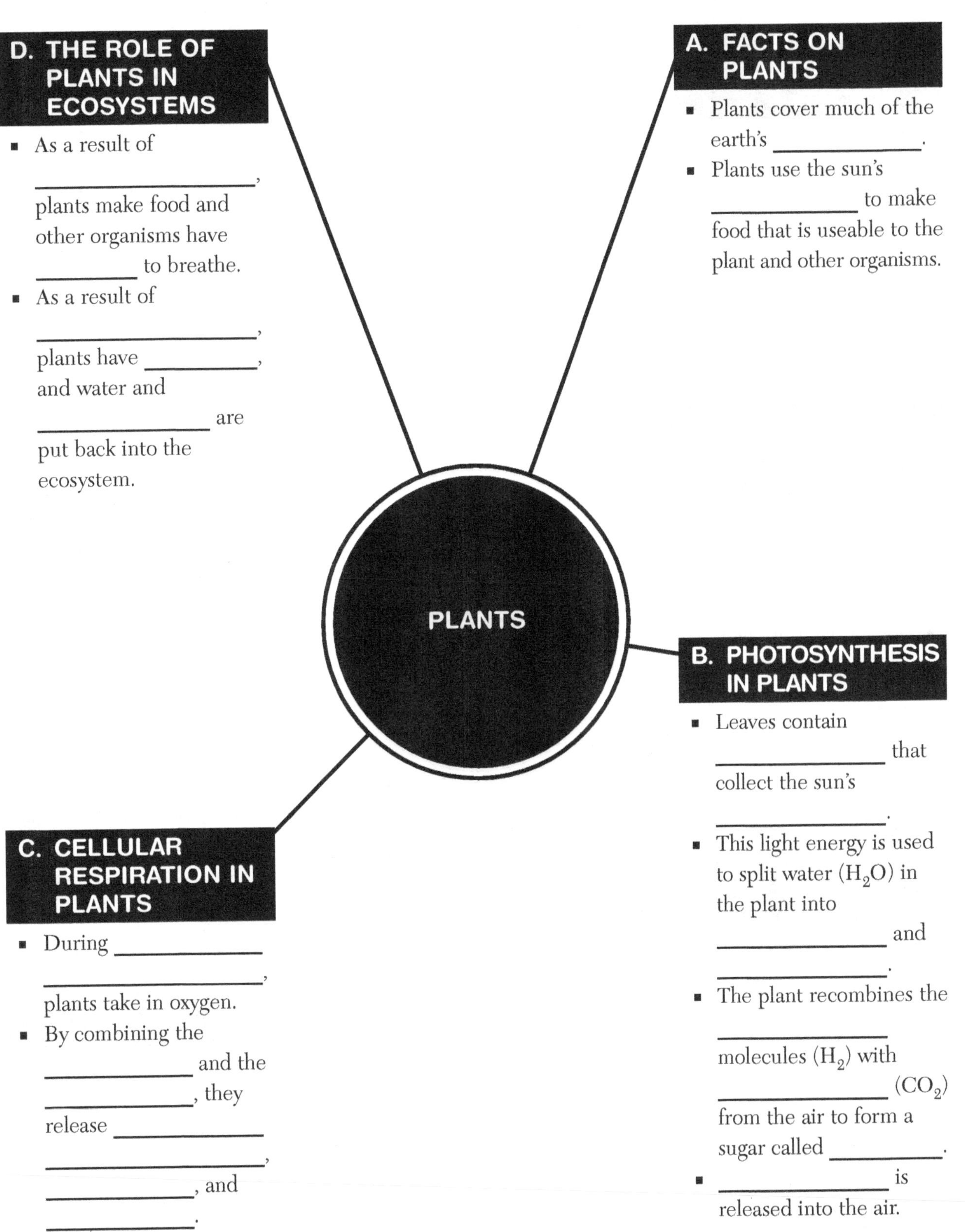
PLANTS
A. FACTS ON PLANTS
Plants cover much of the earth's ____________.
Plants use the sun's ____________ to make food that is useable to the plant and other organisms.
B. PHOTOSYNTHESIS IN PLANTS
Leaves contain ____________ that collect the sun's ____________.
This light energy is used to split water (H_2O) in the plant into ____________ and ____________.
The plant recombines the ____________ molecules (H_2) with ____________ (CO_2) from the air to form a sugar called ____________.
____________ is released into the air.
C. CELLULAR RESPIRATION IN PLANTS
During ____________ ____________, plants take in oxygen.
By combining the ____________ and the ____________, they release ____________ ____________, ____________, and ____________.
D. THE ROLE OF PLANTS IN ECOSYSTEMS
As a result of ____________, plants make food and other organisms have ________ to breathe.
As a result of ____________, plants have ________, and water and ____________ are put back into the ecosystem.

(from Application Lesson 3)

Reproducible C

ACTIVITY C *Passage Reading and Comprehension*

ENERGY & MATTER MOVING THROUGH ECOSYSTEMS

A. FOOD PRODUCERS

- Food producers make their own __________.
- Most are __________.
- In the process of photosynthesis, plants use energy from the ________ to produce food.
- In the process of chemosynthesis, producers break apart simple __________ to get energy.

B. THE ENERGY LINK BETWEEN THE SUN AND ECOSYSTEMS

- Producers capture energy from the ________ and store that ________ in their body structures.
- The energy stored by __________ becomes food for other living things.
- If there are many producers in an ecosystem, the ecosystem is __________.

C. FOOD CONSUMERS

- Food consumers are unable to make their own __________.
- Any organism that eats another __________ is a food consumer.

D. THE ENERGY LINKS BETWEEN PRODUCERS AND CONSUMERS

- In a food chain, one organism eats another __________, who eats another __________, who eats another __________.
- When food chains overlap, they form a __________.

E. SPECIAL RELATIONSHIPS IN ECOSYSTEMS

- __________ are organisms that get their food from living in, or on, other organisms.
- Some organisms, like __________ and ________ live together and help each other.

F. RECYCLING ENERGY AND MATTER

- Decomposers break down and feed on __________.
- __________ and __________ are decomposers.

(from Application Lesson 4)

Reproducible D

ACTIVITY C *Passage Reading and Comprehension*

FOOD PRESERVATION

A. SPOILED FOOD

- Food spoils because ___________ break down or change the food.
- To keep foods from spoiling, you must _________ the microbes, slow their _________, or change the _________ so microbes can't use it.

B. DRYING AND SMOKING

- When a food is dried, microbes can't live without _____________.
- Both _____________ and _____________ are toxic to microbes.

C. REFRIGERATION AND FREEZING

- Refrigeration _________ the growth of microbes.
- Freezing can _________ the growth of microbes.
- These methods of preservation don't change the _______________, _______________, or _______________ too much.

D. CANNING, PASTEURIZATION, AND PICKLING

- When a food is canned, it is _________, and, as a result, the microbes are _________.
- When a food is pickled, an unfriendly place for microbes is created when _________, _________, and _________ are added.
- These methods of preservation do change the ________, ________, and _______________ __________ of the food.

E. CHEMICAL PRESERVATIVES

- Some spices such as _________________ can slow the growth of microbes.
- Today, ___________ are often added to foods to reduce spoilage.
- Adding chemicals to foods is controversial because _________________.

F. IMPORTANCE OF FOOD PRESERVATION

- Because of these food preservation procedures, people are less likely to eat _____________ food and become _________.

(from Application Lesson 5)

Reproducible E

ACTIVITY C *Passage Reading and Comprehension*

THE CARDIOVASCULAR SYSTEM

A. WHAT IS IT?

- Humans have five levels of organization: ________, ________, ________, ________ ________, and the whole ________.
- The cardiovascular system includes your ________, ________, and ________.

B. THE HEART

- The heart is divided into ________ chambers. The upper chambers are the ________, and the lower chambers are the ________.
- The ________ pump blood into the heart and down into the ________.
- The ________ pump blood out of the heart into the rest of the body.

C. THE BLOOD

- Your blood is made up of liquid components called ________ and solid components called ________, ________, and ________.
- Red blood cells carry ________ to the body. White blood cells work hard to fight ________ and diseases.
- Platelets promote ______.

D. BLOOD PATHWAYS

- Two pathways carry ______. The ______ pathway carries oxygen-rich blood to your body and returns the ________ blood back to your heart. The ________ pathway carries the deoxygenated blood from your heart to your lungs, where ________ is released and ________ is picked up.

E. THE BLOOD VESSELS

- The largest type of blood vessels are the ________.
- The ________ and the ________ carry blood away from the ________.
- The blood then flows through ________, ________, and ________.
- The ________ carry blood back to the heart.

F. PROBLEMS

- With high blood pressure, blood vessels are ________, forcing the heart to work harder.
- With arteriosclerosis or atherosclerosis, the ________ must work too hard, or it fails altogether.

(from Application Lesson 6)

Reproducible F

ACTIVITY C *Passage Reading and Comprehension*

HEART TRANSPLANTS

A. WHO IS ELIGIBLE FOR A NEW HEART?

- When a person has a ____________ heart and has NOT responded to prescribed ___________, a heart transplant may be called for.
- People with other ____________ problems are generally not eligible.

B. WHAT MUST HAPPEN BEFORE THE TRANSPLANT?

- The person's names goes on a ___________ until a suitable ___________ heart is located.
- The heart must match in ____________ and ____________ types.

C. WHAT OCCURS DURING THE SURGERY?

- When the donor heart is removed from the body, it is packed in special ___________ and placed on ___________.
- When the surgery begins, the ___________ heart is removed, and the patient is kept alive using a ___________ machine.
- Once the heart is working ______________, the patient is closed up.

D. WHAT IS NECESSARY AFTER THE TRANSPLANT?

- The body may try to ____________ the new heart.
- For this reason, the patient must take special ____________.

(from Application Lesson 7)

Reproducible G

ACTIVITY C *Passage Reading and Comprehension*

VIRUSES

A. WHAT ARE VIRUSES?

- Viruses have some characteristics of ________ things and ________ things.
- In some cases, viruses are ________, but they can live and ________.
- To live and reproduce, viruses must invade a ________ and use it.
- Viruses are NOT ________ but have genetic ________.

B. HOW DO YOU GET INFECTED?

- Different viruses need different ________.
- The ________ coat helps the virus detect the right kind of host cell.
- In adsorption, the virus attaches to the outside of a ________.
- In ________, the virus injects genetic information into the host cell.
- During ________ and ________, the host cell's enzymes obey the virus's genetic instructions.
- During ________, new virus particles leave the ________ in search of new host cells.

C. WHAT DO VIRUSES LOOK LIKE?

- Viruses are smaller than most ________ cells.
- Viruses can only be observed using ________ microscopes.
- Viruses have different ________.
- One common virus is shaped like a ________.

D. HOW CAN WE BE PROTECTED FROM VIRUSES?

- To reduce the spread of viruses, individuals should cover their mouths with a tissue when ________, and they should wash their ________.
- In some cases, a ________ can prevent the virus from infecting individuals.
- Vaccines promote the production of ________ within the body.
- Because the genetic code in viruses can change, ________ also have to be altered.

(from Application Lesson 8)

Reproducible H

ACTIVITY C *Passage Reading and Comprehension*

ANTONI VAN LEEUWENHOEK—FATHER OF MICROBIOLOGY

A. LIFE

- Lived in ________ in 1600s.
- Became interested in microscopes after reading ____________.
- Learned about microscopy (the use of the __________ to investigate tiny ________ things).

B. AN UNUSUAL HOBBY

- Developed a ________ that was different from compound microscopes.
- His microscopes had only ________ lens; however, they were ________ powerful than compound microscopes.
- Became skilled at lens ____________.

C. VAN LEEUWENHOEK'S OBSERVATIONS

- Observed and described small specimens, including ________, ________, and ________.
- Wrote down his findings and sent them to the ______________ ______________.

D. AN IMPORTANT DISCOVERY

- Discovered __________ in a drop of water.
- ____________, a new branch of science, began.
- Provided descriptions of bacteria, algae, and plant and muscle __________.
- Discovered ________ blood cells.

E. RECOGNITION

- After his letters were published, he became quite ___________.
- The field of ___________ is based on his work.
- He kept his lens-grinding technique a _________.

(from Application Lesson 9)

Reproducible I

ACTIVITY C *Passage Reading and Comprehension*

ATOMS

A. WHAT ARE ATOMS?

- Atoms are the building blocks of all ________.
- Atoms are the smallest part of an ________ that behaves like the ________.
- Thus, elements such as carbon and hydrogen are made up of ________.

B. HISTORY

- In 530 B.C., Democritus theorized that all things could be broken into ________ parts and ultimately into ________.
- In 1808, ________ added to the work of Democritus by stating:
  - Every element has ________.
  - All ________ in an element are the same.
  - Atoms of different elements are ________.
  - Atoms of different elements can combine to form ________.
  - In a compound, the number and kind of ________ remain the same.
- These principles formed atomic theory until 1897 when the ________ was discovered.

C. SIMPLE ATOMIC STRUCTURE

- At the center of an atom is the ________.
- The nucleus contains ________ (positive electrical charge) and ________ (no electrical charge).
- The ________ determine how an atom behaves.
- ________ (negative electrical charge) orbit the nucleus.
- If the number of ________ (+) and the number of ________ (–) are equal, the atom is electrically ________.
- If the number of ________ and ________ are NOT the same, it is called an ________.
- Atoms are hooked together to form ________.

D. HOW DO WE KNOW ATOMS EXIST?

- Atoms can't be seen by the naked ________ even when aided by a ________.
- A special microscope called a ________ ________ creates pictures of atoms.

E. IS THERE ANYTHING SMALLER THAN ATOMS?

- ________ particles are smaller than atoms.
- Many subatomic particles exist.
- One such particle is the ________.

(from Application Lesson 10)

Reproducible J

ACTIVITY C *Passage Reading and Comprehension*

RACHEL CARSON, FAMOUS NATURALIST

A. EARLY LIFE

- As a child, Rachel Carson loved ______________.
- At college, she studied ______________ and ______________.

B. PROFESSIONAL LIFE

- Carson taught ______________ at a university.
- She worked for the Fish and ___________ Service.
- She wrote articles and books about ___________.
- Her books were written not just for fellow scientists but also for the ______________.
- Her books made her a famous ______________.

C. HER BELIEFS

- Carson believed that humans were a part of ______________, not in charge of ______________.
- She felt we should NOT drastically change the ______________.

D. CONCERNS ABOUT DDT

- DDT was developed to kill __________.
- Many people became concerned that DDT was causing __________ to living things.
- Carson wrote about the danger of pesticides in her book ______________.

E. CONTROVERSY OVER HER BOOK

- The ______________ industry opposed the positions stated in ______________.
- Their opposition increased the book's ______________.
- President Kennedy ordered research on the effects of ______________.

F. RACHEL CARSON'S LEGACY

- Bills were enacted to regulate the use of ______________.
- The use of DDT was ______________.
- The Environmental Protection Agency ______________ was formed.

(from Application Lesson 11)

Reproducible K

ACTIVITY C *Passage Reading and Comprehension*

DEEP-SEA VENTS

A. WHAT ARE HYDROTHERMAL VENTS?

- When very hot, mineral-rich ________ spews from a ________, a deep crack in the ocean floor, it is called a hydrothermal ________.

B. HOW DO HYDROTHERMAL VENTS FORM?

- Hydrothermal vents can form as a result of underwater ________.
- When hot water is released from a volcano, ________ form where the hot water exits the rock.
- These ________ form hollow, chimney-like ________.

C. HOW DO WE KNOW THEY ARE THERE?

- While exploring a volcanic ridge near the ________ Islands, off South America, a ________ crew discovered a ________ vent.

D. WHY IS THERE ECONOMIC INTEREST IN HYDROTHERMAL VENTS?

- Microorganisms called ________ thrive in the vents.
- These microorganisms produce ________ that might speed up reactions used in industries.
- Some organisms living near the vents might have ________ value.
- The vents also contain ________ that might be possible to mine.

E. WHAT IS LIFE LIKE IN A HYDROTHERMAL VENT?

- The environment near the vents is very harsh: the temperature is ________, there is no ________, and ________ spew out of the earth.
- ________ make food energy through the process of ________.
- Archaea provide food for ________, ________, and ________.

(from Application Lesson 12)

Reproducible L

ACTIVITY C *Passage Reading and Comprehension*

EARTHQUAKES

A. WHAT IS AN EARTHQUAKE?

- Layers of the earth.

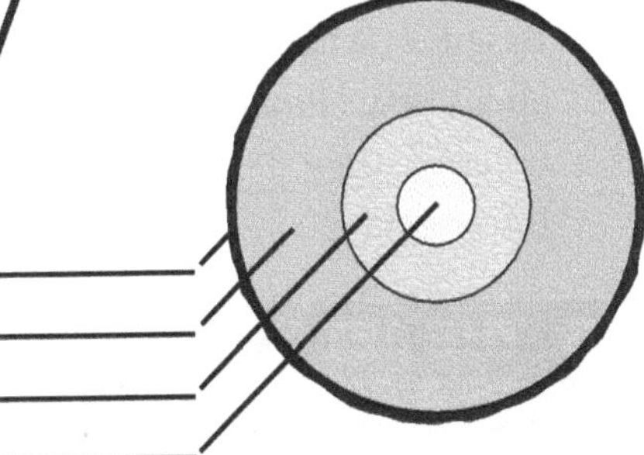

- When a __________ travels through the earth's __________, it is called an earthquake.

B. WHAT IS THE ORIGIN OF EARTHQUAKES?

- According to the ______________, the major cause of earthquakes is the __________ of the earth's plates against each other.
- In some cases, the friction between the __________ is great, and they become stuck. When the plates become unstuck, the force can cause an __________.
- Where the plates meet is called a __________; more earthquakes occur along fault lines.

C. HOW IS AN EARTHQUAKE'S ENERGY MEASURED?

- When an earthquake occurs, it causes __________ waves of energy that spread from the __________, which is right below the __________, a point on the surface of the earth. As the energy travels away from the epicenter, it becomes __________.
- The __________ rates earthquakes from 1 to 10 in magnitude.
- This rating is based on __________ readings and the distance from the __________.

D. HOW DO WE PREPARE FOR THE "BIG ONE"?

- __________ are able to determine where an earthquake might happen.
- However, it is not possible at this time to predict when an __________ will occur.
- People along fault lines can improve their safety by ______________.

(from Application Lesson 13)

Reproducible M

ACTIVITY C *Passage Reading and Comprehension*

WEATHER

A. WHAT IS AN AIR MASS?

- An air mass is a large chunk of ___________ in the atmosphere.
- Warm air masses ___________.
- Cold air masses ___________.

B. THE MOVEMENT OF AIR MASSES AS A FACTOR IN THE WEATHER

- Rising warm air carries ___________.
- When air cools, ___________ occurs, and ___________ are formed.
- When the clouds become heavier, ___________ (e.g., rain, snow) occurs.

C. COLD WEATHER FRONTS

- ___________ moves in and pushes warm air mass up.
- ___________ is produced.

D. WARM WEATHER FRONTS

- ___________ moves in and rises up over the cold air mass.
- When warm air rises high enough, it ___________.

E. THE LAND AS A FACTOR IN THE WEATHER

- An air mass over the land becomes the same ___________.
- Dark-colored areas of earth absorb sun's energy and become ___________.
- Glaciers reflect back sun's energy and surface becomes ___________.

F. THE SUN AND THE SEASONS AS FACTORS IN THE WEATHER

- At different times of the year and in different places, more or less sunlight received, so weather is ___________.

G. THE JET STREAM AS A FACTOR IN THE WEATHER

- The jet stream is a fast-moving river of ___________ that circles the earth.

H. PREDICTING THE WEATHER

- ___________ study the weather.
- Based on what they know about how climate behaves, they ___________ the weather.

(from Application Lesson 14)

Reproducible N

ACTIVITY C *Passage Reading and Comprehension*

TROPICAL RAINFORESTS

A. FACTS ABOUT TROPICAL RAINFORESTS

- Tropical rainforests are located near the __________.
- Though they cover a __________ part of the earth, they contain 50% to 90% of all ________.

B. EMERGENT LAYER

- The emergent layer is the __________ layer.
- The broad leaves of the tallest trees catch a good deal of __________.
- You might see such animals as ________________ at this level.

C. CANOPY LAYER

- Under the emergent layer is the ________ layer, which consists of dense clusters of trees with smooth oval leaves.
- The trees at this level block ________ from lower layers.
- You might see such animals as ________________ at this level.

D. UNDERSTORY

- Beneath the canopy is the ____________. Because of little sunlight, trees are ________ and have broad, flat leaves to catch __________.
- The understory is __________ because moisture collects.

E. FOREST FLOOR

- Because sunlight cannot shine through, the forest floor is __________.
- Few green __________.
- __________ matter provides food for insects.

F. CONCERN FOR THE RAINFORESTS

- With rainforests being destroyed, there are many concerns.
- Because of deforestation, climate is affected, thus affecting ________ and ________ in other areas.
- With deforestation, fewer trees are taking in ____________ and releasing __________. More heat is present in the atmosphere, which may contribute to ______________.
- ________ might lead to _______ breakthroughs if not destroyed.

(from Application Lesson 15)

Reproducible O

ACTIVITY C *Passage Reading and Comprehension*

OIL SPILLS

A. OIL

- Oil is a resource used by all countries, especially ____________ countries.
- Oil takes __________ to form and is found in limited locations.
- Oil is very __________ to remove from the ground.

B. CAUSES OF OIL SPILLS

- Oil is transported on huge ____________.
- Oil spills can be caused by human error, ________ equipment, ________ weather conditions, or ________ dumping.

C. CONSEQUENCES OF OIL SPILLS

- The spilled oil floats on the water, causing an oil ________.
- Marine mammals and birds may lose their ability to repel __________, keep __________, or float.
- They may also be __________ if they swallow the oil.
- The oil also kills ________.

D. RESPONSE TO OIL SPILLS

- The first goal is to __________ the oil spill.
- The next step is to rescue the __________.
- Rescuers try to __________ animals out of the area.
- Rescuers also remove oil from the animals' ________________ ________________.

E. CLEANING THE SPILL

- Using ____________ containment techniques, oil is captured so it can be disposed of properly.
- Using __________ and __________ methods, the oil is broken down faster.
- Using __________ methods, such as wiping and raking, shorelines are cleaned.

F. PREVENTION

- Federal ____________ are designed to prevent oil spills.
- All people can help by proper disposal and ____________ of oil.

Appendix C

Optional Vocabulary Activity: Quick Words

Description of Activity:

Learning and retaining science vocabulary is critical to students' success in science classes. **Quick Words** is a very motivating practice activity for learning and maintaining vocabulary. In this daily activity, students will study their vocabulary words and definitions and then complete a timed exercise where they match the words to the corresponding definitions. This same activity is repeated on subsequent days so that the students can compare their performances.

Preparation:

Before Lesson 1, make a copy of the **Quick Words Chart** found following these instructions. Also, make two or three copies of the blank **Quick Words** activity and a copy of the Answer Key for each student.

Procedure:

Step 1: (Optional) **Setting a Baseline**

Before you even introduce each lesson, you have the option of getting baseline data. Give the students a copy of the lesson's **Quick Words** activity but not the Answer Key. Do not have students study the words and definitions. Time them for one minute. Have the students write the letter of the word next to the corresponding definition. Have them record the total number on the **Quick Words Chart** in the Baseline column.

Step 2: Daily Procedure

On the first day of instruction, do **Quick Words** after Activity A, List 3 (Word Relatives). On subsequent days, do **Quick Words** at the beginning of the period. First, give the students one minute to study the Answer Key. Then, have them put the Answer Key away and give them a blank **Quick Words** sheet. Time them for one minute. Have them write the letter for the vocabulary word next to its corresponding definition. When the minute is up, have the students check their answers with the Answer Key, count up the number of correct matches, and record the number on their **Quick Words Chart** next to the corresponding lesson and in the appropriate column.

Step 3: Varying the Use of the Answer Key

The Answer Key that students will use for studying the vocabulary words can be used in a number of ways. One possibility is to have students read each definition and corresponding vocabulary word with you. Another possibility is to have students work in pairs with one student reading the definition and the other reading the corresponding word. Finally, you could choose to have students take the Answer Key home and study it independently.

Quick Words Chart

Daily Practice on Science Vocabulary

Name ____________________________

Lesson #	Baseline (No prior studying)	Timing 1	Timing 2	Timing 3
Lesson 1				
Lesson 2				
Lesson 3				
Lesson 4				
Lesson 5				
Lesson 6				
Lesson 7				
Lesson 8				
Lesson 9				
Lesson 10				
Lesson 11				
Lesson 12				
Lesson 13				
Lesson 14				
Lesson 15				

APPLICATION LESSON 1

Ecosystems

DEFINITION	MATCH	VOCABULARY WORD
1. matter needed by plants and animals so they can live		A. bacteria
2. all things that exist, including our solar system and beyond		B. requirements
3. very tiny single-celled organisms		C. scientists
4. the end of or the dying out of a type of plant or animal		D. nutrients
5. a living community of organisms and their physical environment		E. predator
6. finally		F. fungus
7. an animal that hunts or kills another for food		G. climate
8. actions or influences on each other		H. extinction
9. all living things, including all plants and animals		I. protists
10. people with expert knowledge of science		J. organisms
11. very humid and hot or having to do with the tropics		K. interactions
12. the pattern of weather conditions in an area or region		L. ecosystem
13. usually single-celled organisms that have both plant and animal characteristics		M. universe
14. things that are needed or depended upon		N. tropical
15. a plant-like organism without leaves, flowers, or green coloring		O. eventually

APPLICATION LESSON 1

Ecosystems—Answer Key

DEFINITION	MATCH	VOCABULARY WORD
1. matter needed by plants and animals so they can live	D	A. bacteria
2. all things that exist, including our solar system and beyond	M	B. requirements
3. very tiny single-celled organisms	A	C. scientists
4. the end of or the dying out of a type of plant or animal	H	D. nutrients
5. a living community of organisms and their physical environment	L	E. predator
6. finally	O	F. fungus
7. an animal that hunts or kills another for food	E	G. climate
8. actions or influences on each other	K	H. extinction
9. all living things, including all plants and animals	J	I. protists
10. people with expert knowledge of science	C	J. organisms
11. very humid and hot or having to do with the tropics	N	K. interactions
12. the pattern of weather conditions in an area or region	G	L. ecosystem
13. usually single-celled organisms that have both plant and animal characteristics	I	M. universe
14. things that are needed or depended upon	B	N. tropical
15. a plant-like organism without leaves, flowers, or green coloring	F	O. eventually

APPLICATION LESSON 2

Plants

DEFINITION	MATCH	VOCABULARY WORD
1. the green substance found in most plants		A. chloroplasts
2. finally		B. molecule
3. a colorless, odorless gas occurring naturally		C. microbes
4. a substance that gives color to plant or animal tissues		D. glucose
5. a very small amount, formed by combining atoms		E. integral
6. necessary for something to be whole		F. chemical
7. related to the properties of substances		G. chlorophyll
8. very tiny living organisms		H. respiration
9. matter needed by plants and animals so they can live		I. carbon dioxide
10. a simple sugar		J. pigment
11. related to cells		K. photosynthesis
12. parts of the leaf in which photosynthesis takes place		L. nutrients
13. the action of breathing		M. cellular
14. the process by which green plants use the sun's energy to make food		N. ecosystem
15. a living community of organisms and their physical environment		O. eventually

APPLICATION LESSON 2

Plants—Answer Key

DEFINITION	MATCH	VOCABULARY WORD
1. the green substance found in most plants	G	A. chloroplasts
2. finally	O	B. molecule
3. a colorless, odorless gas occurring naturally	I	C. microbes
4. a substance that gives color to plant or animal tissues	J	D. glucose
5. a very small amount, formed by combining atoms	B	E. integral
6. necessary for something to be whole	E	F. chemical
7. related to the properties of substances	F	G. chlorophyll
8. very tiny living organisms	C	H. respiration
9. matter needed by plants and animals so they can live	L	I. carbon dioxide
10. a simple sugar	D	J. pigment
11. related to cells	M	K. photosynthesis
12. parts of the leaf in which photosynthesis takes place	A	L. nutrients
13. the action of breathing	H	M. cellular
14. the process by which green plants use the sun's energy to make food	K	N. ecosystem
15. a living community of organisms and their physical environment	N	O. eventually

APPLICATION LESSON 3

Energy and Matter

DEFINITION	MATCH	VOCABULARY WORD
1. slow-growing plants composed of algae and fungi		A. consumers
2. the process by which certain organisms break down energy-rich molecules in order to make their own food		B. alga
3. a killer whale		C. recycling
4. organisms that eat other organisms		D. producers
5. so small as to be seen only with a microscope		E. mutual
6. a simple, nonflowering plant that is usually found in or around water		F. chemosynthesis
7. organisms that break down dead organisms		G. photosynthesis
8. an animal that hunts or kills another for food		H. parasite
9. a living community of organisms and their physical environment		I. lichens
10. organisms that produce their own food		J. fungus
11. changing waste to reusable items		K. decomposers
12. an organism that lives in or on another organism and receives benefits while harming the other organism		L. microscopic
13. the process by which green plants use the sun's energy to make food		M. orca
14. shared		N. ecosystem
15. a plant-like organism without leaves, flowers, or green coloring		O. predator

APPLICATION LESSON 3

Energy and Matter—Answer Key

DEFINITION	MATCH	VOCABULARY WORD
1. slow-growing plants composed of algae and fungi	I	A. consumers
2. the process by which certain organisms break down energy-rich molecules in order to make their own food	F	B. alga
3. a killer whale	M	C. recycling
4. organisms that eat other organisms	A	D. producers
5. so small as to be seen only with a microscope	L	E. mutual
6. a simple, nonflowering plant that is usually found in or around water	B	F. chemosynthesis
7. organisms that break down dead organisms	K	G. photosynthesis
8. an animal that hunts or kills another for food	O	H. parasite
9. a living community of organisms and their physical environment	N	I. lichens
10. organisms that produce their own food	D	J. fungus
11. changing waste to reusable items	C	K. decomposers
12. an organism that lives in or on another organism and receives benefits while harming the other organism	H	L. microscopic
13. the process by which green plants use the sun's energy to make food	G	M. orca
14. shared	E	N. ecosystem
15. a plant-like organism without leaves, flowers, or green coloring	J	O. predator

APPLICATION LESSON 4

Food Preservation

DEFINITION	MATCH	VOCABULARY WORD
1. spoiled		A. pathogens
2. a colorless, odorless gas occurring naturally		B. ingredients
3. the act of making something free from bacteria		C. chemical
4. the physical surroundings		D. dehydration
5. to take away from		E. ancient
6. particular methods of doing things		F. sterilization
7. a longstanding disagreement		G. contaminated
8. the loss of water from an organism		H. nutritional
9. microorganisms, such as bacteria and viruses, that cause disease		I. pasteurization
10. matter needed by plants and animals so they can live		J. carbon dioxide
11. related to the properties of substances		K. techniques
12. the foods or other elements combined to make a mixture		L. nutrients
13. old		M. environments
14. having to do with food so the body functions properly		N. deprive
15. the process of using heat to kill microbes and prevent food from spoiling rapidly		O. controversy

APPLICATION LESSON 4

Food Preservation—Answer Key

DEFINITION	MATCH	VOCABULARY WORD
1. spoiled	G	A. pathogens
2. a colorless, odorless gas occurring naturally	J	B. ingredients
3. the act of making something free from bacteria	F	C. chemical
4. the physical surroundings	M	D. dehydration
5. to take away from	N	E. ancient
6. particular methods of doing things	K	F. sterilization
7. a longstanding disagreement	O	G. contaminated
8. the loss of water from an organism	D	H. nutritional
9. microorganisms, such as bacteria and viruses, that cause disease	A	I. pasteurization
10. matter needed by plants and animals so they can live	L	J. carbon dioxide
11. related to the properties of substances	C	K. techniques
12. the foods or other elements combined to make a mixture	B	L. nutrients
13. old	E	M. environments
14. having to do with food so the body functions properly	H	N. deprive
15. the process of using heat to kill microbes and prevent food from spoiling rapidly	I	O. controversy

APPLICATION LESSON 5

The Cardiovascular System

DEFINITION	MATCH	VOCABULARY WORD
1. a hard substance that builds up in blood vessels and limits the flow of blood		A. arteries
2. the two top chambers of the heart		B. components
3. a condition that happens when the walls of the arteries become thick and not as flexible		C. hemoglobin
4. pieces of cells that prevent blood clotting		D. venules
5. large blood vessels that carry blood away from the heart		E. pulmonary
6. relating to or affecting the body		F. ventricles
7. parts		G. arteriosclerosis
8. relating to or affecting the lungs		H. deoxygenated
9. small blood vessels that connect capillaries to veins		I. cardiovascular
10. a substance in red blood cells that helps carry oxygen throughout the body		J. atria
11. having the oxygen removed		K. plaque
12. the two lower chambers of the heart		L. multicellular
13. diseases caused by germs entering part of the body		M. systemic
14. of the body system that consists of the heart, blood, and blood vessels		N. infections
15. made up of many cells		O. platelets

APPLICATION LESSON 5

The Cardiovascular System—Answer Key

DEFINITION	MATCH	VOCABULARY WORD
1. a hard substance that builds up in blood vessels and limits the flow of blood	K	A. arteries
2. the two top chambers of the heart	J	B. components
3. a condition that happens when the walls of the arteries become thick and not as flexible	G	C. hemoglobin
4. pieces of cells that prevent blood clotting	O	D. venules
5. large blood vessels that carry blood away from the heart	A	E. pulmonary
6. relating to or affecting the body	M	F. ventricles
7. parts	B	G. arteriosclerosis
8. relating to or affecting the lungs	E	H. deoxygenated
9. small blood vessels that connect capillaries to veins	D	I. cardiovascular
10. a substance in red blood cells that helps carry oxygen throughout the body	C	J. atria
11. having the oxygen removed	H	K. plaque
12. the two lower chambers of the heart	F	L. multicellular
13. diseases caused by germs entering part of the body	N	M. systemic
14. of the body system that consists of the heart, blood, and blood vessels	I	N. infections
15. made up of many cells	L	O. platelets

Heart Transplants

DEFINITION	MATCH	VOCABULARY WORD
1. not belonging to		A. anesthetic
2. a person who receives		B. procedure
3. the state of being awake		C. incompatible
4. substances used to treat diseases		D. hemoglobin
5. protected from a disease or infection		E. recipient
6. the removal or repair of injured or diseased parts of the body		F. foreign
7. little by little; slowly		G. suture
8. a drug or other substance that causes loss of feeling, especially pain		H. suitable
9. willingness to give or share freely		I. immune
10. a course of action with steps in a definite order		J. consciousness
11. a substance in red blood cells that helps carry oxygen throughout the body		K. susceptible
12. to stitch together the edges of a cut or wound		L. gradually
13. easily affected		M. surgery
14. meets the requirements of		N. medications
15. not able to work together or get along with		O. generosity

APPLICATION LESSON 6

Heart Transplants—Answer Key

DEFINITION	MATCH	VOCABULARY WORD
1. not belonging to	F	A. anesthetic
2. a person who receives	E	B. procedure
3. the state of being awake	J	C. incompatible
4. substances used to treat diseases	N	D. hemoglobin
5. protected from a disease or infection	I	E. recipient
6. the removal or repair of injured or diseased parts of the body	M	F. foreign
7. little by little; slowly	L	G. suture
8. a drug or other substance that causes loss of feeling, especially pain	A	H. suitable
9. willingness to give or share freely	O	I. immune
10. a course of action with steps in a definite order	B	J. consciousness
11. a substance in red blood cells that helps carry oxygen throughout the body	D	K. susceptible
12. to stitch together the edges of a cut or wound	G	L. gradually
13. easily affected	K	M. surgery
14. meets the requirements of	H	N. medications
15. not able to work together or get along with	C	O. generosity

APPLICATION LESSON 7

Viruses

DEFINITION	MATCH	VOCABULARY WORD
1. a tiny, infectious particle		A. characteristics
2. related to the development of organisms		B. adsorption
3. a dead or weakened virus or bacteria that is used to protect against certain diseases		C. immune
4. given to		D. polyhedral
5. a thin layer of tissue		E. susceptible
6. features, qualities, or functions		F. replication
7. spoiled		G. vaccine
8. easily affected		H. significantly
9. having many sides		I. antibodies
10. keeping something on the surface instead of absorbing it		J. contaminated
11. protected from a disease or infection		K. virus
12. fitting together parts to make a whole		L. genetic
13. a lot		M. membrane
14. a close or exact copy		N. administered
15. proteins in the blood that destroy germs		O. assembly

APPLICATION LESSON 7

Viruses—Answer Key

DEFINITION	MATCH	VOCABULARY WORD
1. a tiny, infectious particle	K	A. characteristics
2. related to the development of organisms	L	B. adsorption
3. a dead or weakened virus or bacteria that is used to protect against certain diseases	G	C. immune
4. given to	N	D. polyhedral
5. a thin layer of tissue	M	E. susceptible
6. features, qualities, or functions	A	F. replication
7. spoiled	J	G. vaccine
8. easily affected	E	H. significantly
9. having many sides	D	I. antibodies
10. keeping something on the surface instead of absorbing it	B	J. contaminated
11. protected from a disease or infection	C	K. virus
12. fitting together parts to make a whole	O	L. genetic
13. a lot	H	M. membrane
14. a close or exact copy	F	N. administered
15. proteins in the blood that destroy germs	I	O. assembly

APPLICATION LESSON 8

Antoni van Leeuwenhoek

DEFINITION	MATCH	VOCABULARY WORD
1. exchange of letters		A. protozoa
2. changed into another language		B. *Micrographia*
3. old, archaic term for tiny swimming animals		C. contemporary
4. finally		D. techniques
5. features, qualities, or functions		E. specimens
6. protection from danger		F. financial
7. a type of bacteria		G. microcosm
8. the branch of biology that studies microorganisms		H. eventually
9. examples		I. characteristics
10. an influential book introducing the use of the microscope		J. microbiology
11. existing at the same time		K. correspondence
12. the little world of microorganisms		L. bacilli
13. single-celled microscopic animals		M. animalcules
14. particular methods of doing things		N. security
15. related to money		O. translated

APPLICATION LESSON 8

Antoni van Leeuwenhoek—Answer Key

DEFINITION	MATCH	VOCABULARY WORD
1. exchange of letters	K	A. protozoa
2. changed into another language	O	B. *Micrographia*
3. old, archaic term for tiny swimming animals	M	C. contemporary
4. finally	H	D. techniques
5. features, qualities, or functions	I	E. specimens
6. protection from danger	N	F. financial
7. a type of bacteria	L	G. microcosm
8. the branch of biology that studies microorganisms	J	H. eventually
9. examples	E	I. characteristics
10. an influential book introducing the use of the microscope	B	J. microbiology
11. existing at the same time	C	K. correspondence
12. the little world of microorganisms	G	L. bacilli
13. single-celled microscopic animals	A	M. animalcules
14. particular methods of doing things	D	N. security
15. related to money	F	O. translated

Atoms

DEFINITION	MATCH	VOCABULARY WORD
1. very small bits		A. nucleus
2. related to an atom		B. neutrons
3. a colorless, odorless, tasteless gas		C. compound
4. finally		D. significantly
5. the center of an atom, containing neutrons and protons		E. ultimately
6. a lot		F. subatomic
7. shared		G. electrons
8. parts		H. electrical
9. fitting together parts to make a whole		I. hydrogen
10. particles with no electrical charge		J. protons
11. having to do with electricity		K. mutual
12. negatively charged particles		L. particles
13. a combination of two or more elements		M. atomic
14. smaller than an atom		N. components
15. positively charged particles		O. assembly

APPLICATION LESSON 9

Atoms—Answer Key

DEFINITION	MATCH	VOCABULARY WORD
1. very small bits	L	A. nucleus
2. related to an atom	M	B. neutrons
3. a colorless, odorless, tasteless gas	I	C. compound
4. finally	E	D. significantly
5. the center of an atom, containing neutrons and protons	A	E. ultimately F. subatomic
6. a lot	D	G. electrons
7. shared	K	H. electrical
8. parts	N	I. hydrogen
9. fitting together parts to make a whole	O	J. protons
10. particles with no electrical charge	B	K. mutual
11. having to do with electricity	H	L. particles
12. negatively charged particles	G	M. atomic
13. a combination of two or more elements	C	N. components O. assembly
14. smaller than an atom	F	
15. positively charged particles	J	

APPLICATION LESSON 10

Rachel Carson

DEFINITION	MATCH	VOCABULARY WORD
1. really liked		A. biology
2. opposing arguments		B. concentrate
3. a branch of biology that focuses on animals		C. naturalist
4. writings on a subject		D. legislative
5. a person who studies nature		E. extremely
6. a chemical used to destroy plants or animals		F. infestations
7. not belonging to		G. ecosystem
8. unchangeable		H. pesticide
9. things needed to do something		I. rebuttals
10. growth in large numbers		J. foreign
11. a living community of organisms and their physical environment		K. zoology
12. the science of living organisms		L. enamored
13. to focus on		M. irrevocably
14. very great		N. materials
15. legal		O. articles

APPLICATION LESSON 10

Rachel Carson—Answer Key

DEFINITION	MATCH	VOCABULARY WORD
1. really liked	L	A. biology
2. opposing arguments	I	B. concentrate
3. a branch of biology that focuses on animals	K	C. naturalist
4. writings on a subject	O	D. legislative
5. a person who studies nature	C	E. extremely
6. a chemical used to destroy plants or animals	H	F. infestations
7. not belonging to	J	G. ecosystem
8. unchangeable	M	H. pesticide
9. things needed to do something	N	I. rebuttals
10. growth in large numbers	F	J. foreign
11. a living community of organisms and their physical environment	G	K. zoology
12. the science of living organisms	A	L. enamored
13. to focus on	B	M. irrevocably
14. very great	E	N. materials
15. legal	D	O. articles

APPLICATION LESSON 11

Deep-Sea Vents

DEFINITION	MATCH	VOCABULARY WORD
1. long, narrow openings		A. crystallize
2. chemical substances produced in the cells of all plants and animals		B. abnormal
3. related to the study of living things		C. chemosynthesis
4. possibly		D. ultimately
5. commonly used		E. volcanoes
6. so small as to be seen only with a microscope		F. enzymes
7. finally		G. fissures
8. hard to believe		H. hydrothermal
9. unchangeable		I. irrevocably
10. to form crystals		J. archaea
11. the process by which certain organisms break down energy-rich molecules in order to make their own food		K. potentially
12. openings in the earth through which molten rock, gases, and rocks are forced out		L. ordinary
13. very different from normal		M. microscopic
14. having to do with the action of hot liquids or gases		N. biological
15. a type of microorganism		O. incredibly

APPLICATION LESSON 11

Deep-Sea Vents—Answer Key

DEFINITION	MATCH	VOCABULARY WORD
1. long, narrow openings	G	A. crystallize
2. chemical substances produced in the cells of all plants and animals	F	B. abnormal
3. related to the study of living things	N	C. chemosynthesis
4. possibly	K	D. ultimately
5. commonly used	L	E. volcanoes
6. so small as to be seen only with a microscope	M	F. enzymes
7. finally	D	G. fissures
8. hard to believe	O	H. hydrothermal
9. unchangeable	I	I. irrevocably
10. to form crystals	A	J. archaea
11. the process by which certain organisms break down energy-rich molecules in order to make their own food	C	K. potentially
12. openings in the earth through which molten rock, gases, and rocks are forced out	E	L. ordinary
13. very different from normal	B	M. microscopic
14. having to do with the action of hot liquids or gases	H	N. biological
15. a type of microorganism	J	O. incredibly

Earthquakes

DEFINITION	MATCH	VOCABULARY WORD
1. a scale for representing the strength of earthquakes		A. seismograph
2. the point on the surface of the earth right above the center of the earthquake		B. earthquakes
3. the size of something		C. probability
4. a line that marks separation		D. satellites
5. a theory that says the earth's crust is broken into plates that move		E. aseismic
6. to focus on		F. Richter scale
7. vibrations traveling through the earth's crust		G. plate tectonics
8. things that happen		H. concentrate
9. likeliness that something will happen		I. magnitude
10. related to cells		J. cellular
11. an instrument used to measure the strength of earthquakes		K. vibration
12. small units of measurement		L. epicenter
13. related to the absence of earthquakes		M. boundary
14. objects that revolve around the earth		N. centimeters
15. a rapid movement back and forth		O. occurrences

APPLICATION LESSON 12

Earthquakes—Answer Key

DEFINITION	MATCH	VOCABULARY WORD
1. a scale for representing the strength of earthquakes	F	A. seismograph B. earthquakes
2. the point on the surface of the earth right above the center of the earthquake	L	C. probability D. satellites
3. the size of something	I	E. aseismic
4. a line that marks separation	M	F. Richter scale
5. a theory that says the earth's crust is broken into plates that move	G	G. plate tectonics H. concentrate
6. to focus on	H	I. magnitude
7. vibrations traveling through the earth's crust	B	J. cellular K. vibration
8. things that happen	O	L. epicenter
9. likeliness that something will happen	C	M. boundary
10. related to cells	J	N. centimeters
11. an instrument used to measure the strength of earthquakes	A	O. occurrences
12. small units of measurement	N	
13. related to the absence of earthquakes	E	
14. objects that revolve around the earth	D	
15. a rapid movement back and forth	K	

Weather

DEFINITION	MATCH	VOCABULARY WORD
1. dark columns of fast-moving air shaped like a funnel		A. atmosphere
2. the size of something		B. accompanying
3. objects that revolve around the earth		C. meteorologists
4. very humid and hot or having to do with the tropics		D. glaciers
5. going along with		E. climatic
6. the change of a gas to a liquid		F. frequently
7. any form of water falling to earth		G. tornadoes
8. thickness		H. alternatively
9. people who study the atmosphere and changes within it—especially the weather		I. magnitude
10. related to typical weather		J. tropical
11. an event that can be observed		K. condensation
12. large, slow-moving masses of ice		L. density
13. the mass of gases surrounding the earth		M. satellites
14. often		N. precipitation
15. on the other hand		O. phenomenon

APPLICATION LESSON 13

Weather—Answer Key

DEFINITION	MATCH	VOCABULARY WORD
1. dark columns of fast-moving air shaped like a funnel	G	A. atmosphere
2. the size of something	I	B. accompanying
3. objects that revolve around the earth	M	C. meteorologists
4. very humid and hot or having to do with the tropics	J	D. glaciers
5. going along with	B	E. climatic
6. the change of a gas to a liquid	K	F. frequently
7. any form of water falling to earth	N	G. tornadoes
8. thickness	L	H. alternatively
9. people who study the atmosphere and changes within it—especially the weather	C	I. magnitude
10. related to typical weather	E	J. tropical
11. an event that can be observed	O	K. condensation
12. large, slow-moving masses of ice	D	L. density
13. the mass of gases surrounding the earth	A	M. satellites
14. often	F	N. precipitation
15. on the other hand	H	O. phenomenon

APPLICATION LESSON 14

Tropical Rainforests

DEFINITION	MATCH	VOCABULARY WORD
1. rising or coming out of		A. canopy
2. plentiful		B. undesirable
3. passing through		C. consequently
4. the clearing of forests		D. portion
5. a living community of organisms and their physical environment		E. precipitation
6. matter needed by plants and animals so they can live		F. penetrating
7. smaller trees that grow beneath big trees in the forest		G. photosynthesis
8. unwanted		H. understory
9. a covering		I. maturity
10. variety		J. emergent
11. as a result		K. nutrients
12. part of a whole		L. abundant
13. any form of water falling to earth		M. ecosystem
14. full growth and development		N. deforestation
15. the process by which green plants use the sun's energy to make food		O. diversity

APPLICATION LESSON 14

Tropical Rainforests—Answer Key

DEFINITION	MATCH	VOCABULARY WORD
1. rising or coming out of	J	A. canopy
2. plentiful	L	B. undesirable
3. passing through	F	C. consequently
4. the clearing of forests	N	D. portion
5. a living community of organisms and their physical environment	M	E. precipitation F. penetrating
6. matter needed by plants and animals so they can live	K	G. photosynthesis H. understory
7. smaller trees that grow beneath big trees in the forest	H	I. maturity
8. unwanted	B	J. emergent
9. a covering	A	K. nutrients
10. variety	O	L. abundant
11. as a result	C	M. ecosystem
12. part of a whole	D	N. deforestation
13. any form of water falling to earth	E	O. diversity
14. full growth and development	I	
15. the process by which green plants use the sun's energy to make food	G	

Oil Spills

DEFINITION	MATCH	VOCABULARY WORD
1. carefully planned		A. aquatic
2. the act of becoming a fossil		B. minimize
3. legal		C. containment
4. watched		D. deliberate
5. something that makes something else dirty or impure		E. similarly
6. to lessen		F. consequences
7. unluckily		G. replenish
8. related to business		H. buoyancy
9. met unexpectedly		I. pollution
10. related to water		J. unfortunately
11. to keep from spreading		K. industrialized
12. being alike		L. fossilization
13. to provide a new supply		M. legislative
14. results of earlier actions		N. monitored
15. the ability to float or rise in water		O. encountered

APPLICATION LESSON 15

Oil Spills—Answer Key

DEFINITION	MATCH	VOCABULARY WORD
1. carefully planned	D	A. aquatic
2. the act of becoming a fossil	L	B. minimize
3. legal	M	C. containment
4. watched	N	D. deliberate
5. something that makes something else dirty or impure	I	E. similarly F. consequences
6. to lessen	B	G. replenish
7. unluckily	J	H. buoyancy
8. related to business	K	I. pollution
9. met unexpectedly	O	J. unfortunately
10. related to water	A	K. industrialized
11. to keep from spreading	C	L. fossilization
12. being alike	E	M. legislative
13. to provide a new supply	G	N. monitored
14. results of earlier actions	F	O. encountered
15. the ability to float or rise in water	H	

Oil Spills—Answer Key

DEFINITION	MATCH	VOCABULARY WORD
1. carefully planned	D	A. [illegible]
2. the act of becoming a fossil	L	B. [illegible]
3. legal	M	C. [illegible]
4. watched	N	D. deliberate
5. something that makes something else dirty or impure	I	E. [illegible]
6. to lessen	B	F. consequences
7. unluckily	J	G. replenish
8. related to business	[illegible]	H. buoyancy
9. met unexpectedly	O	I. pollution
10. related to water	[illegible]	J. unfortunately
11. to keep from spreading	C	K. industrialized
12. being afloat	E	L. fossilization
13. to provide a new supply	G	M. legislative
14. results of earlier actions	F	N. monitored
15. the ability to float or rise in water	H	O. encountered

Appendix D

Fluency Graph: Correct Words Per Minute

In each of the Application Lessons, students engage in repeated readings of Activity C articles in order to increase their reading fluency. A Fluency Graph for recording the student's first timing (Cold Timing) and last timing (Hot Timing) is found on the last page of the *Student Book.* A reproducible version of the Fluency Graph is included on the following page so that you can continue to conduct repeated reading activities after *REWARDS Plus* is completed.

Fluency Graph

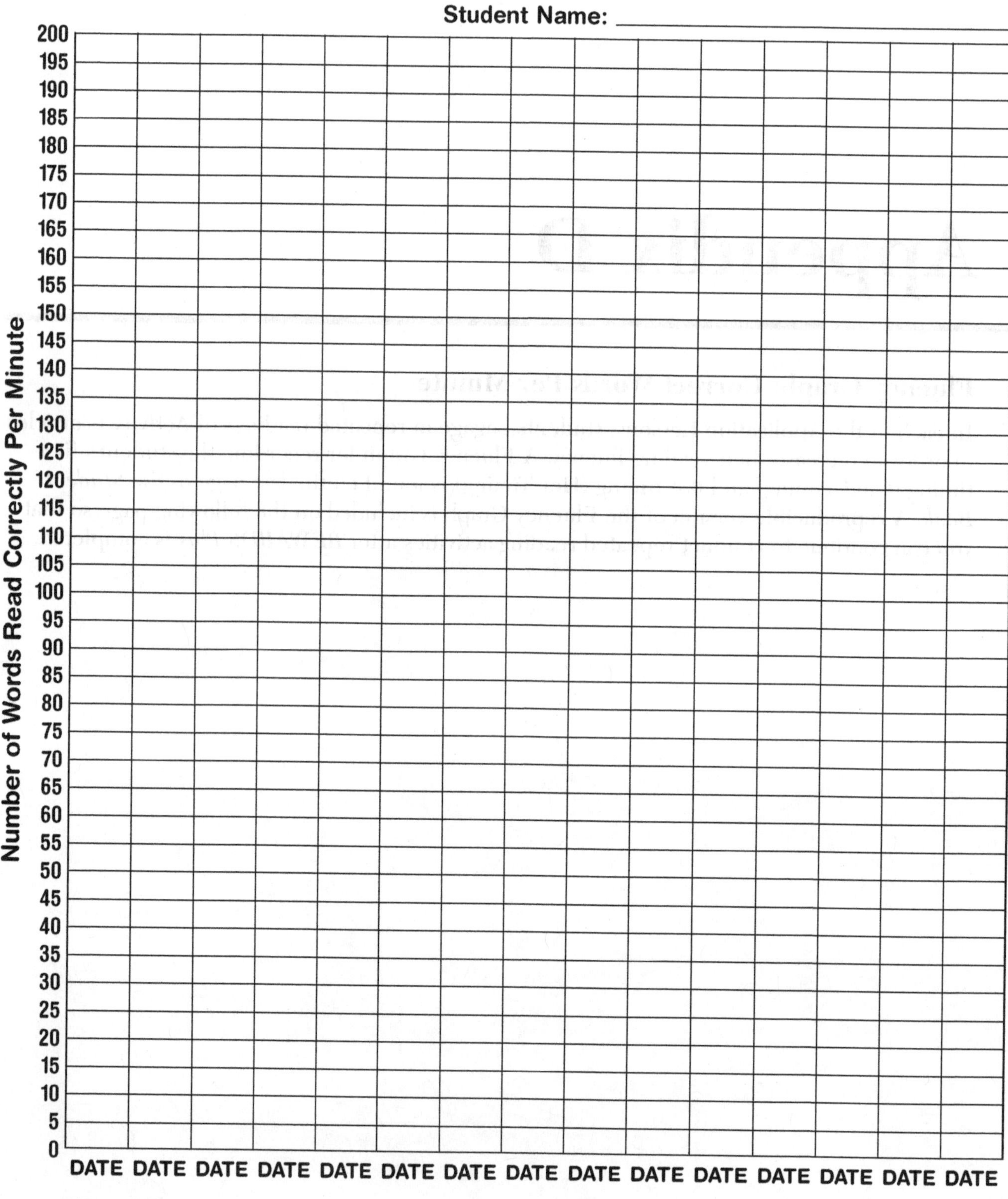

Appendix E

Incentive/Grading System

In some cases, classes will profit from an additional incentive/grading system. This will provide a structured way to give students feedback on their behavior and academic progress. During each lesson, award points for each segment of the lesson as shown in the Review Lessons Chart and the Application Lessons Chart. These points can be used to determine a lesson grade and an overall grade. You may wish students to earn access to special events (e.g., popcorn party, free reading period, video viewing) or prizes (e.g., a book, school supplies, treats) as incentives. Procedures for awarding points during the Review Lessons and Application Lessons are outlined on the following pages.

Incentive/Grading System for Review Lessons

1. Before conducting the first Review Lesson, copy and distribute the Review Lessons Chart (see next page) to students.
2. After students complete the first and second pages in the *Student Book,* award **Participation Points.** If students have followed your behavioral guidelines, paid attention, participated, and responded accurately, award **4 points.** If students perform below your expectations, award **0**, **1**, **2**, or **3** points. Have students record their points on the Review Lessons Chart throughout each lesson.
3. For the Reading Check, ask each student to read one sentence in Activity F. If the student makes no errors, award **4 Performance Points.** Award **3 points** if one error is made, **2 points** if two errors are made, and **0 points** if more than two errors are made.
4. At the end of the Review Lesson, have students add their points to find a subtotal.
5. Award **Bonus Points** for excellent reading and/or behavior.
6. Then, have students total their points.
7. You may wish to award a grade for each Review Lesson. Use the guidelines at right in determining the lesson grade.
8. The total points earned can be used to determine an overall grade for this portion of your reading program. A proposed grading scale is provided at right.

Daily Review Lesson Grade (Possible Points: 12)

11–12 points .... **A**
9–10 points .... **B**
8 points .... **C**
7 points .... **D**
Less than 7 points .... **F**

Overall Review Lessons Grade (Possible Points: 72)

65–72 points .... **A**
54–64 points .... **B**
48–53 points .... **C**
42–47 points .... **D**
Less than 42 points .... **F**

Review Lessons Chart

Name ______________________ Teacher ______________________

	First Page (4 possible Participation Points)	Second Page (4 possible Participation Points)	Activity F Reading Check (4 possible Performance Points)	SUBTOTAL POINTS (12 possible points)	BONUS POINTS	TOTAL POINTS	LESSON GRADE
Review Lesson 1							
Review Lesson 2							
Review Lesson 3							
Review Lesson 4							
Review Lesson 5							
Review Lesson 6							

Participation Points
(Possible Points: 4)

- Following behavioral guidelines
- Paying attention
- Participating
- Responding accurately

Performance Points
(Possible Points: 4)

No errors	**4 points**
1 error	**3 points**
2 errors	**2 points**
More than 2 errors	**0 points**

Incentive/Grading System for Application Lessons

1. Before conducting the first Application Lesson, copy and distribute the Application Lessons Chart (see next page) to students.
2. During the lesson, award **Participation Points** as well as **Performance Points** as listed below.
3. After reading Lists 1 and 2 in Activity A, award **Participation Points**. If students have followed behavioral guidelines, paid attention, carefully practiced the words, and responded accurately, award **4 points.**
4. After the Oral Vocabulary exercise, in which students circle the number of the vocabulary word you give clues about, have students record their tally points (**5 Performance Points** possible).
5. After reading List 3 in Activity A, award **Participation Points**. If students have followed behavioral guidelines, paid attention, carefully practiced the words, and responded accurately, award **4 points.**
6. After the Activity B Spelling exercise, have students record **Performance Points** for the number of correct words (**6 points** possible).
7. After the Activity C Passage Reading, award **Participation Points**. If students have followed behavioral guidelines, paid attention, carefully read the passage, responded accurately to the Comprehension Questions, and filled in their **Information Web** accurately, award **4 points.**
8. After the Activity D Fluency exercise, award **Performance Points**. If a student's fluency increases from the Cold Timing to the Hot Timing, award **4 Bonus Performance Points.**
9. After the Activity E Multiple Choice exercise, award **4 Performance Points** for correct responses.
10. After the Activity F Vocabulary Activities, award **7 Performance Points** for completed responses either orally or written depending on your choice.
11. After the Activity G Writing exercise, award **13 Performance Points** corresponding to the attributes of the rubrics.
12. After the Activity H Writing/Discussion exercise, award **4 Performance Points** for the written paragraph and **4 Participation Points** for the discussion.
13. At the end of the Application Lesson, have students add their points to find a subtotal.
14. Award **Bonus Points** for excellent work and/or behavior.
15. Then, have students total their points.
16. You may wish to award a grade for each Application Lesson. Use the guidelines below in determining the lesson grade.
17. The total points earned can be used to determine an overall grade for this portion of your reading program. A proposed grading scale is provided below.

Daily Application Lesson Grade (Possible Points: 59)

53–59 points .... A
47–52 points .... B
41–46 points C
35–40 points .... D
Less than 35 points .... F

Overall Application Lessons Grade (Possible Points: 885)

795–885 points .... A
705–794 points .... B
615–704 points C
525–614 points .... D
Less than 525 points .... F

Application Lessons Chart

Name ______________________ Teacher ______________________

	Activity A List 1 and List 2 (4 possible Participation Points)	Oral Vocabulary Tally (5 possible Performance Points)	Activity A List 3 (4 possible Participation Points)	Activity B Spelling (6 possible Performance Points)	Activity C Passage Reading (4 possible Participation Points)	Activity D Fluency (4 possible Performance Points)	Activity E Multiple Choice (4 possible Performance Points)	Activity F Vocabulary Activities (7 possible Performance Points)	Activity G Writing (13 possible Performance Points)	Activity H Writing/ Discussion (8 possible Points)	SUBTOTAL POINTS (59 possible points)	BONUS POINTS	TOTAL POINTS	LESSON GRADE
Application Lesson 1														
Application Lesson 2														
Application Lesson 3														
Application Lesson 4														
Application Lesson 5														
Application Lesson 6														
Application Lesson 7														
Application Lesson 8														
Application Lesson 9														
Application Lesson 10														
Application Lesson 11														
Application Lesson 12														
Application Lesson 13														
Application Lesson 14														
Application Lesson 15														

Other Incentives

Group Incentives

You may select to have special events to encourage participation and accurate reading. Oftentimes, it is easier to offer group incentives rather than individual incentives, thus encouraging students to support the academic and behavioral efforts of their peers. Group incentives could be one of the following: popcorn party, ten minutes to visit, a word game, or a special edible treat.

While you may determine your own criteria for awarding group incentives, the following plan can be used:

- Set a goal of all A's or B's in five lessons.
- At the end of each lesson, examine the Point/Grade columns to determine if all students received an A or B. If so, record a group point in a prominent place (e.g., on a bulletin board).
- When all students have earned A's or B's in five lessons, celebrate with the selected treat or event.

Individual Incentives

If you are teaching a small group that includes students with learning challenges, you may wish to award individual prizes when a certain number of A's or B's are earned. For example, an individual student could earn a special treat for five lessons of A or B grades.

Appendix F

Word List for *REWARDS Plus*

The following alphabetized list contains all **Activity A** words that were presented in the Application Lessons. (Additional words found in the science articles are not included in this list.)

Appendix G

Pretest/Posttest Fluency, Writing, and Vocabulary Assessment Procedures

The following procedures can be used to assess students' oral reading fluency, multi-paragraph writing skills, and science vocabulary knowledge before and after participating in the *REWARDS Plus* program.

Fluency Assessment Procedure

1. Administer the following fluency measure to each student before they begin the *REWARDS Plus* program and again after they complete the program.
2. Make copies of the passage on the next page (one copy for each student for recording data and one copy for students to read).
3. Ask each student to read the passage as quickly and as carefully as possible.
4. Have the student read for one minute. Use a stopwatch or timer.
5. Record data as the student reads.
   - Underline all mispronunciations.
   - If the student immediately corrects a mispronunciation, give credit for the word.
   - If the student reverses the order of words, both words are errors.
   - Cross out words that are omitted. They will not be counted.
   - Write in all additions. However, these will not be counted.
6. When the minute is complete, ask the student to stop.
7. Determine the total number of words read. Subtract any mispronunciations. Determine the number of words read correctly in one minute.
8. Keep a record of the pretest score for comparison with the posttest score.

Ecosystems

The universe is a very complex system, in which all things interact with each
14 other. Within this complex system are many different systems called
24 **ecosystems**. An ecosystem is composed of living things interacting with other
35 living things and with nonliving things such as weather, soil, and water. Earth's
48 ecosystems may be as large as an ocean or as small as a drop of water. Forests,
65 rivers, and meadows are examples of ecosystems. (#1)

72 **Energy and Matter in Ecosystems**

77 All organisms within an ecosystem require a steady supply of energy and
89 matter for their life processes. These life processes include growing, developing,
100 reproducing, and responding to their surroundings. (#2)

106 All energy and matter that organisms require must be available within their
118 ecosystem. Most energy comes from the sun. Plants and tiny organisms (protists
130 and bacteria) capture the sun's energy and transform it into food energy (matter)
143 for themselves and other organisms. These other organisms cannot make their
154 own food, so they consume the tiny organisms and plants (or parts of plants). (#3)

168 Eventually, the organisms die. Their dead bodies become food for bacteria
179 and fungi. The bacteria and fungi return nutrients to the soil, where the plants
193 use them, and the cycling of energy and matter begins again. (#4)

204 **Interactions Within Ecosystems**

207 Larger organisms not only consume tiny organisms and plants, larger
217 organisms also interact with other organisms within their ecosystem. Sometimes,
227 these interactions are friendly and benefit both organisms. For example, bees
238 benefit when they gather pollen and nectar from flowers. These substances are
250 food for the bees. Flowers benefit because the bees' gathering activities help to
263 move the pollen from one flower to another so the flowers can make seeds. (#5)

277 Another interaction that benefits two organisms is the special relationship
287 that exists when a type of fungus finds a home in and on the roots of trees. This
305 fungus absorbs water and minerals from the surrounding soil and shares these
317 with the tree. The tree uses these raw materials to make a sugary food, which
332 the fungus feeds on. Large forests depend on this special relationship. (#6)

343 Other interactions appear not to be so friendly. One example is the predator-
356 prey relationship between the snake and the mouse. It seems as if only the
370 snake benefits from eating the mouse, but actually, the population of mice in the
384 ecosystem is helped. Snakes (the predators) keep the numbers of mice in
396 balance with the supply of mouse food available. (#7)

Writing Assessment Procedure

Pretest

1. After teaching Activities A through F of Lesson 1, ask students to write three paragraphs in response to the following prompt: **What are three important things about an ecosystem?**
2. Write the prompt on the board or overhead. Say to students, "Read the prompt with me: **What are three important things about an ecosystem?** You are going to write three paragraphs in response to this question. Be sure that the first sentence of each paragraph contains a topic. The remaining sentences in the paragraphs should include important details. You should take time to plan your paragraphs before you write."
3. When students have completed their paragraphs, proceed to Activity G in Lesson 1.
4. Use the rubric for Multi-Paragraph Answers found on the next page for scoring students' written products.
5. Save each student's scored rubric for comparison with the posttest result.

Posttest

1. After teaching Activities A through F of Lesson 15, ask students to write three paragraphs in response to the following prompt: **Write three paragraphs that describe the causes, consequences, and responses to oil spills.**
2. Write the prompt on the board or overhead. Say to students, "Read the prompt with me: **Write three paragraphs that describe the causes, consequences, and responses to oil spills.** You are going to write three paragraphs in response to this prompt. Be sure that the first sentence of each paragraph contains a topic. The remaining sentences in the paragraphs should include important details. You should take time to plan your paragraphs before you write."
3. If you have selected to have students write these paragraphs as a posttest, skip Activity G in Lesson 15.
4. Use the rubric for Multi-Paragraph Answers found on the next page for scoring students' written products.
5. Compare the posttest results with the pretest scored rubrics.

Rubric—Multi-Paragraph Answer

Rubric— Multi-Paragraph Answer	Student or Partner Rating	Teacher Rating
1. Did the author state the topic in the first sentence?	a. Yes Fix up b. Yes Fix up c. Yes Fix up	a. Yes No b. Yes No c. Yes No
2. Did the author include details that go with the topic?	a. Yes Fix up b. Yes Fix up c. Yes Fix up	a. Yes No b. Yes No c. Yes No
3. Did the author combine details in some of the sentences?	a. Yes Fix up b. Yes Fix up c. Yes Fix up	a. Yes No b. Yes No c. Yes No
4. Is the answer easy to understand?	Yes Fix up	Yes No
5. Did the author correctly spell words, particularly the words found in the article?	Yes Fix up	Yes No
6. Did the author use correct capitalization, capitalizing the first word in the sentence and proper names of people, places, and things?	Yes Fix up	Yes No
7. Did the author use correct punctuation, including a period at the end of each sentence?	Yes Fix up	Yes No

Vocabulary Assessment Procedure

On the next several pages, you will find an assessment of the science vocabulary taught in *REWARDS Plus*. You may select to administer it before your students study the program to gain an idea of their science knowledge and after the program has been taught to determine gains in science vocabulary. You may select to administer the Science Vocabulary Knowledge Test as either a pre- and posttest or as a posttest only. The format of this test is the same as the optional Quick Words activity that accompanies each lesson.

Pretest

1. Duplicate copies of the Science Vocabulary Knowledge Test on pages 455 through 458 for each student.
2. Explain to students that they will be taking a vocabulary test on science words. Explain that they may not know the meaning of all the words, but should try to do their best.
3. Read the directions with the students: **Read each definition in the left-hand column. Find the word in the right-hand column that goes with the definition. Record the letter for the word after the definition. The first one has been done for you.**
4. Have students complete all four sets of match-up items.
5. Score the tests by comparing them to the Answer Key found on pages 459 through 462.
6. A score of 40 is possible.
7. Keep a record of the pretest scores for comparison with the posttest scores.

Posttest

1. Duplicate copies of the Science Vocabulary Knowledge Test on pages 455 through 458 for each student.
2. Explain to students that they will be taking a vocabulary test on the science words that they have learned in *REWARDS Plus.*
3. Read the directions with the students: **Read each definition in the left-hand column. Find the word in the right-hand column that goes with the definition. Record the letter for the word after the definition. The first one has been done for you.**
4. Have students complete all four sets of match-up items.
5. Score the tests by comparing them to the Answer Key found on pages 459 through 462.
6. A score of 40 is possible.
7. If a pretest was given, compare the posttest scores with the pretest scores.

Science Vocabulary Knowledge Test

Directions: Read each definition in the left-hand column. Find the word in the right-hand column that goes with the definition. Record the letter for the word after the definition. The first one has been done for you. (The number in parentheses next to the word indicates in which lesson the meaning is taught.)

Set A

DEFINITION	MATCH	VOCABULARY WORD
1. rising or coming out of	G	A. photosynthesis (2)
2. a simple sugar		B. virus (7)
3. a tiny, infectious particle		C. immune (6)
4. long, narrow openings		D. biology (10)
5. protected from a disease or infection		E. canopy (14)
6. the process by which certain organisms break down energy-rich molecules in order to make their own food		F. nutrients (1)
7. the science of living organisms		G. emergent (14)
8. a covering		H. chemosynthesis (3)
9. the process by which green plants use the sun's energy to make food		I. fissures (11)
10. matter needed by plants and animals so they can live		J. glucose (2)

Science Vocabulary Knowledge Test

Directions: Read each definition in the left-hand column. Find the word in the right-hand column that goes with the definition. Record the letter for the word after the definition. (The number in parentheses next to the word indicates in which lesson the meaning is taught.)

Set B

DEFINITION	MATCH	VOCABULARY WORD
1. positively charged particles		A. antibodies (7)
2. a living community of organisms and their physical environment		B. ecosystem (1)
3. something that makes something else dirty or impure		C. hemoglobin (5)
4. the green substance found in most plants		D. pollution (15)
5. particles with no electrical charge		E. chorophyll (2)
6. proteins in the blood that destroy germs		F. nucleus (9)
7. negatively charged particles		G. protons (9)
8. an organism that lives in or on another organism and receives benefits while harming the other organism		H. electrons (9)
9. the center of an atom, containing neutrons and protons		I. parasite (3)
10. a substance in red blood cells that helps carry oxygen throughout the body		J. neutrons (9)

Science Vocabulary Knowledge Test

Directions: Read each definition in the left-hand column. Find the word in the right-hand column that goes with the definition. Record the letter for the word after the definition. (The number in parentheses next to the word indicates in which lesson the meaning is taught.)

Set C

DEFINITION	MATCH	VOCABULARY WORD
1. a plant-like organism without leaves, flowers, or green coloring		A. alga (3)
2. people who study the atmosphere and changes within it—especially the weather		B. plaque (5)
3. examples		C. epicenter (12)
4. a condition that happens when deposits of plaque build up on the inside of the arteries		D. fungus (1)
5. the point on the surface of the earth right above the center of the earthquake		E. meteorologists (13)
6. an instrument used to measure the strength of earthquakes		F. specimens (8)
7. a thin layer of tissue		G. atherosclerosis (5)
8. a hard substance that builds up in blood vessels and limits the flow of blood		H. seismograph (12)
9. a simple, nonflowering plant that is usually found in or around water		I. molecule (2)
10. a very small amount, formed by combining atoms		J. membrane (7)

Science Vocabulary Knowledge Test

Directions: Read each definition in the left-hand column. Find the word in the right-hand column that goes with the definition. Record the letter for the word after the definition. (The number in parentheses next to the word indicates in which lesson the meaning is taught.)

Set D

DEFINITION	MATCH	VOCABULARY WORD
1. a substance that gives color to plant or animal tissues		A. dehydration (4)
2. having to do with the action of hot liquids or gases		B. pigment (2)
3. the change of a gas to a liquid		C. zoology (10)
4. related to water		D. condensation (13)
5. the loss of water from an organism		E. producers (3)
6. organisms that produce their own food		F. hydrothermal (11)
7. organisms that eat other organisms		G. pasteurization (4)
8. a branch of biology that focuses on animals		H. consumers (3)
9. the branch of biology that studies microorganisms		I. aquatic (15)
10. the process of using heat to kill microbes and prevent food from spoiling rapidly		J. microbiology (8)

ANSWER KEY

Science Vocabulary Knowledge Test

Set A

DEFINITION	MATCH	VOCABULARY WORD
1. rising or coming out of	G	A. photosynthesis (2)
2. a simple sugar	J	B. virus (7)
3. a tiny, infectious particle	B	C. immune (6)
4. long, narrow openings	I	D. biology (10)
5. protected from a disease or infection	C	E. canopy (14)
6. the process by which certain organisms break down energy-rich molecules in order to make their own food	H	F. nutrients (1)
7. the science of living organisms	D	G. emergent (14)
8. a covering	E	H. chemosynthesis (3)
9. the process by which green plants use the sun's energy to make food	A	I. fissures (11)
10. matter needed by plants and animals so they can live	F	J. glucose (2)

ANSWER KEY

Science Vocabulary Knowledge Test

Set B

DEFINITION	MATCH	VOCABULARY WORD
1. positively charged particles	G	A. antibodies (7)
2. a living community of organisms and their physical environment	B	B. ecosystem (1)
3. something that makes something else dirty or impure	D	C. hemoglobin (5)
4. the green substance found in most plants	E	D. pollution (15)
5. particles with no electrical charge	J	E. chorophyll (2)
6. proteins in the blood that destroy germs	A	F. nucleus (9)
7. negatively charged particles	H	G. protons (9)
8. an organism that lives in or on another organism and receives benefits while harming the other organism	I	H. electrons (9)
9. the center of an atom, containing neutrons and protons	F	I. parasite (3)
10. a substance in red blood cells that helps carry oxygen throughout the body	C	J. neutrons (9)

ANSWER KEY

Science Vocabulary Knowledge Test

Set C

DEFINITION	MATCH	VOCABULARY WORD
1. a plant-like organism without leaves, flowers, or green coloring	D	A. alga (3)
2. people who study the atmosphere and changes within it—especially the weather	E	B. plaque (5)
3. examples	F	C. epicenter (12)
4. a condition that happens when deposits of plaque build up on the inside of the arteries	G	D. fungus (1)
5. the point on the surface of the earth right above the center of the earthquake	C	E. meteorologists (13)
6. an instrument used to measure the strength of earthquakes	H	F. specimens (8)
7. a thin layer of tissue	J	G. atherosclerosis (5)
8. a hard substance that builds up in blood vessels and limits the flow of blood	B	H. seismograph (12)
9. a simple, nonflowering plant that is usually found in or around water	A	I. molecule (2)
10. a very small amount, formed by combining atoms	I	J. membrane (7)

Science Vocabulary Knowledge Test

Set D

DEFINITION	MATCH	VOCABULARY WORD
1. a substance that gives color to plant or animal tissues	B	A. dehydration (4)
2. having to do with the action of hot liquids or gases	F	B. pigment (2)
3. the change of a gas to a liquid	D	C. zoology (10)
4. related to water	I	D. condensation (13)
5. the loss of water from an organism	A	E. producers (3)
6. organisms that produce their own food	E	F. hydrothermal (11)
7. organisms that eat other organisms	H	G. pasteurization (4)
8. a branch of biology that focuses on animals	C	H. consumers (3)
9. the branch of biology that studies microorganisms	J	I. aquatic (15)
10. the process of using heat to kill microbes and prevent food from spoiling rapidly	G	J. microbiology (8)

References

The following references provide the research base and validation of the strategies presented in *REWARDS* (Archer, Gleason, & Vachon, 2005). For more information and a synopsis of the validation research, please see Appendix G in the *REWARDS Teacher's Guide*, pp. 351–358.

Adams, M. J. (1990). *Beginning to read: Thinking and learning about print.* Cambridge, MA: MIT Press.

Anderson, R. C., Hiebert, E., Scott, J. A., & Wilkinson, I. A. G. (1985). Conceptual and empirical bases of readability formulas. In G. Green & A. Davison (Eds.), *Linguistic complexity and text comprehension* (pp. 23–54). Hillsdale, NJ: Erlbaum.

Archer, A. L. (1981). *Decoding of multisyllabic words by skill deficient fourth and fifth grade students.* Unpublished doctoral dissertation, University of Washington.

Archer, A. L., Gleason, M. M., Vachon, V., & Hollenbeck, K. (2006). *Instructional strategies for teaching struggling fourth and fifth grade students to read long words.* Manuscript submitted for review.

Canney, G., & Schreiner, R. (1977). A study of the effectiveness of selected syllabication rules and phonogram patterns for word attack. *Reading Research Quarterly, 12*, 102–124.

Cunningham, P. (1998). The multisyllabic word dilemma: Helping students build meaning, spell, and read "big" words. *Reading & Writing Quarterly: Overcoming Learning Difficulties, 14*, 189–219.

Just, M. A., & Carpenter, P. A. (1987). *The psychology of reading and language comprehension.* Boston: Allyn & Bacon.

Lenz, B. K., & Hughes, C. A. (1990). A word identification strategy for adolescents with learning disabilities. *Journal of Learning Disabilities, 23*, 149–158, 163.

Nagy, W. E., & Anderson, R. C. (1984). How many words are there in printed school English? *Reading Research Quarterly, 19*, 302–330.

Perfetti, C. A. (1985). *Reading ability.* New York: Oxford University Press.

Perfetti, C. A. (1986). Continuities in reading acquisition, reading skill, and reading disability. *Remedial and Special Education, 7*, 11–21.

Rayner, K., & Pollatsek, A. (1989). *The psychology of reading.* Englewood Cliffs, NJ: Prentice Hall.

Samuels, S. J., LaBerge, D., & Bremer, C. D. (1978). Units of word recognition: Evidence for developmental changes. *Journal of Verbal Learning and Verbal Behavior, 17*, 715–720.

Share, D., & Stanovich, K. (1995). Cognitive processes in early reading development: Accommodating individual differences into a mode of acquisition. *Issues in Education: Contributions from Educational Psychology, 1*, 1–57.

Shefelbine, J. (1990). A syllabic-unit approach to teaching decoding of polysyllabic words to fourth- and sixth-grade disabled readers. In J. Zutell & S. McCormick (Eds.), *Literacy Theory and Research: Analysis from multiple paradigms. Thirty-ninth yearbook of the National Reading Conference* (pp. 223–229). Fort Worth, TX: Texas Christian University Press.

Shefelbine, J., & Calhoun, J. (1991). Variability in approaches to identifying polysyllabic words: A descriptive study of sixth graders with highly, moderately, and poorly developed syllabication strategies. In J. Zutell & S. McCormick (Eds.), *Learner factors/teacher factors: Issues in literacy research and instruction. Fortieth yearbook of the National Reading Conference* (pp. 169–177). Fort Worth, TX: Texas Christian University Press.

Stanovich, K. E. (1986). Matthew effects in reading: Some consequences of individual differences in the acquisition of literacy. *Reading Research Quarterly, 21*, 360–407.

Stanovich, K. E. (1991). Word recognition: Changing perspectives. In R. Barr, M. L. Kamil, P. B. Mosenthal, & P. D. Pearson (Eds.), *Handbook of reading research* (Vol. 2) (pp. 418–452). New York: Longman.

Vachon, V., & Gleason, M. M. (2006). *The effects of mastery teaching and varying practice contexts on middle school students' acquisition of multisyllabic word reading strategies.* Manuscript in preparation.

Woodcock, R. W. (1973). *Woodcock reading mastery tests.* Circle Pines, MN: American Guidance Service.

Woodcock, R. W. (1987). *Woodcock reading mastery tests* (revised). Circle Pines, MN: American Guidance Service.